Gender History
in China

Gender History in China

Edited by
Masako KOHAMA
and
Linda GROVE

Kyoto University Press

TRANS PACIFIC PRESS

First published in Japanese by Kyoto University Press in 2018 as *Chūgoku jendā-shi Kenkyū nyūmon*.
This English edition published in 2021 jointly by:

Kyoto University Press
69 Yoshida Konoe-cho
Sakyo-ku, Kyoto 606-8315, Japan
Telephone: +81-75-761-6182
Fax: +81-75-761-6190
Email: sales@kyoto-up.or.jp
Web: http://www.kyoto-up.or.jp

Trans Pacific Press Co., Ltd
2nd Floor, Hamamatsu-cho Daiya Building
2-2-15 Hamamatsu-cho, Minato-ku, Tokyo
105-0013, Japan
Telephone: +81-50-5371-9475
Email: info@transpacificpress.com
Web: http://www.transpacificpress.com

© Kohama Masako and Linda Grove 2021.
Edited by Miriam Riley, Armidale, Australia.
Designed and set by Ryo Kuroda, New York, USA.
Printed by Asia Printing Office Corporation, Nagano, Japan.

Distributors

USA and Canada
Independent Publishers Group (IPG)
814 N. Franklin Street
Chicago, IL 60610, USA
Telephone inquiries: +1-312-337-0747
Order placement: 800-888-4741 (domestic only)
Fax: +1-312-337-5985
Email: frontdesk@ipgbook.com
Web: http://www.ipgbook.com

Europe, Oceania, Middle East and Africa
EUROSPAN
Gray's Inn House,
127 Clerkenwell Road
London, EC1R 5DB
United Kingdom
Telephone: +44-(0)20-7240-0856
Email: info@eurospan.co.uk
Web: https://www.eurospangroup.com/

Japan
For purchase orders in Japan, please contact any distributor in Japan.

China
China Publishers Services Ltd
718, 7/F., Fortune Commercial Building,
362 Sha Tsui Road, Tsuen Wan, N.T.
Hong Kong
Telephone: +852-2491-1436
Email: edwin@cps-hk.com

Korea, Taiwan
MHM Limited
1-1-13-4F, Kanda-Jinbocho,
Chiyoda-ku, Tokyo 101-0051 JAPAN
Telephone: +81-(0)3-3518-9449
Email: sales@mhmlimited.co.jp

Southeast Asia
Alkem Company Pte Ltd
1, Sunview Road #01-27, Eco-Tech@Sunview
Singapore 627615
Telephone: +65 6265 6666
Email: enquiry@alkem.com.sg

The publication of this book was supported by a Grant-in-Aid for Publication of Scientific Research Results (Grant Number 19HP6004), provided by the Japan Society for the Promotion of Science.

All rights reserved. No reproduction of any part of this book may take place without the written permission of kyoto University Press or Trans Pacific Press.

ISBN 978-1-925608-09-0 (hardback)
ISBN 978-1-925608-10-6 (paperback)
ISBN 978-1-925608-11-3 (ebook)

Contents

Figures   2
Contributors   3
Acknowledgement   5
Preface: Gender Order in Chinese History – *KOHAMA Masako*   8

PART I

Phase I: Pre-Qin to Sui-Tang: Classical China – The Formation of Patrilineal Society
    Introduction – *SHIMOKURA Wataru*   28
    1. Gender Structure in Pre-Qin China from an Archaeological Perspective
      – *UCHIDA Junko*   43
    2. The Patrilinealization of Society – *SHIMOKURA Wataru*   65
    3. Literature and Women in China – *SATAKE Yasuko*   84
    4. The Family in the Tang Period – *WONG Yu-Hsuan*   102
    Column 1: Introduction of Historical Materials: Wives' Divorce and Daughters'
      Inheritance of Property, Seen in Dunhuang Documents – *ARAKAWA Masaharu*   126
    Column 2: Empress Wu Zetian and Thereafter – *KANEKO Shūichi*   135

Phase II: Song to Ming-Qing: Traditional China – The Strengthening of Gender Norms
    Introduction – *SASAKI Megumi*   144
    5. Livelihood and Gender in the Tang and Song Dynasties – *ŌSAWA Masaaki*   153
    Focal Point: An Overview of Shiga Shūzō's *Principles of Chinese Family Law*
      – *SASAKI Megumi*   173
    6. Traditional Family Ideology and the Chen-Zhu School – *SASAKI Megumi*   184
    7. Marriage and 'Chastity': Structure and Change – *GOMI Tomoko*   199
    8. The Sense of Social Status and Gender – *KISHIMOTO Mio*   208
    Column 3: Court Ladies and Gender – *OGAWA Yoshiyuki*   221

Phase III: Modern and Contemporary China – Changing Gender Order
    Introduction – *TAKASHIMA Kō*   228
    9. Nationalism and Gender – *SAKAMOTO Hiroko*   239
    10. Masculinity in Modern China – *TAKASHIMA Kō*   260
    11. Discourses on the Family, Love and Sex in Modern China – *EGAMI Sachiko*   281
    12. Women's Labor in Modern and Contemporary China – *Linda GROVE*   301
    13. The Founding of the People's Republic of China and the Transformation of
      Gender Order – *KOHAMA Masako*   317
    14. Rearrangement of Gender Order in Post-Mao China:
      Changing Networks of Women's Federations – *OHASHI Fumie*   331
    Column 4: Two Histories of Women in Modern China – *SUDŌ Mizuyo*   351

PART II

    15. The Household Register and the Family in Ancient China – *WASHIO Yūko*   358
    16. Perceptions of 'Talented Women' – *ITAHASHI Akiko*   376
    17. Healthcare, the Body and Gender in Chinese Medicine – *YAO Yi*   390
    18. The History of Women's/Gender Studies and Feminism in China
      – *AKIYAMA Yōko*   413
    Column 5: Sexual Minorities – *TŌYAMA Hideya*   428
    Column 6: Theatre and Gender – *NAKAYAMA Fumi*   437

Bibliography   443
Index   503

Figures

1.1	Tombs of a man and a woman in the Neolithic Age	47
1.2	Relative positions of the royal cemetery and Fu Hao's tomb in Yinxu	50
1.3	Oracle inscriptions on the turtle shell containing references to Fu Hao	51
1.4	The Jin rulers' burial compound at Beizhao (Qucun Locus III), Quwo	55
1.5	Male and female accessories from the Qucun Jinhou cemetery	56
1.6	Guo Meng Ji vessel (*yi*)	58
2.1	Genealogy chart I	69
2.2	Genealogy chart II	71
2.3	Genealogy chart III	71
C2.1	Empress Wu Zetian's family tree	135
5.1	Picture of weeding	156
5.2	Picture of winnowing	156
5.3	Picture of ploughing a field, sowing seeds and covering them with soil	156
5.4	Picture of winnowing	156
9.1	'Changes in the tastes in women's world'	254
10.1	Government officials at the end of Qing (large patterns and rich colors)	265
10.2	Cabinet ministers of the Republic of China (almost uniformly dressed in black)	271
10.3	Chiang Kaishek and Mao Zedong (both dressed in the Zhongshan suit) at the Peace Negotiation in Chongqing	277
14.1	Disparity and changes in average annual income between men and women in urban and rural areas (as a percentage of men's average annual income)	333
14.2	Income brackets and gender in rural areas (2010)	333
15.1	Bamboo slips of Example C. Restored household records in Wu of the Three Kingdoms, excavated in Changsha County	362

Contributors

KOHAMA Masako (Editor, Preface, Chapter 13)
  Professor, College of Humanities and Sciences, Nihon University

SHIMOKURA Wataru (Phase I Introduction, Chapter 2)
  Professor, Faculty of Letters, Tohoku Gakuin University

UCHIDA Junko (Chapter 1)
  Associate Research Fellow, Institute of History and Philology, Academia Sinica

SATAKE Yasuko (Chapter 3)
  Professor Emerita, Tohoku University

WONG Yu Hsuan (Chapter 4)
  Associate Professor, Department of History, Tung Hai University

ARAKAWA Masaharu (Column 1)
  Professor Emeritus, Osaka University

KANEKO Shuichi (Column 2)
  Professor Emeritus, Kokugakuin University; Professor Emeritus, University of Yamanashi

SASAKI Megumi (Phase II Introduction, Focal Point, Chapter 6)
  Professor, Faculty of Law and Literature, Shimane University

ŌSAWA Masaaki (Chapter 5)
  Professor Emeritus, Sophia University; Research Fellow, Toyo Bunko

GOMI Tomoko (Chapter 7)
  Senior Lecturer, Faculty of Liberal Arts, University of the Sacred Heart

KISHIMOTO Mio (Chapter 8)
  Professor Emerita, Ochanomizu University

OGAWA Yoshiyuki (Column 3)
  Professor, College of Literature, Kokushikan University

TAKASHIMA Kō (Phase III Introduction, Chapter 10)
  Professor, Graduate School of Letters, Kyoto University

SAKAMOTO Hiroko (Chapter 9)
  Professor Emerita, Hitotsubashi University

EGAMI Sachiko (Chapter 11)
  Professor Emerita, Ferris University

Linda GROVE (Editor, Chapter 12)
    Professor Emerita, Sophia University

OHASHI Fumie (Chapter 14)
    Associate Professor, Institute for Gender Studies, Ochanomizu University

SUDŌ Mizuyo (Column 4)
    Associate Professor, Faculty of International Relations, Kyoto Sangyo University

WASHIO Yūko (Chapter 15)
    Part-time Teacher, College of Letters, Ritsumeikan University

ITAHASHI Akiko (Chapter 16)
    Assistant Professor, Institute for Advanced Studies on Asia, University of Tokyo

YAO Yi (Chapter 17)
    Part-time Teacher, University of Tokyo

AKIYAMA Yōko[1] (Chapter 18)
    Professor, Surugadai University

TŌYAMA Hideya (Column 5)
    Visiting Researcher, BKC Research Organization of Social Science, Ritsumeikan University

NAKAYAMA Fumi (Column 6)
    Professor, Faculty of Humanities and Sciences, Kobe Gakuin University

---

1 Deceased.

Acknowledgement

This volume is the product of a collective effort by gender history scholars in Japan to consider the special characteristics of the gender order in China from ancient times to the present day. We hope that it will serve as the basis for discussions with scholars sharing similar concerns in other parts of the world.

In 2018, the Japanese edition of this book, which was based on a six-year collaborative research project based at Tōyō Bunko, was published by Kyoto University Press (editors: Kohama Masako, Shimokura Wataru, Sasaki Megumi, Takashima Kō and Egami Sachiko). A small group of Japanese scholars began working on the issues considered in this volume in the early 1970s, and organized the Chinese Women's History Research Association and other research projects. In the early twenty-first century, our research interests broadened, and we began to reconsider the issues from a gender perspective, at the same time moving to incorporate themes and perspectives that had been overlooked when we focused only on women's issues. In 2013, we received a major grant from the Japan Society for the Promotion of Science (JSPS) to support our collective research project, and throughout the years we have had lively and informative exchanges with scholars in both the English-speaking and Chinese-speaking academic worlds.

Over the years we have been inspired by the rapid development of research on Chinese women's and gender history in the English-speaking world. Several years ago we published a Japanese translation (Heibonsha 2015) of our friend Susan L. Mann's *Gender and Sexuality in Chinese History*. We learned much from this volume, which is an outstanding representative of the best scholarship in gender history in the English-speaking world. Susan Mann's book presents a very thoughtful consideration of the fundamental principles of gender order in late imperial and modern China. However, in working on that volume we realized that scholarship in the English-speaking academy on earlier periods of Chinese gender history is not as well developed. We therefore decided to work on this volume, which builds on the rich Japanese scholarship on Chinese history, re-reading earlier studies from a gender perspective.

As researchers on Chinese gender history based in Japan, we believe we can examine developments from an objective perspective. At the same time, Japan has experienced a long and complicated relationship with China and Chinese culture that places scholars based in Japan in a position, different from those of scholars in the European and American intellectual worlds, as partial insiders. For many hundreds of years Japanese society and culture were strongly influenced by China. In more recent times, the relationship has been shaped by a form of colonial modernism which entwined in complicated and complex ways the interactions between China and Japan. These complicated and layered perspectives are reflected in this book. Japan is, of course, a hybrid society, and the authors of the essays in this volume reflect the diversity of the contemporary Japanese academic world. The authors come from various ethnic and cultural backgrounds, including not only scholars from Japan but also from the US, mainland China and Taiwan. We hope that this volume will serve as the starting point for expanded discussions with scholars from the English-speaking world.

Just at the time when we were finishing the editorial work on this volume, the world was struck by the Covid-19 pandemic, and we have been limited to working from home. We all wonder when we will again be able to meet in person with our international colleagues. Under these circumstances, the editorial work on this volume has been conducted through weekly online meetings that brought together members of the editorial team in Tokyo and Kyoto. Linda Grove, an American scholar who has been part of the Japanese research community in Chinese gender studies for many years, has played a major role in the final editing of this volume. Through work on this English edition and a Chinese edition that will be published in Taiwan this year, we have explored the possibilities of new online methods for international scholarly communication, which have allowed us to continue to work despite the pandemic.

We would like to offer our thanks to Suzuki Tetsuya of Kyoto University Press, whose gentle pressure to keep up the editorial work has kept us on track, to Nakamura Reiko, whose English editing skills and attention to detail have contributed much to the completed volume and to Miriam Riley of Trans Pacific Press. We have added supplementary materials to this English edition, including a section on Japanese research on the Tang family which has been added to Chapter Four, and a Focal Point which provides a guide to one of the foundational texts of Japanese scholarship, Shiga Shūzō's *Principles of Chinese Family Law*. Among the translators who have contributed to this volume are Sato Minako, Debby Chih-Yen Huang (Ph.D. candidate, University of Pennsylvania) who translated the new section of Chapter Four and Shinno Reiko (Professor, University of Wisconsin-Eau Claire) and Hasegawa Kenji (Associate Professor, Yokohama National University) who translated Chapter Nine. The publication of this book is supported by a Grant-in-Aid for Publication of Scientific

Research Results (Grant Number JP19HP6004), provided by the Japan Society for the Promotion of Science, to which we express our sincere appreciation. In the months and years ahead, we anticipate major changes in our societies as a result of the world-wide pandemic. We all hope that those future changes in Japan, in China and in the English-speaking world will lead to societies with greater gender equality and equity. As we rethink the gender order regimes that underlay our societies, a deeper understanding of the history of contemporary institutions is important. We hope that the publication of this book will contribute to that deeper understanding.

August 2020
KOHAMA Masako

Preface

Gender Order in Chinese History

— *KOHAMA Masako*

China is currently the second largest economic power in the world and is strengthening its presence in the political arena as well. Gaining a deeper understanding of China, whether to work with it or against it, has become a necessity in the twenty-first century world. At the same time, China boasts the longest history among existing old and advanced civilizations. There is a vast amount of research on its history that has discussed and shed light on a wide range of topics, including philosophy, politics, society, economy and culture. However, for a very long time, little attention was paid to the concept of gender – how masculinity and femininity have been defined and understood. Since gender defines the bedrock of social order, it is impossible to gain a deep understanding of Chinese society without understanding gender dynamics.

In order to understand China with its systems and values that differ from those of Western and Japanese societies (and other civilizations), this book brings together the results of studies on gender history in China published in the Japanese, Chinese and English languages that have made significant contributions. The chapters examine China's gender order from ancient times to today and the processes of change over time in an effort to advance our comprehension of Chinese society while promoting deeper and more active research in the future.

Gender history and gender mainstreaming

What is 'gender'? It has been some time since this term came into wide use in the field of humanities and social sciences, and yet even today gender history is often considered a mere synonym for women's history within the community of historians.

The concept of 'gender' represents an aspiration to reassess and shift all aspects of the knowledge paradigm beyond women's issues. The term 'gender', which originally referred to sex distinctions as expressed in language, came to be used for sociocultural rather than biological sex differentiation during the groundswell of second-wave feminism in the 1970s when it was widely recognized that gender was a cultural construct, and that the characterization of maleness or femaleness varies from one society to another. Upon further analysis, in Joan Scott's (1988) definition, gender is 'based on the perceived differences between the sexes, but is also a way of signifying power differentials'. This way of thinking was later accepted by the international community and reflected in the United Nations' definition: 'Gender is defined as the social meaning given to biological sex differences'.[1] In other words, gender pertains to the way humans are perceived as social 'persons'. While all 'persons' are thought to be characterized by gender, its meaning is assigned by society and varies across communities and times.

The term 'gender mainstreaming' refers to bringing a gender awareness perspective to the mainstream (i.e., generalization) in an endeavor to maintain awareness of how human activities and their meaning vary according to gender in different social classes and ethnic communities in all domains and at all levels, from law and government policy to everyday behavior. Similarly, the 'gender mainstreaming of historical research' entails ensuring that researchers pay attention to gender, which strongly influences all aspects of history along with class and ethnicity.

Previous studies of Chinese history exhibited a conscious and unconscious tendency to focus on men, especially male Han intellectuals who read and wrote in the classical Chinese language, as historical agents. Women were rarely the subjects of Chinese historical studies, since most accounts relied on written historical records, and the volume of writing by or about women was a small fraction of the records by and about men. Research in women's history designed to discover women's untold stories began to gather momentum in the 1970s and gradually revealed their diverse historical experiences. As this has occurred in parallel with the proliferation of studies on how each society has attached meaning to gender distinction itself, the scope of research has deepened beyond women's history to examine history from the perspective of gender.

By advancing research from the viewpoint of gender, the study of Chinese history has been moving away from its overemphasis on male Han Chinese intellectuals, for whom the most important virtue was to marry and produce

---

1 United Nations (1991), *The 1999 World Survey on the Role of Women in Development: Globalization, Gender and Work.*

offspring according to the heterosexual norm. Instead, the field has been reorienting itself towards the reassessment of women, illiterate people, unmarried men and women and 'ethnic minorities' with 'barbaric' customs in male-female relationships as historical actors in order to understand how the social structure that marginalized these people was created and sustained. Other studies are being undertaken to find out how homosexuality, transvestism, transgenderism and other modes of sexuality that have been considered deviant in modern society were perceived historically in relation to current societal values.

From Chinese women's history to Chinese gender history

Let us begin with a broad overview of the evolution of research into Chinese gender history as well as the Chinese women's history that preceded it (to be discussed in more detail in individual chapters).

Among modern studies of Chinese history, the first work that consciously dealt with a particular gender was Chen Dongyuan's *A History of the Lives of Chinese Women* (*Zhongguo funü shenghuoshi*) (1928 [in Chinese]), an overview of the history of Chinese women from ancient times written during the 1920s in the aftermath of the May Fourth/New Culture Movement (see Part I Phase II Introduction). There was no significant book on women's history after that for a long time.

The foremost pioneering work in this genre in the second half of the twentieth century was *Chinese Women in a Century of Revolution* (*Chūgoku joseishi*) by Ono Kazuko (1978 [in Japanese]). Ono, who was the first female student in the Department of Oriental History of Kyoto University, responded to the discourse in second-wave feminism (women's lib) during the 1970s that sharply questioned structural discrimination against women by focusing her research on women in order to challenge male-centrism in the world of Chinese historical science. At that time, both researchers and their subjects were predominantly male. Her research sought to trace the vibrant lives of Chinese women, including their involvement in revolutionary struggles and their fight against sexism. Around the same time, Suetsugu Reiko and other researchers outside academia in Tokyo, and Yanagida Setsuko, who was the first female student in the Department of Oriental History at the University of Tokyo, formed the Society of Historical Studies on Chinese Women and began to unearth the history of Chinese women. Suetsugu focused on the lives of a broad spectrum of modern Chinese women, including the movements and lifestyles of women in Nationalist China as well as under the Communist Party of China, and published her research in Japanese as *History of Chinese Women in the Twentieth Century* in 2009 (see Column Four). In Japan, the historical study of Chinese women has gradually expanded in scope to incorporate gender history centering on modern and contemporary history under the influence of second-wave feminism.

Second-wave feminism stimulated research into Chinese history in the English-speaking world as well. The late imperial period (Song–Ming/Qing) was a particularly noteworthy area of North American research into Chinese women's history that resulted in various studies that challenged the one-dimensional image of women as oppressed people in pre-modern feudal society and shed light on the diverse lives of women in late-imperial China. Patricia Buckley Ebrey (1993) portrayed the diverse lives of Song women with a focus on their standing in the family and the great degree of authority exercised by the legal wife. Susan L. Mann (2007) described the high cultural standards of female poets among Jiangnan elite in the Qing period and their networks. These studies showed that the images of uneducated and helpless pre-modern Chinese women living in a closed world were not necessarily accurate. Above all, Dorothy Ko's studies on footbinding (2001, 2005) gave rise to a revisionist research current inspired by her reinterpretation of the practice of footbinding, arguing that footbinding, which was perceived as the quintessence of Chinese culture, was voluntarily supported by Chinese women at the time. This interpretation stood in opposition to the long-standing view that footbinding was a symbol of the oppression of women in pre-modern China (see Part I Phase II Introduction).

Together with other works, historical studies of Chinese women carried out in the English-speaking world have borne many fruits and evolved into gender history. Since the turn of the twenty-first century, studies on the history of sexuality in China have been under way in response to the third wave of feminism that calls for the social inclusion of even more diverse types of sexuality.

Gender and Sexuality in Modern Chinese History (Mann 2011) is a culmination of this rich array of gender historical studies undertaken in the English-speaking world since the 1980s. This publication looks at gender as an ordering structure permeating society as a whole from the level of one's body to that of the state and depicts changes in the gender/sexuality system of late-imperial Chinese society, showing that the gender system was not a static formation through to modern and contemporary times. This groundbreaking work illustrates the state of gender order in Chinese society as something that prescribes and expresses the structure of an entire society. Perhaps its only weakness reflects the current state of research in the English-speaking world, in that the work does not offer sufficient discussion on changes over the period from pre-Qin times to Ming-Qing.

In the Chinese-speaking world, reform-era mainland China has embraced research on changes in the idea of womanhood and the gender structure in China from ancient times through Ming-Qing to modern times (see Chapter Eighteen). Du Fangqin and Wang Zhen (2004) attempted to follow changes in the gender structure in successive periods, including the shift from prehistoric matrilineal society to Zhou patriarchy, women's activities in the Wei-Jin, Southern and Northern Dynasties and Sui-Tang periods, the Neo-Confucian emphasis on internal and external order in the Song and the great importance placed on chastity in Ming and Qing. In recent years, the research base has broadened with the publication of voluminous works of survey history such as *The General History of Women in China* (*Zhongguo funü tongshi*; 10 volumes) by Chen Gaohua and Tong Shaosu (2010–2011) and *History of the Family in China* (*Zhongguo jiatingshi*; 5 volumes) edited by Zhang Guogang (2007). Nevertheless, a thoroughly systematic overview of women's/gender history in China remains elusive.

In Taiwan, Yu Chien-Ming of the Institute of Modern History (Academia Sinica) and others have been vigorously conducting research on Chinese women's/gender history as they quickly absorb the results of studies from the English- and Japanese-speaking countries. They have accumulated a body of empirical studies based on historical records from various time periods, ranging from a study by Lee Jen-Der (2008) discussing gender order according to the views of the human body during a period from the Qin-Han to the Sui-Tang dynasties, to a wealth of research carried out on the family in Tang as discussed in Chapter Four of this book, and to the publication of multitudes of modern/contemporary historical studies in *Research on Women in Modern Chinese History* (*Jindai Zhongguo funüshi yanjiu*) published by the Institute of Modern History, Academia Sinica (1993–).

As suggested by this brief overview of research into the history of women and gender in China, the combined body of research in the Chinese, English and Japanese languages has accumulated to a considerable level and given us a greater understanding of the gender structure in specific time periods and regions. However, it has not reached the stage of forming a complete schema able to answer the questions of how Chinese gender order is characterized and how it has changed.

Research on Chinese gender history and related issues

Against this backdrop, the Chinese gender history research group in Japan has been conducting collaborative research since 2012.

Although Japanese society belongs to the Confucian cultural sphere in East Asia along with China, its gender order is substantially different from that of Chinese society. Consequently, an analysis of gender order in Chinese society in comparison with Japanese gender order is conducive to an understanding of its deeper and more subtle elements that cannot be achieved in comparisons with the West alone. As we can see from the comparison of family structures below, this approach promotes an understanding of not only the ways in which the Chinese family system differs from the Western model, but also how it differs from other Asian family systems and its internal logic and rules. The internal and three-dimensional in-depth understanding of China's gender order from this comparative approach is very important when we come to consider how to further advance gender equality and justice in Chinese and Japanese societies. At the same time, it offers a meaningful comparative standpoint from which to understand gender order in other societies in the West and in South, South-East and West Asian countries.

Japanese research on Chinese history has much to offer in terms of a systematic study of China's gender history. The collaborative research group has endeavored to paint a comprehensive picture of the characteristics of and changes to gender order in Chinese history and to deepen our understanding of specific phenomena through the critical reassessment of preceding studies and the absorption of new study results into our empirical research on gender.

This book, as the result of our collaborative research, is the group's bold attempt to formulate a comprehensive understanding of Chinese gender history.

In this section, we first introduce the main issues concerning Chinese gender history that emerged in the research process while paying attention to comparisons with Japan and other regions as well as changes across time, that is, spatial and temporal diversity, to serve as pointers for the reader.

Has the Chinese family always been strongly patrilineal?

It is commonly believed that the Chinese family structure has always been strongly patrilineal. Let us examine the characteristics of the Chinese family in early-modern Ming and Qing China – which is generally regarded as 'traditional Chinese society' – in comparison with the early-modern Japanese family and discuss how the patrilineal family has developed and changed in the history of China.

Chinese people inherited their family name from their father which was said to form the core of their self-identity for their entire life. Women did not change their family name upon marriage and their children took their father's family name. People related through the paternal bloodline with the same family name were recognized as kin who shared the same material force.[2] The father's property was divided equally among his sons whereas his daughters were not entitled to inheritance (but they might be given dowries at the family's discretion). If the father had no son, the legitimate option for him was to adopt a male child from his patrilineal bloodline rather than to take his daughter's husband into the family, since daughters were unable to pass on their father's bloodline. The flourishing of patrilineal kin with the same family name was considered as the prosperity of the 'family' (*jia*).[3] Shiga Shūzō (1967) contrasted the Chinese family that emphasized the preservation of patrilineality with the early-modern Japanese 'family' that highlighted the handing down of the family trade, family name and family property to the next generation. He argued that the Chinese divided inheritance equally among male children because the sons shared equal ability to continue the paternal bloodline and called this principle underpinning the family in traditional Chinese society 'Chinese family law'.[4]

While the form of the family in China varies greatly depending on region and social class, many Chinese historians acknowledge that what Shiga called

---

2 Marriage between patrilineal relatives was avoided under the custom of 'no marriage between people bearing the same surname' but no such rule was applied to marriage between matrilineal relatives as they were not considered consanguineous. For example, cousins whose fathers were brothers bore the same family name and therefore could not marry one another whereas cousins who were related on the mother's side or through the father's sisters did not carry the same family name and therefore could marry one another (and such marriage was sometimes seen as the preferred option).

3 Unlike the Japanese early-modern 'family' which was supposed to pass on its family trade, family name and family property for generations, the Chinese patrilineal 'family' had no family trade and was supposed to exploit every possibility to increase the prosperity of its descendants by sending its sons into the imperial/civil service via the examination system, into the field of commerce to make money or into estate management to accumulate land.

4 See Shiga (1967).

'Chinese family law' is a well-considered concept as a fundamental ideal type; we should note that this ideal type is characteristic of families of the Han ethnic group, which was the overwhelmingly dominant ethnic group in Ming and Qing China. Shiga believed it to be the universal principle that held throughout China's history since ancient times. However, in this book we consider that even such central principles of 'Chinese family law' were shaped over the long course of history.

According to recent archaeological findings, there is evidence that allows scholars to describe the sexual division of labor practiced during the early Neolithic Age, proving that gender had great significance in terms of the social structure from such early times. Studies of inscriptions on bones and tortoise shells have found that all Shang kings were men who came to the throne through father–son or brother–brother succession, while succession of the Zhou throne was from father to son in principle. Despite the obvious existence of patriliny, the ancient patrilineal system was not yet sophisticated or strong and hence maternal relatives were also regarded as 'kin' in Han society. Patriliny was eventually given greater priority in the Six Dynasties period, and Chinese society gradually leaned toward 'patrilineality' (see Part I Phase I Introduction and Chapters One and Two). Even the reign of Wu Zetian, the only woman in China's imperial history to rule in her own name, came to be denied in the latter half of Tang (see Column Two). However, it appears that although women's position may have been weakening in China's heartland at that time, women inherited property in the remote province of Dunhuang (see Column One).

In the history of Chinese thought, the system of patriliny was built on the Cheng-Zhu school idea of 'father and son sharing the same material forces' (*fuzi tongqi*) that runs through the paternal bloodline. Only after the emergence of this concept in the Song period did Shiga's logic of 'Chinese family law' under which only the sons were qualified to perform rituals for the father because of possessing the same material force become persuasive (see Chapter Six).

Because Han society in the Ming and Qing dynasties was fiercely competitive due to a high degree of social mobility, patrilineal lineages were developed as mutual aid organizations for survival. On the other hand, connections with daughters and affinal relatives also played a considerable part in social functioning.

Family reforms in the first half of the twentieth century and after the founding of the People's Republic of China improved women's status considerably, but the family institution remained the same in that it was still based on patrilocality. However, China's contemporary society with fewer children under the government's one child policy has made it impossible to reproduce families through the paternal line alone and this has triggered a shift toward a bilateral kinship structure both legally and practically.

China's patriliny is therefore a historical construct and has changed considerably over the years.

Difference between gender order[5] in early-modern China and Japan

It has been said that women in pre-modern and early-modern China were oppressed by stringent gender norms. It has also been said that women could only have a sexual relationship with their husband during their entire life, and not expect a good marriage proposal unless their freedom of movement was constrained by footbinding. How true are these claims?

Confucianism (like many other ethical systems) places importance on female chastity and forbids married women from having sexual relationships with other men. Nonetheless, Chinese society was not always pervaded by the aforementioned stringent gender norms evidenced by the fact that it was normal even for imperial princesses to remarry more than once in the Tang dynasty. During the Song period, one Confucian scholar made the fundamentalist statement, 'To starve to death is a small matter, but to lose one's chastity is a great matter', but even he did not believe that widows should never remarry. In the Ming-Qing period, the spread of the strict gender norms that demanded widows' lifelong faithfulness to their late husband, among other things, led to the commendation of women who remained unmarried after their fiancé's death or committed suicide after their husband's death (see Chapters Six and Seven).

A recent study by Susan L. Mann (2011) points out that the overemphasis on chastity was caused by the use of women's compliance with the gender norms – whether or not they were 'good women' – as an indicator of the family's social status in the basically classless and highly competitive society of early-modern China (see Chapter Eight). In pre-modern China, women had an increased chance of becoming widows due to a higher mortality rate and many widows remarried to survive. However, by the early-modern period, the compelling idea of chastity pervaded all levels of society, as narrated in Lu Xun's novel,

---

5 See Note 2 in Chapter Fourteen for a discussion on gender order.

New Year Sacrifice, in which a widow feared that she might find herself in hell when she was forced to remarry due to poverty. It appears that these gender norms were stronger than those in Japan at the time.

The chief difference between the Ming-Qing gender norms and those in early-modern Japan was the degree of segregation of women. Confucian norms such as 'Men and women should be treated differently' and 'Men work outside, women work inside' not only prescribe the sexual division of roles but also the spatial segregation of men's and women's domains. Chinese society was comprised of genderized spaces as women's place was said to be inside the home. These norms gradually increased in importance from the Song period as the influence of Neo-Confucianism spread.[6]

Gender norms before then were rather loose; for example, it was still possible for a woman to argue with her husband, as we can see in *A New Account of the Tales of the World* (*Shishuo Xinyu*) from the Six Dynasties period. Aristocratic women in Tang routinely went out on their horses and women's free-spirited activities were praised. Historical records from Tang and Song show that women participated in a wide variety of occupations in and out of the home (see Chapter Five). In literature, there was a succession of independent-minded female poets from ancient times and not all female writers were confined to writing about women who waited for men in their inner quarters (see Chapter Three).

In Ming-Qing, however, women remaining inside their home and not being seen by men other than their relatives came to be regarded as proof of the morality and respectability of their family and therefore keeping women hidden in the house became an indicator of a family's social status. In reality, though, many women had to go out to work.

In Ming-Qing society, women with bound, small feet – which meant that it was difficult for them to go out – served as another indicator of the family's social status. Nevertheless, footbound women were not necessarily powerless. Some upper-class women exchanged poems with their relatives and friends while many women contributed to family finances by spinning and weaving at home.

What were the characteristics of 'masculinity' in China?

Just as there are gender norms for women, there are also those for men, or masculinity, that dictate what is expected of men in every society. The masculine

---

6 See Deng Xiaonan (2004).

quality of the mainstream men who hold power in each society is referred to as 'hegemonic masculinity'.[7] Hegemonic masculinity in pre-modern Chinese society was represented by the Confucian model of ideal men. In this model, a high value was placed on filial devotion to parents and marriage to pass on the male bloodline, and the model man pursued book-learning and accumulated virtues to embody 'civility' (*wen* / 文), which was considered the essence of Chinese civilization. In the real world, the hegemonic masculinity model was represented by the scholar-official-class men who mainly hailed from landed families and acquired cultural capital through their effort in Confucian learning to pass the civil service examinations. At the same time, they were literati who wrote poems and appeared as main characters in the scholar and beauty (*caizi jiaren*) genre of romantic novels.

On the other hand, 'military' (*wu* / 武) values were considered inferior to 'civil' values. According to the saying, 'Those who labor with their minds govern others; those who labor with their strength are governed by others' ('Teng Wen Gong' Vol. 1, *Mencius*), the superiority of 'civil' over 'military' was well established in Confucian society. Military heroes in *Records of the Three Kingdoms* and *Water Margin* were heroes in the subcultural world who served gentle and virtuous rulers named Liu Bei and Song Jiang, respectively. They valued the bonds between men (as illustrated by the Oath of the Peach Garden)[8] and showed scant interest in romantic relations with women who might jeopardize male homosociability. In the background of the proliferation of this image of male hero was the presence of a shortage of women caused by such male-chauvinistic practices as female infanticide. Unable to marry and form families, some men turned to vagrancy, and homosexuality also flourished among lower-class men who were unable to marry (called 'bare sticks') (Mann 2011).

This model of hegemonic masculinity changed when China was threatened with national ruin in modern times. The establishment of a new model of masculinity able to save the nation with military strength was sought and the military man was added to the hegemonic masculinity model (see Chapter Ten).

The peak of the predominance of 'military' over 'civil' was reached during the Cultural Revolution. Intellectuals who represented 'civil' values were subjected to political criticism as the 'stinking old ninth' and the value

---

7 See Connell (2005) on 'hegemonic masculinity'.
8 See Sedgwick (1985) on 'male homosociality'.

system of Chinese traditional culture was strongly attacked. During the reform and opening-up period spurred by Chinese aspirations for modernization, the hegemonic masculinity came to entail the possession of money and power as well as flaunting one's power through the sexual control of many women (Song Shaopeng 2016a [Japanese]).

Were 'modern families' formed in China?

In the second half of the nineteenth century, Chinese society began to undergo social changes toward colonial modernization as a result of pressure from imperialistic powers, and the situation surrounding gender and family also began to change. Whereas the gender norm of 'Men go out to work, women work at home' did not spread in the West until modern times, in Chinese society in the early-modern period, the norm of 'Men work outside, women inside' had already taken root and entailed the spatial segregation of women. When late-Qing China was faced with national ruin, however, there was widespread acceptance of the idea that women should also discharge civic responsibility by stepping out of their home to learn and work (see Chapter Nine). Thus, the gender order of the traditional society was headed for radical change while debate raged over new gender norms and the concept of family. During the May Fourth/New Culture Movement, the 'small family' centering on the husband and wife was advocated over the patrilineal 'large family' based on Confucian norms and various arguments were raised as to the concepts of love, sex, marriage and family. The intellectual men and women who had received modern education eventually began to form a consensus that the small family based on love was the ideal family model (see Chapter Eleven). It is possible to say that it followed the 'modern family' model of Western modernity in that it was a nuclear family that combined sex, love, marriage and reproduction.[9]

---

9 The 'modern family' is the concept of family that came to be regarded as a normative model in modern society and is thought to have the following characteristics.
  1. The 'modern family' is a nuclear family comprising a husband, a wife and their unmarried children and does not include non-relatives such as servants.
  2. The husband and wife are united by a bond of love and take care of their children and there is a strong emotional relationship between the family members.
  3. The family home is thought to be a private domain distinct from the public domain outside of it; the husband works in the public domain while the wife performs domestic duties and raises children in the private domain.
This family model is peculiar to modernity and has historicity; see Ochiai (1996 [English]), Ueno (2009 [English]) and others.

Yet, the Republic of China plunged into the age of revolutions and wars without reaching a consensus on the sexual division of labor in terms of whether women should be wise wives and good mothers in a small family or go out to participate in society as citizens. In the meantime, the idea of love-based small families spread in the urban middle class whereas the family form in China's vast rural areas remained almost the same as that before the nineteenth century.

After the founding of the People's Republic of China, family reform was advanced through the promulgation of the marriage law and a national implementation campaign that legitimized the equality of men and women in love-based marriages. At the same time, the government made the gender norm of 'men outside, women inside' a thing of the past and modernized the Chinese family in one stroke by promoting women's participation in the public arena (see Chapter Thirteen).

Did Chinese socialism improve the status of women?

There was a time when people believed in the theory that 'socialism liberates women'. This argument postulated that women would achieve economic independence and liberate themselves from subjugation to men because socialist society warranted women's participation in labor. China's communist government upheld gender equality as one of its major policies and forged ahead with women's participation in labor. It promulgated a law for gender equality in marriage and promoted family reforms through its implementation nationally. This led to a significant rise in the status of women at home and in society and they participated actively as members of the 'masters of the state'. Nevertheless, socialist Chinese society was far from attaining gender equality. Women struggled under the double burden of paid and domestic work as they were required like men to go out and work while continuing to perform domestic duties (see Chapter Twelve).

The expansion of production capacity became paramount for China when reform and opening-up policies were introduced at the end of the 1970s. However, it was not long before women were urged to 'return to the home' when it became clear that there were not enough good jobs for both men and women. Although this idea was not adopted as a policy due to opposition from the All-China Women's Federation and others, the disparity between men and women widened in both urban and rural areas in the course of China's subsequent economic growth (Kohama and Akiyama 2016) (see Chapter Fourteen). This emergence of a torrent of gender issues accompanying economic development has led to a re-evaluation of the consequences of socialism.

Is Chinese society LGBT-friendly?

For the people of pre-modern Chinese society in which passing down the paternal bloodline was of paramount importance, marriage and procreation were unavoidable duties. On the other hand, traditional Chinese society did not see sexual pleasure as a sin in the way that some Christian societies did. Same-sex relationships were common, even within the imperial court, with some emperors' acts expressed in romantic phrases such as 'the divided peach' and 'the cut sleeve' which became euphemisms for homosexual love. Same-sex relationships were not regarded as problematic unless they posed a threat to family norms. There was no distinct category for 'homosexuals' and it was socially acceptable for high status men to dominate other men as well as women sexually. Consequently, like heterosexual relationships at the time, (male) homosexual relationships tended to be asymmetrical between the dominant and the subordinate rather than involving equal parties who were joined in fraternity (Mann 2011).

The 'modern' view that regarded homosexuality as 'abnormal' and homosexuals as 'outcasts' arrived from the West. The propagation of the idea of 'love supremacism' to place heterosexual love as the foundation of marriage played a role in promoting the view of homosexuality and homosexuals as undesirable. There was a period after the founding of the People's Republic of China in which homosexuality was seen as criminal and pathological as well as politically wrong. In recent years, the revision of this situation has been progressing and social movements in support of LGBT rights have become more active (see Column Five) (Shirouzu 2015).

Remaining challenges

While this book attempts to offer a comprehensive picture of the changes in gender structure and gender order in Chinese history as outlined above, many questions are inevitably left unresolved. Some of the remaining challenges are considered below.

Firstly, a majority of the chapters in this book deal with women's situations, even though the book is titled *Gender History in China*. While we set out to provide an overview of gender history, we also have no choice but to take into account the current state of research which has been strongly focused on trying to uncover the hidden history of women. There remains the task of painting a more concrete picture of the entire gender order through an investigation of various paths of gender and sexualities, including the histories of men as gendered subjects as well as LGBTs.

Secondly, China's gender order, once clarified, needs to be analyzed further in comparison with other countries and civilizations. Some of the particularly important discussion points are as follows.

To begin with, what will we find from a comparative analysis of social status and gender between Ming-Qing China and modern Europe? In the West, revolutions broke down the class system and established popular sovereignty under republicanism, but the 'citizens' who were considered as sovereign were only men, and in these societies social status was replaced by gender as a marker.[10] In China, the aristocracy was abolished at the time of the Tang–Song regime change and social power was subsequently held by government officials who had passed the imperial examinations, which almost all men were eligible to take regardless of their social status or ethnicity. In this high mobility society with fundamentally no fixed system of inherited class status, gender functioned as one indicator of social status and the family's social status was symbolized by the seclusion of chaste, footbound women inside the house. This can be regarded as a kind of analog of genderized civil society in early-modern Western Europe where the presence of the virtuous wife who governed the family domain was seen as proof of belonging to the bourgeoisie. Whether in modern or pre-modern times, the demise of a class system brought in gender as an indicator of social status. It seems that such similarity and difference require further consideration.

The next point is that Ming-Qing was a period in Chinese history when particularly strict – highly oppressive by our contemporary standards – gender norms were applied to women, such as intense pressure to maintain chastity and confining women inside the home. Similarly strict rules for women's chastity and seclusion were found in early-modern India and West Asian Islamic societies as well.[11] The strict gender norms for women in these ancient advanced civilizations shortly before the arrival of the modern age formed part of a complex colonial modernity as they were sometimes reinterpreted as the

---

10 See Mitsunari, Himeoka and Kohama (2014) for an overview of the results of many related studies.
11 See Note 10 above.

'essence of a traditional culture' in the subsequent colonization process. There is a need to study the gender norms in other civilizations and those of early-modern China from a comparative historical perspective.

Other points that require further comparative historical analysis include comparison and interaction between China's and Japan's gender orders. While early-modern China's and Japan's gender order and family structure were more different than one might expect, as mentioned above,[12] both societies have lived through their respective forms of colonial modernity.[13] The comparative study of gender order between China and Japan as well as their relationship is indispensable for a multi-dimensional understanding of the history of Japanese gender order since pre-modern times. We must not blame 'tradition' for the existing gender gap without careful empirical research, whether it be in China or Japan. For this reason, we need to understand 'traditional society' empirically and structurally from a comparative historical viewpoint.

Our third challenge is with regard to wartime violence and gender. Empirical research on the Japanese military's 'comfort women' in China has been progressing since the 1990s.[14] At the same time, there have been critical discussions on the social perception of the 'comfort women' issue in Japan and China and the underlying gender order in each society.[15] Although we were unable to include a chapter on this specific topic in this book, we would like to keep it in mind as an important subject for China's gender history in light of current progress in research on wartime violence in many parts of the world.

---

12 One example can be found in The Three Principles and The Five Disciplines of Confucian virtues. Where the Chinese text says 'Intimacy between father and son, faithfulness between sovereign and subject, distinction between husband and wife, precedence of the elder over the younger and faith between friends', the instruction on the husband and wife relationship was interpreted as a teaching to promote amicableness between them in Tokugawa-era Japan (Watanabe 2016).

13 See Koyama (1991), Jin Jung-Won (2006 [Japanese]) and others for the concept of 'good wife, wise mother' in Japan and China in modern times. See Sechiyama (1996) for a comparison of contemporary patriarchies.

14 Ishida and Uchida (2004) is a significant study.

15 Recent studies in Japan include Rekishigaku Kenkyūkai and Nihonshi Kenkyūkai (2014) and Hayashi (2015) and those in China include Qu Yajun (2013 [Japanese]), Jin Yihong (2014 [Japanese]) and Song Shaopeng (2016b [Japanese]).

The composition of the book

This book has been organized in the following manner.

Part One provides an overview and discussion of previous research findings on changes in China's gender order from prehistoric times to today centering on family structure. Shiga's 'Chinese family law' is used as a basis for discussion about pre-modern times while the 'modern family' of Western modernity serves as a springboard for modern and contemporary times. The pre-modern times are divided into two phases – 'Phase I: Pre-Qin to Sui-Tang: Classical China – The Formation of Patrilineal Society', and 'Phase II: Song to Ming-Qing: Traditional China – The Strengthening of Gender Norms'. We have attempted to demonstrate that Shiga's Chinese family law is applicable to the latter half. 'Phase III: Modern and Contemporary China – Changing Gender Order' retraces changes in the characteristics of gender order amid social transformation in the twentieth century before arriving at the current situation. Our discussions go beyond the family to cover various other aspects of gender. Each phase begins with an introduction to offer an overview of the relevant time periods, a brief summary of each chapter and some preceding studies of significance.

Part Two consists of studies that deal with topics that are important for gender history and matters concerning a more comprehensive history. Chapter Fifteen discusses the household registration system used by successive dynastic governments to control people as well as how the governments identified female family members through the male head of the family. Chapter Sixteen examines how talented women were appraised in Chinese society and reveals how chastity became an important criterion in addition to ability in early-modern times. Together with a review of women's literature in Chapter Three, this analysis helps illuminate the realities of China's 'talented women' and their appraisals in a three-dimensional way. Chapter Seventeen focuses on the Chinese view of the body in relation to Chinese cosmology and its shift from the standpoint of gender and considers how this understanding of male and female bodies differs from that in Western societies. Chapter Eighteen discusses the rise of women/gender studies in China during the reform and opening-up period in the context of the time. Column Five retraces the history of the treatment of LGBTs in Chinese society while Column Six introduces transgenderism, gender representation and its limitations in traditional theater forms such as Peking opera and *Yue* opera as well as recent changes in the images of women in theater.

It is our hope that these discussions will convey to the reader that casting a spotlight on gender in diverse fields enriches both historical research as well as the vision of those who live in the present.

Gender History in China

Gender History in China

PART I

Phase I
Pre-Qin to Sui-Tang: Classical China
The Formation of Patrilineal Society

Phase I

Introduction

— *SHIMOKURA Wataru*

The beginning of the gender perspective

It is extremely difficult to find the word 'gender' in studies of pre-Tang history in Japanese research on Chinese history. Publications on the history of the family as well as women's history appear to focus primarily on research into specific areas (such as political or socioeconomic history).[1] It is no exaggeration to say that there has been little impetus for researchers to shift their gaze toward the angle of 'sex-based differences'. This situation is gradually changing, albeit slowly.

In the discipline of pre-Tang history, prehistoric archaeology is perhaps the field in which the term 'gender' has gained the widest currency to date. Numerous prehistoric archaeological sites have been unearthed across China since the country embarked on large-scale domestic development under its reform and opening-up policies. The increasing number of discoveries of burial sites and artefacts has motivated researchers to take more interest in 'sex-based differences'. Needless to say, these burial sites contained the remains of both men and women. Investigations into burial practices have identified various sex-based differences including differences in burial goods; some of the differences may reflect different practices in different time periods and regions. These findings naturally turned researchers' attention toward endeavors to identify gender structures and the process of historical change in those structures in ancient times. The argument in Chapter One revolves around some of these archaeological materials from ancient burial sites.

Let me introduce some findings from research into the prehistoric age. The Peiligang site outside of Xinzheng City, Henan Province, is an early Neolithic cemetery site (10000–5000 BCE) along the middle stretches of the Yellow

---

[1] Examples in women's history include studies about women in positions of power such as Empress Lu of the Former Han dynasty and Empress Wu of Tang or the political status of empress and empress dowager in relation to them. The first thing that comes to mind in the field of family history studies is a debate (between Makino Tatsumi, Utsunomiya Kiyoyoshi and Moriya Mitsuo) over the average Han family configuration of 'a family of five' (*wukouzhijia*). This discussion spawned an argument about family theory that was closely linked with the history of the formation of the Qin-Han empires and the study of powerful clans as a factor that contributed to the transformation of the ancient empires.

River. One distinctive characteristic of this site is the combination of burial goods: this is the only site where stone shovels (hoe blades) and stone querns and rollers (for grinding millet grain) have been found in the same grave. The former were typically found exclusively in male tombs and the latter in female tombs. Based on this fact, Miyamoto Kazuo (2005: 117–118) surmises, 'There was a division of labor between the sexes in that tilling and earthwork were mainly carried out by men while flour milling was mainly performed by women' and that this suggests 'A society in which gender held great significance as a symbolic dualistic concept in social life within the community'.

Miyamoto (2005) also compared the volume of burial goods in individual tombs and found a number of women's tombs that contained higher numbers of items than men's tombs. This suggests that the volume of burial goods did not correlate with sex. Instead, the antemortem social status of the tomb owner – the individual's vocational capability based on the sexual division of labor and the social respect and authority attributed to the individual – determined how many burial goods were entombed. Such a society was a type of 'equal society' that chose its leaders based on their social function rather than heredity.

Next, the Jiangzhai site to the west of Xi'an is a famous archaeological site from the middle Neolithic period (5000–3500 BCE). It is a typical moat settlement of the Yangshao culture with at least three communal burial sites located outside of the moat. The burial sites can be divided into two types on the basis of burial practice. One type contains adult tombs in which the deceased were placed with their head to the west together with burial goods whereas the other type contains adult tombs in which the deceased were laid with their head pointing in various directions with few burial goods. Okamura Hidenori (2008: 33) argues that the former was the burial site for locals while the latter was that for those who had married into the local community from elsewhere, stating, 'Differentiation of burial sites according to one's descent indicates that the blood relationship rather than the matrimonial family relationship was the organizational principle of their society'. Okamura also claims that the society at the time was 'a bilateral descent society where people were able to choose between virilocality and uxorilocality at will after marriage' due to the fact that both male and female bones were found in the communal burial sites of both types.

The unisex placement of human bones in the communal tombs exhibits some changes near the end of the middle Neolithic Age. For example, the excavation of communal tombs (secondary burial sites) at the Shijia settlement site (Weinan, Shanxi Province) found that the multiple remains buried in each grave had been reburied on the basis of the cognate family (consanguinity) rather than the affinal family (affinity) and that there were more male than female bones. However, this bias was found only among adults. In other words, the difference between men and women was found among adults who were probably married.

This means that adult (married) women were no longer buried in the tombs of their consanguineous descent group. Miyamoto (2005: 124–125) explains this phenomenon by referring to an increasing 'tendency for women to marry into other groups while men remained in their descent group and took wives from other groups'. He summarizes the trend of the times where 'the gender-based dual organization characteristic of the early Neolithic Age' was lost and transitioned to the stage that featured the 'agnatic kin group as the basic unit of society'. The historical development from the late Neolithic Age (3500–2000 BCE) onward continued on from this middle Neolithic trend, as discussed in Chapter One.

Impacts from 'underground'

Artefacts unearthed from excavations are important sources not only for understanding prehistoric developments for which there are no written sources, but also for the study of later historical ages where they supplement written sources. A particularly significant impact has been felt by researchers who specialize in the period from the Warring States to the Qin-Han dynasties. For example, a string of discoveries of bamboo or wooden slips and boards buried in excavated tombs has greatly enlarged our base of knowledge. One example is the system of 'household registration' discussed in Chapter Fifteen. During the Han dynasty, the annual door-to-door census was carried out throughout a single state as the basis for the compilation of the so-called '*mingshu*' (name and number) registers. While it was previously supposed based on written historical records that '*ming xian jue li*' (name, residence and title) were recorded in the register, it is now possible to inspect the wooden strips which are believed to be actual examples of the register. Several examples are introduced in Chapter Fifteen.

In Chapter Fifteen, Washio Yūko argues that the 'household' is a unit of 'the sharing of residence and property' and that a married couple had to live in the same household. According to historical documents and unearthed laws and regulations, it was normally the husband's societal role to represent his 'household' as the householder while it was considered preferable for his female spouse to engage in domestic work as the 'wife'. In reality, it appears that in certain cases a divorced or widowed wife became the 'householder' on behalf of her sons as some artefacts have been found that record a woman as the 'householder'. Washio expects that the incidence of '*nühu*' (female-headed households) decreased further from Han to Tang as the Tang dynasty forbade women from becoming the householder if there was any man in the household.

Research into this period of women's history is definitely one of the fields that have been revitalized by the impact of the excavated written artefacts. Relevant research results are detailed in the work of Kotera Atsushi (2008: 15–18), although the emphasis is placed on studies of pre-Qin history. Instead of repeating Kotera's explanation of the overall situation, I shall introduce one extremely important 'new discovery' below.

The Tang Code (penal code) stipulated that the penalty for an assault causing bodily harm to a wife by a husband should be lighter by two degrees than that imposed for a similar offence between other people ('Injury to wife and concubine caused by beating', *Tang Code with Commentary and Explanations*, Vol. 22). It is clear that the husband's sentence was reduced on the basis of the norm of 'husband is superior, wife is inferior' (*fuzun qibei*). This stance remained the same in later dynastic codes, and it was thought to have been the same prior to the Tang Code. However, archaeological discoveries have shown that this was not the case.

Twelve Qin tombs were discovered in a place called Shuihudi in Yunmeng, Hubei Province, in 1975 and over 1,100 bamboo slips were excavated from one of the tombs. The artefacts are known as 'Bamboo Slips from the Qin Tomb at Shuihudi' and contain legal writings that offer a glimpse of the penal code at the time. According to the excavated texts, the Qin Code stipulated that if the husband caned and injured his violent wife, he would be sentenced to the same penalty as in an assault causing injury involving people other than a husband and wife. In other words, there was no distinction between a married couple and other people in terms of the severity of punishment for assault. The 'ethical principal' of a husband's superiority over his wife that we see in the Tang Code is not evident in Qin law. In fact, we must take note of its weak influence.

The new information on the Qin-period code astonished researchers, giving rise to the hypothesis that, unlike in Tang, the idea of setting different degrees of penalty for cases of husband-wife assaults and other assaults did not exist in the Qin Code. Based on the above information, Hori Toshikazu (1996: 86) and Takenami Takayoshi (1995) naturally concluded that wife and husband were treated equally and that their legal statuses were relatively 'equal' at the time. Others such as Yoshida Kōichi (2012: 166–167) put forward the view that this was evidence that at that time the husband's patriarchal authority was yet to be established. Kotera Atsushi (2008) suggests that the progress of research into the excavated artefacts is forcing a revision of the established view that pre-Qin women were 'placed lower in status' than men. This shift is also taking place in the study of the Qin-Han period. It is no exaggeration to say that the perception that 'Women's status had been higher than previously thought' has become a common recognition in the field of ancient Chinese history. Nevertheless, the above view is still at an embryonic stage. The shock of new discoveries has sparked new images and ideas about these societies. It is imperative that the task of verifying the new information and painting a complete picture is taken up. Chapter Two by Shimokura is one such attempt.

Shimokura Wataru examines the cases of maternal half brothers and sisters found in *Records of the Grand Historian* (*Shiji*) and *History of the Former Han* (*Hanshu*) and argues that the sharing of the same father (family name) was not regarded as an absolute criterion to differentiate the relationship between siblings during the Han period because 'non-patrilineal' relations such as this were not necessarily cast aside as irregular relationships at the time. In fact, he suspects that the relationship between a mother and her biological children was treated with importance and hence their awareness, by extension, of other maternal relations was quite high; for example, they would have had a strong a sense of belonging to the same family group as their maternal uncles or sister's sons (nephews).

Dynamic women

Shimokura reviews historical records about princesses (emperors' daughters) through successive periods to demonstrate that their relationships with their husbands changed after the Han dynasty. During and after the Three Kingdoms-Wei period (220–265) for example, an imperial princess lived with her husband and became a member of his family as the 'wife', just as in the case of ordinary women. Shimokura theorizes that as the Confucian family ethics placed more emphasis on male superiority over women, it was considered ideal that even emperors' daughters should abide by the ways of women as dictated by Confucian norms.

On the other hand, Chapter Sixteen by Itahashi Akiko discusses the images of women during the Wei, Jin and Northern and Southern Dynasties period (220–589). In aristocratic society at the time, men began to break free of the late

Han Confucian ethical code in search of new ways of being. In conjunction with the change in men's behavior, aristocratic women were newly motivated to pursue academic and cultural accomplishments and enjoyed a sense of independence that women of the preceding era had not experienced. In her discussion, Itahashi cites Shimomi Takao who explains that 'the women of this period were not necessarily bound by the framework of the family institution and engaged in a wide variety of actions that could not be constrained unilaterally by simple Confucian values such as fidelity and obedience' (Shimomi 1994: 106–107). It is important to note that this view of women is considerably different from that in Shimokura's argument on the women of the Six Dynasties period who became trapped under the Confucian ethical code (patriliny-based family ethics).

Understandings such as Shimomi's have a deep connection with what Kamiya Noriko (1994: 28–31) called the 'Wei-Jin cultural theory', which examines the cultural aspects of the Wei-Jin period (including the Northern and Southern Dynasties period that followed) in comparison with the preceding Han period. The Han (especially Later Han) period was strongly colored by Confucianism-based cultural politics where Confucian teachings governed every inch of the workings of the state and society as well as people's thoughts and behavior. By contrast, non-Confucian spiritual cultures such as the teachings of Laozi and Zhuangzi, Taoism and Buddhism, flourished during the Wei, Jin and Northern and Southern Dynasties period and gave rise to strong criticism that Confucian norms were formalistic.[2] People praised actions that disregarded and diverged from the 'ethics' proselytized by Confucians. Specific anecdotes about these intellectuals can be found in *A New Account of the Tales of the World* (*Shishuo Xinyu*), composed during the Song (420–497), one of the Southern Dynasties. Kamiya describes the book as a 'bible for Wei-Jin culture theory', and some of its stories feature a woman in a central role. The following is one such example.

> Wang Hun and his wife Zhong were sitting together and saw their son Wuzi walking past the garden. Wang Hun smiled and said to his wife, "Having a son like him put our mind at ease". The wife laughed and said, "Had I married your younger brother Wang Lun, I might have had even more outstanding children".

---

[2] The Wei, Jin and Northern and Southern Dynasties period has been regarded as a time of the decline of Confucianism from the perspective of its historical development, but Kamiya defines the Wei-Jin culture theory as a historical view that positively reinterprets such situation.

This account shows no deference to Confucian female virtues or the blind acceptance of women's inferiority. From the perspective of 'Wei-Jin culture', like the change in thought and behavior among male aristocrats, the deeds and words of these women were highly appreciated as an expression of the post-Confucian spirit of the age.

There is a strong tendency for the above view of women to find support among scholars of literature and philosophy perhaps because it originates in 'cultural theory'. On the other hand, the mainstream view in the field of history, especially the history of the family and legal history, appears to differ. For example, Hori Toshikazu (1996: 116–117, 131–135) argues that in China, the patriarch's authority directly extended, since ancient times, to include 'parents, wife and children, as well as siblings'. It was thought that their cohabitation as one family was ideal from the standpoint of emphasizing filiality to parents under what was called the 'three-family system'. This 'three-family system' referred to an enlarged family that had a married adult man at its core and included the man's wife, children, parents and the man's older and younger brothers and their families. The family began to grow in size at the end of Former Han when 'Confucianism flourished and the three-family system probably came to be glorified' and this trend intensified in the Six Dynasties period that saw the appearance of 'the large family form where multiple generations lived together headed by a direct ascendant' (Hori 1996). While the three-family system 'had to maintain harmony between brothers and impose subservience on their wives in particular' to ensure the sustainability of its form, this requirement came to be recognized and enforced by penal law as well as moral codes. The argument presented in Chapter Two of this book that the 'patrilineality' of the family and society in China increased from the Wei-Jin period accords with this historical perspective.

When we survey historical research on the Six Dynasties period with 'women' as the keyword, we find a major contradiction. There are two conflicting views about the attitude of people toward Confucianism at the time. One interpretation argues that the spirit of opposition to the ritual system embodied in Confucianism represents the spirit of the age. The other view takes a directly opposed position, arguing that it was efforts to encode Confucian principles in society that represented the spirit of the age. In the words of Noriko Kamiya (1994), the researchers' historical perspectives are widely split 'between these two views of Confucianism'. As this division is closely aligned with the conflicting views about women, reconciling the two sides is not an easy task.

There is yet another contradiction inherent in this body of research. Previous studies have emphasized the 'dynamism', 'strength' and 'freedom' of Tang women, pointing to people such as Empress Wu Zetian and Princess Taiping. Scholars commonly attributed these qualities to the 'customs that were characteristic of northern equestrian tribes unaffected by Confucian Chinese ethical values' that made inroads into China during the Northern Dynasty period.[3] As Sasaki Megumi states in the 'Phase II Introduction', however, most studies on the Jin and Yuan dynasties claim that the same northern tribal customs were partly to blame for the decline in women's social status at the time. As for the influence of northern tribal customs on the status of women, scholars of Tang history are inclined to stress the positive influence of these customs on women's status, while scholars studying the Jin and Yuan dynasties tend to stress their negative impacts. Is it the case that these totally opposite phenomena grew from the same seed in different times? Again, a contradiction is evident here.

The possibility of a gender perspective

I now briefly look at research on the Tang period. Previous studies have suggested that marriage at the time was characterized by a high incidence of divorce and remarriage. They have explained this fact by arguing that Tang women placed a low value on chastity and this phenomenon was an expression of the spirit of the age, namely, a 'disregard for the Confucian ethical code'. Ōsawa Masaaki (2005a) reflects on this explanation and theorizes as follows. Women (wives) during the period from the Northern and Southern Dynasties to Sui-Tang had the means to support themselves. They engaged in not only domestic work but also activities outside the home to support their husband and sons. Their dynamic activity underpinned their strength and at the same time contributed to the high incidence of divorce and remarriage. Moreover, at the time the wife's parental family – the relatives who the husband would have seen as his 'wife's family' and who she saw as 'her own family' – strongly supported her and her husband's (their son-in-law's) activity. In literary historical materials, there is evidence of cases of weddings being held at the wife's family home or young couples apparently living with the wife's family after marriage. They seem to be clear examples that contradict the patrilineal principle (Ōsawa 2005a: 55–68).

---

3 See Kegasawa Yasunori (2005: 183) for example.

Ōsawa also refers to the Tang-era family, summarizing that 'people in those days had a mentality that was tolerant towards free sexual relationships outside of marriage' and defining attitudes as a reflection of what the nineteenth century anthropologist Lewis H. Morgan described as a 'syndyasmian marriage-level mentality'.[4] It was 'the age when the syndyasmian mentality coexisted with the monogamous moral code' and this ingenuous mentality remained alive in people's consciousness even though the monogamous ideology had already become the state-endorsed moral standard in the Tang period. Accordingly, the 'family' (the small, nuclear family with the husband-wife relationship at its core) as a unit 'had not reached the surface of society and was therefore yet to be normalized in people's consciousness' at this stage. The 'indistinctness of the family union' underwent changes through the dynastic transition from Tang to Song, and 'the family, especially the nuclear family, as a group came to occupy a certain position in people's consciousness' during the Song period (Ōsawa 2005a: 78–86).

According to Ōsawa's understanding, a major change in women's status as well as the notion of family took place in the period from Tang to Song. Chapter Two of Ōsawa's study cited earlier entitled 'Jealous wives' argues that the Northern and Southern Dynasties period was a time when jealous wives 'were societally acceptable, so to speak'. Wives (i.e. officially recognized wives) used jealousy as a weapon in their effort to maintain monogamy in their marriages. In Tang, however, domestic situations such as 'the strong wife, the weak husband' came to be treated as objects of humor that could not be discussed openly. In Song, 'jealous wives' became something to be suppressed both in terms of the state's treatment of them and in the public attitude toward them. The 'freedom to be jealous' was taken away from the wives. In addition, the status of officially recognized wife came to be safeguarded against concubines in efforts toward 'the practical establishment of the small family, the strengthening of cohesion between the married couple and within the family', and 'jealousy' was no longer a necessary weapon used by wives to maintain monogamy in their marriage.

---

4 The American anthropologist L. H. Morgan (1818–1881) sketched a picture of the evolution of marriage types in human history, beginning with a prehistoric pattern characterized by a kind of group marriage, then passing through several stages before arriving at monogamous marriage between one husband and one wife. In Morgan's scheme, the stage immediately preceding monogamy was a stage he referred to as 'syndyasmian marriage', which involved an unstable relationship between a man and a woman, in which either the man or the woman might have sexual relations with someone other than their partner. Morgan's evolutionary theory had a major influence on Engels' *The Origin of the Family, Private Property and the State*, published in German in 1884.

In short, Ōsawa argues that pre-Tang women were dynamic and the nuclear family relationship was not established until the Song period. While this theory has no direct association with the aforementioned Wei-Jin culture theory, both differ from the interpretation put forward by Hori and others in a similar way. Ōsawa himself quotes Hori's view, noting 'There appears to be a minor difference' between it and his argument. He adds that he could not do much about the narrowness of the focus as the scope of his study was the period from the Northern and Southern Dynasties onward (2005a: 134). Nonetheless, is the 'difference' lurking here really a 'minor' one stemming from the 'narrowness of the focus'? As quoted by Ōsawa, Hori (1996: 87) argues that 'The social status differential between the husband and the wife increased greatly from the time of the Qin Code to the Tang. On the other hand, Ōsawa suggests that the nuclear family-type marriage relationship had not yet been established even during the Tang; in making this judgement, Ōsawa uses the social situation in Song as a benchmark and emphasizes the 'strength' of Tang women (wives). While Hori stresses the increasing oppression of women from Qin through successive periods, Ōsawa finds an 'easygoing attitude' in the Northern and Southern Dynasties, Sui and Tang period in comparison with what he sees as the practice during the Song period. In comparing the explanations of Hori and Ōsawa, we can say that the former deals with the history of official state ideology while the latter looks at the actual social atmosphere. It seems that there is an unbridgeable gap between the standpoints of these two explanations.

In previous studies of Chinese women's history of ancient and medieval times there was a tendency to regard the relatively high social status of women (wives) and the weak union between husband and wife as 'hallmarks of the age' that captured the interest of researchers. Hori and Ōsawa are not exceptions to this trend, but the issue here is how they phrase their questions. There used to be a strong tendency to use adjectives to explain these characteristics – women's status being 'high or low' and the marriage union being 'strong or weak'. Let us call this the 'adjectival explanation method' limited to comparisons between a specific period and those immediately before and after it. From Ōsawa's standpoint in the Song period, it is possible to explain the Northern and Southern Dynasties and the Sui and Tang period immediately before it, but it becomes difficult to trace back to the Qin and Han period to discuss its characteristics.[5]

---

5 In fact, Ōsawa (2005a: 68) claims that the Han customs continued to be followed during the Tang. The argument places more emphasis on continuity with the Qin-Han period than difference from it.

Conversely, a challenge for Hori's position is whether it is possible to offer a concrete picture of change from Song onward beyond adjectival explanations (e.g., 'The level of oppression increased further').

Comparative analysis between different historical times is of course an important technique for historical science. However, its primary objective must be to describe conditions during each historical period. A study must go far enough to be able to describe 'forms' peculiar to each period using substantives and not stop at evaluating differences using degrees of adjectives. How can this be achieved? I believe that a gender perspective is an effective approach. Substantively explaining the structure and order of sex distinctions in each period can overcome the problems the adjective-based studies of the history of women and family have had in the past and help us to reach the next stage of comparative historical research.

Accumulated empirical research

The gap between Hori's and Ōsawa's theories stems from a rift in the perceptions and evaluations of women and the family in the Six Dynasties, Sui and Tang period. In fact, the amount of research in this field of Chinese historical research in Japan is far from abundant. In particular, the body of research on the history of the family is rather small, even though the said period has been generalized as the 'age of aristocracy'. In the current state of affairs, we must increase our efforts to accumulate empirical studies while we hammer out our research perspective.

This book has been compiled to inform a wide range of readers interested in China's gender history about the current state of research. In this sense, Phase I chapters should have been devoted to the review and reorganization of preceding studies. Nevertheless, the state of the field as it stands prompted us to include discussions of a more empirical nature. Below is a brief outline of the chapters and columns other than those mentioned above.

Column Two outlines how past studies of Empress Wu Zetian were largely concerned with the history of her 'success story' and paid scant attention to the later stage of her life and thereafter – the political process from the time she named Zhongzong as crown prince to her death, and her treatment during the reigns of Emperors Zhongzong, Ruizong and Xuanzong. How was she evaluated in the period shortly after her death by the courts of her sons Zhongzong and Ruizong and her grandson Xuanzong? This seems to be an important question that should be examined from the angle of women's history and gender history as well as political history. There is a need to clarify not only the forces that pushed her into the position of the only empress in Chinese history but also the process of her 'downfall' – the process in which her increasingly negative reputation led to a general denial of women's right to govern and the eventual infamy of being regarded as an 'unparalleled wicked woman'.

Another set of problems in relation to Tang history that cannot be overlooked is the treatment of the Dunhuang manuscripts as discussed by Arakawa in Column One. The manuscripts include what appear to be model documents (*shuyi*) for divorce bills and wills which suggest the practices of female-initiated divorce and the distribution of family property to unmarried women in this region at the time. These phenomena are clearly 'non-patrilineal' practices but the substance of their peculiarity needs to be assessed cautiously with due consideration of the historical context during the Tang period (i.e., women were in a socially 'strong' position) as well as Dunhuang's unique regional traits (i.e., a largely Han population in a Central Asian oasis city situated on the periphery of China), as Arakawa rightly points out. These considerations must also be taken into account when evaluating the Dunhuang manuscripts as historical resources.

Chapter Three by Satake discusses the old-established form of poetry written on the premise that 'a woman grieves about sleeping alone in the bedchamber'. Many of the works in this 'boudoir lament' genre were written by men who depicted their ideal woman – the delicate and fragile 'waiting woman' who continues to love her man even when he neglects her. Some women's grievance-type poems were written by women, and Matsuura Tomohisa (1986) argues that the Tang women who wrote these poems accepted the stereotypical feminine image favored by men because a majority of their works imitated stories written through the eyes of male poets. By contrast, Satake Yasuko surveys the poems supposedly written by women from the time of the *Classic of Songs* (*Shijing*) to the Song dynasty and argues that while the poems written by women in the latter half of the Six Dynasties period were all about women's grievances, the number of poems about 'waiting women' was surprisingly small in earlier periods. Yu Xuanji of Tang, who was a master of women's grievance poetry, and Li Qingzhao of Song, many of whose works were classified under the women's grievance genre, created 'women's literature' by adopting images of women that differed from men's ideal type and expressing sensibilities that went far beyond men's perspectives at the time. Satake's understanding is considerably different from Matsuura's observations, which focused on the Tang period alone, and is an excellent comparative historical study.

Finally, I shall briefly mention the research situation outside Japan. In the English-language scholarship in this field, Patricia Buckley Ebrey has played a leading role. While Ebrey is best known for her work on gender history in the Song dynasty, her first book, *Aristocratic Families of Early Imperial China: A Case Study of the Po-ling Ts'ui Family* (1978) is on family history from the Han through the Tang. In this book she traces the history of the rise and fall of the Ts'ui family as an example of aristocratic families during this period. In Taiwan, 'gender history' has been established as a research field along with women's history. Researchers have been analyzing various historical materials from different angles and presenting their findings to the world, for example Liu Tseng-Kuei on the Qin-Han period and Lee Jen-Der and Cheng Ya-Ju on the Six Dynasties, Sui and Tang period. In Chapter Four of this volume, Wong Yu-Hsuan introduces current research activity in Taiwan with a focus on studies of the family and kin relations in Tang and considers work by scholars in Taiwan and Japan on the Tang family and gender issues.

Chronology of Chinese Dynasties

Paleolithic Era

Neolithic Era (c. 10000 BCE–c. 2000 BCE)

Shang (商) (c. 1600 BCE–c. 1050 BCE)

Western Zhou (西周) (c. 1050 BCE–c. 771 BCE)

Spring and Autumn Period (春秋) (770 BCE–476 BCE)

Warring States (战国) (475 BCE–221 BCE)

Qin (秦) (221 BCE–206 BCE)

Western Han (西汉) (206 BCE–8 CE)

Xin (新) (8–23 CE)

Eastern Han (东汉) (23–220)

Three Kingdoms Period (三国) (220–280) (Wei 魏, Wu 吴, Shu 蜀)

Western Jin (西晋) (265–316)

Northern and Southern Dynasties (南北朝)

(in the north) Sixteen Kingdoms of the Five Barbarians (五胡十六国) (303–436)

   Northern Wei (北魏) (386–534), Western Wei (西魏) (535–556), Northern Zhou (北周) (556–581), Eastern Wei (东魏) (534–550), Northern Qi (北齐) (550–577)

(in the south) Six Dynasties (六朝)

   Wu 吴, Eastern Jin (东晋) (317–420), Song (宋) (420–479), Qi (齐) (479–502), Liang (梁) (502–557),

Chen (陈) (557–589)

Sui (隋) (581–618)

Tang (唐) (618–907)

The Five Dynasties and the Ten Kingdoms (五代十国) (907–960)
(in the north) Liao (辽) (907–1125)
Song (宋) (960–1127)
(in the north) Jin (金) (1115–1234)
(in the south) Southern Song (南宋) (1127–1279)
Yuan (Mongol) (元) (1206–1368)
Ming (明) (1368–1644)
Qing (清) (1636–1912)

Republic of China (中华民国) (1912–)
People's Republic of China (中华人民共和国) (1949–)

1. Gender Structure in Pre-Qin China from an Archaeological Perspective

— *UCHIDA Junko*

Introduction

Taking an archaeological approach to gender history can shed light on how women lived and their position in society in pre-Qin China. This chapter, based on a careful reading of archaeological research over the last several decades, examines changes in the gender structure of early societies, from the earliest records of the Neolithic era, approximately 10,000 years ago, through the Spring and Autumn and Warring States periods to the pre-Qin era in the third century BCE. Over that long time span, we can trace the development of a social formation beginning from a tribal society to one centered on the patrilineal line, with a gendered division of labor characterized by the phrase 'men till and women weave' and a political system in which core roles were dominated by men. In the feudal society of the Western Zhou period, marriage was regarded as a woman's most important function. Among the aristocracy of that era, although a woman's position was lower than that of her husband, it was still a position with a certain status. Research on pre-Qin women is limited due to the scarcity of written records. On the other hand, archaeology treats extant artifacts and ruins as research materials. While these materials are fragmentary, gathering artifacts and relics in relation to women and carefully assembling and reconstructing more complete pictures can provide clues about their lives. In the late twentieth century, David N. Keightley analyzed materials found in Neolithic era tombs, arguing that there were already hints of a lowering of the status of women. His analysis of oracle bone records found in the tombs of the first dynasty (Shang) suggested that there was a growing gap in status between men and women

Chapter 1

(Keightley 1999). This chapter uses the results of archaeological research on gender in the years since Keightley's path-breaking work to present an overview of the current state of knowledge in this field.

Archaeological materials from tombs

Before moving to a detailed discussion of the archaeological materials, let us begin with a brief review of the social changes during the periods under discussion. The earliest known representations of female figures are from the Paleolithic Age, and it is widely known that Venus figurines have been found in various parts of the Eurasian Continent. It is highly likely that goddess worship also existed in China, as evidenced by the discovery of a notable goddess statue from the Hongshan culture in the middle of the Neolithic Age (Imamura 2002: 1–14). It is believed that matrilineal society was predominant in early civilizations prior to the early part of the Neolithic Age (up to c. 5000 BCE), and it is generally thought that women's social status was high in such cultural contexts.

It is clear from written records that politics was dominated by men during the Spring and Autumn and Warring States periods at the final stage of the age discussed in this chapter, because there is virtually no mention of women who played history-making roles. Accordingly, we can surmise that China's gender structure underwent a significant change over a period of several thousand years from the Neolithic Age to the Spring and Autumn and Warring States periods.

Particular emphasis will be placed on materials found in tombs in order to interpret the circumstances of the change on the basis of information gleaned from archaeological materials. This information is sorted and interpreted using data such as the scale and location of the tombs, the type of burial goods and the estimated ages of the tomb owners based on their remains. These clues are used to discuss the lives, wealth and social status of the people who lived during the different stages of this very long period.

It is thought that the Neolithic Age (from c. 10,000 BCE), when humans began to settle down to engage in cropping and animal husbandry, saw the emergence of a number of cultural patterns in various locations on the Chinese central plain where each community fostered a culture compatible with the local climate. In the late Neolithic Age (from c. 3500 BCE), what we call an urban culture had not yet developed, even though archaeological sites of large communities or villages have been unearthed in the central area of each culture.

Large-scale population centers called 'royal capitals' evolved in the Yellow River Valley during the early states period that began with the Erlitou culture (said to coincide with the Xia dynasty from 2000 BCE). The gap in the cultural standards between the cities and rural villages widened. Writing was invented by the late Shang (Yin) dynasty period (the Yinxu period from c. 1300 BCE to c. 1050 BCE) and used in the strengthening of the system of government, thus transforming the social system significantly. The Western Zhou period (c. 1050 BCE–770 BCE) saw the appearance and development of small-scale cities under feudal rulers in various places along stretches of the Yellow River and began to show clear signs of decentralization that would lead to the Spring and Autumn and Warring States periods (770 BCE–221 CE) that followed. The time period from the Shang dynasty to the Spring and Autumn and Warring States periods was dominated by wars to consolidate these regional city-states. As societies evolved at different speeds at different stages of development, the sizes and contents of tombs diverged greatly between the tombs of citizens of large urban cultures and those in small regional villages.

There are a limited number of excavated tomb sites that are large enough in size and number of materials to allow a comparative study across China over time. Nonetheless, this chapter treats Neolithic burial sites on the assumption that the communities that created these tombs were at similar stages of social development regardless of their difference in size. For the period after the early states period, on the other hand, the level of social development is thought to be a major factor in the discussion of change in gender disparity. Accordingly, the small and large tombs in cities and the regional tombs shall be examined separately.

Gender-based difference in buried tools

This section will consider the development of a gender division of labor during the early Neolithic period (10,000–5,000 years ago) and its expansion during the later Neolithic era (from 3,500 years ago).

There is no marked size difference and hence class difference among tombs from the early part of the Neolithic Age. The Peiligang site in Xinzheng, Henan Province, reportedly yielded stone shovels for tilling and earthwork from its male tombs and stone querns and rollers for grinding grain from female tombs. These variations point to a gender difference in agricultural work. A collective

Chapter 1

burial compound in the Jiangzhai site, Lintong, Shanxi Province, from the middle Neolithic Age shows signs of separation into two family lines, which is considered to be a phenomenon representing a dual organization (moiety) system under which a society is maintained through matrimonial relationships between two moieties.[1] One theory proposes that male kinship groups became the basic units of society in the latter half of the middle Neolithic (Miyamoto 2005: 114–126). This evidence suggests that a transition to patrilineal society occurred as social class distinctions between groups emerged during this period.

Class difference generally became more noticeable in the late Neolithic Age, with many tombs containing varying amounts of burial goods. This time period also features handicraft products such as jade ware, which were manufactured by a special process using materials from specific sources, and earthenware, which were formed on lathes and fired in high-temperature kilns. In other words, professionals appeared and engaged in bulk production and their products were distributed to broader areas during this period.

According to Sun Yan and Yang Hongyu, who analyzed adult male and female tombs of the Majiayao culture and the Qijia culture in the Huangniangniangtai site, Wuwei, Gansu Province, many of the cemeteries with relatively high numbers of tools among burial goods tended to contain axes, chisels, knives and other implements in male tombs and spindle whorls in female tombs, although some male and female tombs contained mostly the same burial goods (Sun and Yang 2004 [English]: 32–38). Spindle whorls have been found in a very small number of male tombs,[2] but these cases are exceptions rather than the rule. This tendency has also been observed widely in other parts of China, including the Zaozhuang burial site of the Dawenkou culture, the Wangyin site (Shandong Province: Figure 1.1) and the Wuxue Gushan site of the Qujialing culture (Hubei Province) (Namba 2005: 78–80). It is likely that women's responsibilities gradually came to be established along with the change in society during the Neolithic Age.

---

[1] Some argue that it was a bilateral descent society (Okamura 2008: 33; see Phase I Part I Introduction).

[2] This suggests that either men were also engaged in spinning or that the spindle whorl was simply regarded as a family asset.

Gender Structure in Pre-Qin China from an Archaeological Perspective

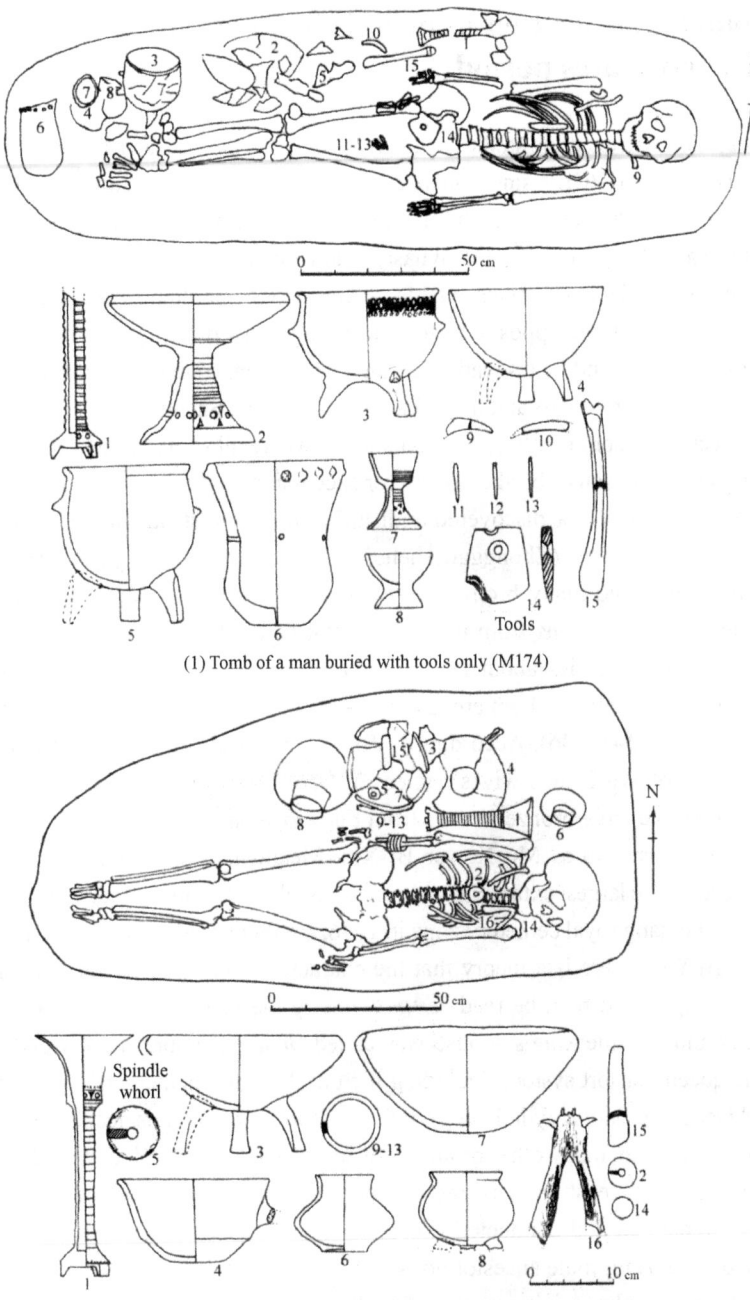

(1) Tomb of a man buried with tools only (M174)

(2) Tomb of a woman buried with a spindle whorl (M2201)

Figure 1.1 Tombs of a man and a woman in the Neolithic Age
Source: Zhongguo shehui kexueyuan kaogu yanjiusuo (2000: Figures 149 and 153).

Chapter 1

Women and written materials from the early states period

This section will examine studies on the roles of women in the later Shang period (1300 BCE–1050 BCE) using evidence from oracle bone records and inscriptions on bronze vessels found in tombs at Yinxu. Yinxu is a large archaeological site, the last capital city of the Shang dynasty, that includes the Xiaotun Palace zone on the bank of the Huan River outside of Anyang City and the Xibeigang royal cemetery zone on the opposite bank. The Shang kings ruled based on portents from turtle shells and bones read by augurs. According to studies of inscriptions on bones and turtle shells and historical documents, the Shang dynasty is said to have been a predominantly patrilineal society where all of its kings were male through father to son or brother to brother succession.

Yinxu Tomb 5 was discovered undisturbed on the west side of the Xiaotun Palace zone in 1976 (Zhongguo shehui kexueyuan kaogu yanjiusuo 1980). Excavations found many bronze vessels inscribed with the words 'Fu Hao'. Oracle bone inscriptions from the time of Wu Ding, the twenty-third king of Shang, record auguries about nearly seventy 'ladies', including Fu Hao, Fu Jing and Fu Wo, all of whom are said to have been the king's wives (consorts) (Ochiai 2015: 141–146). Accordingly, Tomb 5 is considered to be the burial site of one of Wu Ding's wives named Fu Hao. The inscription of 'Simuxin' on some of the large bronze vessels from Fu Hao's tomb suggests that she was formally referred to as Mu Xin or Bi Xin. Meanwhile, the words 'Mu Wu' inscribed on the largest extant Shang bronze vessel, the Simuwu ding, excavated in the Xibeigang royal cemetery zone in 1946, are thought to refer to Wu Ding's queen Bi Wu. There is a theory that the characters '*hou*' (后 / queen) and '*si*' (司 / serve) should both be read as '*hou*' due to the fact that they are mirror-images and that the king's spouse was called '*hou*'. Opinions are divided as to the queen consort system, including the question of whether such a system would lead to monogamy in later periods, and further research is needed on this issue. In addition, many other bronzeware and oracle bone inscriptions indicate that women were enshrined as 'mother' or 'ancestor goddess'. It is certain that people venerated and conducted rituals for female ancestor goddesses to the same degree as for male ancestor gods.

On the other hand, it is supposed that all augurs were men, and female names such as Fu Jing found among carved characters on the edges of turtle shells are thought to be records of shell sorting work. Based on this evidence, some argue that women were engaged in the sorting process at the palace (Miao Lijuan 2013: 21–25). In any case, this shows a phenomenon in which men controlled early writing and held a monopoly over politics while women lacked agency.

Shang kings and their wives from an archaeological perspective

The previous section used evidence from oracle bones and inscriptions on bronzeware; this section will look at the burial goods found in imperial tombs as a way to examine the differences in status between the king and his queen and others among his consorts.

Excavations in the Xibeigang royal cemetery site have found eight large cross-shaped tombs with four sloping ramps, one large partially constructed tomb, three large tombs with two sloping ramps and one large tomb with one sloping ramp (Figure 1.2). The large-scale grave pits with two or four sloping ramps in the royal cemetery are believed to be the tombs of successive Shang kings. Some scholars speculate that Xibeigang HPKM1001 must be Wu Ding's tomb (Liang Siyong and Gao Quxun 1962) due to its temporal proximity to the aforementioned Fu Hao burial goods discovered in the Xiaotun Palace zone, but I believe that Wu Ding's grave is Tomb 1400 and that 84AWBM260, which is situated directly in line with the southern ramp of Tomb 1400 and in which the aforementioned Simuwu ding was discovered, is the tomb of his queen consort Bi Wu.[3] As these three tombs consist of very important materials that allow a comparative study of a Shang king and his queen, we shall undertake a detailed comparison below.

The pit dimensions of Tomb 1400 are 18.3 meters by 15.7 meters, with a depth of 10.6 meters and length of 74.1 meters in a north-south direction and 48.9 meters in an east-west direction if ramps are included. Tomb 260 has a pit of 9.6 by 8.1 meters with a depth of 8.1 meters, about half the size of the Tomb 1400 pit. Including its southern ramp, its length is 33.6 meters. The Fu Hao tomb has

---

3 One theory posits that 'Mu Wu' refers to Fu Jing, Wu Ding's wife (Lin Jialin 2006: 78–88). As Tomb WBM260 in which the Simuwu vessel was reportedly found had been plundered, only a small portion of the burial goods it held are known today. Ying Wang (2004: 98–101) points out that there is a wife's tomb with a single access ramp together with eight cross-shaped tombs of male kings in one section of the Xibeigang royal cemetery and that its configuration is one rank below the kings' tombs.

Chapter 1

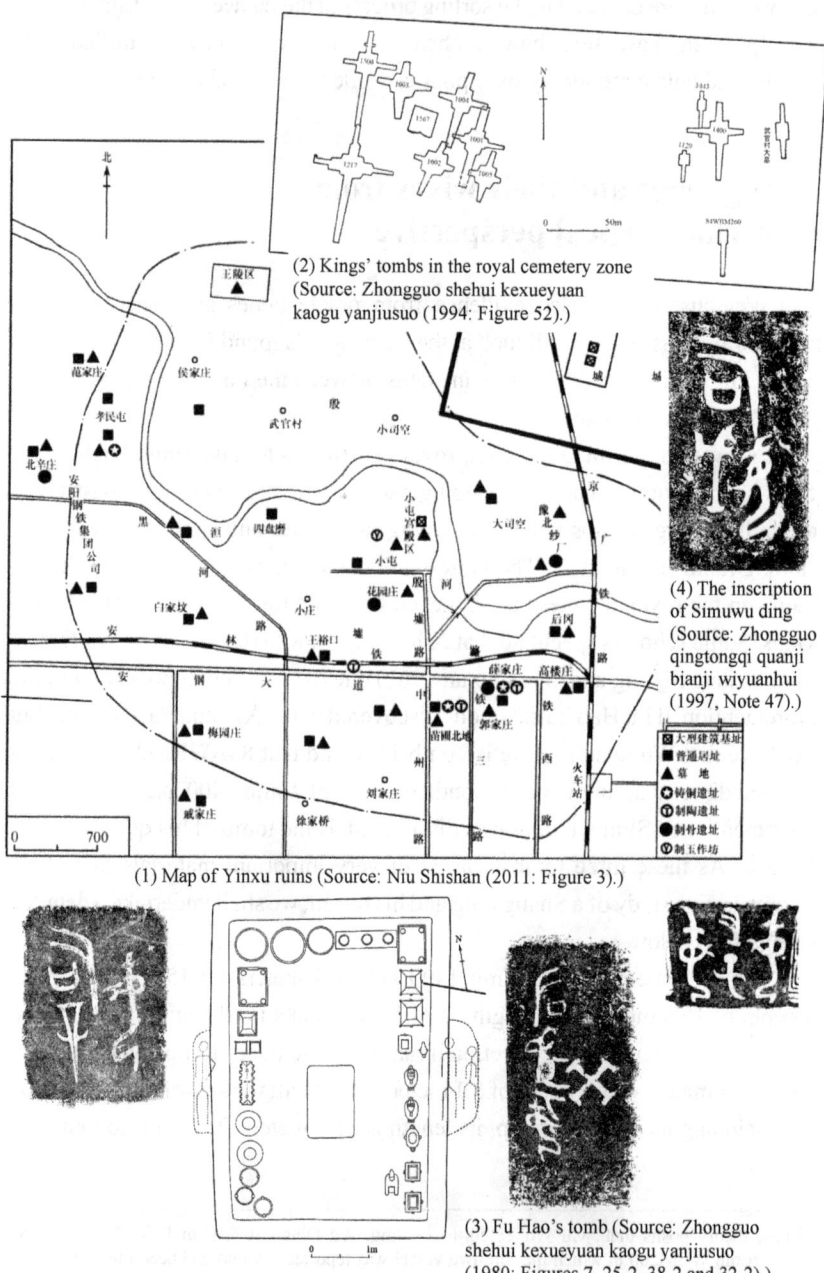

Figure 1.2 Relative positions of the royal cemetery and Fu Hao's tomb in Yinxu

− 50 −

Gender Structure in Pre-Qin China from an Archaeological Perspective

a pit of 5.6 by 4 meters with a depth of 7.5 meters, which is less than one-third of the size of Tomb 1400. The tomb size together with the existence and number of access ramps are considered to indicate differences in social status. It is expected that shrines were constructed on the large tombs in the royal cemetery as well as Fu Hao's tomb to highlight their presence. Tomb 1400 and Tomb 260 are aligned in a north-south direction while Fu Hao's tomb is located in a different area. As Tomb 1400 and Tomb 260 form the only case at the Xibeigang royal cemetery in which a queen's tomb was built alongside a king's, we can surmise that kings' and queens' tombs were generally built on separate sites.

Inscriptions on bones and turtle shells about Fu Hao reveal auguries about such matters as military success, childbearing and toothaches (Figure 1.3). While they provide glimpses into her daily life, the involvement of the king's wife in the military is worthy of attention. Moreover, 134 items of bronze weapons and military objects were found buried in Fu Hao's tomb as if to corroborate the records. It is worth noting that they include many symbolic and practical weapons such as two large axes with the inscription 'Fu Hao', which were regarded as symbols of power at the time, two smaller axes, ninety-one dagger axes and six bow-shaped objects. On the other hand, Xibeigang Tomb 1400 yielded a limited number of burial goods as it had been previously plundered. Accordingly, we shall substitute Tomb 1001 for Tomb 1400 in our comparison with Fu Hao's tomb as the former was built around the same time and provided many surviving artifacts.

Excavations of Fu Hao's tomb found an unprecedented number of splendid bronze ritual vessels (used for ancestral rituals), including forty wine vessels and fifty-three wine beakers, besides the large square Simuxin-ding vessels, stands with three steamers, round and square cups and tripod vessels. Further, three large wine pots in the collection of the Nezu Museum in Tokyo, Japan, are said to have been found in Tomb 1001 and form a set of highly artful and

Figure 1.3
Oracle inscriptions on the turtle shell containing references to Fu Hao
Source: Tsai Mei-Fen et al. (2012: 80, 174).
(1) Academia Sinica R041287 'Delivery could fall on Ding-ri or Geng-ri; unfortunately she gave birth to a girl on Jiayin thirty-one days later'.
(2) Academia Sinica R044577 'When Fu Hao attacks Bafang to defend Zhijia, will they play into her hands if Wu Ding charges from the east'.

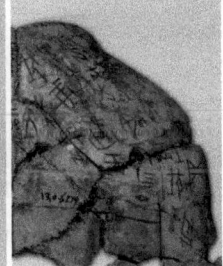

Chapter 1

decorative bronze vessels that are far superior to the Fu Hao tomb artifacts in terms of ornamentation and complexity. When we compare the volume of common types of objects among the excavated materials from Fu Hao's tomb and Tomb 1001 such as bronze and bone weapons, jade ware, inner and outer coffins, pieces of ornamental bone objects, marble carvings decorating tomb ramps and elephant-bone wine vessels, the numbers of items from Tomb 1001 tend to exceed those from Fu Hao's tomb, even though the former constitute the remaining objects that had survived looting. This suggests that Tomb 1001 housed a more lavish and diverse array of burial goods. We can suppose that this difference represents the difference in power and wealth between a king and his wife (consort).

Xibeigang Tomb 1550 from a slightly later period is thought to be a large-scale king's tomb comparable to Tomb 1001 (Liang Siyong and Gao Quxun 1976). Although this tomb had been plundered, two small graves of human sacrifices were discovered on the two-layer platform (*erengtai*) in the outer coffin. Excavations found many decorative bird-hairpins above the buried person's head in one of the graves, M1550:49. It is likely that the remains in this grave belonged to a female servant who wore the hairpins as her distinguishing feature – '妻' (*qi*), the Chinese character for 'wife', is an ideograph representing a woman wearing many hairpins. Her burial goods are clearly different from those of a weapon-bearing male servant in the same royal tomb in that they comprised several items of jade ware and bronze *jue* and *gu* cups with no weapons. We can imagine that the king was served by the male and female attendants with markedly different duties.

Based on the above comparison, it is highly likely that the queens and consorts of the Shang dynastic kings were not given tombs equal to that of their royal husband in terms of size as well as the quantity and quality of burial goods. Furthermore, in most cases they were buried in a different area than their husbands' burial sites. Phenomena such as the construction of the couple's shrines side by side and the flaunting of the wife's family background have not been observed.[4]

---

4 Jonathan Friedman has proposed a model in which prestige goods from higher-ranking lineages are exchanged for non-prestige goods and women from lower-ranking lineages in chieftain society based on ethnological examples (Friedman and Rowlands 1978). While jade ware from the late Neolithic Age and bronzeware from the early states period are thought to have been redistributed as prestige goods in China, it is still unconfirmed that they were exchanged for women.

Analysis of male and female tombs at Yinxu

To this point, I have examined royal tombs. In this section I will examine burial goods from smaller tombs from the late Shang period as a way to understand the gap between men and women among middle-ranking status groups.

Cemeteries containing groups of many small to medium-sized tombs have been found at Yinxu. As each cemetery is composed of tombs from which vessels engraved with the same family emblem have been excavated, these tombs are believed to have belonged to members of the same clan. We can also suppose that people began to clearly recognize family grouping during this period. Men and women were buried in the same cemetery.

An overview of excavations of 1,500 small to medium tombs across Yinxu over a period of four years was published in *Report on Yinxu Excavations (Yinxu fajue baogao) 1958–1961* (Zhongguo shehui kexueyuan kaogu yanjiusuo 1987: 210). The report notes that women's tombs sometimes had weapons and tools among their burial goods but tended to have fewer wine vessel sets or *jue* and *gu* cups for ritual purposes. It is possible to say that ritual bronzeware was rarely given to women of lower social status as items of this nature carried political implications. In other words, women were not heavily involved in politics at the time. On the other hand, the type of burial goods demonstrates the possibility of women's involvement in military matters, as noted in the previous section.[5]

Tang Jigen (2004 [English]) analyzed the difference between men and women in the excavated materials from small to medium tombs in the Yinxu West cemetery, the largest burial zone in Yinxu, distinguishing between men and women using the height range of 156–160 centimeters as a tentative criterion. He found that in many cases a man's and a woman's tomb were placed side by side and concluded that these paired male and female tombs were for married couples in light of burial practices in modern-day Beijing. Tang Jigen argues that while equal numbers of equal types of pottery were found in many of the paired tombs, there was no equality in terms of bronzeware. Moreover, cowry shells (*Monetaria moneta*), which are believed to have symbolized wealth, were found only in male tombs. In the middle class formed though population influx into an expanding city, women's social status was relatively low. While so far

---

5 Thus far, there has been no clear evidence of their participation in military action, such as battle scars on bones.

Chapter 1

there is insufficient information about the owners of these small to medium tombs and the relationships among them due to lack of data on human bones excavated from them, it is hoped that further analysis of burial materials will shed more light on the extent to which the state of patrilineality gleaned from written records about the Shang dynasty was applicable to lower social strata.

Western Zhou to the Spring and Autumn and Warring States

This section will turn to the Western Zhou (1050 BCE–770 BCE) to consider what burial goods from the tombs of aristocrats and the position of tombs can tell us about the relationship between husbands and wives.

Many mid-size tombs from the early and middle Western Zhou dynasty have been found in the Yuguo cemetery site in Baoji, Shaanxi Province, which is considered to have been the cemetery of a local ruling family in the Yuguo area which was on a key transport route to the Sichuan region. Zhuyuangou Tomb 13 contained a man and two women buried in separate pits in the same tomb[6] where a king and his consort were laid together (the consort was sacrificed), with his wife buried in her own pit alongside. Zhuyuangou Tomb 7 and Tomb 4 were also group tombs for married couples. They are notable as examples of the Western Zhou aristocratic burial practice that treats husband and wife equally; however, it should be noted that these tombs were located in what would have been a peripheral region, some distance away from the political center (Lu Liancheng and Hu Zhisheng 1988).

In recent years, there has been a string of discoveries of the enormous tombs of enfeoffed local rulers across China during the period of the Western Zhou dynasty. The Tianma-Qucun Jinhou cemetery in Quwo, Shanxi Province, in particular, offers archaeological materials that are highly valuable for the comparative study of gender in the upper class. There are groups of two to three large tombs with a single access ramp which are thought to be the tombs of Jin marquesses and their wives (and secondary wives), as their remains were placed in different pits in the same tomb from the same time period (Figure 1.4).

---

6 The term 'group tomb' is used in the sense that a group of people were buried on the same site in the same time period.

For example, Qucun Tombs I11M64, I11M62 and I11M63 are the burial sites of a man and two women (Beijing daxue kaoguxuexi, Shanxi sheng kaogu yanjiusuo 1994). Excavations of I11M64, the tomb of a man thought to be Jin Hou Bangfu, found five bronze *ding* vessels and four *gui* bowls as well as weapons and *bianzhong* bells as burial goods. On the other hand, his wife's tomb, I11M62, held three bronze vessels and four bowls, while the secondary wife's tomb, I11M63, contained three bronze vessels and two bowls (from the middle part of the Western Zhou period, the tomb owner's status or class was represented by the numbers of bronze vessels and bowls owned). No weapons were found in either woman's tomb. In the other tomb groups, marquesses' tombs contained five or seven vessels among bronzeware burial goods which were regarded as the benchmark for the ruling class, whereas their wives' tombs generally had three, which was the number for a rank below their husbands'. It is clear from these burial goods that wives ranked slightly lower than their husbands even though they had high social status. Unlike during the Shang dynasty, we can surmise that military affairs were exclusively men's business in this period as we found no evidence of women's involvement in such matters. In addition, musical instruments were discovered in men's tombs only. This indicates that 'music' (*yue*) that formed part of 'ritual' (*li yue*), which had political importance in the Zhou dynasty period, was also monopolized by men. In other words, women were not in a position to administer military or ritual affairs.

The marquesses and their wives wore personal accessories made from precious agate tube beads originating from the western region (Figure 1.5).

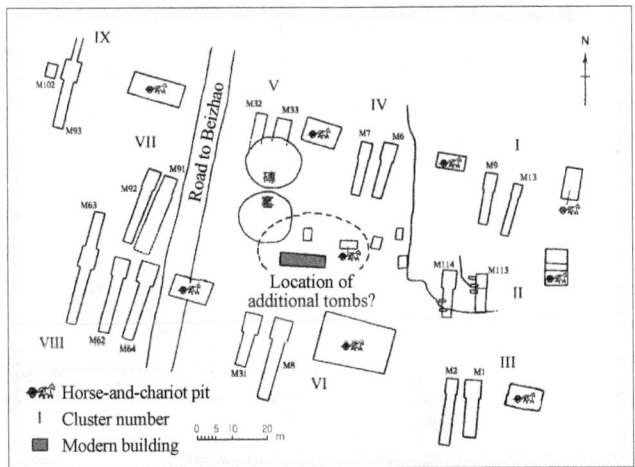

Figure 1.4
The Jin rulers'
burial compound
at Beizhao
(Qucun Locus III),
Quwo
Source:
von Falkenhausen
(2006: Map 4).

Chapter 1

Excavations of the marquess-class tombs in other areas from the middle Western Zhou period found both male and female tomb owners wearing accessories mostly made of similar agate. These accessories are thought to have been worn as the prestige goods of the uppermost class. One point of difference was women's special hair adornments, which were only found in the wives' tombs. These adornments were commonly found in the tombs of marquess-class wives within wide areas centering on the Yellow River basin (Huang Tsuimei 2013: 559–600). We can imagine that ruling-class couples in those days showed off their social status through their appearance by wearing luxury items such as conspicuously red agate tube bead accessories while clearly displaying their gender difference at the same time. They were highly conscious of their personal presentation as a married couple.

This awareness about treating the husband and wife as a pair can also be observed in the side-by-side placement of their tombs. The paired presentation of married couples reveals a change in the attitude toward married couples in the upper class, as this phenomenon was not found in the late Shang tombs at Yinxu. Let us discuss the background to this change in the next section.

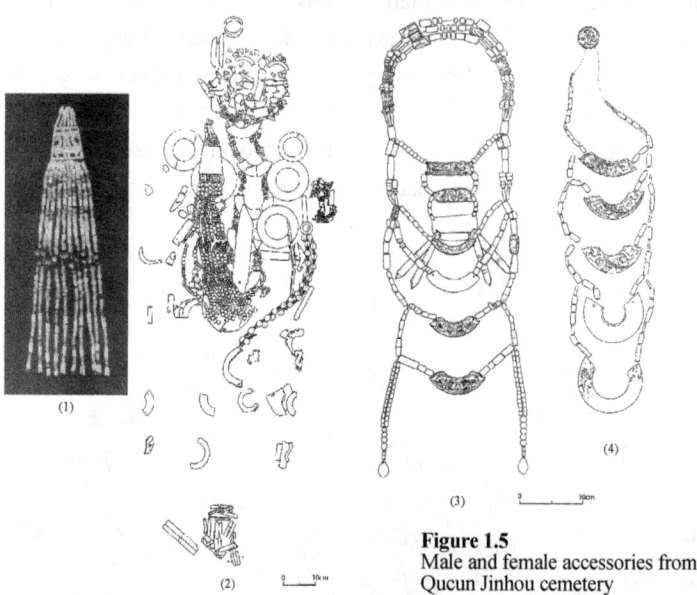

Figure 1.5
Male and female accessories from the Qucun Jinhou cemetery

(1) Necklace with jade plate and beads from M92 (Source: *Wenwu* (1995, Vol. 7: Figure 20).)
(2) Jade articles from the inner coffin of Tomb I11M31, Beizhao (Qucun Locus III), Quwo (Shanxi) (Source: von Falkenhausen (2006: Figure 15).)
(3) Necklace with four jade *huang* pendants and beads (Source: *Wenwu* (1995, Vol. 7: Figure 18).)
(4) Necklace with five jade *huang* pendants and beads (Source: *Wenwu* (1995, Vol. 7: Figure 11).)

Women's role as suggested by bronzeware and accessories

In this section I will look at the same question of what can be learned about marriage relationships in the Western Zhou period, this time focusing on material in inscriptions on bronze vessels.

Lothar von Falkenhausen points out that patrilineal kinship groups constituted the basic units of Western Zhou social-political-military organizations which controlled land and other properties and that the conduct of ancestral rituals was the primary religious act carried out by these groups (2006: 28). In this period, it became more common to mark bronzeware for ancestral rituals with inscriptions and there was an increase in the number of long-form inscriptions and inscribed records clearly stating the actual ritual performers, vessel makers and reasons for vessel-making. Bronze vessels with inscriptions stating that they were made for women are called 'bridal vessels'.

While the lineage (patrilineal kinship group) name is the primary element in determining identity in the case of a man's name in inscriptions, a woman's name always contains the name of the clan[7] into which she was born, followed by the lineage name, rank and personal name (von Falkenhausen 2006: 74–126).

Some of the notable examples of bridal vessels are as follows.

- Xing Ji vessels: The inscription reads, 'Xing Ji Fu also [unknown character] to her ancestors and her deceased father, the [unknown character, an epithet] rulers, a filial *si* sacrifice and a filial *ji* sacrifice at the lineage temple hall. Herewith I, Yu Bo, make tripods and tureens for the use of Xing Ji' (von Falkenhausen 2006: 119).[8]
- Guo Meng Ji vessel: The inscription reads, 'Qi ruler makes a precious Yi vessel for Guo Meng Ji's woman, thrive forever and hand down to her posterity' (see Figure 1.6).[9]

---

7 A clan is a group of people who originate from a common ancestry while a lineage is a subset of people who belong to one clan. Von Falkenhausen follows Keesing (1976: 251) in using this term.

8 邢姬鼎「丼（邢）姬婦■亦■祖／考夌公宗室,／又孝价孝, ■（■）／保■白（伯）, 乍（作）丼（邢）／姬用貞（鼎）、■」(Academia Sinica 02676).
This vessel was excavated from Rujiazhuang Tomb 2, Baoji, Shanxi Province. Bronze vessels gifted by Yu Bo to a Ji clan woman from Xing.

9 虢孟姬匜「齐侯作虢孟姬良母寶匜、其万年無疆、子子孫孫永寶用」
A vessel made for a daughter of the Ji family of Guo (merely called a *liang-mu*) by the Meng family of Qi into which she was to marry.

Chapter 1

To summarize the situations for which these bridal vessels were generally made as explained in inscriptions, they were 'gifted to a daughter upon her marriage', 'gifted by a husband to his wife', 'gifted by a woman to her mother-in-law', 'made by a women for her husband's ancestors', 'gifted by a wife to her husband', 'gifted by the head of a family to an incoming bride' or 'gifted by a wife to her husband who was going on an expedition' (Chen Chao-Jung 2009: 66–85). These bronze vessels were often purposely inscribed with the names of the giver and the receiver. Many inscriptions also recorded the giving and receiving of the bronze vessels, especially in relation to marriage. This suggests that these bronze bridal vessels played the role of verifying marriage alliances, giving the impression that the meaning of women's existence was focused solely on marriage. It is thought that the meaning of existence for women as resources in forming matrimonial relations was established in the elite class at the start of the Western Zhou dynasty period during which local rulers were enfeoffed.[10]

The statement, 'The son's honor increases as his mother's position rises and the mother's honor increases as her son's position rises' (*zi yimugui, mu yizigui*) in 'Yingong', Vol. 1, *Gongyang Commentary on the Spring and Autumn Annals* (*Chunqiu Gongyang zhuan*), represents the notion that the mother's family origins and her son's status have a deep causal link. Some of the examples of inscriptions on bronze bridal vessels also demonstrate that it was very important to clearly state family origins.

Figure 1.6 Guo Meng Ji vessel *(yi)* Source: Chen Peifen (2004: 559); Yan Yiping (1983, Vol. 9: 6866).

10 It is thought that taking a wife with the Ji lineage name was significant and worthy of bronze inscriptions because the Ji lineage name of the Western Zhou dynasty was an important factor that guaranteed one's status under the feudal system.

Life span, life cycle and status among women

This section will turn to a different perspective, examining what we know about the life span of women from the Neolithic period to the pre-Qin era. According to a 2015 World Health Organization (WHO) report, the maternal mortality rate is very high in Africa and other low-income countries at 900–960 deaths per 100,000 people (in Japan in 1899 the figure was 409.8). It is commonly argued that poor sanitary conditions at the time of childbirth account for such high rates. The probability of dying in childbirth increases every time a woman gives birth which can be every few years. The mortality rate is expected to have been even higher in the pre-Qin period. With these statistics in mind, let us look at the life span and life cycle of pre-Qin women based on an analysis of human bones excavated from tombs.

The average life span of the women from 659 tombs at the Dadianzi site in the Inner Mongolia Autonomous Region was in the early thirties range: 61% died between the ages of fifteen and thirty-five and 26% between thirty-six and fifty-five. On the other hand, more men survived beyond the age of thirty-six as their mortality rate was 55% between the ages of fifteen and thirty-five and 35% between thirty-six and fifty-five (Wu Juiman 2004 [English]: 52–55).

Excavations of 101 small to medium tombs were conducted at the southern section of the Qianzhangda site, Tengzhou, Shandong Province, from the late Shang to early Western Zhou period. It was found that the average age was forty among men and 32.5 among women from the late Shang period while it was 34.25 in men and 30.25 among women from the early Western Zhou period (Wang Jianhua and Cao Jing 2014: 530–532).

A large-scale excavation survey covering an area of 100,000 square meters found that the Shangma cemetery in Houma, Shanxi Province, contained around 1,400 small to medium tombs and chariot pits mostly from the early and middle Spring and Autumn period. Of the 1,059 tombs found with human remains, 486 were women's tombs. It is believed that the cemetery was for a locally-based clan for the common people and the slightly higher classes. It is estimated that approximately 60% of men died during middle age (thirty-five to fifty-four) while nearly one-half of women died at a younger age (fifteen to thirty-four) (von Falkenhausen 2006: 134–136).

All of the above examples indicate that women tended to die at a younger age. The primary cause of this is considered to be infection during pregnancy and after delivery.

Chapter 1

Let us next turn our gaze toward life span and property.

M1027 (4 meters long x 2.8 meters wide x 4.2 meters deep, a middle-aged woman) and M1026 (4 meters x 2.9 meters x 2 meters, a middle-aged man) are medium-sized tombs placed side by side at the Shangma cemetery. It is possible that the tomb owners were husband and wife, or at least closely related, based on their side-by-side placement and closeness in age. In terms of burial goods, the woman's tomb had nine bronze vessels[11] whereas the man's tomb contained five bronze vessels and chariot fittings. While it is uncertain if this difference signifies their difference in status, there is no marked disparity between the woman and man at least in terms of wealth. Based on this example, we can surmise that women were able to own as much property as men did if they overcame the risks entailed in childbirth and lived to middle age when their son gained status.

As an aside, no 'bridal vessels' have been found at the Shangma site. This fact suggests that these people as the upper class in a minor city did not proclaim their family origins because the status of the Shangma lineage did not warrant their involvement in important marriage alliances (especially with the Ji lineage) (von Falkenhausen 2006: 150–151).

If we were to imagine the life cycle of ordinary women in ancient Chinese society based on these numbers, we would expect that women would have experienced childbirth multiple times between the ages of fifteen and thirty-five, during which around half of them would have lost their lives. If they survived that life stage and lived to middle age (late forties), they would have become elder women, who were rare in those days. If their adult sons gained status, mothers would have acquired a commensurate level of means and influence, and hence their tombs would contain more burial goods.

While *Zuo Commentary on the Spring and Autumn Annals* (*Chunqiu Zuoshi zhuan*) offers many descriptions of women's matrimonial relationships, it has limited accounts of women's activity. Nevertheless, it conveys a case in which women interfered in politics as mothers. This can be regarded as one manifestation of the aforementioned phenomenon of 'the mother's honor increases as her son's position rises' referred to in *Gongyan Commentary*.

---

11 They are thought to have belonged to the local elite class based on a comparison with the sizes of other tombs at the cemetery.

'Men till the land and women weave cloth'

In this section let us return again to the question of the gender division of labor from the Neolithic to later times, focusing on discussion of the 'men till, women weave' formulation.

As background, we need to briefly consider the technology of weaving. According to Satō Taketoshi (1977), fiber from plants such as hemp was the earliest weaving material in prehistoric times. It is unclear whether silk existed at the time, even though silkworm cocoons have reportedly been discovered in Neolithic ruins. However, artifactual vestiges have confirmed that silk was already in use during the Shang dynasty. Although the silk production process is different from that of plant-based fibers as it involves a silkworm-raising stage, the weaving process after yarn-making is basically the same. Silkworms would have been a precious commodity in the early states to the north of the Yellow River Valley as silk was originally produced south of the Yellow River. There are some bone and shell inscriptions about the worshipping of the god of silkworms, suggesting the existence of silk textile production using both wild and domesticated silkworms (Satō 1977). Excavated artifacts point to the production of a wide range of clothes and woven goods of various levels of quality and decorativeness, including color, contexture and embroidery, by the Shang dynasty period. In light of the situation in the late Neolithic period, it is highly likely that women were involved in such production. In fact, jade spindle whorls were discovered in Fu Hao's tomb.

The Xiaomintun dongnandi cemetery in Yinxu is thought to be for the burial of artisans involved in bronzeware casting. While the sex of the remains was indeterminable due to a poor state of preservation, five spindle whorls were found only in Tomb M1332 out of a total of 132 tombs (Zhongguo shehui kexueyuan kaogu yanjiusuo Anyang gongzuodui 2009: 25). In other words, there is a possibility that women living in the bronze foundry district were engaged in work related to making bronzeware rather than spinning and weaving on a routine basis. I speculate that spinning and weaving was no longer a universal manual occupation for women in this period as manual work became increasingly specialized.

Spindle whorls were also discovered in several women's tombs at the Tianma-Qucun site in Shanxi Province. For example, stone and clay spindle whorls were found in the medium-sized M6080 tomb (Beijing daxue kaoguxuexi Shang Zhou zu et al. 2000: 395–404). However, not all of the numerous small-sized tombs contained spindle whorls; for example, only some of the small tombs of women aged around twenty produced a single clay spindle whorl together with a few earthenware vessels and jade.

There were silkworm-shaped jade objects among the burial goods from Fu Hao's tomb in Yinxu. Large numbers of jade silkworms were combined with agate tube beads as necklace pieces during the Western Zhou period. As they were worn equally by men and women, Chen Chao-jung has suggested that by that time silkworms symbolized reincarnation rather than weaving (Chen Chao-jung 2009: 30–38).

Meanwhile, bronze jars from the Warring States period decorated with the motif of female mulberry-leaf pickers illustrate the symbolic nature of the task as women's responsibility. Some accounts of 'men till the land and women weave cloth' are found in Chinese classic texts such as the *Annals of Lü Buwei* (*Lüshi Chunqiu*), which is believed to have been compiled during the Warring States period, suggesting that the notion of weaving as women's responsibility had been entrenched by that time. According to the *Classic of Songs* (*Shijing*), a collection of mostly Western Zhou songs, men also took part in mulberry-leaf picking in those days. This likely indicates that the task symbolically became women's responsibility during the Spring and Autumn and Warring States periods. Satō Taketoshi states that from these periods spinning and weaving had spread across multiple social classes and included palace workshops, production in urban scholar-official families who produced silk for personal use, farmers' sideline businesses and production by independent handicrafts people. Although women were certainly engaged in handicraft spinning and weaving, the situation may have changed over time in response to further social stratification as not all women were involved in this craft.

The process of change in pre-Qin gender structure

Based on the above review and analysis of burial goods excavated from tombs, it is possible to summarize the change in gender structure over a period of several thousand years from the Neolithic Age to the Spring and Autumn and Warring States periods as follows.

From the Neolithic Age, men's and women's responsibilities became differentiated and the concept of 'men till and women weave' took root while patrilineal society centering on clans was established. Particularly in early economic society where economic activity was dominated by professionals with specialized skills, men gained higher status as they took on responsibility for a wider variety of manual industries.

In the early states period, as represented by the late Qin archaeology site at Yinxu, signs of patrilineality are evident in royal succession. The tombs of queens and consorts were separated from those of kings and not treated equally. Divination by male 'augurs' became an important part of politics during this period and writing at its developmental stage (inscriptions on bones and turtle shells) came into use for this purpose. In other words, from the outset the core of the writing-based political system was operated exclusively by male official historians (*shiguan*) and the monopoly of political activity was handed over to male civil servants (*wenguan*) in later periods. Further, there was a marked expansion of military activity. Women might have been given some military responsibility under special circumstances, but they were gradually excluded from military activity as the specialized position of male military officers was established. It is possible that women's responsibility and social status continued to diminish in relative terms in the urbanized society. This paradigm is thought to have continued and developed further from the Western Zhou period.

A trend to flaunt one's matrimonial relationship through the mode of burial and clothing emerged in the feudal elite society of Western Zhou. It is believed that the need to accentuate matrimonial relationships arose as the formation of marriage alliances between clans became an important political tool and therefore marriage came to be regarded as women's most important responsibility. Although upper-class wives did have social status, it appears that they were ranked lower than their husbands. It is likely that spinning and weaving as women's responsibilities transformed into something symbolic amid the stratification of social structures.

From the viewpoint of life expectancy, an analysis of archaeological materials from commoner's tombs from the Neolithic Age to the Spring and Autumn period indicates that a high percentage of women had a markedly short life span of between fifteen and thirty-five years due to childbirth-related risks and died considerably younger than men, whose average life span was over forty years. This must have been another factor that prevented women's rise in society. On the other hand, some women who did survive into old age managed to acquire wealth as their sons' status rose.

Chapter 1

Women's short life expectancy due to the risks involved in childbearing remained the same through different periods whereas men, who were unburdened by parenting duties, lived a little longer and played central roles in society as military officers in the war-torn era or as civil servants exclusively in charge of the writing-based government system in peace times. Thus, gender structure was dramatically transformed resulting in the differentiation of social responsibilities between men and women and the spread of those norms throughout society.

The interpretations presented in this chapter reflect the author's views. Given the limited sources, both archaeological and written, much of the interpretation is based on suppositions, and it is always difficult to separate one's own contemporary understanding of relationships from one's interpretation of evidence from the past. It can be expected that as archaeological work continues, future scholars will have more evidence to draw upon in revising the interpretations presented here.

2. The Patrilinealization of Society

— *SHIMOKURA Wataru*

Introduction

Han Chinese society is usually classified as a typical patrilineal society. In other words, it was a society that valued relationships between people who shared the same surname. The surname was usually passed down from a father to his sons. It was extremely rare for people to change their surname and even women retained their maiden name after marriage. Marriage between a man and a woman sharing the same surname was avoided, while adopting a son with a different surname was considered a taboo under ordinary circumstances. Kinsmen related through the male line formed a surname group referred to as a lineage (*zongzu*) and women who married into the group (mothers, wives and daughters-in-law) were treated as members, but maternal relatives and relatives by marriage with different surnames were clearly distinguished from agnatic relatives. The category of maternal relatives and relatives by marriage was much narrower than patrilineal kin and positioned lower.

In this patrilineal society, a woman was required to leave her natal family and marry into another family. She was given a social position only when she married and had a son. Once married, she was required to defer to and serve her husband's parents (father- and mother-in-law) as her real parents and to regard her husband as her 'heaven' (i.e., ruler, master) (*tian* / 天). On the other hand, she was revered by her son as the 'mother' and after her husband's death acquired power comparable to that of the 'father' within her household. Nevertheless, her power merely stemmed from the fact that she was the 'wife' of the late father and therefore did not entitle her to make her own decisions on matters of significance to the family's circumstances, such as the disposal of family property.

Chapter 2

A son's body was regarded as a reproduction of his parents, but it was thought that he inherited different elements from each. He inherited the 'bone' (representing an imperishable relationship that would be passed down from generation to generation) from his father and the father-son relationship was described as 'sharing the same *qi*' (*tongqi*).[1] On the other hand, the mother gave her son 'flesh' (symbolizing an impermanent relationship that would vanish over time) as she was thought to give 'form' (physical appearance) to her son who shared the same *qi* with his father. In Chinese society, the concepts of 'father-bone' and 'mother-flesh' were interlocked with the view of kinship – the permanence of patrilineal kinship and the temporary nature of the matrilineal relationship.

Consequently, Han Chinese society was keenly aware of patrilineage (the father's surname) as the marker that separated insiders from outsiders. Within their family and clan, the male parent (husband/father) who remained in his natal family for life was positioned above the female parent (wife/mother) who married into it. In recent years, however, some new discoveries have undermined this commonsense understanding of Han Chinese society in the field of ancient history, as was mentioned in the Introduction to Part I Phase I of this volume.

Regulations written on bamboo slips that are believed to be part of the Qin dynasty penal code, excavated from the Shuihudi archaeological site in 1975,[2] suggest that the penalty imposed on a husband who inflicted an injury on his wife was no different from that imposed on any other offender under the Qin Code. This is markedly different from the Tang Code, which reduced the penalty on the husband by two degrees in comparison with other offenders. The rationale for this discrimination was that the husband's penalty for assaulting his wife was lighter because he was more important than his wife under the principle of 'Husband is superior, wife is inferior'. By contrast, the Qin Code did not provide that the husband should receive a lighter sentence. This leads to the deduction that compliance with the 'Husband is superior, wife is inferior' principle had a significantly low priority in the legal field in the Qin period. From this evidence we can see that the disparity in status between husband and wife in legal codes was not static, and the difference in their relative social positions gradually widened. Research in ancient history must now take this supposition into account.

As demonstrated by the chapters in Phase II of this book, even in early-modern China, the level of priority given to the patrilineal relationship escalated

---

1 For details on *qi*, see Chapter Six.
2 Bamboo slips from a Qin tomb at Shuihudi.

as the years passed. The phenomenon that illustrates this trend clearly is the history of the Chinese lineage, a patrilineal family group that increased in size and became better organized in the Ming-Qing period than in the Song period. Taiwanese scholars have noted that aristocratic family bonds from the Six Dynasties period to the Sui-Tang period (220–970) were not as strong as those of the early-modern Chinese kin. In Japan, scholars have argued that 'The aristocrats saw an individual family or a lineal relation as a family group and a unit of daily activity' (Mizoguchi et al. 2001: 185) (see Chapter Four). The following view is commonly accepted about the Han period at an earlier point in history: while the nuclear family-like small family unit was commonplace in early Han, the extended patrilineal family unit became mainstream in the wealthy class from the latter half of the Former Han to mainly the Later Han dynasty (Satake 1980; Watanabe 1986; Hori 1996, among others). In short, earlier studies have projected an image of an ancient Chinese kinship group that grew larger and developed stronger patrilineal characteristics and had a stronger focus on patrilineal bonds over time. This would seem to reflect the growing strength of a view that prioritized the patrilineal relationship and incorporated it into a moral sense of order. When we trace back through history, we find a stage where the principles of social order such as the norm of 'Husband is superior, wife is inferior', which came to be taken for granted by later generations, were not axiomatic. The discovery of the Qin Code, which suggested a more equal relationship between husband and wife, led to the formation of the above hypothesis, which shall be examined briefly in the remainder of this chapter.

In the next section, based on my earlier studies, I discuss a 'non-patrilineal' aspect found in the Han-period family and kinship relationship. (More detailed discussions can be found in Shimokura 2001, 2005, 2015.) I then look at the husband-wife relationship between imperial princesses (*gongzhu*) and their husbands that changed over time. Together with the conclusion, this section will show that from the Six Dynasties period onward, even women of a special standing such as emperors' daughters were required to have relationships that conformed to the principle of 'Husband is superior, wife is inferior' (albeit at a highly superficial level). In other words, it is possible to say that the level of 'patrilinealization' certainly deepened in Chinese society through the transition from the Han dynasty to the Six Dynasties period.

Chapter 2

Uterine siblings and the maternal uncle-nephew relationship

Having stated above that people in Han Chinese society were highly aware of patrilineage (surname) as the indicator separating insiders and outsiders, it is now necessary to examine whether this socially accepted belief remained unchanged in Chinese society. In this section, I look at the uterine sibling relationship and that between maternal uncle and nephew,[3] both of which are kinship relationships among individuals with different surnames, mediated by a woman. I address the above question by examining these relationships in ancient times.

The Qin bamboo slips, *Shuihudi Qinjian*, record that uterine siblings who are found to have engaged in incest are to be sentenced to death. In China, sexual relationships between men and women outside of marriage had long been regarded as a criminal offence and the penalty for incest in particular was heavier due to the close nature of the blood relation between offenders. According to the bamboo slips, the Qin Code imposed the death penalty on uterine siblings of both sexes who engaged in a sexual relationship and would also have applied the same penalty in the case of incest between agnate siblings.[4]

Let us compare this provision in the Qin Code with one in the Tang Code. The Tang Code imposed the death penalty on incest between agnate siblings. It is likely that a death sentence had consistently been applied to that crime. The question is how were incestuous uterine siblings punished? The Tang Code imposed three years of forced labor,[5] which is clearly lighter than the death penalty that was applied in the case of agnate siblings.

Uterine siblings were half siblings with different surnames. A uterine sibling relationship came into existence when a mother remarried and gave birth to another child in the new matrimonial relationship. As her children inherited the surnames of their respective fathers, these siblings had different surnames.

---

3 In Han Chinese society, different terms are used to distinguish paternal and maternal uncles as well as a brother's child and a sister's child. While a paternal uncle and a brother's son are called the equivalent of father/son, a maternal uncle is called *jiu* and a sister's son is called *sheng*. These kinship terms derive from the fact that one has the same surname as one's paternal uncles and brother's sons whereas one's maternal uncles and sister's sons have different surnames. This is regarded as a phenomenon that directly represents the patrilineal nature of Han society.

4 Regulations from the early Han period, which were unearthed in Hubei Province in 1983, clearly stipulate that 'Agnate siblings who have a sexual relationship shall be punished by death'. It is safe to suppose that the Qin Code prior to Han had the same rule.

5 'Miscellaneous rules' (*Zalü*), *Tang Code with Commentary and Explanation* (*Tanglüshuyi*), Vol. 26.

The Patrilinealization of Society

The Tang Code provided different degrees of punishment as it placed priority on the question of whether the parties had the same father (surname). This clearly demonstrates that the Tang Code was based on the principle of the primacy of patrilineality.

However, penalty stipulations regarding incest between siblings were not immutable in the history of Chinese legal codes. This fact was revealed by the discovery of the Qin bamboo strips. The penalty for a sexual relationship between siblings was death under the Qin Code, whether they were from the same father or different fathers. The surname was not treated as a categorical determinant of kinship. It is possible to say that the underlying idea in this case cannot be described as 'patrilineal'.

Based on this finding, I next examine examples from well-known classical history books, *Records of the Grand Historian* (*Shiji*) and the *History of the Former Han* (*Hanshu*), and briefly introduce a few examples of the uterine sibling relationship. The first features Empress Wang of the Former Han (173 BCE–126 BCE).[6]

Empress Wang was the official wife of Emperor Jing (r. 157 BCE–141 BCE), the sixth emperor of Han, and the birthmother of the seventh, Emperor Wu (r. 141 BCE–87 BCE). She had married a man named Jin Wangcun before joining the concubinage of Emperor Jing, the crown prince at the time. It was her mother, Zang Er, who offered her already married daughter to the crown prince. It is said that Zang Er snatched her daughter from her then husband and

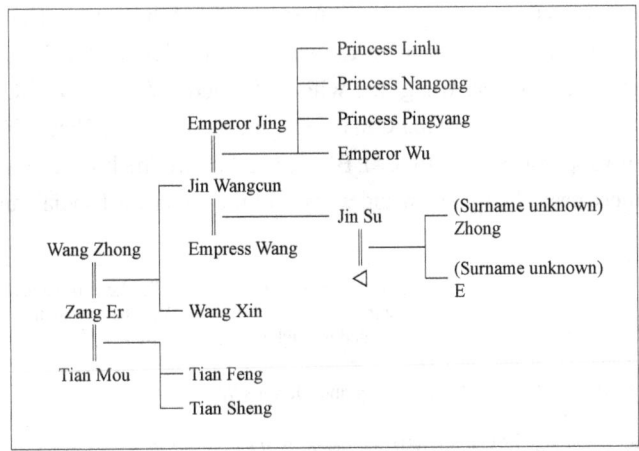

Figure 2.1
Genealogy chart I

---

6 'Biography of Empress Wang of Emperor Jing', *History of the Former Han* (*Hanshu*), Vol. 97.

Chapter 2

sent her to the crown prince because she had been told by a fortuneteller that her daughter would become a woman of very high standing (see Figure 2.1).

Empress Wang had given birth to a daughter by Jin Wangcun whose name was Jin Su. Emperor Wu was not aware of the existence of his half-sister early on, but once he discovered this fact, he personally went to meet her and brought her to his palace. Upon their first meeting, Emperor Wu called Jin Su 'Daijie', which is a form of addressing one's eldest sister. According to the historical accounts, he returned to his palace with his half-sister of a different surname and 'presented' his three agnate sisters (imperial princesses) to her. Jin Su had a son and a daughter who moved to the capital with her and received special treatment.[7]

Empress Wang herself had two uterine brothers named Tian Fen and Tian Sheng. Following Emperor Wu's enthronement, Tian Fen (?–131 BCE) was appointed as prime minister and went on to wield considerable influence.[8] We can find a similar example in the Warring States period involving Wei Ran (see Figure 2.2). Wei Ran was the uterine younger brother of Queen Dowager Xuan, who was the birthmother of King Zhaoxiang of Qin (r. 306 BCE–251 BCE). He facilitated the accession of King Zhaoxiang and managed the affairs of state under the king.[9] It is supposed that Tian Fen and Wei Ran were able to gain power because of their positions as the maternal relatives (the empress's brother and the queen dowager's brother) of the emperor and the Qin king respectively. As they were uterine brothers of the women in power, it is conceivable that the idea of discriminating insiders and outsiders on the basis of surname was considered insignificant in Chinese society of the Former Han and earlier eras.

Other examples after Emperor Wu's reign in the Former Han dynasty include Empress Wang, the wife of Emperor Yuan (r. 49 BCE–33 BCE), and her uterine brother Gou Can (see Figure 2.3), and Fu Zhaoyi,[10] the grandmother of Emperor Ai (r. 7 BCE–1 BCE), and her uterine brother Zheng Yun. Each of these cases feature men and women of the uppermost social rank close to that of

---

7 The son's name was Zhong and the daughter's name was E. Their surname (their father's surname) cannot be found in the history book. For Emperor Wu, they were his relatives mothered by a woman (Jin Su) who was related through his mother (Empress Wang) and hence twice removed in terms of their surname.

8 'Biographies of Marquis Weiqi and Marquis Wu'an', *Records of the Grand Historian (Shiji)*, Vol. 107.

9 'Biography of Marquis of Rang', *Records of the Grand Historian (Shiji)*, Vol. 72.

10 *Zhaoyi* is a rank given to a consort and not her name. A consort was positioned one rank below the empress.

The Patrilinealization of Society

an emperor or king. It is likely that they had no idea about the 'irregularity' of their 'non-patrilineal' kinship bond. Emperor Wu's behavior clearly illustrates his understanding of this matter. If an emperor who belonged to the uppermost class of society acted in such a way, it is easy to imagine how it was in the rest

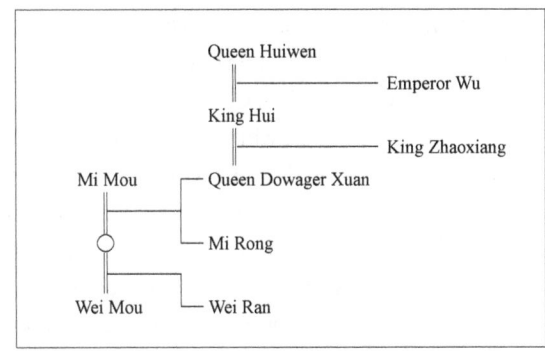

Figure 2.2
Genealogy chart II

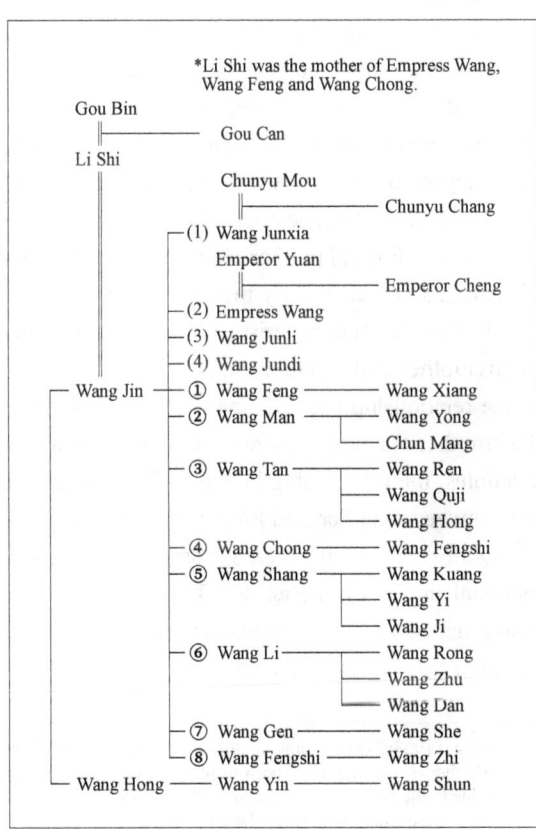

Figure 2.3
Genealogy chart III

of society. We can infer the 'non-patrilineal' social norm of that time sufficiently from these examples.

In concrete terms, the 'non-patrilineal' relationship refers to the consanguineous relationship that originates in the 'mother' (a woman who married into a particular family). We can surmise that the 'uterine' relationship, or the 'mother-child' bond, was given more importance in inverse proportion to the agnate relationship in ancient China. When it came to the mother-child relationship in early-modern China, the legal wife of one's father was regarded as one's official 'mother', while one's birthmother (the biological mother-child relationship) was treated as a secondary issue. The distinction between the legitimacy and illegitimacy of children was very relaxed under the patrilineal principle,[11] whereas children were strictly required to make the above distinction toward their mothers. If this assumption about the mother-child relationship in early-modern society is correct, then it was far removed from the situation in ancient society.

Uterine siblings are brothers and sisters who are related because they have the same biological mother. It is reasonable to suppose that the mother-child relationship was not regarded as inferior to the father-child relationship in ancient China because at that time incest between uterine siblings attracted the same degree of punishment as that between agnate siblings. As a result, it is difficult to think that one relationship was considered superior or inferior to the other. The biological mother-child relationship was thus yet to be relativized or disregarded, unlike in early-modern society.

The 'ancient' characteristic is also found in a kin relationship as an extension of this mother-child relationship. Here I am referring to a phenomenon observed in the relationship between maternal uncle and nephew. They are related via the 'mother' (a woman who was married out). Among the aforementioned examples, the relationship between Wei Ran and King Zhaoxiang of Qin and that between Tian Fen and Emperor Wu fall under this category.

Quite interestingly, there is commonality between the two cases. The older maternal uncles (Wei Ran and Tian Fen) provided political support to their young nephews (King Zhaoxiang and Emperor Wu). If we call this political situation 'regency by maternal relatives', we find the highest incidence of it in

---

11 As Shiga (1967: 248) explains, a father's property was equally divided between his sons, regardless of whether or not they were born of his legal marriage, in near-modern and modern times. This was due to the belief that it is unreasonable to discriminate between sons on the basis of who their mothers were when they shared the same material forces with their father.

Chinese history during the Han dynasty. The phenomenon in which the brother (the maternal uncle of an emperor) of an empress (the mother of the emperor) takes charge of state affairs as the young emperor (his nephew) ascends to the throne has drawn the interest of researchers as a major characteristic of the political history of the Han dynasty. While various views have been put forward as reasons for the high incidence of maternal relative regencies during this period, the 'maternal uncle-nephew' relationship should probably be considered as one of the factors. Where the biological mother-child relationship was considered important, people's sense of relationship with their maternal family was bidirectionally stronger than in subsequent periods. The sense of relationship between the maternal uncle and nephew was naturally strong and this strength likely spurred the prevalence of regency by maternal relatives.

The hypothesis that the maternal uncle-nephew relationship was more solid in Han than in subsequent periods is supported by another example.

Upon the enthronement of the fifteenth emperor of the Former Han, Emperor Cheng (r. 33 BCE–7 BCE), Wang Feng (?–22 BCE), who was the elder brother of the emperor's mother, Empress Wang (71 BCE–13 BCE), was appointed as prime minister. Thereafter, the post of prime minister was occupied by a succession of members of the Wang family throughout Emperor Cheng's reign. It appears that the emperor planned to appoint Empress Wang's brothers (his maternal uncles) to the position in order of age. When Wang Gen, her seventh brother, eventually took the prime ministership, the line of succession was switched to the next generation as the emperor ran out of suitable men in Wang Feng's generation. The leading candidate at the time was Chunyu Chang (?–8 BCE), the son of the elder sister of Empress Wang (see Figure 2.3).

According to the biography of Chunyu Chang,[12] Prime Minister Wang Gen was prone to illness and offered to resign from the post many times. For this reason, Chunyu Chang began to think of himself as the prime candidate for the position in view of the pecking order among the emperor's 'maternal relatives'. While the surname of Emperor Cheng's maternal relatives was generally 'Wang', Chunyu Chang was regarded as the emperor's maternal relative because his mother was a Wang even though he had a different surname.

---

12 *History of the Former Han* (*Hanshu*), Vol. 93.

Chapter 2

The biography presents the following anecdote.

> Then Wang Feng fell ill. Chunyu Chang devotedly kept vigil day and night by his uncle's sick bed demonstrating the nephew's deep sense of gratitude and obligation towards his maternal uncle. At the point of death, Wang Feng asked Empress Dowager Wang and Emperor Cheng to treat Chunyu Chang favorably.

Let us compare the above with the next account found in the biography of Wang Mang.[13] Wang Mang (45 BCE–23 CE) was Wang Feng's nephew with the same surname.

> When his uncle Wang Feng fell ill, Wang Mang stayed by his side and nursed him. He tested medicine before administering it to his uncle and did not fix his own hair, wash himself or change his own clothes for months as he looked after his uncle at his bedside. On his death bed, Wang Feng asked Empress Dowager Wang and Emperor Cheng to treat Wang Mang favorably.

These two accounts are almost identical. Together they suggest that by the sickbed of Wang Feng was a nephew with the same surname and one with a different surname. Uncle Wang Feng told his younger sister (Empress Dowager Wang) and her son (his nephew Emperor Cheng) his dying wish to favor the two nephews. We observe three uncle-nephew relationships centering on Wang Feng here – Wang Feng and Wang Mang with the same surname, Wang Feng and Chunyu Chang with different surnames and Wang Feng and Emperor Cheng with different surnames.

It is likely that the different surnames of the two nephews did not mean much to Wang Feng. He would have felt that both Chunyu Chang and Wang Mang were two of his relatives of his child's generation who had nursed him hand and foot. The two nephews might have stood side by side as they kept vigil by their uncle's bed. Chunyu Chang was subsequently ousted on the basis of accusations brought by Wang Mang. As the former was probably older than

---

13 *History of the Former Han* (*Hanshu*), Vol. 99.

the latter,[14] Wang Mang would have seen Chunyu Chang as his biggest rival among his family group – his contemporary who had an edge over him among the maternal relatives of the emperor.

The relationships between Wang Feng, Chunyu Chang and Wang Mang appear to symbolize the characteristics of the uncle-nephew relationship in the Han dynasty. At the risk of oversimplification, it can be generalized that maternal uncles and nephews had a strong sense that they belonged to the same family group. While the aforementioned uterine sibling relationship was one between half-siblings with different surnames centering on the same mother, the maternal uncle-nephew relationship was one between relatives with different surnames connected by the 'mother' (a woman who had married out of her natal family). Just as the former was not distinguished from the agnate sibling relationship, it is possible that the latter was regarded as no different from a same-surname relationship. It is at least possible to speculate that these relationships directly represent the 'non-patrilineal' aspect of this age.

The history of imperial princesses

This section approaches the question of the strengthening of the patrilineal system by looking at the relationships between imperial princesses, their husbands and their husbands' families. This relationship presented a major contradiction, since as members of the imperial lineage, the princesses were of highest status but as daughters-in-law, they were expected to provide respect and service to their parents-in-law. This section examines the way this relationship was treated in different periods, beginning with the Ming-Qing period for which we have the best records and then working back in time to look at earlier eras.

Imperial princes were given the title of *wang* when they reached adulthood, while imperial princesses were given the title of *gongzhu*. According to historical records from the Tang and later dynasties, the ceremony to confer the title was normally conducted as part of a wedding immediately before the marriage ritual.

Needless to say, these married imperial princesses existed in Chinese society throughout the history of imperial China. As their history is examined diachronically in this section, special attention is paid to changes from the Han

---

14 The mother of Chunyu Chang was the eldest of the four daughters of Wang Jin. It is unclear whether she was older or younger than his eldest son, Wang Feng, but it is likely that the eldest daughter married and had a child before Wang Feng did so. There is a strong possibility that Chunyu Chang was the eldest of his generation (to which Wang Mang belonged).

dynasty to the Six Dynasties period. I begin with an examination of the Ming-Qing period and go back in time in order to ascertain what changed and how the changes came about.[15]

The Six Dynasties seen from the perspective of the Ming-Qing

In historical accounts from the Six Dynasties period on, the husband of an imperial princess was called '*fuma*', because the emperor's son-in-law was given an official position called '*fumaduwei*'. Ordinarily, a woman would move in with her new parents-in-law at the husband's family home and hence 'to marry' was synonymous with 'to take [her] to wife'. This situation did not apply to the marriage of an imperial princess, which was literally described as 'to meet a princess as a wife' or 'to be given a princess as a wife' but never 'to take a princess as a wife'.

So, where did an imperial princess and her husband live after marriage? According to a Qing-era essay, her father, the emperor, would give his daughter who was an imperial princess a residence to live in upon her marriage. She would not live with her husband's parents who, when they wanted to meet their daughter-in-law, had to undergo a ritual similar to that to receive an audience with the emperor. Her husband lived in a building constructed outside of the imperial princess's residence and could not sleep with his wife unless he was summoned to do so. Movement in and out of the residence was managed by the princess's female wet-nurse/house-manager to whom the husband had to pay large sums of money in order to gain entry.[16] The high-handedness of house-manager ladies was mentioned in essays from as early as the Ming dynasty.[17]

When the imperial princess died, her residence along with all its contents, daily necessities and clothing was forfeited as the property of the palace and her widowed husband was evicted from his dwelling.[18] It can be inferred from this account of the husband's eviction and forfeiture of her residence that the building in which the husband lived was an outbuilding of the imperial princess's

---

15 Preceding studies on imperial princesses include Fujikawa (1968), Gao Shiyu (1988), Zhang Bangwei (2003), Wang Shou-Nan (1992), Yi Jo-Lan (1999), Chen Gaohua and Tong Shaosu (eds) (2010–2011), Lee Jen-Der (2001), Huang Chih-Yan (2013) and Kawai (2015).

16 'No consideration for the blood-relation in the royal family' (*Huangshi wu gurouqing*), in *A Sketch Story from the Qing Dynasty* (*Qingdaiyeji*), Vol. 1.

17 'Restrictions on the fuma' (*Fuma shouzhi*), *Unofficial Matters from the Wanli Period* (*Wanliyehuobian*) Vol. 5.

18 See Note 17.

The Patrilinealization of Society

residence and hence to outward appearances, the wife and her husband were cohabiters who lived on the same grounds.

In other words, imperial princesses and their husbands during the Qing dynasty (and probably the Ming dynasty as well) lived together in the sense that they resided on the same grounds even though they lived in separate buildings and led their everyday lives separately. This relationship between the imperial princess and her husband appears to be unchanged from preceding periods. In the Northern Song dynasty, a man named Wu Yuanyi married an imperial princess. The year after his wife's death in 990 CE, he was asked to hand back the residence he had been given. At the same time, he offered to resign from all of his official positions and return to his homeland.[19] The residence in question would have been given to him when he married the imperial princess. We can suppose that Wu lived in that residence with his wife (on the same grounds but not in the same building) and continued to live there after her death. Nevertheless, the case of Wu Yuanyi seems uncommon and the residence given to the husband had to be returned when the imperial princess died according to historical records from that time.[20]

Looking further back to the late Tang dynasty (in the late ninth century), the sons of gentleman scholars at the time were averse to marrying imperial princesses because members of the imperial family were known to be very domineering. The matrimonial estate of the imperial princess was partitioned by walls into exclusive zones and the wife held parties with her own relatives inside her own zone. The husband did not see his wife on many of his visits because she was out 'playing', and her maids simply ignored him when he visited.[21]

In the late Tang period, the imperial princess and her husband led their separate lives in partitioned zones and saw one another infrequently even though they were a married couple. However, they still lived on the same grounds rather than setting their respective homes on separate sites. Instead, they occupied separate territories within the same area. This spatial arrangement was no different from the layout within the imperial princess's residence during the Qing dynasty.

---

19 'The imperial house: The miscellany of the chief-commandant of attendant cavalry' (*Fumaduwei zalu*), in the *Draft Recovered Edition of the Essential Documents and Regulations of the Song* (*Songhuiyaojigao*), Vol. 8.

20 *Supper Discussions of the Stone Forest* (*Shilinyanyu*), Vol. 3.

21 *Stories from Amidst the Court* (*Zhongchaogushi*), Vol. 1.

Chapter 2

Going back even further in time, the imperial princesses of the Song of Six Dynasties (Liu-Song) were reportedly very jealous women, a fact which troubled the King of Xiangdong (later Emperor Ming of Jin). When a man named Jiang Xiao was selected to marry an imperial princess, the king wrote a petition to turn down the marriage in Jiang's name and sent it to the then emperor, hoping to enlighten the imperial princesses and their father. The king criticized their problematic behavior as follows.

The husband is made to run around in confusion to his wit's end as he comes and goes when summoned by the imperial princess. He is stopped as he tries to enter and not allowed to exit either. If he turns back because he can't enter, the wife feels like he is alienating her, and if he asks to be excused, she suspects that he wants to get away from her. When she calls for him, she always orders him to come in the evening and only allows him to leave after sunrise. The husband cannot gaze at the Moon in the evening or twinkling stars in the morning.[22]

Entry to and exit from the imperial princess's daily living space was strictly controlled in this period as well, and the husband's frustration about the difficulties involved in coming and going was no different from the situation in the Ming-Qing period.

Imperial princesses in the Han dynasty

Let us go further back in time to the Han dynasty, to a time when the situation looked rather different from later periods. The imperial princess and her husband set up their respective residences in different locations, and the husband commuted and served his wife. In other words, the relationship between the Han princess and her husband was the complete opposite of the 'Husband is superior, wife is inferior' principle. Historical records report that the following reform was undertaken immediately after the fall of the Han dynasty for this reason.

> According to the Han dynastic convention, the imperial princess lived in her own residence and her husband-to-be came to her residence for the conduct of a marriage ritual. This tradition was changed as Prime Minister Wang Lang of the Wei dynasty raised an objection.[23]

---

22 'Biography of Empress Wang Xiaowu Wenmu', *Song History* (*Songshu*), Vol. 41.
23 'Treatise on rituals' (*Lizhi*), *Song History* (*Songshu*), Vol. 14.

Wang Lang[24] (?–228) was not the first person to express opposition. During the reign of Emperor Huan of the Later Han dynasty (r. 146–167), Xun Shuang (128–190) criticized the convention as 'The husband controlled by his wife' and called for rectification.[25] Wang Lang proposed a revision based on Xun Shuang's advice.[26]

So, what was changed on that occasion? In Han Chinese society, a marriage ritual was normally held at the husband's home. The bridegroom would go to the bride's home and bring her back to his home to perform the wedding ritual. Although I am inclined to think that the imperial princess's wedding venue would have been changed from her residence to her husband's home as a result of Wang Lang's proposal, this does not appear to have been the case.

Reviewing the marriage ritual for imperial princesses in the Song and Ming dynasties we find that the husband-to-be would attend the palace and escort the imperial princess into a palanquin at a designated place. He would then return to the wedding venue ahead of his bride and wait for her arrival. This venue was none other than the imperial princess's residence that had been gifted by the emperor for her marriage.[27] In other words, the imperial princess's marriage ritual was still performed at her residence in the Song and Ming dynasties, in line with the Han-period marriage ritual. Was the 'reform' proposed by Wang Lang at the beginning of Wei (220–265) of the Three Kingdoms a temporary change that reverted to the previous practice? The answer to this question is no, because things were different after the conduct of a marriage ritual between the Han and subsequent dynasties.

The first noteworthy change was in relation to the criteria for selecting the imperial princess's husband. In Han, the candidates were selected exclusively from among marquises. From the Wei of the Three Kingdoms on, this criterion was discarded and any man who married an imperial princess was given the title of '*fumaduwei*'.[28] In Han, each marquis was normally granted a residence in the imperial capital when his title was conferred. Accordingly, any marquis

---

24 Wang Lang was the prime minister during the reign of the first emperor of Wei of the Three Kingdoms (220–226) and therefore the marriage reform concerning imperial princesses is considered to have taken place shortly after the fall of the Han dynasty.
25 'Biography of Xun Shuang', *History of the Later Han* (*Houhanshu*), Vol. 62.
26 Fujikawa (1968).
27 'Blessed Rites/Rituals', *History of the Song* (*Songshi*), Vol. 115; 'Marriage rite' (*Hunli*), *Collected Statutes of the Great Ming* (*Daminghuidian*), Vol. 70.
28 'Fuma', *Notes for Young Beginners* (*Chuxueji*), Vol. 10.

Chapter 2

who married an imperial princess already had his own residence in the capital and commuted to the princess's residence to serve her after marriage. Xun Shuang would have criticized these Han traditions on the basis that 'The husband [was] oppressed by the wife', including this so-called 'commuter marriage' after the wedding.

Into the Six Dynasties period, imperial princesses continued to live in their own residences for life.[29] This situation remained the same in Tang and subsequent periods. What changed was the place of residence of the husband rather than the princess. After the early Wei of the Three Kingdoms 'reform', the husband began to 'cohabit' by living on the grounds of the imperial princess's residence. The venue for their marriage ritual was a 'new residence' for both of them and the husband technically did not go to the wife's residence for the conduct of the ritual. This measure glossed over the flaw in the ritual that could be construed as the oppression of the husband by the wife by staging the 'couple's space of cohabitation' after their wedding. It can be supposed that the removal of the marquis status as a necessary criterion for an imperial princess's husband was an inevitable consequence of resolving the state of 'living apart'. However, the staging of a form of 'cohabitation' had little impact on the couple's actual relationship.

The separate living arrangement influenced not only the marital relationship but also the couple's relationship with their children, resulting in a particularly marked difference in the area of inheritance between different dynastic periods.

Under the Chinese system, each imperial princess was granted an estate together with her title of *gongzhu*, just as an imperial prince was made a king and granted a state. Just like a princely state, an imperial princess's estate was inherited by her heir and during the Han dynasty, the right to inheritance was limited to her biological male children – sons who were born of the princess.[30] This restriction on successors can be regarded as a succession rule that was unique to the Han dynasty, as it was distinct from the regulations of later dynasties. In the Western Jin period for instance, Wang Ji and his imperial princess wife did not have a biological son. Consequently, the husband's *shuzi* was made her heir.[31] '*Shuzi*' refers to a son born of a consort other than the man's wife, indicating that it was possible during this period for the husband's son to

---

29 Zhou Yiliang (1985).
30 'Annals of Empresses', *History of the Later Han (Houhanshu)*, Vol. 102.
31 'Biography of Wang Ji', *History of the Jin (Jinshu)*, Vol. 42.

inherit the imperial princess's estate even though he had no blood relation with her. It is likely that the idea to prioritize patrilineality (the husband's bloodline) became more entrenched in society in the process of transition from Han to the Six Dynasties period.

Why was inheritance limited to the biological son of an imperial princess in the Han dynasty? There is no doubt that this was based on the separate residential arrangement between the princess and her husband. Among the husband's children, only the biological children of the imperial princess would have lived in her residence; his other children by other women would have been raised elsewhere, such as in his residence. In the latter case, there was nothing to prove their biological relations with the imperial princess nor evidence of parenting by her or cohabitation with her. It would have been impossible to qualify someone as an heir in a case like this where not even a social parent-child relationship existed.

On the other hand, the imperial princess and her husband began to 'live together' in the Six Dynasties period. As a result, the imperial princess 'cohabited' with her husband's children whether she was their birthmother or not. Consequently, it became unacceptable to treat children differently depending on who their mother was, even in the case of the imperial princess.

It became possible for non-biological sons to inherit the imperial princess's estate in the Six Dynasties period and the main reason for this change was 'cohabitation of the parents'. Although it was largely a matter of formality, the relationship between 'husband and wife' was established when the princess and her husband began to live on the same estate. This had a strong impact on the 'parent-child' relationship.

The actual rank relationship between the imperial princess and her husband did not change in the Six Dynasties and subsequent periods. It was impossible for the husband to act as such toward the daughter of an emperor and this situation continued for the duration of the Chinese monarchy. However, a change can certainly be identified if we shift our gaze from the husband-wife relationship to the parent-child relationship. With the transition from Han to the Six Dynasties period, the real mother-child relationship between the imperial princess and her biological son was relativized and the expansion of her progeny through her husband became a matter of priority. The imperial princess was taken into her husband's line of succession as his 'wife', just as was any ordinary wife. Although Princess Taiping (c. 665–713) of the Tang dynasty is the most renowned powerful princess in Chinese history, Han imperial princesses were

Chapter 2

treated with far more deference from the viewpoint of the principle of rank order within the family. Their position was detached from the bounds of the normal family hierarchy in which the husband was in a superior position and was far higher than the status afforded to princesses in later periods.

In closing

Fujikawa (1968) concludes that the ritual and institutional history surrounding the marriage of imperial princesses represents a history of struggle between the lord-vassal order and moral principles embodied in the family system. When an imperial daughter was married off to a vassal and an attempt was made to apply the family moral principle of 'Husband is superior, wife is inferior' to such a marriage, contradictions arose in terms of the rituals involving the husband's parents or in-laws as well as in the husband-wife relationship.

In an ordinary marriage ritual, the bride was presented to the bridegroom's parents the day after the wedding and the parents-in-law reciprocated her salutation. The bride was acknowledged as a formal member of the husband's family through the completion of this ritual. In the case of an imperial princess, however, this ritual was not performed until the beginning of Tang and the ritual procedure was not followed strictly even after the practice was initiated. Still, all dynasties from Tang onward contrived ways to avoid conflict with the traditional ritual system. A particularly novel idea was put into practice in the Northern Song dynasty.

The following story (which may seem rather farcical from today's viewpoint) is reported in a history book from that period. Wang Pu (922–982) was a senior vassal in the early Northern Song who had four sons. Their names were *Yi*sun, *Yi*zheng, *Yi*qing and *Yi*xu. The second son, Yizheng, had a son who went on to marry an imperial princess. His personal name, *Ke*ming, included the character '*Ke*' which was used by all males of his generation. He changed it to *Yi*yong upon his marriage to the princess,[32] intentionally choosing a new name with the character '*Yi*', which was the common character indicating generation in the names of his father's brothers.

This change in name was a strategy that reflected the idea common in the early-modern Chinese lineage-based society of seniority between generations, which was seen in the system for selecting personal names. Under this system,

---

32 'Biography of Wang Pu', *History of the Song* (*Songshi*), Vol. 255.

the members of a family who belonged to the same generation used a common character in their names. Sons were not allowed to use the character that identified the names of their father's generation, as this was denounced as a barbaric act that undermined the seniority order in the family. Despite this rule, Wang *Ke*ming changed his name to Wang *Yi*yong when he married an imperial princess, breaking the taboo of the day in doing so. What does this strange story suggest about the relationship between gender and patrilineal lineage?

The purpose behind Keming's change of name was to upgrade his position by using the character that appeared in the names of a senior generation of his family members. This act raised his position to the level of his father's brothers, where his father was no longer his 'father'. As a result, the imperial princess as his bride was no longer required to greet the bridegroom's father with respect due to his change in status. This name change was an expedient way for the imperial princess to avoid the ritual audience with the groom's parents. According to the historical record, this practice continued until the latter half of the tenth century.

Did Northern Song scholar-officials try to circumvent the situation that required the emperor's daughter to bow to his vassals (the bridegroom's parents) in order to avoid compromising the primacy of the emperor? Or did they dutifully contrive to maintain the exact performance of the Confucian ritual to which they were so devoted? It is hoped that further scholarly research will reveal their motivations.

Let us return to the discussion at the end of the previous section. During the transition from Han to the Six Dynasties period, the real mother-child relationship between the imperial princess and her biological son was relativized and she was incorporated into her husband's lineage as his 'wife'. This change represents the greatest shift in the history of imperial princesses. From the Six Dynasties period onwards, even the women of a special class such as imperial princesses were required to abide by the principle of 'Husband is superior, wife is inferior' (albeit on a very perfunctory level) in their spousal relationships. Accordingly, it can be concluded that the level of patrilinealization in Chinese society deepened further as time progressed from the Han dynasty to the Six Dynasties period.

3. Literature and Women in China

— *SATAKE Yasuko*

Introduction

This chapter considers women's contributions as writers, beginning with China's first collection of poetry, the *Classic of Songs* (*Shijing*), and continuing through to poets in the Tang (618–907) and Song (960–1279) dynasties. One difficulty in approaching this subject is the question of how we, as readers, can know whether a specific poetic work was written by a woman. The earliest collection of poetry, the *Classic of Songs*, does not provide the names of authors, male or female, and efforts to attribute particular poems[1] to a female writer on the basis of a 'feminine style of writing' fall back on our own contemporary understanding of what we imagine a women might have written.

    The attribution of authorship, and whether a specific poem was written by a woman, is an important question, since the answer to that question plays an important role in tracing the literary genealogies of women writers. Chinese classical literary culture relied very directly on literary precedents. Later writers read the works of earlier writers and followed models and themes taken up in earlier works in composing their own poems. Earlier works that were formally attributed to female authors provided strong support to women poets of later times as models and justifications. Women poets of later times modeled their works on poems that were believed to be the work of earlier female poets. Since there is no way for us to be absolutely certain of the gender of a poet from the earliest times, in this chapter I have followed Chinese practice and included works that were commonly regarded in the Chinese poetic tradition as works

---

1 Poems in Chinese literature are categorized as follows: *fu* (賦) – rhymeprose or rhapsodies; *ci* (詞) – lyrics of unequal lines composed to a tune; *shi* (詩) – classical poetry.

'authored by women'. While women writers, as well as male writers, tended to model their works on earlier precedents and themes, there is no question that truly talented women were able to add and innovate in new dimensions. This chapter will examine the ways in which women inherited and enriched the ongoing Chinese literary tradition. There is one further complication with regard to authorship that we need to consider. From late Han times on, some male writers who dominated the literary world in the overwhelmingly male-centered society of the time produced works in a genre known as 'boudoir lament' (*guiyuan*).[2] In this style of poetry, a male writer assumed the persona of a woman complaining about being abandoned by her lover. Poems in this genre first appeared in the *Nineteen Old Poems* (*Gushi shijiushou*) collection in the late Han period. The first poets to write in this style were Cao Pi (187–226 CE) and Cao Zhi (192–232 CE), accomplished poets who were also the sons of the famous general Cao Cao (155–220 CE). Following in this tradition, later male writers continued to produce poems in which they assumed a female voice. The female character depicted in this genre was usually a graceful and fragile woman who continued to wait for her lover, even though he had deserted her.

'Swallow song' (*Yan ge xing*)[3] by Cao Pi is an example of an early *guiyuan* poem.

> Why do you stay elsewhere?
> I, a humble woman, guard the empty room alone
> I feel a rush of melancholy as I cannot forget you
> Tears flow and soak through my dress

Another example is Cao Zhi's 'Seven sorrows' (*Qi ai shi*).[4]

> It's been more than ten years since you left me
> I'm a lonely woman always on my own
> [...]
> I wish I could be a southwesterly wind
> And rush into your arms in a far-away land
> If you don't open your arms
> Is there anything this humble woman can depend upon?

---

2 'Boudoir lament' (*guiyuan*) is an expression of distress by neglected, offended or simply unhappy women.
3 *Selections of Refined Literature* (*Wen xuan*), Vol. 27; *Song History* (*Songshu*), Vol. 21.
4 *Selections of Refined Literature* (*Wen xuan*), Vol. 23.

Although Cao Pi and Cao Zhi had completely different poetic styles, they penned very similar *guiyuan* poems. We can imagine that the image of the 'waiting woman' depicted in these works represented an ideal type for men of that time.[5]

The women depicted in these classical poems, written by men in a female voice, cast the woman as a meek and melancholy figure, stripped of her multifaceted personality and turned into a sexual object patiently waiting for the man who has deserted her. We can but wonder if women poets of the time assumed that their own works would be more acceptable if they portrayed stereotypical 'waiting women'. The question is, however, what did women poets actually write?

The pre-Qin period (before 221 BCE)

The *Classic of Songs* (*Shijing*), the oldest existing collection of poems and the oldest literary work in China, is thought to have been compiled before the sixth century BCE. As it is mentioned as a classic in the *Analects* (*Lunyu*), it is clearly older than the latter. It is difficult to interpret the *Classic of Songs* due to its antiquity and the extreme economy of language contained within. There are no surviving records of interpretations from the time of its compilation.

Fortunately, however, there are a substantial number of mainstream interpretations from the period from the Later Han dynasty to the Tang dynasty[6] that can be regarded as contemporaneous.

According to the analyses, eight of the some 300 poems in the *Classic of Songs* were written by women, all of whom were the wives of feudal nobility in the Zhou dynasty. The first verse of 'Swallows' (*Yan yan*) among the Odes of Bei (*Bei feng*) reads as follows.

> Swallows fly about with their wings spread
> The lady was returning and I escorted her far into the country
> I looked into the far distance until I could no longer see her
> And my tears fell down like rain

---

5 For example, see Matsuura ([1982] 1986: 78) and Kusamori ([1973] 2013: 459).

6 Interpretations by the School of Mao Edition of the Songs. According to the *Four Branches of Literature Collection* (*Sibu congkan*) and the *Thirteen Classics with Commentaries* (*Shisan jing zhu shu*).

Because 'return' can mean 'marry', this poem is often interpreted as a song of lost love where a lover who is marrying another man is being seen off. According to the contemporaneous interpretation, however, the poem is about Zhuang Jiang, the legal wife of Lord Zhuang of the state of Wei, sending off Dai Wei, Lord Zhuang's concubine. As Zhuang Jiang did not have a son, she adopted Dai Wei's son, Wan. After the passing of Lord Zhuang, however, the son of another concubine killed Wan, and Dai Wei had to return to her native state of Chen. Zhuang Jiang left her compound and accompanied Dai Wei to the country.

In the poem, Zhuang Jiang laments Dai Wei's departure as if sending off a lover. Zhuang Jiang praises her in the last lines.

> Dai Wei is wonderful, with her deeply sincere heart
> Always calm and docile, a gentle and virtuous person
> Thinking of my late husband, comforted and supported me

The poem is a song of farewell and friendship between the two women caught up in a family feud.

'Bamboo' (*Zhu gan*) in the Odes of Wei (*Wei feng*), a poem about a neglected wife yearning to go home, features the following phrase.

> The beautiful smile shines
> The worn gemstones make a measured sound

Here the smile and the jewelry are not of her husband: the wife is writing about herself. She takes pride in acting genially and courteously without hating her husband, even while he continues to neglect her. Nevertheless, the poem is infused with criticism of her husband who treats her poorly.

Classical China has a history as a literary genre that denounces the injustice of the poor treatment of blameless people, such as the well-known 'Encountering sorrow' (*Lisao*) in the *Songs of Chu* (*Chuci*).[7] 'Bamboo' is similar to the *guiyuan* poems of Cao Pi and Cao Zhi mentioned in the previous section. Nevertheless, unlike the style adopted by the male authors that makes a woman call herself a 'humble woman' (*qianqie*), it asserts her righteousness rather than self-deprecation and is closer to the lineage of 'Encountering sorrow'.

---

7 'Book catalogues in the standard histories' (*Yiwenzhi*) in the *History of the Former Han* (*Hanshu*) by Ban Gu.

Chapter 3

As shown by the two leading examples, the motifs of the eight poems allegedly authored by women in the *Classic of Songs* have surprisingly few elements of woman's grievance or sexual love, at least according to the interpretations of the time.

The Han dynasty period

Of the three female writers who represent the Han dynasty period, the works of Ban Jieyu (c. mid-first century BCE to early first century CE) and Cai Yan (c. 177–249 CE) have been plagued by suspicions that they are fakes created in a later era. However, based on the prevailing view of the time, we shall treat the works credited to them in the official histories as their own works.

According to the *History of the Former Han* (*Hanshu*), Ban Jieyu became a concubine of Emperor Cheng (r. 33–7 BCE) and gave birth to a son who died when he was a few months old. As the emperor subsequently favored the Zhao sisters, Ban chose to protect herself by becoming a lady in waiting to the Empress Dowager and died in semi-seclusion. The 'Rhapsody of self-commiseration' (*Zidao fu*) in the *History of the Former Han* is comprised of a main text containing Ban's life story and a short conclusion, beginning with 'I say again'. Halfway through it, she declares that she learned from classical paintings and literature, took a leaf out of history books, avoided bad examples and single-mindedly followed good examples. This self-assertion is similar to that in 'Bamboo' in the *Classic of Songs*. In the conclusion, however, the 'waiting woman' aspect comes to the fore. 'As I look down at the bright red ground of the inner palace, I remember your shoes / When I look up at the roof as high as a cloud, two strings of tears flow out'. A strong *guiyuan* element has crept into this part.

Ban Jieyu's great niece was Ban Zhao (mid-first century to early second century CE). She was the daughter of Ban Biao (3–54 CE), Ban Jieyu's nephew and historian, and the sister of Ban Gu (32–92 CE), known as the editor of the *History of the Former Han*, and Ban Chao (32–102 CE), a military commander of the Western Regions.

Ban Zhao had three personae; the first was as a scholar and court literati. After her brother Ban Gu died in prison, Ban Zhao wrote the unfinished part of his *History of the Former Han* and lectured Ma Rong (79–166 CE), Later Han's leading scholar, about the book. In the court, she composed poems in the rhapsody (*fu*) style and ode (*song*) style in response to imperial commands. This is corroborated by the fragments of these works left in ancient records.

Her second persona is evident in her 'Rhapsody on the journey to the east' (*Dongzheng fu*), contained in the *Selections of Refined Literature* (*Wen xuan*), an anthology of poetry and literature compiled in the sixth century, along with her father's 'Rhapsody on the journey to the north' (*Beizheng fu*). In her rhapsody, Ban Zhao states, 'My late father embarked on a journey and composed a rhapsody / Incompetent as I am, how could I not emulate his work?'. Thus, her 'Rhapsody on the journey to the east' was consciously written as a sequel to her father's 'Rhapsody on the journey to the north'.

Ban Zhao's third persona is that of an educator. The seven chapters of her *Precepts for My Daughters* (*Nüjie*) are included in the official *History of the Later Han* (*Houhanshu*).[8]

The above three aspects of Ban Zhao are not unique to women and are in fact no different from the roles traditionally assumed by men. The subject matters explored in her writing are not confined to home life. In this sense, there is little difference between Ban Zhao's literary work and that of her male contemporaries.

Cai Yan, who lived at the end of the Later Han period, was one of the daughters of Cai Yong (c. 132/133–192 CE), who was the most prominent scholar and author at the time. When Cai Yong's collection of some 4,000 volumes of ancient books was lost in the ravages of war, it is said that Cai Yan recited 400 of them from memory and wrote them down without 'omission or error'. Unlike Ban Zhao, however, there is no record of Cai Yan's activity as a scholar or court literati. Cai Yan is defined by two poems under the title 'Poem of grief' (*Beifen shi*) contained in the *History of the Later Han*. The poems narrate her own experience.

According to the *History of the Later Han*, Cai Yan was kidnapped by a northern tribe in the midst of the turmoil of the war at the end of that period and held in captivity for twelve years during which she gave birth to two children. However, Cao Cao, a close friend of her father Cai Yong, paid a ransom to secure her release and arranged her remarriage so she could continue Cai Yong's bloodline. The first 'Poem of grief' describes this course of events. It begins with an account of the devastating chaos at the end of the Han, followed

---

8 A prior educational book for women is *Biographies of Exemplary Women* (*Lienü zhuan*) compiled by Liu Xiang (77–6 BCE).

by the invasion of nomadic tribes, Cai Yan's abduction to the northern land, the maltreatment she suffered as a captive, the drastic change of culture and climate, nostalgia for her homeland, being allowed to return home, parting from her beloved children and the ruinous state her homeland was in when she arrived home, written in a long-form epic poem. The second poem ends with Cai Yan's separation from her children as the climax of the story. If the 'Poem of grief' had been recognized as Cai Yan's work through to the Tang dynasty period, it would have had the effect of expanding the motifs of women's literature.

The Wei, Jin, Southern and Northern Dynasties

Zuo Fen (?–300 CE) of the Western Jin dynasty was a successor to Ban Zhao as a court literati during this period. She was the younger sister of Zuo Si (?–308 CE), a leading scholar of literature in that dynasty. According to the official record in the *History of the Jin* (*Jinshu*), Zuo Fen composed rhapsodies by imperial command, dedicated eulogies (*lei*) upon the passing of the empress and princesses and presented odes when the empress entered the palace. Every time the court received precious tributes from local regions, she composed rhapsodies and odes. Fragments of these works were quoted in ancient books, as was the case with Ban Zhao's works.

Several poems about Zuo Fen's life have survived. They describe her misgivings about leaving her family to enter the court as follows: 'My beloved family have turned into strangers and we shall be apart forever'[9] and 'two years have passed in a flash since I left my parents' home'.[10] No extant *guiyuan* poems are attributed to Zuo Fen.

Xie Daoyun (mid-fourth century to early fifth century) of the Eastern Jin dynasty was a renowned 'talented woman'[11] and added a new dimension to the lineage of female poetry writing. She composed metaphysical philosophical poems in a genre called 'arcane-words poetry' (*xuanyan shi*) that became fashionable in the Eastern Jin poetry world. The *Classic of Changes* (*Yijing*), *Laozi* and *Zhuangzi* were hailed as the three metaphysical classics (*san xuan*)

---

9 'Rhapsody on longing in separation' (*Lisi fu*), *History of the Jin* (*Jinshu*), Vol. 31.
10 'Rhapsody of thoughts on separation' (*Ganli fu*), *Literature Arranged by Topic* (*Yiwen leiju*), Vol. 29.
11 See Chapter 16, 'Perceptions of "Talented Women"'.

and their words and phrases were actively used in discourses and poetry. Xie An (320–385), 'artistic' prime minister and Xie Daoyun's uncle, and Wang Xizhi (303–361), a famous calligrapher and Xie Daoyun's father-in-law, were highly skilled in this genre.

Xie Daoyun's works are included in an early Tang book as 'Compositions by Wang Ningzhi's wife by the surname of Xie of Jin'.[12] One poem praises Mount Tai (Shandong Province) as follows.

'Among its cliffs is a quiet empty space
It's still, subtle and profound
Not the work of artisans
Its cloud-like structure came about spontaneously'

'Physical things, what right do they have
To move me in all sorts of ways'

'If I live in this space away from them
I shall be able to live out my natural life'

The expression 'physical things' was borrowed from the *Classic of Changes*. She also incorporated words from *Laozi* and *Zhuangzi* freely.

Her only other poem is 'Imitating Ji Kang's poem' (*Ni Ji Zhongsan shi*).[13] It emulates the style of Ji Kang (223–262), who lived some 150 years before Xie Daoyun, telling of her yearning for a supramundane world. Ji Kang was one of the seven sages of the bamboo grove who was versed in metaphysical philosophy.

In short, Xie Daoyun composed intellectual poems on the cutting-edge of the male-centered world of poetry of the time. There is of course no shadow of *guiyuan* in her poetry.

In the late Six Dynasties period about half a century after the time of Xie Daoyun, however, the works of a handful of female poets became almost completely steeped in *guiyuan*. Bao Linghui, the younger sister of Bao Zhao (c. 414–466) of the Liu-Song dynasty, wrote that her beloved was far away: 'Shedding a lifetime of tears, I wait for him through the autumn into the spring'.[14]

---

12 *Literature Arranged by Topic* (*Yiwen leiju*), Vol. 7.
13 *Literature Arranged by Topic* (*Yiwen leiju*), Vol. 88.
14 *New Songs from a Jade Terrace* (*Yutai xinyong*), Vol. 4.

Chapter 3

The younger sisters of Liu Xiaochuo (481–539) of Liang and the granddaughter of Shen Yue (441–513) wrote many poems in the *guiyuan* genre as well as romantic poems (*yanshi*).[15]

The Tang dynasty

Shangguan Wan'er (664–710) of the early Tang dynasty is considered to be the woman who changed the situation that prevailed in the latter half of the Six Dynasties period. According to official histories such as the *Old History of the Tang* (*Jiu Tangshu*) and the *New History of the Tang* (*Xin Tangshu*), Shangguan Wan'er was the granddaughter of Shangguan Yi (?–664), a scholar and court poet. Her grandfather and father were executed as a result of a political conspiracy when she was a baby, and she and her mother were enslaved in the inner palace. As she grew up, she distinguished herself with her brilliance and wielded influence over court poetry while Empress Wu Zetian and Empress Wei held the reins of power.

Shangguan Wan'er was killed when Empress Wei was deposed. In her prime, she was in charge of drafting imperial orders, presented poems at banquets at the imperial palace and constantly ghostwrote poems for the emperor, empress and princesses, often working on several poems at a time. Almost all of her thirty-odd extant poems[16] are works that praise the gardens of the emperor or of court women and can be seen as classical examples of court poetry. On this aspect, Shangguan Wan'er inherited the tradition of Ban Zhao of the Later Han and Zuo Fen of the Western Jin. Shangguan Wan'er is also considered to be the last female court poet who emerged under the reigns of Empresses Wu Zetian and Wei before the civil service examination system was strengthened. Once the civil service exams were consolidated as the route to official positions, most of the court poets were men who had passed the civil service exams. Since women were not eligible to take the exams, this undoubtedly led to the exclusion of women as court poets in later years.

---

15 *New Songs from a Jade Terrace* (*Yutai xinyong*), Vols. 5–10; *Literature Arranged by Topic* (*Yiwen leiju*), Vol. 92; *Collection of Music Bureau Poems* (*Yuefu shiji*), Vols. 68, 77, 86.

16 *Tang Poetry Chronicle* (*Tangshi jishi*), Vol. 3. '*Cai shu yuan*' at the beginning of the book is the only *guiyuan* poem. According to *Notes on Poetry from Four Seas* (*Siming shihua*), Vol. 4, by Xie Zhen of Ming, it was composed by Mrs. Shen of the Six Dynasties.

Although women were pushed out of the world of court poetry in the central court, they were still allowed to function in the regional government context. One such poet was Xue Tao (c. 770–c. 832), who lived in the middle Tang period. Xue Tao is simply referred to as a 'concubine-entertainer from Shu' in the earliest record from the end of the ninth century.[17] According to later records, she was the daughter of a government official who accompanied her father to his posting in Sichuan Province (Shu). When he died there, she remained and became a concubine-entertainer. Although she was a concubine, less than half of her existing ninety or so works are typical *guiyuan* poems. A majority of her poems are the kind of poems that would have been exchanged on social occasions, or poems about things (*yong wu shi*). Many are moderate and clear-cut short poems which hide the composer's personality and serve as examples of the way in which the qualities of court poetry were continued in a regional context. In this case, Xue Tao's contribution to traditional female poetry is not immediately apparent.

An additional element is more conspicuous in the poetry of Yu Xuanji (c. 844–c. 871) of the late Tang period. According to the earliest record by Huang Fumei (late ninth to early tenth century?),[18] Yu Xuanji was a daughter of townspeople in Changan who was ordained as a Daoist nun sometime after the age of sixteen. Because of her talent for poetry, she constantly mixed with scholars. She was executed for allegedly strangling her maid who she suspected was having an affair with her lover. The Japanese novel *Gyo Genki* by Mori Ōgai was based upon Huang Fumei's work and later records.

Some fifty poems by Yu Xuanji, another Tang period poet, are still extant. Although one half of them are *guiyuan* poems, the character portrayed in them is no longer a conventional 'waiting woman'. Instead, the female subjects of the poems throw sarcasm at men as well as provocations and attacks. '*Zeng linnü*' is one example.[19]

---

17 'Foreword to the *Anecdotes of the Northern Quarter*' (*Beilizhi*) by Sun Qi.
18 '*Sanshui xiaodu*' in *Extensive Records Assembled in the Taiping Era* (*Taiping guangji*), Vol. 130.
19 Its subtitle is 'Dedicated to vice director Li Yi' (*Ji Li Yi yuanwai*). The poems of Yu Xuanji in the section below are based on the *Three Women Poets of Tang* (*Tang nü shiren ji san zhong*) by Chen Wenhua (1984).

Chapter 3

> Priceless jewels are easy to obtain
> But a man with a heart is hard to find
>
> [...]
>
> I could look for Song Yu[20]
> Why would I hold a grudge against the man who broke my heart?

Like Xie Daoyun, Yu Xuanji incorporated the fashionable poetry style of the day. While it was 'arcane-word poetry' for the latter, for the former it was 'poetry about freedom and comfort' (*xianshi shi*),[21] proposed by Bai Juyi (772–846), which prizes a quiet and leisurely life. Yu Xuanji's 'Qian huai' reads as follows: 'In self-seclusion, I have nothing to do / Wind and light play as they please / Scattered clouds, the moon's reflection on the river's surface / An unmoored boat in the ocean / The thicket of bamboo is my companion / Stone pieces are my good friends'. She ends the poem by saying, 'My bed is covered with books / Half-drunk, I get up and comb my messy hair'. As readers already know that the poem was composed by Yu Xuanji, they understand that it portrays a woman readily seen as a libertine in the eyes of conservatives.

'Bamboo' in the *Classic of Songs* and Ban Jieyu's 'Rhapsody of self-commiseration' discussed above asserted the authors' sobriety and legitimacy, while Ban Zhao's *Precepts for My Daughters* advised other women to maintain such qualities. Yu Xuanji's transgression is remarkable in comparison. Her self-portrait with poetry and alcohol as her companions is represented in such verses as 'I am drunk with poetry and wine mornings and evenings'[22] and 'I got drunk and fell asleep, woke up and composed poems / While I took no notice of anything else, my boat drifted away and I found myself near the bank of the Han River this morning'.[23]

---

20 Song Yu is a legendary handsome man from around the third century BCE associated with the following anecdote. Song is said to have refuted an accusation of lechery, stating, 'The most beautiful women in China are all in our state of Chu. The most beautiful women in Chu are all from my hometown. Even they are no match for the daughter of my east neighbor. [...] This beauty has been eyeing me over the hedge for three years, but I have yet to surrender myself to her desire'. ('Rhapsody on the lechery of Master Dengtu' (*Dengtuzi haose fu*) attributed to Song Yu, *Selections of Refined Literature* (*Wen xuan*), Vol. 19.)
21 'Letter for Yuan Jiu' (*Yu Yuan Jiu shu*), *Collected Works of Baishi* (*Baishi wenji*), Vol. 28.
22 'To Guoxiang' (*Ji Guoxiang*).
23 The second poem of 'Travelling on the river' (*Jiang xing*).

In reply to her western neighbor, she writes, 'I have recited one hundred times the lovely poem you gave me, [...] When I look to the west, I'm tempted to look over the hedge as Song Yu's beautiful eastern neighbor did, [...] People feel homesick in the cold months but please don't drink alone if you have good wine'. Here she is inviting her neighbor to drink with her as she liked his poem.

On a fine spring day, she is vexed at the sight of a noticeboard listing the names of those who have passed the civil service examination and complains that women are not allowed to sit the test: 'I resent that the thin silk feminine dress hides my talent for poetry / I can only look up at the noticeboard with envy'. In a poem about her feelings toward a lover, she says, 'We have had sex, but we have never had a union of our hearts'.

In Yu Xuanji's poems lives a free and daring woman who deviates from the stereotypical womanhood found in the conventional female norms and *guiyuan* poems.

Li Qingzhao of the Song dynasty period

Li Qingzhao (1084–mid-twelfth century) is thought to represent the consolidation of the literary works of the women discussed in the earlier sections. She was the daughter of Li Gefei (c. 1045–1105), a Northern Song scholar-official who wrote the *Famous Gardens of Luoyang* (*Luoyang mingyuan ji*). At the age of eighteen, she married Zhao Mingcheng (1081–1129), three years her senior, and avidly studied epigraphy (*jinshixue*)[24] with her husband.

Unfortunately for them, the demise of the Northern Song dynasty was imminent. The Jin forces invaded from the north and forced the court to move to the south. Emperor Gaozong soon assumed the throne in Nanjing and the former government officials moved south in droves, including Li Qingzhao. Then, her husband died of an illness and while she moved from place to place in Jiangnan, she lost most of the study materials she and her husband had collected. She described this course of events in her 'Afterword' to her husband's posthumously published work, *Record of Inscriptions on Bronze and Stone*

---

24 Epigraphy is the field of study combining archaeology and literature that involves analysis of inscriptions and writing carved into metals such as bronzeware as well as stone tablets and epitaphs.

Chapter 3

(*Jinshilu*).²⁵ However, let us begin our discussion with Li Qingzhao as a renowned composer of the *ci* form of poetry.

Ci poetry is distinct from the so-called *shi* poetry, including old-style poetry and regulated verse, in that it consists of more complex tonal, rhythmic and line length patterns. It emerged in the middle of the Tang dynasty period and flourished during the Five Dynasties and Song dynasty periods. Li Qingzhao's *ci* poetry was praised in the most authoritative Qing bibliography, *Catalogue of the Complete Library of the Four Branches* (*Siku quanshu zongmu tiyao*; completed in 1782),²⁶ which states, 'She composed only a small number of *ci* poems but they must be cherished as rare treasures; she was one of the greatest *ci* poets of her generation'. She proved her talent in the new literary style just as Xie Daoyun did in the arcane-word poetry style and Yu Xuanji did in the poetry of freedom and comfort genre.

For instance, her '*Yu jia ao*' is a poem on an almost cosmic scale.²⁷ In it, the protagonist crosses the Milky Way amid the dance of a thousand sails, talks to the Lord of Heaven and commands the powerful winds to 'send my little boat to the Mountain of Immortals in the eastern sea just like the Peng bird'.

On the other hand, she recounts as follows in '*Ru meng ling*', where she vividly depicts a scene from her memory as if it were a dream she has just had.

> How many evenings in the arbor by the river
> When flushed with wine we'd lose our way back.
> Our revels ended, returning late by boat
> We'd stray off into a spot thick with lotus
> And rowing, rowing through
> Startle a shoreful of herons by the lake.²⁸

---

25 This and the poems quoted below are based on the *Collected Works of Li Qingzhao* (*Li Qingzhao ji jiaozhu*) by Wang Zhongwen (1979) as well as the *Collected Works of Li Qingzhao* (*Li Qingzhao ji jianzhu: xiudingben*) by Xu Peijun (2013).
26 Reprint, Beijing: Zhonghua shuju, 1965, Vol. 196.
27 The *ci* poetry was originally written as the lyrics for a particular musical tune and the title of the original tune became the title of the poem and was unrelated to its content.
28 Most of the translations of the works by Li Qingzhao that are included here are taken from the translations by Eugene Eoyang and included in *Women Writers of Traditional China: An Anthology of Poetry and Criticism* edited by Chang Kang-i Sun and Haun Saussy (1999: 89–99).

Just like Yu Xuanji, Li Qingzhao does not try to hide her overindulgence in wine and poetry as we can see in the above poem and in the following extracts: 'I work out a few tricky rhymes, Raise my head, clear my mind of wine' ('*Nian nu qiao*'); 'With whom can I share my drunken conviviality and poetic sentiment?' ('*Die lian*'); 'I'm sorry, my drinking friend and my poetry companion' ('*Yong yu le*'); 'Last night, a bit of rain, gusty wind / A deep sleep did not dispel the last of the wine' ('*Ru meng ling*'); 'My recent weight loss has nothing to do with my drinking' ('*Fenghuang taishang yi chui xiao*'); 'I cannot forgive the darkness of amber [euphemism for wine] in the deep cup / It would dissolve my heart before I sink into inebriety' ('*Huan xi sha*'); 'Why not accept our portion, and be drunk before the cup?' ('*Zhe gu tian*'); 'The wine's finished, pleasant the bitter taste of tea' ('*Zhe gu tian*'); 'Where is my home? / I forget except when I'm drunk' ('*Pu sa man*').

In addition to portraying herself in this manner, she criticizes successive *ci* poets in the fragmented remains of her 'Theory of *ci* poetry' (*Ci lun*). Another reason behind her somewhat poor reputation is her alleged remarriage after the death of her husband that ended with divorce just 100 days later. She was criticized along these lines as follows: 'She scrabbles imprudent street language as she pleases. I have never seen this degree of wantonness in a talented woman from a good lineage' (Wang Zhuo in *Biji manzhi*;[29] early twelfth century); 'Skillfully composed poems but not fit for formal occasions' (Chen Tingchuo in '*Baiyuzhai cihua*' Vol. 8;[30] late nineteenth century); 'She cannot begin to compare to Ban Zhao whose talent and conduct were seen as the exemplar of the inner palace and whose writing and scholarship did her father and brother honor' (Yang Weizhen in 'Foreword of *Caoshi xuezhai xiangeji*';[31] fourteenth century).

Yang Weizhen is referring to Ban Zhao for comparison. However, Li Qingzhao did have two of the three personas of Ban Zhao discussed in an earlier section of this chapter – first as a scholar and second as her father's successor. The first persona is clearly apparent in the thirty volumes of the *Record of Epigraphy*.[32] The first ten volumes contain a database of 2,000 examples of epigraphy from several centuries BCE to the tenth century. The remaining twenty volumes provide commentaries on and appraisals of some

---

29 *Collection of Ci Comments* (*Cihua Congbian*) by Tang Guizhang (1986: 88).
30 Chen Tingchuo's manuscript reprint edition, Shanghai: Shanghai guji chubanshe, 1984.
31 The *Collected Works of Dongweizi* (*Dongweizi ji*), Vol. 7 in the *Four Branches of Literature Collection* (*Sibu congkan*)
32 Based on Zhao Mingcheng, Jin Wenming's correction edition ([n.d.] 1985).

500 selected examples and correct errors in earlier studies and traditions. The face of the successor appears in the 'Afterword' to the *Record of Epigraphy*, written by Li Qingzhao herself. Chen Jingyun lauded it in the eighteenth century, saying, 'Her writing is full of power, complexity and variety comparable to [her father] Li Gefei'.[33] Li Qingzhao was a writer who followed in her father's footsteps just as did Ban Zhao.

Her 'Afterword' reveals the persona of a scholar immersed in the joy of research. Let us look at some of her accounts below. She begins by recounting her life as part of a newly married couple. Her husband, Zhao Mingcheng, was a student of the national university at the time and only came home on the first and fifteenth days of the month.

> On the first and fifteenth days of each month, we took off work and went out. We got 500 qian by pawning some clothes, strolled to the Temple of Xiangguo, bought some epigraph impressions and fruit and went home. As we sat face to face to appraise and eat fruit, we felt as if we had been the people of the mythological golden age.

After Zhao Mingcheng found a civil service job, they were able to collect more valuable research materials.

> As I copied intently, I was even more excited and could not stop. If I came across a painting by a great master or a rare piece of ancient bronzeware, I would take off my coat on the spot to pay for the work.

Their research took priority over everything else.

> We decided at the start to have only one meat dish, only one piece of embroidered clothing, no accessories and no luxurious furniture. If we found a book free from missing characters or errors in any genre, we always acquired it and made a duplicate copy.

---

33 *Catalogue of Jiangyunlou* (*Jiangyunlou shumu*), Vol. 4, by Qian Qianyi, annotated by Chen Jingyun ([n.d.] 1969).

They even spent their relaxation time after meals in the following way.

> After a meal, we always sat in our study room, made tea and pointed at a pile of books. We would ask one another, "In which line of which page of which volume of which book do you find such and such?" We decided on who would drink the tea based on this guessing game. When one guessed correctly, we would raise our cups and laugh out loud so much so that tea spilled on the chest and we had to stand up to drink it. We were deeply satisfied to grow old together in this way.

As mentioned earlier, however, the Northern Song dynasty fell when Li Qingzhao was forty-three and then her husband passed away. As the couple could not transport their vast collection of research materials in its entirety, they left much of it behind at home or dispatched it to their relatives inland to protect it from the ravages of war. Yet, all was reduced to ashes. The small number of artefacts Li Qingzhao carried with her were also lost while she moved from place to place in Jiangnan. The latter half of the 'Afterword' consists of her accounts of tragic losses in the maelstrom of war. Cai Yan's 'Poem of grief' discussed in the second part of this chapter was also about the chaos of war, but Li Qingzhao's 'Afterword' is a far more specific and heartfelt record based on her personal experience.

Her '*Sheng sheng man*' is believed to have been composed after her southward move. It is generally very difficult to estimate when a poem was composed, but the deep sense of loss permeating the entire *ci* verse certainly echoes the latter half of the 'Afterword'.

> Search ... seek
> Dreary ... desolate
> Dismal ... downcast ... disconsolate
> A warm spell – then it's back to winter
> Hard to find rest.
> A few swallows of weak wine
> Can hardly fend off the urgent wind towards evening.
> The wild geese have gone –
> Breaks one's heart! –
> They are acquaintances from the old days.

The poem begins with fourteen syllables of reduplication ('*Xunxun mimi, Lengleng qingqing, Qiqi cancan qiqi*'[34]). It is an innovative opening of which it was said that it seemed 'as if pearls of various sizes are falling on a jade saucer' (Xu Qiu 1636–1708) in *Ciyuan congtan* (Vol. 3).[35] Despite liberal use of colloquial words of the time, the poem is without a hint of vulgarity or frivolity. An overwhelming sense of loss percolates through her plain and steady words and filters down to the poem's core.

In closing

As I stated in the introduction, the men who controlled the literary world of Classical China composed *guiyuan* poems masquerading as women and created their ideal type in the 'waiting woman'. Although this ideal image from the male perspective was also represented in the works supposedly composed by women, a significant fraction of a small pool of female writers went beyond the bounds of such view.

In the *Classic of Songs*, those attributed to the wives of feudal nobility by the interpretations in the heyday of *guiyuan* poetry exhibited a strong sense of pride or dignity at odds with the typical 'waiting woman'. Possibly emulating these examples, Ban Zhao of the Later Han dynasty had success as a scholar, educator, inheritor of her father's style and court literati. Zuo Fen of the Western Jin dynasty and Shangguan Wan'er of the early Tang followed in this tradition claiming identities as court literati. Meanwhile, the 'Poem of grief' reportedly composed by Cai Yan of the Later Han broadened the scope of subject matters for poetry by depicting the desolation of war in the lead up to the fall of a dynasty. Xie Daoyun of the Eastern Jin dynasty composed metaphysical philosophical poems in vogue at the time and Yu Xuanji of late Tang incorporated the *xianshi shi* style of poetry that became fashionable from the middle Tang period. While Yu Xuanji was a master of *guiyuan* poems, her heroine was a non-conventional, provocative and aggressive woman.

---

34 尋尋覓覓、冷冷清清、悽悽慘慘戚戚
35 Xu Qiu, corrected and annotated by Tang Guizhang ([n.d.] 1981: 57).

Li Qingzhao of the Song dynasty combined all of these different identities, including scholar, father's successor, recorder of a war-torn world at the end of a dynasty, practitioner of new literature and narrator of a non-conventional self. The works of this excellent *ci* poet are often placed in the *guiyuan* genre. Yet, her 'Sheng sheng man', for example, smashes through the *guiyuan* poems written by men and extends into the vast emptiness beyond.

Classical literature written by the hands of women scintillated as it rushed through many different fields and outstripped the 'women's literature' created by men.

4. The Family in the Tang Period

— *WONG Yu-Hsuan*

Introduction

This chapter introduces numerous studies on Tang-period family and kinship published in Taiwan and Japan. As I begin discussion of questions related to studies of Tang family history, it is necessary to clarify the meaning of several key terms and how they have been used by scholars researching Tang history. These key terms are household (*jiating*), family (*jiazu*) and lineage (*zongzu*). Tu Cheng-Sheng, a leading expert on Tang history at Academia Sinica, has defined the terms as follows: the household is a group that includes three generations that live together and share a common budget, or in some cases those who share the same grandfather and live together and share the same budget; 'family' refers to a broader group that also includes those outside the direct line of descent who share shorter mourning obligations but do not live together and share a common budget; and 'lineage' refers to a still larger group that also includes those who share the same surname but are beyond the five ranks of mourning (Tu Cheng-Sheng, 1992). However, a survey of studies by historians of the Tang shows that Tu's formulation has not been universally accepted. This is because many scholars work from a model of the lineage based on practices developed during the Song and later dynasties, and connections to the Tang lineage are unclear. As a result of a lack of sources, and lack of clarity in the sources that do exist, the line between the 'family' and the 'lineage' is blurry, and there has been no way for historians in the field to deal with this issue.

Given this difficulty, we can at least assert without much question that the term 'household' refers to a group sharing common descent and living together, that family includes a broader group of people than the household encompassing collateral, blood-related kin and that the lineage is broader than the family, including those who share a common ancestor.

Although the subject of this chapter is research on the Tang family, it includes references to research that considers the household and the lineage, as well as work on the family. The first section is on research by scholars in Taiwan, and the second section features work by researchers in Japan.

Studies of local prestigious families and the family/kinship

The first section of this chapter introduces research in Taiwan, collated under the following three headings: 'Studies of local prestigious families with aristocratic lineages and the family and kinship', 'Studies of women's history and the family and kinship' and 'Studies of the *li* and legal systems and the family and kinship'.[1]

Let us begin with Tu Cheng-Sheng (1992). Tu divides pre-Tang family configurations into the 'Han family type' and the 'Tang family type'. The former is a small family with four to five members, while the latter is characterized as a 'three-generational co-resident unit' (*sandai tongtang*), where grandparents, their children and grandchildren lived under the same roof. In reality, this latter type would have entailed multiple patterns such as the cohabitation of grandparents with all of their married and unmarried children or with just one married child and his family. In any case, the trend of increasing family size is observable in the Tang period.

Tu's study was originally published in 1982 and a further substantial study on a similar subject did not appear until Lo Tung-Hwa (2000) analyzed the Tang family configuration. Lo's understanding was developed in papers published in 2015. Lo divides the Tang family formation into detailed categories with emphasis on relationships pertaining to the ownership of family property. I shall not go into detail here, but like Tu, Lo considers that the typical Tang

---

1 I would like to stress the following point. All of the studies cited above are published papers and hence a vast number of master's and doctoral theses have not been included. In reality, many of the published monographs and articles above were originally written as master's or doctoral theses or their revised versions. Master's and doctoral theses tend to deal with a diverse array of themes. It goes without saying that such studies can power innovations in academic circles. It is my hope that future master's and doctoral theses will continue to open up new horizons and spark new research movements in this discipline.

family was characterized by the co-residence of multiple married adults (e.g., brothers with their respective wives).

Regarding the family in the Six Dynasties and Sui-Tang period, a vast majority of researchers have concluded that it was larger than the family in the Han period that preceded it. This is because the period is regarded as the age of local prestigious families with aristocratic lineages. While research in this subfield has a long history and tradition in Taiwan, Kan Huai-Chen (2012) criticizes the conventional studies by pointing out that they exhibit a strong tendency to explain the kinship group of an aristocratic lineage by superimposing the concept of early-modern lineage on it. It is conceivable that when researchers applied the early-modern concept, they subconsciously assumed that group members shared the same residence and joint family property and that there were devices for family unification such as the family genealogy and ancestral hall. As these features were the historical products of the Ming-Qing lineages, we must refrain from trying to understand Six Dynasties and Sui-Tang aristocratic lineages based on the concept evoked by the later model. Kan proposes that we pay attention to the difference between the aristocratic lineages and the Ming-Qing lineages even if we find some commonality between them. For example, Kan states that while the Ming-Qing lineage members are known to have gathered at one place to conduct rituals to collectively worship their ancestors, it is difficult to find evidence in the historical resources that aristocratic lineages conducted similar joint rites.

It seems that in the past, studies of aristocratic lineages were not interested in the aspect of family relationships and kinship organizations. Research on matrimony (the human connections made in this way) was actively pursued from the viewpoint of how the social stratum of aristocratic lineages was formed and how they maintained their status. On the other hand, there have been few monographs that have dealt squarely with issues such as the relationship between patrilineal kin. I suspect that the view that equates the 'aristocracy' with the 'lineages' has stemmed from this deficiency.

Nevertheless, it is undeniable that aristocratic lineages are an important subject deserving of analysis in the study of the history of the family and kinship in this period, and we do find in the research history numerous valuable studies that must be consulted. I shall introduce some of them next.

Firstly, Mao Han-Kuang (1988) brought a breath of fresh air to the study of aristocratic lineages by scholars in Taiwan offering a wide-ranging analysis of inscriptions on Tang epitaphs (copies based on stone rubbings held by Academia

Sinica). Epitaph inscriptions are of very high research value and are treated as key historical resources in the contemporary study of Tang history. Many of the tomb owners named in these inscriptions are lower-ranking government officials not mentioned in China's standard histories. For this reason, studies using epitaph inscriptions are able to examine not only the aristocrats occupying high positions but also the middle- to low-ranking officials.

Mao analyzes the 'social base' and 'social status' of the then ruling class by reconciling these epitaph inscriptions with standard historical records and applying statistical analysis, making reference to their families and relatives in the process. What is notable is the introduction of the concepts of '*fang*' (房) and '*zhi*' (支) to the analysis. These words refer to a subgroup within a family formed with a certain figure as the ascendant (originator). The splitting of a lineage into these houses and branches was ubiquitous among the Tang aristocracy. Mao argues that the fortunes of these subgroups were linked to the rise and fall of their political and social status.

Lu Chien-Lung (1993) and Wang Jing (2015) also highlight the divisions within a family group such as *fang* and *zhi*. Lu looks at one branch of the Pengcheng Liu family[2] and traces its transition during the Tang period in a concrete way. The branch family secured posts in the central bureaucracy at the beginning of the Tang dynasty and moved from Pengcheng to Luoyang. In middle and late Tang, however, the clan members drifted apart and the unity of the family disintegrated. Wang points out that even a Tang aristocratic lineage that resembles an enormous organization according to its genealogy was actually an ensemble of *zhi*-based small kinship groups bristling with numerous branches. Incidentally, Ch'en Chieh-Hsien (1989) argues that genealogies had been used exclusively by the aristocracy since Wei and Jin, but the weakening of the hereditary aristocracy prompted the common people to compile their own genealogies. This 'democratization of the use of the genealogy' gave rise to a new current from Northern Song onward.

In the Tang period, increasing numbers of aristocratic lineages began to move their residences away from their native land to take up posts in the central government, like the Pengcheng Liu family in Lu's study. Kan Huai-Chen (1995) explained that many of these officials wished to remain in Luoyang after retirement and hence gradually lost their connection with their homeland and

---

[2] A prestige family since the Northern Dynasties and a member of the Liu family of Pengcheng County, Shandong Province, which had split into seven branches before Tang.

Chapter 4

contributed to the 'urbanization' of Luoyang. On this point, Cheng Ya-Ju (2010) also examines the trend toward 'centralization' using one branch (the lineage of Lu Baosu) of the Fanyang Lu family. Cheng found through an analysis of epitaphs that Lu Baosu's descendants moved to Luoyang during the heyday of the Tang dynasty and stopped using their native land as their home base even though they never changed their registered domicile after their move. Another study on this phenomenon is Hu Yun-Wei (2008). As officials' family members frequently travelled back and forth between the places of their new posts and usual residence and the capital, Hu considers the impact of this migration on their lives.

Studies on women's history and the family/kinship

A considerable number of studies on Tang women have been published in Taiwan. However, the number of purely historical studies is small as many of the researchers approached the subject through literature. This field of study experienced a new development with the rise of gender history research in the 1990s. As a relatively significant change, the issues of gender and the family began to draw attention.

While I mentioned the high research value of Tang epitaph inscriptions in the previous section, many such inscriptions found on women's tombs opened a new horizon for women's history research in addition to the study of aristocratic lineages. Again, Mao Han-Kuang was a pioneer in this field. Mao (1995) divides the life of a woman into four stages based on the lives of tomb owners described in epitaphs, namely, the 'premarital stage' (*zaishi*), 'marital stage' (*jieli*), 'mistress of the house stage' (after the mother-in-law's death; *zhujia*) and 'widow stage' (after the husband's death; *guaju*). Mao argues that Tang wives had a closer relationship with their husband's family than their natal family and rose in status within the family because they took on greater responsibilities as they moved through these stages.

Following Mao, Lu Chien-Lung and Chen Jo-Shui studied women-related issues using epitaph inscriptions as their main historical resource. Lu (1997) states that many of the writers of the Tang-period epitaphs of unmarried women were their fathers or brothers whose messages expressed a deep affection for the entombed. It appears that men and women had an equal right to education at the time as the inscriptions suggest that the women buried in the tombs received the same education as their brothers. Lu points out that these two characteristics have not been found in the Song-period epitaph inscriptions of unmarried women.

Chen Jo-Shui (1997) considers the relationship between married women and their natal families on the basis of numerous accounts quoted from epitaph inscriptions that imply that aristocratic women stayed at their natal home for extended periods and that some husbands lived with their wife's natal family. Chen (2004) continues to analyze the associated subjects using brush-note style novellas as the main historical resource. The two studies have been rewritten as Chen (2007), which finds that because aristocratic families were large in size and complex in composition, they had no problem if married daughters returned after their husband's death or stayed for an extended period for some other reason. Accordingly, married women were able to choose to return to their natal home as they wished, depending on their own circumstances, and this was an important factor in promoting a close relationship between a woman and her natal family. Chen (2007) also discusses the relationship between married women and their natal families as well as matrimonial and family issues in the aristocracy by analyzing the novel *Tang Xuan* that narrates the story of a man named Tang Xuan who saw the ghost of his late wife.

In addition to the above empirical studies, Chen Jo-Shui proposes new directions for the field of women's history research in Taiwan. Chen (2007) presents two approaches, one of which is about the relevance of the history of the family. The family and home would have been the primary domain of activity for women. However, in the past, Taiwan's historians have not been sufficiently aware of the need to delve into women's lives. Chen argues that one approach for future studies would be to undertake concrete examinations of, for example, shifts in women's roles within the family – as mothers, wives, daughters-in-law, daughters and mothers-in-law – and the relationships between women in these different roles.

The next generation of researchers eventually responded to this proposal and began to dig deeper into this field. While historical resources make reference to types of women such as 'stern mother, jealous wife, virtuous wife and filial daughter',[3] Liao Yi-Fang (2009) examines the families in which these women

---

3 The 'stern mother' is one who uses harsh punishments in educating her sons. The 'jealous wife' is one who adamantly refuses to raise her husband's son by another woman out of jealousy. The 'virtuous woman' is a widow who maintains her loyalty to her late husband and raises their children singlehandedly despite pressure from her natal family to remarry. The 'filial daughter' is a woman who is prepared to leave her family and children to search for the remains of her missing father.

lived, their human networks and the sociocultural and historical environment surrounding them from the viewpoint of the mother-son relationship.

Cheng Ya-Ju (2001) also focuses on the mother-son relationship. In 330 (during the Eastern Jin dynasty), a woman named Mrs. Yu petitioned for the official recognition as her own child of a child of her husband's brother who had been in her care from a young age. Cheng (2009) reviews the findings of historical studies of the family from Han to Tang and points out that from the third to the tenth century, the notion that 'the father deserved supreme venerability' had not yet gained predominance while it was believed that the ethic that 'the mother was closest emotionally' could not be disregarded. As various ethical values derived from Buddhism and the northern pastoral tribes coexisted and competed with each other, the Confucian norms became fused and aligned with other cultural ideas and principles to possess a considerable degree of flexibility.

Lee Jen-Der (1999) discusses wet-nurses from the second century BCE to the sixth century, using historical records to examine the original social ranks of wet-nurses for the imperial and aristocratic families of the day, their appraisals and the relationship between wet-nurses and their charges during power struggles between the imperial court and the aristocracy. Hu Yun-Wei (2014) discusses the relationship between a stepmother and a child in early Tang from a case study of the relationship between Wang Wan from the Wang family of Langya, who married into the Wei family, and Wei Chengqing, the son of her husband Wei Siqian and his previous wife. This provides a realistic portrayal of the stepmother-stepson relationship complicated by moral principles and realities.[4]

Lo Tung-Hwa (2015) also discusses stepmothers and stepsons, looking at not only the stepmother-stepson relationship but also at that between paternal brothers – the stepmother's biological son and her stepson – and describes in detail a conflict of interest between them in employment and marriage. On the other hand, Lo (2015) deals with the relationship between wife and mother-in-law. This study points out that the relationship between these women was often represented as mutually hostile in the world of popular literature such as novellas, even though it was generally described as 'The mother-in-law was

---

[4] In more specific terms, 'moral principles' refer to Confucian morals or norms for mothers and sons in patrilineal society such as 'The stepmother must treat her own sons and stepsons equally' and 'The stepson must exercise filial piety to the stepmother as if she were his biological mother'. In reality, however, there were social tendencies such as the harsh treatment of stepsons by their stepmother and stepsons not getting along with their stepmother.

deeply affectionate towards her daughter-in-law and the daughter-in-law was very dutiful towards her mother-in-law' (*guci fuxiao*) in epitaph inscriptions. Lo (2015) examines the system of mutual aid within a family and reveals that it was less organized in Tang than in later periods because the joint ownership of family property to service financial assistance was yet to be established and the recipients of the assistance went beyond paternal kin and included maternal and affinal relatives.

Cheng Ya-Ju (2016) offers an interesting case study on the positive effect of affinal relationships, analyzing the 'Epitaph of Chen Zhao' that carries a calendar year in the mid-eighth century. Chen Zhao was related to the imperial family of the Chen dynasty (Southern Dynasties) who first married into the Xu family of Donghai and later remarried into the Fanyang Lu family. Her two marriages rescued her natal family from predicaments and her own cultural accomplishments made a major contribution to the education of girls in her husbands' families. In short, Chen argues that Chen Zhao's marriages conferred great benefits to both her cognate and affinal families.

I mentioned above one of the two approaches for future women's history studies proposed by Chen Jo-Shui (2007). The other approach is cooperation with the fields of research on childbearing and medicine. While the history of medicine is one of the emerging research fields in Taiwan, the pool of researchers working in this area has begun to expand steadily. When it comes to ancient history in this field, however, Lee Jen-Der is the only researcher making significant headway. Lee (2008) is a culmination of such effort and presents China's childbearing culture, methods of praying for fertility, gestation and delivery and means for contraception and abortion. It also explains the history of the development of Chinese women's medicine and areas where women were able to exercise their medical skills.

These studies are not simple studies of the history of medicine because ancient gynecology was deeply linked to childbirth and in turn childbirth and childrearing had a close and inseparable connection with the notion of the family. Moreover, they deal with a relatively long period of time from Han to Tang. Lee's studies deserve high regard for this point as well.

Chapter 4

Studies on the ritual and legal systems and family/kin

The first study worth mentioning in this area is Lee Jen-Der (2001). It is a good guide that uses examples from the Northern Wei period to introduce general readers to a specialized historiological discussion with a succinct and easy-to-understand writing style and explanations. During this period, Princess Lanling of the imperial family (?–c. 520) miscarried and subsequently died after she was assaulted by her husband. The study examines the crime of adultery under the traditional Chinese legal system, domestic violence and women's status through the debate sparked by this incident between Empress Dowager Hu and government ministers.

On the subject of studies on the ritual system in Tang, Kan Huai-Chen (1991) deals with the question of ancestral temples. Although only families belonging to the feudal lord class and above were permitted to construct ancestral/lineage shrines to worship their ancestors, the ancestral temple system was developed during the Tang dynasty, which gave officials in the fifth and higher grades permission to establish ancestral temples. Chang Wen-Chang (2012) discusses family rituals. From the middle Tang period, books on Confucian ritual principles underwent some significant changes. One of them is a phenomenon associated with privately compiled ritual rulebooks,[5] commonly known as family rituals, where scholar-officials vied with each other to compile their own family ritual books for the purpose of educating their family and relatives. This trend became even more pronounced during the Song period, but *Wen Gong Family Rituals* (*Wen Gong Jia Li*) compiled by Zhu Xi was published and eventually circulated widely. In Yuan and Ming, Zhu Xi's privately compiled family rituals began to influence the ritual study principles of the state to the extent that these rules were eventually incorporated into the state-designated book of rituals.

Pan Wei-He (1965), in an early study in the field of legal history, argued that the Tang Code was deeply colored by Confucian ethics, which were a set of ideas centering on familism in the name of bloodline. In this area, collective research led by the research group on the Tang Code and individual studies

---

[5] A book of family rituals is a collection of prescriptions for ritual practices within the family and corresponds to a manual for ceremonies and rites.

published by its members have flourished in recent years. I shall introduce some of them in subgenres, starting with the subject of the patriarch.

Kao Ming-Shih (2003) examines the patripotestal system and argues that the status of the patriarch involved not only the rights granted by the state but also the obligations and responsibilities. Guei Chi-Shun (2005) looks at the provisions relating to 'family complicity in crime' – only the 'head of the family' was subject to punishment in this type of crime under the Tang Code. Guei argues that this rule aimed to impose on the patriarch a duty to maintain 'domestic order'.

As the Tang Code used terms such as 'the master of the house' (*jiazhang*), 'family patriarch' (*zunzhang*) and 'household head' (*huzhu*) to signify the head of a family, Lo Tung-Hwa (2015) attempts to clarify the difference between them. Lo argues that the household head and the master of the house are intrinsically different concepts and cannot necessarily be equated based on the clause in the statutes on households (*huling*) that 'Every master of the house shall be designated as the household head'. The government generally questioned the responsibility of 'the master of the house' who had the ability to control the family and very rarely subjected the 'household head' to punishment for crimes (Lo Tung-Hwa 2015). Similarly, 'the master of the house' and 'family patriarch' were clearly distinguished as the responsible entity under the law: the former concerning matters in connection with the interests of the state such as taxes and duties and the latter concerning other matters such as social and private interests. The 'family patriarch' originally referred to the most senior person in a family. Once the father had reached the age of exemption from tax and compulsory labor, the family would have a master of the house (adult son) and a family patriarch (elderly father) at the same time. Lo argues that in this case the authority of the master of the house and of the family patriarch would be complexly intertwined as the former did not necessarily have the highest degree of authority and hence the power structure within the family was not always pyramidal with the master of the house at the apex (Lo Tung-Hwa 2015).

Lo has also published a study on household registration. The Tang statutes used an age-based classification system to determine the size of farming land and taxes or labor duties: 'infants' for age zero to three, 'children' for four to fifteen, 'youth' for sixteen to twenty, 'adult' for twenty-one to fifty-nine and 'the old' for sixty and over. Lo (2015) analyzes population registers excavated in northwestern China and points out the following about the women recorded in them. The adult-age women who appeared to have returned home after losing their husbands were never noted as 'widows' and rarely recorded as 'adult females'. They were most often classified just as 'youth' and so on in the registers. Li Zheng-Yu (2005), in another study that uses the documents discovered at Dunhuang, shows that according to census returns (declarations of the number of household members and house and land ownership) during the Tibetan empire (Tufan) period, family sizes were relatively large. Li argues that this was a result of an increase in the number of joint families (where a set of lineal relatives such as grandparents, parents and children lived together with collateral relatives such as brothers and their wives and children) as well as the recording of non-consanguineous members such as bondservants in the register.

In the field of domestic order, Chen Hwei-Syin (2005) compares the Tang Code and the family and kinship clauses of contemporary laws and argues that there is a clear structural difference between them, as the former mainly centered on the relationship between parents and children whereas the latter revolve around the husband-wife relationship (marriage). Wong Yu-Hsuan (2005a) points out that although the household and marriage section of the Tang Code was built on the family order that conformed to the principles of kindred law thoroughly tinged with Confucianism, it is highly doubtful that these rules were followed closely in reality. Wong (2012a) analyzes laws concerning the crime of illicit sexual relationship and its legal precedent to examine how the concept of adultery changed from Tang to Song, stressing that the research will not only help us understand the interrelation between men and women in traditional Chinese society but also contribute to the reconstruction of the traditional family order.

In the field of the family and kin relationships, Hsiang Shu-Yun (1991) is a pioneering study on the husband-wife relationship. Hsiang notes that while Tang society observed matrimonial rituals closely, it also gave married women more leeway to remarry as they wished. Liu Yen-Lih (2003) is a monograph about the husband-wife relationship in the Tang Code, and Liu (2007) is an expanded version that includes a discussion about the husband-wife (including concubines) relationship from the viewpoint of rituals in addition to laws. Under the Tang Code, the relationships between husband and wife, husband and concubine and wife and concubine were treated as fictitious patrilineal kin relationships similar to those between father and son or elder and younger brothers and were incorporated in the kinship framework even though they were not real blood relations. Liu argues that the Confucian standards between husband, wife and concubine subsumed the women (wives and concubines), who were major contributors to the preservation of the family, under the patrilineal kin system tactfully and went on to form an unshakable Confucian family institution through the Tang Code. Liu (2005a) examines the husband-wife relationship in the subordinate class. When a woman from a commoner family married a man of the subordinate class ranked just above the bondservant class, the woman's status was downgraded to the subordinate class as the Tang Code had the underlying idea that 'the wife obeys the husband'.

Lee Shwu-Yuan (2005a) discusses what is termed 'domestic violence' today. Under the Tang Code, physical assault of the wife or concubine by the husband was treated as 'battery causing injury' (*oushang*) and violence was not regarded as abuse. Because such acts of violence were considered equivalent to the disciplining of a child by a parent, divorce was the only option if the woman wished to escape from domestic violence. Lee (2010) examines divorce, explaining that legal provisions for divorce such as 'seven reasons for divorce' (*qichu*: husband-initiated divorce) and 'compulsory divorce' (*yijue*: authorities-initiated divorce) were means for the government to wield public authority by law to intervene in marriage, which was basically a private matter. They were formulated for the ultimate purpose of protecting the interests of men. Lai Liang-Chun (2011) analyzes the 'form for divorcing the wife' (*fangqishu*) among the Dunhuang manuscripts. Lai suspects that the form intentionally adopted ambiguous phrasing to avoid conflicts and confrontations in the process of marriage dissolution for the sake of a peaceful conclusion of the divorce procedure.

In the field of the parent-child relationship, Huang Mei-Yin (2003) analyzes the concept of 'three fathers, eight mothers' (*sanfu bamu*)[6] in rituals and laws. Huang states that the actual blood relationship was given more importance than bonds of love and obligation in one's upbringing and therefore in the case of conflict between the birth mother and the stepmother or the biological parents and the adoptive parents, the former always prevailed. Liu Yen-Lih (2005b) also looks at the mother-son relationship, especially the birth mother, the remarried mother and the son under the Tang Code and draws a similar conclusion to Huang's.

Lo Tung-Hwa (2015) reports that when a government official went into mourning for his parent, the type of the mourning clothes to be worn, the period of mourning and the period of leave to organize a funeral varied depending on his

---

6 The term refers to non-biological fathers and mothers and includes stepfather, stepmother, divorced mother (*chumu*), remarried mother (*jiamu*) and concubine mother (*shumu*).

relationship with the deceased (e.g., a biological father or mother or otherwise). Lo (2015) is a monograph on adoption that analyzes the two types of child adoption found in historical records, namely 'general' and 'special'. Lo points out that rules concerning adoption were provided in both the ritual and legal aspects because adoption gave rise to mutual rights and obligations under the law as well as according to Confucian rules to both the adoptive and natal family.

Guei Chi-Shun (2003) discusses other aspects of kinship under the Tang Code. Guei explains that under the Tang Code, those who were 'cohabiting relatives' were among the two types of relatives who were, because of closeness of blood links, exempted from punishment or subjected to reduced penalty in cases where they concealed knowledge of a crime. However, this provision was not applicable to major crimes. Wong Yu-Hsuan (2005b) offers an overview of court actions over disputes between family members and observes that a majority of cases involved senior members (fathers and grandfathers) or senior siblings (older brothers) as plaintiffs suing members of younger generations (sons and grandsons) or juniors (younger brothers). In Song, officials presiding over these cases took a more liberal approach and guided the parties to settlement with flexible advice and guidance such as exhorting them to practice the Confucian doctrine of filial piety rather than strictly applying the standard penalties. Consequently, these cases rarely developed into major social incidents. Lee Shwu-Yuan (2005b) points out that the provisions for collective punishment of the family were much more lenient in Tang than in previous periods and that the revised penalty clause for women excluded the death penalty and instead recommended seizure of assets (*meiguan*)[7] as a penalty. In reality, however, Lee adds that there were cases that did not adhere to this rule in which women were put to death.

Under the Tang Code, privately subordinated people[8] were treated as family members under the control of the master of the house even though they were not related. Wong Yu-Hsuan (2003) analyzes provisions concerning subordinate people and reveals that the severity of punishments was significantly greater for offences committed by the lower (servants) against the upper (masters) than in the reverse situation. Lo Tung-Hwa (2015) explains that the master of the servants who was called the 'master' or 'master of the house' under the Tang

---

7 The person is seized by the authorities and enslaved.

8 There were two types of privately subordinated people under the Tang Code: male and female subordinated people and bondservants. The latter ranked lower in status than the former (more subordinated).

Code had to fulfill three legal requirements to be recognized as such: being in the same register as the servants, having status as a commoner and having a right to a share in family property (*caifen*).⁹ The master of the house was not necessarily the only family member who satisfied these requirements and the position was not limited to men. Nonetheless, Lo argues that the eligibility was generally limited to the close family members of the master of the house (*qiqin*: requiring one year of mourning).[10]

Finally, I shall touch on Kao Ming-Shih (2009). Through an analysis of the Tang Code, Kao argues that the relationships between lord and vassal, superior and subordinate, teacher and student, friends, and monks/priests[11] in addition to husband and wife were supposed to be *yihe* relationships based on a 'debt of gratitude' (*yi* / 義). In other words, all bilateral relationships between individuals and groups outside of blood relationships were defined as those mediated by a debt of gratitude. For example, the state of marriage between a man and a woman was referred to as an '*yihe*'[12] relationship, while a compulsory divorce enforced by authorities was called '*yijue*' under the Tang Code. These expressions were used because the marriage relationship was believed to be a bond mediated by a 'debt of gratitude'. Moreover, the Tang Code provided a standard concerning 'disloyalty' (*buyi*), which was counted among the 'ten abominations' (*shiyi*).[13] Kao argues that a compulsory divorce (*yijue*) was an act of disregarding *yi* just as was disloyalty (*buyi*) and was regarded as a very serious crime that violated the value system of Confucian society.

Characteristics of Taiwan research on the Tang family

In Taiwan, research on Tang-period family and kinship used to be a subfield of the study of aristocratic lineages. It began to gain recognition as a separate genre when studies on family configurations appeared in the 1980s. After an apparent cessation of activity, more researchers emerged in the 2000s to resume studies on similar topics. Today, research into the Tang-period family and kinship is

---

9 Family members such as concubines had no right to a share in the 'division of family property'.
10 They include the grandfather, uncles, brothers and sons.
11 The master-disciple relationship between monks or Confucian priests.
12 '*Yi*' is pronounced 'ɪ' in the International Phonetic Alphabet.
13 The ten most heinous offenses that attracted particularly heavy penalties as crimes that disturbed the order of society and the state.

Chapter 4

deepening in knowledge in conjunction with study in the areas of 'aristocratic lineages', 'women's history' and 'the history of the Confucian ritual and legal systems'. While new horizons such as the history of medicine have opened up, the traditional area of aristocratic lineage research is being re-examined from the viewpoint of the history of the family and kinship. Conventional studies largely dealt with the establishment and maintenance of the aristocratic social class and the interpersonal connection through marriage networks, but family and kinship are drawing more attention today. It is expected that in the future an increasing number of researchers will aspire to investigate topics such as the condition within the family, the relationship between women and the family and the relationships within the family and kin.

Legal documents are one of the fundamental historical resources for the study of the family and kinship and the Tang Code is a particularly important document that offers us a glimpse into the legal framework of the day. Research from this angle has also made significant progress since 2000. As a result of long-term and focused efforts made by academic groups such as the Society for the Study of the Tang Code, research in this area has accomplished a great deal while advancing in the direction of refinement and specialization. Studies on the master of the house and domestic order not only highlighted the characteristics of the family in traditional China but also played a role in the reconstruction of the family order during the Tang period. Studies on the family and kin relationships looked deeply at the subject by examining the law and clarified how the husband-wife relationship and the parent-child relationship were positioned. They provide information that helps us understand the family issues facing today's Chinese society.

Despite these achievements, there are still some issues that are yet to be resolved. One is the issue of the social stratum under investigation. It is undeniable that people and women of the aristocracy remain the main subject of studies in the field of women's history as well as the history of the family and kinship. This inevitably creates the impression that the scope of research is limited to a particular social class. Another issue relates to the fact that there are not very many Tang-period judicial cases in the historical records. For this reason, studies from a legal angle are limited to examining codes and statutes. Regrettably, researchers are currently unable to find sufficient materials to attempt to meet the need to approach issues from a legal practice viewpoint.

Japanese studies of the Tang family

Scholarship on the family during the Tang dynasty in Japan began in the pre-war period. The themes of these earlier studies continued post-war and became one of the major areas of academic study in Japan. These studies have been complemented by more recent Japanese scholarship which addresses new research questions. This section lays out the historiography of the Tang family in Japan in three parts: (1) family property, family forms and the Tang family; (2) great clans and the Tang family; and (3) reflections on recent research trends.

Family property, family forms and the Tang family

Nakada Kaoru (1926) was the first to explore issues related to 'common property' in the Tang family, such as the scope of a joint household and property management and its distribution, through cases of 'common living, common property' in joint households as depicted in dynastic histories and legal codes. Then Niida Noboru and Shiga Shūzō both advanced research on similar topics by expanding the field from the Tang dynasty to all dynasties in China, specifically focusing on the legal history of the family and household. In particular, Niida (1937) primarily examines documents from the Tang-Song period, such as divorce papers, adoption certificates, deeds of family settlement for the division of property, last wills and testaments, and household registers. He also enumerates five kinds of legal documents in Dunhuang manuscripts, such as family settlement agreements, last wills and testaments, adoption certificates, divorce papers and manumission certificates, and analyzes their formats (Niida 1959).

Also contributing to the legal history research on Tang families is Okano Makoto (1976), who examines the legislative history of the Tang marriage law article on 'marriage prohibition'. Examining cases under the section of the Tang Code banning marriage between those who were close kin, Okano explores the background conditions that led to an interpretation which included under this statute those related by marriage who had no mourning obligations, but were bound by hierarchical relations of superior and inferior. Okano (1990) also compares articles in the Tang Code and similar articles in Japanese law dealing with 'violating the law by not selecting the eldest son of the principal wife to be heir' to explicate a legislative change from 'the oldest son of the principal wife becomes heir' in the Tang dynasty to 'the oldest son of a concubine becomes heir' in the Song dynasty.

Chapter 4

Other Japanese scholars began debates about the forms of the family in the Han dynasty from the pre-war period. Moriya Mitsuo proposes a model of the 'three-relationship family' (in which a family consists of parents, wives and brothers as the three relationships). Utsunomiya Kiyoyoshi and his cohorts revisited the model in the post-war period. Hori Toshikazu (1996) summarizes the preceding research and extends scholarship from family types in the Han dynasty to the Tang. Hori argues that small-scale families were standard and commonly found, and that the 'three-relationship family' form and the composite family form were both derived from the simpler, small-scale model. He points out that the 'three-relationship family' is worth studying because: (1) the well-known Chinese family form in which successive generations reside together without splitting the patrimony emerged from the 'three-relationship family'; and (2) this latter family form was long-maintained not only because it was regarded as morally correct but also because it had been enforced by law (namely the Tang Code).

In terms of Dunhuang household registers, Kitahara Kaoru (1980) reconstructs various family forms preserved in the Dunhuang household registers based on Yamamoto Tatsurō's hypothesis about the records of the heads of households. Kitahara infers that the division of households did not take place all at once in the Dunhuang rural areas. Instead, the division of property took place individually after each sibling came of age. Initially, minor siblings lived with the eldest brother; however, one's coming of age entailed another division of the household, and the land share of the eldest brother shrank as a result. Due to this situation, the patrimony was not always divided equally among brothers. If these individual families went on to face worsening economic conditions, it was more than likely that local officers would come to request them to combine their households.

Regarding the history of the family during the Period of Division, Ochi Shigeaki (1997) investigates joint households in which a father and his sons dwelled together and had property in common from the Han dynasty to the Six Dynasties. He points out that this joint household model was not standard in the lower Yangtze region; the Wang and Liu families' 'duplicated patrimony' and the division of property in the Xie family all prove this point.[14]

---

14 The duplicated patrimony, in Ochi's definition, refers to the patrimony – entirety of property belonging to the family – being divided several times after the death of the parents. In such a case, a portion of the patrimony has been divided yet the rest of it remains in common. Therefore, a member of the family can be both an owner of the divided property and a possessor of the undivided property.

Okano Makoto (1976) examines the ritual system and the practice of family extermination as a penalty from the Han dynasty to the Northern Wei dynasty. The scope of Okano's study includes the 'three *zu*' (kinsmen of a given individual from their father's clan, mother's clan and wife's clan) and also the more complex kinsmen categories delineated by the 'nine *zu*'. He reinforces the idea that 'the husband and wife are of one body' in his research. Katsumura Tetsuya (1974) also contributes to the discussion by analyzing Ren Fang's impeachment of Liu Zheng with his own interpretation of events.

Great clans and the Tang family

Many scholars in post-war Japan persistently undertook research into the great clans (the technical term used by Japanese scholars is more accurately translated as 'aristocratic families', *kizoku*).[15] They have conducted detailed and specialized studies to construct and arrange the genealogies and pedigrees of the great clans from the Six Dynasties to the Northern Song dynasty, intermarriage between great clans and the tendency of clan members to serve in the bureaucracy. However, as I discussed in the first part of this chapter on studies in Taiwan on the family during the Tang period, the scholarship on the great clans is not necessarily related to the topic of the family.[16] Therefore, in this section I only introduce studies of great clans that intersect with the research on aristocratic lineages, the family and the home.

Moriya Mitsuo (1968) examines 'family instructions' written in the Six Dynasties and shows that these instructions, in both the Northern Dynasties and the Southern Dynasties, were written with some regard for family welfare. Unlike the Tang family admonitions which were formulaic, the family instructions written in the Six Dynasties varied in style. After investigating the genealogy, family traditions and life career of Yan Zhitui, a refugee to the north, Moriya (1968) points out that the *Family Instructions of the Yan Clan* used examples from Yan's own observations to highlight successes and failures in the north and the south. Yan compared and contrasted advantages and disadvantages of the northern and southern cultures for his children and

---

15 In English, David Johnson uses 'great clans', Patricia Buckley Ebrey uses 'aristocratic families' and Dennis Grafflin uses 'great families'. I use 'great clans' in this article in order to avoid confusion between *jiazu* and *shizu*. The former refers to lineage groups, the latter class identity.

16 Here, I mean that the scholarship on the great clans covers a wide range of topics and the family history of the great clans is just one subfield.

grandchildren, who were born and raised in the north. Takeda Ryūji (1955) contends that the great clans had conduct standards embedded into family codes. The old clans raised awareness of the family practice when faced with the emergence of new bureaucrats. Tanigawa Michio (1976) takes the great clans of the Northern Wei, such as that of Yang Chun, as his research subject and explores one of their family forms in which successive generations resided together, describing their style of life and their relationships with township and ward residents during the Northern Dynasties.

Osabe Yoshihiro (1990) examines the family education of the great clans from the Six Dynasties to the Tang dynasty. He argues that junior members of the great clans depended little on the government school for their education: instead, they learned at home, where their fathers, clan elders and even those related through marriage were responsible for teaching the junior members. Female members of the great clans also received an education. When there was no suitable male member in the family to assume the teaching role, the women would be responsible for educating orphans. Nakasuna Akinori (1993), using epitaphs as a source, enumerates the efforts an elite family would make and the difficulties they would encounter when taking the body of a deceased person home for burial. He argues that these practices reflect the changing concept of 'the family' to the Tang elite.

In addition, Taga Akigorō dedicated himself to research that used genealogies during the post-war period and has also contributed to the field of genealogies and pedigrees written before the Song dynasty. Taga (1981) explicates the particularities of the genealogies and pedigrees compiled before the Song dynasty (referred to as 'ancient genealogies' in Taga's research). He proposes that the 'ancient pedigrees' were products of great clans (literally 'renowned families' in Taga's article), and most of them were official genealogies. This suggests that the compilation of pedigrees and genealogies was state-sponsored. The state allocated different ranks to the great clans for management and governance. Along with the decline of great clans at the turn of the tenth century, the compendium of genealogies of all the elite clans gradually disappeared. The element of family pedigrees was later incorporated into gazetteers in the late imperial period. During the Tang dynasty, many genealogies were titled *jiapu* instead of *zongpu* or *zupu* (genealogies of lineage groups). This shows that the ancient genealogies differed from those compiled in the late imperial period. The former did not include lineage members on a large scale.

In terms of ritual systems, Fujikawa Masakazu (1960) argues that aristocratic society formed in the Wei and Jin dynasties reinforced family bonds. Discussions and reforms about the regulations on mourning garments and rituals, which represented the norms of family relations, received much attention during the Wei and Jin dynasties. The debates often resulted from conflicts between ritual prescriptions and real-life situations, reflecting changes in this period. Fujikawa (1958) also contends that the reforms to the regulations on mourning garments under Empress Wu and Empress Wei elevated the status of mothers and maternal relatives. He attributes the reforms not only to female rulers but also to the openness of contemporary society.

New research trends

From the late 1990s onwards, scholars diverged from traditional scholarship and made advances in the understanding of the Tang family by adopting new approaches or probing new topics, such as issues related to women, marriage and the family. Ōsawa Masaaki (2005a) uses divorce cases to discuss the interrelationship between women and the family. He argues that Tang women enjoyed privileges in marriage alliances and freedom of action.[17] However, the monogamous relationship was not the ultimate stable male/female relationship.[18] While small-scale families became ingrained as a social norm in the Song dynasty, the marriage alliances between great clans receded into the background. Ōsawa (2005a) also examines different opinions about 'jealous women' based on textual evidence ranging from the Six Dynasties to the Song dynasty. He contends that the marriage and family system of Han Chinese people was influenced by Xianbei culture. As the Xianbei elements in the marriage system faded, it was later transformed and reborn into a new system. Ostensibly, the problem of 'jealous women' was no longer a concern in the Tang dynasty, but there remained traces of jealousy in the domestic sphere, which led to the origin of the term 'henpecked husbands'. Wong Yu-Hsuan uses demographic information provided by epitaphs, such as ages of the entombed and his/her

---

17 Ōsawa suggests that Tang women sometimes took a firm line on divorce partly based on the ties with their strong natal families and partly because of the Tang people's open-mindedness about women's behavior.

18 Ōsawa argues that Tang people were open-minded about sexual relations outside marriage because they married less based on fond feelings and more due to political needs. This mentality made their monogamous relationships unstable.

partner and records of their children, to argue that elite men's average age of marriage rose from the mid-Tang period onwards. The age disparity between husbands and wives also increased during that time. It was common for an elite man to collect concubines and produce offspring before he took a spouse. Surprisingly, instead of legally marrying wives, some elite men gave their unmarried concubines the power to manage domestic affairs, even though the concubines could not be regarded as wives. The case reflects actual experiences in aristocratic society. Wong Yu-Hsuan (2003b [Japanese]) also uses epitaphs written in the Tang and the Northern Song dynasties to examine widowhood and the frequency of remarriage. She points out that, in the Tang epitaphs, there were few examples of remarriage, showing that Tang men often celebrated chaste widows who fulfilled the important task of burying their husbands or kinsmen. In contrast, based on the Northern Song epitaphs, many tomb occupants were widows whose husbands died before the women were thirty, indicating that Song men commemorated mothers who dedicated themselves to family education and helped their sons become civil officials.

On the topic of family forms, Ōsawa Masaaki (2005a) examines family structures based on fictional short stories, such as the *Extensive Records Assembled in the Taiping Era (Taiping guangji)* and the *Records of the Listener (Yijianzhi)*. He contends that the minimum size of households in the Tang-Song period consisted of four to six persons, and the average size of households consisted of five to seven persons. He also points out that the upper classes tended to have smaller-size households with more men than women. Wong Yu-Hsuan (2000 [Japanese]) combs through the Tang epitaphs for records of the genealogies, residences and family tombs of thirteen great clans. She finds that stem families, in which parents, the wife and siblings all dwelled together, were most common in the elite class.

As for examining the domestic order, Ōsawa Masaaki (2005a) uses the *Extensive Records Assembled in the Taiping Era* and the *Records of the Listener* to investigate the relationships between masters and their hereditary laborers, such as debased-status groups and indentured servants, from the perspectives of the perpetrators and victims of domestic violence respectively. During the Tang dynasty, the patriarch's family members and bondservants were all submissive to his authority. By contrast, there was a tendency during the Song dynasty to transfer part of the patriarch's authority to his wife. Lineage groups were less influential at the individual or family level, and state intervention was instead more powerful. Wong Yu-Hsuan (2012b [Japanese]) examines the actual state of the master-servant relations based on fictional short stories and epitaphs. She employs the approach of social history and looks at the issue from three different aspects, including the afterlife, freed bondservants who gained commoner status and trials and sentencing in the netherworld.

In addition, recent research trends related to the family and tombs emerged in ritual studies. Egawa Shikibu (2010) points out that the *Ceremonials for the Grand Tang under Emperor Xuan* (*Da Tang Kaiyuan Li*) incorporated tomb-sweeping practices during the Cold Food Festival in the name of tomb-visiting rites. This incorporation reflects how widely tomb-sweeping practices had spread; it also suggests that, contrary to old ritual canons that only allowed the representative chief of the clan to make offerings, it was now acceptable not only for the representative chief but also other family members to offer sacrifice to ancestors. Based on the Tang Code of the law in which the Cold Food Festival was an official holiday, the tomb-sweeping practice had already become a sanctioned festival activity, observed by both elite men and ordinary people. Egawa (2013) also uses the scholar-official Quan Deyu as an example to study the reburial procedures of such officials' families in ritual and legal systems. She argues that the new class of scholar-officials sent petitions for posthumous titles and moved family graveyards to better places in order to elevate the social status of their families.

Characteristics of Japanese research on the Tang family

The field of Tang family studies began quite early in Japan. As early as in the 1920s, a legal history scholar named Nakada Kaoru published research regarding family property. Subsequent scholars continued to pay attention to issues related to family property. Their efforts laid the foundations for this field. However, even as these Japanese scholars long dedicated themselves to studies of family property, they made much more positive contributions to research on a later period, the Southern Song dynasty, rather than the Tang dynasty.

Another area of scholarship that was initiated in the pre-war period was the debate over family forms of the Han dynasty. This controversy continued into the post-war period, and subsequently led to the acceptance of the model of the 'three-generational family'. At first, the debates on the family forms of the Han dynasty were limited to that dynasty. Hori Toshikazu subsequently

Chapter 4

incorporated the Tang dynasty into his research on the three-generational family. Recent scholars working on this topic have also assessed fictional short stories and epitaphs.

Some primary sources, such as Dunhuang household registers, are actually the most relevant sources for research into family types, in particular, those of ordinary people. However, this kind of study is particularly rare, likely because most studies focus on the 'equal-field',[19] with their emphases very much on the state and the political sphere. Thus, issues related to the family remain understudied. Similarly, research on great clans generally focuses on the social class to which they belonged, correlating with political and state issues but seldom paying attention to the domestic sphere.

From the 1990s onwards, the frontiers of knowledge in Tang family studies have extended to gender history. Ōsawa Masaaki's research based on fictional short stories and Wong Yu-Hsuan's scholarship on epitaphs are representative of these new research trends. Nevertheless, only a few scholars have seriously engaged in the topic of the family, leaving the door open for the participation of other scholars.

Conclusion

As we can see from the survey of research on the Tang family by scholars from Taiwan and Japan, one of the major sources for research in this field is the 'Miscellaneous rules' (*Zalü*) in the Tang Code. Legal history approaches have been at the center of both the early research by Japanese scholars and more recent research by scholars in Taiwan. One of the special characteristics of research in this field has been a focus on the complex relationships between individuals who live together and share a common budget.

Although this chapter has surveyed work by scholars from Taiwan and Japan, I would like to add a brief reference to that by scholars from China. Scholars in China, beginning from the 1980s, have published much research on women's history and the history of marriage. When Ōsawa Masaaki investigated questions related to 'jealous women', he discovered that

---

19 The 'equal-field' system refers to the land-reallocation policy implemented from the Northern Wei dynasty to the mid-Tang dynasty. Based on the system, each peasant farmer notionally gained eighty *mu* of land for grain and twenty *mu* for hemp (one *mu* was approximately 0.06 hectare).

many works published in China had been strongly influenced by the Chen Dongyuan's 1930s study *A History of the Lives of Chinese Women* (*Zhongguo funü shenghuoshi*) (Ōsawa 2005a).

How are traditional studies of women's history related to contemporary studies of gender history? I believe that recent studies based on tomb epitaphs represent an important new research approach. Chen Jo-Shui's research on new family forms in the Tang has not only provided inspiration to young scholars in Taiwan but has also had an important impact on the work of scholars in China (Chen Jo-Shui 2007). We can catch glimpses of his influence in the recent work of Chinese scholars.

Finally, I would like to briefly refer to the work of Yao Ping, a Chinese scholar based in the U.S., and her book, *Life Histories of Tang Women*, which was published in Chinese in 2004. Yao's research was inspired by the work of Patricia Buckley Ebrey, and takes tomb epitaphs as a major source in its examination of the life histories of Tang women. Many of the examples are focused on the household. Professor Yao has continued her research using tomb epitaphs, and published *Tang Society and Gender Culture* in 2018.

As noted above, there is a vast volume of research from Chinese scholars, and we can anticipate that there will be many new works that deserve serious scholarly attention in future.

Column 1

Introduction of Historical Materials: Wives' Divorce and Daughters' Inheritance of Property, Seen in Dunhuang Documents

ARAKAWA Masaharu

Historical materials relating to divorce in Dunhuang

This column uses materials that are usually referred to as the 'Dunhuang Documents' to explore a number of issues related to divorce and women's inheritance status in early and medieval China. Dunhuang is an oasis city located in the northwestern part of China (contemporary Gansu Province). From early times until the tenth century, Dunhuang was a prosperous town on the Silk Road that linked China with the Western world. The famous world heritage site, the Mogao Buddhist Caves are located in the suburbs of Dunhuang, and it was there that the famous documents were discovered in the early twentieth century when a local priest found the documents which had been sealed up in one of the caves. The early twentieth century was a period when foreign scholars and adventurers were carrying out exploratory missions in that part of Western China and Central Asia, and most of the documents were taken out of China by explorers from England, France, Germany, Russia, America and Japan. This vast collection of documents dating from the Tang dynasty and earlier numbers in the tens of thousands. While most of the documents are Buddhist scriptures and classics, there are also a significant number of secular documents that provide a detailed picture of life in the Dunhuang region in the ninth and tenth centuries.

Among the many documents found at Dunhuang are numerous items that can be called 'bills of divorce'. However, most of these are not actual bills of divorce, but ones that have been handed down as templates. Moreover, the compiling of large numbers of 'models' of bills of divorce in a similar manner to the writing of letters and the like suggests that divorce was by no means rare in Dunhuang society at the time.

Bills of divorce handed down as such can be roughly divided into the following three categories, in light of their contents.

1. Bills of divorce that should be called 'Bills of husband-led divorce' (*Fangqi shu*) – P.3536; P.3730v (model documents); P.4525; S.343v (model documents); S.6537v (model documents).
2. Bills of divorce entitled 'Bills of wife-led divorce' (*Nüren ji zhangfu shoushu*), and 'Bills of marital equality divorce' (*Fufu xiangbie shu*) – P.3212v (model documents); P.4001 (model documents).
3. Untitled bills of divorce – S.6417v (model documents); S.5578 (model documents); S.6537v (model documents).

Of these, the 'Bills of husband-led divorce' are those in which the husband takes the initiative and are similar to the following.

[Historical materials I] 'Model documents for bills of husband-led divorce (ninth century)' (P.3730v; TTD III: 155)

Translation (based on Umemura 2007: 17–18)
    (a) An anonymous bill of husband-led divorce from an unnamed village.
    (b) A married couple is one where they compassionately respect justice, exchange the cups pledging their coupledom and share both joy and suffering. The manner in which husband and wife relate to each other is just like that of mandarin ducks that fly in tandem; and the way they join knees and gaze at each other's face is akin to the beautiful aligning of two virtues. They love each other, live together as one in body and soul, and after death, they sleep in the same coffin in the same grave.
    (c) If there has been a three-year connection in a previous lifetime, in this lifetime they will be an amicable couple. However, if there were three years of mutual hatred in a previous lifetime, they will become mutual enemies in this lifetime. One imagines

that the souring of the relationship between the two now probably stems from a grudge between their families in a previous lifetime. Developing mutual hostility and dislike will mean hating each other even as far as the afterlife.

(d) As I cannot remain married for life through such an evil connection, I divorce you.

(e) The parents of both parties will be present, and will investigate the assets of husband and wife, and write these out.

(f) After the divorce, please choose the sort of husband that would hold the additional post of a high official and present the appearance of a happily married couple in the lane and garden. Now that we have dissolved our relationship, henceforth we will probably not even have occasion to speak.

(g) I shall give you money for three years of food and clothing. I pray that you will be happy forever.

(h) X year   X month   X day

Offerings

These historical materials appear to have been compiled by the male (the husband's) side, and their contents comprise elements (a)–(h).

(a) Title... records the husband's address and full name.
(b) Introduction... describes the ideal image of a married couple.
(c) Reason for divorce... discord arising from a connection from a previous lifetime.
(d) Pronouncement of divorce.
(e) About disposition of the couple's assets... survey in the presence of relatives.
(f) Permission for the wife to remarry.
(g) Settlement of spousal maintenance... the husband to bear the wife's expenses including for food and clothing and medical expenses for the next three years.
(h) Conclusion... date of compilation.

Among the abovementioned items, from the contents of (f) and (g), etc., it can be thought that these bills of divorce were documents the man's (husband's) side basically should compose, and the woman's (wife's) side should keep.

By contrast, the group in (2) 'Bills of marital equality divorce' differ greatly in character from those in (1). Specifically, they are as follows.

> [Historical materials II] 'Model documents for women's and men's bills (tenth century)' (P.4001; TTD III: 154)
>
> > 1. A bill that a wife hands to her husband (bill of divorce in her own hand) 'Seal'.
>
> According to what one hears privately, apparently if [a couple] who have not had their karmic connection from a previous life enter into a relationship of marriage too lightly, then after several years they will start to fight like cat and mouse. In the home, they will make no effort meekly to yield, and having hurt [each other], will each have different sentiments. If one considers the feelings of their close relatives, it will be necessary for them to take a new husband or wife. Before compiling this 'Bill of Divorce', they met and exchanged words, but they each treated the other like a bird or animal, and it is not a situation in which they could accept each other. Now, with parents and relatives as witnesses, they each express their own desire to separate, and make it possible for them to seek happiness and open a door [anew]. As today it has come to the point where they can separate cheerfully [?] like clouds [flowing away], and finally divorce their partner, even if they should again be joined with a splendid partner, thereafter they must not further hinder [remarriage] or be jealous, or impose their own feelings, or the like. Now, face-to-face with [their respective] closest relatives, they [mutually] divorce [their partner]. All have compiled this document [bill of divorce] with pleasure. Certified by fingerprint.[1] 'Seal'

---

1 In general, the position of the tip and joints of the forefinger were marked with black dots and used as a substitute for a signature.

From the perspective of their content, it can be seen that these historical materials were those that wives compiled in an equal position to husbands. Naturally, they do not contain such items as (f) 'Permission for wife to remarry', and (g) 'Settlement of spousal maintenance'.

Judging from the title, these could even be termed 'Signed certificates of divorce' that the wife's side was likely to have compiled, and it can be assumed that the husband's side would have kept them. Moreover, bills of divorce that carry the title 'Bills of marital equality divorce' also do not have items such as (f) or (g), and from the entire contents it can be seen that couples compiled these from a position of equality.

In the final remaining untitled bills of divorce (3), only S.6417v has the item 'Settlement of spousal maintenance', but the others comprise a collection of model texts with an emphasis on literary embellishments.

In the first place, in Tang legal codes and statutes, three types of divorce can be deduced: 'Divorce that a husband can unilaterally implement for certain reasons', 'Forced divorce by a political power' and 'Consultative divorce with permission of the husband'. (1) 'Divorce that a husband can unilaterally implement for certain reasons' is that by a husband who expels his wife; (2) 'Forced divorce by a political power' is that compelled by the state – this can also be said to have been an expression of the will of the state that did not allow married couples who defied 'proper conduct' (Tang Statutes, Article 31: Section on residence units). The words of (3), 'Consultative divorce with permission of the husband', only appear in 'Tang Code, Article 41: Section on the household and marriage', but it can be considered to have been a divorce by discussion, with the husband's permission being obtained.

In relation to the actual conditions of divorce in Dunhuang, the main focus has been previously directed towards (1) 'Bills of husband-led divorce' that are compiled from the man's position, and 'Bills of divorce' have been collectively termed 'Bills of husband-led divorce'. It can, however, be inferred from the existence of such model documents as (2) 'Bills of marital equality divorce' that in Dunhuang it was not always the case that the husband's side would compile the bill of divorce and hand it to the wife – there were also bills of divorce that the wife's side would sign and hand to the husband. This suggests that there was also female-initiated divorce (see Nie Xiaohong 2009: 73).

Column 1

Historical materials relating to the inheritance of property in Dunhuang

Previously, in relation to women's inheritance of property among the Han in China, the question of whether women had the right to inherit family property has been a significant issue. Many debates have accumulated to this day, such as the dispute between Shiga Shūzō and Niida Noboru around the Song dynasty 'daughter's half-share law'. Since then, debate on daughters' rights of inheritance of family property has expanded and split into an affirmative faction (Niida, Yanagida Setsuko, Itabashi Shin'ichi, Aoki Atsushi, B. Birge, et al.), and a negative faction (Shiga, Nagata Mie, Takahashi Yoshirō, K. Bernhart, et al.). For detailed contents and history of these discussions, see Aoki (2003).

As there are documents that afford a glimpse of the situation of daughters' inheritance of family property in Dunhuang, even though they are models for wills, I would like to introduce one below.

> [Historical materials III] 'Model wills' (Дх.02333В, *Dunhuang Documents held in Russia*, 9: 153)

> Now, on the occasion of dividing [family property] among close relatives, I catalogue the 'desires' [will] of the party in question [who bequeaths the family property] in relation to each of the sons and daughters [who will inherit the family property].[2]

> The division of the above will be determined based upon my Will and Testament, and distributed. I will not allow those who have committed [?] or any of the five heinous crimes [killing one's lord, father, mother, grandfather or grandmother] to take advantage of my Will. If they ever imprudently complain and quarrel, even if I die, I will not allow the granting to them of the 'bounty' [from the division of family property]. If there are any errors in these articles of agreement, then this Will document must be submitted to an official and must be dealt with in accordance with regulations.

---

2 Actual wills specifically listed the contents of family property that is going to be divided (rice fields, buildings, livestock and so on) and the inheritors (eldest son, second son, daughter, etc.).

From this document, it is clear that in Dunhuang around the ninth to tenth century, inheritance of family property, at least by unmarried daughters, was permitted. However, to understand how far such concrete examples – including the previously introduced female-initiated divorce – exerted influence upon Han society in inner China at the time, there is a need to consider the area called Dunhuang along with the historical circumstances comprising the Tang dynasty.

The historical materials introduced here belong to the Tang dynasty, in which it is said that women historically had a socially 'strong' presence. Yet, what we must first consider above all is that Dunhuang was both a society where Han people who maintained Han culture accounted for the majority of the population and also an oasis belonging to Central Asia. For example, in terms of the previously introduced divorce issue, in Sogdian society,[3] an oasis situated similarly in Central Asia, divorce in which women took the initiative was guaranteed (see reference materials in Yoshida and Arakawa 2009: 348–350). What particularly cannot be overlooked is the fact that in an oasis like Dunhuang where only limited agricultural land was available, women existed as a crucial labor-force that supported the livelihoods of the majority of general households. Of course, whether this directly links to elevation of the status of women is a question for further investigation, but in any case, in order to utilize Dunhuang's documents widely for historical research, it is first necessary to clarify how 'special' their contents are.

Abbreviations

TTD = Yamamoto Tatsurō et al. (1978–1987, 2001), *Tun-huang and Turfan Documents Concerning Social and Economic History I–IV & Supplements*. Tokyo: Toyo Bunko.
Dunhuang Documents held in Russia = Eluosi kexueyuan dongfang yanjiusuo, Sheng Bidebao Fensuo, Eluosu kexue chubanshe dongfang wenxue bu, Shanghai guji chubanshe (ed.), *Eluosi kexueyuan dongfang yanjiusuo Sheng Bidebao*

---

[3] Sogdiana was an important early kingdom on the Silk Road in Central Asia, west of the Pamir Mountains. The kingdom was created by people related to contemporary Iranians. The Han dynasty began to conduct trade with the Sogdians in the first century and the kingdom was under Chinese influence in politics, military affairs and culture through the eighth century.

fensuo cang Dunhuang wenxian [Dunhuang Documents held at the St Petersburg Branch of the Russian Academy of Sciences Eastern Studies Institute], 1(17). Shanghai: Shanghai guji chubanshe, 1992–2001.

Reference Material

On the day of Asmānwāč in the month of Masβōγīč in the tenth year of King Tarxūn's[4] reign (25 March 710 CE), Ot-tegin,[5] nicknamed Niδan, takes to wife a woman named Dhγutyōnč who was under the guardianship of Čēr, the lord of Nawēkat.[6]

This woman, called by the nickname Čat, was the daughter of Wiyūs. And Čēr gives his ward [Čat] to him [Ot-tegin] in accordance with traditional law, and with the following conditions. Ot-tegin must give this Čat food, clothing and ornaments as his beloved wife; and as his wife with full authority, he must behave [towards her] with affection in a manner appropriate for a noble man making a noble woman his wife. And in future, if Ot-tegin has any other wife or concubine or similar woman without the permission of Čat, and places Čat in an unfavorable situation for that reason, then Ot-tegin, the husband, must pay thirty pure, good-quality silver dirhams to his wife, Čat. And, in future, if Ot-tegin decides that he will no longer have this Čat as his wife, then, besides food, he must give her the goods she had during her married life and the money she received, and set her free. And he shall have no obligation to give any more compensation, nor to pay anything, above this. After that, he can marry any woman whom he likes. And similarly, if Čat decides that she is no longer Ot-tegin's wife, she should leave his place. In this case, she should return to him the wearable clothing and ornaments and the goods she received from Ot-tegin. However, she may take away her own personal items and what she has worked [?] herself. And she shall have no obligation to pay any more dirhams above this.

---

4 The king of Samarkand. In 709, he surrendered when Arabian troops invaded Sogdiana. The next year, the inhabitants of Samarkand forced Tarxūn to abdicate and revolted; and it is variously claimed that he committed suicide or was killed by Ghūrak, his successor to the throne.

5 A Türkic name, or else a title, meaning 'Prince of fire'.

6 A Sogdian people's colonial town in Semireč'e.

Phase I

After that, she may take any man whom she desires as her husband… [omitted hereafter]…

Source: Document of marriage contract in Sogdiana (Sogdian document).

Column 2

Empress Wu Zetian and Thereafter

KANEKO Shūichi

China's sole female emperor

Empress Wu Zetian is known as one of China's 'three great heroic women', along with the Han dynasty's Empress Lü (Empress Dowager Lü) and the Qing dynasty's Empress Dowager Cixi. However, in contrast to Empress Dowager Lü and Empress Dowager Cixi, who held power in their positions as emperors' mothers, Empress Wu Zetian became the sole empress[1] who reigned under her own name in China's history, and the fact that she wielded power as an official emperor made a huge difference. When an emperor died and the next took his place, the former emperor's empress became an empress dowager (*huang tai*

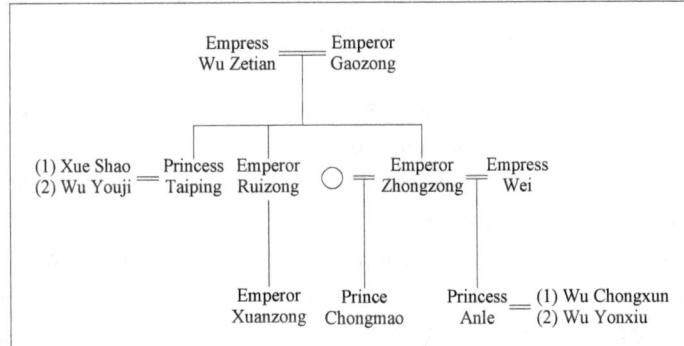

Figure C2.1 Empress Wu Zetian's family tree

---

1 'Empress' has been used to translate several different Chinese titles including those that refer to reigning emperor's wife (*hunaghou*) and the widow of a former emperor, i.e. a dowager empress. Some dowager empresses acted as regents for a minor emperor, often acquiring significant political power. The same term is also used to refer to Empress Wu, the only woman who reigned in her own name. Empress Wu served as *de facto* ruler of China, first as a regent for her ailing husband and minor sons from 665 to 690, and then seizing the throne, changing the name of the dynasty to Zhou and ruling in her own name.

hou, abbreviated to *tai hou*), regardless of whether or not the new emperor was her biological son. In cases where an emperor was a child, he could not directly rule immediately, and in some such cases the empress dowager and her family assumed political leadership. This so-called 'rule by consort kin' appeared most markedly in the Later Han dynasty – Emperor He's empress, Empress Dowager Hexi (81–121 CE), took control of the government, and one sees text praising her administration here and there in later historical materials. Emperor Shun's empress, Empress Liang (116–150 CE), was present at the imperial court at the times of Emperors Chong and Zhi, making decisions in the names of the infant emperors. Empress Dowager Liang's elder brother, Liang Ji, who was a member of the Liang lineage which is said to have been the largest consort lineage in history, poisoned Emperor Zhi. For that reason, Empress Dowager Liang is not highly esteemed, but her efforts at good governance were made at the imperial courts of Emperors Chong and Zhi. As for the Early Han Empress Dowager Lü (?–180 BCE), she was present at the imperial courts of Emperor Hui, Young Emperor Gong and Young Emperor Hong, assisting the young emperors. Although the later evaluations of her activities are not positive, I think that at the beginning of Han state-building, none but a person like Empress Dowager Lü, with her strong temperament, would have been able to maintain stable government. In the Han dynasty, when the empress system itself was underdeveloped and incomplete, there might not have been as much resistance to an empress taking political control as in subsequent ages.

From early times there was a strong tendency to avoid women's direct involvement in imperial court government. The term that is used in historical records to describe the practices briefly described above is 'regency' (*linchao chengzhi*), which refers to an empress attending imperial court and leading the imperial government. The '*zhi*' in '*chengzhi*' means an emperor's commands, and issuing commands in place of an emperor is termed 'saying commands' (*chengzhi*). The word for regency dates from the time of Empress Lü, and in that respect, the official stance that the emperor would take control of government existed from Early Han. In the 'Speech at Mu' (*Mu shi bian*) chapter of the Confucian classic text, the *Book of History* (*Shujing*), we find the phrase 'a hen's crowing' (*pinji zhi chen*); because it is a rooster that announces the hour of dawn, it would be an evil omen for a hen to implausibly announce the hour. This is employed idiomatically as a metaphor for women disrupting politics by speaking out of turn. There is also the phrase 'governing from behind the screen' (*chuilian ting zheng*), meaning that without showing herself in front of vassals in the imperial court, the empress issues instructions to the emperor from behind a hanging screen, which he receives and hands down as commands to his vassals.

Amid such a tradition, Empress Wu Zetian became the sole female emperor. She became empress in 655, six years after the accession of Emperor Gaozong to the throne, and after that, she started to take political control in place of Gaozong, who suffered from paralysis. In 690, she became emperor and founded the Zhou to replace the Tang, thirty-five years after becoming empress and nearly a decade after the death of Gaozong in 683. According to the standard practice during the Tang dynasty, when the previous emperor died, the next emperor would accede to the throne after several days of mourning, and during that blank period of government, he would appoint, as a formality, a 'temporary minister' (*she zhongzai*). This title came from earlier dynastic practice: 'minister of state' (*zhongzai*) was an official title originating in the Zhou, meaning 'to assist the emperor in ruling over all the officials', while '*she*' has the sense of a 'temporary official'. Gaozong died on 4 December 683, and Zhongzong, who was the son of Gaozong and Empress Wu, was enthroned seven days afterwards on the eleventh. During that time, Tian-hou ('Empress of Heaven', Empress Wu's title at the time) directed the administrative and military matters. This is recorded in Gaozong's last will and testament, 'Posthumous edict of the Great Emperor' (*Dadi yizhao*), in the *Great Collection of the Edicts and Commands of the Tang* (*Tang da zhao ling ji*, Vol. 11), which outlines the process by which Empress Wu took power. This position of temporary minister of state became institutionalized in Tang emperors' enthronement ceremonies after this time, but it is important to be aware that it was this pretext for avoiding a political vacuum while the new emperor was in mourning that played a role in Empress Wu's seizure of power.

Empress Wu Zetian and her heir

Numerous research papers and literary works have outlined Empress Wu Zetian's strategy for becoming empress, her moves to crush the opposing

Phase I

faction centered on others in the Tang imperial Li lineage and her proactive appointment of administrative officials through civil service examinations in place of the traditional nobility. However, what has received unexpectedly little notice is the political process in her later life after she installed Zhongzong as crown prince, and the treatment of Empress Wu in the respective reigns of Zhongzong and his younger brother Ruizong, and then Ruizong's son Xuanzong, who was Empress Wu's grandson.

In her later years, Empress Wu summoned Zhongzong (whose accession to the throne she performed after the death of Gaozong and who abdicated in 684 and was exiled to Fang-zhou, now Fang County in Hubei Province) to Luoyang in 698 and made him crown prince. Empress Wu placed Ruizong on the throne after Zhongzong's abdication, but when establishing Zhou in 690, she placed Ruizong, who until then had been emperor as a mere formality, into the position of the emperor's successor (*huang-si*), and kept him in Luoyang, which Empress Wu had renamed Shendu (the capital of god), as the effective capital. In the following year, 699, Empress Wu gave the title King of Xiang to Ruizong. The 'emperor's successor' title was probably discontinued at this time. In May 700, Empress Wu renamed the era and revised the title to 'Emperor' (*huangdi*). In October of that year, she amended the Zhou dynasty calendar which had designated the November following the establishment of Wu Zhou (Empress Wu's Zhou-dynasty) as the beginning of the year (classical Zhou dynasty calendar), returning to the conventional calendar (Xia dynasty calendar) with January as the New Year. Zhongzong was the son of Empress Wu, but his surname was Li, and making Zhongzong the crown prince demonstrates Empress Wu's resolve to return rule to the Li clan. Empress Wu's subsequent moves can be understood to have been what laid the groundwork for the transfer of government to the crown prince by gradually diluting the characteristics of Wu Zhou rule. In that regard, what should be noted are the empress's visit to Chang'an, which had been the capital city of the Tang dynasty, in October 701, and the change of the era name to Chang'an.

From 682 in Gaozong's latter years, Empress Wu continued to remain at Luoyang. Then, after almost two decades, she went to Chang'an, and the fact that she also made Chang'an the era name shows the importance of her move to that location. In November the next year, Empress Wu performed the Rituals for Heaven at the Altar of the Southern Suburbs in Chang'an, but this altar had been a ritual altar of heaven since early Tang, and the Rituals for Heaven at the Southern Suburbs Altar had been the most important rituals for emperors not only in Tang, but also for each dynasty from Han onwards. Accordingly, Crown Prince Zhongzong also took part in the Rituals for Heaven at this time, and Zhongzong's investiture as crown prince itself is presumed to have been reported to the Celestial One (*Haotian shangdi*) and to his Tang ancestors. It is interesting to note that the eighth Japanese envoy to the Tang court, Awata-no-Mahito, arrived in Chang'an one month earlier in October, and he and his group probably took part, as guests from a distant foreign country, in the Rituals for Heaven at the Southern Suburbs Altar where Empress Wu, Zhongzong and Ruizong were all present. After their defeat by the Tang army in the Battle of Baekgang in 663 in Gaozong's reign, Japan (then called Woguo) had severed relations with Tang for a period of thirty years, the seventh Japanese envoy to the Tang court in 669 having been the last previous visitor.

During those years in which there were no visits, the Japanese court studied Tang legal codes via Silla (Korea), changed the name of their country to Nihon (Japan) and promulgated the *Taihō ritsuryō* (Legal codes of the Taihō era) which collectively laid down laws and ordinances. At the same time, the Japanese court decided to send an envoy to China. To Empress Wu, who had expressly visited Chang'an and was about to perform the Rituals for Heaven at the Southern Suburbs Altar, the arrival of the eighth Japanese envoy to the Tang court turned into superb promotional material certifying the correctness of her own political judgement.

We can see this reflected in the epitaph of a person called Du Sixian who served Empress Wu and died in 713, which states, 'As the emperor's virtue has extended far, Japan has come to the court'. It is significant that the Japanese visit to the court for the first time in thirty years was especially mentioned. It is no mistake to see Empress Wu's performance of the Rituals for Heaven during her visit to Chang'an in connection to Zhongzong's investiture as crown prince as being included in the emperor's virtues, but it means that the correctness of such a series of actions was certified by the court visit of Awata-no-Mahito and others. In 703, Empress Wu entertained Awata-no-Mahito and others at Chang'an's Linde Residence of Daming Palace ('Record of Woguo and Riben', in the *Old History of the Tang* (*Jiu Tangshu*), Vol. 199), but in Du Sixian's epitaph it is clearly recorded that Li Huaiyuan, Doulu Qinwang and Zhu Qinming attended as well as Awata-no-Mahito. Of these, Li Huaiyuan and Doulu Qinwang were ministers around that time, and Zhu Qinming became one after that. From this, too, one can imagine the cordiality of Empress Wu's welcome to the eighth Japanese envoy to the Tang court. From Du Sixian's epitaph, it is also indicated that a Ritual Ceremony of the New Year (*Chaohe zhi li*) was held on New Year's Day in 702. This ceremony was an important ritual in which central officials, regional officials who came to the capital to make annual reports and emissaries from other ethnic groups gathered at the imperial court. Not only did they congratulate the emperor on the new year, they also gained a real sense of the extent of the emperor's dominion. Although it cannot be determined from the description in the epitaph whether the Ritual Ceremony of the New Year was held in 703, as Empress Wu returned to Luoyang in October of that same year and Awata-no-Mahito and others were also in Chang'an, it is probably permissible to assume that the ceremony was held on New Year's Day in 703. Du Sixian's epitaph is a gratifying historical record that conveys the reality of rituals and rites in the latter half of the Wu Zhou reign.

Wu Zetian and her sons and grandson

At the New Year in 705, Empress Wu was made to abdicate through a coup d'état while she was bedridden, and Zhongzong acceded to the crown. Steps were taken to return to Tang dynasty practices, such as returning Wu Zhou official titles to their former Tang names. Empress Wu died in November of the same year. However, the Wu clan gradually made a comeback, and perhaps because she felt anxious about that, Emperor Zhongzong's wife, Empress Wei, conspired with her daughter Princess Anle, who had married into the Wu clan, to poison Zhongzong in 710. Empress Wei made the youngest son of Zhongzong (not Empress Wei's biological child) by the name of Wen Wang (King Wen) Li Chongmao into the emperor, took the unprecedented step of installing Princess Anle as a female crown prince, and attempted to establish her own regime modelled on Empress Wu. However, Xuanzong, who was the fourth son of Ruizong by the name of Linzi Qunwang (Semi-king of Linzi) Li Longji, killed Empress Wei and Princess Anle, after which Ruizong was crowned and Xuanzong became crown prince. Soon after, hostility between Ruizong and

Xuanzong became evident, and Ruizong's sister, Princess Taiping, who had also played a role in the abdication of Wen Wang, urged abdication upon Ruizong in the form of his seizure of power of administrative and military regimes. In 712, Xuanzong became emperor and Ruizong became 'Retired Emperor Taishang' (*Taishang huangdi*). However, antagonism between Princess Taiping and Xuanzong immediately intensified, and the following year, Xuanzong purged the main ministers of Princess Taiping's party and ordered the princess to commit suicide. Ruizong relinquished his political mandate, and Xuanzong commenced direct imperial rule. Princess Taiping had also married into the Wu clan, and at this point the Wu clan withdrew from the political limelight.

In this last section, I consider the attitude of Zhongzong, Ruizong and Xuanzong towards Empress Wu. One way to measure the attitudes of the emperors is to consider the ways in which they refer to Empress Wu in the documents known as 'emperors' commands' (*zhaochi*). If we look at examples of the commands of all of the emperors before the current one – in the case of Zhongzong, his ancestors: Emperor Gaozu, Taizong, Gaozong and Empress Wu – we find that there are references to Empress Wu until Ruizong; but they completely disappear after Xuanzong became emperor. From Xuanzong's successor Suzong onwards, references are only to the numbers of generations in imperial succession of previous emperors but there are no examples that are believed to include the existence of Empress Wu Zetian. In other words, Ruizong and Xuanzong mark the boundary at which the treatment of Empress Wu in Tang emperors' commands completely changes. Nevertheless, out of the two commands mentioning Empress Wu from Zhongzong, and the one from Ruizong, the only one that makes Empress Wu an emperor is the 'Pardon on the Accession of Zhongzong' in 705. In the other two, Empress Wu is treated as an empress, but in the first year of Ruizong's reign, 712, in the 'General amnesty at the northern suburban sacrifice', in the *Great Collection of the Edicts and Commands of the Tang* (*Tang da zhaoling ji*), Vol. 73, Empress Wu's rule is explained as having been a matter of extreme urgency, to save a crisis in the Tang dynasty. This kind of justification of Empress Wu's rule is common to both of Zhongzong's emperor's commands. What is impressive is the fact that Empress Wu is described as having been a compassionate mother to Zhongzong and a wise ruler of her subjects, found in Zhongzong's emperor's command thought to date from May in 705 which can be seen in the 'Biography of Wu

Yanyi' in the *Old History of the Tang* (*Jiu Tangshu*), Vol. 183. Empress Wu, who was the biological mother of Zhongzong and Ruizong, was a presence that absolutely could not be publicly denied.

However, when the cloistered ex-emperor Ruizong died in 716, Xuanzong amended the inscription that had hitherto been on Empress Wu's spirit tablet, 'Empress Wu or Holy Emperor of Heaven' (*Tianhou shengdi Wu-shi*) to 'Empress Wu Zetian' (*Zetian huanghou Wu-shi*), and the following year, 705, in an imperial visit to Luoyang, he demolished the Hall of Light (*Ming tang*) which Empress Wu had deemed the authentic palace of the 'capital of god', reconstructed it and turned it back into the Qianyuan palace that had existed until Gaozong's reign. In addition, he scrapped the altar for prayer to receive favorable signs in the River Luo, which Empress Wu had erected in order to enhance her own authority upon acceding to the position of emperor, and so on. In short, he erased the structures in Luoyang that were connected with the celebration of Empress Wu's authority. In light of the exclusion of Empress Wu's existence from emperors' commands from Xuanzong onwards, it is probably clear that from the very start of Xuanzong's accession to the throne, he took a negative attitude towards Empress Wu. Nevertheless, the fact that it began immediately after Ruizong's death indicates that even after his abdication, the presence of Ruizong had been significant for Xuanzong. Various questions surface, such as why Empress Wu, who had banished Zhongzong to Fangzhou, kept Ruizong in Luoyang, and how the presence of Ruizong appeared in the eyes of Empress Wei, who poisoned Zhongzong, and suchlike, but I would like to reserve these for future discussion. In this column, I want to stop at pointing out that the stance towards Empress Wu differed markedly among her own sons – Zhongzong and Ruizong – and from the time of her grandson Xuanzong onwards.

Gender History in China

PART I

Phase II
Song to Ming-Qing: Traditional China
The Strengthening of Gender Norms

Phase II

Introduction

— *SASAKI Megumi*

Tang-Song Transition Theory and gender

There is a widely known theory which postulates that Chinese society underwent a major qualitative change over the period of the Tang and Song dynasties: this so-called 'Tang-Song Transition Theory' was first put forward by Naitō Konan (1866–1934) and argues that there was a shift from the aristocracy and aristocratic society that prevailed during the Wei, Jin, Northern and Southern and Sui-Tang dynasties period to monarchical authoritarianism. Monarchical authoritarianism was based on the notion that there was 'One emperor and all of the other people are commoners', producing a classless society symbolized by the imperial examination system from the Song dynasty onward. The broader transition also involved the change from a predominantly barter-based economy in Tang and earlier periods to the Song period that saw the development of a money economy that promoted further urbanization and commercialization, as well as the shift from the pre-Tang aristocratic and formalistic culture to the popular and more open culture in Song and onwards. Naitō also defined the birth of the Cheng-Zhu school in Song as a change from pre-Tang Confucianism which featured exegetics with no room for new theories to a new framework that allowed free interpretation of Confucian classics. We need to turn to the work of other Japanese scholars to see how they have treated gender issues during this crucial transition period. For example, Seo Tatsuhiko has suggested that there were major changes in gender-related issues when 'romance (literature)' emerged in ninth-century Tang; this was a time when scholars reliant on their own knowledge and poetry-writing skills began to look to courtesans as women of beauty who were able to understand their talent and respond to their witty poems at a time when even hereditary aristocrats started taking imperial examinations in droves (Seo 2002, 2003). Ōsawa Masaaki argues that the family and marriage up to the Tang period were characterized by the predominance of lineage-like associations, freedom of conduct for women, indistinct family relationships and fluid relationships between husband and wife (in the poorly defined state of marriage), whereas a sense of family togetherness and a small family mentality and environment emerged during the Song. Ōsawa also analyzes the way jealous wives were depicted and found a change in the institution of marriage from monogamy with equality between husband and wife during the Northern Dynasties to a system in the Song that was formally monogamous, but in which men were allowed to have concubines (Ōsawa 2005a, 2005b). Satake Yasuhiko (2007) explains the near absence of women in *Traveling Upstream at the Qingming Festival* (*Qingming shanghe tu*), a landscape painting depicting the Northern Song capital Kaifeng, explaining the absence of women as related to the notion of 'Men work outside, women work inside' and the sexual division of labor in the context of the history of the family under the development and expansion of the imperial examination system in the Song period. Kinoshita Tetsuya (2007) argues that the patripotestal attitude of Song scholar-officials was fostered to countervail the matriarchal society that had persisted since Tang.

Studies on women's history and gender history are actively being pursued in China, Taiwan and the United States. I would like to introduce *The Inner Quarters: Marriage and the Lives of Chinese Women in the Sung* by Patricia Buckley Ebrey (1993) as a comprehensive study with the Tang-Song Transition Theory in mind for the purpose of presenting an overview of the gender situation in the Song period. Ebrey characterizes the Song period as an epoch of transition on the assumption that Tang was a time of women's activity while Qing was an oppressive era for women, and describes gender variation in the historical phase where the class system vanished under the imperial examination system and the trend toward urbanization and commercialization continued to intensify. The following list is taken directly from Ebrey's summary in the final chapter of her book with supplementary explanations added in parenthesis by the author as required.

General changes in women's situations

- Increased commercialization of textiles
  (which were mainly produced by female workers).
- Increased literacy among women.
- Growth in the market for women as maids, concubines, courtesans and prostitutes.
- Revised notions of both masculinity and femininity
  (i.e., from horse-riding, vigor and hunting to literati,
  literary classics and antiques for men and more emphasis
  on petiteness and delicateness for women).
- The spread of footbinding.

Phase II

Changes in the rhetoric on family, marriage, and gender associated with the growing importance of neo-Confucianism

- More attention to the segregation of the sexes.
- Higher evaluation of women's roles as family managers.
- Encouragement of women's literacy when used to educate their sons, but discouragement of it for writing poetry.
- Increased emphasis on patrilineality.
- More stringent questioning of widows' remarrying.

Changes in marriage practices from Tang to Northern Song

- More emphasis on choosing sons-in-law for their likelihood to rise in the bureaucracy and less on their ancestry.
- Escalation in the size of dowries.
- Increased evidence of sororal marriages (to a deceased wife's younger sister).
- Increased evidence of uxorilocal marriage.

Changes in marriage practices from Northern to Southern Song

- Decline in cross-regional marriages among the families of higher officials.
- Greater legal recognition of daughters' claims to dowries.
- Some questioning of widows' claims to dowries.
- Greater recognition of the property claims of uxorilocal sons-in-law.

Ebrey explains each point in terms of its association with the characteristics of this historical phase such as the development of the imperial examination system and the increased urbanization and commercialization. Some of the points contradict one another: for example, increased emphasis on patrilineality seems inconsistent with phenomena such as the rise in uxorilocal marriage, greater recognition of the property claims of uxorilocal sons-in-law and escalation in the size of dowries. However, these contradictions can be regarded as manifestations of the transition that took place during Song. The Song period was characterized by the coexistence of, and the interaction between, remnants of the Tang period and embryonic Song elements, which went on to predominate in the Ming-Qing period.

In relation to Chapter Eight of this book, I would like to take note of Ebrey's point: 'More attention to the segregation of the sexes'. Using the accounts of Sima Guang and other Confucian scholars as well as paintings and drawings as historical resources, Ebrey states: 'Thus gender distinctions were intimately connected to class distinctions; or, to put it another way, one way the upper class made its distinctiveness visible was by making its women invisible'. Although it is not expressly mentioned by Ebrey herself, it is easy to infer that the full introduction of the imperial examination system increased social mobility and in turn elevated people's interest in climbing the social ladder and maintaining their social status. Dorothy Ko and Susan L. Mann have been working hard to study the Ming-Qing period from this perspective, focusing on the increase in social mobility of people and families when compared with the Song period (see Chapter Eight).

Chen Dongyuan's *A History of the Lives of Chinese Women*

The view outlined at the beginning of this introduction that there was a major transition from Tang to Song is in fact not new, especially in relation to women's history, but has been an established theory since the discourse on the history of Chinese women was initiated. Chen Dongyuan's (1928) *A History of the Lives of Chinese Women* (*Zhongguo funü shenghuoshi*) has continued to be a seminal work in Chinese women's history since its publication in the early days of historical research into Chinese women; Chen was among the first to demonstrate that the transition from Tang to Song represented a major change in the status of women. Chen's work was inspired by the thinking behind the New Culture/ May Fourth Movement of 1919. In other words, it aimed to explore the historical origins of the oppression of women by the feudal code of ethics (Confucian family ethics) for the purpose of establishing modern individuality and breaking down the feudal code that was hindering that change. The study explained that women were able to engage in dynamic activities without being constrained by Confucian ethics during the Sui-Tang dynasties, which had been influenced by the northern non-Han people, whereas the Song dynasty of Han Chinese turned toward the oppression of women, which escalated through the Ming-Qing period.

Chen saw the emergence and spread of Neo-Confucianism in the Song period as the primary cause for the oppression of women. Cheng Yi of Northern Song stressed the importance of fidelity by saying, 'To starve to death is a small matter, but to lose one's chastity is a great matter' (*Esi shi jixiao shijie shi jida*). In the Yuan, Ming and Qing periods that followed, each dynasty promoted the notion of chastity by the increasingly liberal use of awards – '*jingbiao*' (旌表) – through a state system to commend chaste widows who refused to remarry, unmarried women who remained single after the death of their fiancé, female martyrs who died defending their chastity and loyal wives who committed suicide after the death of their husband. The custom of footbinding also spread to the general female population in the Ming-Qing period. Thus, Chen depicted the history of Chinese women as one of oppression and emancipation in that women were increasingly oppressed under the feudalistic Confucian ritualistic religion that dogmatized predominance of men over women from Song through to Ming-Qing before their liberation in modern times.

After the publication of this 'gold standard' for women's history in China, research activities on subjects such as women and families were sluggish from the 1940s to the 1980s. Since the 1980s, however, historical studies of the Chinese family and women in China, Taiwan and the U.S. have been livelier than ever before thanks to the effect of the revival of historical research in mainland China as well as the advancement of gender studies in the West. Indeed, recent studies can be described as attempts to relativize and enhance the picture of the history of Chinese women painted by Chen Dongyuan. The issue of the feudal code of ethics or chastity that oppressed women has attracted a large share of research due to the availability of historical resources in this area. See Chapter Five for the scarcity of historical resources about women and the problem of biases found in extant materials and Chapters Seven and Eight for studies surrounding the issue of chastity.

There are two main viewpoints from which Chen's picture of the history of Chinese women can be relativized: 'Is it accurate to identify a major transition in the history of Chinese women during the Tang-Song period?' and 'Is it right to portray women's history in China as one of oppression?'. Let me introduce some studies on Song and Yuan in relation to the former question and recent studies on the Ming-Qing period regarding the latter.

Introduction

The Song dynasty period

Academic trends for and studies on the history of women in the Song in China and Taiwan have been concisely discussed in Chen Jo-Shui (2003), Deng Xiaonan (2004), Yen Ju-Ting (2005), Cheng Yu (2006), Tie Aihua (2011) and Wang Shen (2012) (all in the Chinese language). To summarize the recent research trend, studies are finding that it is inappropriate to uncritically assume that the oppressive conditions experienced by women in Ming and Qing can be automatically applied to the Song period because many aspects of the situation of Song women and families were found to have existed in the Tang period when women enjoyed more freedom. Many researchers share the view that remarriage was common for women in Song as it was in Tang, whether they were from government official families or commoner families, that remarriage was not seen in a negative light and that Cheng Yi's comment, 'To starve to death is a small matter, but to lose one's chastity is a great matter', was not socially influential at the time.

Zhang Bangwei is a driving force behind this research current (1989, 2003) and discusses the Tang-Song Transition Theory in his broad introduction to the history of Song society in China (Zhang Bangwei 2011). While Zhang himself takes a passive stance toward the exploration of the link between the issue of women's status and the Tang-Song transition, he thinks highly of research from the perspective of the Tang-Song transition (Ebrey 1993). On the other hand, Ōsawa Masaaki (2005b) explores the academic trend with regard to gender from the viewpoint of the history of the family.

The Yuan dynasty period

In recent years there has been a significant increase in scholarly reconsiderations of the timing of the shift to more restrictive regulations on women's activities, and the importance of changes during the Yuan dynasty under the Mongolian empire. Beverly Bossler (2002) and Sakai Keiko (2006) discuss a change in the *jingbiao* (state's system of commendation) for faithful wives and identify the turning point for women's status during the Yuan period while Ōshima Ritsuko (1997) and Mori Noriko (2005) examine 'Collected biographies of women' in the *History of the Yuan* (*Yuanshi*) and place the transition point in the period from the end of Yuan to early Ming. Although it is commonly believed that the propagation of the Cheng-Zhu school of Confucianism and its influences were the reasons for the declining status of women in these periods, Bossler and Sakai argue that people turned their attention toward the idea of 'faithful wives' and applied for *jingbiao* rewards in large numbers in Yuan as a means to obtain the privilege of exemption from corvée labor in the context of the suspension of imperial examinations and civil service cutbacks. Bossler's and Sasaki's findings are also noteworthy in association with gender as a representation of social status in an age devoid of a social status system, as discussed in Chapter Eight.

There is a string of studies that attribute the decline of women's status in Jin and Yuan to the influences of the customs and practices of the northern nomadic peoples. Yu Hui-Yuan (2003), Wang Xiaoqing (2005) and Chen Gaohua (2011) all make the following points.

- The practice of levirate marriage (a younger brother of the deceased husband marries his widow and prevents her from marrying into another family) spread to Han society during the Yuan period. This was an expression of the view that women were the property of the agnate family.

- This view of women changed the way women's dowries were treated in the Yuan period. While dowries were regarded as women's personal property which they were able to take with them when they remarried in Song, new rules were introduced under the Yuan dynasty preventing women from doing so because they were considered the property of the husband's family.

The lower status of women in nomadic society is an established theory among Jin and Yuan specialists and has been widely introduced to the public (Uno 2014). On the other hand, the view attributing women's 'strength' and 'freedom' observed during the Northern Dynasties and the Sui-Tang periods to the absence of Confucian ethical constraints in northern nomadic society seems to contradict the commonly accepted view stemming from the work of Chen Dongyuan. As this contradiction does not appear to have been explained in a coherent manner, further research in this area is much anticipated.

The Ming-Qing dynasties period

The history of China entered a new stage from the sixteenth century in late Ming. The beginning of the Age of Exploration led to the rise of global trade and a massive influx of silver from Japan and the New World changed China's silver-based monetary system. Against this historical backdrop, social mobility increased further, and cities experienced an unprecedented level of prosperity as economic and cultural centers. Vast numbers of women were commended for engaging in extreme acts of chasteness – e.g., becoming a martyr to their deceased husband or remaining single for their deceased fiancé – which had been unanticipated during the Song period, while the practice of footbinding spread to commoner women. The issues surrounding chastity and fidelity are discussed in Chapters Seven and Eight and the research trend for women's history in China and Taiwan is introduced in Lin Liyue (2005) for Ming and Cheng Yu (2003) for Qing.

In the U.S., Dorothy Ko and Susan L. Mann have published studies that are critical of Chen Dongyuan's depiction of the history of Chinese women as a history of oppression and propose a reinterpretation that states that many of the phenomena that have previously been considered as examples of oppressive practices involved choices made by women themselves (see the 'Preface' by Kohama and Chapter Eight). Mann (2007) describes the lives of the daughters of an elite Jiangnan family named Zhang whose mother encouraged them to engage in poetry composition; the daughters of the family married and lived uxorilocally, maintaining strong bonds between sisters and maternal relatives (see Chapter Sixteen). The study overturns the conventional image of Chinese families as having a history of intense and persistent patrilineal family principles. Ko and Mann used collections of poems written by these women as historical sources. The specific conditions at the end of Ming which meant that their poetry collections were compiled and published by their families and survived to the present day have been combined with incisive analysis by Ko and Mann to produce these studies. The availability of historical sources from Ming and Qing is different from the Tang-Song situation mentioned in Chapter Five. Matthew H. Sommer's (2015) work based on judicial records portrays the family and women in the lower strata of Qing society where wife-selling and polyandry were rife. Li Zhongqing et al. (2000), Ding Yizhuang and Guo Songyi (2005) and Wang Yuesheng (2003) are statistical studies based on a large volume of archival records. We shall wait and see how the unparalleled

Phase II

availability of pre-modern historical resources can be utilized to add more richness to the portrayal of this history.

Column Three shows that the system of female court officials as career bureaucrats actually continued to function into the Ming period in spite of a general belief that it was limited to the Tang dynasty. Chapter Seventeen examines the Ming-Qing view of the human body which has emerged as a new research focus since the 1980s.

5. Livelihood and Gender in the Tang and Song Dynasties

— ŌSAWA Masaaki

Introduction

I was once asked to give a lecture on Chinese history at one of China's National Key Universities to a class of students of the general education course. One student raised his hand in the middle of my lecture, looking as if he wanted to ask me a question. This kind of situation was very uncommon in the Japanese university context, but since I was in China, I listened to what he had to say. His question was as follows: 'Given the scarcity of historical records from ancient times, how can we understand all aspects of ancient societies?' This is an acute and fundamental question to historical science, just what I would expect from a Key University student. Feeling unnerved as much as impressed, I responded as follows: 'Historical records are certainly scarce and highly biased. However, a large volume of records does not necessarily guarantee a clear understanding of history. For example, it is very difficult to get close to the essence of modern history because there are too many historical records. What is important is how to decipher the biased historical records and extract as much information as possible'. The student must have accepted my answer as he asked no further questions.

We do find many limitations and biases in historiographies in general, not only in relation to Chinese history. The primary reason is that writing was monopolized by a small section of the population in ancient times largely comprised of upper-class intellectuals and political rulers, the great majority of whom were men. Their thinking was driven by the dominant values of the time. In the case of China, for example, Confucian values formed a large

Chapter 5

part of its culture and led to the androcentric point of view, which became the starting point for male chauvinism. These values also added authority to the sexual division of labor that would have existed prior to Confucianism (Ueda 1979). In addition, the elite class entertained the idea of the populace as 'ignorant people' who needed proper guidance as well as the notion that mental labor was superior to physical labor. The Chinese historical records contain many layers of these biases. Those who study these historical records as research materials are tasked with taking these biases into account in order to get to historical truths. In this chapter, I explore ways to draw a clear picture of the reality of historical societies through identifying biases in the historical records. As the theme of the discussion – 'livelihood and gender' – suggests, an examination of women's livelihoods naturally directs us to the problem.

The concept of 'livelihood' is very broad. Occupations such as prostitutes and professional female entertainers (singer-dancer-companions) are livelihoods that involve women working individually. Any labor undertaken by women as members of a family can also be regarded as their livelihood. This chapter treats any labor carried out by a family or an individual in order to make a living as a 'livelihood' and limits the scope of the discussion to livelihoods in production and distribution. In China, women were traditionally not permitted to undertake labor outside of their home. This inside/outside (or private/public) distinction pertains to the ideology of the sexual division of labor which requires men to work outside the home and women to stay inside. I examine the link between women and livelihood in the Tang and Song periods in relation to the nature of historical records.

Historical records in Tang and Song: Limitations and possibilities

Let's begin with some examples of biases manifest in ancient visual and written records and examine what we can learn from them. Visual records such as paintings, which supposedly depict reality, are great examples. Although paintings tend to be regarded as faithful representations of reality, they are biased as far as women's labor is concerned. For instance, there are two sets of famous Song paintings entitled *Traveling Upstream at the Qingming Festival* (*Qingming shanghe tu*) and *Pictures of Tilling and Weaving* (*Gengzhi tu shi*). The former is a long scroll painting that depicts the city of Kaifeng during the Song dynasty and is often reproduced in world history textbooks. It vividly portrays the landscape extending from the downtown area to the manors on the outskirts of the city and the life of the people who lived around the city's inland port. A close study of its details, sometimes with the aid of a magnifying glass, is a very interesting activity; it is surprisingly difficult to find women in this image of the downtown precinct. Satake Yasuhiko (2003 [Chinese]) put the spotlight on the ideology of the sexual division of labor at play in the painting – the male/female ratio of the depicted figures is 'one thousand to one'. In other words, a great majority of the population featured in the painting are male. Most of the women are shown to be in their homes or courtyards with children and there are very few female workers in the town. Is this image faithful to an actual street scene and ways of life at that point in time? It is highly unlikely. Multiple historical records describe the presence of women in the town in those days, indicating that the image depicted in the painting reflects a certain intent: the tacit understanding on the part of the painter that women were supposed to stay inside their homes. This was a principled stance taken by the painter who made the decision not to paint women working outside of their homes or walking about the town in the belief that women should not be in the public domain.

The second set of paintings is a visual record that fails to depict farm labor undertaken by women. As its title suggests, *Pictures of Tilling and Weaving*[1] by Lou Shu consists of images and poems about tilling (farming) and weaving (sericulture and weaving). While the original Song period paintings have been lost, the existing copies that were repeatedly remade between the Yuan and Qing dynasties are thought to reflect the original composition. A majority of the people depicted in the tilling pictures are men, while mostly women are shown in the weaving pictures. Setting aside the weaving images for now, a closer inspection of the tilling pictures finds that a small number of women and children are portrayed, but those engaged in farm work are all male. Let us look at the pictures of weeding and winnowing (*fengxuan*), for example (Figures 5.1 and 5.2), from a Qing-period version (reprinted edition).[2] The weeding picture depicts a woman and children delivering lunch to the men who are pulling out weeds. In the winnowing image, women and children are removing chaff

---

1 Watabe Takeshi (1978) is a detailed study of *Pictures of Tilling and Weaving*. The relevant pictures are also contained in *Zhongguo nongye bowuguan* (China Agricultural Museum) (ed.) (1995).

2 Peiwenzhai reprint of *Pictures of Tilling and Weaving* (*Peiwenzhai gengzhitu*), Kangxi Year 35, with foreword (1892), Tokyo: Tōyōdō.

Chapter 5

and foreign objects from the grain behind the winnowing men. These pictures portray women as the providers of service or ancillary support to men rather than as the main performers of labor. These are two of only three pictures that include women among a total of twenty-three tilling pictures in *Pictures of Tilling and Weaving*. In terms of real-world farming practices, however, at the time women did participate in some of the main physical tasks as mentioned below. Yet, such scenes were not depicted in these paintings, suggesting that *Pictures of Tilling and Weaving* is a visual representation of China's traditional idea of 'men till and women weave' – the sexual division of labor in terms of livelihood. Despite clear evidence of women's participation in agricultural labor in the real world, it was not shown in the visual records from the Song period.

Conversely, visual records from the Wei-Jin period show women actually performing agricultural labor. The pictures of farming painted on tomb walls in Jiayuguan (in present-day Gansu Province) (Gansu sheng wenwu dui [Gansu provincial heritage research team] et al. 1985) depict women's

Figure 5.1 Picture of weeding
Source: Peiwenzhai reprint of Pictures of Tilling and Weaving (Peiwenzhai gengzhitu), Kangxi Year 35, with foreword (1892), Tokyo: Tōyōdō.

Figure 5.2 Picture of winnowing
Source: As for Figure 5.1.

Figure 5.3 Picture of ploughing a field, sowing seeds and covering them with soil
Source: Jiayuguan tomb wall paintings, Gansu sheng wenwu dui et al. (1985).

Figure 5.4 Picture of winnowing
Source: As for Figure 5.3.

involvement in seeding after tilling (Figure 5.3) as well as a woman passing a bundle of wheat to a winnower (Figure 5.4). From these paintings we can infer that women were incorporated in the processes of agricultural labor, although they may not have undertaken primary farming tasks. In other words, the clear intent to depict the sexual division of labor evident in the *Pictures of Tilling and Weaving* cannot be detected in the mural paintings of Jiayuguan. This comparison reveals that over time paintings came to depict scenes that contradicted reality and conformed to certain gender-based ideas.

Turning to the written historical records, the situation is basically the same. Good examples of this include official histories such as the *New History of the Tang* (*Xin Tangshu*) and the *Old History of Tang* (*Jiu Tangshu*) from the Tang dynasty and the *History of the Song* (*Songshi*) of the Song dynasty. These are authoritative histories commissioned and approved by the subsequent dynasty. The annals section in each contains the annals of the emperors; the treatise section covers various themes, including rituals, geography and economy; and the biographies section records the biographies of individuals. Only a very small part of these books is devoted to women. Besides some records of Empress Wu Zetian, who took the reins of the Tang dynasty for a period, the so-called 'collected biographies of women' (*lienü zhuan*) about empresses, imperial princesses and renowned virtuous women forms the only substantial record. Men are placed at the center of an overwhelming majority of these historical accounts. Their mothers, wives and daughters may appear in relation to the men's activities but their records are mere side stories.

Needless to say, we encounter a similar situation when we study other 'orthodox' historical records; however, we can glean information on women's activities if we pay attention to non-orthodox historical records. For example, there are books of collected 'insignificant stories' (*xiaoshuo*) such as the *Extensive Records Assembled in the Taiping Era* (*Taiping guangji*) and the *Records of the Listener* (*Yijianzhi*). The *xiaoshuo* genre contains myths, legends, oral biographies, essays and fiction. The *Extensive Records Assembled in the Taiping Era* is known for its compilation of stories and anecdotes covering the period from ancient times to the Tang dynasty and the Five Dynasties as well as the 'section of women' (Shio and Kawamura 2004). The *Records of the Listener* is notable as a Southern Song compilation of stories about strange or fantastical (*zhi guai*) events. The number of stories about women's activities in these historical records is large if only in comparison with the orthodox records. I discuss some examples later in the chapter.

Chapter 5

In any case, there is no doubt that a great obstacle lies in the path of identifying women's activities from our reading of the historical records. Nevertheless, some studies have attempted to overcome the issues, as outlined below.

One is a study on the female/male ratio cited in written historical records that presents a statistical analysis of the percentage of women who appeared in the aforementioned *Records of the Listener* as well as a Southern Song book called *Collection of Enlightened Judgments by Celebrated Judges* (*Minggong shupan qingming ji*). I shall discuss these lesser-known historical records before moving on to examples taken from the *Collection of Enlightened Judgments*. The former is a collection of anecdotes heard and written down by Hong Mai (1123–1202) of the Southern Song. It is a compilation of tabloid reports, so to speak, and historical records of this type are very different from the official histories which are highly valued as orthodox accounts. As a result, the book was not taken seriously in the process of transmission and only about half of the originally published scrolls have survived. It is actually a precious source of information for the study of society in general as it contains numerous stories about common people in addition to those featuring the intellectual and social elites of the time. On the other hand, the *Collection of Enlightened Judgments* is a categorized scrapbook of court judgments and draft judgments of the day whose compiler is unknown. The purpose of this book was to organize the judgments handed down by the regional officials (administrative officials who also presided over courts of law) considered to be 'eminent' for the purpose of assisting in judgment writing. The book is at the opposite end of the spectrum in terms of orthodox value from the *Records of the Listener*, but only partial copies were known until a complete Ming edition was discovered in the 1980s.

Kami Yuki's study (2009) of the *Records of the Listener* found that of the 5,470 people appearing in 2,753 titles, 339 were women. The preponderance of men is overwhelming, and this ratio could easily lead one to conclude that the book's perspective was biased. However, there is a catch: the number included only those who were named. 'Nameless' commoners were not counted. The author decided to include all 'nameless' women in order to reflect the reality more accurately; this included women who were cited merely as someone's mother, wife or so on. As a result, the author counted 2,193 real-life women who appeared in 48.7% of all titles. The number is still less than half the number of men, but it is a significant figure not normally found in any historical record other than the *Records of the Listener*. Unfortunately, the author did not count the number of 'nameless' men, perhaps because he expected this figure to be smaller than the number of 'nameless' women because men were generally identified by their names, whether proper names or nicknames. What this exercise uncovered was the fact that a far larger number of women appear in the *Records of the Listener* than in any other historical record but that men still account for the great majority of characters on a superficial level, despite women's participation and activity. The book is a special historical record in the sense that it portrays a considerable number of women. It is expected that a study of this record will help us paint a more realistic picture of society at the time with a significantly reduced gender bias.

Prior to Kami's study, I conducted a statistical analysis of the *Collection of Enlightened Judgments* (Ōsawa 1997). As part of the study, the number of women was counted on the basis of their names, because plaintiffs, defendants and witnesses were named (by nicknames in many cases) in the judgment documents even if they were women. The analysis found 284 women, or just over 10%, among a total of 2,380 people. The number was a reflection of the status of women found in official sentencing documents of the time. Based on this citation ratio in the original court documents, we can assume that the actual courts were dominated by men. This is understandable as women were not treated as household heads in principle and therefore seldom made an appearance in court. In fact, the said ratio seems rather high in view of this situation. A closer look at the breakdown reveals yet another picture.

Let us examine individual categories (seven 'sections' in total) in the *Collection of Enlightened Judgments*. There was a large difference in the percentage of women between the sections. The highest female ratio was found in the human relations section (*renlun men*) at 22.8% followed by the household and marriage section (*huhun men*) at 14.4%. The human relations section contained judgments concerning ethics and morality with titles such as 'A divorce is granted as the wife is found guilty of disobeying her husband and opposing her father-in-law' and 'The woman conspired to avoid charges by maligning the reputation of her father-in-law' (both from Vol. 10). In these court cases, women – wives and daughters-in-law – who acted against the morals of the time were punished. There were of course many cases in which men were punished, but the percentage of women was markedly high in the human relations section. What does this imply?

A more detailed examination of the records found that not all the women were defendants: many were plaintiffs, witnesses or involved parties. This accounts for the high ratio of women. As the judgments in the human relations

Chapter 5

section mostly concerned family troubles, the women cited in the judgments were family members. It has generally been thought that in patriarchal society family problems are resolved by the patriarch of the family. In other words, family troubles in principle should not be brought to court. However, court challenges between members of the same family or patrilineal group was a frequent occurrence during the Song dynasty period. In short, the patriarch of the family was actually unable to control female family members even though they were supposedly living in a patriarchal society. The patriarch had no choice but to rely on state power to bring women under control through the court process. This was the reality reflected in the court judgments in the human relations section.

This line of reasoning can also explain the high percentage of women in the household and marriage section. This section contains the court judgments concerning property disputes within the family or patrilineal group as well as family succession issues. The high percentage of women's involvement in such cases points to the fact that either women were parties to these property and succession disputes or that their presence could not be ignored. According to the prevailing ideology of the time, women had limited power to designate a successor and no property rights. However, women were able to exert strong pressure behind the scenes and this fact was reflected in laws to a certain extent. For example, a widow was permitted to assume the role of the family patriarch after the death of her husband. Under such circumstances, women asserted their presence when inheritance or succession disputes broke out and their names ended up in the court judgments.

As we have seen above, books like the *Records of the Listener* and the *Collection of Enlightened Judgments* can help us understand the lives of women, who are rarely mentioned in other historical sources. However, as we have already seen, the visual and written records that survive from the Song period are not always a true reflection of reality. The same can be said about the historical records from the Tang period. In reviewing the sources, we need to constantly remember that both visual and written sources often presented a picture based on accepted norms of women's activities, rather than a picture of what they actually did.

Women's livelihoods

Despite the strong bias found in the historical records, there is some information about what kinds of labor women engaged in. Glimpses of women's activities can be gained from the Tang poems discussed by Gao Shiyu (1988) as well as Tang and Song historical records discussed by Yu Hui-Yuan (1998), Tajima Miki (1999) and Ning Xin (2003).[3] Regrettably, however, these studies simply focused on listing articles about women and failed to contextualize the historical records they were dealing with. For example, recorded events or people can be interpreted completely differently depending on whether the cited record is a legal document of the state or a record of stories and anecdotes. Further, women's labor is likely to be different depending on whether they were Han or of another ethnicity, and the place of women's labor within a household needs to be taken into consideration. With these points in mind, a limited number of historical records will be discussed in this section. Most of them are inevitably records of stories and anecdotes.

Livelihoods and family businesses in general

First, I examine a historical record about livelihoods in general – a book of family precepts entitled *Yuan Clan Hereditary Rules* (*Yuanshi shifan*) written by Yuan Cai (the late twelfth century) of the Southern Song dynasty.[4] It contains the following statements that point to women's active participation in the real world. The first is about the relationship between women and 'outside work' (*waishi*), which means work outside of one's home and is synonymous with 'livelihood' here, as follows:

> 'Women shall not engage in work outside of the home unnecessarily' (Vol. 1).

---

3 Of these preceding studies, Gao and Tajima quote numerous poems. However, using poems for the study of history is riddled with pitfalls. Of course, some poems are factual representations and Furukawa Sueki (2008) successfully used such poems to study the reality of agricultural life. On the other hand, some poems make copious use of classical verses while others were created out of their authors' imagination. It is difficult to determine whether a particular poem depicts scenes from the real world without further analysis. Accordingly, I have decided not to quote poems in my discussion here.

4 I have discussed the question of women described in the *Yuan Lineage Hereditary Rules* in more detail in Part 2 of Ōsawa Masaaki (2015). Further, 'A wife with an incompetent husband' (Ōsawa 2008) in the *Yuan Lineage Hereditary Rules* is a version I rewrote for a general readership.

Chapter 5

In my view, the statement means that a woman should not need to go out of the home to work if her husband and sons are capable of earning a living. What would happen to her if her husband and sons were not capable of earning a living but hid the fact from her? The argument goes as follows: when her husband is incompetent, when her sons are incompetent, it is a great misfortune in a woman's life; the best course of action is for the husband and the sons to take pity on their wife/mother and immediately regret what they have done.

This circuitous argument is unavoidable in an age pervaded by an androcentric ideology. In essence, it revolves around the question of what to do when one's husband and sons, who should be responsible for the family's livelihood, are incompetent. In this case, the wife has time to take things into her own hands. If the men of the family do not realize it, the entire family will end up in misery. It is likely that the above statement is based on actual cases known to Yuan Cai. In fact, such cases would have been quite common. Men were forced to become heads of households and be responsible for the family's livelihood just because they were male. It must have been difficult for those who were not suited to such responsibility. Yet, the family would starve if they did not earn a livelihood, and thus women would be forced to go out to work.

The statement implies that there were women who had fulfilled the role of providing for their family admirably, whether or not they had been pushed into doing so by hardship. About family businesses (*jiaye*), Yuan Cai says as follows:

> 'It is difficult for a widow to entrust her family business to a stranger' (Vol. 1).

Here are some examples from the book. There was a woman who operated her family business, managed money and crops and was not deceived by others simply because her husband was foolish and weak. Another woman managed her family trade with her sons to avoid bankruptcy because her husband was incompetent. Yet another woman educated her children well, maintained good relations with her relatives and managed the family business so that it flourished, even though she had lost her husband when the children were very young. They were all 'wise women'.

These are specific cases of women who managed their family businesses – probably involving the operation of their manors. They were respectable business managers who ran and protected their family businesses on behalf of their incompetent or absent husbands and were what Yuan Cai called 'wise women' (*xian furen*).

These articles written by Yuan Cai raise doubts about the prevalence of the ideology of the sexual division of labor at the time. People were faced with realities that did not accord with the ideological framework. Yuan Cai's stories paint a picture, albeit slightly abstract, of the livelihood of the upper class and the actual position occupied by women in that social stratum. After all, society did not operate in accordance with ideology.

It is impossible to know the size of the female population considered worthy of praise by Yuan Cai. However, the existence of the term 'a household headed by a woman' (*nühu*) indicates that a considerable proportion of households were headed by women with property (Yanagida 1993). The state recognized the households managed by head women and taxed them accordingly precisely because they represented a significant proportion of households in the real world.

Divorced women are discussed next in relation to the question of women's independence. There are some surviving historical records that show the existence of women who sought divorce during the Tang and Song periods.[5] I am curious about what they thought about livelihood security after divorce but the records are silent on this subject. One can imagine that some would have returned to their parental home while others would have sought opportunities for a better marriage or financial independence. An anecdote about Yan Zhenqing (709–786), a famous Tang calligrapher, from his younger days piques my curiosity. It can be summarized as follows:

> When Yan Zhenqing was a Jiangnan county official, the wife of an impoverished scholar petitioned for a divorce. Yan pronounced a judgment. He sentenced the wife to caning as her action was an affront to public morals and permitted the wife to divorce and remarry after the punishment was carried out. Following this case, <u>no woman dared to desert her husband in Jiangnan for a decade or so</u>. (Underline added; 'Intelligence of Duke Yan of Lu', *Yunxi youyi*, Vol. 1)

---

5 See Chapter 1, 'Wives are strong', in Ōsawa (2005a).

Chapter 5

The last sentence (underlined) is interesting. It implies that many wives had deserted their husbands before that point in time. It is possible to infer that wives behaved well for a decade or so after Yan's judgment, but then the situation reverted to the previous state. In other words, it was common for wives to abandon their husbands if they displeased them for some reason. It follows that the wives in question must have had no trouble making a living without their husbands and had independent means or the prospect of making a living on their own. Perhaps some of them had some sort of livelihood. While the intent of the historical record was to celebrate Yan's achievement, the article reflects the underlying reality that wives of a certain economic status enjoyed much freedom and independence at the time.

Similarly, the *Collection of Enlightened Judgments* also contains some judgments relating to wives who petitioned for divorce. I shall not mention individual cases due to limited space here, but in most cases a divorce was granted after a punishment had been meted out to the wife in question. It is unfortunate that the women's financial backgrounds are not stated in the records. However, it is reasonable to suppose that they had some means to secure their own independence. This point will be examined later in relation to another historical record.

Thus, the actual circumstances surrounding women's livelihoods and independence can be gleaned even from the limited number of historical sources. Let us try to decipher these few records in order to ascertain the relationship between women and livelihoods in more detail.

Women's agricultural labor

Historical records of agricultural labor are very limited due to the aforementioned reasons. Nevertheless, it is possible to gain a glimpse into the reality by reading historical accounts such as the following even in fragmented form.

Firstly, the *Extensive Records Assembled in the Taiping Era* includes the following account about a woman engaging in rice planting.

> The daughter of the Shi family in Wutan Cun, Lishui County [in present-day Jiangsu Province] became tired from rice planting work and lay down under a tree to rest. Then, a monster with scales, horns and claws appeared and mounted the woman. ('The daughter of the Shi family', *Jishenlu*, Vol. 471)

After mentioning the woman's rice-planting work, the fantastical story goes on to its main subject. Since no other person is mentioned in this scene, it can be assumed that the daughter was working alone. The Shi family must have been a small-scale farming family.

The *Records of the Listener* (*Yijianzhi*) also contains several stories that include mention of rice planting performed by both men and women.

> Dongtasi Temple in Poyang township [in present-day Jiangxi Province] owned farming land in Chongde County along with Zhishan Chanyuan Temple to the north of the town. Their fields adjoined each other and the homes of the farmers who tilled the lands were scattered nearby. On 1 May of the third year of Qingyuan (1197), men and women from all of the farming families were out in the fields planting rice. Only young children stayed home with their elderly or disabled relatives. Rain started falling during the day and the sound of thunder shook the sky. The homes of the four servants of the Dongtasi Temple were damaged by the strong winds. ('Major wind damage at the estate of Dongtasi Temple', *Zhigui*, Vol. 9)
>
> The Li family, who were the residents of Taigong Cun, Huangpo County, Huangzhou [in present-day Anhui Province] [...]. One day in the early summer, all of the men, women and children of the family were out in the field planting rice. Only one girl stayed home to prepare lunch. There was a voice from outside, 'Is Yige [Brother Yi] home?' The girl replied, 'He is out in the field'. Yige was the twelve-year-old son of Mr. Li. [...]. ('A woman in a red dress in Huangpo', *Sanzhiren*, Vol. 6)

The subject of the first story is the storm damage to the servants' homes at the estate of a Buddhist temple. The last sentence says, 'It is rumored that the servants paid for their penchant for killing cows'. The rice planting involving men and women was merely a setting for the mysterious karmic event. Perhaps women's involvement in rice planting was mentioned because it was part of the narrative. Similarly, agricultural labor has no direct bearing on the storyline in the second story. All the men, women and children (aside from one girl) were engaged in rice planting. Thus, the *Records of the Listener* shows glimpses of women's involvement in rice planting labor. No other account of women's involvement in rice cultivation can be found in the book. Still, the above descriptions demonstrate that there was no division of labor between men and women in rice planting in the real world even

Chapter 5

though it was depicted as men's work in the *Pictures of Tilling and Weaving*. Tajima (1999) reports that women played an important role in irrigation and drainage work in paddy fields. This is corroborated by a story included in the *Records of the Listener*.

> In the drought season in the seventh year of Qiandao [1171], Zhu Qi, a Wanchun Xiang farmer, and his wife went to Chengzi Tang near the village to irrigate the paddies. The reservoir was twenty *li* [approximately ten kilometers] square and supplied irrigation to one thousand *qing* of paddies. ('Aquatic animal of Chengzi Tang', *Sanzhixin*, Vol. 7)

In the above the husband and wife engaged in paddy irrigation together, although there was no mention of the agricultural implements they used in doing so. We cannot know if the couple worked together because it was an emergency situation in a drought year.

On the other hand, there are some historical records about the labor involved in silk farming, which was supposedly women's work, such as mulberry-leaf harvesting. Four stories are found in the *Extensive Records Assembled in the Taiping Era* and they all describe the way women climbed mulberry trees to pick the leaves. It seems that at the time mulberry-leaf harvesting was carried out high in mulberry trees. Nowadays mulberry trees are managed so that they only grow to a reachable height whereas in those days they were left to grow very tall (over ten meters high in some cases). One of the stories narrates as follows:

> [...] a wicked thought entered the mind [of a man who was transformed into a tiger]. He looked up and saw a lone woman picking mulberry leaves up on a tree. He watched her through the blades of grass and thought [...]. ('A scholar-official [*shi-ren*] in Nanyang', *Yuanhuaji*, cited in Vol. 432)

The tiger was looking up at a woman who had climbed a mulberry tree to harvest leaves on her own. Although stories about mulberry-leaf harvesting by women are more common than those about men, it was not performed exclusively by women, as shown in the following story.

> There was a thirteen-year-old boy in a village adjoining Jizhou [in present-day Hebei Province] at the start of the Kaihuang era of the Sui dynasty [at

the end of the sixth century]. [...] The southern part of the village used to be a mulberry field. Spring ploughing had finished but seeding had not been carried out. [...] the villagers were out in the field and picking mulberry leaves and many men and women were working. They all saw the boy running around the field crying loudly. [...]. ('A child in Jizhou', *Mingbaoji*, cited in Vol. 131)

Both men and women engaged in mulberry-leaf picking in this village. Silk farming was a key industry in this region and there was no sexual division of labor as we can see from the fact that both men and women engaged in leaf picking. The local reality of livelihood requirements must have outweighed the ideological concerns.

The *Records of the Listener* also contains a story surrounding mulberry-leaf picking.

Wu Nianjiu, a resident of Jinxi [in present-day Jiangxi Province], was about to transplant rice seedlings in the spring of the second year of Shaoxi [1191]. [...] There were more than ten mulberry trees on his land, one-half of which were owned by his wife and the other half were owned by his mother. His mother picked mulberry leaves from his wife's trees by mistake and the wife told Wu about it. He dragged his mother out of her room and said [...]. ('Wu Nianjiu', *Zhiding*, Vol. 4)

In the above, a conflict arose because the mother harvested mulberry leaves owned by her daughter-in-law. It is rather interesting to note that the ownership of mulberry trees was divided between the wife and the mother within the same family. That said, mulberry-leaf picking was an agricultural task performed by the women of this family.

In addition, this farming family had rice paddies. Wu Nianjiu was trying to secure workers for rice planting while his mother and wife managed their respective mulberry trees. In short, the family was involved in rice cropping and mulberry growing at the same time. It is likely that they raised silkworms to sell their cocoons as well as mulberry leaves or woven silk fabric. Although these commodities might have been used to pay part of the family's tax, they were valuable sources of income for a farming family. Women contributed to their family's farming operation in this way. It is important to pay attention to

Chapter 5

the role played by women within this type of family-run farming business in discussing women's livelihoods.

Family farm operation, women and commerce

The unit for the imposition of tax and labor service by the state was the household, which was in effect the married couple. The Sui dynasty's tax system clearly stipulated that 'Adult men aged eighteen or older must turn in three *shi* of millet for the payment of grain tax, and silk fabric in the mulberry production area and hemp fabric in the hemp growing area for the payment of in-kind tax, per married couple' ('Treatise on economic matters' (*Shihuozhi*), the *History of the Sui* (*Suishu*)). In other words, the unit of state control was the married couple, perceived as one entity by the government. The state took it for granted that farming in those days was operated by a husband and a wife together. The ideology of the sexual division of labor was brought into the picture at a later stage. Consequently, the woman must be considered as a partner in the family's collective endeavor when thinking about women's livelihoods. A Tang example can be found in the *Extensive Records Assembled in the Taiping Era*.

> A wife named He Shi lived in a private home in Yanzhou [in present-day Shandong Province]. The villagers called her 'weaving maid' [*zhinü*]. Her parents-in-law farmed the land while her husband travelled between the village and the town as a peddler. [...] The husband spent all his earnings on keeping a mistress elsewhere and did not bring any money home. ('He Shi', *Yutang Jianhua*, cited in Vol. 271)

The above refers to a farming family of four members from two generations. The parents farmed while their son worked as a peddler and his wife wove for a living. Role-sharing in running a household in this way is thought to have been common practice in a typical small-scale farming family, and it is unlikely that there was a strict division of labor along gender lines. Each family member assumed whatever role they could in order to support the household. In the real world, a man cannot necessarily be the main breadwinner. The difference in the incomes of the parents and the son and how much the wife earned from her weaving work cannot be ascertained. Nevertheless, we can surmise that all components of the family's labor were indispensable. We tend to think that family farming operations would not have been viable without the male family head because of the state law that designated a man as the family head. However, it was a system based on an androcentric ideology and did not reflect reality.

The son's trade is worth noting here. From the early Han period, the state proclaimed its agriculture-based national ideology that regarded farming as the primary or root industry and commerce as the secondary or branch industry. The ruling class directed the 'ignorant people' to focus on the main industry and not to touch the secondary industry. However, this was merely a goal to strive for and far from reality. Conversely, the state directed farmers to stay in agriculture perhaps because many of them were switching to commerce. In my view, farmers were inseparably linked to commerce. The aforementioned farming family was a very ordinary farming family and not a special case. Moreover, many farmers went to work for wages in cities. Commerce and wage labor were activities pertinent to the currency-mediated distribution of goods, and the operation of farms could not be separated from commodity distribution.

With this nature of commerce in mind, let us look at how it relates to women and, in particular, the relationship between divorced women and commerce mentioned earlier in the chapter. While Yu Hui-Yuan (1998) refers to an actual example, the *Records of the Listener* tells a story about how a divorced woman started a business.

> Wang Balang, a wealthy man from Tangzhou, Biyang County [in present-day Henan Province], went to the Jianghuai district every year to conduct business extensively. He became intimate with a prostitute and lashed out at his wife every time he went home as he wanted to drive her out. His wife was a wise person who had given birth to four daughters, three of whom were already married. She felt she could not leave home yet as the youngest daughter was not even ten. [...] The wife held her husband by the sleeve and went to petition the local authority. The county office approved their divorce and equal division of their assets. [...] decided to take custody of their daughter and live in another village. She bought pots and jars and displayed them out in front of the house for sale. [...] the daughter grew up and married into the Tian family in Fangcheng County.

Chapter 5

> She already had 100,000 *min* [one min = 1,000 bronze coins] in savings.
> ('Wang Balang', *Bingzhi*, Vol. 14)

Wang's wife sold 'pots and jars' to raise her daughter after divorcing her husband. She was likely financially secure as she had received one half of the husband's property upon divorce. Nevertheless, she was able to give a large sum of money to her daughter probably because earnings from her trade covered their day-to-day living expenses, and she was able to live independently as a divorced woman. There are other stories about divorced women who went into business to lead independent lives.

> The wife of a bowman [*gong-shou*] of the county police chief [*dongwei*] of Poyang County [in present-day Jiangxi Province] was a divorced woman who sold drinks to make ends meet. Chen Xiaoyao frequented her bar and drank on credit but the woman served him drinks regardless. ('Chen Xiaoyao', *Zhigengzhi*, Vol. 9)
>
> Fang Wu, a soldier in Yongnian Jian, died and his widow made illicit liquor to make a living. She always hired a fishing boat to transport her goods to a liquor shop in town during the night and received payment a few days later. She always accompanied Wu Liu to help her. Three years ago, Fang's wife went out with her eight-year-old son. She received over ten *guan* [one guan = 1,000 bronze coins] of money and left it inside the boat. ('Wu Liu's boat race', *Zhikuizhi*, Vol. 9)

These stories tell us that divorced women with seed money could easily start and continue a business and that they could make a decent amount of money from it. These characteristics of commerce provided conditions that guaranteed security for women after a divorce and promoted independence. A woman was even able to support her husband on her own, evident in a case portrayed in the *Records of the Listener*.

Dong Guoqing [...] was appointed to the position of Registrar of Laizhou-Jiaoshui County [in present-day Shandong Province]. There was some military activity along the northern border and he left his family behind to work there. Later on, the Central Plains fell into enemy hands and he was unable to return home. He abandoned his position, fled to a village and became friends with the owner of an inn. The inn owner took pity on him and bought a mistress for him. The woman's origin was unknown but she was a wise and beautiful woman. She saw how poor Dong was and felt that it was her duty to bolster their livelihood. She invested all she had in the purchase of several donkeys and ten *hu* of wheat to mill flour. She rode her donkey to transport flour and sell it in the town as she produced it. She returned home with the day's takings in the evening. She went to sell flour every few days and increased her profit over the next three years enough to buy farming land and a house. Dong had been separated from his mother and wife for so long and did not know their whereabouts. ('Chivalrous woman', *Yizhi*, Vol. 1)

In this story, a former mistress started a flour milling business singlehandedly and not only supported Dong but also bought a house and land within three years. We cannot confirm the veracity of the story, but it tells us that a flour milling business could be operated by a woman alone and be rather profitable.

These narratives demonstrate that commerce and flour milling offered more prosperous conditions as livelihoods. There was no reason for farmers not to try them. Someone in a farming family would likely have been involved in trade such as the aforementioned silk farming, weaving and peddling. We need to remember that family farm operations as a livelihood had a composite nature. Examining the roles assumed by women in this setting can reveal the picture of women that has been hidden behind the surfaces of historical records and foster an understanding of the important parts they played.

Chapter 5

Conclusion

This chapter has discussed the question of gender and livelihood in relation to a review of historical records from the Tang and Song period. The nature of each historical record has been clarified and contextualized, highlighting the importance of deep reading, and a small part of women's livelihoods that have been concealed beneath the surface has been uncovered. Chinese historical records are in a sense profound and written brilliantly. The skills forged by legions of intellectuals over millennia are awe-inspiring. On the other hand, they are tinged with ideologies both overtly and covertly. We the readers have often been mesmerized by the cleverly expressed colors. However, it is important not to overlook the presence of people who have been relegated to the background of history by ideology. It is necessary to develop a critical gaze through which to examine historical records and learn to constantly question their intent.

Focal Point

An Overview of Shiga Shūzō's *Principles of Chinese Family Law*

SASAKI Megumi

Introduction

Shiga Shūzō's *Principles of Chinese Family Law* (*Chūgoku kazokuhō no genri*) (hereinafter referred to as 'Shiga's *Family Law*') is the most important study to consult when researching pre-modern Chinese family/gender history. While the book is well-known in Western academic circles, its contents are not easily accessible to English-speaking readers due to the absence of an English edition. This supplementary article has been included for the purpose of providing an overview of Shiga's *Family Law* for information and reference.

Shiga Shūzō was a giant in the field of Chinese legal history. He was a scholar who had come from the discipline of jurisprudence and produced major studies in historical textual research on successive legal codes as well as analysis of mainly Qing-period trials.[1] However, his focus in the first half of his academic career was on the study of family law in traditional China. Shiga's research culminated in the study which defined the period of over two thousand years from the Han dynasty to the Qing dynasty as the 'imperial period', and hypothesized and analyzed the principles of Chinese family law that he believed had existed consistently throughout that period. The logical coherence of his theory running through the entire book that treats the property

---

1 Here is a list of some of Shiga's works (in Japanese): 'Tang Code with commentary and explanations translated and annotated 1 (Penalties and application rules)' (1979); *Law and Trial in Qing China* (1984); *Essays on the History of Chinese Law: Legal Codes and Penalties* (2003); *Law and Trial in Qing China, Supplementary Volume* (2009); and as an editor, *History of the Chinese Legal System: Study of Basic Materials* (1993). He also published numerous other theses and essays. Shiga's studies are referred to in Philip C. C. Huang (2006 [English]).

Part II

rights and ritual rights of individual family members as one radiates beauty akin to a very sharp Japanese sword, and it is no wonder that Shiga's *Family Law* became a commonly accepted theory especially among Japanese researchers of Chinese history. It has not lost its position as a prevailing orthodoxy five decades after its publication. Legal historian Terada Hiroaki recently made the following comment about the book.

> Professor Shiga set his eyes on the idea of consanguinity, which is the idea of human being peculiar to traditional China [the Han], and explained all sorts of special phenomena in family relationships as manifestations of the idea of consanguinity so thoroughly [...] that he managed to end almost all of the long-standing debates and controversies. In this sense, his study was a groundbreaking work in the history of traditional Chinese family law studies in the world and still wields an almost decisive influence today. (Terada 2018)

The study has been published in the Chinese language (Shiga 2003), but it has not been translated into English. The only English-language thesis published by Shiga (1978) mainly focuses on property inheritance and the father's authority and does not touch on the subject of female family members, to which considerable space is devoted in *Family Law*. For this reason, I provide an overview of Shiga's *Family Law* in this Focal Point, paying special attention to gender-related discussions.

In his theory, Shiga viewed the principles of Chinese family law as immutable throughout the period of over two thousand years from the Han to Qing dynasties. In contrast to Shiga's claim, as stated by Kohama Masako in the 'Preface' (page 15), the present volume proposes that these principles were shaped over the long course of Chinese history rather than being immutable. We have decided to include this supplementary article in the English edition as we believe that the historical research value of our attempt at a critical revision of *Family Law* will be better appreciated by our readers if they have sufficient information about Shiga's work.

Common living/budget and principles of Chinese family law

This section offers a brief explanation of the Chinese family structure and the principles theorized by Shiga in *Principles of Chinese Family Law* (1967). We encourage our readers to read this section in conjunction with Shiga (1978).

Chinese families were stringently required to lead a communitarian life with the participation of all family members. As the historical term '*tongju gongcai*' (common living, common budget) signifies, a family was a communal living entity with a combined family budget. Each family member was required to put all earnings in a family purse (household budget) and was not allowed to keep any of it for themselves. All necessary expenses of the family members were paid from the family budget. Any goods paid for by the family budget formed part of the family property owned jointly by all family members. A death in the family simply meant the loss of one constituent member from the common living and budget relationship. The family relationship would continue as it was unless any special problem arose, and therefore property inheritance was not something that would happen automatically upon someone's death. It was no different when the father as the family head passed away. Property division was carried out if family members wished to dissolve the common living and budget relationship, but the Chinese ideal was to continue to grow into a larger family that involved the cohabitation of multiple generations of family members without property division.

A brief summary of Shiga's views suggests that China's family law is about the question of rights in which three relationships, namely, that between father and son, between husband and wife and between brothers, manifest at the scene of common living and budget. As he analyzes the details of the property rights and ritual obligations of each family member, Shiga proposes the following as the principles of Chinese family law: 'father and son forming one body', 'husband and wife forming one body' and 'equality of brothers', together with the concept of 'father and son(s) sharing the same material forces' or 'divided form but of the same material forces' that underpins these principles.

Shiga explains this concept as follows.

> It is the idea that a human bloodline is passed from father to son and that the bloodline does not lose its identity no matter how many generations it is passed through; moreover, that such lineage is the origin of life and life itself by which each person's true nature is defined [...]. The bloodline in this sense is signified by the word *qi* in Chinese rather than "blood". Father and son are materialized as two individuals (of divided form) but life forces residing within them are identical (the same material forces) and therefore the son is considered to be none other than an extension of the father's life. (1967: 35)

The phenomenon of communal living that underpins the Chinese family system is said to be a natural consequence of the idea that father and son share the same life form and the same personhood: 'Where the father and his son are of the same personhood, all assets acquired through their labor – or if he has more than one son, the labor of all his sons – must be combined to form a property of assets; in other words, the father and his son(s) are destined to be united by the common living and budget relationship' (1967: 130). Where the father and his son(s) are of the same material forces, the brothers are of the same material forces as well. This relationship of shared material forces spreads over many generations to form a lineage (*zongzu*) like tree branches growing out of a single trunk. The term '*zong*' refers to all branches of a patrilineal lineage descended from a common ancestor and is a kinship concept that excludes matrilineal descent.

The relationships between the property rights and ritual obligations of each family member based on Shiga's *Family Law* can be summarized as follows. One of the features of his principles is the close link between property and ritual.

- Father and son forming one body: This notion was almost synonymous with 'father and son sharing the same material forces' as mentioned above. A father and his son(s) were of the same personhood and the son inherited from the father comprehensive property rights in consideration of his ritual obligations as a consequence of the continuity of personhood. Shiga specifically called it 'succession'. The son inherited his father's property, memorialized his ancestors, was buried in the grave of his natal family upon passing and was memorialized by his descendants. Although a mother was the giver of life to her son in the same way that a father was to his son, the word *qi* was never used in the context of succession from a mother to her son because it was the father who determined the true nature of the son's life. There was no succession relationship between the mother and the son in terms of property and ritual rights.[2]

- Husband and wife forming one body: A daughter did not have social status within her natal family. Only when she got married and became a wife did she acquire social status within her husband's family. The wife and husband formed one personhood as the wife's personhood was absorbed into the husband's personhood. Accordingly, a wife had no share of her husband's family property separately from her husband and she had no separate existence as she remained hidden behind her husband as long as he lived. When she became a widow upon his death, however, she came to the fore as the custodian of her husband's property rights because she represented her husband's personhood. For rituals, wife and husband formed one body and conducted rituals for the husband's ancestors together. When she died, she was buried in her husband's grave and her mortuary tablet was paired with his and she was memorialized by their descendants as a mother.

- Brothers forming one body: Brothers formed one body in the sense that they recognized their father's being in each other based on the principles of 'father and son sharing the same material forces' and 'father and son forming one body'. Family property was equally divided among brothers regardless of their birth order or whether their mother was the legal wife or a concubine. This is because brothers were regarded as equal in succeeding their forefathers – brothers memorialized their father as an ancestor in an equal capacity.

---

2 See Chapter Six and Sasaki (2020).

The rights of female family members

This section offers a summary of the rights of female family members, which were not mentioned in Shiga (1978).

Wife

A wife was a formally wedded spouse tied to her husband as one entity and occupied an inviolable position within the blood relationship on the husband's side. A husband could not have more than one wife at once, but he was permitted to have any number of bedchamber partners other than his wife as concubines. This is why China's marriage system was called 'monogamy with many concubines'. When a concubine gave birth to a son, the legal wife had the primary parental rights and there was a clear distinction between the wife and concubines.

The wife's dowry

A dowry which the wife brought to the marital relationship (marital furniture, land if her natal family was wealthy and so on) remained the property of the couple (which was never pooled with the household property belonging to a larger group that included the husband's parents and brothers). The power to manage and dispose of the dowry rested with the couple only and the dowry was excluded from the family property for division between the husband and his brothers. The dowry became the exclusive property of the marital couple because there was a concrete rule that what was gifted to an individual by another became the exclusive property of that individual, whereas family members had to put all of the earnings gained by their labor into the family budget under the common living and budget system. Any land included as part of a dowry was usually owned in the husband's name according to the principle of 'husband and wife forming one body' and could be disposed of by the husband with the wife's consent. The wife's dowry was eventually combined with a share of the family property that the husband acquired through division to form the family property of a new household. The significance of its dowry origin was lost when it was inherited by subsequent generations.

The wife after the husband's death

When a husband died without leaving a son, all of the property and rights of the husband were transferred to the wife based on the principle of husband and wife forming one body. Unlike a succession relationship between patrilineal family members, the wife's custodianship was of an intermediate nature on behalf of an heir whom she would adopt in future. The widow was unable to dispose of her property freely under these circumstances. It was the right and obligation of the sonless widow to resolve this anomalous situation by adopting an heir from among patrilineal kin. The wife had the power to choose an adopted heir. Where one of the brothers living in the same house died without leaving a son, his share of the family property was transferred to his wife. When family property was divided among brothers who lived in the same household, the widow was entitled to receive the share of property that her deceased husband would have received on an equal basis with his brothers.

When a husband died leaving sons, the husband's share of property would be passed on to his sons. In reality, however, it meant the establishment of a household where one or more sons lived in the same dwelling with a common budget under their widowed mother as the head. The mother was often called the family head and took charge of family finances. In order to dispose of the family property of the household where the mother and her son lived together, both parties needed to agree to the transaction. A contract of sale had to be signed by the mother as the principal party. The mother had the right to cancel the contract if the family property was disposed of without her consent such as in the case of forged signature. The mother was not allowed to dispose of the family property without her son's consent either.

Concubine

A concubine did not have a position within the husband's family. She was not regarded as a person representing the husband's personhood as the principle of husband and wife forming one body did not apply to her. Yet, she was recognized as a member of the household and her relationship with the husband was different from a clandestine sexual relationship in that sense. When a man died and his only surviving relative was a concubine, the right to choose an adopted heir or to manage his property belonged to the husband's lineal ascendant or the head of his cognate family. Where the husband had a successor, whether he was a biological or adopted son, the concubine only had the status of mother to her biological son. If the husband was survived by his wife, the concubine did not have a primary parental right even to her biological son. Once the sons came of age, disposal of family property could be carried out by the consensus of the legal wife and her biological and acknowledged sons and the concubine's consent was usually not required. On the other hand, the husband's successors were obligated to support their father's concubine for life on his behalf.

Unmarried daughter

An unmarried daughter had no social status within her natal family and no entitlement to inherit the property of her natal family either. She was given a dowry upon marriage, but the amount of dowry was determined by her parents at their discretion rather than as a matter of her right. Matrilocal marriage (where a married couple lived in the home of the wife's parents) was a form of marriage used to allow a daughter to inherit the property and ritual rights of her native family, but it happened only in exceptional circumstances such as poverty and was not permissible in principle. A daughter was required to marry into her husband's family. If an unmarried daughter died, she was neither buried in her natal family grave nor memorialized in her natal family.[3] For this reason, there was a custom called 'ghost marriage' by which a deceased unmarried daughter was buried in the grave of a deceased man who was chosen as her suitable spouse.

---

3 In reality, the building of tombs for daughters was practiced by their natal families. Neo-Confucianists such as Cheng Yi and Zhu Xi, who were supposedly strict observers of principles and precepts, built graves for their daughters. See Chapter Six.

Women's personal property

Women were able to keep earnings obtained by their labor as their personal property. Under the common living and budget system, all family members were supposed to put their earnings in the family purse. This main principle was applied strictly to male members whose primary role was to provide income, whereas it was not so strict for female members. Women's primary role was homemaking and they were not required to contribute monies they earned in their spare time between household chores. It was very common for women to have some private funds which they used to buy cosmetics and other goods for themselves or spend on education and clothing for their daughters who were generally less favored in family budgetary allocation. Besides the dowry the daughters received from the family budget upon marriage, their mother gave them part of her personal property. When the mother died, her personal property was transferred to her unmarried daughters, or her son's wife or her husband's sisters if she didn't have a daughter. Women's personal property was passed from women to women in a separate line of succession from family succession.

The debate on women's right to inheritance in Song China

Shiga's *Family Law* had a major impact on the study of Chinese history in Japan. This is reflected in the fact that a massive body of research was accumulated on the single subject of Song Chinese women's right to inheritance. The latest developments in this debate are summarized in Aoki Atsuhi (2014) and Ogawa Yoshiyuki (2015) which discuss over twenty Japanese studies.

The debate on Song Chinese women's right to inheritance centers around a passage in a court judgment from the Southern Song period: 'The law states that when family property is divided between a son and a daughter upon their parents' death, the daughter can acquire one half of the son's share'. There was a heated debate between Niida Noboru, who considered this clause important as it reflected a Southern Chinese practice at the time, and Shiga, who criticized Niida's theory as absurd. Shiga's *Family Law* developed out of this intense debate. Since a daughter was not entitled to a share of the property of her natal family under Shiga's family law principle, the said law to allow distribution of family property to a daughter contradicted Shiga's 'principle' completely. Shiga maintained the integrity of his theory by giving the law dismissive assessments such as 'Not a universal rule about daughters' status'.

In other words, the existence of the Song Chinese law about women's right to inheritance came to be seen as a small chink in the armor of Shiga's *Family Law* and hence Shiga and his supporters perceived it as a problem that had to be resolved. During the 1980s, a full copy of the *Collection of Enlightened Judgments* (*Minggong shupan qingming ji*) containing a reference to the customary practice about women's right to inheritance was discovered in Beijing and sparked much interest as well as instantly reigniting the debate which drew in the voices of many scholars. Naturally, scholars of Song history in other countries began to discuss this ruling. A common characteristic among the discussions involving Japanese scholars, whether they took a positive or negative stance on this issue, was that they started their arguments by stating that the judgment contradicted the principles of Chinese family law, demonstrating the extent of the influence of Shiga's *Family Law*.

Conclusion

What was interesting for me personally after rereading Shiga's study for the present volume was that Shiga had already pointed out that women were able to own personal property which men were not allowed to own under the common living and budget system and that property was passed from women to women independently of family property under this system. Shiga would have thought that women's personal property was allowed because it was a very small amount and was acquired by the labor they engaged in during their spare time between household duties. However, it is conceivable that women contributed significant amounts of income to the household budget in some situations or that they were expected to do so in families of certain social strata. In such situations, how did people deal with women's earnings when the rule stated that women's labor income was their personal property? Was the rule applied differently depending on the family's economic circumstances? What was the role played by the customary practice of treating women's labor earnings as their personal property when women's paid labor became commonplace in modern times? What was the relationship between the custom of women's property being passed on to female members of the family and the matrilineal family in Qing China recently described by Susan L. Mann (2007)?

As I mentioned earlier, this book offers an alternative view to Shiga's conceptualization of the principles of Chinese family law as remaining unchanged for over two millennia (see Chapters Two and Six in particular). On the other hand, Shiga's *Family Law* contains numerous points of argument which must continue to be upheld and deepened and others which continue to inspire various interests. I recommend that our readers use Shiga's *Family Law* as the starting point for their own research.

6. Traditional Family Ideology and the Cheng-Zhu School

— *SASAKI Megumi*

Introduction

It is commonly thought that the decline in women's status and restrictions on activities began during the Song dynasty, and this decline is often linked to the development of the Cheng-Zhu school of Neo-Confucianism. This chapter will consider these arguments and propose that the decline in women's status – as seen in such practices as restrictions on widows' remarriage, the spread of footbinding, and sex-based segregation – only appeared in the Ming dynasty. Our reconsideration of these issues will begin with a critical view of one of the leading Japanese works in this field, Shiga Shūzō's *Principles of Chinese Family Law* (*Chūgoku kazokuhō no genri*) (1967). (For more on Shiga's arguments see 'Focal Point'.)

Principles of Chinese Family Law by Shiga Shūzō

The content of Shiga's celebrated book is explained in a separate section of this book entitled 'Focal Point'. In his book, Shiga proposes three principles of Chinese family law, namely, 'father and son forming one body' (*fuzi yiti*), 'a husband and his wife forming one body' (*fuqi yiti*) and 'equality of brothers' (*xiongdi yiti*), accompanied by the concept of 'a father and his son(s) sharing the same material forces' (*fuzi tongqi*) that underpins these principles.

He theorizes that they functioned trans-historically for over two thousand years and states in his 'Preface' as follows.

> [...] to treat so-called traditional China, or a China before modernization, as a temporally and geographically vast social regime, to analyze the condition of the family under the regime from a juristic perspective, to formulate a conceptual framework and to describe it systematically. [...] I shall call the period through to the Spring and Autumn era the ancient period, the period from the Republic of China to the modern period and the long period between them the imperial period for want of a better label. This book is intended to deal with family laws in the imperial period. [...] I consider the period from the Han dynasty to the Qing dynasty as one period [...] because I would like to argue that certain fixed patterns under the regime remained the same in their most fundamental aspects from a macroscopic view, regardless of what advances were made.

In other words, Shiga discusses China from Han to Qing as a fundamentally static entity called 'traditional China'. Because Shiga was a scholar of law rather than history, it is understandable that he focused on the continuity of legal principles that existed throughout the ages rather than examining changes over time. When legal scholars try to understand the underlying principles, they are not looking at law codes but rather at practices, some of which are revealed through the small number of surviving records of legal cases. Although it is reasonable to expect that historians would feel uncomfortable with Shiga's approach as change over time is very important in their discipline, they did not offer much in the way of critique.

One of the reasons for their reticence was that the study was an attempt to identify 'the oughts etched in the minds of Chinese people', to borrow Shiga's own words, and not a study of the history of codified laws. In Shiga's book, rituals, codes and statutes are not principles in themselves. Any stipulations that are temporarily inconsistent with the said principles are treated as exceptions that do not diminish the fundamental nature of the principles. Since even the ritual and legal rules are not seen as principles in some cases, it is all the more so with real-world cases. It is thus no surprise that some of Shiga's principles cannot be put into action in reality, despite the many cases that are incongruent with the principles. Thus, in Shiga's understanding everything in the real world

Chapter 6

can be fitted into the framework of 'principles and realities' or 'principles and exceptions'.

This is a very strong framework, but one which troubles the minds of social historians who see their mission as painting a picture of society based on surviving records of actual practice. Even if they demonstrate how different the realities were from Shiga's principles and identify real world changes over time, these phenomena can be brushed aside as mere exceptions.

Ōsawa Masaaki (2005b) expresses a sense of uneasiness about Shiga's reasoning that categorically treats records of practices that do not conform to Shiga's theory as 'exceptions', collecting and systematizing examples in order to identify the existence of the Tang-Song transition in the conditions of the family and women. In comparing the work of Ōsawa and Shiga, we can clearly see the difference between the approaches of a legal historian and a social historian. The legal historian is likely to critique the work of the social historian as a 'mere collection of exceptional cases'. As Ōsawa has suggested in Chapter Five, Chinese gender history suffers from constraints associated with the availability of historical resources. Even if a study overcomes such constraints and discovers various historical phenomena that do not fit into Shiga's principles, they are treated as exceptions and their implications go unrecognized.

In light of the above, what stance should we take on Shiga's principles? One of the ways to negotiate them is to examine them from the viewpoint of the history of thought. This entails the task of questioning whether it is possible from an ideological standpoint to assume that Shiga's principles continued to be transhistorical principles for Chinese people and whether any ideas similar to Shiga's principles existed in each historical period and if so identifying where they were positioned.

Despite its seemingly solid structure, Shiga's *Chinese Family Law* actually appears surprisingly insubstantial from the angle of the history of thought. The primary feature of his work is that it treats property and rituals as one entity. Property rights have been a key theme in Chinese legal history while rituals have constituted a major research subject in the field of Chinese philosophy and the history of Chinese thought. As a work in legal history, *Chinese Family Law* offers remarkably scant discussion on rituals compared with property in terms of reasoning and analysis (Sasaki 2015a, 2015b). It is thus necessary to distinguish between property and rituals and re-examine Shiga's principles in relation to the latter. The shortest route to enable us to move beyond Shiga's principles would be to liberate social history from the framework of said principles if the result of the re-examination warrants us to do so.

'Traditional family ideology' and the Cheng-Zhu school

When historians encounter Shiga's proposition that the long span from Han to Qing should be treated as a single historical period, they immediately raise questions. They recall Chen Dongyuan's classical masterpiece *A History of the Lives of Chinese Women* (*Zhongguo funü shenghuoshi*), which locates the beginning of the suppression of women's status in the Song dynasty and associates it with the emergence of the Cheng-Zhu school of Neo-Confucianism that occurred during the same period. Chen attributes a further increase in the oppression of women during the Ming-Qing period to the strengthening of the feudal code of ethics caused by the spread of the teachings of the Cheng-Zhu school. While many of the more recent studies are cautious about locating the historical change in the Song period, arguing that the Neo-Confucian discourse had not yet reached society in general (see Part I, Phase II Introduction), many scholars still subscribe to the idea that the Cheng-Zhu school was the cause of the subsequent oppression of women.

Conversely, Shiga does not make particular reference to the Cheng-Zhu school in *Chinese Family Law*. This is because Shiga sees no need to mention the Cheng-Zhu school that emerged as a new type of Confucianism in Song as long as he refers to the fact that the patrilineal kin principles were already established in Confucian classics from pre-Qin to Han, such as *Observances and Rituals* (*Yili*) and *Records of Ritual* (*Liji*). In his view, this shows that the principles remained unchanged for over two millennia from Han to Qing.

From the viewpoint of the history of thought, however, Confucianism did not always throughout the two millennia provide behavioral principles to Chinese people. In particular, Buddhism and Taoism were far more prevalent in the periods immediately before Song, namely, in the Wei-Jin, Northern and Southern Dynasties, and during the Sui and Tang periods. The Song period saw the birth of the Cheng-Zhu school, which was a Confucian revival and reform movement aimed at injecting new breath into Confucianism and returning it to its ancient spirit by constructing a new metaphysical philosophical base that earlier Confucianism lacked, and integrating it with Confucian doctrines

Chapter 6

about politics and society in the physical world. Kinoshita Tetsuya has clarified the continued presence of a strong maternal authority from the previous era into Song society and places the Cheng-Zhu school in the lineage of the history of ideology that resisted that reality and sought men's independence (Kinoshita 2007).

In this chapter, we examine the discourse of the Cheng-Zhu school on the question of ritual rights – one of the pillars supporting Shiga's principles. What is the relationship between Shiga's principles and the rituals that were conceptualized and practiced by the scholars of the Cheng-Zhu school who sought to return to the 'transcendental reason' of Confucianism? This is an essential task in our re-examination of the theory of ritual rights posited by Shiga's principles.

Shiga's principles and the Cheng-Zhu school

Ancestor worship by the son

According to Shiga's principles, father and son share the same personhood and therefore only the son inherits ancestral property rights and ritual responsibilities on the grounds that 'Father and son are of one material force' (*fuzi tongqi*). While Shiga offers no detailed commentary on or analysis of '*qi*' (氣), it is of course a fundamental concept of Chinese philosophy that is often described as 'material force' or 'vital energy'. *Qi* is believed to be a gaseous material with vital energy which acts and solidifies spontaneously to form elements that constitute all things and injects life and vitality into the world. In short, the concept of the 'oneness of the material forces of father and son' means that their bodies are made of identical constituent elements.

How does the sharing of the same material force in this context relate to the idea that only the patrilineal male descendants are qualified to conduct rituals for their ancestors? Why are people prohibited from performing rituals unless they share the same material force?

Zhu Xi, the founder of the Cheng-Zhu school of principle and material (*li* and *qi*) dualism, dealt with this question. The following is a very simple summary of his exposition. All things in the world are different from one another because they are made up of different material forces. Ancestral spirits are essentially material forces. The ancestral spirits can feel and sympathize with the rituals performed by their descendants because the same *qi* has been transmitted from the ancestors to successive generations of their descendants ('Spiritual force', *Classified Sayings of Master Zhu* (*Zhuzi yulei*), Vol. 3).

Zhu Xi, as the one who perfected the *li-qi* theory, was the first scholar to offer a clear exposition on this question.

As I have shown in my earlier work (Sasaki 2020), there is no evidence that the notion of 'Father and son are of one material force' was used in or before Han. Prior to this period, the term 'one material force' (*tongqi*) was used in either the saying 'Father, mother and son are of one material force' or 'Mother and son are of one material force'. In fact, the *qi* relationship was believed to be stronger between mother and son than between father and son indicated by the context even when the former expression was used.

In the Wei, Jin, Northern and Southern Dynasties and Sui-Tang periods, the expression 'Brothers are of one material force' came into common use after Cao Zhi stated that he and his older brother Cao Pi were of one material force in his 'Memorial seeking to prove myself'. Shiga's principles regard this relationship between brothers to be predicated on the father-son relationship. Although 'Brothers are of one material force' is certainly one of the principles provided by Shiga, the relationship between brothers cannot exist before the father-son relationship comes into existence under Shiga's principles. The notion that father, mother and son are of one material energy continued to be used, especially in the literature of Taoism.

The use of the concept of the sharing of the same material force between parents and son or between brothers certainly existed before Song. However, the concept was never used in explanations of ancestor rituals before Song. A precursory view that equated spirits with material forces existed in the Han dynasty and subsequently faded away. While Zhang Zai and the Cheng Brothers (Cheng Hao and Cheng Yi) posited that spirits were material forces when Neo-Confucianism rose in Song before Zhu Xi, the latter was the first scholar who used the concept of material forces in relation to rituals.

While the above arguments have been used to stress the importance of the male line of descent and its links to ritual practice, another approach is to consider whether the early Neo-Confucian practices conformed with these theories. It may be relevant here to examine the practice of matrilineal ancestral rituals around Neo-Confucian scholars. Cheng Yi applauded his mother for performing rituals for her natal ancestors and it is likely that he himself practiced rituals for his mother's ancestors. Some of the disciples of Zhu Xi conducted rituals for their ancestors on their wife's or mother's side.

In short, the logic in Shiga's principles that explains the father-son transmission of ritual obligations by reference to 'one material force' is the same logic used by the Cheng-Zhu school that established itself in the Southern Song period. It goes without saying that we must not trace its origin back beyond Zhu Xi because this ritual theory was first established by Zhu Xi. Moreover, we cannot suppose that this logic had become a generally accepted understanding among the intellectual class prior to the spread of the Cheng-Zhu school – all the more so regarding common people who were yet to be acquainted with Zhu Xi's philosophy of *li* and *qi*. Of course, the patrilineal kin principle itself had existed for a long time as it was written in classics. However, the strengthening of the philosophical grounding by linking rituals to *qi* did not happen until Zhu Xi of the Southern Song. We must take this into account and understand that the patrilineal kin principle before Zhu Xi was a fragile one due to a lack of grounding in a metaphysical theory.

Rituals for and by daughters

Under Shiga's principles, daughters have no right to their natal family property or to perform rituals for their ancestors. Daughters are unable to obtain social status within their natal family; if they die as unmarried women, they are not buried in their natal family tomb nor worshipped as ancestors. Daughters gain social status only when they marry and become incorporated into their husband's kinship group.

What did Zhu Xi think of rituals for and by daughters? In short, Zhu Xi believed that it would be reasonable for daughters to perform ancestral rituals in their natal family and to be buried by their natal family if they died.

Let us look at a chapter about the general principles of rituals (general ancestral rituals performed in an ancestral hall) in a manual for the capping, wedding, funeral and ancestral rites entitled *Family Rituals* (*Jia Li*, written by Zhu Xi). It does not emphasize the superiority of men because the rite takes the format of men offering tablets to male ancestors and women offering tablets to female ancestors. The men and women of the family line up separately on the eastern and western sides of the ancestral hall and the front row of the male group is occupied by the master of the house and his eldest son while the mistress of the house (wife) and her eldest daughter or the wife of the eldest son stand in the front row of the other group, playing a central role in the ritual. The unmarried eldest daughter is assigned a much more important role than the family's younger sons and collateral uncles who merely stand behind and follow the leaders. On the other hand, Zhang Zai was praised for letting his daughters conduct ancestral rituals properly (Zhang Zai's biography written by Lü Dalin). In this context, the conducting of rituals by unmarried daughters for their natal ancestors was considered correct behavior.

When unmarried daughters died, it was considered normal to bury them in their natal family tomb. The Cheng brothers as well as Zhu Xi buried their unmarried daughters in their family tombs as a matter of common practice. Zhu Xi's daughter died while engaged to be married. Zhu Xi buried her in his wife's (her mother's) grave and he himself was buried in the same grave when he died, even though according to Shiga's principles the daughter should be buried in the tomb of her fiancé's family (Sasaki 2015a, 2015b).

There is no rule against offering ancestral tablets to unmarried daughters in an ancestral hall. Zhu Xi's *Family Rituals* have a provision for rituals for young people who die prematurely which prescribes making tablets for them and placing them next to those of their parents so that they can receive a family rite. It does not specify that this practice pertains to males only.

Shiga's principles suppose that young sons as well as unmarried daughters who die prematurely are not recognized as full family members and hence not buried in their family tomb or honored with rituals. It must be said that the rules proposed by Shiga's principles are clearly far more restrictive than those found in Zhu Xi's *Family Rituals* or in the actions of Cheng Yi and Zhu Xi themselves.

One of the bases for Shiga's depiction of rituals for daughters was provided by *Rural Customs and Practices of China*, which was a survey conducted jointly by the Manchurian Railway Investigation Department and the East Asia Institute in the 1940s. The pioneering legal historian, Niida Noboru, was a participant in the survey compilation and the materials from the surveys were used as an important source by Japanese legal historians in early attempts to understand Chinese customary legal practice. However, it is inappropriate to extrapolate from the rural customs and practices of North China in the 1940s back to the Song period, let alone the Han period, without critical analysis. If one is to claim that the rules denying daughters' rights to perform ancestral rituals or natal families' rights to bury and honor their unmarried daughters became common practice in the post-Zhu Xi era, one must provide an explanation as to when and why it happened. This issue warrants further investigation.

Chapter 6

Oppression of women and the Cheng-Zhu school

The theory that the Cheng-Zhu school of Neo-Confucianism led to the oppression of women has been widely accepted since Chen Dongyuan. This is based on Cheng Yi's statement about the remarriage of widows with young children that 'To starve to death is a small matter, but to lose one's chastity is a great matter' and Zhu Xi's support for this statement.

Researchers who attempt to dig deeper and understand more about the oppression of women from the writings of Cheng Yi and Zhu Xi are likely to be bewildered and frustrated because they will be unable to find any commentary directly relevant to the oppression of women other than the above statement.

Bettine Birge's work (1989), for example, is a sincere attempt to examine women's oppression in the teachings of the Cheng-Zhu school based on Zhu Xi's writings. However, the only materials Birge analyzed were *An Anthology of Excerpts from the Classics* (*Xiaoxue*) jointly compiled by Zhu Xi and his disciples and women's tombstone epitaphs written by Zhu Xi. The former is a collection of aphorisms about etiquette and decorum extracted from classics compiled for children, but the policy behind its editing is unclear as some inclusions make one wonder whether Zhu Xi really thought they should be put into practice. As epitaphs were normally commissioned by the family of the deceased and written as a laudatory statement, they cannot be considered robust material for the purpose of examining Zhu Xi's philosophy.

Deng Xiaonan's 2004 work is a study on the idea of male/female segregation during the Song and quotes only one short comment from Zhu Xi's explanatory note to the text: 'What is most advantageous is that the wife be firm and correct; to make things right in the family, inner order will naturally produce outer order'.[1] Deng Xiaonan simply offers an explanation of this sentence along the lines of Zhu Xi's comment, 'It was perceived that making things right within the family would not only result in good family management but also develop the rightness of the outer world'. This comment is hardly a basis for drawing conclusions on the segregation or oppression of women. If Zhu Xi wished to segregate and suppress women, his explanatory note to 'The regulation of the family' would have been an ideal place to expound his view, but he did not do so.

---

1 'Divinatory trigrams', in 'The regulation of the family' in *The Original Meaning of Zhouyi*.

Zhu Xi's commentary on the familiar classical text associated with the oppression of women reads as follows: 'There are three unfilial matters and to have no posterity is the greatest of them' (*buxiao yousan, wuhou weida*) ('Li Lou', Vol. 1, *Mencius*). Although Zhu Xi valued *Mencius* as one of 'Four Books' and put much effort into annotating it, he actually paid no attention to this particular section and did not comment on it at all. In *Family Rituals*, Zhu Xi provided some rules for rituals such as using memorial tablets for not only those who died prematurely but also for collateral relatives who died without progeny. In other words, Zhu Xi formulated his family rituals on the assumption that some family members would have no children and no posterity. He did not believe that producing progeny was the essence of filial piety and that therefore one had to have children.

In the case of Cheng Yi, he wrote a laudatory epitaph for an unmarried niece (his brother Cheng Hao's daughter) who had failed to find a suitable husband and died in her natal home, stating that she had been good to her mother and had been better off remaining unmarried than marrying an unworthy man (Sasaki 2015a, 2015b). We must remember that this is the man who said 'To starve to death is a small matter, but to lose one's chastity is a great matter'. He also applauded his own father for allowing his aunt to remarry as a 'righteous deed' and thus it would be surprising if he believed that women should starve themselves to death rather than lose their fidelity. I suspect that his extreme comment about remarriage was related to a particular incident in the Cheng family. Cheng Hao's son died young and his wife left the Cheng family to remarry Mr. Zhang, a friend of her dead husband. Cheng Yi's fury at Mr. Zhang for 'stealing a friend's wife' echoes the vehemence of the above statement. It is possible that Cheng Yi's statement was of a personal and coincidental nature sparked by the case of the remarriage of his nephew's wife rather than his general belief.

Zhu Xi has been accused of supporting Cheng Yi's statement. However, Zhu Xi clearly stated that remarriage was acceptable for widows in financial difficulty and that not everyone could afford to maintain their faithfulness. This is a more orthodox interpretation in accord with the meaning of the text. Zhu Xi's support for Cheng Yi's statement is based on the fact that he once quoted it in a letter he wrote to urge someone to maintain their fidelity. This was a completely isolated case in which the person in question was a high official's daughter with no financial difficulty at all (Sasaki 2000b). For both Cheng Yi and Zhu Xi, it is reasonable to say that the statement against remarriage was

Chapter 6

merely a short comment written regarding individual cases which was later taken out of context and emphasized. If negative sentiment toward remarriage spread in the Ming-Qing period, it was not caused by the popularization of the teachings of the Cheng-Zhu school; it is more logical to think that there were forces in Ming-Qing society that strove to negate remarriage and sought support for this position in the writings of Cheng Yi and Zhu Xi. The question that must be asked is what was happening in Ming-Qing society that created this pressure against the remarriage of widows.

The same can be said about various phenomena that appeared in the Ming-Qing period such as widows martyring themselves for their deceased husband and unmarried women moving to live with the family of their deceased fiancé where they remained chaste. Some argued at the time that the actions of these chaste widows and chastely martyred wives and daughters were excessive (Yuasa 1981; Mori 2005), and that if Zhu Xi and other Song scholars had found out about this situation, they would have been shocked and critical of such practices. Both Cheng Yi and Zhu Xi understood that a daughter would gradually become a wife as she sequentially passed through the stages of a marriage rite (negotiating the marriage, presenting the betrothal gift, presenting the valuables, welcoming in person, presenting the bride to her parents-in-law and presenting at the family shrine). The act of a daughter 'marrying into the family of her deceased fiancé' without going through a proper marriage rite would be an irreverent act that they would not have anticipated. Above all, Song Neo-Confucians would not have expected widows to martyr themselves to their deceased husbands, and never offered praise for martyred wives.

Patricia Buckley Ebrey notes the spread of the rumor in modern times that Zhu Xi recommended footbinding while he was a regional official and argues it is foolish to criticize Song-period Confucianism on the grounds of what happened in the Ming-Qing period (Ebrey 1992). As Ebrey claims, we must not look to the doctrines of the Cheng-Zhu school and their diffusion to identify the cause of the rash of chaste daughters and martyred wives in Ming and Qing. The oppressive situation for women in the Ming-Qing period occurred to an extent that far exceeded anything that the theories of Cheng Yi and Zhu Xi might have suggested. The cause of this phenomenon in the Ming-Qing period must be analyzed in the context of the history of Ming-Qing society. In this sense, Mann's study is interesting as it argues that gender served as a practical indicator of social status from the end of Ming onward when the old class system was dismantled and social mobility increased markedly in comparison with the Song period and explains segregation between the sexes in relation to law and order issues (see Chapter Eight).

The descent-line system and the Cheng-Zhu school

The previous section explained how Cheng Yi's and Zhu Xi's comments were used to reinforce the oppression of women far beyond their intent and noted that a number of groundless claims were attributed to the Cheng-Zhu school of thought. Conversely, we now look at some family-related matters that were not put into practice by later generations even though Neo-Confucian scholars had repeatedly emphasized them.

Song scholars who were affiliated with the Cheng-Zhu school such as Zhang Zai, Cheng Yi and Zhu Xi preached that the descent-line system (*zongfa*) should be revived and practiced. The patrilineal kin groups or lineages that were found across China during the Ming-Qing period, especially in the southern region, professed that their kinship organizations conformed to the descent-line system. For this reason, the Neo-Confucians' argument for the revival and implementation of the descent-line system was thought to have been aimed at a broader association and mutual aid among patrilineal kin (Inoue 2000).

In reality, what the Song Neo-Confucians aspired to revive by promoting the restoration of the descent-line system was the establishment of the primacy of the first-born legitimate son and the rule of primogeniture concerning ritual rights. In other words, their goal was to return to the feudal kinship concept and kinship organizations of the Zhou dynasty period. However, they also knew that it would be difficult to spread and entrench the kinship concept to limit hereditary ritual rights to the first-born legitimate son in a society where the concept of equal division between brothers ('Brothers are of one material force' in Shiga's language) was well established. Zhang Zai tried to realize this primacy by granting the first-born legitimate son an official rank and economic advantage while Cheng Yi attempted to achieve this by slightly toning down the primacy of the first-born legitimate son. Zhu Xi considered various forms of rituals to allow younger sons to preside over lesser rituals on the basis that if only the first-born legitimate son inherited ritual rights, younger sons would not be able to perform rituals once they set up separate residences (Sasaki 1998, 2000a). Confucian scholars of the

Chapter 6

Joseon dynasty in Korea correctly understood that the goal of the Song Neo-Confucians' attempt to revive the descent-line system was to restore primogeniture. They changed the property inheritance law from equal division between sons and daughters in the Goryeo dynasty and the early Joseon dynasty to equal division between sons and then to preferential treatment of first-born legitimate sons. They also created lineages on the basis of the rule of primogeniture for ritual rights and developed the Yangban society that emphasized the practice and transmission of rituals (Miyajima 1995). While some scholars have attempted to explain the cause of the change from a socioeconomic viewpoint, there is no doubt that the Cheng-Zhu school played the role of at least legitimizing and invigorating the change.

Meanwhile, Zhu Xi's theory was not received with such sincerity in the home of the Cheng-Zhu school. In Chinese society where the practice of equal division between brothers was thoroughly entrenched, it was believed to be impossible to gain public acceptance of the kinship concept that gave first-born legitimate sons special status and hereditary rights. *Propriety of Family Rituals*, written by Ming scholar Qiu Jun, was a revised version of Zhu Xi's *Family Rituals* and enjoyed a much wider circulation than the original version. In this book, all of the rules in relation to the descent-line system were shelved because they were considered too difficult to put into practice (Sasaki 2009).

What we can learn from a comparison of Korea and China with regard to the revival and practice of the descent-line system is that the latter society did not change no matter how loudly Zhu Xi called for it or how well the Cheng-Zhu school became established as a teaching system. Teachings can only spread when there is an element of desire to change on the part of the society that receives them. In other words, the strengthening of gender norms in the Ming-Qing period was the result of forces in Chinese society that favored the adoption of the teachings of the Cheng-Zhu school and used them to enforce gender norms well beyond those teachings rather than to simply diffuse Neo-Confucianism (the Cheng-Zhu school). It is this societal element that we must investigate. If the diffusion of the Cheng-Zhu doctrines alone was the cause of the change, the rule of primogeniture would have been revived and practiced as it was the linchpin of the school's ideology.

In terms of a comparison between the lineage-related norms of Song and those of Ming-Qing, it is very interesting to compare the rules of the Fan Clan's Charitable Estate and the lineages of the Ming-Qing period. The Fan Clan's

Charitable Estate was founded by Fan Zhongyan, a famous mid-eleventh century political figure who was regarded as an exemplary scholar-official. Although he was not a Cheng-Zhu scholar, the rules he established continued to be seen as a model for lineage organization for many generations. However, the mutual aid rules established by Fan Zhongyan stipulated that men and women were to be provided with the same amount of basic rice allowance and that a marrying woman was to receive ten *guan* more than a man taking a wife as an allowance. They also provided that even relatives by marriage were eligible to receive aid in needy circumstances such as famine ('The rules made by Fan Zhongyan'). Thus, women received generous support and in-laws were not excluded from mutual aid in the early form of lineage organization in the Song dynasty period. If mutual aid by lineage organizations came to be limited to patrilineal kin or men in the Ming-Qing period, we must examine its timing and social background.

In closing

Returning to our title, 'Traditional Family Ideology and the Cheng-Zhu School', when looking back from a modern or more recent perspective, are we able to identify a specific point in time when what has been believed to be the family ideology of traditional China was put together and began to function as a unitary system? As discussed above, Zhu Xi is recognized as the first scholar who successfully rooted the patrilineal family principle in a metaphysical theory, but he himself was hardly interested in sex-based segregation or the oppression of women. Moreover, the gender norms that pervaded in Ming-Qing society were altered and fortified beyond those discussed in Zhu Xi's ideology. In view of these points, this chapter puts forward the hypothesis that what was considered the family ideology of traditional China by modern people was born not during the Han period over two millennia ago as Shiga argues and not during the Song period about 1,000 years ago as Chen Dongyuan claims but instead was established sometime after the beginning of the Ming period about 400 years ago.

At this stage in the development of this hypothesis, I have only considered the theories of Zhu Xi and several Neo-Confucian scholars before him; as yet I have not conducted a chronological analysis of the ideas on gender norms developed by the thinkers of each historical period after Zhu Xi. People may

Chapter 6

think that an ideology is a publicly declared set of concepts that are set in stone, but in reality, it is actually more fluid and mirrors the conditions of the time and place when examined in the context of the thinking that generates and structures the ideology. Once we set aside the assumptions that have been regarded as given, such as Shiga's principles and the Cheng-Zhu teachings as a feudal code of ethics, we can find a large opening for further development of the study of Chinese gender history.

7. Marriage and 'Chastity': Structure and Change

— *GOMI Tomoko*

Introduction

The Chinese family placed a high value on preservation of the patrilineal line, which was the fundamental building block of the Chinese family and the larger lineage unit. Since the chastity of a woman marrying into a family was a precondition for the preservation of the purity of the family's male bloodline, there was a strong association between chastity and marriage. Thus, from early times, a wife's involvement in illicit sex was seen as one of the seven grounds for divorce.[1]

Female chastity has been considered important since ancient times in China, but the concept of 'chastity' has not remained consistent. While affairs involving a married woman and a man other than her husband have drawn criticism since ancient times, the scope of chastity in China went beyond adultery. One of the crucial issues in later times was the question of the remarriage of widows which came to be regarded as a violation of chastity. A second, and related, issue was the proper behavior for a woman whose fiancé died before their marriage: should she remain loyal to him, or was it acceptable

---

1 '*Qiqu*' refers to the seven grounds for divorce, including disobedience to parents-in-law, childlessness, unfaithfulness, jealousy, terminal illness, gossiping and thieving. However, a wife could not be divorced if she met one of the following three conditions: if the wife had completed three years of mourning for one of her parents-in law; if the husband's household had been poor before the marriage but became rich after the marriage; if the wife had no family to return to. The seven grounds for divorce and three conditions blocking divorce appeared in a number of classical texts, including: 'Benmian pian' (*Dadaili*), 'Benming jie' (*The School Sayings of Confucious*), 'Zhuanggong twenty-seventh year' (*Chunqiu Gongyangzhuan*) and *He Xiu's Commentary*.

Chapter 7

to marry someone else? The key task of this chapter is to examine the varying definitions and importance of chastity throughout history.

From a global perspective, the Chinese focus on the remarriage of a widowed woman as a violation of chastity is unusual. Remarriage of a widow was not regarded as a violation of the 'chastity' norm in many regions or ages in the Islamic world, in Japan or in the Christian world. This chapter will trace the changes in ideas of chastity and the conditions and ideas that supported varying views of chastity, revealing that the situation varied greatly from one period to another. For example, remarriage was a very common occurrence even for princesses during the Tang dynasty period (Gao Shiyu 1988). The stricter idea of chastity that abhorred women's remarriage emerged during the Song period but had not yet become a widely prevalent view (Yuasa 1981: 150–156). The idea of the chastity of unmarried women also changed significantly across the ages. An unmarried woman's act of staying single out of loyalty to her deceased fiancé against her parents' wishes was at times considered unfilial, while the act of following her fiancé to death was at times regarded as devaluing one's life. These acts were not always seen as commendable. Accordingly, this chapter analyzes the concept of chastity in relation to marriage with a focus on its variability over time.

Changes in the concept of chastity and the awards system

The emergence of the notion of scorning women's remarriage is said to have been symbolized by the statement made by Cheng Yi of the Northern Song dynasty: 'Too starve to death is a small matter, but to lose one's chastity is a great matter'.[2] However, there are broadly two different views when it comes to how to position this statement within the development process of the chastity concept. One view argues that people such as Cheng Yi and Zhu Xi expressed their disapproval of women's remarriage which gradually strengthened to become a social-moral rule that reached its peak in the Ming-Qing period (Gōyama 2006: 166). The other position contends that Cheng Yi's statement was a reconfirmation of the 'official stance' or 'principle' formulated in a social

---

2 'Remnant books' (*Yishu*) in the *Complete Writings of the Two Cheng Brothers* (*Er Cheng quanshu*), Vol. 25.

climate that widely permitted women's remarriage (Sasaki 2000b: 127–128), and that the spreading of the chastity concept was instead driven by the state's system of commendation (Sengoku 2011: 14). Sakai (2006: 49–50) has argued for the increasing awareness of the system of rewarding chaste widows, which developed out of a Yuan system of court awards that provided for the cancellation of the labor service owed by a chaste widow's household. The number of women rewarded in this way rapidly increased during the Ming dynasty and this trend did not stop even after the regime change to the Qing. Generally speaking, the honoring of widows who stayed alive and kept their chastity ('chaste widows') was accepted with less reluctance than the honoring of unmarried women who martyred themselves or stayed single for the sake of their deceased fiancé.

The discussion now turns to how the concept of, and rewards for, unmarried women who pledged to remain faithful to their fiancé ('faithful maidens') changed over time. The Southern Song dynasty clearly praised unmarried women in this category (Lu Weijing 2008 [English]: 27). The phenomenon of following one's fiancé to death was first reported in the Yuan dynasty, which responded with caution to requests to commend such acts (Lu Weijing 2008 [English]: 28–29). It was not until the Ming dynasty that the government began to reward unmarried women who remained single or committed suicide after the death of their fiancé (Lu Weijing 2008 [English]: 32–33). More dramatic expressions of chastity such as committing suicide after the death of one's fiancé were applauded in the latter half of the Ming period and the number of court commendations for such women increased (Lu Weijing 2008 [English]: 32–36). Emperor Kangxi (r. 1661–1722) and Emperor Yongzheng (r. 1722–1735) of the Qing dynasty banned chastity suicides for 'taking life lightly', but the prohibition policy was not consistently implemented. Women who followed their fiancé to death were often commended, and the rule to confer honor to such women was established during the Qianlong era (r. 1735–1796) (Yamazaki 1967: 50–51, 58–60; Lu Weijing 2008 [English]: 71).

The mass commendation of chaste women, be they widows or unmarried maidens, began in earnest during the Ming dynasty. The conferring of honor to virtuous people by a dynastic court can be traced back to the Han period, and the focus of the court awards shifted during the Yuan period from filial sons to chaste widows and chastely martyred wives and daughters, especially those widows who remained single without remarrying (Sakai 2006). This tendency intensified and the number of such cases increased markedly during the Ming and Qing periods.

Chapter 7

The act of sacrificing one's life to preserve chastity was praised in most cases, but a question was raised as to how far one should go to do so. In 1753, there was an incident in Shanxi where a man took a knife to the home of another man who had insulted his sibling's wife, and stabbed a female family member, leading to her death (Theiss 2004: 167–175). The county magistrate blamed both the insulted woman's overreaction and the insensitivity of the people around her. A perennial argument revolved around the contention that women who committed suicide to avoid being raped might be praiseworthy, whereas being mocked was not a strong enough reason to motivate one to commit suicide; moreover, such acts conflicted with the virtue of protecting one's life. Nevertheless, women's suicides following acts of men taking liberties with them or making sexual advances towards them came to be honored by the court during the Qianlong era. The importance of chastity must have outweighed criticisms about 'taking life lightly'.

Punishment for sex crimes

One of the chief yardsticks for understanding what was involved in 'unchaste' behavior is an examination of laws related to sexual crimes. The diversity and temporal shift in the concept of 'chastity' can be clarified by examining the circumstances under which chastity was thought to have been 'lost'. In other words, what are the actions to which varying degrees of 'unchasteness' are assigned? In the Ming-Qing period, a widow's remarriage was perceived as a loss of chastity, as mentioned above, but of course a widow's illicit sexual intercourse drew harsher criticism.

The Qing dynasty instituted numerous rules concerning sex crimes which were even more detailed than the Ming rules. In an effort spearheaded by Matthew H. Sommer, researchers from the U.S. have considered this change to be significant and studied it intensively (Ng 1984; Sommer 2000; Theiss 2004), arguing that dynastic policy change would be expressed in laws and regulations.

Sommer analyzed rules related to sexual activity with a focus on the Qing-period laws. According to his study, the policy for the control of sexual activity changed dramatically from the Yongzheng era. This involved a change from 'status performance' that had regulated sexual behavior based on social status since the Tang dynasty to 'gender performance' that imposed gender-based sexual morality regardless of status. The major concern during the Tang period was the raping of the master's wife by his bondservants, whereas the most dreaded crime in the Qing was the raping of female family members and young men by ruffians outside of the family institution. The population expansion as a result of the prosperity of the Qing dynasty exacerbated the gender imbalance due to increased female infanticide and trafficking in women, leading to a rise in the number of men unable to find spouses. It has been argued that the serious promotion of female chastity during the eighteenth and nineteenth centuries was an indication of the authority's effort to protect the bounds of the family institution from the growing number of miscreant men at the bottom of society by turning women into the 'moral police' and asking for 'wifely behavior' from all women (Sommer 2000).

Opinion is divided on this point, but my current view is as follows: while it is true that there is significant difference between Tang and Ming laws, the impact of the series of new laws promulgated during the Yongzheng and Qianlong reigns does not seem as great as Sommer suggested. The change in thinking was a gradual process that began in the Ming period and the ongoing shift in social norms would have been taken into account in decision-making in actual courts of law. We can surmise that these variations in thinking happened to be written into law during the said eras. The establishment of such laws is of course significant; and it is clear that the revision of sex crime laws and the award system was actively pursued during these eras. It is also possible that the Qing rulers actively sought to reward chaste women while trying to punish offending men and unchaste women. The Manchu rulers of the Qing may have adopted this view as a way to show that they were as 'civilized' as the Han population over which they ruled. In fact, honors were given not only to Han women, but also to Manchu women.

Firstly, let us look at differences in punishment for an act deemed 'consensual illicit sexual intercourse'. In Ming-Qing China, consensual sexual intercourse between an unmarried woman and a man was also defined as illicit sexual intercourse, but the punishment for the act was lighter than that for a sexual liaison between a married woman and a man other than her husband. The latter involved eighty strokes of the heavy bamboo rod for the unmarried woman whereas ninety strokes were meted out to the married woman. It should be noted that the level of punishment did not depend on the marital status of the man. The man's crime was having sex with another man's daughter, wife or concubine; betraying his own wife or concubine was not considered a crime. Illicit sexual intercourse by the connivance of the husband carried ninety strokes of the heavy bamboo rod to the husband, the adulterer and the wife/concubine. If the husband forced his wife/concubine to have illicit sexual intercourse, he received one hundred strokes while his wife/concubine was not charged. These rules were applied in both Ming and Qing.

Rape was taken seriously and carried the death penalty by hanging during the Ming period. Female victims were not charged. In the Qing period, rapists were sentenced to strangulation subject to review while female victims were not charged. However, a rape charge could not be substantiated unless there was violent coercion or other circumstances that prevented the victim from escaping. It was stipulated that death by strangulation was applicable only if there were witnesses or evidence such as physical injuries and torn clothes. In fact, a sign of change manifested earlier during the Ming period when it was stipulated in the fifteenth year of the Wanli era (1587) that rapists should be hanged only if there was clear evidence that they had threatened their victims with weapons, tied them up, prevented them from escaping and so on.

The level of punishment for spousal killings depended on the sex of the offender.[3] If a wife or concubine conspired with an adulterer to murder her husband, she was sentenced to death by slow slicing while her male co-conspirator was sentenced to beheading subject to review. If her illicit relationship was connived by her husband, her punishment was mitigated. If the man with whom she engaged in adultery killed her husband, she was sentenced to strangulation subject to review even if she had no knowledge of the killing. On the other hand, there was no specific article of law for cases in which the adulterous husband killed his own wife/concubine or those in which the woman with whom the husband engaged in adultery killed his wife. The same laws for spousal killings were used in the Ming and Qing periods.

In the Ming period, forcing a widow to remarry attracted eighty strokes of the heavy bamboo rod, but her grandparents and parents and her husband's grandparents and parents were exempt from punishment if they were the perpetrators. The punishment on her relatives needing a one-year mourning period was reduced by two degrees.[4] In the Qing, heavier punishments were imposed on the act of forcing a widow to remarry. Her grandparents and parents and her husband's grandparents and parents were subjected to eighty strokes while the punishment was increased by one degree for her relatives needing

---

3 See Kita (2010), Gōyama (2006), Gomi (2015) and Sasaki (2008) for details of spousal killings.

4 Under Confucian mourning rituals, relatives were divided into five ranks with different mourning obligations. So, for example, a son was required to do three years of mourning for a parent, while a more distant relative was obligated for only a few months. These same standards were used for the reduction of punishment in cases where a superior inflicted injury on an inferior.

one-year mourning time and by another degree for her relatives needing nine months or less mourning time. If the woman was widowed prior to the consummation of a marriage, she was allowed to go back to the husband's home to maintain her chastity and the bride price was returned. The punishment for forced remarriage of a widow became heavier in Qing than in Ming.

In the process of revising the criminal code as one step in the process of regaining full sovereign rights at the end of the Qing period, a controversy arose over 'sexual intercourse by unmarried or widowed women'. This crime was not included in the draft criminal code of the great Qing or in its second draft, but it was introduced into the interim regulations annexed to the second draft after objections were raised (Ono 1992). Moreover, although the original intent of this charge was to punish both men and women who engaged in illicit sexual intercourse, it was decided that the penalty was applicable only to husbandless women; no question was raised about the culpability of their male counterparts (Ono 1992: 40). Under the Provisional Criminal Code Supplementary Regulations of the Republic of China proposed by the Yuan Shikai government, the crime of fornication by husbandless women was revived with conditions while concubines were given status equivalent to wives. Becoming a concubine was not regarded as bigamy or fornication by a husbandless woman (Ono 1992: 58). In other words, the rules concerning fornication by husbandless women were revised at the end of the Qing, but the underlying ideology remained unchanged and still required chastity only on the female side while permitting men to have concubines.

The women's dowry

Another approach is to examine cases related to the legal handling of a woman's dowry in the case where she did, against some of the norms discussed above, remarry. The laws of Tang and Song provided that the part of the husband's property that had been gained from the wife's family should be exempted from the equal division of assets between his brothers that occurred when they became independent and left their parents' house.[5] It was ruled that the wife's dowry was the couple's property.

---

5 *Huhunlü, Beiyong sishan yongcai* in *Tang Code with Commentary and Explanations* (*Tanglü shuyi*), Vol. 12. *Huhunlü, Beiyong sishan yongcai* in *Criminal Laws of the Song Classified by Category* (*Song xingtong*), Vol. 12.

Chapter 7

During the Yuan period, a clause was added concerning the treatment of the dowry upon remarriage. The *Statutes and Precedents of the Yuan* (*Yuandianzhang*) contains the following provision.

> Henceforth, if a woman wishes to remarry someone, whether she has been divorced while her husband was alive or widowed upon her husband's death, her previous husband's family shall have complete disposal of the dowry she brought to the previous marriage and she shall not be permitted to take it with her as was permitted previously.[6]

This change forbade the wife from taking her dowry to her next marriage, forcing her to leave it behind with her previous husband's family. In the Ming period, the law provided that 'When a woman remarries, her previous husband's property and the dowry she brought to the marriage shall remain the property of the previous husband's family'.[7] This rule continued into the Qing period.[8]

A gradual erosion of women's dowry rights is evident beginning from the Song period. What caused this change? As mentioned above, there was a growing tendency from the Song period to praise and honor widows who remained single while criticizing those who remarried. It appears that the erosion of women's rights to their dowry upon remarriage occurred in step with this trend. We can surmise that the rising criticism of women's remarriage led to the curtailing of their rights.

Aside from the legal changes, analysis is needed in terms of whether these rules of law were applied in actual court cases. Were remarrying women actually barred from taking their dowry with them in the Ming-Qing period? Takahashi Yoshirō (2007: 34) states as follows.

> While I assume that the wife had less freedom to take her dowry with her than during the Southern Song period, I suspect that there was very little change in people's perception of a dowry being the wife's property. Nevertheless, we are yet to understand many aspects of how a dowry was treated in the Ming-Qing period and must await further studies.

---

6 *Fuwang, Liantian ting fujia weizhu, Hubu*, Vol. 4, in *Statutes and Precedents of the Yuan* (*Yuandianzhang*), Scroll 18.

7 *Huling* in *Statutes of the Great Ming* (*Daming ling*).

8 *Hulü, Huyi*, '*Li dizi weifa*,' Ordinance No. 2, *Great Qing Code with Substatutes* (*Daqinglüli*), Vol. 8.

Raijō Kōhei (2013) examined a range of cases found in novels and various records of judgments and found no evidence that this rule was effectively used in Ming law courts or that the wife's dowry was retained by the husband's family upon her remarriage or return to her natal lineage. For this reason, he surmised that the wife took her dowry property with her in most instances despite the existence of the basic rule that the divorced wife should leave her dowry behind when she returned to her natal home. No study has been undertaken on the situation in the Qing period. Although further analysis of historical records is required in relation to the Ming period, these studies point to the possibility that the ban on the withdrawal of the dowry by the wife failed to become a socially accepted idea, even though it was established as a rule of law.

Conclusion

In this chapter, we have examined changes in the concept of chastity in relation to marriage and women's status in the family. The discussion has shown that while men's unfaithfulness to their wives and concubines was hardly viewed as an issue in the public arena, regardless of its morality, women's chastity was emphasized in laws and the encouraged by the system of court awards for virtuous behavior. Female chastity was regarded as the foundation of marriage. This way of thinking was reinforced in successive periods from the Song dynasty and had repercussions on women's property rights. Looking at the actual cases in which remarrying women took their dowry with them, however, the change in law does not appear always to have resulted in an immediate change to social norms and practices.

The act of trying to stay 'chaste' sometimes impinged on other virtues. One of them was filiality (Sengoku 2015). Other considerations included protecting one's own body that was given by one's parents and deferring to one's husband. These virtues were relevant to actions such as unmarried women's suicide or staying single against one's parents' wishes, women's suicide in response to mocking or teasing and wives resisting coercion by their husband to prostitute themselves. The treatment of these women in the dynastic award system was a troublesome problem, but in general we have seen that in later dynasties chastity tended to outrank the other virtues.

8. The Sense of Social Status and Gender

— *KISHIMOTO Mio*

Introduction: The concept of 'the sense of social status'

This chapter discusses trends in research on gender history in China from the angle of 'the sense of social status'. This term is not necessarily in common usage, but it shall be used here to represent the following viewpoints in the study of gender history.

First is a 'holistic' perspective. The approach of seeing individual phenomena as part of a total picture of the world rather than as discrete elements has been advocated in the concept of 'total history' proposed by the Annales School (Harsgor 1978), and it appears to be an effective viewpoint for gender history as well. As stated in Kohama Masako's 'Preface' to this volume, the original connotation of the term 'gender history' involves reassessing all of history from the perspective of those who have been rendered invisible or objectified in conventional history rather than reserving the field of 'women's history' as a separate genre or focusing on the 'male-female relationship'. While the term 'status' brings to mind the image of hereditary and fixed social stratification in pre-modern times, it is broadly interpreted here as a structure made of vertical relationships thought to be the ideal state of social order. In the traditional Chinese lexicon, *'fen'* (分, lit. 'division') is used more commonly than 'status'. The various divisions that signify interpersonal relations between superiors and inferiors, such as those between masters and bondservants, elites and commoners, the good and the debased, seniors and juniors and so on, are entwined and cover the entire Chinese society.

Second is an 'internal' viewpoint. With regard to certain historical phenomena that are considered oppressive of women from a contemporary perspective, gender historical studies have revealed that women of that time were in some cases active participants and made independent choices to take part. What was the motivation behind women's conduct when, for example, they actively complied with the Confucian gender norm of chastity? In order to develop more than a superficial understanding, we need to question how women perceived the world around them, where they placed themselves and others in it and how they aspired to achieve upward mobility and lifestyle stability, in addition to applying contemporary concepts such as patriarchal ideology. Although few would disagree that the goal of the study of gender history is to look at history from the viewpoint of women instead of men, the so-called women's viewpoint is not monolithic and the question of whether the perspective of today's women is the same as that of women in days gone by raises further questions. These questions make up the important unresolved problems at the heart of the study of gender history, including the conundrum about whether we can truly gain an insider's understanding of how people of the past viewed their society.[1]

Third is a 'sensory' factor. People's choice and behavior are not necessarily guided by a clearly conceptualized perception of social structure or morality. In fact, it is possible to think that the senses that have been corporealized to a barely conscious level – the sense that something is 'abnormal', 'grotesque', 'refined', 'civilized' and so on – form the deep-rooted foundation underpinning social order as Norbert Elias (2000) argues in relation to post-medieval Europe.

Having defined the 'sense of social status' approach as above, I now offer an overview of studies that are relevant to these questions. While some of the studies mentioned in this chapter are discussed in more detail in other chapters of this book, the use of the 'sense of social status' viewpoint may uncover some previously hidden aspects. Or, the nebulous nature of this perspective may enable us to deal with specific issues that other chapters cannot fully discuss.

Although the scope of research from the approach outlined above is of course not limited to the period from the Song dynasty to the Ming-Qing, this chapter shall focus on that period as defined by the needs of this book. This focus is meaningful given that Confucian gender norms grew stricter during

---

1 For example, Clifford Geertz (1983) questions whether we can 'understand' the Balinese practice of *suttee* (the old custom of a widow sacrificing herself by burning to death on her husband's funeral pyre).

Chapter 8

this period and that this change took place concurrently with increased fluidity in social stratification, which is considered an 'early-modern' characteristic in terms of the social status system as a whole. I apologize for any deficiencies in my discussion of the Song to early Ming period, which falls outside of my realm of expertise.

'Social status' in traditional China

The definition of 'social status' is a relatively difficult question when it is discussed in the context of Chinese history. For example, Japanese would generally think of a 'class system' such as the warrior-peasant-artisan-merchant (*bushi-hyakushō-chōnin*) system in post-medieval Japan or the clergy-nobility-commoner system at play during the Ancien Régime in France. Social status under these class systems was characterized by the hereditary and fixed nature of the social standing or occupation, where one's social standing was determined by the family into which one was born. In imperial China (221 BCE–1911 CE), however, ordinary society did not have a hereditary social status system in principle, outside the imperial household and governing groups such as the Eight Banners (*baqi*). Japanese legal historian Mizubayashi Takeshi defines 'class society' as 'a society in which the social division of labor is organized according to the groups to which individuals belong by birth (e.g., family)' and argues that Chinese society from Song onward was already an 'individualistic post-class society or state' where hereditary ruling families no longer existed (and neither did families that succeeded to the fixed occupation of farming, craft or trade) (Mizubayashi 1987, 1992).

When reference is made to 'status law' (*shenfen fa*) in the field of Chinese legal history on the other hand, its main concern seems to be the norms on the relative social standing between individuals within blood-related (and fictive kinship) connections, which were refined and strengthened throughout China's imperial regimes, rather than the overall structure of group-based society. It is interesting to note that the contents of Niida Noboru's work, *A History of Chinese Status Law* (*Shina mibunhōshi*), one of the early Japanese publications on 'social status' in China from a legal historical viewpoint, deals with laws concerning lineages, relatives, family, marriage, the parent-child relationship and guardianship, as well as laws concerning slaves and servants as fictitious dependent family members (Niida 1942). In terms of a hierarchy of status under the law, there is no doubt that the superior-inferior and senior-junior relationships within kinship groups were the primary focus. In view of these strict hierarchical rules for kin (and fictive kin) relations between individuals, it also becomes apparent that what Mizubayashi called China's 'individualistic post-class society' was never based on the principle of 'the equality of all persons'; it was rather a society transpierced by a crisscrossed mesh of strict dominant-subordinate relations.

The status relationships between elite and commoners (*shi* / 士 and *shu* / 庶) and the good and the debased (*liang* / 良 and *jian* / 賤) were the legally designated hierarchical relationships in a broader society based on these morality relations within kinship groups. Since the issue of gender in terms of family relations is discussed in other chapters of this book, this chapter will consider the gender issue in these two status relationships. I would like to begin with brief explanations of these two relationship categories.

The division between elite and commoners refers to the relationship between the ruling elites who were required to be intellectuals and the subordinate class comprised of common people. The oft-quoted characteristic of the ruling class in traditional China is that it was not a hereditary class like the English aristocracy or the Japanese warrior class. Instead, it consisted of bureaucrats selected from among the general public through the civil service examinations, especially from the Song dynasty onward. Although this dominance relationship can be considered a relationship between 'officials and the public', the authority of the bureaucrats was ascribed to the individual's ability to pass the civil service examinations – a moral capacity involving the acquisition of proper human behavior through the study of Confucianism rather than a mere academic capability. Consequently, those who did not enter into the civil service after passing the examinations and those who retired from the civil service were granted privileges and powers equivalent to those of the serving bureaucrats as well as preferential tax and legal treatment comparable to government officials. In this sense, it would be closer to the truth to say that the hierarchical relationship between these people and the general public was a division between elite (intellectuals) and commoners rather than between officials and the general public. The widely used terms such as 'gentleman' (*shenshi*) and 'literati' (*shidafu*) in China broadly referred to the ruling elites, including serving and retired bureaucrats, successful candidates in the imperial examinations and those regarded as having the capacity to pass the examinations. Women were not allowed to take the examinations and hence barred from joining the 'elite', but they were able to earn due social respect by belonging to a gentleman's family.

Chapter 8

The coverage of the term 'the debased people' in the division between the good and the debased varied in different periods, but the main constituents of the category during the Ming-Qing period included 'bondservants' (*nubi*: enslaved servants who have served their master's family for generations; an umbrella term including men (*nupu*) and women (*bi*)), 'entertainers' (*changyou*: performers such as actors and singers; implies 'prostitutes' in the case of women) and 'manservants' (*lizu*: servile physical laborers such as gatekeepers at government buildings; male only). While no clear explanations have been found in historical documents as to why they were considered 'debased', it is possible that working under a service obligation and having a servile attitude to subjugate oneself to others underpinned the perception of 'debasedness' in those days (Kishimoto 2003). Those who were not 'debased' were regarded as 'the good', but people in this category also engaged in labor service at times. Thus, the boundaries of the debased were not clear-cut and the legal definition of 'debased people' did not necessarily correspond to the social perception of debasedness. Significant inequalities between the good and the debased under the law included some difference in the degree of penalty imposed on assault cases between the good and the debased, a ban on marriage between the good and the debased and the barring of the debased from taking the civil service examinations, i.e., blocking their path to rise to the 'elite' class.

Whether the division was between the elite and commoners or the good and the debased, it was a social class distinction which differed from the relative standing of individuals such as parents and children. However, affiliation to these classes was not determined hereditarily or by birth; it was largely determined by people's behavior and practice later in life, as those who succeeded in the civil service examinations would become elites while those who worked in servitude would become the debased. Consequently, competition for upward mobility (or competition for not being downgraded) was very fierce. From the point of view of social recognition, it was important to 'act becomingly'. Those who belonged to a family of the gentry were required to exhibit behavior expected of members of such a family. Conversely, debased people who were recognized to be noble-minded could be applauded (for their honorable deeds, in spite of their debased status). The competitive nature of China's 'social status' conferred some peculiar characteristics to Chinese people's social choices. For instance, a Chinese phenomenon in which an increase in social mobility leads to the tightening of gender norms instead of their loosening can be considered in the context of this competitive aspect.

Gender and the elite/commoner divide

Women's education and an upward mobility strategy

By law, the distinction between elites and commoners was established by the civil service examination degrees (or former official posts) held by individuals. In this sense, women were excluded from the elite status from the start as they were ineligible to take the examinations. In terms of a more general perception, however, the gentry in regional communities were recognized according to relatively vague criteria such as family members' cultural accomplishments and lifestyles. The personal qualities of female family members also formed an important part of these criteria. For this reason, women's personal qualities such as cultural accomplishments, morality and deportment drew attention from gentry families (and those who aspired to join the gentry class) as a strategy for social climbing or securing a stable standing in society when social mobility increased from the end of the Ming to the Qing period. Susan L. Mann's 'Grooming a daughter for marriage' (1991) is an early study that focused on this point. She quotes family instruction books mostly written by male literati and points out that their discourse on women's education demonstrates their effort 'to protect the existing class hierarchy' in the face of competition. At the same time, Mann refers to the aspect of women's education itself that tends to shake up the existing gender order and outlines the possibility of historical research on Qing women based on books written by women.

Upper-class women

The heralded research based on the writings of elite Ming and Qing women was presented in *Teachers of the Inner Chambers* by Dorothy Ko (1994) and *Precious Records* by Susan L. Mann (1997). The former focuses on Jiangnan (lower Yangzi region) in the seventeenth century (late Ming to early Qing) and points out that the 'talented women' (*cainü*) of the time renowned for their literary skills reinterpreted the traditional feminine virtue (*fude*) of modesty and displayed their talents in a broader sphere of activity beyond their home. Ko also suggests that their fame added to the cultural resources of their families. In the preface of her book, Ko sharply criticizes the prevailing notion that women of Old China in general were victims as this view was formed by a peculiar confluence of 'the May Fourth-New Culture movement, the Communist revolution, and Western feminist scholarship' (Ko 1994: 3). She advocates the need to understand the choices made by women in response to the circumstances of the time within the 'dynamics of the functioning of Chinese society as a whole' (Ko 1994: 4). This attitude constitutes one of the powerful currents in the study of Chinese gender history in the West. Mann's study, while sharing Ko's perspective, begins where Ko's work ends and deals with the Jiangnan region in the eighteenth century (middle Qing). While Mann considers that the trend of female education and literature pointed out by Ko continued into the Qing dynasty, she argues that the middle Qing period was characterized by elite women who empowered themselves by wielding their literary skills mainly at home. Their studies shed light on the lively cultural activity of elite women in Ming-Qing Jiangnan and at the same time reveal a gaping social rift between elite women and other women.

The introductory chapter of a more recent publication by Mann (2011), *Gender and Sexuality in Modern Chinese History*, offers a sketch of the gender system in China's traditional patrilineal society by juxtaposing two expressions of the day – 'cloistered ladies' (*guixiu*) and 'bare sticks' (*guanghun*). In other words, the chastity and purity of the insulated daughters of good families (cloistered ladies) were of central significance to the preservation of this system while at the opposite end were marginalized and impoverished unmarried men (bare sticks) who were regarded as a potential threat to the political and gender order. This picture adopts a perspective that portrays gender history in the context of a broader social hierarchy rather than the confines of gender dominance relations within a family. In the former, the dominance of elites over commoners and gender relations are interlocked and form a three-dimensional system. It is possible to appreciate that the words 'cloistered ladies' and 'bare sticks' convey a sensuous quality accompanying a physiological fear of intrusion into this system. They express value judgments rather than social classes seen from an objective viewpoint.

Footbinding as a culture

Within this trend in historical research, footbinding is also being studied from perspectives other than the oppression of women. *Cinderella's Sisters* by Dorothy Ko (2005) with the subtitle *A Revisionist History of Footbinding* challenges the common belief that footbound women were helpless victims and proposes to understand their choice to participate in this practice from their standpoint – 'in her shoes' in Ko's words. She argues that the interpretation of footbinding in terms of miserable victimhood is a one-sided view that directly reflects the perspective that has persisted since the end of Qing when there was a significant shift in the image of the practice. Ko meticulously demonstrates that footbinding was generally a symbol of women's social standing and self-respect in the Ming-Qing period, although individual circumstances varied. In *Every Step a Lotus*, Ko (2001) puts a spotlight on various cloth shoe designs for footbinding crafted by women themselves, including many beautiful pictures of the shoes, and points out that shoe-making was a culture inherited in the context of the close relationship between a mother and her daughter.

Another noteworthy point about Ko's study is that it makes mention of the meaning of footbinding in the Chinese world order – with China as the center of civilization and its neighbors as barbarians – beyond the sense of class inside the nation. She states that the practice of footbinding took on the meaning of a symbol of Han civilization contrasted with the Manchus in the Ming-Qing transition period when the Manchu 'barbarians' conquered China proper inhabited by the Han Chinese (Ko 1997a [Japanese]; Ko 1997b). While Han men were forced to wear the Manchu *queue* hairstyle, women's footbinding survived through Qing even though the practice was banned by the dynasty. Xia Xiaohong (2002) discusses the question of how the discourse of 'Men surrendered, women did not' (*Nan xiang nü buxiang*) was revived in the late Qing as a form of praise for women, describing it as consistent with the revolutionary movement that was campaigning against footbinding.

Conferring honors on faithful widows

The state's system of commendation (*jingbiao* / 旌表) to faithful widows and chastity martyrs drew attention from early on in relation to state policies for gender order. Among many studies of the commendation system celebrating women's virtue, here we shall look at those which focused on the issue of social standing or status. According to a study by Susan L. Mann (1986 [Japanese]; 1987), increasingly fierce competition surrounded the civil service examinations as the degree quotas remained the same despite population growth in late Qing. This led to an enthusiastic response to the commendation system for faithful widows as an alternative means to enhance family honor among commoners and the lower-gentry class. The number of applications was so great that the Board of Rites was unable to process them all and was forced to delegate the job to individual counties in 1851. According to Mann, by that stage the widow's virtue of remaining chaste had lost its meaning as a status symbol among upper-class elites but was actively promoted in the lower-class social groups.

Looking at it from another angle, widows in poor lower-gentry families were forced to live a hard life because of their inability to remarry, fettered as they were by family pride and pressured to stay faithful. The activities of charitable halls (*shantang*), established to help the widows of gentry families (and called by such names as 'halls of pure chastity' (*qingjie tang*) and 'associations for the relief of widows' (*xuli hui*)), are detailed in *A Study of the History of Charitable Halls and Associations in China* (*Chūgoku zenkai zendō shi kenkyū*) by Fuma Susumu (1997: Chapter 7). The associations for the relief of widows provided modest financial support and freedom of conduct whereas the halls of pure chastity imposed stringent control with little freedom in exchange for respectable facilities. This difference points to the widows' predicament brought about by tensions between social climbing strategies and the need for survival.

Gender and the good/debased divide

Literati and courtesans

Adherence to the gender norm was used as a social climbing strategy whereas deviation from it led to lower social standing. For women, the act of going to work outside of their homes constituted a departure from the gender norm according to the standards of a good family.[2] Becoming a courtesan was regarded as an ultimate transgression. Regardless of whether they engaged in prostitution or not, the act of providing entertainment services to men was considered a 'demeaning occupation' for women and courtesans were regarded as 'debased people' who were the polar opposite of 'cloistered ladies'. Generally speaking, however, a person's 'debased' social status and moral rectitude or cultural accomplishments were not necessarily mutually exclusive. There were high-

---

2 A category of women who were collectively called '*sangu liupo*' (三姑六婆, lit. 'three spinsters and six dames') can be regarded as professional women at the time. The 'three spinsters' refers to nuns, Daoist adepts and female diviners and the 'six dames' includes procurers, matchmakers, female exorcists, brothel madams, female drug peddlers and midwives. They were depicted and criticized by literati as wily women who used their eloquence and a variety of means to gain access to good families and trick naïve young girls in the inner quarters (Yi Jo-Lan 2002; Katsuyama 2007).

minded people among the debased and dishonorable people among literati. Tensions surrounding the sense of social status produced by this ambivalence became more evident especially at the end of the Ming period when social mobility increased and became a ready subject in literature. Let us now look at some examples of gender-related issues.

So-called 'romantic love' became fashionable in late Ming as discussed in Ko (1994) and love affairs between literati and courtesans were problematic in terms of the sense of social status. In late Ming Jiangnan, affairs between literati and courtesans such as Chen Zilong, Qian Qianyi and Liu Rushi (Chen Yingke 1980) and between Mao Xiang and Dong Xiaowan (Ōki 2010) were talked about widely. As the social status of courtesan falls under the debased class, the attempt by Qian Qianyi, who was a famous literati-official, to marry Liu Rushi after their love affair was reportedly met with vigorous opposition from the local gentry for breaking the taboo against marriage between the good and the debased. Nevertheless, the actions of Liu Rushi – who had achieved cultural distinction despite her humble origin – such as exchanging poems and discussing current affairs with the literati of the Restoration Society (*Fushe*)[3] dressed in men's clothing and trying to persuade Qian to join the anti-Qing movement out of loyalty to Ming at the time of the regime change were glorified in stories. These records do not signal any negative feelings toward her 'debased' status.

How should the admiration for courtesans at the end of Ming be interpreted? While it is possible to understand it as a sign of the decline of Confucian gender norms (McMahon 1994 and others), the popularity of what we may call the 'virtuous underclass' concept among a wide spectrum of people in the background of this phenomenon at the time must be taken into account. For instance, a widely read genre of novels in late Ming had a *yipu* (righteous and faithful servant) as the protagonist who had stronger Confucian moral fiber than the average literatus. Amid the current of increased social mobility, the conventional social status diverged from people's ideological standards and came to be questioned. Be it a righteous servant or a righteous courtesan, the ambivalent existence of the 'virtuous underclass' became the central concern here. (See Kishimoto (2005) for the above view of the debased at the end of Ming.) Although many of the courtesans whose love affairs with literati became

---

3 The Restoration Society was a reformist association set up by young literati-officials in 1628 which aspired to 'restore ancient learnings' in the field of literature while actively engaging in political criticism.

the talk of the town were praised at the time largely for their physical beauty or skills as entertainers, we must remember that there were people such as Liu Rushi who were admired for their morality that surpassed that of literati. It is possible to say that a love affair between a courtesan of 'debased' class and a literatus could demonstrate the integrity of their love in a more dramatic fashion in comparison to the romance between a son and daughter of gentry families. This orientation can be seen as a move to reorganize the Confucian norms in a morally purer form in response to increased class fluidity rather than the decline of these norms.

Prostitution and social norms

It appears that the Qing dynasty's social status policy also tended to respond to social mobility. Matthew H. Sommer uses the expression 'From status to gender' to sum up the shift in sexual norms which began in the Song dynasty and took a definitive form in the middle of the Qing (Sommer 2000). It is well known that Emperor Yongzheng (r. 1722–1735) abolished the *jian* category of household registration and allowed the *zixin* (lit. 'self-renewal', or joining the 'good' category by quitting demeaning jobs) of those who had been forced to engage in 'debased occupations' as members of hereditary debased groups. According to Sommer, this policy accompanied a move toward a total ban on prostitution, which debased groups such as *yuehu* (lit. 'music households') had been permitted to engage in. In other words, the various sexual norms that had been applied to different social statuses were consolidated to cover all people; this in turn resulted in the spreading of the gender norms of the elite class to the lowest class of society (Sommer 2000).

Sommer's view seems to point to the dismantlement of hereditary debased groups along with the increase in class mobility and the resultant change in the treatment of prostitution from a pejorative attitude based on 'debasedness' to prohibition based on 'criminality'. As Sommer acknowledges, however, the Qing dynasty was unable to eradicate prostitution by the poor, and after the Yongzheng era, even tolerated it in practice unless it became a social problem. It should be noted that society's view of prostitution as a 'debased occupation' did not disappear.

In his latest work, *Polyandry and Wife-Selling in Qing Dynasty China*, which draws on a large number of central and local government archives, Sommer (2015) attempts to reinterpret polyandry, wife-selling, prostitution and other acts that were placed in the category of 'illicit sexual intercourse' (*jian* / 姦) at the time more coherently and internally, locating these acts as part of a survival strategy. He identifies the proliferation of polyandry due to a shortage of women in the lower class as the flip side of upper-class polygamy. Broadly speaking, polyandry entails one woman having sexual relationships with multiple men, and Sommer positions its various forms on a spectrum according to the degree of disconnect between the woman and her family. At one end of the spectrum is a form called '*zhaofu yangfu*' (lit. getting a husband to support a husband) where the wife stays at home and invites other men to come and support her family while at the other end is 'wife-selling' where the wife is sold to another family and moves out of her home. Various patterns of prostitution are placed between these extremes, including husband-managed prostitution and pledging the wife to a brothel in payment for a debt. According to Sommer, people made independent choices from a series of strategies according to their circumstances and the wives had a strong voice in the matter. He stresses the women's pragmatism in their strategy selection and explains that their pride was held up by the preservation of a utilitarian man-woman relationship which was valued in monetary terms as opposed to romantic love.

Just as in the work of Ko and Mann noted above, Sommer attempts to explain the internal logic of women's agency from a position that criticizes the view of Chinese women as passive victims. Ko and Mann attempt to listen to women's voices in the writings of elite women whereas Sommer endeavors to understand the choices and attitudes of lower-class women based on judicial documents and testimonies. While all three have their sights set on society as a whole beyond the family's internal dominance relationships, it is rather interesting that they happen to describe the gender system from the complementary standpoints of the voices of upper-class and lower-class women.

Conclusion: A comparative historical view

The above points may seem disjointed, but each reflects a certain aspect of the sense of social status in China. Let us make comparisons with early-modern Japan and Europe. As mentioned earlier, 'class systems' such as the warrior-peasant-artisan-merchant system in post-medieval Japan and the clergy-nobility-commoner system that functioned during the Ancien Régime in France were characterized by the hereditary and fixed nature of social standing or occupation,

Chapter 8

where one's social standing was determined by the family into which one was born. In short, the main unit of social status order was the family in both Japan and Western Europe. By contrast, social standing and occupation had no hereditary or fixed nature in China as a general rule. The bedrock of social status in China was formed by morality relationships between individuals within a family, such as between parents and children and between brothers, or within a fictive kinship group. A married couple also played an important part in this morality-based 'status' system along with the parents-child and male sibling relationships. Strict adherence to these morality relationships was deeply linked to upward social mobility. China's gender norms had a profound connection with a hunger for higher status and a fear of downfall in a competitive and fluid society in contrast with the sense of social status in a fixed and hereditary society.

In my view, China's gender history needs to be studied in the context of not only male-female relations but also in terms of the comprehensive structure of status relations. This will enable us to make productive comparisons with other eras and regions.

Column 3

Court Ladies and Gender

OGAWA Yoshiyuki

In the inner courts of successive Chinese dynasties, in addition to the emperor and the empress and concubines who were in conjugal relationships with him (empresses, consorts and so on), there were also court ladies who were female court officials of various statuses who undertook such practical business as the management and handling of archives, clothing, food and accommodation. These female officials were controlled by a different mechanism from that which governed the empress and concubines. In a broad sense, the term 'court ladies' has on occasion included empresses and concubines, but here I wish to focus upon court ladies in a narrow sense to the exclusion of empresses and concubines.

What kind of work might these women have undertaken in the imperial palace? To what extent were they involved in civil service related to politics? What was the interrelationship between their work and that of male officials and eunuchs? Can differences from dynasty to dynasty and historical changes be seen in their roles? Pondering such questions is an important issue relating to gender history.

In ancient Japan, in emulation of the Tang system, twelve offices were established in the imperial court's inner palace, headed by a female courtier, and high-born women served there. In reflection of the social conditions in Japan in those days, however, where there was scant social disparity between men and women in the first place, there was much everyday collaborative work involving court ladies and male officials. Furthermore, court ladies of higher rank are assumed to have conveyed the emperor's orders verbally to male officials and had them compose drafts.

After the Heian period, one can also see a tendency for official duties to shift to male officials, but the institution of court ladies is presumed to have been maintained until its dismantling after the 1868 Meiji Restoration. So, what was the situation in China? There were no eunuchs in Japan, but in China the relationship with eunuchs seems to have become more important. In that case, what was it like?

The history of the court-lady system in China is long, but in the Sui and Tang dynasties, an official system of six boards and twenty-four offices was implemented together with the official system of the highest administrative office (central administrative mechanism) in the outer court.[1] This system exerted great influence upon the court-lady systems in later times, and also upon those of Japan and the Korean peninsula.

The *Shanggongju*, the highest level of these offices staffed by women, were in charge of such matters as overall financial management, rituals and education, clothing, meals, bedding and sewing work, etc. Below these were established twenty-four 'offices'. There were also officials who managed and trained staff who were in charge of conveying documents between the emperor and male officials. In the Tang dynasty, there were also women such as Song Ruozhao (761–828) whose scholarship was esteemed, and who were appointed as court ladies.

This system was further improved once the Song dynasty began. An organ called the 'inner court secretariat' was established, and under its head, the secretary of the inner court secretariat led the court ladies of the six boards.[2] Moreover, in the Song dynasty, high-ranking court ladies were given titles that reflected their status, such as *Gu Furen, Jun Furen* or *Jun Jun.*

In addition, not only were female secretaries installed in each of the boards, but some in the positions of official scribes were promoted to the position of secretary of the inner secretariat.

Furthermore, during the reign of Emperor Huizong (1101–1125), a tendency was observed that could be termed the 'imperial secretarialization' of court ladies, where court ladies were proactively involved in the administration of documents by means of the establishment of departments in the inner court secretariat to deal specifically with reports to the throne from each of the highest administrative offices of the outer court.[3]

---

1 On Tang court ladies, see, for example, Gao Shiyu (1988); Zhu Ziyan (1998); and Otagi (2002).
2 On Song court ladies, see, for example, Zhu Ruixi (1994); Gong Yanming (1997); Zhu Ziyan (1998); Tokunaga (1998); Deng Xiaonan (2009); and Tao Jing-Shen (2013).
3 *Collected Grand Edicts and Decrees of the Song Dynasty* (*Song dazhao lingji*), Vol. 21.

Court ladies who thus took on a 'secretarial' role for the emperor dressed in male clothing, served at the emperor's side and conducted the confirmation, organization and classification of reports to the throne, the compilation of drafts of the emperor's replies and the ghost-writing of the emperor's mandates (see Tokunaga 1998 and Deng Xiaonan 2009). The image of court ladies in male garb can be appreciated from the Song-dynasty colored clay figurines in the Hall of the Sacred Mother in the famous Jinci temple in Taiyuan.

The influence at court of the palace women who served as secretaries and dealt with the highest-level secrets of the state was huge: one source reports that an older woman of high rank called Madame Zhang, for one, who was active during the reign of Emperor Zhezong (r. 1086–1100) and into that of Emperor Gaozong (r. 1127–1162), 'had previously taught Emperors Zhezong (1076–1100) and Huizong (1082–1135) how to read, and all the written words in the imperial court passed through her hands. There was nothing she did not know about what was going on in the palace'.[4]

Furthermore, if we examine the role of eunuchs in the Song dynasty, we will see that compared to the Tang dynasty, in general a variety of restraints were added in Song. In relation to the administration of documents, eunuchs basically only had the role of delivering them, so their duties were limited (see, for example, Yu Huaqing 1993; Tokunaga 1998).

Details on the position of court ladies in the Liao and Yuan dynasties are unknown, although they seem to have been impacted by the customs of northern nomadic peoples.

Furthermore, during the Yuan dynasty, women of various tribal backgrounds such as Khitan, Jurchen and Goryeo became court ladies, and Empress Qi (the consort of Emperor Shundi) herself had been a court lady with a Goryeo background, with many court ladies hailing from Goryeo apparently under her command.[5] On the other hand, it can be ascertained that the Jin dynasty fundamentally adopted the official system of six boards and twenty-four offices.[6]

---

4 Li Xinchuan, *Record of Important Events in Chronological Order since the Jianyan Era* (*Jianyan yilai xinian yaolu*), Vol. 21.
5 On Yuan dynasty court ladies, see Chen Gaohua (2008).
6 'Baiguan zhi, Gongren nüguan', *The History of Jin* (*Jinshi*), Vol. 57.

Phase II

In the Ming dynasty, a court-lady system was set up in the reign of Emperor Hongwu (r. 1368–1398) in emulation of the Tang system, but it was reduced in scale and turned into six boards and one office (the one office being the *Gongzhengsi*), and the *Shanggong* controlled the former.[7]

From the era of Emperor Yongle (r. 1403–1424) onwards, however, the influence of eunuchs intensified, and work relating to imperial edicts began to be undertaken by eunuchs called *silijian* (see Noda 1993, for example). Although the court-lady system of early Ming was maintained until the end of the Ming dynasty, it appears that its function declined.

In one sense, the work undertaken by court ladies of the inner court secretariat in the Song dynasty began to be handled by eunuchs such as those with the title of *silijian* from the era of the Ming dynasty's Emperor Yongle onwards – in short, a tendency for the role of 'emperor's secretaries' to shift from court ladies of the inner court secretariat to *silijian* eunuchs.

However, Ming court ladies in the ministry of ceremonies and education (*libu*), regardless of physical attractiveness, were chosen from among unmarried civilian females of around the age of fifteen, or from among women under forty who had no husband, and who could read and write. It is noteworthy that these were different selection criteria from those of empresses and concubines, in which importance was attached to appearance.

After arriving at court, they would learn the Confucian classics and court rules and regulations in the training facility inside the palace, and those with excellent grades would be given the title of *Nüxiucai* that corresponded with the first degree in the imperial examination system, or *Nüshi*. For example, Shen Qionglian, the daughter of Shen An, a *juren* ('gentleman' – one who had passed the second rung of the Chinese higher civil-service examinations) from Huzhoufu in Wucheng Province, served at court during the reign of Emperor Tianshun (r. 1457–1464) due to her thorough knowledge of the Confucian scriptures and history books in spite of her very young age, and at thirteen she was promoted to *Nüxiucai*.[8]

---

7 On Ming dynasty court ladies, see Wang Yun (1997); Zhu Ziyan (1998); Hu Fan and Wang Wei (1999); Maeda (2009); and Qiu Chung-Lin (2012).

8 Chong Zhen, *Wucheng xianzhi*, Vol. 7.

Considering that literacy was thus esteemed, these women could be considered to hail from the intellectual class. Whether they returned to their natal home and married after working for a set period or remained at court, money and the privilege of exemption from statute-labor service were granted to the families of such court ladies.

However, apart from such court ladies (*gongnü*), there were also numerous female servants called 'palace people' (*gongren*) or 'palace slave-girls' (*gonge binü*) in the inner palace. The emperor's wet-nurse was one of these. While on the one hand there were some among them who gained power by colluding with eunuchs and suchlike, as did the wet-nurse of Emperor Tianqi (r. 1605–1627), Ms Ke (?–1627), who conspired with the eunuch Wei Zhongxian and carried out misdeeds, there also seem to have been many who were placed in a difficult situation. There was one incident known as the Renyin plot (1542) in which the female palace servant Yang Jinying (?–1542) and others allegedly attempted to strangle the sleeping Emperor Jiajing (1507–1566).

The Qing dynasty differed greatly from all of the earlier dynasties in that it did not employ the court-lady system based on the Tang official system of six boards and twenty-four offices. Instead, the imperial household agency (*Neiwufu*) managed the serving-women of the inner palace.[9] Furthermore, eunuchs were also placed under the management of the imperial household agency (see Yu Huaqing 1993, etc.).

'Excellent' female palace servants (*xiunü*) were chosen by a process of selection conducted by the imperial household agency from among the girls and women in the group directly attached to the emperor known as the agency's 'Three Banners' (*Baoyi sanqi*) that did the housekeeping, and the target for selection was fairly limited. The majority of these women left the palace after having worked for about a decade, and it was also permissible for them to marry.

To this point, we have examined the state of court ladies and female palace servants mainly from Song to Qing, but as a major trend, the institution of court ladies comprising an official system of six boards and twenty-four offices was instituted, and a tendency was seen to involve court ladies proactively in the administration of documents and turn them into 'emperor's secretaries'.

---

9 On Qing dynasty female palace servants, see, for example, Zhu Ziyan (1998); Zhao Lingzhi (2006 [Japanese]); Zhao Lingzhi (2008); and Qiu Chung-Lin (2014).

Once the power of eunuchs had expanded from the reign of Ming dynasty Emperor Yongle onwards, however, the role of court ladies began to decline.

Furthermore, importance was attached to the fact that, unlike empresses and concubines, court ladies were intellectuals able to undertake practical business, and women who hailed from the intellectual class were hired, regardless of their marital history.

The Qing dynasty, however, did not adopt an institutionalized Tang-like court-lady system such as that described above and did not appoint intellectual women from the Han ethnic group, and the role of court ladies – placing them under the control of the imperial household agency, and so on – was limited in comparison with the practices of the Song and Ming dynasties.

I have examined the work and roles of court ladies, focusing upon their connection with the administration of documents, but while there are studies such as Qiu Chung-Lin's (2004) on cooking-related duties in the Ming-dynasty court, it is likely that there are still many areas yet to be examined, such as the extent of the other duties over which court ladies presided (work to do with cooking and medical care, music, clothing and adornment, etc.) in each era, and specifically what the situation was in relation to the division of roles between women and eunuchs or male officials. Shedding light upon these issues could be considered a way of bringing consciousness of female courtiers' roles to the fore.

Furthermore, it appears that court ladies and female court servants in dynasties from the Song to the Qing were able to leave the palace after a certain period of time, and also to marry, unlike court ladies in the Korean Joseon dynasty (those ranking from *Shanggong* down fundamentally never left the palace, nor were they allowed to marry) (see Kim 1987).

Tao Jing-Shen's (2013) examination of court ladies in the Song dynasty indicates that there may have been an extension of the court atmosphere to the civilian population, but there is more scope for future investigation in terms of what kind of impact these women who entered the court exerted upon society.

A careful comparison of the similarities and differences among the court-lady system in Japan, the Korean peninsula and Vietnam, and in China from Song to Qing, would be very interesting, but research along these lines has not progressed very far, so I look forward to seeing the results of future research.

Gender History in China

PART I

Phase III

Modern and Contemporary China
Changing Gender Order

Phase III

Introduction

Modern and Contemporary China: Changing Gender Order

TAKASHIMA Kō

What do you picture when you are asked about the traditional attire of China? Many people would think of *qipao* or the colorful costumes of ethnic minority women. If we qualify the question with 'Han Chinese' or 'Chinese men', how many of us would visualize the ordinary clothes worn in the real world rather than costumes depicted in historical dramas? In modern and contemporary China, 'the traditional' has been equated with 'the feudal' and therefore destined for eradication. Han Chinese men have been at the center of the movement away from traditional dress while ethnic minority women have been at its periphery. The adoption of Western-style clothing, especially by men, has always occurred in the modernization process of non-Western nations (Ross 2008), yet rarely has it been enforced so thoroughly as in modern and contemporary China. The 'absence' of traditional attire is a result of the bio-power exerted by modern and contemporary Chinese governments on people's bodies and gender. Now that China has become a global superpower in both name and substance, however, there is an increasing appetite for traditional costumes among Chinese people (of which Han Chinese account for a vast majority). Since the turn of the twenty-first century, Tang-style costumes (*Tang zhuang*) and Han-style clothes (*Han fu*) have been newly 'created' and are drawing broad support from people mainly from younger generations. Phase III chapters in this book provide an overview of modern and contemporary China from the viewpoint of changing gender order to aid our understanding of a country that is approaching a major turning point.

China's modernity began with an asymmetrical encounter with the West. When the Qing dynasty was defeated by Meiji-era Japan in the midst of the latter's vigorous push to modernize, the West was transformed from a heterogeneous other in the minds of Chinese to a model for emulation. On the other hand, China continued to perceive the West and Japan as threats. Modern and postmodern China has been trying to determine what kind of relationship it should maintain with the West and Japan in view of this ambivalence.

To borrow the words of the philosopher Li Zehou, modern and contemporary Chinese history can be seen as a double variation set in which the first theme of enlightenment (*qimeng*) is the goal and the second theme of national salvation (*jiuguo*) is a threat (Li Zehou 1987).

Opening the stage curtain: Nationalism and gender

Given these conditions, China's traditional gender order underwent a transformation as Western modernity-style gender and its variation, militaristic-nationalistic gender, competed with one another. According to a concise and succinct summary by Susan L. Mann, this shift can be characterized as a change in China's sex/gender system from the imperial-age goal of the seclusion of women to the twentieth-century focus on moving women into public spaces outside the home (Mann 2011). Chen Dongyuan argues that the shift began with the anti-footbinding movement and the campaign for women's education around the time of the Hundred Days' Reform (Chen Dongyuan 1928: 316); the former corresponds to the emancipation of the body and the latter to that of the mind. For Liang Qichao, an advocate of the movements, the strengthening of women was needed to effect the strengthening of men and the state. Thus, a new sex/gender system was required to form a foundation on which to build a new state and a proper nation (Liang began to use the term 'citizens' (*guomin*) in 1899 after he took refuge in Japan).

National salvation was the theme that first came to the fore. In the early 1900s, the term '*shangwu*' meaning 'martial spirit' became a buzzword among Chinese students in Japan. The government embarked on nation-building founded on soldier (*junren*)-citizens by abolishing the civil service examination system and developing an elementary education system for men and women. While male intellectuals led the argument that sought to place women outside of the citizenry by calling them 'mothers of the citizens', women put forward the notion of 'female citizens' (*nüguomin*). This was not unrelated to the matter of national salvation. Women's rights were left on the backburner for a long time as national salvation took precedence. The first example of this policy was the denial of women's suffrage by the newly founded Republic of China, which gave priority to the unity of men under the banner of 'Five Peoples Under One Union' (*Wuzu gonghe*) (see Chapters Nine and Ten).

Phase III

As Western nations could no longer afford to interfere with East Asian affairs due to the outbreak of the First World War, the threat of the West diminished (although the threat of Japan increased) and the theme of enlightenment came to prominence. Chinese intellectuals turned their attention to domestic affairs such as Yuan Shikai's move to restore the monarchy and conflicts between warlords. The Republic of China at the time diverged widely from what they had tried to 'envision' and rescue from destruction at the end of the Qing dynasty. The question of the relationship between the state and its citizens was raised once again and all sorts of ideas were envisioned. Confucianism, which continued to maintain a firm grip on China's social and family relations, was not spared from criticism, which stimulated people's imagination surrounding gender. This period saw the emergence of the most diverse arguments and debates about love, sex and family in the history of China. The notion of the Western-style modern family that sought to connect love, marriage, sex and reproduction was not only proposed but also scrutinized for potential problems and significant effort was made to resolve them (see Chapter Eleven). The conditions of manhood and womanhood, especially the latter, were becoming diversified not only in discourse but also in the real world. Women's economic independence was advocated, and some women made their way into white-collar occupations such as lawyers, doctors, journalists and civil servants in addition to roles as factory workers and prostitutes (see Chapter Twelve). However, we must remember that the 'person' assumed by the enlightenment movement was male and not an asexual being. A woman was recognized as a 'person' only if she played the role of a man. This way of thinking was reflected in a person's appearance. A section of women thought that women became liberated by wearing men's clothes and began to keep their hair short and dress in the long gowns worn by male intellectuals (Takashima 2010).

With the rise of nationalism and the ascendancy of national salvation over enlightenment in the latter half of the 1920s, the legacy of the May Fourth Movement was carried on to meet the needs of national salvation. *A History of the Lives of Chinese Women* (*Zhongguo funü shenghuoshi*) by Chen Dongyuan published in 1928 was the first book about the history of Chinese women from ancient times to the 1920s. Chen posited that Chinese women were victims or people in need of rescue as they were the human beings who suffered most in the world and depicted their history in the basic context of their liberation (Chen Dongyuan 1928). His account of the period after the May Fourth Movement focuses on politics and the theory behind the movement rather than on historical investigation, with the Kuomintang of China located as the agent of women's liberation (Chen was a party member). This view of the history of women's liberation continued to define the women's movement in China until recently, although the Kuomintang was replaced by the Communist Party of China along the way.

China's prolonged war with Japan that started with the Manchurian Incident pushed militaristic and nationalistic notions of gender to the forefront. The Nanjing government attempted to increase the population of soldiers and workers through the introduction of conscription and the initiation of the New Life Movement and altered the sex/gender system to fit this purpose. Its military uniform and tunic suit (Zhongshan suit) were visualizations of a citizenry the Kuomintang was trying to create (the Communist Party version of the tunic suit was similar) (see Chapter Ten). Conversely, the women's liberation movement was forced to make a compromise as the 'modern girl' was criticized and women were told to 'return to the home'. After the turn of the twentieth century, women were sometimes encouraged to leave home and at other times were urged to return home. Each time, women had to face the contradiction and conflict between being an individual (a woman) and being a mother. The relationship between women and the family was a barometer for the situation of gender at the time (see Chapters Nine and Eleven). The problem of wartime violence arose between two competing nation-states which were militaristic and nationalistic and hence patriarchal. The ability to protect women became a question of survival for the masculinity of each nation-state. In this context, rape became a symbolic act of displaying the dominance of the nation-state's masculinity. The Japanese military's 'comfort women' system was a mechanism to practice rape in an organized and ongoing fashion. Chinese women were sometimes sent to the Japanese army by their countrymen in areas where the war had reached a stalemate such as Shanxi Province.

New China: Socialism and gender

After the founding of the People's Republic of China in 1949, the powerful Communist Party government forged ahead with the reorganization of the gender order from a socialist standpoint. The party and state claimed that women had been liberated and gained equality with men in New China. The change in women's status manifested clearly in the areas of marriage and labor. The Marriage Law promulgated on 1 May 1950 was a 'modern' marriage law based on the principles of marital freedom, monogamy, equality for men and women and the protection of the interests of women and children. Together with land reform, it formed a set of policy measures to dismantle the traditional family that underpinned the feudal system and to create a new family institution as the bedrock of New China. However, the movement for the full implementation of the Marriage Law was frustrated half-way through as it collided with the interests of men who were the beneficiaries of both traditional society and New China. The Communist Party chose to secure the support of men as the bedrock of nation-building instead of challenging their resistance to new ideas about marriage and the family as 'feudalistic attitudes'. Although the Marriage Law advocated marital freedom, this was designed to impose the concept of the 'modern family' as the quaternity of sex, love, marriage and reproduction rather than permitting diverse forms of marriage. The Anti-Prostitution Movement was the flip side of the new marriage law and the Communist Party also had an intolerant stance toward homosexuality (see Chapter Thirteen and Column Five).

The Communist Party's policy decision in 1943 that women's liberation would be effected by their economic independence through productive activity largely defined its approach to the women's liberation movement in New China (see Chapter Thirteen). According to official party lines, the formation of New China as the result of a triumphant class struggle was to almost automatically bring about women's liberation. As this was, of course, not the case in reality, the party needed to put together a more realistic picture of women's liberation. According to the 1943 Decision, women's liberation was supposed to be demonstrated by the level of their participation in productive activity. The Great Leap Forward built momentum for the mass mobilization of women into the workforce in both cities and rural areas and it was the All-China Women's Federation (ACWF) that connected the government and women in grassroots communities. As demonstrated by the history of the 'Silver flower contest' campaign outlined by Ohashi Fumie (see Chapter Fourteen), there was an initial influx of women into male-dominated workplaces in response to the publicized 'equal pay for equal work' doctrine, but men eventually stopped doing the same work as women and moved to other occupations that could earn them more work-points. The ideal of equality for men and women turned out to be a gendered division of labor and resulted in the preservation of male dominance.

The Communist Party's position on women's labor oscillated. The push for gender equality escalated and women's participation expanded markedly during periods of mass-mobilization ('Red' phases) whereas pressure to force women back into the home became stronger in periods of economic pragmatism ('Expert' phases) (Mann 2011: 49). Thus, women continuously found themselves on uncertain ground.

Gender equality in New China was achieved by increasing the burden on women – requiring women to replicate men (the masculinization of women). Women were required to carry out the same work as men while continuing to shoulder the burden of household labor (which in many cases was not regarded as productive activity). This situation both improved the status of women and increased their workload. The emphasis on class struggle and supposed equality for men and women concealed many problems surrounding gender (see Chapter Twelve).

The Cultural Revolution saw the peak of China's 'Red phases' and the existence of gender differences was denied in the face of the brutal class conflict. Turning women into an issue was criticized as bourgeois thinking and the ACWF was forced to suspend its activity (see Chapter Fourteen). The denial of gender differences manifested in the unilateral masculinization of women. Moreover, women were required to emulate the most masculine of men, the 'iron girls' movement being a typical example. This gender view was 'accepted' without strong resistance not only because of its coercive nature but also because the women's liberation movement after the May Fourth Movement had been demanding that women should be allowed to behave like men in exchange for their enjoyment of men's privileges (whereas in the West, it did not demand that women become men as women were not given men's privileges). While Mao Zedong declared, 'Whatever men comrades can do, women comrades can do, too', Wang Zheng points out that he failed to ask, 'Can men comrades do what women comrades can do?' (Wang Zheng 2004). This gender uniformity appeared most prominently in clothing. Men and women were dressed in the same style of Mao suits while Western-style or traditional clothes were regarded as symbols of enemies of the people (i.e., capitalism and feudalism). For example, Wang Guangmei, the wife of Liu Shaoqi, was forced to put on a *qipao* dress when she was interrogated at a rally.

Whether on the subject of gender or otherwise, the study of Cultural Revolution-period China has been slow to develop, as Kohama Masako points out in Chapter Thirteen. There is a need to examine why the Cultural Revolution happened in the way it did, rather than rejecting it outright or dismissing it as an aberration. In one sense, the Cultural Revolution may have been the ultimate form of a militant nation that China had pursued since the end of the

Qing dynasty. Nonetheless, the Cultural Revolution certainly had an aspect of emancipating women and we must not overlook its impact on the women's liberation movement in the rest of the world at the time. It is significant that *Chinese Women in a Century of Revolution* (*Chūgoku joseishi*) by Ono Kazuko was published in Japan in 1978 shortly after the Cultural Revolution. It was also at this time that the study of Chinese history began in earnest outside of China (see Column Four).

Reform and opening-up: Economic development and gender

China steered a course from class struggle to economic development after the end of the Cultural Revolution and developed a market economy under the so-called reform and opening-up policies. State power that had exerted centralized control over society had taken a step back, allowing an expansion of the space 'outside of the system' where economic and social activities could be carried out more freely, with a resulting increase in the diversity of society. Gender differences were also on the rise after they were reduced to a minimum during the Cultural Revolution. This shift has brought to the surface all the contradictions that used to be concealed behind the notion of class struggle. Against this backdrop, one of China's most prominent feminists, Li Xiaojiang, came to be conscious of being a 'woman' and raised the issue of feminine subjectivity: 'For our generation of educated women who had the experience of playing "men's roles", it was no easy task to appreciate our unification with "femininity"' (Li Xiaojiang 1998 [Japanese]). Li blazed a trail for gender in the new society by linking research and activism (see Chapter Eighteen).

The one child policy was initiated when the level of freedom was generally increasing in Chinese society (although a birth planning policy had been implemented intermittently since the 1950s). Although it seemed like a regressive policy from the point of view of individual freedom, it was consistent with the overall policy of the Communist Party in the sense that it was designed to help achieve modernization. The policy continued for a whole generation despite heavy criticism before transitioning to the current two child policy. State control over reproduction continues to date. The resulting population sex imbalance and aging population combined with the diminishing number of children are having a profound impact on China's sex/gender system (see Chapter Thirteen).

Politically, liberalization led to a growing demand for democratization among students. However, political control has been tightened since the Tiananmen Square protests of 1989. Deng Xiaoping's Southern Tour in 1992 accelerated China's shift to a market economy and subsequent rapid economic growth. Massive numbers of farm workers migrated from poverty-stricken inland villages to coastal cities for work. This mass population migration shook the social structures of both cities and rural villages to their foundations and led to a surge in social problems such as the abandonment of children in villages. The reform of state-owned enterprises and other factors further intensified an already competitive labor market and female workers who were constrained by childbirth and the traditional domestic role were marginalized and experienced a growing wage gap with men (to put this in perspective, the gender wage gap has been wider in Japan) (see Chapter Twelve and Jin Yihong 2016 [Japanese]).

Women's studies in China have seen major progress since the 1990s. Exchanges with Western scholars began while women's research centers were established at universities across China and various projects were initiated, including the Oral History of Chinese Women of the Twentieth Century (*20 shiji Zhongguo funü koushushi*). The 'women boom' peaked at the world conference on women hosted by the ACWF in 1995. Women's studies (women's history) has subsequently evolved into gender studies (gender history) more broadly (see Chapter Eighteen).

In the aftermath of the 1989 Tiananmen Square incident, the Communist Party embarked on the so-called 'patriotism education campaign'. The basis for the legitimacy of the Communist Party shifted from Marxism-Leninism to anti-Western and anti-Japanese nationalism (Wang Zheng 2012 [English]). In 1996, a book by Song Qiang et al. (1996) entitled *The China That Can Say No* (*Zhongguo keyi shuo bu*) became a bestseller, reflecting a rising sense of national greatness among the Chinese people. China completed its recovery of European colonies when Hong Kong and Macau were returned to it in 1997 and 1999 respectively. The International Olympic Committee General Assembly decided in July 2001 to stage the 2008 Olympics in Beijing and the APEC (Asia-Pacific Economic Cooperation) forum was held in Shanghai in October of the same year. It is customary for APEC participants to wear the traditional costume of the host country for a group photo. However, there was no traditional costume of the Han people acceptable to all and hence the organizers had to 'create' Tang clothing for this occasion. In response to the rising nationalism, Tang clothing is gaining the status of new traditional clothes along with Han attire.

Phase III

Around the same time, the Communist Party began to trumpet the 'Great Rejuvenation of the Chinese Nation' and the 'comfort women' issue received widespread publicity in China. As Song Shaopeng points out, the humiliation of the loss of chastity experienced by 'comfort women' under masculinist culture was redressed through nationalism (Song Shaopeng 2016c [Japanese]). Nevertheless, it does not follow that 'masculinist culture' has waned. The current 'comfort women' controversy in China serves to help drive nationalism but does not call on Japanese society or the Chinese males (society) who supplied women to the Japanese army in Shanxi to reflect on their actions. Under the Xi Jinping government, the slogan of the 'Great Rejuvenation of the Chinese Nation' has become the Chinese Dream (*Zhongguo meng*). In the meantime, China has built up its economic and military presence in the international community. These government actions are exerting enormous influence on China's sex/gender system in various forms such as the revival of traditional morals and a crackdown on feminists. Nationalism has always been associated with masculinity and China is no exception.

Abridged Chronology of Modern Chinese Gender History

1840	First Opium War begins (lasting until 1842); opening of the first five treaty ports
1884	Empress Dowager Cixi (b. 1835, d. 1908) gains a stronger role in Qing court politics
1897	Anti-footbinding movements in Shanghai, Guangdong and Hunan
1898	Opening in Shanghai of the first Chinese-run girls' school
1903	Jin Tianhe publishes *Bell of the Women's World*, launching discussions on issues including women's role as 'mothers of the citizens'
1907	Qiu Jin founds the *Chinese Women's Journal*, while Yan Bin and others found the *New World of Women in China*, discussing topics such as women citizens; creation of the system of women's teacher training schools; anarchists including Liu Shifu and He Zhen found *Natural Justice* and argue for the abolition of the family
1911	Xinhai Revolution; fall of the Qing dynasty
1912	Founding of the **Republic of China**; promulgation of the Provisional Constitution of the Republic of China, clearly establishing popular sovereignty, but with no clear specification of equal rights between the sexes
1915	Founding of *Youth Magazine* (later *New Youth*) which becomes the center of the New Culture Movement
1919	May Fourth Movement
1921	Establishment of the Chinese Communist Party (CCP)
1926	2nd National Congress of the Nationalist Party of China adopts a resolution on the women's movement
1927	Along with the development of the national revolution, the women's movement flourishes
1931	Implementation of the National Government Civil Code on the family and succession; Chinese Soviet Republic established, promulgation of marriage regulations

1933	National government announces the Military Service Act, making military service obligatory for men
1934	Chinese Soviet Republic publicly proclaims the Marriage Law; Chiang Kai-shek proposes the New Life Movement; beginning of debates over 'Women go home' (continuing until 1937)
1937	Beginning of the Sino-Japanese War (ending in 1945); many instances of sexual violence, including forcing women to serve as 'comfort women'
1943	CCP promotes women's labor participation in anti-Japanese bases (1943 Decision)
1949	Establishment of the All-China Democratic Women's Federation; establishment of the **People's Republic of China**
1950	Promulgation of the Marriage Law and Agrarian Reform Law
1950s	Promotion of female labor
1958	Great Leap Forward and establishment of People's Communes
1966	Beginning of the Cultural Revolution (continuing until 1976); popularization of the slogan 'Women hold up half the sky'
1973	Anti-Lin Biao Anti-Confucius movement attacks Confucian patriarchy
1978	Beginning of the reform and opening-up policy
1979	Beginning of the one child policy
1979–82	Spread of the system contracting agricultural labor to the household
1980	Amendment of the Marriage Law; Women go home' official policy blocked by the Women's Federation
1992	Passage of the Law of the People's Republic of China on the Protection of Rights and Interests of Women
1995	Fourth UN World Conference on Women held in Beijing
2012	First LGBT parade in Hubei Province follows multiple art performances nationwide by young feminist activists
2016	End of the one child policy: all couples allowed a second child

9. Nationalism and Gender

— *SAKAMOTO Hiroko*
(Translated by Reiko Shinno and Kenji Hasegawa)

Introduction: Modern nationalism

The word 'nationalism' came into common use only toward the end of the nineteenth century. Moreover, it was only in the recent past that nationalism came to gain serious scholarly attention and that outstanding studies began to appear in large numbers. According to Ōsawa Masachi, scholarly works on nationalism first appeared in the 1980s (Ōsawa 2002: 4).[1] For example, Ernest Gellner's representative work, *Nations and Nationalism*, published in 1983, defined nationalism as 'primarily a political principle, which holds that the political and the national unit should be congruent' (Gellner 1983: 1) and argued that it was generated by industrialization. Such development coincided, if not interacted, with the social changes outside of academia, including the Tiananmen Incident in China followed by the revolutions in Eastern Europe in the late 1980s, the collapse of the Soviet Union in 1991 and the resultant tectonic shift toward globalization spurred by U.S. hegemony. To this day, in the age of globalization, nationalism has changed forms but shows absolutely no sign of abating.

The conceptual difficulty surrounding nationalism derives from its multiple meanings, reflecting the complexity of the ways each example of nationalism was formed and the fact that it cannot be generalized across regions in the world. A representative study on nationalism in the 1980s that pertains to Asia is Benedict Anderson's *Imagined Communities: Reflections on the Origin*

---

1 See Ōsawa (2002), in which over forty authors introduce fifty representative essays on nationalism written since the nineteenth century.

Chapter 9

and Spread of Nationalism. A specialist in Southeast Asian studies, analyzing the wars that erupted after the Second World War, Anderson characterized nationalism as an 'uncomfortable anomaly to Marxist theory' (Anderson 1983: 3) and sought to provide tentative interpretations of this anomaly. He described nationality and nationalism as 'cultural artefacts' and defined the nation as 'an imagined political community – and imagined as both inherently limited and sovereign' (Anderson 1983: 6). Unlike the 'religious community' and the 'dynastic realm' that preceded it, the nation often encourages self-sacrifice and is 'always conceived as a deep, horizontal comradeship' (Anderson 1983: 7). As the factors that enabled this new system, Anderson emphasizes an idea of 'homogeneous, empty time' that can be 'measured by clock and calendar' and the print capitalism that promoted vernacularization and the Reformation. Also, looking at the modern factors that shaped nationalism, Eric Hobsbawm pointed out that many of the key elements in the ideological construction of nationalism and its integrative forces were artificially invented after the beginning of the modern period as 'traditions' (Hobsbawm and Ranger 1983).

In contrast to such modernist theories of nationalism, Anthony D. Smith posited the existence of nation-like groups in the pre-modern period and termed the ethnic community with shared myths, symbols and memories an 'ethnie' (Smith 1986). Ōsawa (2002: 312) argues that Smith's scholarship 'shed light on the nation's convoluted process of reverting to the past to realize its innovation'. Although I question whether or not the ethnie existed in the pre-modern period, I agree with Ōsawa that Smith's scholarship pointed to the complex relationship between modern nationalism and pre-modern concepts.

A critique of the above arguments was formulated by Étienne Balibar, who in his joint study with Immanuel Wallerstein deepened the analysis of the relationship between nationalism and racism ('race' is also a social construct) only superficially presented in Anderson. Balibar argued that racism 'makes visible the invisible cause of the fate of societies and peoples' (Balibar and Wallerstein 1991: 55) and emphasized that racism 'supplements' nationalism. In the field of the history of the common people in Asia, Partha Chatterjee, known for his scholarship in colonial/post-colonial studies and subaltern studies based on the Indian case, argued that the nationalism forged in India's anti-colonialism also lacked the ideological means to combat 'the legitimacy of the marriage between Reason and capital', with the 'conflict between metropolitan capital and the people-nation' being absorbed by the state (Chatterjee 1986).

This analysis opened new pathways for the study of nationalism in the 'Third World' (Sakiyama 2002: 292–293).

However, a critique of subaltern history emerged, pointing out that it remained entrapped in gender discrimination with the tendency to limit the agents of historical change to males. This argument was put forward by Gayatri Spivak, also known for her critical feminism. While not a historian, Spivak analyzed the rite that came to be called *sati*, which had been mostly abandoned by the beginning of the eighteenth century but saw a revival under British imperial rule from the end of that century (Spivak 1988). Analyzing this ritual, in which the Hindu widow sacrificed her own life at the cremation of her husband, she argued that it was overdetermined by the multiple factors of race, class and gender.

Although *sati* is often misunderstood to have been a long-established 'tradition' based on a specific Hindu canon, it is simply the feminine form of the word *sat*, which signified high-level existence – the Truth, the Good and the Right – and *sati* meant 'good wife'. The ritual was not practiced universally, and neither was it specific to caste or class. Having established these points, Spivak offers commentary on two attempts related to the rite. First, there was the effort by 'white men' of the Dutch East India Company and missionary groups to outlaw the practice, based on multiple linguistic misunderstandings, to 'save brown women from brown men'. Second, there was the perception of Indian nativists that 'the women actually wanted to die' (Spivak 1988: 297). Spivak criticizes both groups on the following grounds. On the one hand, the white males misunderstood the meaning of the word *sati* and 'imposed a greater ideological conscription by absolutely identifying [...] good wifehood with self-immolation on the husband's pyre' (Spivak 1988: 305). On the other hand, Indian nativists conducted 'skillful manipulation' by constituting women's subjectivity in perceiving the ritual as their own suicidal aspiration. While following the husband to the pyre as a good wife (backward customs) and the women's subjective (courageous) suicide seemed to be conflicting understandings, Spivak contends that they 'go a long way to legitimize each other' (1988: 297) and lose opportunities to encounter 'women's voices – consciousness'. In this sense, the women as sexual subalterns 'cannot speak' (their voices are not heard). These points also offer many useful insights in considering the Chinese cases of 'chaste widows and female martyrs' (*jiefu lienü*) and footbinding and anti-footbinding movements in China.

Chapter 9

Ann Laura Stoler's interesting book on the plantation belt in northern Sumatra Island, Indonesia, from the late nineteenth century clearly integrated gender analysis in the study of nationalism within the context of colonial studies. She conducted an in-depth analysis of the contradictions between capital, class, race, ethnicity and gender to understand the labor management strategies arising from multilayered interactions between 'white' plantation owners, locals, Chinese coolies and Javanese immigrants (Stoler 1995). She then elucidates 'why connections between parenting and colonial power, between nursing mothers and cultural boundaries, between servants and sentiments, and between illicit sex, orphans, and race emerge as central concerns of state and at the heart of colonial politics' (Stoler 2002: 8).

The brief historiographical survey above shows that the emergence of rigorously gendered scholarship on nationalism is a relatively new phenomenon. We may even be able to say that gender problems tended to manifest themselves in conspicuous fashion in the 'typical' colonies, and that this is partly the reason why pioneering scholarship on gender and nationalism appeared in the field that studied those colonies. In contrast, the historiography of modern China has tended to treat foreign concessions and leased land as 'alien' regions. Moreover, the ways in which China was semi-colonized varied from one place to another. Thus, as I will show below, it has been hard to define nationalism and identify the complex processes through which it was formed, let alone to incorporate gender as a tool to analyze nationalism.

Scholarship on *minzu zhuyi* in modern China

Studying *minzu zhuyi* in China, often translated as 'nationalism', is thus a difficult task. The non-Han rule of the Qing dynasty drastically expanded the territory from the Ming dynasty and conducted multiethnic rule, while also complicating the problem of distinguishing between the civilized (*hua* / 華) and the barbaric (*yi* / 夷). This was amplified by the split between the anti-Qing revolution faction and the constitutional monarchy faction at the end of the Qing dynasty. In addition, as a result of the 1911 Xinhai Revolution, far from achieving an anti-Qing revolution, there was the complicated historical, political and cultural context that led the revolutionaries to construct the Republic of China, which inherited the Qing dynasty's territory and demographic composition. The republic promoted the principle of 'Five

Peoples Under One Union' (*wuzu gonghe*). The Five Peoples referred to the Han, Man (Manchus), Meng (Mongols), Hui (Muslims) and Zang (Tibetans). Further complicating the situation was the introduction of the five-race classification theory of 'white, yellow, red, brown and black', which spread from the West after the eighteenth century. This theory was introduced amidst the late nineteenth century crisis of the threat of imperial incursions, adding yet another layer to the complications.

Realizing these complexities, Wang Hui, one of the most influential scholars in China today, has been searching for ways to understand China and Chinese political culture in the context of the dynamic interactions between heterogeneity and homogenization. In his long-term vast scholarship that remains an 'unfinished inquiry', he states:

> Far from being completely modern creations, this 'imagined community' and its identity are the products of a nation forming over a long period of history through continuously changing derivations of language, institutions, faiths, myths and ways of living. It is a mode and force through which national struggles and the modern party politics of national movements bind local culture to the demands of nationalism. (Wang Hui 2014 [English]: 109; 2008 [Chinese]: 77–78)

Unlike the European nation-state model, 'In structural terms, there are obvious continuities between China as a modern, sovereign state and the Chinese empire (*Zhonghua diguo*)' (Wang Hui 2014 [English]: 132; 2008 [Chinese]: 93). From this perspective, Wang states, 'seeing the "imagined community" as a purely modern phenomenon offers no way to explain the transformation that China has undergone' (Wang Hui 2014 [English]: 111; 2008 [Chinese]: 79). Both the Republic of China and the People's Republic of China (PRC) were born from 'revolutions' but also inherited the territory and ethnic demographic structure of the Qing. Thus, it is hard to characterize them as 'completely new modern creations', and they were certainly unique in world history.

Note, however, that it is not the case that the 'territory' of the Chinese empire was enclosed within the Great Wall, and its peripheral borders were often determined through complex negotiations in the modern period. For example, the Qing court prohibited migration into the region which later became Yanbian Korean Autonomous Prefecture as the place of origin of the Manchu people. However, after Korean farmers entered to cultivate the land

Chapter 9

and the migration of Han people was eventually permitted, a border dispute arose between Korea and China. Japan's imposition of a protectorate in Korea amidst this dispute and subsequent intervention further complicated matters. Song Jiaoren (1882–1913), who was exiled in Japan as a revolutionary in the late Qing period, learned of Japan's intention to advance into the Asian mainland in 1905 based on its actions against Korea, made a risky journey to the region close to Yanbian and conducted a survey based on old maps and books on the shifting course of the river and the location of border monuments in an effort to determine the 'national boundary' in the area. The result was his 1908 report, *On the Gando Issue* (*Jiandao wenti*), in which he sided with the Qing dynasty on the territorial issue. This was one year before the dynasty and Japan signed the Gando Convention. Song had been a major critic of the Qing dynasty and that was why he was in exile. However, Japan's imperialist intention sparked his nationalist passion and turned him into a Qing ally on this boundary issue. He would later become the *de facto* leader of the Nationalist Party (Guoming dang) at the time of the founding of the Republic of China. This was one of the beginnings of national consciousness in China.

In his preface to the Japanese translation of the *Rise of Modern Chinese Thought* and his essay in *Perspectives on Asia*, Wang Hui proposes the understanding of China as a political regime transversed by ethnicity, religion, language and civilization, as a 'system transversal society' and a social network that is structurally 'different from the intellectual framework of nationalism' (Wang Hui 2010 [Chinese]: 283–284; 2011 [Japanese]: xix, 299). However, while the people who composed 'All-Under-Heaven' (*tianxia*) in the 'empire' felt no need to be cognizant of the 'outer', 'national citizens' (*guomin*) were at least gradually forced to imagine the 'Chinese people' (*Zhonghua minzu*) as a nation and became strongly aware of not only other 'nation-states' but also female national citizens (*nü guomin*). Thus, I believe analyzing nationalism in China as a 'modern creation' can offer a key to our explorations in this volume.

Although the sense of unity or belonging encompassing the present regional scale of 'China' was not quick to emerge, the formation of a sense of unity was underway during the late Qing period. Yoshizawa Seiichirō notes, 'It is not possible to make a clear argument by simply applying terms such as *kokumin shugi*, *kokka shugi* and *minzoku shugi*'. All of these three Japanese terms can be translated as 'nationalism' in English, with different connotations. He adopts the concept of 'patriotism' (Japanese: *aikoku shugi*; Chinese: *aiguo zhuyi*), frequently used since the late Qing period to discuss the origin of the discourses on modern history (Yoshizawa 2003).

Despite the scholarly debates, the national history of the PRC considers the Opium War against Great Britain, along with the resultant unequal treaties and opening of its ports to Western powers, to be the origin of modern China. The PRC viewed nationalism as resistance against foreign aggression at that point and characterized it as 'patriotism'. However, it is widely understood in academia in China and elsewhere that at the time, such sense of national identity was not widely shared beyond the court and the officials leading the central government as well as their assistants.

The military defeat to the small country of Japan in the First Sino-Japanese War (1894–1895) shocked the intellectuals who finally began to fear the demise of their empire. The Treaty of Shimonoseki (1895) spurred officials-to-be, who had gathered in Beijing from all regions to take the civil service examinations, into organizing the submission of a joint memorial to the emperor, protesting the treaty and begging for political reforms. Their action had the effect of spreading the news of the movement for political change through newly published newspapers and magazines, not only in the big coastal cities, but also inland cities such as Changsha in Hunan Province.

At the end of the nineteenth century, social Darwinism began to make a major impact around the same time that the concept of the 'five race' categorization entered China. As the hierarchy that placed 'blacks' at the bottom and 'whites' at the top emerged, the discourse regarding the crisis of the defeat of the 'yellow races' arose. Around this time, Germany's rule over the Shandong Province, the Boxer Rebellion and the Siege of the International Legations in Beijing led to widespread and intense 'national' consciousness sprouting in numerous facets.

After this point, literati like Zhang Binglin (1869–1936) gave up on the Qing government's ability to reform itself and expressed their defiance of the dynasty by cutting their *queues*. By around 1903, anti-Qing revolutionary societies had been formed in various regions and began inventing 'tradition' by arguing that legendary figure Huangdi (the Yellow Emperor) was the common ancestor of the Han, drawing his portrait and creating what they considered the 'Chinese calendar', which started with either the assumed year of his birth or his enthronement. According to the anti-Manchu theory of revolution advocated by the revolutionary groups, the Han was either the main group or leader of 'yellow races', to be distinguished from ethnic groups such as the Manchus, whom they called Tartar slaves (*dalu*) or northern slaves (*hulu*) who supposedly smelled like sheep (*yangchou*). Against such views, the constitutional monarchist Liang Qichao (1873–1929), for example, provisionally accepted the theory that the Han were the descendants of Huangdi, with the caveats that it was difficult to definitively determine whether the Han shared one common ancestor and to distinguish them from other ethnic minorities due to the history of intermarriages. Liang writes,

> The Han refers to us, the inheritors of the so-called civilization and the descendants of Huangdi, who are currently present across the entire country. Huangdi came from the Kunlun Mountains and his descendants headed east from the Pamir Mountains to enter China, living along the Yellow River; the population expanded for thousands of years and gained a glorious reputation in the world. The so-called Asian civilizations all began with our race/ethnicity planting its seeds and cultivating its harvests. (Liang Qichao 1901: 6)

Further, he stated that if one were to categorize, 'We are clearly the yellow race vis-à-vis [the foreign] white, brown, red and black races. As to the [domestic] Miao, Tibetan, Mongol, Xiongnu and Manchu, it would not inconvenience anybody to generally consider them as the Han and refer to ourselves as the four hundred million compatriots'. He thus advocated the view that equated the yellow race with the greater Han as compatriots. While the revolutionary faction later emerged victorious, it can be said that Liang Qichao's 'greater Han' became the model of the 'Chinese people' (*Zhonghua minzu*) as a nation in the Republic of China (Sakamoto 2004a).

During the same period, intellectuals made attempts to conceptualize the traditional scholarship. Following Meiji Japanese who coined the term '*kokusui*' (*guocui* in Chinese) to translate the English word 'nationality', or national character, some Chinese intellectuals called traditional scholarship *guocui*. Others adopted the word '*guoxue*', which referred to schools or lecture halls in texts such as *Rites of Zhou* (*Zhouli*). This movement placed a renewed emphasis on traditional scholarship as an oppositional strategy after having acquired the West's scholarly knowledge. Traditional scholarship became an object of 'preservation', as seen in the establishment of the Society to Preserve National Scholarship (*Guoxue Baocun Hui*). *Guocui xue bao* (*Journal of National Scholarship*) was published in this context. Zhang Binglin, the revolutionary also known as the Great Master of National Scholarship, was inspired by the nationalist thought of Indians living under asylum in Japan due to their involvement in anti-British movements, among others. Zhang's and other Chinese intellectuals' interactions with political refugees from India and Vietnam in Japan as well as Japanese socialists and anarchists such as Kōtoku Shūsui (1871–1911) led to the establishment of the Asian Solidarity Society (*Yazhou heqin hui* [Chinese] / *Ashu washin kai* [Japanese]), which had great potential to promote the international communist movement as it aimed to foster solidarity to fight against imperialism and to achieve independence of the oppressed peoples (Sakamoto 2001). Yoshizawa also recognizes the historical significance of the rapid changes in social thought from the 1898 Wuxu Reform to the 1911 Xinhai Revolution and identifies various kinds of nationalism. He argues, 'The view that considers China as one indivisible unit was forcefully formed in the anti-Qing movement' (Yoshizawa 2003: 118).

One chapter of Yoshizawa's book entitled 'Militant citizens and physical education' discusses physical education groups such as *Tiyushe*. According to Yoshizawa, the establishment of this organization shows that 'the concept of patriotism along with the need for regional defense promoted changes in the concept of the body', and that '[i]n the context of the discussion on ethnicity and military consciousness, the attention on the body resulted in the reconstruction of the gender division of labor' (Yoshizawa 2003: 43). He points out that men cutting their *queues* and dying patriotic deaths have gender implications, but he does not offer any in-depth gendered analysis. In contrast, Takashima Kō discusses physical education during this time from the viewpoints of masculinity studies (see Chapter Ten of this book).

Yoshizawa and Karl Gerth analyze anti-imperialist boycotts termed the National Products Movement, which started in 1905. While the former analyzes it as a mere part of the formative process of patriotism, the latter explores it also from the perspective of consumer culture. By looking at the National Products Movement at the center, Gerth demonstrates that nationalism and consumerism developed in tandem in China from the late Qing to the 1930s (Gerth 2003). His book points to the complex relationships between capitalism and nationalism, while discussing changes in men's appearance, especially hairstyles and clothes (Chapter 2: 'Nationalizing the appearance of men') and gendered manifestations of female consumers' nationalism (Chapter 7: 'Nationalizing female consumers'). His work analyzes essays that criticized the 'Modern Girls' (see below) and collects

Chapter 9

interesting relevant visual materials such as cartoons and advertisements from the 1930s, especially 1934, the year the Nationalist regime designated as the Women's National Products Year.

Onodera Shirō studied concrete cases – the national flag, national anthem, party anthem, holidays, calendars, etc. – not as objects but as political symbols (Onodera 2011). His study elaborated on how these symbols were used as tools to evoke nationalism after the 1911 revolution. He is aware of gendered perspectives but does not make full use of them. This problem may arise from the fact that only male politicians were obsessed with the 'national flag, national anthem and national holidays', but if that were the case, Onodera and others could have analyzed them from perspectives of masculinity.

Japanese scholars have conducted more research that pays attention to Chinese nationalism in the twentieth century. One example is a collected volume edited by Nishimura Shigeo (2003), and another is the four-volume series edited by Iijima Wataru, Kubo Tōru and Murata Yūjirō (2009), which deals with nationalism since the end of the Qing period. In particular, Murata's chapter, 'Genealogy of discourses on Chinese people as a nation', gives a clear overview and analysis of the complex negotiation process that led to the 'Five Peoples Under One Union', one of the major principles of the Republic of China, which I mentioned above.

Unfortunately, however, studies that focus on political processes tend to lack gendered perspectives. Even the abovementioned Wang Hui, who examines theories broadly inside and outside of China, does not explicitly point to the gender axis in his 'system transversal society'. In Japanese academia, in which over 90% of China historians are male, I continue hearing the argument that gender is irrelevant to revolutions and wars. Where does such a misunderstanding come from? Could it be because women's history has at times only aimed at filling the gaps in male-centered history without looking at the social construction of gender as a whole? Could it be because women's history (especially that of socialist nations) has often turned into the 'history of women's liberation' due to limited primary sources? Or is it simply because male historians cannot move beyond the misconception that studies on women equal gender studies?

The exclusion of women from politics may appear to give historians a license to engage in genderless analysis. It is true that studies in the realm of social and cultural history that completely ignore gender are, as expected, becoming increasingly rare. However, for example, when historians discuss 'nationals' in analyses of the 'nation-state' in the Republic of China, they do not thoroughly investigate the significance and structure of the claim to a 'republic' even when it excluded women. Note that women just like men were mobilized in the revolutionary movement. Zhang Zhujun (1876–1964), one of the few female medical doctors at the time, led a group of Red Cross medical staff to the site of the 1911 Revolution and subsequently participated in the female suffrage movement. Then, why were women excluded? Historians must discuss the quality of 'national integration' at the time. Some may simply say that women were excluded in the process of the former revolutionary faction and the old guard compromising for the purpose of integration as they worked toward the establishment of a political party. But is it true that only ideology or the logic of the 'desire for power' shaped the construction of the new republic? Putting aside the historical constraints of the time, I believe studies on socialism and liberalism also require analyses from gendered perspectives.

Bodies and gender: Bound feet and anti-footbinding movements

'[N]ationalism was related to reproductive heteronormativity as a source of legitimacy' (Spivak 2010: 13). The issues surrounding 'citizens' bodies' and reproduction in modern China are also closely linked to nationalism. Here, the biggest topic is the problem of the abolition of footbinding, the practice of forcefully changing the body by folding the feet and binding them so that even the bones are deformed. The practice had become a female gender norm as the strongest weapon in the competition to enter a 'good marriage' and thereby escape heavy labor.

The practice of footbinding began perhaps around the Song dynasty as an upper-class fashion of wearing beautiful specialized shoes. During the Ming dynasty, the practice spread as a custom for Han women. In the ensuing Qing dynasty, it was initially prohibited, but eventually the ban was rescinded. Lower-class women also bound their feet as long as they did not need to engage in physical labor. Particularly in cities, women with 'big feet' came to be looked down upon as 'village girls or barbaric women'. Small feet were a *sine qua non* for entering good marriages, even in the late nineteenth and early twentieth centuries. 'Cry first and laugh later. Crying is just for a short time but laughing is for a lifetime. So even though we often say, "A pair of

Chapter 9

bound feet and a barrel of tears", in reality, it is usually, "A pair of big feet and a barrel of tears"', said Zou Ying (d. 2001) in the Republican period (cited in Yao Lingxi 1936b: 271–272).[2]

Until recently, with the exception of those by Orientalist dilettantes, studies on footbinding characterized the practice as barbaric and grotesque, framing it within the 'history of pain' symbolizing the victimization of Chinese women. Dorothy Ko has shown how the image of pre-modern Chinese women within the framework of the 'feudal, patriarchal, repressive image of "traditional women of China"' was the product of interactions among the May Fourth/ New Culture Movements, the communist revolution and Western feminism. Ko re-evaluated the practice of footbinding and the production of shoes for bound feet as a women's culture, generated in the processes of their achieving femininity that demonstrated 'women's efforts and pride' within the Confucian world (Ko 1994, 2001). Inspired by Spivak among others, she argued 'the current views on bound feet as "crippled" came from modern teleological views linked inseparably with the identity exploration of the men traumatized by imperialism"', based on the writings of missionaries, anthropologists, medical doctors and enlightenment intellectuals after the nineteenth century (Ko 1997a [Japanese]: 469; also see Ko 2001 [English]).

Takashima Kō has surveyed the historiography on modern anti-footbinding movements in his works that analyze the activities and problems surrounding the records of the Natural Foot Society organized by British women and the Anti-Footbinding Society (*Buchanzu hui*) run by Chinese intellectuals (Takashima 2003, 2004). Thus, I will not elaborate on these issues here. Through extensive archival research, Xia Xiaohong established the shifting views of late Qing literati on footbinding from 'a symbol of feminine beauty' to 'an archetype of deformity and disability' and from 'national essence to national shame' (Xia Xiaohong 1995). Xia's research gains even more significance if seen from the abovementioned theoretical perspectives.

---

[2] Zou Ying was a pen name of Zhu Chengyu (Ko 2011: 71, 253 n. 5). Yao Lingxi (1936a, 1936b) collected a large number of primary and secondary sources on footbinding throughout history. Also, Ke Ji-Sheng, a medical doctor and famous collector of shoes for bound feet, has published a valuable sourcebook with photos of his collected items, including footbinding paintings (e.g., *chungong hua*, a genre of pornography), shoes, tools, certificates and other relevant materials (Ke Ji-Sheng 2013).

From the late nineteenth century, criticisms of the customs of footbinding and female infanticide were published in missionary journals such as *Church News* (*Jiaohui xinbao*, later *Wanguo gongbao*). Western medical doctors also voiced their opinions about the harmful effects of footbinding. Chinese intellectuals such as Zheng Guanying (1842–1922), who worked for the Qing government and was also an entrepreneur, also joined in the criticisms. He lamented that cases of footbinding were widespread in the cities, where 'the limbs are lost, joints and bones are restricted, the qualities of natural endowments are marred and the way of nurturing small children is lost'. He said that it was a vice only seen in China (Zheng Guanying 1880: 164) and the source of 'Westerners' mockery' (Zheng Guanying 1895: 65).

As Kang Youwei (1858–1927), Liang Qichao and others led the 1898 Reform Movement (*bianfa yundong*), anti-footbinding became part of the agenda along with women's education. This group also established the Anti-Footbinding Society. Liang Qiachao's famous *General Discussions on Reform* (*Bianfa Tongyi*, 1897) argued for the necessity of education for women as follows. In his view, Chinese women had traditionally been considered as beings who only 'took part of other people's profits' (*fenli*: consume) and did not produce. For women, Liang reminded readers, talentlessness (*wucai*) was considered a virtue. However, he argued, because mothers taught their children, education for women was the 'great origin of survival and extinction, strength and weakness for all under heaven'. Other nations were thus strengthening their military while having all women learn to exercise, which enabled them to bear strong and healthy children. In other words, according to Liang, women's learning (*fuxue*) was fundamental to the protection of the race. Despite women's education being such an urgent task, Chinese women were trapped and isolated in their homes and had no way of learning practical studies (*shixue*). Moreover, they were turned into 'cripples' (*feiji*), into disabled people, as a result of footbinding. To continue with his argument, without first changing footbinding, female education would not be possible, and China would be 'the object of mockery by other peoples outside China' (Liang Qichao 1897). Liang thus portrayed Chinese women as ignorant beings that 'took part of other people's profits', who had 'seriously disabled' bodies as the result of footbinding, were unable to perform their duties of 'protecting the race' and were a 'disgrace to the nation' (see Sakamoto 2004c [English]).[3] In other words, as Qiao Yigang and Liu Kun (2010) say, male intellectuals began advocating for the prohibition of footbinding and the promotion of female education in order to produce women with the 'dual human resource value of "labor force/producer of surplus value" and "reproducer of humans"'.

Women were subsequently redefined from 'takers of other people's profits' to 'mothers of the citizens', in other words from a 'negative value' to a 'positive value'. The 'mothers of the citizens' discourse began to spread after around 1903 when, inspired by the 'women's rights' theories of John Stuart Mill in Shanghai's revolutionary movement, it was introduced in the male elite Jin Tianhe's (Jin Yi, 1874–1947) *Nüjie zhong* (*Bell of the Women's World*).[4] Jiang Weiqiao's (1873–1958) contemporaneous lamentation appeared in *Nüzi shijie* (*Women's World*) (1903–1906): 'The people of our nation are being laughed at by all the nations of the earth' as a 'weak race'. The less populous 'white race' was stronger and Japan, the 'same race' (*tongzhong*), was treating them as barbaric. 'Our racial inferiority is no doubt caused by the lack of knowledge, but it is also because of our physical weakness. Isn't our physical weakness being caused by all the mothers of the citizens practicing footbinding?' (Jiang

---

3 Liang was certainly exaggerating when he said that all Chinese women were taking part of the profits. He did that to emphasize the significance of the reform. At the same time, intellectuals had begun discussing the issue of footbinding as a women's physical issue, but as far as we can tell from the excerpt from Liu Dapeng's (1857–1942) diary, more entries on the harms of opium smoking can be found than other entries on women. Liu was from Taiyuan in Shanxi Province, serving as a teacher in the family school of a wealthy merchant in the same province beginning in 1886. For example, on the fourth day of the tenth lunar month in 1891, he deplored that when a woman smoked, her husband and children followed her example. As a result, he claimed that they did not weave as much as they did earlier and thus the family became more impoverished. On the second day of the second month in 1894, he cited an elderly man who said 70–80% of all the residents in his village, and 50–60% of the women, smoked opium. He said only 10–20% of 200 or so households were able to survive the starvation and coldness, and other families were all in absolute poverty. In other words, the primary cause of the physical and economic disasters in Liu's view was opium smoking. It has been said that footbinding was popular in Shanxi. Could it have been that footbinding and smoking opium were correlated?

4 Jin also wrote the first part of a popular novel, *A Flower in a Sinful Sea* (*Niehai hua*). Zeng Pu is known to be the author of the entire novel. Wang Zheng, Gao Yanyi (Dorothy Ko) and Liu He (Lydia H. Liu) (2004 [Chinese]) argues that the *Bell of the Women's World* should be called the *Bell of the Men's World* because in this work, Chinese men's sense of crisis is expressed as their desire to be white Western men. According to them, 'a similar mindset can be observed in societies that have been colonized/conquered by the West'. Although the *Bell* is often considered to be the pioneer of Chinese feminist writings, Wang, Ko and Liu argue that it blames women for turning China from the great empire into 'the second citizen'. In other words, they argue that even though the work advocates 'gender equality', it constantly reproduces male chauvinistic thought. In their view, it is a utopian literary work, which depicted men's desire for, or attraction to, a nation-state from the male perspective.

Weiqiao (Zhuzhuang) 1904: 3–5).[5] Clearly, the issue of footbinding was recast as the exceedingly national problem of reproductive subjects – the 'mothers of the citizens' who should give birth to a 'strong race' and a 'superior race' that would determine the fate of the nation-state – from the problem of its reputation as the 'shame of the country'. This process simultaneously gave rise to new discrimination against indigenous and minority peoples as 'weak races' (Sakamoto 2004a).

However, from around this time, women's voices began questioning the male-centered calls for women's education and rights. For example, Chen Xiefen (1883–1923), the daughter of the publisher of *Su bao* (*Jiangsu Daily*), who herself published *Nü bao* (*Women's Journal*), later retitled *Nüxue bao* (*Journal of Scholarship on Women*) (1902–1903), stated that even though the abovementioned intellectuals argued for the promotion of women's education and rights, 'It was the same old story of women's education and rights. They are just to suit male needs, and their arguments did not necessarily reflect the standpoint of women'. Thus, Chen was aware of the need for 'Independence!' (Chen Xiefen 1903; Qiao Yigang and Liu Kun 2010). The discourse of the 'mothers of the citizens' literally recognized women as mothers who gave birth to citizens. In this view, women could become a resource for nationalism, but this did not signify that they were recognized as citizens with rights themselves.

Upon the foundation of this 'mothers of the citizens' discourse based on biological sex, the positive aspects of women's status were further defined, giving rise to the discourses on female citizens (*nü guomin*) (Qiao Yigang and Liu Kun 2010). By 1907, following in the wake of journals by male intellectuals, women's journals with titles including the characters '*nü*' (女) or '*fu*' (婦) began to be published by Chinese women, especially by those studying overseas. He Zhen (1886–?), also known as He-Yin Zhen, advocated for women's liberation and anarchism. She published the journal *Tianyi bao* (*Natural Justice*) in Tokyo. Qiu Jin's (1875–1907) *Zhongguo nü bao* (*Chinese Women's Journal*) was published in Shanghai, calling for the abolition of footbinding,

---

5 Shimoda Utako (1854–1936) made a similar argument as she emphasized the significance of girls' education from the viewpoints of nationalism, the Sino-Japanese relationship and the Asian yellow race, in a lecture published in *Dalu bao* (*The Continent*) (Shimoda 1902 [Chinese]). Shimoda was a pioneer in modern Japanese women's education and founded Jissen Joshi Gakko, the first school in Japan to accept female exchange students from Qing China. *Dalu bao* was published by Zuoxin Publisher in Shanghai, which had a close relationship with Shimoda. I think her lecture and Liang Qichao's argument influenced each other. Jiang Weiqiao as well as Qiu Jin and Yan Bin, whom I mention later, all seem to have also been influenced by Shimoda's argument.

Chapter 9

promotion of women's education and state revolution. In the same year, Yan Bin's *Zhongguo xin nüjie* (*New World of Women in China*), which discussed 'female citizens', was also published in Tokyo. One can see in the essays contributed to *Zhongguo xin nüjie* aspirations toward the North American white middle- and upper-class women's calls for 'women's rights', which were free from issues surrounding colonial rule and ethnic relations. The editor of this journal, Yan Bin, and her group argued, 'There are many bodies of female citizens in China, but not many souls of female citizens. Such being the case, it is as if the existence of the citizens has no substance' (Yan Bin (Lianshi) 1907a: 2). She called for new theories and civilization for women and ethics education to attain the goal of acquiring female citizens. Footbinding, 'an act of inhumanity unparalleled in the world' against the women of Chinese society, was 'plunging the lives of young girls into despair', depriving them of the ability to walk properly and causing illnesses due to the stagnation of the vital energy (*qi*) and the blood (*xue*) of the whole body. 'This sick girl will become a sick wife and will surely reproduce sick offspring through her sick genes'. If the two hundred million women in such a degraded state were not reformed, 'the health of the race will not be attained and that epithet of the Sick Man of East Asia will be confirmed as true and justified' (Yan Bin (Lianshi) 1907b: 3). The colonial and national discourse of the 'Sick Man of East Asia' (Takashima 2016b) is thus also attributed, and inextricably linked, to footbound women. Around this time, also starting in the cities, natural feet (*tianzu*) began to be seen as a symbol of 'progress'.

Figure 9.1
'Changes in the tastes in women's world'

This cartoon, drawn by a male artist, satirizes that women's favorite activities change over time: footbinding in the past, reading in public in the present and serving as soldiers in the future. He was aptly observing and predicting the process of women's nationalization.

Source: 'Changes in Tastes in the Women's World' (*Nüjie fengshang zhi bianqian*) in *Tuhua ribao* (*Daily Pictorial*) (1909, Vol. 12). Also see Judge (2008: 10).

A 'female citizen' was thus imagined, but in the Provisional Constitution of the Republic of China (1912), the principle of 'equality of the sexes' was excluded. It stated that 'the people of the Republic of China are all equal regardless of ethnicity (*zhongzu*), class or religion'. A newspaper at the time even cited a reader's letter which argued that some of the suffragists held a 'philosophy of no husband' (*wufu zhuyi*) and that it would lead to the eradication of the Chinese people (Zhang Renlan 1912). When female activists of the women's suffrage movement 'trespassed' into parliament, a newspaper reporter argued in 1912 that the act of demanding women's suffrage through such 'barbaric methods' was shameless and would 'leave a stain on the republic and make it a laughing-stock of foreigners', particularly because in his understanding even women in the West had not yet gained the right to vote (Menghuan 1912). While footbound women were labeled a 'national disgrace' in the late Qing period and the practice was prohibited in the republic, this time the female citizens taking part in the women's suffrage movement were criticized as a 'stain' on the republic.

With the rise of nationalism after the May Fourth Movement, as women participated in the student movement, labor movement and nationalist revolution after the First United Front of 1924, the equality of the sexes came to be approved in principle. Women, however, were repeatedly disappointed by the fact that the realization of true gender equality was always placed behind other political adendas and faced further problems as their bodies came under state control. As a result of the time lag between the order to unbind their feet and resulting changes to their bodies, women's bodies and minds were once again subjected to excruciating pain (Sakamoto 2000). This problem was especially salient during the period of the Nanjing Nationalist regime (1928–1949), when there was a grand campaign to ban footbinding in the provinces, giving rise to terrorizing scenes of 'bound-feet hunting'. Bound feet that had already been deformed could not be healed by unbinding, which only exacerbated the pain. Despite this, the immediate unbinding of feet was unreasonably enforced, with the result that women were 'once again subjected to excruciating pain'. Women looked down upon their unrecoverable feet that metamorphosed into a different deformity as 'feet of failure', desiring their own 'psychological reformation' and comfort. Men mercilessly castigated such feet as 'not a donkey nor a horse, a strange and grotesque shape, unbearable to look at', as seen in Yao Lingxi's essay ('Pinping') (Yao Lingxi 1936a: 148).

Chapter 9

In-depth studies on footbinding by Chinese scholars have been few due to the deep-rooted perception that it was a horrible custom, but Yang Xingmei has published her findings on 'the struggle between footbinding and anti-footbinding', drawing inspiration from scholars active in North America, led by Dorothy Ko, while simultaneously reconciling her findings with Chinese perspectives that place the practice in the history of 'women's liberation' (Yang Xingmei 2012). It is a valuable empirical study based on wide-ranging sources including local newspapers, magazines and archival materials.

Yang focuses on two different methods in the anti-footbinding movement: 'prohibition' (*jin*) and 'promotion' (*quan*). There was a mixture of prohibition and promotion in the late Qing and early Republican periods. The Beijing government suppressed demands from intellectuals and shifted toward promotion, but the regime was unstable and there were regions where local warlords pushed forward with prohibition. With the establishment of the Nanjing Nationalist regime after the reunification of China, an ordinance prohibiting women's footbinding was issued in 1928. At that point, the state-led prohibition movement spread to many provinces. However, the effects were limited due to the lack of cooperation between the government and the people and the failure of the measures to take the realities of footbound women into account. As the ideals of anti-footbinding were 'politicized' in the shift from 'barbarism' and 'dropouts from progress' (*luowu*) to 'national disgrace', the movement became burdened with difficult responsibilities such as national strengthening and honor, the achievement of the revolution, the struggle against feudalism, military mobilization in the anti-Japanese resistance and the advancement of industrial productivity. Punishments for footbinding came to include violent coercion, including fines, mandatory unbinding of feet, forced labor and dragging footbound women through the city streets. Despite these developments, the aesthetic consciousness of the masses that valued small feet for marriage remained unchanged until at least the eve of the war of anti-Japanese resistance. Many women refused to unbind their feet despite the punishments they faced. Footbound women were thus long made to represent 'backwardness', leaving them without a voice. However, Yang stresses that one must not deprive footbound women of their right to speak by branding them as barbaric and backward from the standpoint of 'women's liberation' and 'social progress'. The problem of 'politicization' that Yang raises has opened possibilities to further research from the standpoint of gender and nationalism.

From May Fourth/New Culture Movement to 2nd Sino-Japanese War

As we have seen above, the social Darwinist nationalist discourse based on the sense of crisis brought about by the aggression of the great powers after the late Qing had a tendency to merge with the anti-footbinding movement, or the politics of the 'citizens' body', finding expression in terms such as 'strengthening the race' (*qiangzhong*), 'mixing races' (*hezhong* and *tongzhong*), improving the race (*youzhong* and *shanzhong*), preserving the race (*baozhong* and *liuzhong*) and propagating the race (*jinzhong* and *chuanzhong*). This process evoked the notion of 'reproductive subjects' and was thus gendered. The May Fourth/New Culture Movement was influenced by the philosophy of the Fabian Society established in late nineteenth-century London, which aimed for gradual social changes toward socialism and gender equality. Some of the society's members turned to Neo-Malthusianism, which promoted birth control as a way to control the population and to resolve the issue of poverty. Their ideas eventually merged with eugenics, sometimes translated as *shanzhong xue* (studies to improve race), and eugenics theory seeking to protect the 'good race' (*liangzhong*) and end the 'bad race' (*ezhong*).

It goes without saying that theories of eugenics led directly to issues surrounding state control over reproduction in the form of the population problem and birth control amidst social changes such as industrialization. In addition, after the emergence of the modern model of love marriage and small families in the New Culture Movement (see Chapter Eleven), the intellectuals seeking to resist the traditional family system and the notion that valued having many children, especially the women seeking women's liberation, believed they could use eugenics thought with its emphasis on demographic 'quality over quantity' as an intellectual weapon. Zhou Jianren (1888–1984), a younger brother of Lu Xun (1881–1936), went so far as to proclaim that it was love marriages that fit with eugenics thought (Sakamoto 2004a, 2004b [English]).

Pan Guangdan (1899–1967), who received specialized training in the U.S., 'correctly' transmitted cutting-edge eugenics theories to China (Pan Guangdan 1924). According to Pan, as human civilizations modernize, the rate of cultural and social selection outpaces natural selection, with the result that racial extinction may come about from the inability of biological survival of the fittest to function. For example, he characterized celibacy, late marriages, fewer children, the social advancement of women and public health policies

Chapter 9

and medical care that lengthened the lives of the weak based on Western individualism and urban modernism to be, from a biological standpoint, contrary to eugenic principles. While he did not go so far as to advocate a negative eugenics policy of forced sterilization for those deemed 'unfit', as was starting to be practiced in the U.S., he leveraged eugenics as a 'scientific' discourse to oppose the New Culture Movement, specifically the discourses based on principles of human equality such as individualism, socialism, democracy and feminism. From the standpoint of 'national eugenics', Pan continued being critical of women's social advancement even amidst the discourses on national rejuvenation in the 1930s and until the establishment of the PRC, becoming the target of criticism by feminists such as Huang Biyao (Huang Biyao 1948).

During the 'Golden Decade' (*Huangjin shinian*) of the interwar period (1927–1937), with the development of capitalism under the Nanjing Nationalist regime came the emergence of a mass middle-class society in the big cities (Iwama 2012) and the 'Modern Girl' (*modeng nülang/xiaojie/ guniang*) phenomenon appeared with varying degrees of connections with colonial modernity (Sakamoto 2010). With their ostentatious display of a feminine and modern lifestyle, they became the object of aspiration for some. Simultaneously, they became the object of scorn and mockery for both men and women fearing the transgression of traditional gender norms and self-proclaimed 'progressive' intellectuals, much like the footbound women after the late Qing period. With the militarization of society after the Mukden Incident (1931) and Shanghai Incident (1932), they were further criticized as useless and luxuriously wasteful.

In 1934, the Nationalist regime started the 'New Life Movement' based on the Confucian morality of proper right (*li*), righteousness (*yi*), honesty and cleanliness (*lian*) and shame (*chi*). The goal of this movement was to reform irregular lifestyles, unsanitary bodies and minds and 'barbaric manners' and to rejuvenate the culture specific to China. In this context, along with the discussions on the rejuvenation of the Chinese people, the discourse ordering women to 'return to the home' and attacks on the Modern Girl intensified.

It was not the case that, during the war against Japan or at the time of revolution, 'gender ceased to be relevant', nor that gender retreated to the background. During the war against Japan, the gender politics of the mobilization of women and the repression of femininity by both Nationalists and Communists strengthened (see Chapter Thirteen). A national plan to mobilize and train all women was formulated. While there were cases of women soldiers going into battle, the government created the 'new wise wife and good mother' model for most women and promoted the gendered division of labor on the front lines and in the home.

These developments connected with the issues surrounding Chinese female survivors who had been made into 'comfort women' by the Japanese military during the Japanese occupation, victimized by atrocious acts of sexual violence. These women victims 'kept themselves from committing suicide for their children or parents, but were mocked and labeled as "Modern Girls who engaged in sexual relations with Japanese" by cruel neighbors and continued to be subjected to derisive laughter and mockery after the war' (Peng Hui 1948: 8). Perspectives of both nationalism and gender are indispensable if we are to confront the histories of these multilayered and deep wounds and elucidate the gravity of the assaults and damages.

10. Masculinity in Modern China

— *TAKASHIMA Kō*

Introduction: What is masculinity?

What is 'masculinity'? Readers know that 'gender' is 'knowledge about sexual differences' which is generated as a social construct (Scott 1999). The categories of 'male' and 'female' (are believed to) exist in this world and each human supposedly identifies with one or the other. In reality, each human is raised as a male or a female by the people around them from birth (or before birth these days) and generally comes to identify with one sex. However, one cannot become a man or a woman by self-identification alone. Society dictates that men and women be a certain way and behave in a certain way (and therefore it is a question of ideology). One is recognized as a man or a woman only when one conforms to the expectations of the society. These social expectations constitute masculinity and femininity. Alternatively, the process by which individual humans become constituent members of the social categories of 'men' and 'women' can be described as masculinity and femininity. The relationship between masculinity and femininity is asymmetrical in that the former confers authority and power on those who have a male body and male identity.

The masculinity that is described in contrast to femininity – for example, 'Men are more aggressive than women' or 'Men are more rational than women' – is not an inherent quality. Different masculinities exist in different societies at different times. Masculinity is 'constructed' and varies according to culture, race, class and changes in the course of history. There are multiple masculinities in each society with hierarchical relationships between them. The most dominant masculinity in any given society which subordinates, marginalizes and feminizes the other masculinities is called 'hegemonic masculinity', and corresponds to what is generally called 'manliness' (Taga 2001, 2006; Bederman 1995; Connell 1995).

This chapter first discusses men's history as a historical field of inquiry and its relation to theories of nationalism, imperialism and colonialism. The second section then outlines Chinese traditional constructions of masculinity, before turning to the third section which traces the historical development of ideas about masculinity from the late Qing dynasty through to the establishment of the People's Republic of China. This discussion focuses on how the traditional construction of masculinity in which highly literate officials (*wen*) held a hegemonic role was transformed into a modern understanding of masculinity.

What is men's history?

Men's history or the history of masculinity is the historical study of men as a genderized category. Masculinity is inseparably linked with politics, economy, culture and society and intricately intertwined with categories such as race, class, sexuality, religion and ethnicity. Consequently, men's history must be treated as a study covering all aspects of history rather than one specific area (Sinha 1999).

According to Thomas Kühne (1996), men's history must be studied simultaneously at three levels:

1. cultural image;
2. social practice and the practical reproduction of a gender system;
3. subjective perception, experience and identity.

The first level involves discovering historical changes, or more specifically, examining how and why a particular masculinity is constructed, transformed and dismantled. While this level involves the study of masculinity as a norm or ideology, the third level entails the study of the realities of masculinity. The male body is not a blank canvas on which to reproduce masculinity as the norm. How does one establish one's male subjectivity when one recognizes a gap between the norm and the reality? This mutually dependent but strained relationship between society and the individual is studied at the third level. The first and third levels mainly focus on masculinity, whereas the second level sheds light on the relationship between men and women. The history of gender has exposed the distinction between 'male' and 'female' as a political categorization designed to grant power and authority to men (as a whole regardless of internal differences between men) rather than a cultural categorization. While women's history approaches gender from the women's side, men's history approaches it from the men's side.

Men's history was born out of a re-evaluation of the monolithic view of men as the victimizer in women's history and gender history that emerged during the 1970s, and a considerable body of research has since accumulated largely in the English-speaking world.

Men's studies on China began in Taiwan and Hong Kong in the late 1990s and in mainland China in the late 2000s (Fang Gang 2008). Men's history lags further behind, with very few significant studies being produced in mainland China. In the English-speaking world, Kam Louie (2002) discusses Chinese masculinity from the viewpoint of the *wen-wu* (文武) dyad (cultural attainment versus martial valor), while Song Geng (2004) and Martin W. Huang (2006) look at pre-modern Chinese masculinity from a literary historical standpoint. Although research on each historical period remains scarce, Bret Hinsch (2013) attempts to write a complete history of masculinity. Research on homosexuality is very active and significant studies include Hinsch (1990), Wu Cuncun (2000), Kang Weiqing (2009 [English]) and Giovanni Vitiello (2011). There is a strong interest in contemporary masculinity and major studies on the Han include Zhong Xueping (2000 [English]), Kam Louie and Morris Low (2003), Chou Wahshan (2009 [English]), Marc L. Moskowitz (2013), Song Geng and Derek Hird (2014) and Kam Louie (2015). On the masculinities of ethnic minorities, Jay Dautcher (2009) discusses the Uyghurs while Ben Hillman and Lee-Anne Henfry (2006) studies the Tibetans. The relationship between ethnicity and gender adds an interesting dimension to the discussion on masculinity among ethnic minorities – as pointed out by Emma Jinhua Teng (2004), masculine traits predominate in the north (the Mongol and the Jurchen) of the Han-dominant region (in the center) but become increasingly effeminate to the south (the Miao and the Thai). There are not many studies on Chinese masculinity in modern times in the English-speaking or Chinese-speaking countries other than Wang Shih-Ying (2011) and Hee Wai-Siam (2015); a general overview can be found in Chapter Seven of Bret Hinsch (2013).[1] In light of the scarcity of empirical studies, this chapter sketches an overall picture of modern Chinese (especially Han Chinese) masculinity from

---

[1] For Chinese masculinity in modern times, Louie (2016) and Schillinger (2016) are well worth a perusal although I have not read them.

the *wen-wu* dyad viewpoint proposed by Louie, focusing mainly on the first of Kühne's (1996) three levels: cultural image.

Nationalism, imperialism and colonialism

Before we discuss Chinese masculinity, let us briefly look at the characteristics of modern masculinity in the West.

Mosse locates the origin of modern masculinity in the Napoleonic Wars period, the time when nation-states were forming in Europe (Mosse 1996). Modern masculinity and nationalism were indivisibly connected from the outset (Enloe 1990). While Sikata Banerjee (2012) named this type of nationalism 'muscular nationalism', it can also be called 'nationalized' or 'militarized' masculinity. The heroic citizen-soldier who was brave, physically strong and disciplined and willing to bear arms to dedicate his life to the nation represented hegemonic masculinity at the time (Nagel 1998). The idea of strong masculinity was reinforced further by social Darwinism, which likened masculinity to biological evolution and turned physical strength into a privilege. The notion of survival of the fittest was applied to the competition between nations and used to justify imperialism (see Chapter Nine).

In the colonial context, the rulers maintained their dominance by subordinating and feminizing the masculinity of the ruled. On the other hand, the ruled attempted to restore their masculinity (remasculinization) through various means, ranging from defeating the rulers in sport to gaining political independence. The struggle over masculinity between the colonial ruler and the ruled is described as 'colonial masculinity' (Sinha 1995). Masculinity in modern China, which was a semi-colony of imperialist powers, should be considered as a type of colonial masculinity in the sense that it was constructed on the premise of the existence of another masculinity that always had predominance over it (Takashima 2013). Modern Japan also suffered from an inferiority complex in relation to the West, but it managed to hold on to a positive self-image. By contrast, modern China attempted to build a nation through reactions against negative self-images such as the 'sick man of East Asia' (Takashima 2016b). This 'sick man of East Asia' trope was a description often used by late Qing and early Republican intellectuals to conceptualize the state of their country and people after they had been invaded by the great powers. From the perspective of men's history, we can see the use of this phrase in one sense suggesting that

Chinese masculinity had become 'unmasculine'. At the same time, it was used as a rallying cry to fellow Chinese in their struggle to regain a more healthy masculine identity.

Traditional masculinity: Hegemony of *wen*

China's traditional masculinity is composed of *wen* (cultural attainment) and *wu* (martial valor). *Wen* and *wu* were not mutually exclusive categories: having both *wen* and *wu* was considered an ideal. China's successive dynasties conferred power, status and wealth on those who were equipped with these qualities through the imperial examinations. These examinations functioned as a device to institutionalize *wen* and *wu* as ideal masculine qualities as women were not eligible to take the examinations. Greater weight was placed upon *wen* and the imperial examination generally meant the civil service examination; even the imperial military examination included written tests (while the civil service examination did not include practical tests).

The disparity between *wen* and *wu* became definitive during the Song dynasty. (Although the image of Song as a state governed by *wen* is being overturned by recent studies of its military history, it is conceivable that the state placed greater importance on *wen* to compensate for its limited military power in competing against garrison states.) The lower standing of *wu* can be gleaned from a popular saying of the time: 'Good iron is not made into nails, good men are not made into soldiers'. The practice of footbinding spread among upper-class women in this period. Fragile-looking women were considered to be suitable partners for the literati. While the literati kept many concubines, other men who were alienated from marriage and power – vagrants, 'bare sticks' or single men and bandits – found manliness in the *haohan*, the brave men depicted in popular novels like *Water Margin*. *Haohan* was demonstrated by excessive eating and drinking, violence and extravagant spending (Huang 2006 [English]). The fearless rogues who swaggered about in nineteenth-century Tianjin dressed in distinctive clothes were descended from the *haohan*. By contrast, Guan Yu who was enshrined in martial temples represented the martial valor of the ruling class. While Wu Song in *Water Margin* lacked self-control and had no cultural attainment, the deified Guan Yu exhibited masculinity heavily tinged with *wen*. However, Wu Song and Guan Yu shared a common ground in misogyny, as it was feared that women might undermine homosocial relationships between

Masculinity in Modern China

men ('Brothers in Mt. Liang' in the case of Wu Song and 'Oath of the Peach Garden' in the case of Guan Yu) (Louie 2002; Sedgwick 1985). While women enhanced *wen* masculinity, *wu* masculinity was reinforced by shunning women. The eunuchs, men who had been castrated and assigned tasks within the inner quarters of the imperial household, are often regarded as the third sex, but it is more appropriate to see them as a subordinate masculinity similar to *wu*. Some impoverished underclass men chose to become eunuchs as a way to gain access to power and wealth (Mitamura 1963; Inohara 2014) (see Chapter Nine).

The regime change from Ming to Qing brought a deep humiliation to Han Chinese men. Apart from the military defeat, they were forced to wear their hair in *queues*, the Manchu hairstyle, as a symbol of their submission. The Han Chinese leaned farther toward *wen* as a way to distinguish themselves from the Manchus, who took pride in their military valor. Han Chinese believed that rather than standing in opposition to the Manchus, the shortest road to power, status and wealth was to enter the bureaucracy by passing the civil service examination. The masculinity of beardless, delicate and scholarly men became the hegemonic masculinity of the Han Chinese. Women were required to be even more delicate. The seclusion of women was strengthened and the practice of footbinding spread outside of the elite class. As we can see in the scholar-beauty genre of romantic novels, masculinity and femininity were not contradictory in Han Chinese society during the Qing dynasty (Edwards 1994).

Manchu society was segregated from Han Chinese society administratively, occupationally, spatially and socially. For the minority Manchu to achieve dominance over the Han, who accounted for an overwhelming majority of

Figure 10.1
Government officials at the end of Qing (large patterns and rich colors)
Source: Wang (2003: 25).

the population, they had to rely on their military valor, whereas civilization = Sinicization meant feminization. Successive Qing emperors showed a strong interest in the language and mounted archery skills of the Manchu people. Even the civil service examination included archery tests in the case of Manchu candidates. The emperors who ruled the Manchu and the Han Chinese justified their sovereignty by flaunting their *wen* and *wu* qualities. Nevertheless, the martial ethos continued to wane and Emperor Jiaqing (r. 1796–1820) became the last emperor who tried to stop the decline (Rhodes 2000: 52–63).

The shock of the Sino-Japanese War: The rise of *wu*

The defeat in the First Sino-Japanese War delivered a savage blow to China's masculinity. Its navy was almost annihilated and China had to confront world powers virtually unarmed. All of the previous foreign wars were fought against others outside of the Chinese world order, but Japan was different. Japan's victory smashed from the inside not only the China-centered world order but also the underlying Confucian world order as well as *wen* masculinity. The loss of both *wen* and *wu* masculinities forced the Chinese elite to recognize China's castration and feminization and to begin the search for a path to remasculinization.

Shortly before a ceasefire was declared, Chinese scholar Yan Fu (1854–1921), famous for introducing Western ideas, published 'On the origin of strength' (*Yuan qiang*) and proposed the improvement of intelligence, physical fitness and moral virtue of the people as a way to remasculinize China. In his essay, Yan related an episode in which a Westerner visiting an examination hall (*Gongyuan*) in Beijing had commented derisively that government officials were being selected in a building filthier than a prison or animal barn and Yan wrote that he had to acknowledge that the comment was very irreverent but true. Scholar-officials, who embodied China's ultimate masculinity ('superior people' in Yan's words), existed in worse conditions than prisoners and livestock animals – an anecdote quite symbolic of the feminization of China.

Chinese philosopher Kang Youwei, who led the Reform Movement of 1898, proposed that cutting the *queue* would be one means for remasculinization. In his 1898 essay, 'Memorial for cutting the *queue*, changing official uniforms, and revising calendars', Kang argued that Westerners, who had originally also had *queues*, had cut their *queues* along with industrial and military advancements and, therefore, Chinese should also cut their *queues* and change their unmanly customs. He claimed that China was weak because of the *queue* and the *queue* was ridiculed because China was weak, and that the *queue* was the cause and effect of China's feminization. To remasculinize itself, China had to cut the *queue* and increase its wealth and military strength just as the Westerners had done. Thus, Chinese masculinity was denied and replaced by Western masculinity as the goal. The same can be said about women's footbinding. Gender and sexuality were reconstructed under this semi-colonial situation.

Kang Youwei and his disciple philosopher Liang Qichao, who produced *Discourse on the New Citizen* (*Xinmin shuo*) as a journalist, emphasized the reform of the civil service examination in the 'Hundred Days' Reform' in an attempt to reconstruct the kind of *wen* befitting the new age. The career switch from civil service to business made by Zhang Jian, who won the highest rank (*zhuangyuan*) in the 1894 civil service examination, became a symbol signifying the destabilization of *wen*. The attempt to reconstruct *wen* was interlinked with ideological changes sparked by multiple and sometimes conflicting intellectual tides, including the Gongyang and Hundred Schools of Thought schools of interpretation of the Chinese classics, resurgent Buddhism and Western studies (Shimada 1967). The commitment of Kang and other Gongyang scholars to Buddhist studies led to a high regard for the moral values of Buddhists that transcended life and death and self-interest (Mori 1999). The reappraisal of 'knight-errantry' (*renxia*) indicated a new relationship between *wen* and *wu*. While ancient Chinese philosopher Han Feizi saw the scholar (*wen*) and the knight-errant (*wu*) as opposites, others such as Tan Sitong, one of the martyrs of the 1898 Reform Movement, had no trouble unifying them without incongruence. Zhang Binglin (1869–1936) discussed similarities between the scholar and the knight-errant in *Qiu Shu* while Liang Qichao sought the origin of the warrior's way in Confucius in *Bushido of China*. The union between *wen* and *wu* was also used to justify cooperation between revolutionaries and secret societies.

After the First Sino-Japanese War, as railroad and steamship networks expanded, colonial powers found their way into the interior from their original bases in the coastal regions. Wang Guimei described the situation as follows: '[they] set foot on the eastern land in a violent manner and China under the Dragon Flag immediately lost its nerve and peace just like a virgin' (Wang Guimei 2008). This exactly represented the relationship between the West and China surrounding masculinity. The Boxer (Yihetuan) Uprising can be understood as a challenge to an all-out confrontation with Western masculinity. Railways were targeted for destruction and canons lost their power in front of

Chapter 10

female fighters such as the Red Lanterns (*Hongdengzhao*). After the failure of the uprising, Chinese masculinity was set to be constructed through negotiations rather than direct confrontations with Western masculinity.

Liang Qichao who took refuge in Japan after the failed Hundred Days' Reform tackled the issue of national identity reform. His *Discourse on the New Citizen* (*Xinmin shuo*) was a manifesto about a masculinity which China should aim for. He argued that the 'new citizens' who are bound to the state through the relationship of rights and duties constitute a free and independent nation filled with a spirit of enterprise and mental and physical strength. While this masculinity was a mixture of English, American, German and Japanese masculinities, it was generally closer to the German or Japanese soldier-citizen who was bound tightly to the state via conscription than to the English or American citizen-soldier (Liang used the term 'soldier-citizen'). The soldier-citizen was a new masculinity designed to mobilize (male) citizens for the remasculinization of China and its formulation was greatly influenced by Japan (Yoshizawa 2014). Chinese students in Japan experienced many humiliations, including being mocked by children as '*chanchan bozu*' (a derogatory expression for a Chinese man with the *queue*). These experiences made them realize the extent of China's feminization. It is hardly surprising that the idea of the soldier-citizen arose in none other than Japan (Takashima 2016b). The revolutionaries advanced on the path to militarized citizenry and the Association for Soldier-Citizen Education was formed in 1903 and evolved into the China Revival Society (*Huaxinghui*), the Restoration Society (*Guangfuhui*) and the Chinese Revolutionary Alliance (*Tongmenghui*). We need to examine from the perspective of masculinity why the revolutionaries rallied around Sun Yat-sen (courtesy name, Zhongshan), who was completely different to the image of a typical traditional Chinese intellectual, and why many women participated in the movement unlike in the case of the constitutionalists. The answer to the latter question can be found if we recall that the Chinese Nationalist Party (the Kuomintang) denied women's suffrage as soon as they took the reins of government. Patriarchy did not disappear even when the dynasty vanished.

The *wen-wu* reconstruction that had begun with the Hundred Days' Reform continued under the New Policies of the late Qing. The imperial military examination was abolished in 1901; the mounted archery test in the examination had been the last bastion of Manchu masculinity. The new Western-style military smashed the traditional image of soldiers reflected in the saying 'Good men are not made into soldiers' and began to turn soldiers into embodiments of masculinity.

Even intellectuals no longer shunned military service. In fact, a considerable number of Chinese students in Japan studied military science, Chiang Kaishek amongst them. China introduced conscription into some provinces in 1905 on its way toward the implementation of universal conscription (Takashima 2015b). On the *wen* front, China introduced a modern education system in 1904. The imperial examination was abolished in the following year and the traditional *wen* masculinity lost its hegemonic position. However, the removal of the imperial examination caused disaffection among Han elites rather than increasing the number of citizens loyal to the Qing dynasty.

Women's education was excluded from the new education system as it had traditionally been regarded as belonging to the domain of individual families. However, the Qing dynasty had to respond to a rapid increase in the number of private schools for girls. It acknowledged the need to redress progressive girls' education by incorporating girls' education into the regular education system and promulgated new rules for girls' schools in 1907. The objectives for women's education included the cultivation of female virtues, acquisition of knowledge and skills and development of a healthy body for the ultimate purpose of producing wise mothers who would manage their families to provide a good foundation for the state. Together with the conscription system, the single-sex education system was an attempt to nationalize and militarize gender (Takashima 2015b).

Birth of the Republic and the May Fourth Movement

Conflict between modernity and tradition became apparent in various ways during the Republican era. Unlike in Japan, the meaning of the traditional was never clear-cut in China. This had major implications for masculinity.

On the evening of New Year's Day of 1912, the inauguration of the provisional president took place in Nanjing. Many of the attendees were dressed in frock coats or military uniforms and none wore the *queue*. The presidential decree issued on 5 May ordered all people to cut their *queues*, making *queue* cutting the duty of the 'people of the new state'. For many men, cutting their *queue* was their first experience of the Xinhai Revolution. It was often carried out violently and accompanied by a sense of confusion and humiliation. While there were some who clung to the *queue*, in reality the custom had already lost its connection with hegemonic masculinity. When the puppet state of

Chapter 10

Manchukuo was established in the early 1930s and Pu Yi, who had been the last emperor of the Qing dynasty, was put on the throne, he did not try to revive the *queue*, nor did anyone propose reverting to the hairstyles of the last dynasty ruled by an ethnic Han, the Ming. While there was no revival of hairstyles, there was an attempt to revive Han-style fashion immediately after the Xinhai Revolution. For a brief period of time it seemed as though stage actors had left the theaters and were walking in the streets (Li Jingheng 2014). On the other hand, Beijing government ministers all dressed in Western clothing (tailcoat) or military uniform. The new political culture signaled the arrival of a new political regime. The choice between Western clothes and military garb was relevant to the image each politician wished to project. For instance, Yuan Shikai, first president of the new Republic of China, wore either the official uniform of the Qing dynasty or Western-style military clothes before the revolution but exclusively wore the latter after the revolution. When he attempted in 1915 to restore the monarchy, he also tried to revive Han-style clothes. At the time of the Xinhai Revolution, modernity and (Han Chinese) tradition were not seen as contradictory, but they became incompatible when Yuan revived the monarchy and replaced tradition with a new empire. Military uniforms served to reconcile this conflict. The Beijing government had a succession of ex-military presidents (Yuan Shikai, Li Yuanhong and Feng Guozhang) while in Guangdong, even Sun Yat-sen wore a military-style uniform (but later came to regret it; Epstein 1993). One of the reasons that military uniforms came to symbolize authority was the ongoing militarization of the nation following the fall of the Qing. The Qing dynasty, the revolutionaries and the constitutionalists were all supporters of soldier-citizens. The outbreak of the First World War further increased the need to create a militarized citizenry.

In September 1915, philosopher Chen Duxiu, who was a revolutionist at the end of the Qing dynasty and later co-founded the Chinese Communist Party, launched *Qingnian zazhi* (*Youth Magazine: La Jeunesse*; the title was changed to *Xin qingnian* (*New Youth*) in 1916). At the time, Chen had been estranged from political power following the failure of the Second Revolution. Just as Liang Qichao called for a reformation of the nation in *Discourse on the New Citizen* (*Xinmin shuo*) after the failure of the Hundred Days' Reform, Chen tried to achieve the remasculinization of the nation (which had been feminized by the acceptance of the Twenty-One Demands) by calling for the reform of the young people. Chen regarded the traditional ideal of the literati, which he saw as producing weak and pale students, as the main cause of the nation's problems and advocated 'animalism' in education.² Physical strength became a vital element of masculinity. For instance, a popularity contest among students at Hunan No. 1 Normal School used various criteria in three categories to evaluate contestants: moral (integrity, self-governance, diligence, self-restraint, prudence, service); physical (boldness, health, gymnastics, athleticism); and intellectual (ability, language, literature, science, art). It is notable that Western criteria such as health, sport and science were listed alongside Confucian morals. Incidentally, the highest-ranking student in 1917 was Mao Zedong (Li Rui 1993). In the same year, Mao published 'A study on physical education' (*Tiyu zhi yanjiu*) in the journal *Xin qingnian* (*New Youth*) (Uberoi 1995), in which he quoted 'Civilize one's spirit, barbarize one's body' from Cai E's 'On military citizens' (*Jun guomin pian*). Mao was strongly influenced by the militarized citizenry ideology.

Xin qingnian (*New Youth*) levelled criticisms at Confucianism which it viewed as the core of *wen* while advocating *wu*. It aspired to release people from the constraints of Confucian rules and build a society based on new human relationships by criticizing the three principles and five virtues including filiality and chastity; with regard to political questions, it argued against attempts to restore Manchu rule, as well as moves to make Confucianism a state religion. The 'new youth' was to be the new masculinity of the new society. It is noteworthy that *Xin qingnian* (*New Youth*) also supported a literary revolution, entailing the deconstruction of the traditional *wen* from a masculinity point of view. This was akin to Liang Qichao's proposal for the reform of fiction

Figure 10.2
Cabinet ministers of the Republic of China (almost uniformly dressed in black)
Source: Wang (2003: 93).

---

2 Chen Duxiu, 'Today's educational policy', *Qingnian zazhi* (*Youth Magazine*), 1(2); 'New youth', *Xin qingnian* (*New Youth*), 2(1).

and promotion of the practice of what he called the 'New Citizen style' in his writing.

Young people (men) put much effort into reforming the family around that time. Those who left their homes and lived in the city were faced with the issue of marriage. For them, an ideal family was a small family – a two-generation family – of a couple and their children united by a bond of love. The small family was supposed to contribute to social development and national strength by making individuals happy and increasing their productivity. However, even if the small family ideal was achieved, it would not directly lead to women's liberation as it did not change the conventional gender roles that assigned production to men and reproduction to women (Glosser 2003) (see Chapter Eleven).

Nevertheless, the proposed new family ethics brought changes to the ways of being a man and a woman and the relationship between them. To choose one's marriage partner, one needed to live in an environment that allowed men and women to meet freely. This gave rise to calls for the removal of restrictions on social intercourse. Modern public spaces such as parks, movie theaters and museums offered places where the previously segregated young men and women could get together (Hinsch 2013). A handful of universities, including Peking University, opened their doors to women. Libraries initially set aside women-only reading rooms or women-only days but eventually abolished them (Huang Shaoming 2007). Organizations and movements such as the New Citizen Academic Society of Mao Zedong's group, the Enlightenment Society of Zhou Enlai's group and the Diligent Work Frugal Study Movement were open to members of both sexes. Men's behavior changed in response to the presence of women and romance became a major matter of concern for young men.

The relationship between cities and rural areas was also changing on a fundamental level. The advance of capitalism widened the gap between cities and villages and the abolition of the civil service examination disrupted the circulation of human resources between urban and rural areas. Consequently, there was a one-way outflow of people and capital from villages to cities. The ascendancy of cities transformed masculinity. Confucian masculinity had been founded on rural values that respected harmony, but the urbanized capitalist society attached higher value to competition and material success and regarded traditional male virtues as worthless and unproductive. Successful businessmen became not only manly but also patriotic and sexually desirable (Hinsch 2013). The development of sports also reflected the new values that emphasized competition. The secretaries of the YMCA responsible for physical education made an effort to replace militaristic school physical exercises with more democratic sports (Takashima 2016a). Even some traditional martial arts were subjected to scientism (i.e., systematization, universalization, standardization), urbanization, modernization and internationalization and attempts were made to move away from their rural base and adapt to the urban environment (Morris 2004; Ching May-Bo 2012 [Japanese]; Takashima 2016b).

In China, the first YMCA was established in 1895, which coincided with the start of the reconstruction of Chinese masculinity. While the conventional Christian churches spread among the lower class and included many female parishioners, the YMCA comprised mostly urban middle-class men. The YMCA drew progressive Chinese men as the organization emphasized social reform rather than the salvation of individual souls. YMCA buildings were equipped with gymnasiums, showers and lecture rooms and hosted a variety of activities in addition to religion. The homosocial space created by the YMCA came to symbolize a new masculinity in modern cities (Dunch 2001).

While scholars were severed from the center of power and marginalized as mere intellectuals after the abolition of the civil service examination (Luo Zhitian 1999), the scholar-official tendency steadfastly persisted through modern times and manifested in the form of the popularity of liberal arts (especially law) among university students. For instance, 42% of students at Peking University majored in law in 1918 while 21% studied liberal arts and sciences respectively, and 4% engineering. The student ratio between liberal arts and science/technology was 2.5 to one.³ The influence of traditional education meant that students developed their knowledge centering on humanities (for example, Mao Zedong and literary historian/philosopher Hu Shi were inept at mathematics) and placed greater value on taking political responsibility while paying little attention to other forms of knowledge that more directly trained individuals for roles in contemporary society. The concentration of students in the military and political domains resulted in a mismatch between university graduates and the needs of society and not only created massive unemployment

---

3 Around the same period, the student ratio between liberal arts and science/technology at the Tokyo Imperial University was 1:1 (law 41%, medicine 16%, engineering 15%, literature 9%, science 5% and agriculture 13%) (Tokyo Teikoku Daigaku (ed.) 1919). The tendency of Chinese students to concentrate on humanities and social sciences continued through the 1920s; the number of students enrolled in those fields in 1931 was 9,511 as against 4,222 enrolled in science/technology. The science/technology courses gained more ground by securing 6,204 enrollments as against 5,430 in liberal arts in 1926 after the Nanjing government put greater emphasis on education and training in science and limited the number of liberal arts enrollments and courses. Still, the liberal arts have enjoyed an enduring popularity among the Chinese (Zhang Yumu 2005).

Chapter 10

but also impeded the development of versatile human resources that were essential for modernization (Zhu Zongzhen 2000).

During the three decades after the end of the Qing, 'science' was the only noun that drew broad support from all segments of society (Hu Shi 1923). Science was a masculine enterprise that enabled the remasculinization of the nation through increasing wealth and military power. Chen Duxiu and Hu Shi, who were flag-bearers for the New Culture Movement, pursued their respective brands of science. Hu Shi proposed the reorganization of national heritage in an attempt at the remasculinization of China through the scientific re-evaluation of previously derided traditions. Conversely, Chen Duxiu accepted Marxism, which presented an alternative path to China's remasculinization without submitting to the West or returning to tradition.

Germany's defeat in the First World War resulted in the decline of the soldier-citizen ideology. Clashes between warlords and a spate of internal insurrections damaged the reputation of the military, while the new school system that was established in 1922–23 substituted sports for military drill. The Japanese educational model was replaced with the American model with the aim of cultivating a spirit of democracy in Chinese citizens. However, this did not mean that the citizens were no longer required to have military capabilities. Cai Yuanpei, the president of Peking University, urged his students to receive military training while arguing for provincial autonomy and troop cuts in an effort to transition from the discredited central government with its armed forces to autonomous provincial governments with their own militias. Although the soldier-citizen ideology had lost its appeal, China was still groping for a new vision to replace it. Although various discourses of the May Fourth/New Culture Movement freed young people from tight-knit communities such as the family and the village, there was as yet no new nation to accept them, leading to much dysphoria among them. The 1923 debate on science and the philosophy of life among notable intellectuals took place in the context of this sense of loss of direction.

The Nationalist Party and the Communist Party: The age of *wu*

Domestic troubles and external threats did not permit China's young people to remain in this state of dysphoria for long, and many of them began to commit to new ideologies (Wang Fansen 2013). In particular, the May Thirtieth Incident in 1925 played a major role in emancipating youth from their state of unease to rally for nationalism. A national revolution driven by the Nationalist Party and the Chinese Communist Party became the receptacle for these young men. Members of the New Citizen Academic Society and the Enlightenment Society also tilted toward the Communist Party. For others, an 'academic and ideologist military organization', the Huangpu Military Academy, offered a new militaristic masculinity which was different from that of the warlords' forces (Wang Shih-Ying 2011; Takashima 2015a). As the National Revolutionary Army swept across China, peasants, workers and women broke out of their political alienation and participated in the national revolution. Now the 'individuals' were released from tradition and tied to the state as 'citizens'. Nevertheless, women's status was still lower than that of men, as exemplified by the priority given by the Nationalist government in Wuhan to the activities of the farmers' association over the women's association.

The Nationalist government began to advance nation-building in the face of internal struggles, conflict with the Communist Party and Japanese invasion. While the government strongly urged its citizens to make military contributions, (some sections of) its citizens expressed their desire to participate in nation-building through military contributions. One example was the introduction of military training to high schools and tertiary institutions in 1928. The government promulgated the Military Service Act in 1933 and imposed compulsory military service on men aged eighteen to forty-five and implemented training for conscription candidates for men other than students. Training for lower-school students was carried out through the boy scouts (*tongzijun*) (Takashima 2015a; Culp 2006). However, the Nanjing government did not have enough power to extend these measures to every corner of society.

Threats of Japanese invasion and conflicts with the Communist Party prompted the Nationalist Party to aim for its unique masculinity. According to Fukamachi Hideo, the New Life Movement was an attempt to create modern citizens through 'physical discipline' and 'formed part of social orchestration designed to cultivate diligent and fit soldiers and workers in order to maximize the military and economic potential of the nation-state' (Fukamachi 2013). It was another form of the soldier-citizen ideology which was intended to turn young Chinese men into 'tens of thousands of Chiang Kaisheks'. Women were required to make indirect contributions to the state through childbirth and child raising under this scheme. Commands such as 'Fasten buttons properly', 'Conduct business fairly' and 'Do not expectorate indiscriminately' were expressions of the new masculinity which were drawn from the history of physical reformation since the end of Qing and incorporated elements of Confucian tradition, Japanese military school practices and the social reform movement of the YMCA. Yet, this attempt to militarize and nationalize masculinity ended up as empty slogans. From the perspective of the relationship between *wen* and masculinity, it is curious to note that the campaigns for and against the revival of classical Chinese were mounted around the same time.

The Greater Shanghai Plan, which was promoted by the Nationalist government for the purpose of marginalizing the concessions governed by foreign powers, and the Nanjing Capital Plan for the creation of a new capital to replace Beijing were devices to set the stage for the masculinization of the nation. New buildings were constructed in a mixture of the traditional and modern styles according to the principles used in the design of the Zhongshan suit, named after Sun Yat-sen's courtesy name, as discussed below. While the Nationalist Party tried to turn the masculinity of urban modern men into a hegemonic masculinity, the Communist Party idealized the masculinity of workers and farmers. The Diligent Work Frugal Study Movement and the New Village Movement which were pursued at the time of the New Culture Movement were attempts to find a masculinity to replace *wen*. For the Communist Party that had taken up the challenge, workers and farmers were simultaneously the ideal of and the subject for liberation. The difference between the two parties is evident in their differing attitudes toward health. Health was a central issue for the New Life Movement whereas it was considered as 'bourgeois expression' in Yan'an. This difference was also a reflection of the different personality traits of their leaders (Chiang's fastidiousness and Mao's indifference to health). The Communist Party criticized tradition as feudalistic, but it had to accommodate the traditions of farmers in their support base. The exemplary figure embodying the ideal masculinity sought after by the Communist Party was called the 'principal graduate', drawing on the traditional term that had been used to designate the man who ranked first in the imperial examinations (*zhuangyuan*). The party thus used the traditional *wen* masculinity to enhance its own masculinity to facilitate political mobilization (Maruta 2013). On the other hand, inheritors of *wen* – students who moved from cities to Yan'an with the dream of national salvation – were classified as 'intellectuals' and subjected to political remolding; they had to try to learn to behave like farmers (Lei Sean Hsiang-Lin 2011).

Nevertheless, the Nationalist Party and the Communist Party had much in common. They both aimed for China's remasculinization through modernization. The Zhongshan suit, often referred to in the West as the 'Mao suit', was a visual representation of this. The suit was reportedly invented by Sun Yat-sen and adopted a unique non-Western, non-traditional style (Zhang Yu 2014). The use of domestically produced fabric was its only Chinese element, while the rest of the suit was barely distinguishable from Western garb if not for some minor elements. It was the very expression of Chinese modernity, or Westernization-modernization with some Chinese configurations made by the Chinese. We can also find overlap between it and Sun himself, who was a Chinese armed with Western cultural knowledge and deportment. The Zhongshan suit matched the image of a citizen idealized by both parties in that it symbolized discipline and loyalty rather than freedom and individualism. For this reason, increasing numbers of party members (of both parties), government officials and education workers who were required to be model citizens chose to wear the Zhongshan

Figure 10.3
Chiang Kaishek and Mao Zedong
(both dressed in the Zhongshan suit)
at the Peace Negotiation in Chongqing
Source: Wang (2003: 152).

suit. The suit was designed for men alone and this was not surprising in view of what 'citizens' referred to at the time.[4]

About 50,000 people entered military service in December 1936, marking the start of China's conscription. However, the Sino-Japanese War broke out in the following year and China had to fight the war before completing the militarization and nationalization of its masculinity. Consequently, it was extremely difficult to build up troop strength unlike in the case of Japan which was able to draft its citizens with draft notices printed on sheets of red paper. A strong fear of being labelled 'unpatriotic' compelled many young men to join the military in Japan whereas the label of 'Traitors to Han Chinese' (*Hanjian*) did not exert the same level of influence in China. Forcible measures such as kidnapping and bribery were often used to recruit Chinese soldiers (Sasagawa and Okumura 2007).

The war gave impetus to the militarization and nationalization of Chinese masculinity. As shown by Lydia Liu in her brilliant analysis of *A Place for Life and Death* by Xiao Hong, nationalism was a patriarchal ideology that qualified the fighting men as 'citizens-subjects' and allowed even an impoverished village man to acquire a new identity as a citizen-subject and enhance his masculinity by participating in the war against Japan (conversely, he would damage his masculinity if he was seen as a 'traitor to Han Chinese'). A lame man (hence lacking masculinity) called *Erliban* was no exception. On the other hand, widows in rural villages were left with only two options: to shed their female identity to participate in the war or to be objects of exploitation or rape. Unlike real men, however, women were unable to feel any enhancement of their status through connection with the state even if they participated in war. As Xiao claims, the sufferings of Chinese women were inflicted not only by the Japanese military but also by Chinese men (Liu 1995 [English]). Nationalism (and militarized and nationalized masculinity) was built upon the exploitation and control of women and the division of men (between citizens and traitors).

Finally, let us touch on the relationship between homosexuality and masculinity using Peking opera as an example. The male actors specializing in female roles, the '*dan*', often had homosexual relationships with the elite men who patronized them. The act of penetrating the *dan* boosted elite men's sense

---

4 The close resemblance between the Zhongshan suit and men's civilian uniform in wartime Japan was not coincidental. While the Zhongshan suit had no female equivalent, Japan had a few designs of standard women's clothing (Inoue 2001). In both China and Japan, women were excluded from 'citizens' even in terms of clothing.

of masculinity. The popularity of the *dan* coincided with the rise of Peking opera from the end of the eighteenth century to the early nineteenth century. However, China's crises from the end of the nineteenth century and the importation of sexual morality and the concept of homosexuality from the West turned male homosexuality into an unmanly practice and a national embarrassment. Ba Jin portrayed his grandfather who was enamored with a *dan* despite being a strict moralist. To his Westernized sensibility, his grandfather's behavior felt contradictory.

Mei Lanfang, one of the most famous *dan* actors of the twentieth century, endeavored to maintain the separation of his artistic feminine persona on stage and his image as a masculine, heterosexual modern citizen with social status outside the theater. To construct a strong nation, all Chinese men, including *dan* actors, had to be manly. Following the occupation of Hong Kong by the Japanese military, Mei grew a moustache while he was there. He would have understood the meaning of playing a feminine role under the Japanese occupation. After Japan's defeat, Mei immediately shaved off his moustache and returned to the stage (Hinsch 1990; Kang 2009 [English]; Vitiello 2011) (see Column Six).

Conclusion

China's defeat in the First Sino-Japanese War made Chinese intellectuals keenly aware of the loss of masculinity, and the remasculinization of feminized China became the central issue for modern China. As China grappled with this issue, the traditional masculinity comprised of *wen* and *wu* was restructured and the relative importance of *wen* over *wu* was reversed. Although modern Chinese intellectuals consistently pursued the ideal of a soldier-citizen type nation-state (Onodera 2011: 328), their efforts did not lead to the establishment of a hegemonic position for *wu* as a modern militaristic masculinity. There was no clear form of nation that people could identify with or pledge their loyalty to. China was crowded with powers that asserted their own brands of masculinity, including the Nationalist Party, the Communist Party and many warlords. Moreover, China had to deal with external pressure from imperialist nations. Their colonies such as India and Vietnam configured their masculinities in ways to countervail the masculinities of their suzerain states. On the other hand, semi-colonial China which pursued a number of different goals had difficulty building a specifically

Chapter 10

Chinese masculinity to rival Western modernity due to a lack of clarity about the differences between them (Takashima 2016b).

Nevertheless, there is no doubt that China's masculinity evolved around the rebuilding of *wen* and *wu*. Mao Zedong tried to fill China with his clones through the Red Guards. The Red Guards were mere shadows of the soldier-citizens because they were born out of the process of personal power struggles rather than a sincere effort to build a nation. While Mao deprived China's intellectuals of *wen*, he tried to monopolize *wen* by creating his own verses and calligraphy. Moreover, he downgraded the authority of *wen* by praising the *wu* of farmers and workers and at the same time reinforced his own *wu* as their leader. After the founding of the communist state, Mao often publicized images of himself swimming in order to emphasize his *wu* as well as his relatability. Mao reigned over China as a figure equipped with cultural and martial accomplishments just like the emperors before him. The enthusiasm for swimming and sports shown by China's successive leaders after Mao seems to confirm that the *wen-wu* masculinity continues to maintain its effectiveness in China.

11. Discourses on the Family, Love and Sex in Modern China

— EGAMI Sachiko

Introduction

A flurry of active discussions about the family took place in China from the end of the Qing dynasty to the 1920s. Reasons behind this phenomenon included the country's existential crisis after the Opium War, the transition from a family-based small farming economy to a modern economic structure, the diminished authority of Confucianism and the influx of Western culture (Lin Jiling 1999; Li Guimei 2008). In the context of the urgent need for national salvation at the end of Qing, family reform was called for to provide a foundation for national reform while various flaws arising from the 'traditional family system' (see Chapter Six) were highlighted and women were expected to assume new roles in this family reform initiative. These debates reached a peak over the period from the Xinhai Revolution to the May Fourth/New Culture Movement. A number of visions were proposed for the new family that would support China's modern nation-building endeavor, sparking active debates on women's liberation, marriage, romance and sexual morality (see Chapter Thirteen).

A considerable number of studies on these discussions have generally offered praise for the arguments that contributed to the fall of the 'traditional family system' and the construction of the 'modern family system'. In this chapter, I review the results of these studies and shed light on the arguments that were largely overlooked. There is a need to reassess the arguments that opposed the 'modern family'[1] ideology that prevailed in Western nations and

---

1 See Note 9 in the 'Preface' by Kohama Masako.

Chapter 11

Japan and became the main prototype of the new family as the 'small family' in the formative phase of post-May Fourth China. Reassessing these arguments can illuminate the views of modern elites on the state, society and gender/sexuality and help us find a way to reform the 'modern family' ideology that has so far failed to resolve gender disparity, despite various efforts made on this front.

The first section provides an overview of the debates about the disintegration of the traditional family system and construction of a modern family system from late Qing to the 1920s. The second part looks at widespread objections to the modern family ideology, especially those voiced by women during the 1920s. The discussion then turns to ideas about the abolition of the institution of marriage raised shortly before the Xinhai Revolution and introduces relevant arguments, mainly from the 1920s, using historical sources. Despite being the most conspicuous objection to the modern family ideology, the argument for the abolition of the marriage system has received scant attention thus far, and the third part of this chapter aims to fill this gap.

Discussions about the old and new family systems

Criticism of the traditional family system

Various criticisms were repeatedly raised regarding the traditional family system from the end of Qing to the 1920s. Although the point of contention changed over time and in accordance with different perspectives, the following were commonly pointed out as the main problems.

Firstly, criticisms were levelled at arranged marriage (where a marriage was organized by the parents of a man and a woman who had never met), polygamy, concubinage, bride-buying, early marriage, cumbersome rituals and the involvement of matchmakers. It was argued that these types of marriage denied a person's value, restricted personal freedom and hindered the development of individuality. Moreover, it was claimed that the goal of family reform was a political revolution because marriage made people dependent, frustrated economic independence, stymied the nation's economic development and underpinned autocratic governance (Chang Yu-Fa 1992; Liang Jinghe 1994, 1998, 2011; Chen Wenlian and Li Guimei 2003).

Another point of contention was that the traditional family system was an agnate system that prioritized male heirs and deprived women of their human rights, inheritance rights and freedom to divorce while the concept of 'chastity' continued to oppress them. Critics called for a rejection of the Confucian order and morality at the root of male chauvinism (Shen Shaogen and Yang Sanping 1999; Li Guimei 2008).

Calls for a modern family system

These criticisms prompted a search for a modern family system that led to the development of four main propositions. The first was to modify the traditional family relationship and lifestyle while retaining some positive elements of China's traditional family system.[2] The second proposal advocated for the 'small family', living in a separate dwelling and with separate property, to replace China's traditional 'large family'. The third plan supported the 'small family' idea but argued that such reform would be achieved as part of broader social reform, i.e., the dismantling of private ownership and the class system. The fourth proposal rejected even the 'small family' and advocated for the abolition of marriage and family altogether. The second proposal gained mainstream acceptance at the time, while the first tended to draw negative comments even though it incorporated changes such as equality between family members, personal independence and the discontinuation of extravagant spending. Many scholars in mainland China considered the third proposal to be the 'correct' idea, and this view continues to hold sway even today. The fourth proposal has largely been seen as a biased and puerile utopian vision, a view that is also evident in recent publications (Liang Jinghe 1991, 2009; Chen Wenlian and Li Guimei 2003).

The prevailing view of the 'small family' system outlined in the second proposal can be generally summarized as follows: the small family comprises a husband and a wife, who married according to their own will based on love, and their unmarried children; faithfulness is required of the husband and the wife equally and freedom of divorce and remarriage is afforded to both equally as well; the family is not governed autocratically by the patriarch; family members are equal and the husband and wife share the burden of caring for the young and the elderly; women are not the private property of men and the wife

---

2 According to Olga Lang (1946), Pan Guangdan was the leading advocate of this idea.

must be independent rather than dependent on her husband and therefore needs economic independence. Along with the proposed small family system came the abolition of footbinding, the introduction of school education for women and opportunities for social intercourse between men and women. Calls for women's legal rights, suffrage and employment also increased. These changes have been highly regarded to this day for laying a foundation of morals and ethics grounded in liberty and equality centering on 'love' as well as for promoting women's liberation and individual freedom (Chang Yu-fa 1992; Shen Shaogen and Yang Sanping 1999; Chen Wenlian and Li Guimei 2003).

The 'small family' proposal certainly emancipated women from the constraints of the traditional family system in certain respects. The arguments put forward by modern elite men formed the foundation for some of the achievements of the women's liberation movement in the 1930s: legislation banning 'new concubinage', applying the offence of adultery equally to men and women and giving women inheritance rights. However, the small family system did not entail 'equality for men and women'. Tai Guangdian and Bao Zhen argued that the 'new family' was a 'small family' comprising 'a father, a mother and children' and 'marriage is formed on the basis of love between a man and a woman'. Unlike the traditional 'large family' in which the master of the house 'limits the freedom of his progeny', the small family offers 'equality' to its members and the father 'represents the family' while the mother 'is in charge of domestic affairs' (Tai Guangdian and Bao Zhen 1921). In other words, the small family system shared many features with the aforementioned 'modern family' ideology that advocated for the image of a woman as a 'new wise wife and good mother' with emphasis on 'maternal love' and the 'mission' of home management and childrearing.

Women's new role in 'helping the husband and educating children' was proposed as early as late Qing China as it was supposedly modelled on the 'good wife and wise mother' ideology of Meiji Japan. While the woman's role in the small family is often prefixed with 'new' to distinguish it from the late Qing 'wise wife and good mother' in the traditional family system, it failed to redress China's traditional gender role norm of 'Men work outside, women work inside'. This type of small family system entrenches a system of gender roles that assigns 'the public domain to men, the family domain to women' and at the same time prescribes that 'the husband governs the family' and ranks the wife below him (Egami 2013).

Discussions on love and sex in relation to the small family system

Along with the proposal for the small family system, there were active discussions about love and sex as its preconditions. It has often been argued that the propositions considered at that time led to women's liberation in China (Egami 2014). Firstly, in the 'chastity debate' of 1918–19, criticisms were raised against the imposition of the chastity rule on women while men were allowed to be sexually 'loose'. It was also argued that sexual desire and marriage without love was immoral and that the 'unification of spirit and flesh' connecting chastity and love was needed. It is of great significance that the debate led to the rejection of the loveless marriage and the inequality of sexual morality between men and women. On the other hand, it also resulted in an overemphasis on the spiritual side of love which turned love-based fidelity into a moral principle as well as on the view that romantic love should lead to marriage. These became new norms that in some sense gave rise to new constraints. Next came the 'discussion on love' of 1922–23, which argued that romantic love was neither immoral nor mysterious, that true romantic love was spiritually sublime and that the goal of heterosexual relationships was the preservation of the species. As romantic love-based marriage fit the purpose of the evolution of the species and the science of eugenics (see Chapter Nine), sexual relationships in the absence of romantic love violated the fidelity principle and morals.

A debate known as the 'sex education debate' broke out in 1923, focusing on the claim that there had not been sufficient discussion on the 'flesh' when the 'unification of spirit and flesh' was postulated in the previous debate. It was argued that sexual desire was natural, not immoral, and it was wrong to suppress or hide it. However, this had not been well understood in China and the male-centered oppression of female sexuality had been rife. Consequently, sex education was needed in order to prevent the adverse effects of promiscuity and abstinence. Unlike prurience, the notion of 'romantic love' was sacred and respected the partner's personality. Marriage for money or status is not romantic love, which should be a spiritual and carnal love. Still, spirit was given precedence over flesh despite the legitimacy afforded to sexual desire as it was argued that sexual desire should be humanized, sanctified and spiritualized into noble and pure love. Although there was some attention on sexuality at that point, the debate gave greater importance to the state and species than individuals and continued to neglect sexual diversity.

By the mid-1920s, the 'new sexual morality debate' (1925) emerged, calling into question some of the preceding arguments. The editors of *Funü zazhi* (*Ladies' Journal*) asserted that 'A polyfidelitous form of marriage between, say, one husband and two wives or two husbands and one wife consented to by all spouses cannot be regarded as immoral as long as it does no harm to society or other individuals' and that men 'should pay attention to their partner's desires and ensure she gains complete satisfaction'. This newly emerged view giving approval to romantic love and sexual relationships that would not lead to marriage received more censure than support at the time. Many in China still believe that this argument was too progressive for its time.

Around the same time, an argument put forward by Zhang Jingsheng sparked a 'discussion on the rules of love' (1923) and the 'debate on *Sex Histories*' (1926). Zhang proposed that love was chosen on the basis of criteria such as feelings, personality, ability, appearance, honor and wealth; love could change over time and the love between a married couple should evolve through mutual encouragement and betterment. Zhang's argument was severely criticized by modern elite men and was for many years cast aside as being immoral, a view which was not reassessed until the end of the twentieth century. Zhang's proposal had been meant as a warning that the over-sanctification of romantic love would create a new form of constraint, i.e., a modern form of the chastity rule. Yet, it received an overwhelmingly negative reaction and critics largely argued that love was noble, pure and unconditional.

Zhang Jingsheng wrote *A Way of Life Based on Beauty* (*Mei de rensheng guan*) (1925) and *Sex Histories* (*Xingshi*) (1926) in an attempt to deepen the discussion on sexuality. He asserted the importance of spiritual and physical 'sexual pleasure' over sexual intercourse 'for reproduction' and opposed men's promiscuity and forcible intercourse. He stressed the importance of women's sexual satisfaction as well as their independence in sexual conduct and proposed specific means to achieve it. Zhang contended that the marriage system oppressed women and would eventually transition to a 'lover system' when women gained social status, and that the criterion for the union of a man and a woman was 'affection' and hence there was no need to tie partners down with marriage (Egami 2014).

Women's objections to the 'modern family' ideology

Chinese students in Japan at the end of Qing

As noted above, criticisms of the traditional family institution and the new role of the 'wise wife and good mother' who 'helped her husband and educated her children' were proposed in late Qing China before the discussions on the 'small family' system took place and before the 'new wise wife and good mother' concept was proffered.

In the midst of this shift, Yan Bin and other Chinese women who were studying in Meiji Japan voiced their opposition toward 'good wife and faithful lady' education and raised their demands for the equality of education for men and women in all fields including the military, law and industry and for equal participation in politics. The voices of these female students eventually led to Gao Susu's rejection of the 'wise wife and good mother' concept as well as the development of the women's suffrage movement driven by Tang Qunying and others in the early days of Republican China. Despite the strong demands of women, the Provisional Constitution at the time of the founding of the Republic of China in 1912 did not provide for equality between men and women, or women's suffrage or monogamy (Suetsugu 2009: 33–36; Egami 2013; Xia Xiaohong 2014).

Arguments for unmarried life

In the love debate of 1922–23 discussed above, one of the participants, Fengzi, was a leading advocate for singlehood. She argued that people did not live for romantic love alone and that they should have the freedom to become involved in romantic relationships or to remain single. Marriage was the root of all evil because when people married, had a family and owned private property, women became private property as their father's daughter, their husband's wife and their son's mother. Whether it was romantic love due to sexual or spiritual desire, the emphasis on romantic love would trap women in a doll's house. Fengzi claimed that her idea of 'freedom of romantic love' emphasized freedom rather than romantic love and so she opposed matrimonial union. She also related her own experience of a difficult divorce involving numerous court actions in her essay 'My divorce' published during the same period.

However, Fengzi's argument failed to win support and her critics rejected her interpretation of the 'freedom of romantic love' as an error. They maintained that the 'freedom of romantic love' was a spiritual and carnal unification of a man and a woman by their own 'free will' and marriage through romantic love could not be the 'root of all evil'. Once romantic love was established, the husband and wife should remain a couple until their romantic love failed; romantic love with a third party was not permissible and the couple should have a family and take responsibility for their children. Fengzi's critics argued that her idea was incorrect because singlehood was different from the freedom of romantic love. She insisted on a woman's freedom to stay unmarried and her right to make decisions, based on her own painful experience, and her arguments served as a criticism of the small family system that sanctioned the superior-inferior relationship between men and women on the premise of love. Her name has been all but forgotten by subsequent generations in China (Egami 2014).

Zhang Ruoming, a member of the Tianjin Awakening Society, was another supporter of the right to be single, stating that 'True advocacy for "women's liberation" would need someone who dedicated her life to it [...] and it would be most appropriate for those in the vanguard of "women's liberation" to pursue singlehood' (Zhang Ruoming 1920). A considerable number of women chose to stay unmarried to avoid marriage-related constraints or to strive for women's liberation at the time. For example, only 16% of the 105 graduates of Ginling Women's College from 1919 to 1927 got married. The proportion of unmarried women was higher among women with higher education. This phenomenon fomented controversy as a 'troublesome trend', with prevailing opinions in the press asserting 'Women should not be stubborn about staying unmarried. [...] those who wish to stay single should do so after discharging their childbirth responsibility' and 'Singlehood not only makes society imperfect but also makes individuals imperfect' (Yu Ping 2010 [Japanese]: 188–196).

From the works of women writers

Even in the 1920s, women's opinions tended to be disregarded by the world of commentators. Under these circumstances, it was in the fictional world of novels that women were able to express their gender-related pain and suffering. Male authors wrote novels about the problems of the small family system, including *Aching for the Departed* and *Ni Huanzhi*, many of which depicted the wife's 'backwardness' from the husband's viewpoint. Among the works of female authors, on the other hand, *Separation* (1924) by Feng Yuanjun voiced an objection to the mythologization of 'maternal love' from a daughter's perspective.

The novels that followed depicted the suspicion, anguish and dissent harbored by women toward the role of 'new wise wife and good mother' who had built their 'small family' through love-based marriage. Many of the women writers had received higher education at institutions such as Beijing Women's Higher Normal School and Yenching University and pursued the ideas of spiritual freedom, personal independence, the disintegration of marriage traditions, sacred love, gender equality and social activism. Once they had fulfilled their love according to their free will, they inevitably became trapped in the family, failed to keep their ideals alive and fell 'behind the times'. The first novel that dealt with this subject was *Old Friends from the Seaside* (1923) by Lu Yin which described a sense of anxiety, grief and emptiness about the loss of a network of female school friends after marriage. She later depicted the regrets, frustrations and loneliness of the wife in a small family in *After Victory* (1925) and other works. Although Lu Yin's novels won the hearts of young readers with their boldness and frankness, they were harshly received by literary circles for 'the narrowness of the subject' and 'trifling with life'.

In *Question of Rogers* (1924) by Chen Hengzhe, China's first female professor at Peking University, the heroine broke off her engagement with her romantic partner out of fear that the burdens of home and childrearing duties would adversely affect her academic life. However, Chen had conflicted feelings because of the importance of the mother's role and wrote a work about a widow who gave up a new love for the sake of her child. Chen Ying wrote about the woman's role with an even more incisive pen. The wife in *After the Wedding Reception* (1929) experienced a sense of hopelessness when she realized that her husband still acted in an old-fashioned manner in their small family. The heroines in *Old Friends* (1934) reunited with their old friends as married women and lamented that 'The family is a graveyard for women'. They confessed that 'Marriage does not pose an obstacle to men, but it holds women in bondage, stops them from speaking up and corrodes their minds until they feel dead'. The women, who had once pursued ideals side by side with modern elite men, were marginalized again and these works also missed out on accolades for many years (Shirouzu 2001, 2003; Egami 2013).

Ding Ling expressed her confusion about the love and sex that underpinned the small family. She portrayed women who agonized over their sexuality as well as gender in her early works, including *Miss Sophie's Diary* (1928). She raised questions from a women's point of view about equality between men and women and 'sacred' love and sex, which were used as the new basis for marriage in the May Fourth era theories of the 'unification of spirit and flesh'. She examined 'female sex', boldly described women's sexual desires, asserted women's independence in sexual intercourse and approved of romantic love and sexual relations that would not lead to marriage. Although her works were highly rated by literary circles at the time, Ding Ling was later criticized and purged as a 'writer who dallied with men' (Egami 2014).

Rejection of the 'family faction' women

As calls for the 'small family' system increased, the wife's economic independence became the most controversial issue. In China, the acquisition of economic power by women had been considered important since the end of Qing when the 'wise wife and good mother' idea was promoted. The 1920s saw greater demands for women's economic independence in addition to being a 'new wise wife and good mother' (see Chapter Twelve). A strong push for 'career women' came from women as well. Xiang Jingyu, Head of the Communist Women's Bureau, nominated the 'small family faction' as one of the 'three factions of Chinese intellectual women' and described their idea that the gender norms were a graveyard where women were buried alive forever. She saw higher value in the 'career women faction' (Xiang Jingyu 1923). However, career opportunities for women were limited at the time, while increasing numbers of women received intermediate education in China. It was extremely difficult to balance life as a career woman with a small family. Many men demanded that their wife be a 'new wise wife and good mother' while criticizing their economic dependence as 'parasitic'. The move to ask the 'new wise wife and good mother' to also have a career was a revision of the 'modern family' ideology observed in China and something that did not occur in Japan. While it placed a double burden on women, their inability to balance their work and family was used as justification for their inferior status. Tan Sheying, a GMD-feminist activist, hit back at this unfair position by stating that women were saddled with 'family responsibility' and given fewer employment opportunities compared with their male counterparts (Egami 2013).

Against this background, an increase in the number of so-called 'modern girls' became a social problem from the mid-1920s to the mid-1930s. They were met with criticism from all quarters of society for desiring freedom and material/sexual fulfillment, pursuing 'love is everything'-ism and shunning even a new system of marriage (see Chapter Nine). However, a large section of those who were regarded as modern girls were women who deviated from the 'modern family' ideology in that they were highly educated and valued the individual's freedom, independence and sexuality more than the state or the family. Xiang Jingyu called them the 'romanticists faction' and hoped that they could become 'a vanguard of women's liberation and social reform' if awakened.

On the other hand, *Funü gongming* (*Women's Sympathetic Understanding*) magazine, edited by Tan Sheying and others, called 'modern girls' an 'impediment to women's movements' and asked women to value motherhood and the nation while proposing the concept of 'new wise husband and good father'. This proposition was based on the argument that both men and women should play roles in the family and participate in society at the same time. In this sense, it was another revision of the 'modern family' ideology. However, it hardly received any support and in fact drew severe criticism from communists claiming that it was a 'reactionary' opinion arguing for 'Women's return to the home' (Egami 2007). This criticism still persists in present-day China (Zhonghua quanguo funü lianhehui 1989: 341).

In the mid-1930s, as international tensions that would lead to the Sino-Japanese War increased, discourse surrounding the small family and the new wise wife and good mother ideology transmuted into one dominated by nationalism (see Chapter Nine).

The argument for the abolition of the marriage institution

Anarchists in the Xinhai Revolution era

Shortly before the Xinhai Revolution, Chinese anarchists based in Tokyo and Paris put forward an argument for the abolition of the family/marriage in their magazines *Tianyi bao* (*Natural Justice*) and *Xin shiji* (*New Century*) (both launched in 1907). They asserted that 'The family is the worst of all evils which makes people selfish, allows men to shackle women on a daily basis and creates useless and harmful little problems', 'puts child raising on the shoulders of a woman alone although it is supposed to be the responsibility of the whole community', and hence, 'When the family is destroyed, human beings become citizens and private individuals disappear, extinguishing any reasons for men to abuse women'. They posited that 'social revolution' would start with 'the destruction of the family' and claimed that 'The family was established on the basis of coercive power rooted in the system of private property rather than spontaneously occurring according to human physiology' and therefore it was the 'fruit of autocracy' and a 'burden on society'. They asserted that women's 'economic independence' through the 'dissemination of education' would spare them from 'oppression by men' and 'the family revolution' would be needed because 'otherwise the family would privatize education'.[3]

They also made more specific recommendations: 'The conjugal relationship should be abolished first' because 'The marital home is a prison of inequality'; both men and women should enjoy a limited amount of sexual intercourse in a pleasant environment; and facilities such as 'nursery schools', 'aged-care homes' and 'leisure centers for young men and women' should be provided.[4] Another argument claimed that 'Human beings are inherently equal' and require 'independence' and 'benevolence', and therefore they should destroy the institution of marriage and provide occasions and places where men and women could gather according to their emotional needs as well as 'mutual societies' to offer care during childbirth, aging, sickness and death and charitable enterprises including maternity hospitals, convalescent hospitals, old people's homes, nursery schools and kindergartens.[5]

One of the central figures in this movement, Liu Shifu, argued that 'The marriage system is a tool for the strong to oppress the weak' and that the burdens of childbirth and childrearing adversely affected women's economic potential and contributed to their oppression by men. Moreover, the reality of 'monogamy' was 'unequal' and even 'women in the West' were 'men's playthings'. He advocated for 'free love' (i.e., based on love and physiology rather than

---

3 See the articles on the abolition of the marriage system written by Hanyi in *Tianyi bao* (*Natural Justice*), 4 (1907) (Zhang Nan and Wang Renzhi 1963), and 'Family and education' in 11 and 12 (1907) (Zhonghua quanguo funü lianhehui funü yundong lishi yanjiushi 1991a).

4 See the article on the abolition of the marriage system written by Gao Yabin in *Tianyi bao* (*Natural Justice*), 11 and 12 (1907) (Zhonghua quanguo funü lianhehui funü yundong lishi yanjiushi 1991a).

5 See the article on the abolition of the marriage system written by Jupu in *Xin shiji* (*New Century*), 49 (1908) (Zhang Nan and Wang Renzhi 1977).

money or coercive power; sexual intercourse according to the free will of a man and woman for their mutual pleasure, not by coercion) because love was the only thing needed for the union of a man and woman and the marriage system and related laws had nothing to do with love. Liu argued that 'The family should be abolished first' because the existence of the family was 'an impediment for progress' that made people 'lose their independent personalities' and 'only care about their private property' as 'The world evolution would soon extinguish borders between countries and races'. In his view, the family would become obsolete if 'Father and son and men and women were equal' and people were 'independent and free' in the 'evolution of happiness' (Liu Shifu 1912).

These anarchists claimed that the family system should be abolished because it had a wide range of negative effects, including oppressing women and the weak, damaging people's personalities and producing harmful trivialities. They attempted not only to reject the traditional family system but also to overcome the 'modern' one while advocating for the need for women's education and economic independence. They offered specific recommendations for the purpose of improving marital relations and replacing the family function and pre-emptively put forward the arguments about love and sex described above. Unlike the nationalists who sought 'the wealth and power of the state', the anarchists proposed 'social revolution' involving the rejection of capitalism's system of private ownership. Their ideas were unique in many aspects (Nakayama 1983: 98–107; Saga 2001: 120–127). However, for a very long time they were viewed as 'childish dreams', 'unrealistic' and 'absolute fantasies' (Liang Jinghe 1994; Zhonghua quanguo funü lianhehui 1989: 46; Li Guimei 2008) until a reassessment finally began in the 2010s (Liu Renfeng 2012; Liu Huiying and Chen Yangu 2012).

He-Yin Zhen, one of the leading female anarchists, edited and published *Tianyi bao* (*Natural Justice*), the journal of the Women's Rights Recovery Association in Tokyo. While the movement had been seen in Japan as a form of 'women's lib that suddenly appeared in late Qing Chinese society', He-Yin Zhen drew little attention in China until the beginning of the twenty-first century (Ono 1978: 96; Liu Huiying 2006; Xia Xiaohong 2006). However, it has been pointed out that He-Yin's argument differed from those of male anarchists as she herself did not propose the abolition of the family. Her argument about the family featured the following points. Firstly, she sought 'absolute equality' between men and women and supported the use of 'violent' means towards men for that purpose. He-Yin insisted on monogamy, denounced 'promiscuity' and even suggested that marriage should only be between two people who have never been married before while remarriage should be between two people who have been previously married. She took a cautious stance on sexual freedom and emphasized equality more than 'freedom of marriage'. She also proposed that the wife should not take the husband's family name and children should take the family names of both their father and mother but that family names should be abolished after an anarchist revolution (He-Yin Zhen 1907a; Xia Xiaohong 2006; Zarrow 1988).[6]

He-Yin did not argue for women's employment and suffrage. She explained that the recent proposition for women's 'occupational independence' would merely serve society 'monopolized by a small number of wealthy people' and that even if a handful of women were elected to congress, it would only bring 'unfair class discrimination into women's society' as far as lower-class women were concerned. She dismissed the women's liberation movement of the time as 'the product of men's self-interest and greed' and argued that 'Men pushed women into toil and trouble day after day' even though they claimed to give women 'independence' and 'civilization'. He-Yin expressed her disappointment at the state of gender equality in the West and claimed that it was only 'false freedom and false equality'. She was also critical of men's advocacy for women's education, claiming that men wished that 'civilized women' would take charge of 'family management' and 'children's education' in place of 'uncultivated women' (He-Yin Zhen 1907b; Xia Xiaohong 2006). A similar criticism is found in 'Problems in women's education' by Zhida in *Tianyi bao* (*Natural Justice*), Vols. 13–14 (1907), which states 'women's education of late' turns women into 'slaves to the nation' by encouraging them to be 'patriots' as well as 'slaves to the family' by telling them to 'help the husband and educate children' (Xia Xiaohong 2006; Liu Huiying and Chen Yangu 2012). These criticisms of women's education and the aforementioned rejection of the 'wise wife and good mother' ideology by women have something in common.

The difference between the arguments made by male anarchists and those by He-Yin was that the former stressed the ideal of abolishing the private ownership system and tended to raise women's issues in order to free themselves from the shackles of the family whereas He-Yin prioritized women's

---

6 See also 'The Women's Rights Recovery Association General Regulations' in *Tianyi bao* (*Natural Justice*), 1, 8–10 (1907).

interests in dealing with the actual problems that they encountered (Liu Huiying 2006, 2013; Liu Huiying and Chen Yangu 2012). Another study has pointed out that He-Yin's uniqueness lies in her emphasis on taking the power to oppress women away from men rather than 'giving women rights/power equal to men', distinguishing her from many other women's rights advocates (Song Shaopeng 2016b). There was a general tendency to propose feminism as part of nationalism at the time, but He-Yin stressed the distinction between them (Zarrow 1988). He-Yin's observation that 'Men's dominance over women would not disappear even in modern capitalist society' has been recognized as 'significant' in Japan while her ideas have been receiving attention in the U.S. in recent years (Suetsugu 2009: 56–57; Liu, Karl and Ko 2013).

The argument for the abolition of the marriage system in the 1920s

Anarchist organizations and publications numbered over seventy each in the May Fourth/New Culture Movement period due to the influence of Liu Shifu (Liang Jinghe 1999). In the first half of the 1920s, the argument for the abolition of the marriage system regained strength amid the active discussions on the family, love and sex as well as propositions for the small family and the new wise wife and good mother ideology described above. While the arguments during the Xinhai Revolution period had been put forward by a limited number of Chinese nationals living overseas, this time the issues were debated by a much larger number of people within the country. Let us look at the early 1920s argument for the abolition of the marriage system with a focus on the difference between these discussions and those of the Xinhai-era.

In 1919, the abolition of the family was proposed in *Xin qingnian* (*New Youth*) and *Xingqi pinglun* (*Weekly Review*). In 1920, a 'debate on the marriage system abolition issue' was initiated in *Juewu* (*Awakening*), a supplement of *Minguo ribao* (*Republican Daily News*), and attracted widespread attention. This debate involved the proposal for the abolition of the marriage system made by Ma Zhemin and dozens of articles for and against the argument in response. Ma made the proposal on the grounds that inequality between husband and wife made the dissolution of marriage difficult in reality, even though marriage was supposedly free and could be dissolved if either spouse was dissatisfied.[7] Around the same period, debates took place in other publications such as *Shaonian Zhongguo* (*Young China*), *Jiating yanjiu* (*Family Studies*) and *Funü zazhi* (*Ladies' Journal*). The main points of these arguments can be summarized as follows, although there are some ambiguities due to varying definitions of common terms such as 'free love' and 'economic system reform' in the debates.

The most fundamental question was whether the small family was a satisfactory model. The opponents of the abolition of marriage argued that when 'a man-woman couple' 'developed affection for one another through companionship' that developed into love and married 'by mutual consent', such a marriage would not constitute 'unfreedom'; and that there was nothing better than this 'free marriage' at present and those who did not want it should choose to stay unmarried.[8] Some acknowledged the 'ills' of the family institution and went on to argue that there should be a change from large to small families because it would be difficult to abolish marriage and it would become less restrictive once 'men and women have education and careers' (Lin Zhensheng 1920). On the other hand, abolition proponents argued that the monogamous small family based on free marriage would still restrict freedom in two main areas as follows. One was a restriction on women's freedom – many articles referred to this problem and contended that even the small family still kept 'men outside and women inside' and held on to the wise wife and good mother ideology, preventing women's independence and entry into society.[9] The most specific and pointed argument was put forward by Xiang Jingyu who insisted that gaining the rights to vote and inherit property were not sufficient to achieve women's liberation. Xiang wrote:

> The family is still headed by a man who leaves most of the family matters to a woman to deal with according to his instructions while he works for

---

7 Ma Zhemin's proposal was published in *Juewu, Minguo ribao* (*Awakening, Republican Daily News*) on 8 May 1920. According to Liang Jinghe (1999), 'The debate on the marriage system abolition issue' took place in May and June 1920 with fifty to sixty articles contributed by over twenty people, mostly published in *Juewu, Minguo ribao* (*Awakening, Republican Daily News*).

8 See the article written by Xiaofo as part of 'The debate on the marriage system abolition issue' in *Juewu, Minguo ribao* (*Awakening, Republican Daily News*) dated 22 May 1920.

9 See the article written by Li Chuo as part of 'The debate on the marriage system abolition issue' in *Juewu, Minguo ribao* (*Awakening, Republican Daily News*) dated 26 May 1920. See also Li Chuo (1920), Chen Dezheng (1921) and Yi Jiayue (1921).

society, so the woman works for her family as if she is commissioned by her husband [...] to perform many miscellaneous tasks, including taking care of her home, the aged and the young, [...] the reality of the small family is no different from that in the traditional family, [...] and the small family proponents are simply trying to send women into a new enclosure. [...] The tasks of taking care of food, clothing, housing, the aged and the young are necessities for the family, [...] and even if a woman is competent all around, she is forced to reduce her activity in society. [...] Women will never be liberated unless the family system is completely destroyed. (Xiang Jingyu 1920)

The second area of restriction was related to 'true love' and 'legitimate sexual desire'. The abolitionists argued as follows: romantic love that would not lead to marriage was not regarded as 'legitimate' or 'sacred'; love could be 'transient' but a 'constraint' in the form of remaining 'monogamous would arise' once a couple was married; people were supposed to have 'freedom to divorce' once love evaporated, but it was actually difficult to do so; those who stay in a loveless marriage would miss out on legitimate 'sexual satisfaction' while those who choose to stay unmarried would also miss out on sexual satisfaction.[10] Thus, the abolition proponents considered that there should be more freedom in the way men and women conducted their romantic relationships and thus they supported the 'free love' proposed by Liu Shifu. They further argued that the large family should be destroyed but even the small family could place constraints on love and sexuality; that many problems were being experienced by the family system in the West as well; that family reform should be furthered by the abolition of the marriage system and the removal of the titles of husband and wife; that the oppression of women would decrease and 'true love' would be easier to achieve; and that the 'free union' between a man and a woman should not need 'legal' protection and the family could be formed in various 'configurations' with 'flexibility'.[11]

---

10 See the articles written as part of 'The debate on the marriage system abolition issue' in *Juewu, Minguo ribao* (*Awakening, Republican Daily News*) by Shi Cuntong dated 23 May 1920 and by Zhu Zhian dated 12 June 1920. See also Shi Cuntong (1920).

11 See the article written by Zhu Zhian as part of 'The debate on the marriage system abolition issue' in *Juewu, Minguo ribao* (*Awakening, Republican Daily News*) dated 12 June 1920. See also Li Chuo (1920), Shi Cuntong (1920), Chen Guyuan (1920) and Huangshi (1923).

The removal of constrains in this second area, however, sparked much opposition and concern. Firstly, the abolition opponents retorted that abolition would allow people to overindulge in lust because 'people's desire has no limit' and that sexual desire was 'legitimate' but 'abstinence was necessary' because otherwise sex-related 'conflicts' would increase as well as 'sexual promiscuity' and 'animal impulses'.[12] The abolition proponents countered that the proposed abolition was not for the purpose of 'sexual fulfillment'; that it was a mistake to see 'free love' as 'dangerous' and overemphasize 'chastity'; that 'free love' was 'love and not carnal desire' and it was 'questionable to see sexual intercourse as a prime condition for romantic love'; and that what was pleasurable was 'sincere love' and not 'carnal desire'.[13] Nevertheless, concerns were raised by many who were not necessarily opposed to the abolition. They cautioned against hasty arguments about free love out of fears that lack of consideration for 'historical society and customs' would cause 'turbulence' in society; that 'the result would be bad if young people acted on it'; and that it could lead to various misconceptions such as 'heterism' (women-sharing) and the 'nationalization of women'.[14]

The next major point of contention was whether the abolition of the marriage system could be implemented promptly. Shao Lizi and Shi Cuntong argued that immediate abolition was not feasible, asserting that it would be impossible unless 'society's economic infrastructure was fundamentally altered' and that the family would remain necessary unless 'communal childrearing' was provided as 'fulfillment of sexual desire would produce children'.[15] On the other hand, Beiying, Li Chuo and Ma Zhemin argued that 'economic revolution was the fundamental solution' but the marriage issue should be dealt with 'complementarily and in parallel to it'. Moreover, they

---

12 See the articles written as part of 'The debate on the marriage system abolition issue' in *Juewu, Minguo ribao (Awakening, Republican Daily News)* dated 11 May 1920 by Baohua and by Zanping dated 28 May 1920.

13 See the articles written by Shi Cuntong and Yitai as part of 'The debate on the marriage system abolition issue' in *Juewu, Minguo ribao (Awakening, Republican Daily News)* dated 29 May 1920. See also 'To those who advocate for "small family" and oppose "marriage system abolition"' by Li Chuo in *Juewu, Minguo ribao (Awakening, Republican Daily News)* dated 10 July 1920.

14 See the articles written as part of 'The debate on the marriage system abolition issue' in *Juewu, Minguo ribao (Awakening, Republican Daily News)* by Shao Lizi dated 8 May 1920 and by Jinglu dated 23 May 1920. See also Shao Lizi (1920).

15 See the articles written by Shao Lizi as part of 'The debate on the marriage system abolition issue' in *Juewu, Minguo ribao (Awakening, Republican Daily News)* dated 20 and 23 May 1920 and those written by Shi Cuntong dated 20 and 25 May 1920.

stated that the perceived 'infeasibility without public institutions to provide food, clothing and housing' would bring 'inertia' instead of progress and therefore 'determination' was important. They declared that they would continue to call for the abolition while promoting 'independence' and 'employment' because 'communal childrearing could not be realized if no one called for the abolition of marriage'.[16]

In the debate on the feasibility of the abolition of the marriage system, communal childrearing was considered to be 'the most important key' in addition to the need for 'public kitchens', 'cleaning specialists' and 'childcare centers and kindergartens'. Some maintained that the abolition was feasible only after the removal of the private ownership system as 'common people' had no money to pay for communal childrearing and the privately-owned communal childrearing bodies would 'disrespect personalities'. Xiang Jingyu proposed that 'aged care and childcare as well as food, clothing and housing for people' 'should be organized communally by society as a whole' and 'specific' measures would include the establishment of 'organizations to study and promote women's issues', 'associations to support self-determination on marriage' and 'banks to lend money for women's education', and that communal childrearing 'should be organized without delay' because it 'could be implemented by groups of ten or more people'.[17]

The argument for the abolition of the marriage system in the 1920s is worthy of re-evaluation as it elucidates the problems of the 'modern family' ideology that continues to impose restrictions even today and explores ways to overcome them. Now that the destruction of the private ownership system that was supposed to precede the abolition has become an unrealistic idea and that some of the communal/public organizations that were considered unrealistic at the time have been realized, the merits of re-evaluating this argument have increased. In fact, the abolition of the marriage system is already part of a historic trend. However, many Chinese studies scholars continue to dismiss it as 'unrealistic', 'extreme' and 'childishly utopian' (Zhonghua quanguo funü

---

16 See the articles written by Ma Zhemin as part of 'The debate on the marriage system abolition issue' in *Juewu, Minguo ribao* (*Awakening, Republican Daily News*) dated 23 May 1920 and those written by Li Chuo dated 26 May 1920 and Beiying dated 1 June 1920. See also 'To those who advocate for "small family" and oppose "marriage system abolition"' by Li Chuo in *Juewu, Minguo ribao* (*Awakening, Republican Daily News*) dated 10 July 1920.

17 See the article written by Shi Cuntong as part of 'The debate on the marriage system abolition issue' in *Juewu, Minguo ribao* (*Awakening, Republican Daily News*) dated 25 May 1920. See also Shao Lizi (1920), Huangshi (1923) and Xiang Jingyu (1920).

lianhehui 1989: 106–107; Shen Shaogen and Yang Sanping 1999; Lin Jiling 1999; Chen Wenlian and Li Guimei 2003). Even an argument for a very limited re-evaluation merely stresses that the debate was raised with 'an earnest and serious-minded attitude' and not out of lasciviousness (Liang Jinghe 1999). This level of discussion cannot lead to a revision of the existing marriage system or gender structure. In fact, it may contribute to the strengthening of state power through state control over the family and people's sexuality. Together with further discussions about the small family and the new wise wife and good mother ideology, a further deepening of research to re-evaluate commonly accepted views is much anticipated.

12. Women's Labor in Modern and Contemporary China

— *Linda GROVE*

There was a dramatic change in women's work in China over the course of the twentieth century. In 1900 very few women, whether they lived in rural areas or in towns or cities, worked outside the home; by the end of the century work outside the home was the norm, and women who chose to be full-time housewives felt they had to defend their choice. This chapter will look at how this radical change in norms and practice occurred and the consequences for women's lives. The shift, as we will see, was brought about by changes in attitudes, as well as by changes in economic conditions and social organization.

This chapter will examine the shift from the traditional gender division of labor in which most women worked primarily within the home, to the situation we see in the late twentieth to early twenty-first centuries in which most women work outside the home, while also bearing most of the burden of housework. The discussion will look at three stages in the process of change. The first stage, from the late nineteenth century to the 1950s, was characterized by a gradual transformation at both the upper and lower ends of the social scale. The advent of formal education for women created a new stratum of women who wanted to pursue careers, while at the lower end of the social scale the establishment of light industrial factories created a demand for cheap factory labor and led some poorer families to send their daughters to work outside the home.

The second stage, from the mid-1950s to the 1980s, brought a radical transformation in both norms and practices; in the cities women became a regular part of the work force, with stable jobs and much improved working conditions, while in rural areas the creation of communes and a system of collective work mobilized the labor of women who were compelled to join in what was seen as economically productive work.

Chapter 12

Finally, we will look briefly at the transformation of work in the reform era. The third stage which began with the break-up of the communes and China's 'second industrial revolution' has transformed a formerly socialist, inward looking economy into the 'factory of the world', creating a huge demand for low wage labor. Millions of young women have left their rural villages to take up jobs in coastal area factories. At the same time, the end of state-assigned jobs in the urban areas has created a new, competitive labor market that offers both opportunities and risks. The spread of higher education and the rapid growth of new manufacturing and service industries have created new opportunities for well-educated women, and women as well as men are involved in previously unimagined global careers. In recent years, changes in the family system and new demands on an emerging middle class have led some well-educated women to turn away from the challenges of a career and choose instead to become full-time housewives.

Although work – inside or outside the household – has occupied most of the daily schedules of women in both rural and urban China over the long twentieth century, there are relatively few studies of women's working lives, especially with reference to the early decades of the twentieth century. While the pioneering work of Nishijima Sadao on the traditional Chinese cotton industry in the Ming-Qing period gave a great deal of attention to the roles of women in cotton producing households, studies of the rise of modern industry have focused on markets, entrepreneurial histories, managerial techniques and international competition. Labor historians have looked at strikes and the relationship between labor organizing and the rise of the Communist Party, while party historians have focused on women's roles in the revolutionary movement rather than on their daily activities. There is thus a surprising lacuna in research on women's work for the earlier two stages. Thus, the major sources for understanding women's work in this period come from contemporary reportage and studies by sociologists and anthropologists. Let us then turn to look at the beginnings of change in women's work in the late nineteenth century.

First stage of change: Women work outside the home

As many of the chapters in this book have shown, traditional norms established a gendered division of labor in which 'men tilled and women wove'. Until the late Ming dynasty, tax was assessed in kind on the product of the labor of both men and women, so households paid a land tax collected in grain and a tax on the product of women's labor in bolts of cloth. According to Francesca Bray, whose study *Technology and Gender: Fabrics of Power in Late Imperial China* (1997) provides a comprehensive exposition of changing patterns of women's work in the Ming-Qing period, the gradual commercialization of textile production beginning from the late Song period led to a new formation in which production for the market of fancy silk fabrics was taken over by male weavers, while subsistence production of plain weave silks – and by the late Ming-early Qing of cottons for home use – remained in the hands of women. Bray argues that the combination of these changes – the professionalization of some parts of the weaving industry and the tax reforms that ended the collection of taxes in kind on cloth – led to a major shift in the social meaning of women's work. While the 'inner realm' of the home had originally been viewed as a site of production and a woman's contribution to the state was seen in her work at the loom, by the late Ming-early Qing the 'inner realm' had come to be viewed primarily as a site for reproductive labor which contributed to the nurturing of the family but added little to the income of the family. Thus, Bray argues, the material value of the work of women involved in the production of cloth was 'veiled' from view, and a woman's worth came to be seen in her moral virtue and her role providing moral education for her children, rather than in her productive activities.

While the material value of women's productive work may have been 'veiled', there is little question that women of all social classes continued to spin and weave to provide clothes for their families, and in some specialized regions to also send the product of their looms into the market. Nishijima Sadao's pioneering research, first published in Japanese in the late 1940s (Nishijima 1984 [English]), combed through a wide range of sources to create a picture of the work of women in the domestic production of cotton cloth in Jiangnan during the late Ming dynasty. He discovered poems from the period describing the difficult life of women who worked long hours spinning and weaving in order to support their families. In recent years Kenneth Pomeranz, whose work on the Great Divergence touched off a heated debate among global historians on when the West began to pull away developmentally from East Asia, has argued that the income a family would have received from a women's weaving activities in the early eighteenth century exceeded the income earned from her husband's farming activities (Pomeranz 2013). However, after 1750, the gradual spread of cotton cultivation, spinning and weaving to areas that had previously purchased fabrics from Jiangnan led to a downturn in the market and a decline in income from weaving activity. Despite the decline in income, women continued to spin, weave and sew to provide for family consumption. However, except for those who worked in regions that produced large volumes of textiles for the national market, the material value of their productive activities would have been – as Bray has suggested – 'veiled' and counted as part of reproductive labor. This was true even for the wives and daughters of gentry families who had to pursue income generating activities to supplement the unstable incomes of their husbands. Susan L. Mann's *The Talented Women of the Zhang Family* (2007) provides a vivid description of the Zhang daughters who produced fancy embroidered piecework, which they sold to help support their family when fathers and husbands were far away pursuing education, serving as tutors in wealthy families or taking exams.

The beginning of changes that led to the transformation of gendered patterns of work can be traced to the mid-nineteenth century. China's defeat in the Opium Wars (First Opium War 1840–1842; Second Opium War or Arrow War 1856–1860) led to the establishment of the first treaty ports and the opening of the interior to missionary activities. Foreign goods and new ideas began to enter the Chinese empire, inducing a number of changes at both ends of the social scale. At the upper end of the scale the first formal schools for women were opened and some members of the enlightened elite began to argue for new ideas of women's roles in society. A small elite of women who graduated from the new schools began to pursue careers, the numbers increasing by the second and third decades of the twentieth century. At the lower end of the social scale, the opening of the treaty ports for foreign trade led to a rapid expansion in the import of cotton cloth and cotton yarn, leading by the late nineteenth century to a reorganization of the indigenous system of cloth production. Cotton spinning and weaving mills, modeled on the factories of England and America, were established in Chinese coastal cities and home weavers in many parts of the country gave up home spinning and began to use machine spun yarns on their looms. While the early factories used male labor, it was not long before women also began to enter the labor force, working in light industries including cotton spinning and weaving, silk filatures and silk weaving, cigarette factories, match factories and various other light industrial enterprises.

First generation of professional women

As the number of graduates of the new women's schools increased in the early twentieth century, a new group of women with modern education began to seek jobs outside the home. The most common occupations for educated women were school teaching and nursing. Most of the school teachers taught in elementary schools or in schools for women, with only a very few finding positions at the university level. By the 1920s, women began to enter white-collar fields like banking, commerce, editorial work in publishing houses, journalism and administrative work in the civil service. In some cases, the women worked in institutions that had been set up to serve them, like the women's bank in Shanghai and women's department store in Tianjin, and some occupations came to be seen as particularly appropriate for women, for example work as telephone operators.

From the time of the 1911 revolution gender equality had been one of the major features of the progressive agenda. From its origins the Chinese Nationalist Party (the Kuomintang) had supported women's rights but was not strong enough to block the conservative Beiyang government (1912–1928) when it passed legislation that denied women the right to manage their own property and run businesses. When the Nationalist Party established a new government in Nanjing in 1928, it vowed to realize equal rights for women and opened the door for women to enter the bureaucracy and other professions. By 1933 there were 457 female civil servants in the central government, out of a total of 16,990 (2.7% of the total). The Shanghai Municipal Government started to recruit women civil servants after it came under Nationalist Party control in 1927, and by 1934 there were 214 women, comprising 6.05% of the total. The city of Beijing appointed its first policewoman in 1931, and in larger cities across the country small numbers of women began to work in government offices as well as in some private enterprises.

Shanghai was China's largest and most modern city in the 1930s, and the subject of numerous studies of China's new middle class. The city was also the center of China's lively media and publishing worlds, and as a result the life of the new middle class was regularly reported in the newspapers and magazines published in the city. The Japanese Shanghai history research group has edited a series of books on Republican era Shanghai that provide a portrait of the rapidly changing city and its inhabitants. A volume on various occupations in Shanghai by that research group offers short essays on fifty different occupations in 1930s Shanghai (Kikuchi 2002). Some of those – like dancers, courtesans and workers in the silk filatures – were exclusively open to women, but many other professions, from lawyers, doctors and journalists to employees of the post office and civil servants, were positions open to both men and women. This richly illustrated book provides a good introduction to the diverse employment opportunities in Shanghai. Iwama Kazuhiro, a member of the Shanghai research group, has published several books about the new middle class in Shanghai in the Republican period. Chapter 5 of his book on white-collar occupations in Shanghai examines the roles of 'white-collar' women, looking at both housewives and professional women (Iwama 2011).

While small numbers of women, backed by the support of Nationalist Party-sponsored women's organizations, were entering new occupations in the 1930s, more conservative forces were not happy with the situation and took every opportunity to try to promote a return to more traditional gender norms. Just as women were beginning to make progress in entering professional occupations in the late 1920s to early 1930s, the global depression began to affect the Chinese economy. Conservatives saw the downturn as an opportunity to call on women to 'return to the home', surrendering their positions to men who needed the jobs to support their families. Maeyama Kanako (1993) and Egami Sachiko (2007) have written about the debates around the question of whether women should withdraw from the labor force and return to work in the home.

A second round of debate about women in the work force was touched off in the early war years. The Japanese occupation of the coastal provinces sent a flood of well-educated refugees out of the coastal cities and into the interior, putting great pressure on the job market. In response, many again began to argue that women should surrender their jobs to men. Although the Nationalist Party government had established a record of supporting the advance of professional women, provincial governments began to put limits on the number of women in civil service positions and forced many married women civil servants to quit their jobs. In Shanghai in March 1939 these movements came to a head when the Shanghai Post Office prohibited women from sitting for employment examinations. This move was a shock to the women's movement since the post office, along with the telephone company, had been one of the leaders among public institutions in employing women. While women's groups rose up in protest over the shift, under the pressure of wartime conditions, they were not able to overturn the decision (Grove 2020 [Japanese]).

The first generation of women factory workers

As we have seen earlier, in the traditional gendered division of labor women were responsible for the production of textiles to clothe the family. As China began to enter the modern world this traditional division of labor was shattered. Imports of cheap machine-made fabrics and yarn began to flood the Chinese market competing with the product of handlooms and leading to the establishment of mechanized cotton spinning and weaving factories and modern silk filatures. Textile production began to shift out of the home. While most of the early-modern factories employed only male labor, slowly women also began to join the factory labor force. By the mid-1930s, on the eve of the war with Japan, women comprised more than half of the labor force in cotton and silk spinning and weaving mills. The following discussion will focus on studies of women cotton mill workers, but it is important to note that women also played an important role in mechanized silk filatures, as Soda Saburō's important study of the silk industry shows (Soda 1994), as well as in other light industries including food processing factories, match factories and cigarette factories.

Research on this first generation of women workers has focused on a number of key issues, including when and why factories began to employ women, how workers were recruited and managed, the lifestyles and experiences of the first generation of female workers and comparisons of the working experiences in Chinese and foreign owned mills.

The first modern cotton mills were established in China in the 1890s. The early mills were Chinese owned but following the Treaty of Shimonoseki (1895), foreigners gained the right to invest in manufacturing, and by the 1920s there were many foreign-owned mills in China. The major centers of cotton textile production were in Shanghai and other Yangzi region cities, and in the north in Qingdao and Tianjin. In the early years, all of the mills used only male labor, but gradually the mills in the Shanghai and the Yangzi region began to recruit female workers. By the early 1930s, some 70% of the work force in Shanghai cotton mills was female. At the same time, 95% of the workers in silk filatures were women, with the figure just under 60% in cigarette factories and about 55% in match factories. There is a general consensus that mill owners began to recruit large numbers of female workers because they were less likely than their male counterparts to join strikes, were more docile and could be paid lower wages.

However, mill owners did not always find it easy to recruit female workers. Traditional norms had restricted work outside the home. It was commonly believed that a woman who worked outside the protected domestic environment risked her reputation if she went to work in a mixed gender environment, and the life stories of early female workers include descriptions of various forms of sexual harassment. As a result, most of those who entered the early factories were daughters of poor rural families for whom the promise of extra income overcame the worries about reputation. Many of the women entered the factory in a relationship that resembled indentured servitude: labor recruiters offered an advance payment to the woman's family which was paid off through her work in the factory. Working hours in the factory were long, with most factories operating two twelve-hour shifts. Women normally lived in dormitories, either provided by the factory or by the labor recruiter.

Let us now look at the literature on this first generation of female factory workers. One of the earliest studies on female workers was carried out by Okabe Toshiyoshi, who worked as a young researcher for the Tōyō Keizai Shinbunsha from 1932–1937, specializing in analysis of the cotton textile industry. His study of women workers in the Chinese textile industry, which was first published in 1942, examined the reasons for the switch from male to female workers, looking at the regional differences in timing and labor recruitment (Okabe 1992). Okabe examined cultural factors including gender norms that made recruitment of women workers difficult, and also considered the impact of footbinding on the ability of women to work in a factory. He concluded that many of the early female workers did have bound feet but were still able to work for long hours on the factory floor. Okabe argued that although the women had bound feet, footbinding practices in rural Yangzi valley villages resulted in a relatively loosely bound foot, leaving the women with greater mobility and thus an ability to undertake factory work.

While there were numerous contemporary reports on women workers in the popular press of the 1930s and 1940s, serious scholarly work in China on women workers only began in the 1950s and 1960s, when some historians and social scientists began to chronicle the experiences of the first generation of female factory workers. Some of the earliest work along these lines was begun in the 1950s in both Shanghai and Nantong, which was home to Da Sheng, one of China's earliest modern cotton mills. While much of the interview material collected has never been published, more than 200 short oral histories of workers at Da Sheng that were collected in the 1960s were published in 1994 by Mu Xuan and Yan Xuexi. From those biographies we can see that most of the female workers first entered the factory as child laborers and continued to work even after they married and gave birth to children, in some cases taking their children with them when they worked. The Mu and Yan collection and analysis of the oral history materials has made available the 'voices' of members of this early generation talking about their families, the work environment, hierarchical relations on the factory floor and much more about their daily lives.

Emily Honig's *Sisters and Strangers: Women in the Shanghai Cotton Mills, 1919-1949* (1986), is the best academic study of the first generation of Chinese female workers. Honig's research was conducted in Shanghai in the early 1980s, and she made use of unpublished interviews with workers that had been collected by the Shanghai Academy of Social Sciences, documentary and archival materials, her own interviews with former workers and interviews with labor organizers from the YWCA. Honig's rich portrait of the lives of mill workers in Shanghai uncovered the impact of localism among women workers, many of whom were recruited from the area known as Jiangbei, a relatively poor area in Jiangsu Province north of the Yangzi River. Suffering from discrimination at the hands of native Shanghainese, who looked down on those from the Jiangbei region, female workers preferred to work in the Japanese-owned mills where supervisors were free of such prejudice and generally provided better working conditions. Honig's account of localism in the Shanghai mills of the 1930s and 1940s is echoed in some of the work on contemporary female workers in southern Chinese factories, where Cantonese-speaking supervisors oversee the work of '*putonghua*-speaking' migrant workers (see the later discussion of the work of Leslie Chang).

Finally, I would like to briefly mention studies on women workers in the major northern industrial center of Tianjin. Gail Hershatter's pioneering study, *The Workers of Tianjin, 1900-1949* (1986), includes a chapter on cotton mill workers, both male and female. As she notes, Heng Yuan was the first Tianjin mill to hire female workers, beginning in the early 1930s. Some years ago, the archives of the Heng Yuan mill were opened, and I used those archives, including a daily record of the personnel department as well as a dormitory diary, to explore the life of women workers in Tianjin in the late 1930s (Grove 1997 [Japanese]).

Chapter 12

Another site of female labor – the entertainment trades

Before moving on to consider the status of female workers after the establishment of the People's Republic of China, let us briefly refer to another site of female labor outside the home: the entertainment trades, including the sex trades. The late nineteenth and early twentieth centuries saw an explosion in employment of women in the entertainment trades. The development of the treaty port cities and the influx of male migrants had created a demand for all kinds of sex and entertainment services. By the 1920s, Shanghai and other treaty port cities offered a range of entertainment options including dancers in modern dance halls, high class courtesans who provided entertainment and companionship as well as sex services to carefully selected clients, mid-ranking courtesans who dealt with a wider range of customers in the city's brothel district and the 'street chicken' prostitutes who offered quick services to poor men. Christian Henriot's study of Shanghai prostitution estimated that there were about 30,000 prostitutes in that city before the Anti-Japanese War, and as many as 50,000 after the beginning of the war (Henriot 2001). In Tianjin there were at least 500 registered brothels at the end of the Qing dynasty, and in Guangzhou 30% of the municipal revenues came from taxes on houses of prostitution (Remick 2014).

By the 1920s and 1930s, prostitution had spread from the treaty ports and large cities to smaller towns in the interior; any place where commerce or industry flourished, one would find women providing sex services to the mobile male population of merchants and workers. My own work, based on unpublished 1930s social survey notes, has looked at prostitution in one small North China town (Grove 2018). All of this sex work was, of course, stigmatized, and after the Communist Party came to power in 1949 there were nationwide efforts to rescue women from the sex trades and provide them with job skills – and in some cases with husbands – so that they could become productive members of the new society. At least officially, sex work disappeared from the Chinese scene for several decades, only to make a strong resurgence following the initiation of the economic reform policies in the early 1980s. In contemporary China, sex services are available everywhere – from the high-class call girls who often become the 'mistresses' (*er-nai*) of prosperous officials and businessmen to the women offering sex services in massage shops in small towns and in restaurants along the main highways. While sex work is still stigmatized – as we can see from the fact that women rarely engage in sex work in their own hometowns

– new discourses have also appeared in which some young women flaunt their status as mistresses of the wealthy and the rewards of choosing a life of leisure and consumption.

There have been a number of works on women and the sex trade. The work of French scholar Christian Henriot provides a social history of prostitution in Shanghai (2001), while that of Gail Hershatter provides a sophisticated exploration of the discourses surrounding Shanghai prostitution (1997). The work of Iwama (2011) and other members of the Japan Shanghai research group provides a window onto the Shanghai entertainment world, including the world of the dance halls, and the volume on Shanghai occupations includes several short chapters on other aspects of the entertainment trades. Elizabeth Remick's study *Regulating Prostitution in China* has examined the ways different cities attempted to control the entertainment trades (2014). In the last several years, there has been an explosion of interest among Chinese social and cultural historians in the pre-liberation sex trades, and a number of histories of prostitution have been published. Finally, one of the many studies of contemporary sex work in China is the work by anthropologist Tiantian Zheng, *Red Lights: The Lives of Sex Workers in Postsocialist China* (2009), based on fieldwork among karaoke bar hostesses in Dalian, which shows how poor rural women are struggling to make a living in reform-era China.

Women's work in the Maoist era

Chapter Fourteen by Ohashi Fumie introduces the Communist Party's approaches to gender equality and its efforts to see those approaches implemented through top-down policy changes. This section will look briefly at the impact of those policies on women's work. In terms of timing, the beginning of the Great Leap Forward in 1958 marked a major turning point. Under the household registration system of 1958, Chinese citizens were assigned either an urban or rural residence status. From that time on the state took responsibility for assigning jobs to those with urban residence status; jobs in state factories and organizations were reserved for those with urban residence status and the flow of workers from the countryside into urban factories stopped. In the countryside women's labor was mobilized for work in agriculture, a story that Ohashi covers in her chapter.

In the cities, the socialization of commerce and industry in the early and mid-1950s transformed private enterprises into state-run organizations with

Chapter 12

much more stable working conditions, creating what the Chinese refer to as the 'iron rice bowl'. Once assigned to a job, a worker was virtually guaranteed 'lifetime employment'. The individual worker (either in a factory or in a business) was attached to a 'work unit' that provided work, social services and retirement benefits. For women factory workers, the Maoist years brought the most stable working conditions since the company provided housing, maternity leave and nurseries for young children, which made balancing work and family life easier. Moreover, from the early 1950s on the state began to honor model workers; this marked a major shift from the situation two decades earlier when society had questioned the virtue of women who worked outside the home in mixed gender working environments.

A major study by Tong Xin, a sociologist at Peking University who specializes in gender studies and studies of women and labor, provides a vibrant portrait of women workers from the early 1950s to the early twenty-first century (Tong Xin 2003). Tong collected forty detailed life histories from several generations of women factory workers, most of whom worked in state-owned enterprises in North and Northeast China. Almost all of her informants had long working careers from the time they entered the factory in their late teens or very early twenties until retirement at the age of forty-five or fifty, and the interviews show the changes in their work and lives from the early years when they were still unmarried through the early years of marriage and childrearing to maturity and retirement. Tong notes that the experiences of different age cohorts varied significantly, not only because of changing conditions within Chinese factories, but also – and maybe more importantly – because of the changing expectations of the women and their families.

The earliest cohort includes the women who began working in factories before 1949. Most of this cohort had gone to work in a factory to help support their families at a time when working outside the home was not the norm and factory work was not socially valued. This was the cohort who most directly experienced the 1949 revolution as 'liberation': workers, who were formerly part of an impoverished underclass, came to be regarded as the 'masters of society' and along with that new social status came more stable working conditions. Hours were shortened, more attention was paid to safety, and by the late 1950s factories began to provide nurseries, maternity leave and other support activities to make it easier to manage work and family obligations. While there is no question that the lives of women workers were greatly improved after 1949, Tong argues that the explanations for how and why that happened give much more importance to class than gender. Women workers were viewed primarily as members of the working class with all the privileges that ensued from that class status, while questions of gender equality were 'veiled', only to reappear again in the 1990s.

Later cohorts of women workers who came to adulthood after 1949 were raised in a new society that assumed that women's work outside the home was an important part of a family's strategy for survival. Tong uses the life history interviews to examine questions of subjectivity, looking at the ways in which individual women pursued their careers, acquired additional skills and were able to move from apprentice factory workers to positions of greater responsibility, finding meaning in their lives through their work. Work outside the home not only gave women greater economic independence; if the women Tong interviewed are in any way typical, it also seems to have produced more equitable relations within the family. Tong presents one telling set of interviews with a husband and wife who seemed to represent a kind of ideal: both were employed, and the husband participated fully in housework, including cooking, laundry and childcare. However, in the late 1990s the wife lost her job when the state factory where she formerly worked downsized, and she was unable to find other work. At that point her husband not only stopped sharing housework, but also began to make major purchases without consulting his wife since he felt she was no longer contributing economically to their household.

One of the interesting revelations of this study is the way in which women workers viewed the relationship between factory work and reproductive work, what in Western societies is the highly contentious issue of 'work-life balance'. The women and men Tong interviewed did not see paid work and reproductive work in opposition, but rather as parts of a common life structure that encompassed both. Tong suggests that this perception is the result of a historical evolution quite different from the pattern we see in Western societies. In Western societies economic development led to the rise of a middle class, resulting in an era when middle class women were most commonly full-time housewives. In China, as a result of the socialist revolution, women got the right to be workers with a wage, and that wage, like that of their husbands, was an important part of family income. Thus, both men and women came to see women's work outside the home as the norm. However, she argues, patriarchy and the ideas associated with it did not completely disappear. When working class families were faced with conflicts between the careers of husband and wife, almost all of her informants said that it was natural for a woman to sacrifice her own chances for advancement if they conflicted with her husband's career progression.

Tong's study shows a very clear demarcation between the working lives of women under the planned economy and since the introduction of the economic reforms. While the changes did not come immediately, by the mid- to late 1990s many of the large state enterprises in the old northeast industrial heartland went bankrupt and large numbers of workers, overwhelmingly female, were laid off. As the old centers went into decline, new industrial centers based on private investment rapidly developed in the southern part of China, and a new generation of migrant women workers, drawn from rural villages in the interior, flocked to the coastal factories. While the women workers in Tong's study thought of themselves as members of the working class, with the respect that went along with that status during the latter half of the twentieth century, the new generation of migrant workers are almost always referred to as '*dagongmei*', a category that the sociologist Pun Ngai in her award-winning book *Made in China: Women Factory Workers in a Global Workplace* (2006) argues is a new concept that contrasts with the history of Chinese socialism. Labor, especially alienated labor, supposedly emancipated for more than thirty years, is again sold to capitalists, this time under the auspices of the state machine. In contrast to the term *gongren*, or worker, which carried the highest social status in the rhetoric of Mao's day, the new word *dagong* signifies a lesser identity – that of a hired hand – in a new context shaped by the rise of market factors in labor relations and hierarchy.

Leslie Chang's *Factory Girls: From Village to City in a Changing China* (2009), follows this new generation of women workers, examining their motivations for leaving the countryside, their working experiences in private factories under a regime characterized by long hours and rigid rules, their struggles to improve themselves and move ahead and their changing relations with the families they left behind in the villages. The author was a reporter for the *Wall Street Journal* when she began this study, and many of the themes she discusses reverberate with the experiences of earlier generations of Chinese factory workers. This new generation of factory workers were born and raised in rural villages, and most left to seek employment in southern China after finishing junior high or high school. Unlike the earliest generation of rural women workers who often entered the factories as a result of arrangements made by their impoverished parents, the new generation, bored by the prospects of staying at home where there was nothing to do, made conscious decisions to look for work and a more exciting life. Just as Tong described the strong motivations of socialist-era women workers to improve their skills and move up in the factories, Chang describes the young women's efforts to improve their skills and appearance so they can get off the assembly line and into clerical or managerial work. The factories where they work, however, are run according to rules that more closely resemble those of the pre-1949 factory world than those of the planned economy era. Few factories offer long-term benefits, and young and ambitious women frequently jump from factory to factory, seeking higher wages, better working conditions or employment in a factory with others from their hometowns.

The thirty years that have passed since the beginning of the economic reforms have produced a transformation in the lives of women workers in China and attitudes toward work. As a result of the one child policy, the total number of workers in China's labor force has reached a peak and started to decline. Wage levels in China are rising; workers in the southern Chinese industrial zone are becoming more assertive, organizing work stoppages and demanding better working conditions. We can only wonder what changes these new circumstances will bring to labor markets and the choices that new generations of women will make in planning their careers and family lives.

Recent developments do seem to call into question the once proud Chinese socialist claim that 'Women hold up half the sky'. At the upper end of the labor market we see highly educated women forced to make difficult choices between career and family life. For some, parents or parents-in-law take over childcare so a woman can continue to work. Others turn to the full-time care workers whose lives have been studied by Ohashi Fumie (2011). But some make the difficult choice to quit working and devote themselves to childcare. For women making this choice, the issues are similar to those cited by highly-educated professional women in America who choose the 'mommy track'. The Chinese women making this choice are motivated by pressure to see that their one child is given all possible advantages for the future but have also been pushed to this choice by the collapse of public childcare for children under the age of three. While most of this cohort do not want to permanently become full-time housewives, there is no assurance that they will be able to re-enter the labor market as full-time employees in jobs that make use of their skills.

At the lower end of the labor market there are other problems – long working hours and the instability of work arrangements are complicated by the lack of support for working mothers. One of the consequences of the new work arrangements for rural migrant laborers has been the problem of 'left behind' children, the millions of children sent back to live in the countryside with grandparents while their parents work. The carefully constructed institutions of the planned economy era that supported women working outside the home were swept away under the economic reforms, leaving behind a working environment that resembles that of pre-1949 China. The post-socialist era has thus revealed problems with socialist-era policies, policies that focused on women workers as members of the working class, neglecting issues of basic gender equality that have again re-emerged. It is thus left to a new generation to carry on the struggle for gender equality and to create new institutions to support women in their endeavors to find a way to effectively combine productive and reproductive work.

13. The Founding of the People's Republic of China and the Transformation of Gender Order

— KOHAMA Masako

Introduction

The founding of the People's Republic of China (PRC) brought a major change to gender order in Chinese society. This chapter explores two major questions: the first considers and evaluates efforts by the PRC system to control the gender order in Chinese society, while the second examines how those efforts define the conditions of present-day Chinese society primarily in terms of the issues surrounding the family.

I first review the family-related laws and policies during the Republic of China period, and then examine how the Marriage Law of the PRC, which was promulgated in 1950, and its early policies, including the campaign for its implementation, altered China's gender structure and provided a new base for administration. Then, I look at policy changes in relation to gender order from the 1950s to the Cultural Revolution before investigating how the PRC government created a system to control birth through its birth planning policy and the one child policy that followed.

Thus, in this chapter I identify the way the family system and human birth in the PRC has been transformed by the state as a form of what Michel Foucault (1976) calls 'bio-power'. I observe the characteristics of the change of the family during the PRC era and consider its position in historical context since pre-modern times, which has been examined in preceding chapters.

Chapter 13

Laws and policies on gender and the family in modern China

China began to prepare the ground for the enactment of modern laws at the end of the Qing dynasty and some of the statutes concerning family relationships implemented at the time were precursors to the modern reform of the family institution. In particular, a heated controversy that arose over the removal of the *wufu jian* provisions (regarding penalties against unmarried women and widows who engaged in sexual relationships) in the penal code in the first years of the Republic of China indicated how sensitive Chinese society was to women's sexual freedom (Ono 1992) (see Chapter Seven). On the other hand, reform-minded intellectuals came to the view that the extent of women's liberation served as a barometer for modernization and that the reform of the traditional family characterized by the dominance of men over women (*nanzun nübei*) was an important challenge for China's modernization reform. The New Culture Movement proposed family reform as a major issue. A wide range of discussions took place in the 1920s and 1930s about the ideal family (see Chapter Eleven). The Chinese Nationalist Party (the Kuomintang) and the Chinese Communist Party (CCP) both put forward the equality of men and women and women's liberation as their major goals. According to Suetsugu Reiko (2009), the alliance between political reform and women's liberation promoted the women's liberation movement from above while creating a tendency for women's own demands to be overshadowed by the political agenda of the time.

The Civil Code, which was promulgated by the National Government in 1930, emphasized monogamy and that the decision to marry should be made by the man and woman involved, while recognizing women's right to property and allowing them to initiate divorce. Ironically, the law resulted in an unfavorable outcome for women in some aspects because it treated women as independent legal entities and removed the protection previously available to them, even though it failed to thoroughly apply the gender equality principle (Mann 2011).[1] Above all, the effect of China's first modern civil law was only felt by a section of urban intellectuals and had no bearing on the reality of rural villages.

---

1 The main provisions and characteristics of the Republic of China Law and the Chinese Soviet Republic Marriage Code mentioned below are explained in Chūgoku joseishi kenkyūkai (2004: 115–118).

Meanwhile, in 1931 the Chinese Soviet Republic (CSR) under the CCP promulgated the Marriage Code that emphasized women's interests. Its anti-patriarchal characteristics were attenuated slightly in the Marriage Code of the Border Area, which was later enacted during the Anti-Japanese War period under the Second United Front (cooperation between the Nationalist Party and the CCP). The CCP adopted a policy of mobilizing women for production under the party's guidance on the grounds that women's liberation would be achieved through their economic independence by their participation in production activity as part of the 'Year-43 decision'. This continued to form the basic party policy for women's mobilization and resulted in the inhibition of women's movement outside production participation as well as the subordination of their movement within the party (Egami 1993).

Gender reform and the Marriage Law campaign

The People's Republic of China was founded in October 1949. In the Common Program of the Chinese People's Political Consultative Conference, which can be regarded as the new nation's provisional constitution, Article 6 declared, 'The People's Republic of China shall abolish all feudal institutions that restrict women; women have equal rights with men in all areas of political, economic, educational-cultural and social lives; it shall implement freedom of marriage between a man and a woman'. It positioned gender equality as one of its national principles. Seven months later in May 1950, the PRC Marriage Law was promulgated and implemented on the same day. In addition to the legislation, a campaign for the implementation of the Marriage Law was rolled out nationally in 1953 and contributed to a major transformation of the gender order in Chinese society.

The Marriage Law was a 'modern' law based on principles such as marital freedom (*hunyin ziyou*: autonomous decision to marry and divorce), monogamy, gender equality and the protection of women's and children's interests, and promised to eliminate 'feudalistic' practices such as marriage arranged by parents (*baoban hunyin*) and bride-buying involving large sums of betrothal money. Ono Kazuko values the nature of the law and the campaign highly as they promoted women's liberation by abolishing feudal marriage practices. Ono Kazuko (1977) vividly depicts the process in which the principle of matrimonial freedom gradually took root in Chinese society, despite opposition which included the deaths of reportedly 70,000–80,000 women a year, some at the hands of village chiefs who were upholding feudal values and others the result of suicide when their efforts to exercise their right to freely marry or divorce were thwarted. Ono examines the way the law, together with the Agrarian Reform Law that came into operation around the same time, made it possible for impoverished farmers with no bride-buying money to marry; they increased their productive effort as they thanked 'Chairman Mao for giving a wife to a poor man' and built the foundation for the construction of New China. At the same time, Ono points out that the 'winding-up of the feudal system' came to a premature end when the central government suppressed the movement.

Judith Stacey (1983) has argued that through the processes of land reform and the family revolution the Communist Party actually enabled the reproduction of small peasant families. By stabilizing the small peasant family, which had been struggling to survive, the party consolidated support for the government. Stacey found that the radical policies in the early years of the Chinese Soviet Republic had led male farmers to worry that they might be deprived of land and women, which were their most valuable possessions, so the CCP backed down and switched to a policy for active family protection. The safety of the family foundation was more important than freedom of divorce for a great majority of peasant men and many peasant women. As the government removed patriarchs from certain social classes, including landowners, based on the view that the patriarchy had derived from a 'feudal' social structure, the new and more democratic patriarchal family structure came within reach of all men. The point emphasized by Ono and Stacey that the family reform in conjunction with the land reform revived peasant families, which formed a power base for the Communist Party government, should be given more significance in understanding the Chinese Revolution. Along these lines, Takahashi Nobuo states that the way the revolutionary regime dealt with gender relationship reform was of crucial importance in securing peasants' support (Takahashi 2010).

It is also important to pay attention to the difference between the rural and urban areas in considering the effects of the campaign for the implementation of the Marriage Law. The challenge for the campaign in rural villages was the strength of 'feudal forces'. Many women lost their lives in suicides or murders under the oppression of their family and village CCP cadres who were charged with responsibility to promote the campaign but did not themselves support freedom of marriage. On the other hand, the main problem in cities where the relatively modern idea of the link between romantic love and marriage had spread by the Republican era was an increase in the number of married men who left their wives of many years for other women under the pretext of 'marriage freedom'. The phenomenon in which revolutionary cadre left their wives in the country and married younger women in the city became a social problem (Jin Meilan 2011; Diamant 2000).

In any case, the Marriage Law and the campaign for its implementation greatly upset the gender order of the time and the law was mocked as the 'divorce law' due to the unprecedented number of divorce petitions it inspired. The Communist Party ended the campaign in mid-1953 out of fear that it might push the implementation too far. Many of the divorce petitions filed after the end of the campaign were rejected and the divorce rate stayed at very low levels until China adopted the reform and opening-up policies. After reforming the feudal family with the Marriage Law and the campaign for its implementation, the government moved to protect and maintain the family as the bedrock of social order. Nevertheless, the changes to the family in the early years of the PRC encompassed many aspects, ranging from the improved status of the wife and the reduced authority of the mother-in-law within the family (Suetsugu 2000) to the resumption of intra-lineage marriage which had previously been avoided (Anita Chan et al.1984).

In reviewing this process, we can reach several conclusions about the Marriage Law. Firstly, the form of marriage it envisioned was a type of 'modern family' based on a compulsory heterosexuality that united sex, love, marriage and reproduction.[2] All other forms of relationships were criticized in many respects. For instance, the Guangdong custom for unmarried women to form an alliance and live together was suppressed as 'feudalistic'. In Huian County, Fujian Province, the custom of the wife not moving into the husband's home immediately after marriage had to be changed. Homosexuality became a punishable offence, although it had never been suppressed in traditional Chinese society (Mann 2011; Evans 1997) (see Column Five).

The second point concerns the relationship between the state and the family, that is, how government policies control and involve the family. Under the Marriage Law, the bride and the groom had to register their marriage themselves as a requirement for the completion of a marriage (Article 6). While this was a simple and easy way to ascertain that bride and groom were marrying according

---

2 It was different from the typical 'modern family' in that it did not adopt the gendered division of labor principle of 'Men work outside, women work at home'. See the 'Preface' by Kohama.

to their own will, it also signified the infiltration of state control into the family in that for the first time in Chinese history, the completion of a marriage was approved by the state in the form of Communist Party cadre rather than deities, ancestral tablets or regional communities.[3] Registration of any marriage that did not conform to the spirit of the Marriage Law was prohibited. In fact, 1.5% of marriage applications in 1954 were rejected for the reason of 'arranged or forced marriage' (Ono 1977). In this way, the state actively intervened in the modality of marriage and the family. The Marriage Law prescribed that the husband and wife should 'love, respect and help one another, stand together harmoniously, strive for production, raise children and make a great joint effort for the family's happiness and the development of New China' (Article 8). As the family was required to strive for the production of goods and the reproduction of people as the bedrock of nation-building, marriage was a public affair that formed the basis of the state rather than a private matter between individuals. Although marriage was underpinned by love, a marriage based on romantic love alone was considered 'bourgeois' and romantic love was required to have a class perspective. Married couples who were prepared to sacrifice their family life for national production were commended as model couples while unmarried women were forced to undertake self-criticism for avoiding their duty to marry and bear children (Jin Meilan 2011). Premarital and extramarital sexual relationships were considered to come from an immoral bourgeois mentality and the concept of marrying within the same social class replaced the practice of 'marriage between equal social status families' (*mendang hudui*). The new sexual ethics under socialism established the principle of equality between men and women but it led to the retrogression and denial of the freedom of the individual's body, which had been pursued since the New Culture Movement (Liao Xichen 2012).

A study of prostitutes in Shanghai by Gail Hershatter (1997) posits that the campaigns for the liberation of prostitutes and the abolition of prostitution, which were undertaken decisively in cities across the country at the beginning of the PRC period, can be regarded as part of the movements to create a gender order that keeps sexuality within the confines of marriage. The implementation process of these campaigns varied from one region to another, but Lin Hong (2007 [Japanese]), in her detailed study of documents and interviews about

---

3 In traditional China, a marriage was considered effected upon completion of the six ceremonies of betrothal and marriage (*liuli*). They were often performed in a very simplified form in practice.

the situation in Fuzhou, reveals that the sexual activity of Communist Party members in particular was strictly controlled by the party and the extramarital relationships of party cadre were subjected to administrative punishments. This serves as an example of how the government tried to manage and control people's sexuality.

Social reform and change of gender construction

After the founding of the PRC, women's participation in society and labor was promoted and the number of women workers in state-run and public 'units' in the cities nationwide increased according to the principles of the 'Year-43 Decision' (Chen Yan 2006) (see Chapter Twelve). China also tried to redress its traditionally low education and literacy rates by developing primary education as well as through the adult education campaign to eliminate illiteracy that mainly targeted women (Liu Xiaoli 2014).

Together with family reform, the social reform undertaken shortly after the founding of the PRC dramatically transformed the gender order in Chinese society. The CCP mobilized and organized people in the traditionally disadvantaged strata of society into its power base and women as the largest group of the socially vulnerable were organized under the All-China Women's Federation (ACWF) (see Chapter Fourteen). The ACWF had seventy-six million members in 1953, far exceeding the size of other mass organizations such as the All-China Federation of Trade Unions with a membership of 10.2 million people (Liu Xiaoli 2014: 305), and vigorously promoted work concerning women and programs to organize women. Zhang Jishun (2015) describes the way Shanghai women were assembled into neighborhood committees and labor unions and became political actors. Although that process took a complex path, there is no doubt that these policies greatly empowered many women and other previously disadvantaged sections of society as a whole.

Nevertheless, the period in which many women and men were encouraged to exuberantly participate in the movement from above was short-lived. The history of the women's movement prior to the Cultural Revolution written by the ACWF is divided into two phases: from 1949 to 1956 and from 1956 to 1966 (Gu Xiulian 2013). The 'General Line for Socialist Construction' started in 1956 and supported the broad participation of women in production. In the following year, however, the Central Committee of the CCP proposed a policy of dual responsibilities (*liangqin*) in which women were called upon to 'support the family and contribute to the nation's socialist construction through thrift and side work at home' in its work concerning women. The party encouraged women to stay home and contribute towards nation-building when it became increasingly obvious that it was impossible to provide employment to all women. There was a strong push for women's employment during the period of the Great Leap Forward policy from 1958, but the party reverted to the dual responsibilities policy when the failure of the former became apparent in 1960.

This tendency for the women's mobilization policy to fluctuate according to changes in the political situation of the time, as pointed out in Suetsugu (2009), is also apparent from the assessment of household labor. Song Shaopeng analyzes changes in the opinion of unemployed women in urban families based on articles published in *Renmin ribao* (*People's daily*). At the time of the founding of the PRC, they were criticized as 'parasites' who depended on workers. Once the First Five-Year Plan was initiated, women were expected to manage family life well and provide rearguard support for productive labor. The promotion of the Great Leap Forward policy from 1958 to 1960 saw the emergence of the argument that women should step out of the home and participate in production labor. In the early part of the 1960s, after the failure of the policy, women's role within the family was once again seen as important (Song Shaopeng 2011).

The household registration (*hukou*) system was introduced in 1958 to establish a mechanism to control the populace based on the family which severely limited freedom of movement. Birth planning was introduced in the mid-1950s (to be discussed below). Thus, China's Foucauldian bio-power began to tighten its grip on people's daily lives. Kohama Masako (2016) provides an overview of historical materials concerning the gender history in China in the 1950s.

The Cultural Revolution and gender

The Cultural Revolution that began in 1966 is now perceived as a decade-long social upheaval caused by Mao Zedong's attempt to regain political power. China's gender order also experienced 'upheaval' during this period.

When the journal of the ACWF, *Zhongguo funü* (*Chinese Women*), started a 'debate on women's value' in 1963–1964, it received criticism on the grounds that discussing women's value was a reflection of feudalism and the bourgeois perspective as well as the bourgeois 'women's viewpoint' that erased class distinctions. This controversy provides a glimpse of the Cultural Revolution-era trend to lump all issues with class struggle. This trend, which strengthened in the late 1960s, is clearly reflected in the publication of an article in *Renmin ribao* (*People's daily*) newspaper on 11 March 1968 in the midst of the Cultural Revolution titled, 'Condemnation for China's Khrushchev anti-revolution revisionist line on the women's movement', which completely rejected the women's movement since the foundation of the PRC on the following grounds.

> China's Khrushchevs used a bourgeois "women's viewpoint" and "welfare viewpoint" to hide the class struggle nature of the women's movement. [...] They turned their back on political struggle and tried to keep women within the confines of the family and revive capitalism under the banner of "I".

It also argued that the dual responsibility '*liangqin*' policy was an assertion that class struggle had ended, whereas 'the substance of the women's movement ought to be class struggle' (Gu Xiulian 2013).

During the Cultural Revolution, there was a tendency for the gender gap between men and women to be minimized under this logic. Mao Zedong's slogans such as 'Women hold up half the sky' and 'Whatever men comrades can do, women comrades can do, too' were popularized while women dressed in clothes that minimized gender differences, and young women referred to as 'iron girls' (*tie guniang*) were celebrated for engaging in hazardous physical labor such as high-voltage powerline work and oil excavation, which had traditionally been considered as exclusively men's occupations. In recent years, this phenomenon has been viewed as an attempt to conform women to men's standards under the slogan of gender equality which imposed unreasonable demands on women, disregarding their physiology, even though it did broaden their opportunities and reform the gendered division of roles (Jin Yihong 2010 [Japanese]; Egami 2015).

One of the visual representations symbolizing the Cultural Revolution era is the poster of 'barefoot doctors' who worked in the field of primary healthcare in rural areas. Although a majority of the barefoot doctors were men, most of the posters featured women because the barefoot doctor symbolized rural villages, women, ideologies and Chinese medicine that were upheld in that period. Yao Yi (2016 [Japanese]) points out that the propaganda endorsed the existing patriarchal norm that a woman's body was the property of its male owner even though it popularized female therapists.

The percentage of women in state leadership positions, including the deputies of the National People's Congress, was the highest in the history of the PRC in the latter half of the Cultural Revolution period when Jiang Qing (Mao Zedong's wife) and the other members of the Gang of Four wielded power. What is the significance of the prominence of women during this period? In China, the Cultural Revolution-era phenomena have been dismissed as radical and preposterous and research into the situation at that time has stagnated as it has been treated almost as taboo. However, there is a need to deepen studies on phenomena and representations surrounding gender in this historical context. It seems impossible to avoid research into this period if we wish to understand the outcomes and limitations of the gender order reform undertaken during the Chinese Revolution.

The state, family and individual regarding birth planning

Another major change to the family resulting from government policy on par with the Marriage Law was a dramatic reduction in the number of children due to birth planning (*jihua shengyu*), including the so-called 'one child policy'. The one child policy refers to a basic state policy that had been operating since 1979 under which the state coercively controlled the number of births basically to one child per couple. However, while the post-Cultural Revolution 'one child policy' has received great attention, the implementation of 'birth planning' or a birth control policy began much earlier in the mid-1950s. Unlike in Western society where modern birth control spread privately rather in defiance of the state during the first half of the twentieth century, family planning was implemented from above as a government policy in Asian countries after the Second World War. Although China's one child policy is often considered unique due to its large scale and coercive means, it ought to be seen as part of the bio-politics employed in contemporary Asian nations (Kohama and Matsuoka 2014). Let us trace the course of the implementation of the birth planning policy to tease out some issues.

The Founding of the People's Republic of China and the Transformation of Gender Order

Before the one child policy

Chinese families in the pre-PRC era tried to control generational reproduction by regulating the number of children, but they were basically left to their own devices with no state intervention. When the Central People's Government came to power, it actively intervened in reproduction and implemented its population policy from an early stage (White 2006; Kohama 2020).

Initially, childbirth was encouraged, and maternal and child health was studied on the grounds that New China's superior social system would allow people to produce and raise children safely while abortion was criticized for reasons of 'protection of the health of women and children'. However, when the 1953 Census found that the population had grown faster than expected and reached 600 million, the government reversed its stance and began to promote birth control beginning in the mid-1950s. In order to turn public opinion around, it added higher goals such as 'the prosperity of the nation' and 'the swift construction of socialism' to 'women's health'. The evolution of this argument led to the gradual formation of a structure in which a discursive space concerning sex and reproduction was controlled by politics rather than ethics. While the PRC's population policy has had many changes in direction since then, political control over reproduction has continued to this day (Kohama 2020).

The birth planning program was interrupted during the Great Leap Forward from 1958. When the second baby boom in the early 1960s saw China's total fertility rate exceed six, however, the government resumed the birth planning program in an attempt to curtail rapid population growth. In Shanghai, the vigorous efforts of its administrative and health authorities had by this time made birth control accessible to working-class women. The program at the time was run on a voluntary basis but women actively used it as they were carrying a double burden of work and home/childrearing duties. As Shanghai women increased their agency to choose and decide whether or not to have children, the birthrate decreased markedly during the 1960s. Due to the gender structure with many men reluctant to accept birth planning and the technological constraints, however, tubal ligation and abortion became the main methods of birth planning despite placing considerable stress on women's bodies (Kohama 2010 [Chinese]; Kohama 2020). Tubal ligation and abortion were again used as the main methods when the birth planning program was later extended to rural areas. In any case, birth planning was not utilized in most rural villages where a majority of China's population lived at the time and the effect of the program on demographics was limited through to the 1960s (Scharping 2003).

The practice of planned birth penetrated the entire country, including rural areas, in the 1970s. Thanks to the work of the barefoot doctors and other improvements in the rural system of primary healthcare discussed earlier, the mortality rate among infants and small children dropped dramatically. It was this improvement in primary healthcare infrastructure that laid the base for the penetration of birth planning in the countryside. China's total fertility rate dropped most rapidly between 1971 (5.44) and 1979 (2.75). The slogan 'Late marriage, late childbirth, two children per couple' was publicized in each village. The Women's Heads (see Chapter Fourteen) of the production brigades in each village played a major role in mobilizing rural women to receive tubal ligation surgery. In this way, reproductive management by the state spread nationwide through the administrative power of the grassroots cadre (White 2006). Kohama (2011 [Chinese], 2020) examines the status of one village in the Chinese northeast that was recognized as a model village for birth planning and reports that the decline in the birthrate was the outcome of a complex power negotiation between state policy, patriarchal rural families and women as the primary agents of childbirth.

The evolution of the 'one child policy'

In the late 1970s, the period of class struggle under the Cultural Revolution came to an end, and with the launching of the reform and opening-up policies, birth control policy entered a new stage with the beginning of the 'one-child policy'. The decision to enforce the universal policy of stringently limiting each couple to one child was driven by the 'scientific' argument put forward by a group of scientists led by cybernetics scientist Song Jian that China's rapid population growth had to be stopped in order to advance modernization. Susan Greenhalgh (2008) states that Deng Xiaoping-era China saw the construction of a 'knowledge framework' in which a theory asserted in the name of 'science' had a decisive influence over politics. This policy, which was positioned as a 'basic state policy', provoked a major backlash[4] and resulted in a great number of cases of the abuse of female infants and the women who gave birth to girls because,

---

4 Steven Westley Mosher (1990, 1993) gathered much attention by reporting on the realities of the one child policy inside China in the early phase of the reform and opening-up policies.

with the introduction of the contract responsibility system for individual farming households, farming families preferred to have a son. Thomas Scharping (2003) points out that resistance and opposition to the one child policy came from China's traditional families rather than modernized individuals, while Kohama (2020) describes the complex process of policy implementation in a farming village in South China.

As the stringent universal one child policy caused a major backlash and confusion, it was relaxed slightly from 1984 in an effort to reduce the turmoil. After the plateauing of the birthrate during the 1980s, the government began to enforce the planned birth policy more rigorously from 1991 amid rising tension, causes of which included a serious imbalance in the sex ratio (White 2006; Greenhalgh and Winckler 2005; Wakabayashi 2005). The birthrate declined from the mid-1990s and fell below the population replacement level by the end of the twentieth century. It is debatable as to whether this was the result of the rigorous policy implementation or an upturn in China's economic development. Since the United Nations Fourth World Conference on Women in Beijing in 1995, China has been 'brought into the orbit' of the rest of the world (see Chapter Eighteen) and the introduction of new concepts such as 'population and development' and reproductive health and rights led to the promotion of the linkage between birth planning and the betterment of people's lives and interests as well as the use of gentler birth control methods (Wakabayashi 2006).

Since the turn of the twenty-first century, there have been growing calls within China for a policy shift after it became apparent that China's population was rapidly aging with a dwindling number of children and that the one child policy has distorted its population composition from a demographic point of view (Tian Xueyuan and Wang Guoqiang 2004). Questions have also been raised from a human rights perspective. However, according to Chen Guidi and Chun Tao (2004), it has not been easy to alter the birth planning policy because of the existing vested-interest structure surrounding its operation. In 2016, the government finally decided to transition to a two child policy that allows all couples to have a second child. Nevertheless, China intends to maintain state control over childbirth for the time being and the state shows no signs of relinquishing its power to manage human reproduction even though the nation has shifted to a market-based economy.

Chapter 13

In closing

The Marriage Law was revised in 1980 after the start of the reform and opening-up policies and the one child policy. The revision sought to increase compatibility with the one child policy by lifting the legal age for marriage, making birth planning compulsory for both spouses and preparing to transition to a bilateral descent system allowing a child to take the family name of either parent. It also accommodated social conditions by introducing divorce for reasons of marriage breakdown (Katō 2001). Then, the Marriage Law was amended in 2001 to respond to a diverse range of situations that came along with the progression of reform and opening-up, including provisions to ban polygamy, family abuse and abandonment and domestic violence. The divorce rate jumped in the reform era from a very low rate in the socialist era. While the state's stance to protect order in the marital home as the bedrock of society has been maintained, as demonstrated by the inclusion of a clause about a culpable spouse's obligation for compensation, government policy-making seems to have had trouble keeping up with the speed of change in the family landscape.[5]

In present-day China, expectations for the mutual aid function of the family are rising amid increasing social mobility and social divide promoted by the growth of the market economy and the weakening of social security which was previously supported by 'units' in cities and 'people's communes' in rural villages. The re-evaluation of kinship networks is under way, including maternal and matrimonial relatives in addition to the traditional paternal family and lineage system (Kohama 2015).

Families in contemporary China are still highly controlled by the state. As demonstrated by the initiation of the one child policy alongside the reform and opening-up policies, from the end of the twentieth century the Chinese government continued to strengthen its grip on people's bodies and lives while it liberalized its economy. Now that the policy has transitioned from one-child to two-children, I watch with interest to observe how bio-power will change.

---

5 An overview of issues surrounding marriage and its system in contemporary China is found in Kansai Chūgoku joseishi kenkyūkai (2014: 10–15).

14. Rearrangement of Gender Order in Post-Mao China: Changing Networks of Women's Federations

— *OHASHI Fumie*

Introduction

Post-Mao China has achieved steady development through a major structural change involving its transition from a planned economy to a market economy and engagement with the global economy. It recorded an average real economic growth rate of more than 10% in the 1990s and 2000s, although its year-on-year growth has been decelerating in recent years. It is possible to say that the Chinese economy has managed to make a soft landing macroeconomically. However, this economic restructuring has eroded the basic foundation of life for many people. Amid changes such as the dismantling of the public ownership-based economy, a decline in agriculture producing a growing number of migrant workers and land-grabbing for development projects, a large number of people have found themselves unable to find work or housing, form intimate relationships, have children or enjoy old age.

A gender perspective is essential for an accurate understanding of this situation. The impact of poverty amid economic growth manifests more strongly in women than men as pointed out by feminist economics and social policy studies under the concept of the 'feminization of poverty'.[1] As the changing

---

1 'Feminization of poverty' is a concept that was introduced by the Fourth World Conference on Women in 1995 to indicate that the proportion of women among the poor is increasing and that the poverty rate among women is rising faster than for men.

socioeconomic structure rearranges the gender order[2] that has historically been embedded in society, the situation is becoming even less favorable for women.

In order to find out how the status of women and men has changed since China's transition to the reform and opening-up policies, I look at data on changes in economic disparity between women and men found by the Survey of the Social Status of Women in China, a national sample survey conducted by the All-China Women's Federation (ACWF) and the National Bureau of Statistics of China once per decade.[3]

Figure 14.1 shows the change in women's average annual income in urban and rural areas represented as a percentage of men's average annual income. It fell from 77.5% in urban areas and 79.0% in rural areas in 1990, shortly before Jiang Zeming announced the 'socialist market economy' during the 14th National Congress of the Chinese Communist Party, to 70.1% and 59.6% in 1999 and to 67.3% and 56.0% in 2010 respectively. The data indicate:

1. the existence of economic disparity between men and women before the introduction of the market economy;
2. the overall economic gap between men and women has been widening;
3. the economic disparity between men and women in rural areas was smaller than in urban areas but it rapidly increased from the 1990s.

When we look at the 2010 rural data by income bracket in Figure 14.2, we can clearly see that higher income brackets were dominated by men whereas there were more women in lower income brackets. Liu Bohong et al. (2014 [English]) detect occupational gender segregation behind this phenomenon. Male workers who migrate from rural villages to urban cities tend to concentrate in the high-income construction industry while women tend to work in relatively low-income occupational fields such as in beauty salons, hair salons and housekeeping (domestic workers) (Liu Bohong et al. 2014 [English]).

---

2 'Gender order' is a historically constructed pattern of power relations among women and men in a society which institutionalizes various gender regimes that affect people's relationships (such as policies, laws, beliefs, norms etc.), but it is at the same time reorganized through the everyday practices of women and men (Connell and Pearse 2014)

3 The data from the Survey of the Social Status of Women in China were compiled by Liu Bohong et al. This survey is a nationwide sample survey conducted by the All-China Women's Federation and the National Bureau of Statistics of China and has so far been conducted in 1990, 2000 and 2010.

In order to explain the background of this change, this chapter discusses the network of the ACWF as the meso-level actor with local Women's Federations under its umbrella which mediates the socioeconomic structure on the macro-level and individual women on the micro-level. The Women's Federation network functions as the linchpin when the Chinese Communist Party (CCP) mobilizes women for political purposes such as rural development projects and community activities as well as the messenger who informs women about government policies concerning gender equality, women's rights, the family and children. Although the ACWF and local Women's Federations are supposedly non-governmental 'people's organizations', they are a de facto national/local machinery that wields powerful influence on the construction of gender order in Chinese society on the national and local levels.

The first section provides a brief overview of the history of the Women's Federations through to the early phase of the reform and opening-up period and summarizes the research trends in the history of women and the women's movement in China and the English-speaking world. In the next section,

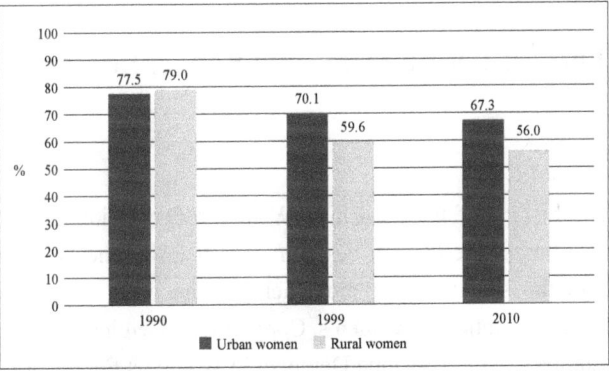

Figure 14.1
Disparity and changes in average annual income between men and women in urban and rural areas
(as a percentage of men's average annual income)

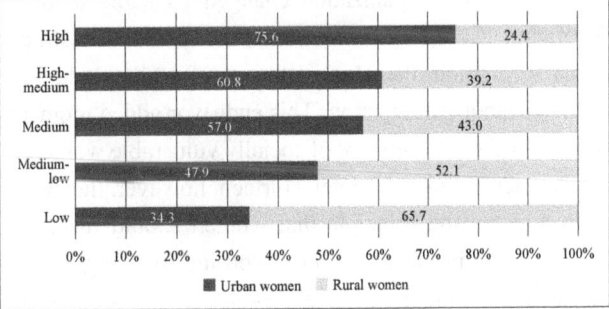

Figure 14.2
Income brackets and gender in rural areas (2010)

Chapter 14

I discuss the organizational structure of the Women's Federations today and its change in the context of China's transition to a market economy. This change is heavily involved in the question of the mobilization of women in economic development. Nevertheless, this section draws attention to the point that the existence of a national/local machinery for women's policy such as the Women's Federation network does not necessarily mean the top-down formation and maintenance of a gender order. While paying attention to this point, the final section discusses the association between the Women's Federation network and the grassroots women's movement for gender equity.

Chapter Thirteen of this book touches on the activity of Women's Federations in China in its discussion on how government policies concerning gender order have changed since the foundation of the People's Republic of China (PRC). Chapter Eighteen considers the trend in feminism and women's/gender research in post-Mao China, including the active and passive involvement of the Women's Federation network. The combined reading of these chapters will help the reader gain a deeper understanding of the relationship between the Women's Federation network and gender order in China.

The All-China Women's Federation and its change

History

The history of the All-China Women's Federation dates back to before the founding of the PRC. It began in March 1949 when women who sympathized with the social reform movement of the early twentieth century convened the First National Women's Congress in Beiping (present-day Beijing) and established the All-China Democratic Women's Foundation. After the founding of the PRC, the organization changed its name to the All-China Women's Federation (ACWF) in 1957. Under the socialist construction project, the CCP began to promote the Marxist theory of women's liberation and encouraged women's labor participation. This endeavor added momentum to the economic and political empowerment of socially vulnerable women.

As mentioned in Chapter Thirteen, however, the party's central committee often adopted the principle that women should focus on their role at home rather than in productive labor according to changing political and economic conditions. During the Cultural Revolution, any women-specific ideologies and arguments were denounced as bourgeois and the ACWF was forced to suspend its operation from 1966 to 1976. The ACWF resumed its activity at the Fourth National Women's Congress in September 1978.

History of the women's movement: Early post-Mao period

During the 1980s, when the dust had settled after the major upheaval of China's political regime through the reforms, studies on the history of the women's movement were undertaken by CCP historians and ACWF researchers while studies on the history of the party were compiled one after another. A notable study published at the time is *History of the Chinese Women's Movement* (*the New Democratic Era*) (Zhonghua quanguo funü lianhehui 1989). As mentioned in Chapter Eighteen, this book was compiled with the awareness that the Women's Federations were the legitimate bearers of the Chinese women's movement and paid attention to the activities of not only the CCP affiliates, but also Christian activists and the women activists of the Chinese Nationalist Party (Kuomintang) as it reviewed the development of the women's movement alongside the history of the communist revolution from the May Fourth Movement to the founding of the PRC. Yet, its focus was limited to 1919–1949 and women's history after the founding of the PRC was not included. There was no attempt to explore deeply how women had lived through the political and economic conditions of the socialist regime.

Reviews of the conditions of women's lives and the activity of the ACWF in the PRC progressed faster overseas than in China. In the English-speaking world, the 1980s saw the appearance of studies that re-examined the history of the mobilization of women under the Communist Party regime, including the Cultural Revolution period, from a feminist point of view.

Patriarchy and Socialist Revolution in China by Judith Stacey (1983), mentioned in Chapter Thirteen, offered a very perceptive critical discussion. Stacey regarded the ACWF as an organization that supervised women under the direction of the CCP as 'public patriarchy' and argued that it was 'created by the party partly to enhance the power of formerly subordinate social groups, operate in formal subordination to the CCP and exist only at its pleasure' (Stacey 1983: 228). This assessment has validity in view of the fact that the ACWF was barred from even discussing women's social subordination amid the radicalized class struggle of the Cultural Revolution era and forced to suspend its operation.

Still, Stacey's discussion does have limitations. Much of her argument relies on ethnographic records made by the Western intellectuals who stayed in China during the 1950s to 1960s to whom changes in gender relations on a micro-level were not very visible. In other words, there is no detailed report on specific activities undertaken by local Women's Federations, how women responded to them or on how they changed the roles and awareness of men and women in the community and the family as a result during the period. This type of constraint due to limited information was common to overseas studies of China at that time.

From the 1980s to the early 1990s, the compilation of records concerning the history of the women's movement in modern and contemporary China was undertaken. Major works include *Chinese Women's Movement Documentary Records Edition* (Zongguo funü guanli xueyuan 1987, 1988, 2 volumes), containing past decisions and directives concerning the women's policies of the CCP and reports written by women cadres, and *Historical Records of the Chinese Women's Movement* (Zhonghua quanguo funü lianhehui funü yundong lishi yanjiushi 1986, 1991a, b, c and d, 6 volumes) putting together a variety of documents concerning women's liberation in modern and contemporary China ranging from discourses hinting at women's liberation in the Ming-Qing transition period, the Opium Wars period and the Taiping Rebellion period as well as Qing-period recommendations against footbinding and in favor of women's education to the women's policy documents of the CCP.

Narratives on the ACWF from oral histories

Among studies from a feminist perspective, attempts to construct an oral history were initiated in the 1990s by analyzing and re-evaluating various activities of the Women's Federations based on stories told by the women who were involved in them.

In 1993, Gao Xiaoxian, who worked in the Research Office of Shaanxi Provincial Women's Federation, began an interview survey of women aged sixty and older (at the time) about their memories of mobilizations of rural women in places such as Xi'an and Weinan in Shaanxi Province during the 1950s. Amid increasingly active international exchanges between Chinese and Western researchers in the field of gender studies around that time (Wang Danning et al. 2014 [Japanese]), American historian Gail Hershatter collaborated with Gao in the project on Chinese women's oral histories from the 1950s.

Gao's study, 'The silver flower contest: Rural women in 1950s China and the gendered division of labor', was published in 2005 and analyzed the impact of the cotton production competitions held by the Women's Federation in rural Shaanxi villages on local gender relations by reference to the accumulated oral history records taken from rural women and Women's Federation cadres as well as archival records and publications (Gao Xiaoxian 2005).

In 1950s China, cotton production took on increasing importance in the industrial sector. New technologies necessitated a finer division of work in cotton production and gave rise to demand for a massive injection of labor. In response to the government's call for labor mobilization into cotton production, the Shaanxi Provincial Women's Federation initiated the 'Silver flower contest' campaign to actively encourage women to learn the required skills and compete for larger output. While it had previously been uncommon for rural women to work outside of their homes, there was much publicity about 'equal pay for equal work' at that time and women were able to earn the same number of work points as men. Thus, the number of female workers increased in cotton production, which had been dominated by men until the early 1950s.

When women's work participation expanded, men moved out of cotton production that utilized complicated new technologies and streamed into industries where they were able to gain more work points for labor contribution such as sideline production (*fuye shengchan*), irrigation and steel production. Gao Xiaoxian points out that 'With the disappearance of "equal work" for men and women, the struggle for "equal pay" disappeared and women's work points slumped' (2005: 168). Men returned to cotton production when the contract responsibility system was adopted in the reform and opening-up period, but a gender gap between men and women was reintroduced to the work-point system (ten points for men and seven points for women). This course of events is likely to have had relevance to the change in income disparity between rural men and women mentioned earlier.

Hershatter carried out a survey of oral histories for her joint research with Gao Xiaoxian in Shaanxi villages during the 1990s and reported her findings in *The Gender of Memory: Rural Women and China's Collective Past* (2011). The study asked what socialism meant for women who were born before 1949 and spent their youth through agricultural collectivization in the 1950s. Hershatter states 'All socialism is local' by reference to the phrase, 'All politics is local', made by Tip O'Neill who was speaker of the house in the U.S. from 1977 to 1987 (2011: 31). In other words, her analysis focuses on the meaning of the changes to the gender relations brought about by socialism to the women who lived in various local communities in various circumstances across Shaanxi Province rather than on painting an overall picture of the socialist gender regime in the framework of 'China'.

Hershatter's interviewees include a broad spectrum of women ranging from non-local cadres on secondment from urban Women's Federations who resided with local families to train local women leaders (*dundian*),[4] rural women selected as campaign activists to promote the Marriage Law, full-time women workers in collective farming and midwives caught between the traditional childbirth practices trusted by rural women and the new 'safe' and 'hygienic' midwifery practices recommended by the Communist Party, to women who were made 'labor models' in cotton production as highlighted by Gao Xiaoxian's study. Individual oral histories shed light on how the network of Women's Federations organized under the socialist regime intersected with the everyday lives of local women and men.

With a growing body of oral history-based new studies such as this, there has been some change in the current of Women's Federation studies linked with the study of CCP history. *The Twentieth-Century History of the Chinese Women's Movement*, recently published in three volumes by the ACWF, discusses the period from 1949 to the Cultural Revolution in volume two, and from the reform and opening-up period onward in volume three (Gu Xiulian 2008, 2013). Although like *The History of the Chinese Women's Movement* it still carries the tone of the history of the women's movement defined by the Communist Party regime, it is underpinned by a body of research accumulated by gender historians in and outside China. Volume three also casts light on the endeavors of regional Women's Federations. This is likely to have been influenced by a growing number of regional studies that paid attention to the history of local women's movements. The use of oral histories is spreading in this field of study as well. *The History of Women's Work in the Chinese Communist Party 1921–1949* compiled by Geng Huamin, who specializes in the history of the CCP, makes reference to many memoirs of former Women's Federation cadres and people around them as well as interviews conducted by Geng.

---

4 '*Dundian*' refers to the embedding of cadres into rural grassroots society to facilitate an understanding and resolution of front-line issues.

Organizational structure and governance of Women's Federations

The organizational structure of the Women's Federations

As mentioned in the previous section, the Women's Federations were forced to suspend their activity during the Cultural Revolution and reactivated during the reform and opening-up period. I now look at the organizational structure of the Women's Federations since the resumption of their activity to date and at how their governance influences the rearrangement of China's gender order.

Today, the ACWF is referred to as one of the 'social organizations' on the website of the Central People's Government of the People's Republic of China. A 'social organization' has a similar status to that of an NGO but it is actually subjected to guidance and control by a superagency according to the rules set out by the Regulation on Registration and Administration of Social Organizations. In reality, many of them operate under administrative or government agencies. According to the overview of social organizations on the webpage of the State Council of the People's Republic of China, 'There are approximately two-hundred social organizations that have been established under administrative agencies and institutions and receive state funding of which the All-China Federation of Trade Unions, the Communist Youth League of China, the All-China Women's Federation and others perform governmental functions to a considerable extent despite their non-governmental nature'.[5] In this sense too, the ACWF can be regarded as a de-facto national machinery for women's policy in China.

The organizational structure of the Women's Federations is under the strong guidance of the CCP. Their network spread throughout society in a manner reminiscent of the capillary network based on the vertical relationship from the local Women's Federation in each province, autonomous region, municipality, county and district to the grassroots women's federation in each township and subdistrict as well as the women's committee in each of the women's workplaces such as administrative agencies and business units. A committee for women workers as part of the trade union is set up in each corporation and school and affiliated with the local Women's Federations on the county

---

5 See the website of the Central People's Government of the People's Republic of China, 'Main Social Organizations', http://www.gov.cn/test/2005-05/24/content_18314.htm (accessed 4 August 2020).

Chapter 14

level and above. The organizational network of the Women's Federations is controlled by the party committee on each level, including personnel matters. On the other hand, their representatives participate in the People's Congress, the People's Political Consultative Conference and their standing committees at each level. The chairperson of the ACWF also serves as vice-chairperson of the Standing Committee of the National People's Congress. Under this structure, the Women's Federations are deeply involved in the legislative process in the domain concerning women and children.

The highest authority of the ACWF is the National Women's Congress, which is held every five years. It carries out important tasks, including decision-making on its operational policies and responsibilities, the deliberation and ratification of reports it receives from the ACWF's executive committee and the election of the executive committee. A similar system has been set up for all of its suborganizations; the congress of women meets every five years on the local level and every three to five years on the grassroots level. The residential committee in every urban residential district and the village committee in the rural village convene the congress of women every three years and elect a women's head (*funü zhuren*) and other local leaders.

The women's head is the official within the network who has the closest involvement in people's day-to-day lives. As the women's leader in the community, she undertakes tasks such as moral education for women and children, the provision of health and hygiene information including that on sexual health and the propagation of new laws and government policies according to the ACWF's action plan. Projects such as the 'Two studies, two competitions' (*Shuangxue shuangbi*) campaign, as discussed below, are planned and implemented in concrete terms on the initiative of the women's head in each community.

In rural villages, the women's head of each village often serves as the head of the local family planning commission. Chapter Thirteen notes that women's heads who were assigned to production brigades were involved in the dissemination of family planning in rural villages during the 1970s. Women's heads still play the central role in reproductive management in rural villages today. The involvement of the grassroots women's power agents in the network points to the organizational broadening of the women's federations since the reform and opening-up era.

Women's Federations' initiative for gender equity

We have seen above that the Women's Federations operate under the guidance of the CCP, including their personnel matters, despite their NGO status as 'social organizations'. However, they have not been following the party's political moves completely and have actively taken the initiative in decision-making on party policies that impact on gender equity.

For instance, the Women's Federations took action and stopped the 'Women go home' (*funü huijia*) ideology from being adopted as a government labor policy when it was proposed in 1980. Movements on the theme of 'Women go home' have been repeatedly debated among Chinese intellectuals since the 1930s. Such movements, which most commonly occur during economic downturns, argue that women should withdraw from the labor force where they compete with men for jobs and return to the home where they can contribute to the domestic realm for the improvement of society and the nation. But when looking back on the early stage of the reform and opening-up policies, it is necessary to understand how the debates were associated with the socioeconomic condition of the time. By the 1980s, China was grappling with the presence of 'youth waiting to be employed' (*daiye qingnian*) who were unable to find employment upon completion of intermediate education due to the effect of Cultural Revolution-era programs such as the Sent-down Youth Movement. In this situation, it was argued that encouraging women to engage in domestic work and childrearing would create job vacancies and improve people's domestic lives at the same time. It won the support of many at the Ministry of Labor (presently the Ministry of Human Resources and Social Security), an administrative division of the State Council of the PRC. On the other hand, the cadres of the ACWF, which had always been supporters of women's participation in productive labor, became concerned about this move.

Political scientist Xu Jialiang analyzed the function of social organizations in the process of decision-making on public policy and shined a light on the action of ACWF cadres at the time. The Ministry of Labor submitted a report to the Central Committee of the CCP that recommended the adoption of 'Women go home' as a policy in 1980. When the ACWF cadres found out what was happening, they raised an objection with the Central Secretariat of the CCP. Nevertheless, their argument was not heard because the ACWF had no authority to take part in the resolution on this report. Luo Qiong, deputy chairperson of the ACWF at the time, telephoned Peng Chong who was involved in the labor, youth and women matters at the central secretariat and demanded to be included in the decision-making process. In the end, Luo Qiong managed to obtain approval from Hu Yaobang, the then secretary general of the central secretariat, and succeeded in swaying the committee to reject the recommendation at the meeting (Xu Jialiang 2003).

This episode illustrates how the cadres of the ACWF, as a non-governmental organization, use its position as a part of the machinery of the CCP power relationship to engage in active lobbying concerning gender-related policy decisions. As we will see in our detailed discussion on the process of the enactment of the Anti-Domestic Violence Law of the People's Republic of China (Anti-DV Law) below, the political negotiation capability of the ACWF rooted in its strong ties to the CCP and the government also carries significance in the legislative process.

Women's Federations and local gender order in the shift to the market economy

The ACWF and local Women's Federations on all levels have initiated various projects mainly for women in post-Mao China.

Volume three of *The Twentieth-Century History of the Chinese Women's Movement* mentions the following among their nationwide projects:

1. 'Two studies, two competitions' (learning culture and technology and competing for grades and contributions: a project to stimulate the rural economy through improved literacy and women's learning of farming technology);

2. 'Heroine's contributions' (*Jinguo Jiangong*: a project to encourage women's contributions to their workplaces and communities through training and commendation);

3. 'Five good families' (*Wuhao Jiating*: a project to commend families that excel in five aspects – spirit of supporting the elderly, good childrearing through family planning, equality of men and women, diligence and frugality at home and environmental protection).[6]

---

6 The 'Five good families' project has been launched frequently under the CCP's women's policy. The five conditions vary from time to time.

The volume explains the history of each project and how they were implemented in various regions. It is difficult to understand from these documents how the Women's Federation projects operate on a local level. Official documents and reports may give the impression that the ACWF gives top-down political guidance to its vertical network of women's organizations down to workplaces and grassroots communities. In reality, observations in communities such as villages and subdistricts have found that their system does not necessarily entail the total obedience of the women's head and other women to unilateral communication from the ACWF.

The Chinese Women's Movement between State and Market by Ellen Judd is a study on the way grassroots level rural women's movements have been implemented in and around Dezhou, Shandong Province (Judd 2002). Judd observed how rural women recognized their own needs and engaged in social reformist practices from the mid-1980s to the 1990s. While the 'Two studies, two competitions' campaign was launched nationally in 1989, the local Women's Federations in the area were supporting the implementation of the women's 'Courtyard economy' (*tingyuan jingji*) by 1984.

The 'Courtyard economy' is an endeavor to make use of land around the house to grow cash crops and raise livestock. It became a valuable means for women in this region to earn cash income without infringing on the 'Men till and women weave' (*nangeng nüzhi*) tradition too much as they were able to engage in economic activity without leaving the home. Judd considers that this type of local political activities to support the practical needs of women were subsequently incorporated into the national 'Two studies, two competitions' campaign that emphasized the importance of women's role in the rural economy. While the 'Two studies, two competitions' campaign promoted the mobilization of women for economic development with a top-down policy, it began as a bottom-up project in the rural villages of Dezhou, Shandong.

Judd's ethnography portrays the women in the position of women's head as non-homogeneous individuals who make different decisions depending on their personal background, interests and the changing expectations of the local Women's Federation and the government. In Huaili village, the women's head was replaced many times between 1988 and 1995. The local Women's Federation in the area maintained that a young and educated woman who put her energy into the 'Two studies, two competitions' campaign would be ideal for the position of women's head. In reality, however, women in their twenties who were interested in economic activity and capable of leading the campaign eventually chose to

Chapter 14

leave the village and pursue business opportunities in the city amid the national shift toward a market economy. In the mid-1990s, the county government put the women's head in charge of a family planning-related project and offered remuneration. Consequently, the women who took on the position around that time spent much of their time promoting administrative programs such as family planning and tax payment and had little involvement in activities such as the 'Two studies, two competitions' campaign (Judd 2002: 88–90).

The ethnography highlights the agencies of rural women who attempt to meet their own needs based on their realistic political and economic considerations while getting involved in the organizational network of the Women's Federations stretching from the ACWF to grassroots communities. The cases of former women's heads who chose to pursue economic self-fulfillment in the city rather than promote the 'Two studies, two competitions' project in the village also remind us that the impact of China's drive toward a market economy has been spreading throughout society.

The Women's Federation projects such as 'Two studies, two competitions' and 'Heroine's contributions' reflected the idea of training women with the capabilities required to perform in a market economy in the first place. When I conducted interviews to collect life histories from the women who worked as domestic workers in Beijing from 2005 to 2007, I noticed that in many cases the Women's Federations and other local administrative agencies were involved in the system of sending and receiving rural women as migrant labor. The ACWF and the State Council Leading Group Office of Poverty Alleviation and Development have been recommending women's employment in domestic service in cities as part of the government policy for rural development (Ohashi 2011). In many regions of China during the 2000s, vocational training and employment for rural women were promoted in the fields of babysitting, elderly care, beauty therapy and hairdressing as well as domestic service under the 'Two studies, two competitions' and 'Heroine's contributions' campaigns. As I mentioned at the start of this chapter, there is occupational gender segregation among migrant workers in the background of the recent economic disparity between men and women in rural areas. It is reasonable to say that this phenomenon has been underpinned by both economic development and women's policy.

Women's needs have become more diverse than ever before due to changes in China's socioeconomic order triggered by the introduction of the market economy system. Under these circumstances, the Women's Federations are not only utilizing their extensive network spreading to the fringes of society as they have done in the past but are also turning their eyes to the activities of grassroots women's organizations. The Federations themselves are more than ever before putting forward their own policies that are different from the wishes of the CCP or the government while maintaining their basic stance that they are 'the bridge and link between the Party and the Government and women, as well as the important pillar of the State power' (ACWF Mission Statement, partly revised at the Eleventh National Women's Congress, 31 October 2013). We shall discuss further changes in the activities of the Women's Federations next.

Today's gender order and changing women's movements

Diversification of women's movements

Women's movements in Chinese society have traditionally been regarded as 'legitimate' when carried out under the guidance of the Women's Federations. Even when projects were implemented bottom-up rather than top-down as we have seen in the previous section, the presence of women leaders such as the women's head and village committee members at the grassroots level was important.

Today, however, the 'women' who are the target of the Women's Federations' activities are not monolithic. With the advance of the market economy, there are increasing numbers of women who engage in informal forms of work such as temporary hiring or seasonal work without a formal employment relationship, female migrant workers from villages or women who have no permanent address due to all sorts of family circumstances. These women slip out of the grasp of Women's Federations' networks at workplaces and in grassroots communities. An increasing number of women work in realms that are less accessible by the Women's Federations such as in foreign-affiliated companies, private-sector businesses or self-employed businesses. Under these conditions, there has been a growth of grassroots women's organizations that dealt with women with different needs from the late-1980s to the 1990s.

Jude Howell has revealed that the Women's Federations were searching for a road map amid the diversification of women's movements at that time based on the interviews and collected writings of ACWF cadres and activists during the period. According to her study, the Sixth National Women's Congress in 1988 became an arena for heated debates on the direction of the Women's Federations. Some argued that they should be autonomous of the CCP and others held that they should become a government ministry or department. Some asserted that they should turn the organization into an NGO while others urged close cooperation with the new women's organizations (Howell 2003).

In reality, the Tiananmen Square incident of June 1989 put all non-governmental activist entities under strict control. Once the Regulation on Registration and Administration of Social Organizations was promulgated by Order of the State Council No. 43 in October of that year, each social activist organization had to be affiliated with its superagency called its 'supervisory unit' (*guakao danwei*) and operate under its management and supervision. Grassroots organizations formed in response to the diverse needs of women were also affected by the regulations. Many of the women's research groups, hotlines and salons that had operated from the late 1980s ended up suspending their activities.

Nevertheless, the United Nations Fourth World Conference on Women/NGO Forum, for which preparations were underway at the time, built a momentum for a common understanding of the importance of a gender viewpoint among many women. The grassroots women's organizations mentioned in the next section launched their gender perspective-based activity in this context. In addition to grassroots women, some Women's Federation cadres and university academics actively pursued interchange under this understanding and built up the subsequent trend of gender research and social practice in China. This development is detailed in Chapter Eighteen. Many case reports contained in *Chinese Women Organizing: Cadres, Feminists, Muslims, Queers* edited by Hsiung Ping-Chun et al. paint concrete pictures of the activities of various women's activist entities during the 1990s (Hsiung et al. 2001).

Strengthened governance and flexible networks

Grassroots organizations came to be subjected to even more stringent control when the Regulation on Registration and Administration of Social Organizations was revised and new rules such as the Interim Regulations on Registration and Administration of Private Non-Enterprise Units and the Regulation on Foundation Administration were created at the end of the 1990s. While social organizations, private non-enterprise units and foundations are NPOs with slightly different characteristics, all are required to 'affiliate' (*guakao*), i.e., attach themselves to, a superagency and receive its supervision.

Has the strengthening of governance placed contemporary China's gender order under a top-down system? In reality, women's activist entities have maintained their networks in an adaptable manner by making flexible choices when caught in the dilemma between the need to solve practical problems and the reinforced rules and regulations. Some women launched their NGOs by complying with the registration regulations while others continued their activities unofficially without 'affiliation'.

Some of China's well-known women's activist entities have continued to maintain a certain level of independence in their operations without affiliating with a superagency that has strong backing. One such case is the Migrant Women's Club (*Dagongmei zhi jia*), which was established in 1996.[7] This organization was formed as an associated project of the *Nongjianü baishitong* (*Rural Women Knowing All*) magazine, which began publication in 1993 under the *Zhongguo funü bao* (*China Women's News*) national newspaper. One of the founders, Xie Lihua, explained that the Beijing Civil Affairs Department had advised them that the organization was not required to register as it was similar to a readers' club of a magazine (Hsiung et al. 2001: 227). For this reason, the Migrant Women's Club was operating without affiliation to a superagency even though it was a grassroots organization. The Migrant Women's Club and the Practical Skills Training School for Rural Women, a separate organization in the same group, are no longer unregistered as they went under the umbrella of a superagency called the Cultural and Developing Centre for Rural Women in 2001. However, the Cultural and Developing Center for Rural Women is a corporation registered with the Bureau of Industry and Commerce and not officially an NGO.

The Center for Women's Law and Legal Services of Peking University was founded by women lawyers and legal researchers only two months after the World Conference on Women and began its activity by forming an affiliation with Peking University. The organization continued to operate as an NGO that conducted legal counselling and research from a gender perspective for over

---

7 The Migrant Women's Club is known as an organization that offers practical social support for rural women living in cities, such as counseling, legal aid and emergency relief funds. In the mid-2000s, they also organized a network of migrant domestic workers who were socially isolated, in cooperation with UN agencies and international NGOs. See Ohashi (2011) for more details on their support for domestic workers.

a decade and built up a reputation in China and overseas. Li Jun has summarized the organization's history based on interviews with the people involved (Li Jun 2014 [English]).

When the center's affiliation was cancelled by Peking University in 2010, it changed its name to the Beijing Zhongze Women's Legal Consulting Services Center under the registration of the Bureau of Industry and Commerce. The official reason for the cancellation was that the center did not meet the university's requirement for an affiliated organization to have a representative and at least five staff members in the employment of the university. According to Li, however, the real problem lay in the fact that the center received funding from a foreign source to engage in public-interest activity (Li Jun 2014 [English]: 5). Amid further tightening of the regulations under Xi Jinping's regime, Zhongze was closed in February 2016. It is obvious that those organizations without strong backing are vulnerable to political pressure, although the human-rights lawyers who used to work at the Peking University center and the Zhongze are continuing their activities at a private law firm called Beijing Qianqian Law Firm.

Have the women's organizations that chose to accept governance from above been subsumed into the top-down gender order? It seems that simple generalization is impossible on this point, even regarding the Women's Federations 'within the system'. Women's Federations are exposed to a regulatory burden more than any other women's organizations as they are closely aligned with the CCP and the government. Yet, they have strong political bargaining power precisely because they are inside the system as mentioned earlier. On the other hand, it is not entirely correct to say that grassroots women's organizations operating under governance from above are weak activist entities with no political negotiation capability either. Some of the grassroots women's organizations that are officially registered according to the regulations are affiliated with 'social organizations' with a certain level of political influence, including government agencies, Women's Federations, education and research institutions and academic societies, and are capable of using their networks for policy lobbying.

Let us look at the development of women's activism surrounding the Anti-Domestic Violence Law, which was enacted in December 2015 and implemented in March 2016. The legislation was realized through solidarity between the ACWF, regional Women's Federations and grassroots women. During the process, Women's Federations at all levels got involved in investigative research and political coordination from the 1990s with an eye toward the submission of their proposition at the National People's Congresses and the Chinese People's Political Consultative Conferences. At the same time, a grassroots women's organization called the Anti-Domestic Violence Network was established with affiliation with the China Law Society and worked effectively inside and outside the state apparatus. It is said that the network tackled the issue of domestic violence using wide-ranging approaches from policy and legal recommendations to model-building for DV intervention, provision of psychological counselling and legal advisory services that were unavailable in the public service and organizing training for the judiciary, the police, lawyers and Women's Federation cadres (Feng Yuan 2016 [Japanese]).

Lastly, it is not necessarily the case that the women's activist entities that have been eluding reinforced governance have no connections with the Women's Federations which operate 'within the system'.

Xie Lihua of the Migrant Women's Club mentioned above used to be a deputy editor-in-chief of the *Zhongguo funü bao* (*China Women's News*), which is the official organ of the ACWF. Guo Jianmei, a representative of the former Peking University Center and Zhongze Center mentioned above, worked in the legal consultant office of the ACWF during the 1980s and took part in the drafting of the Law of the People's Republic of China on the Protection of Rights and Interests of Women, which was promulgated in 1992. The leaders of these women's movements have made a conscious decision to remain grassroots and searched for solutions to gender-sensitive issues even though they were in a relatively close position to the Women's Federations and the government.

In closing

In this chapter, we have laid out changes in China's gender order at the junction between economic marketization and economic globalization as well as in the recent tightening of regulations for civic movements with a particular focus on the history of the Women's Federations and changes in their endeavors before and after reform and opening-up.

The oral history studies of Gao Xiaoxian and Gail Hershatter and the ethnography of Ellen Judd highlight the fact that China's gender order has been reorganized in response to the practical needs of the women who live in local social relationships and has not necessarily been prescribed in a top-down manner. On the other hand, many rural women were placed in an even weaker economic position amid occupational gender segregation after reform and opening-up as shown by the data presented in the introduction to this chapter. While the women might choose to leave home villages as migrant workers according to their practical needs to support their family and pay for their children's education, the projects that were undertaken by the Women's Federations in step with economic marketization contributed to the occupational gender segregation trend considerably.

In the meantime, Chinese women can no longer be regarded as a monolithic entity. Post-Mao China has spawned many grassroots women's movements as if to echo their diverse voices. The Women's Federations 'within the system' and the grassroots activist entities appear to operate under completely different principles. However, it is clear that the women activists of the latter are not necessarily disconnected from the Women's Federations network but instead sometimes collaborate in a flexible manner as demonstrated in the move to achieve anti-DV legislation.

Thus, today's Chinese gender order is influenced by an intricately constellated relationship. It is unclear how the recent move to tighten control over civic movements will transform this relationship in the future. As mentioned in Chapter Eighteen, since the mid-2010s the government has been suppressing grassroot activists who spread critical feminist views through performance art on the streets, at university campuses and on internet media. Despite the growing pressure, women's voices calling for gender equity still resonate under the condition of top-down governance.[8] The most thrilling aspect of gender studies is its capacity to detect the possibility of change in their voices as we critically discuss structural disparity and oppression.

---

[8] For example, in early 2020, Guo Jing, a feminist activist and social worker based in Wuhan, started reporting on ordinary people's everyday life during the COVID-19 lockdown by posting articles on 'Matters', a Chinese-language online public space that bypasses government censorship. In her report, Guo sharply described her feminist concerns during the lockdown period, such as increasing cases of domestic violence and the heavy burden of housework on women. She also interviewed the people on the street, often rural migrants, who had to risk their lives to continue to work during the pandemic. Guo's report was published as *Diary of the Wuhan Lockdown* (*Wuhan fengcheng riji*).

Column 4

Two Histories of Women in Modern China

SUDŌ Mizuyo

It goes without saying that research on 'women's history' deepened consideration of the question of women in history before the emergence of the field of gender history studies. At present, analyses that introduce the concept of gender are mainstream, but this does not mean that these are based on a repudiation of 'women's history' research in its entirety. Research into modern Chinese women's history, in particular, is a field in which there is a rich accumulation of studies, and current gender-history research has inherited much from it.

Ono Kazuko (b. 1932), a researcher who studies the history of the Ming and Qing dynasties, was the first Japanese scholar to seriously direct a spotlight upon modern Chinese women's history. In 1978, Ono published a pathbreaking book, *Chinese Women in a Century of Revolution, 1850–1950* (Ono 1978). That was over forty years ago, and at the time, there was hardly any research relating to modern Chinese women even in China, let alone in Japan.[1] For that reason, when the book was published, it attracted international attention, and was translated first into Korean (Ono 1985) and then into Chinese (Ono 1987) and English (Ono 1989).[2]

What significance might be found in reappraising Ono Kazuko's achievements from the perspective of present-day gender history research? And what impact has this work had on research today? Two aspects are identifiable – a positive legacy and a negative legacy.

---

[1] Apart from Ono's own paper (1968), there had only been a few works on the period prior to the Xinhai Revolution, namely Chen Dongyuan (1928) and Tan Sheying (1936), penned in the 1920s and 30s.

[2] Even today, this is referred to as 'the most comprehensive history of modern Chinese women to date' (Judge 2008: 2). At an international conference held jointly by Fudan and Michigan Universities in June 2004, Ono Kazuko, who took the podium as a presenter, was given a special introduction by the organizers as a pioneer in this field. Some of the papers presented at that conference (including Ono Kazuko's 'Ma Junwu's translations and Japan') are contained in UM-Fudan Joint Institute for Gender Studies (2005).

In terms of the positive, one could cite the fact that Ono's *Chinese Women in a Century of Revolution* became the foundation for the later growth of individual and specific research groups in Japan on women's history in modern China. The major feature of the book was its excavation of traces spanning the over 120 years from the Taiping Rebellion to the 1970s of the women who lived their lives in a broad range of fields, including politics, thought, society, literature and labor. The book is unparalleled in its full use of diverse historical materials such as newspaper and magazine articles, laws, songs and literature, and in terms of its empathic depiction of each of the women, whether urban or rural, ranging from the intellectual class to the poverty-stricken. Furthermore, its venture into women's sexuality through the word 'eros' is noteworthy. After the book's publication, much research on such specific issues started to accumulate.[3]

The negative legacy can be seen in its uncritical use of the Chinese popular 'revolutionary history' narrative as a framing for the book. Ono's *Chinese Women in a Century of Revolution* is one of women's liberation that aligns with the historical perspective of the Chinese revolution, and in the preface to the English version, Ono herself states that there was 'a tendency [in the book's content] to idealize the Cultural Revolution and superficially to accept its rhetoric' (Ono 1989: xvi; Suetsugu 1995: 229).[4] Underpinning this description lay such historical limitations as a dearth of information about China in that same period. In Ono's subsequent research, as such problems as human rights abuses towards women that had occurred in parallel with the advancement of women's liberation progressively came to light, it was natural that a reappraisal of the relationship between women's liberation and revolution became a significant point of contention (Suetsugu 1995: 229).

From the 1980s onwards, numerous studies focusing on approaches from both history and literature have examined the ways Chinese women relate to the state, and research from a gender perspective became more common from the 1990s.[5] What such research elucidated was that the path to transforming women

---

3 On research in Japan, see Akiyama (2016b), as well as Fujii (1995) and Sudō (2002, 2007b [English], 2012 [Chinese]). For research published in Chinese, see Wang Shu-Hwai (1995).

4 The Korean edition was banned because of its positive description of Chinese revolutionary history and critical account of the family system. See Ono (2005).

5 There are, for example, the following studies: Maeyama (2000); Shirouzu (2004a); Egami (2003); Sakamoto (2004a); and Sudō (2007a).

into 'citizens' had headed in the direction of emphasizing women's contribution to the revolution and the state, and as a consequence, this arguably hindered the development of feminism in China.

A study that reappraised and comprehensively discussed the relativization of the connection between women's liberation and the Chinese revolution is Suetsugu Reiko's (1929–2016) *History of Chinese Women in the Twentieth Century* (*20 seiki Chūgoku joseishi*), published in 2009. Its author was a scholar from the same generation as Ono, who served for a long time as the representative of the Tokyo-based Society of Historical Studies on Chinese Women. This book represented a new historical overview published around thirty years after Ono's *Chinese Women in a Century of Revolution*.

In Suetsugu's book, again, one can identify a legacy from Ono's scholarship in two respects. Firstly, in Suetsugu's volume, a great deal of further historical material has been added, taking into account the advancement of research over the three decades, as well as the author's own exhaustive investigations. Changes in fashions, women of ethnic minorities, female students who went to Japan to study and both Japanese and Chinese women in Manchuria were among the new themes considered, and this was significant in the sense of supplementing areas that had received inadequate research attention. The volume has a strong interest in the Sino-Japanese relationship, and mention is also made of the fact that women who had been subjected to sexual violence from the Japanese army had begun to raise their voices in the early 1990s.

Furthermore, while aware of the gender perspective in the Chinese Communist Party's historical view of the revolution, Suetsugu critically questions it anew, pointing out:

> While there were significant accomplishments as a result of strong government leadership, the strong government role meant that demands of the women's movement were always deemed subordinate to the regime's central goals, and whenever the government's definition of its central goals changed, policies with regard to women's issues also changed. (Suetsugu 2009: 327)

In other words, she argued that even though women's liberation and revolution might have appeared to have progressed in alliance, in fact there was always tension between them, and the interests of the revolution and the regime's central goals tended to take precedence over women's liberation.

Conversely, a look at research in modern Chinese women's history conducted in China shows what we might call China's 'official' view of women's history which regards the revolution and women's liberation as a single entity. In other words, this 'official' view emphasizes women's contribution to the revolution and the state, and discusses the process by which women were 'liberated' from a subordinate position by the revolution, leaving 'the home' to go out into society and gain economic independence.[6] With the advent of the 1990s, oral history studies began to appear and there was great diversity in research, visible in terms of topics and methodology, including the introduction of the concept of 'gender'.[7] However, positive appraisals of the revolution are fundamental, and there has been no overall reconsideration of the connection between the revolution and the women's movement and women's lives.

If one takes into account such tendencies in China, it could be argued that the progress of Japanese research into modern Chinese women's history from Ono to Suetsugu did deepen the investigation, while maintaining a certain distance from the Chinese historical view of women's liberation.

However, the meaning of researching modern Chinese women's history as Japanese female scholars is complicated. This is because while on the one hand Japanese women scholars' own life experiences have led them to share empathy with Chinese women, they also have had to acknowledge their position as scholars from the country that had once invaded China. Both Ono and Suetsugu were extremely aware of their own positionality, and Ono described her motivation for writing *Chinese Women in a Century of Revolution* as follows:

> It is my heartfelt wish that [my research] will be useful to the women of both Japan and China whose countries for these several decades were in

---

6 On this point, see Maeyama (2005) and Du Fangqin (2011 [Japanese]).

7 On the issues of the introduction of the concept of gender to China and its translated terms, see Wang Zheng (2016 [Japanese]: 96–126).

an especially unhappy relationship, so that they will deepen their mutual understanding and strengthen their solidarity. (Ono 1978: 282)

As mentioned above, Suetsugu, too, devoted many pages to relations between Japan and China. The question of how to understand such consciousness is a task for future scholars.

Gender History in China
PART II

15. The Household Register and the Family in Ancient China

— WASHIO Yūko

Introduction

Imperial China ruled its people through the use of a registration system that recorded population using the household as the basic unit. This record is called the household register. In the Spring and Autumn period, the traditional clan system of society slowly fell apart and agricultural work increasingly took place in smaller independent family units. The territorial states that emerged during the Warring States period as well as the subsequent empires of China gathered demographic data on families as household units which were regarded as the economic foundation of the polity. For imperial China (the Qin and Han dynasties in particular), the compilation of household registers was essential. Household registers are still used in China and Japan today.

The primary purpose of household register compilation was to allow the regime to gather information on its people as a state resource. It was intended to comprehensively assemble information, including each person's place of residence, economic condition and cohabiters. In addition, the regimes attempted to entrench marital order underpinned by the husband's superiority over the wife through the household institution. Because the order of the household as the family unit was primarily based on kinship, the proper functioning of family order was a major factor in the safeguarding of the household as the smallest constituent unit of the state. Because the household institution placed certain constraints upon the male-female relationship, a discussion of the actual conditions and significance is useful in ascertaining the state of this relationship at the time as well.

The Household Register and the Family in Ancient China

This chapter explains briefly why household registers were established and why the household unit was created for the purpose of registering people.

Humans as a resource

The origin of household registration traces back to the Warring States period (fifth to third centuries BCE), an age of hardship for ordinary people. Jia Yi stated in his *Essay Faulting the Qin* (*Guoqinlun*) that the war-weary people at the end of this period simply accepted Qin rule in hope of peace and quiet. According to Jia Yi, one million lives were lost in battles against the Qin. From this statement we can see that it was common to deploy hundreds of thousands of infantrymen to battles in large-scale conflicts during the Warring States period; there is little question that wars consumed vast numbers of human lives.

Large-scale conflicts require not only many soldiers but also food to feed them as well as a wide variety of goods such as weapons, clothing and vehicles. The importance of military manpower and financial muscle was acknowledged by the thinkers of the day.[1] Mobilization of non-military labor was also essential as the transportation of food required manpower. The people were the resource supporting this military force, financial power and labor force and regimes endeavored to gather accurate information on people's whereabouts, including their age, sex and whether or not they had disabilities, in order to efficiently secure control over human and financial resources. The following examples are Qin-era registers of residents (census registers) excavated in 2002 from the ruins of an ancient castle in Liyezhen located on the western edge of northern Hunan Province. Personal information about all household members was found on each wooden slip.

Example A[2]:

Nanyang, householder, Jing [origin], *bugeng* [rank], Manqiang [name].	Wife named Qian.	Child [son], lesser *shangzao* [rank], □[name].	Minor daughter, Tuo [name].	Bondservant named Ju. Head of the group of five.

---

1 'Waging war', *Sunzi: The Art of Warfare*, among others.
2 Artefact No. k11/k27, Color illustration No. 36, 1 and 2 in Hunansheng wenwukaogu yanjiusuo (2007).

Chapter 15

Example B[3]:

Nanyang, householder, Jing, *bugeng*, Songwu. Younger brother, *bugeng*, Xiong. Younger brother, *bugeng*, Wei.	Xiong's wife named □□. Wei's wife named □.	Child [son], lesser *shangzao*, Chuan. Child [son], lesser *shangzao*, Zhu. □'s son, lesser *shangzao*, □. Xiong's son, lesser *shangzao*, □.	Wei's child, minor daughter, □.	Bondservant named □.

While a majority of bamboo or wooden slips documenting official records measure around twenty-three centimeters long (one *chi*), these slips are twice as long at forty-six centimeters. The writing space is divided into five sections by four horizontal lines. The beginning of the first section always records the householder who is responsible for the household. Example A indicates that it was a Nanyangli householder who was formerly a subject of Chu, followed by his rank (*bugeng*) and name (Manqiang). As I will explain in more detail later, ancient China bestowed merit or honor ranks on many adult men to indicate their positions. The ranking system included twenty ranks, in which the rank of *bugeng* was fourth lowest.

Entries for other household members included their relationship with the householder followed by their name, as shown in the second-section entry of 'wife named Qian', the householder's wife. The second section in Example B shows each member's family relationship with a member other than the householder as in, for example, Xiong's wife. The third section in Example A shows his son with a rank of lesser *shangzao* and the fourth section indicates that his daughter was a minor. Thus, the relationship, name, rank and whether the individual was an adult or child were recorded for each household member.

---

3 Artefact No. k11/k2, 23, Color illustration No. 39, 19 and 20 in Hunansheng wenwukaogu yanjiusuo (2007).

The Household Register and the Family in Ancient China

Incidentally, age (adult/child) and sex were not always recorded. This is probably because it was possible to deduce such information on the basis of the section in which an individual was recorded. In this format, the first section contained entries concerning adult men, the second section adult women, the third section minor men, the fourth section minor women and the final section elderly adults without corvée obligation (for example, a bondservant named Ju in Example A). These sections represent the degree of levy imposed by the state: military service as well as corvée labor were imposed on the adult men recorded in the top section whereas the adult women recorded in the second section were obliged to provide corvée labor only. The elderly people in the last section were exempted from levy. In short, this was a list that categorized people according to the level of their service obligations.

The list was established by the Qin dynasty, a short-lived regime lasting for just over a decade after its unification of the central parts of what we now know as China, but the practice of collecting accurate personal information was also observed by subsequent dynasties. As the household register formed the basis on which state resources were properly quantified, it was thought that 'Having a thorough grasp of the population is fundamental to the running of a state'.[4] It is said that Cao Cao was delighted to discover the number of soldiers in the newly acquired territory of Jizhou thanks to its household registers.[5]

One concrete example of this type of population data collection is the census register excavated in the city center of Changsha, Hunan Province, in 1996. This Three Kingdoms-period list recorded the names of residents in units of families. The register was excavated at the site of the former administrative office of the fiefdom of the Lord of Linxiang in Changsha County, in the state of Wu. The bamboo slips had originally been strung together in book form, but it is now largely impossible to figure out how individual slips were connected to one another as they have come apart due to broken strings. Consequently, there are very few cases where complete restoration has been achieved for records on all members of one household. The following are examples of partially restored household records.

---

4 'The numbering of people', *Balanced Discourses* (*Zhonglun*) by Xu Gan.
5 'Biography of Cui Yan', in *Records of the Three Kingdoms*.

Chapter 15

Example C[6]:

Village of Pingyang, householder, *gongsheng* [honorary rank], named Zheng Ping, thirty-two years old, one *suan*, legs swollen. (Bamboo slip 10480)

Ping's mother, adult female, Qie, seventy years old. (Bamboo slip 10479)

Ping's wife, adult female, named Qu, twenty-eight years old, one *suan*. (Bamboo slip 10481)

Ping's child, minor male, named Ge, seven years old. (Bamboo slip 10488)

Example D:

Village in Dongyang, householder, *gongsheng*, □ Zan, twenty-one years old, one *suan*, *geixianzu*. (Bamboo slip 10308)

The format of this list was different from that of the aforementioned Qin registers in that information about one person was recorded on one bamboo slip. The first slip was for the householder beginning with the name of the village where he lived, his position within the household, honorary rank, name, age and *suan* recorded in that order. The *suan* was the unit of calculation for adult men and women who were subjected to corvée labor, capitation and other levies. The slip was followed by other bamboo slips carrying information about the other members of the household. They generally began with the name of a person and the

10488   10481   10479   10480

Figure 15.1
Bamboo slips of Example C.
Source: Restored household records in Wu of the Three Kingdoms, excavated in Changsha County.

---

6 Examples C, D and E. 'Bamboo slips One', in Changsha jiandu bowuguan, Zhongguo wenwu yanjiusuo and Beijing daxue lishixuexi (2003).

family member's kin relationship with that person, followed by the member's name, age and corvée obligation (*suan*). The majority or minority (age) or sex of each person were not always recorded, just as in the case of the Qin slips. It would have been possible to determine whether a person was an adult or a minor based on the recorded age.

In Example C, we can see the comment 'swollen legs' at the end of the entry for the householder, Zheng Ping, indicating some kind of disability due to illness. In this way, disabilities or illnesses were often recorded in the register (Fukuhara 2015). The term *geixianzu* in Example D indicates that this man served as a county soldier. Information about people's involvement in certain forms of military service, labor service or government service was recorded in this way which exempted them from other service obligations.

Example E:

> Village in Yinyang, householder, *gongsheng*, named Hengyi, thirty-five years old, *zhenli* [official title]. (Bamboo slip 9143)
>
> Yi's mother, adult female, named Qie, fifty-five years old. (Bamboo slip 9149)
>
> Yi's daughter's, minor female, named Hua, six years old. (Bamboo slip One 9431)
>
> Yi's younger brother, named Yi □ □, twenty years old. (Bamboo slip 9081)
>
> Yi's sister, named A, thirteen years old. (Bamboo slip 9079)
>
> Yi's bondservant, named Shi, sixty-three years old. (Bamboo slip 9134)
>
> Yi's bondservant, Jian, fourteen years old. (Bamboo slip 9135)
>
> Yi's family has ten members, *zi* one hundred. (Bamboo slip 9055)
>
> (Machida 2007)

In the household shown in Example E, the householder, Hengyi, was a government official. The last slip (9055) tallied up the number of household members and indicated *zi*, which showed the amount of tax on their assets. Corvée obligation was not recorded in this register format. From this we can see that the state of Wu used various census registers for different target populations at different times and recorded in different formats.

Chapter 15

It is clear from the Wu census register that the name, age, rank and familial relationship along with disability or illness and official duty (public service and particular types of corvée labor or military service) of each person were important items for the record. The maturity or minority and age of the person were not always recorded as they could be inferred from the age and relationship. The age was relevant to the collection of the capitation tax while the age, rank, illness and duty related to military and labor services.

It is evident from the aforementioned registers from the two different time periods that the name, maturity or minority or age (to determine if the person was an adult), merit rank and familial relationship (which also indicated sex) of each member of the household constituted important information. In short, it was important for the regimes to know the familial relationship between people besides their resource value (age and sex) and position in the state (rank) as it had a bearing on control over human relationships within the 'household' (to be discussed later).

The 'household' and household registration

In fact, we cannot be certain that the above two census registers of residents were household registers per se, even though they would have pertained to household registration. One example that illustrates the contents of a household register more directly is the following change-of-address notification addressed to the land of the dead. This document was found among the burial goods of a woman who was buried during the reign of Emperor Wen of Han, excavated in 1992 from Former Han tombs near Gucheng of Chu in Jiangling County, Hubei Province (present-day Jingzhou District, Jingzhou City, Hubei Province).

Example F[7]:

> In the seventh year [of the reign of Emperor Wen, i.e., 17 BCE], in the tenth month, in which the first day was *bingzi* [the thirteenth day], <on *gengzi* [the thirty-seventh day]>, Qi, [Bailiff] of Middle Township respectfully reports the following: [A resident of] Xin'an, an adult woman, Yan, personally reported that together with [her] adult male bondservants Jia and Yi [A & B], and <adult> female bondservant Fang,

---

7 M18:35 A, B, C and D. See Jingzhou Museum, Hubei Province (2000) and Huang Shengzhang (1994).

[they would] move to [the Underworld] Andu 'City of Peace'. [Yan requests that her document] be presented to [the Underworld] Deputy of Andu. [Ask the Underworld bureaucracy to] accept [the] recorded names and related accounts [of Yan's household] [i.e., the household register]. When [these] documents arrive, send a receipt back. [Qi] respectfully reports above.

In the tenth month, on *gengzi*, Deputy of Jiangling [County] from the Long lineage respectfully transfers [these documents] to the [Underworld] Deputy of Andu. / Handled by Ting [M18:35 B front side].

Handled by Chan [M18:35 B reverse side]
    Xin'an [Village], head of the household, adult woman,
    Yan, widow of *guannei hou* [the nineteenth rank]
Adult male bondservant Jia
Adult male bondservant Yi
Adult female bondservant Fang
This household is privileged and not levied poll taxes and corvée service [M18:35 C].

The notification comprises four wooden slips, A, B, C and D. They were stacked in that order with B facing downward so that the written surfaces of B and C faced each other. A functioned like the front of an envelope and indicated that the notification was from the assistant officer of Jiangling County to the assistant officer (of the county) of Andu. B was a cover letter stating that the bailiff of Middle Township, Jiangling County, reported to the county assistant officer the transfer of a household of four members headed by an adult woman named Yan in October of the seventh year of the reign of Emperor Wen of Han and their household register was being sent to Andu (another name for the underworld). It is supposed that the information written on C (and possibly D) was the contents of their household register. The first entry included the householder's village name (address), position in the household, age/sex (adult woman), name and the merit rank of her deceased husband, followed by entries about the other three household members (bondservants) who were moving with her stating that they were 'adult', and their names. The last entry stated that they were *husuan*, meaning that they were exempted from state levies. D contained a list of burial goods, which is thought to be an inventory of the possessions the householder intended to take with her when she moved from the world of the living to that of the dead.

Although the document was a burial item and not an official document, it is considered to have been modeled on the official format. Its contents suggest that the official household register would have recorded the householder's local village, name, majority or minority and merit rank (that of her deceased husband in this example).[8]

The fact that the residents recorded on the lists were registered with local government offices in units of households gives rise to the question of what the 'household' was. Why were people registered in households rather than individually?

Firstly, the household was the unit of land ownership. According to an early-Former Han regulation,[9] people other than the householder were barred from registering the ownership of any agricultural or residential land. In other words, land was owned by households. It is unknown how chattels were treated, but the total asset ownership was recorded for each household as in the example of the Wu slip cited earlier.

The registration of residential land for each household meant that people in the same household lived on the same grounds. Under the Qin Code, the bounds of a household were determined by the bounds of cohabitation based on the understanding that the household register was defined by the sharing of a residence and should correspond to the place of residence (Liu Hsin-Ning 2011 [Japanese]). In short, the household register was the unit of cohabitation and co-ownership of real property, which was a major asset.

Based on this attribute, the household overlapped with the 'family' (*jia*) as the unit for 'common living and budget' as well as the unit of livelihood. According to one historical document,[10] a person received 100 *mu* (4.368 hectares) of paddy field when he turned thirty years of age and supported a family of five (parents, himself, wife and child) who belonged to the same household.

---

8 It is debatable whether the property inventory on D was part of the household register or not, because opinions are still divided on the question of whether the household register at the time recorded people's land and other assets.

9 'Statutes on households', *Statutes and Ordinances of the Second Year*, 323–324.

10 'Commentary on well-fields' quoted in *Comprehensive Meanings of Popular Customs* (*Fengsu tongyi*) by Ying Shao, cited in 'Biography of Liu Chong', *History of the Later Han* (*Hou Hanshu*), Vol. 76. Also, 'Year 15 of the reign of Duke Xuan', *Gongyang Commentary on the Spring and Autumn Annals with Etymological Commentary* (*Chunqiu Gongyang jiegu*) by He Xiu states: 'Therefore the saint established the nine-square land ownership system to distribute arable land. A plot of 100 *mu* was distributed to each married couple to support their parents, wife and son in a family of five'.

The Household Register and the Family in Ancient China

As the household was the unit for the sharing of residence and wealth, the arrangement was dissolved when an individual gained independence and set up a separate household. A historical document about property disputes in the Qin period reports a case in which a man was given a house and part of a field for his livelihood when he broke away from a household and set up on his own. A wealthy Qin person named Pei allowed a bondservant named Shi to marry in the fifteenth year of King Zheng of Qin (232 BCE). One year later, Pei spent 5,000 coins on buying a house for Shi and settled a horse and twenty *mu* (0.87 hectares) of field on him so he could split from Pei's household and set up his own household register.[11] The purchase of a residence (to allow Shi to live separately) and the division of livelihood occurred simultaneously with the splitting of the household.

In this way, the household played an important role as a unit of people living together. For this reason, the state endeavored to maintain and develop households.

The political discourse at the time emphasized the importance of protecting any *jia* (household as the unit of living) that fell into crisis due to overburdening or a natural disaster.

Example G[12]:

> In a farming family of five, at least two members are obligated to perform labor service these days. One farmer is capable of cultivating 100 *mu* at most, which can yield only 1,940 liters of crop. Tilling in spring, weeding in summer, harvesting in autumn and crop storing and tree felling for firewood in winter. The repair and maintenance of the local office and other compulsory services [...] no time to rest one's body throughout the year. Tasks such as attending to private visitors, making condolence visits, visiting sick people and caring for orphans and infants add to one's burden. Such is their hardship. In addition, they suffer natural disasters such as flooding and drought. The government comes to collect taxes at short notice and irregular intervals and issues decrees in the morning and begins to enforce them in

---

11 According to 'Four documents on the criminal lawsuits' (Slip numbers 0040 and 0089) in Zhu Hanmin and Chen Songchang (2013), 'Shi was a former bondservant of Pei who lived in the same residence [belonged to the same household]. Pei let Shi marry three years ago and bought him a house worth 5,000 *qian*, settled a horse and twenty *mu* [0.87 hectares] of rice field on him, and released him from Pei's household to set up for himself a year later'.

12 'Treatise on economic matters', Vol. 1, *History of the Former Han* (*Hanshu*), Chao Cuo's memorial to Emperor Wen.

Chapter 15

the afternoon. The haves must sell necessities at half the market value while the have-nots are forced to borrow money at an interest rate of 100%. Some people have to sell their cropping land or house and even their children or grandchildren to repay their debts.

The above statement assumed a family of five who cultivated their fields to make a living. The household had at least two income providers but they were extremely busy with their year-round farming work and corvée labor while caring for children and the sick and organizing funerals for the dead. When struck by a disaster or other unforeseeable situations such as a sudden tax demand, their farming income was not enough to support their family: they lost their land or children and the family fell apart and the household disintegrated. The household was a place of residence for those involved in production, which was the economic cornerstone of the state. Policy-makers had to enforce measures and policies with the protection of households in mind because the regime's economic foundation could not be sustained unless the viability of vulnerable households was maintained. With regard to state-imposed levies in particular, it was important to survey the condition of households as units of livelihood and prevent excessive burden on them by making requisitions in an efficient, fair and measured manner based on the collected data.

The system thus reflected the necessity of avoiding excessive levies. For a household to be maintained, there had to be income earners within the household to support it economically. For this reason, authorities were prohibited from drafting more than one member of a household into military service at the same time.[13] Registration for individual households was required so that levies were imposed according to their circumstances and assistance was provided according to the level of hardship for the purpose of preserving the household as a dwelling and economic unit.

Those deployed to battlefields as soldiers were granted merit ranks according to their military service. They were given an 'incentive' to distinguish themselves in battle whereby they could gain higher ranks that promised more privileges and property, a system designed to increase their willingness to fight. For the populace, going off to war was a life-threatening high-risk act but it

---

13 'Miscellaneous excerpts of Qin's statutes' 39, the Qin bamboo slips from Shuihudi. The statute concerning garrison service states, 'Members of the same household shall not be conscripted at the same time. If Prefectural Overseer, Commander and Warrior Official fail to obey this rule, they will face a fine of two sets of armor.

also came with the possibility of high returns. Any improvement of their rank as the result of meritorious military service was recorded in the household register. Household registration functioned to record and guarantee the benefits pertaining to one's position gained through service and at the same time acted as a means to draft people into such service.

It was essential for the government to know the whereabouts of its people if it were to conscript soldiers. All residents had to keep the authorities informed about their whereabouts, and this was done by registering the individual as a member of a household attached to a specific local administrative unit, the 'village'. This mechanism was further supported by the five-households system, in which neighboring households were held jointly responsible for crimes or corvée evasion.[14]

As the household was the unit for daily life, it was also the place where the next generation of the workforce was nurtured. The regimes developed systems to encourage childbirth that targeted, first of all, women as the child-bearers, and secondly their husbands, by releasing them from some obligations or offering rewards.

At the time, some people thought that married couples should recognize their responsibility to raise children.[15] It was believed that the responsibility for the growth and development of the next generation of the labor force rested solely upon the shoulders of each married couple. Regulations stipulated that the married couple must belong to the same household, and as we will see later, the household was expected to function as the site of labor reproduction.

Household registration and the concept of 'inside and outside'

Chinese regimes not only paid attention to sustaining the economic viability of the household = family, they also looked to order within the household. This can be observed in the institution of 'husband and wife'. The husband and wife had to belong to the same household and the wife was prohibited from becoming the

---

14 'Miscellaneous excerpts of Qin's statutes' 32–33, the Qin bamboo slips from Shuihudi. 'People who commit fraud such as pretending to be elderly and making a false declaration in their old age shall face a fine of two sets of armor. If the heads of the village fail to report such offense, they shall face a fine of one set of armor each. The heads of the five households will be fined one set of armor per household. All will be sentenced to banishment [The statute concerning registration]'.

15 'Biography of Wang Ji', *History of the Former Han* (*Hanshu*). 'In the community at large, people marry at a young age and have children before they learn how to be their father and mother; because they are not educated adequately, many of the people die young.'

householder. Consequently, in cases where the household included only members of a nuclear family, the husband was always named as the householder.[16]

In fact, *huren* (householder) is not a term that we often encounter. Students of Chinese history are more likely to have encountered the Tang term *huzhu* to indicate the 'person who represents and takes responsibility for a household'. The *huzhu* in the Tang period was responsible for the accuracy of information in his household register and subjected to heavy punishment if entries such as the number and ages of its members were found to be incorrect. As the head of the family was always named as the head of the household, he was able to control the members of his household based on his position as the most respected member of the family. On the other hand, the *huren* had less responsibility and was not punished for incorrect age entries in the register. Thus, the *huzhu* and the *huren* were both household heads but there was a slight difference between them.

Nevertheless, the *huren* was the representative of his household and responsible for observing formalities in dealing with the state. As we saw in the above example (Example F) regarding notification to move to another world, if a family moved to another township, the householder had to report to local authorities. The householder also had a duty to declare their household property.[17] In one case reported in the aforementioned accounts of property disputes in Qin, the mother of a minor household member declared property on his behalf and was punished for impropriety. This suggests that the householder was supposed to make the declaration and receive punishment if it was incorrect. Although the *huren*'s measure of responsibility was less than that of the Tang *huzhu*, he still had some degree of responsibility and suffered punishment if he failed to fulfill it.

The *huren* was also expected to assume the duty of acting as a village elder (*fulao*), a group that represented the village and was expected to participate in the administrative tasks of higher administrative organs such as the township and county.

From these descriptions we can see that the householder assumed the role of representing the household in various activities that involved interaction between the people and the state, such as official registration and administrative assistance. The householder was the only person in the household permitted

---

16 'Statutes on households', *Statutes and Ordinances of the Second Year*, 345.
17 A Han-period slip (V 1210③: 96) from Xuanquanzhi, Dunhuang, recorded a declaration made by a female householder about a private vehicle (Hu Pingsheng and Zhang Defang 2001).

to own land. For this reason, the wife's dowry was absorbed into the property of the husband or the husband's household by law as she had no capacity to become the householder.[18] While she remained a wife, it was impossible under the law for a woman to become the main entity for land registration. In short, the householder represented his household in dealing with the state (the 'official') and acted as the point of contact between the official and the household as the unit of livelihood. The wife was barred from acting in this capacity. Moreover, in general, a large majority of adult women were wives. For instance, the archaeological evidence from the state of Wu found at Changsha indicates that an overwhelming majority of women in their twenties to fifties were wives (Washio 2015). The state also encouraged, and sometimes forced,[19] women who had reached a certain age to marry as it was believed that adult women, in principle, were meant to be wives. Thus, adult women were generally and in principle excluded from the position of the householder and distanced from the official realm of the state.

The distancing of women from officialdom is a feature observed in the merit ranking system as well as the household registration system. The Han dynasty established a system of twenty merit ranks, each of which had a specific name such as *gongshi* for the first rank and *shangzao* for the second rank. The general population were able to achieve up to the eighth rank (*gongsheng*) and receive benefits, according to rank, such as reduced penalties and an age limit for exemption from corvée labor. These state-awarded ranks were in principle only available to men and their wives were only able to enjoy the benefits through their husbands (Hoshina 2002). This is consistent with the rule, 'Women acquire no ranks; they are governed by their husbands' ranks' found in a Confucian textbook.[20] One benefit afforded to a wife according to her husband's rank was a reduction in criminal punishment. The penal code of the day provided that the wives of men ranked *shangzao* and above would receive reduced sentences even when found guilty and would escape physically damaging punishments.[21]

Moreover, wives were, to a certain extent, able to continue receiving the benefits associated with their husband's rank after the passing of their husband.

---

18 'Statutes on the establishment of heirs', *Statutes and Ordinances of the Second Year*, 384.

19 It is mentioned in 'Annals of Emperor Hui' in the *History of the Former Han* (*Hanshu*), Vol. 2, that unmarried women between the ages of fifteen and thirty were levied five times more poll taxes than women over the age of thirty.

20 'The border sacrifices', *Records of Ritual* (*Liji*).

21 'Statutes on the composition of judgment', *Statutes and Ordinances of the Second Year*, 83.

Chapter 15

In the aforementioned Qin document about property disputes, a discussion about the sentencing of a wife who had concealed her assets revolved around the question of whether she was recognized as the widow of a man with the rank of *shangzao* or above (whether she was in a marital relationship with a ranked man while he was alive). This suggests that wives were able to enjoy the benefits of their husband's rank after they were widowed.

It is clear from the household and merit rank systems that wives were separated from the official realm of the state and only able to access it via their husbands. The exclusion of wives from direct access to official positions was tied to the division of roles between wives who worked inside the house and husbands who worked outside. This was explained according to the logic that there were no merit ranks for women because they worked in the house,[22] which was first and foremost domestic work. Han intellectuals stated that the proper role for a woman was preparing food and clothing and looking after parents-in-law and therefore women should be trained for domestic affairs and not hold aspirations outside of the home.[23] Thus, women were separated from the state outside of the home because their principal occupation was domestic work.

However, women's exclusive engagement in domestic labor was not always associated with spatial segregation, since the definition of 'household labor' as women's principal occupation included management of other family enterprises and income-generating labor to earn a living also fell under the category of household labor. Women worked in diverse occupations other than in government service and were never criticized or despised for working outside their home. Although the spatial division between inside and outside became stricter and women were increasingly secluded from the outside from the early modern period onward, it was much less pronounced during this period. Nonetheless, household labor was a relatively 'private' occupation which was segregated from the state as the 'official-outside' and direct contact between women and the state was, in principle, non-existent as they were supposed to engage primarily in domestic labor.

There were, however, some exceptional cases of direct contact between women and the 'official-outside' involving women who became householders, as we can see from excavated records of a small number of households with

---

22 'Rank', *Comprehensive Discussions in the White Tiger Hall* (*Baihu tong*).
23 'Matronly models', *Biographies of Exemplary Women* (*Lienü zhuan*) by Liu Xiang.

female householders. One example was the female householder who declared her assets in the Han slips from Xuanquanzhi, Dunhuang.

How did these women become householders? As mentioned earlier, a woman in the position of a wife could not become a householder. An opportunity to become one arose in the case of divorce or the death of the husband. On these occasions, the wife's dowry was returned to her and she could legally become the owner of her property.[24]

In some cases, the wife inherited her deceased husband's property as the heir to the householder status (*huhou*) although she was low in the order of succession. When the male householder died with no surviving son, parents or wife, his daughter was able to become the heir.[25]

Divorce, the death of the husband and other events provided opportunities for women to become householders. Some examples are found in the Zoumalou tablets and slips from the state of Wu.

Example H[26]:

> An adult female, named Tang Shan, seventy-four years old. Shan's son, *gongsheng* [honorary rank], named Hu [?], fifteen years old, left leg swollen. (Bamboo slip 1741)

Example I[27]:

> Village in Pingyang the head of the household, adult female, Liu Qie, thirty-seven years old, *zi* fifty [poll tax]. (Bamboo slip 4292)
>
> Qie's family has five members, of which four are male and one female. (Bamboo slip 4288)

Tang Shan in Example H was seventy-four years old and far too old to perform state duties such as corvée labor. Her fifteen-year-old son would have been eligible to take on service duties, yet she was recorded as the householder. This was probably due to the fact that her son was incapable of carrying out

---

24 'Statutes on establishment of heirs', *Statutes and Ordinances of the Second Year*, 384.
25 'Statutes on establishment of heirs', *Statutes and Ordinances of the Second Year*, 379–380.
26 'Bamboo slips Two' in Changsha jiandu bowuguan, Zhongguo wenwu yanjiusuo and Beijing daxue lishixuexi (2007).
27 'Bamboo slips Three' in Changsha jiandu bowuguan, Zhongguo wenwu yanjiusuo and Beijing daxue lishixuexi (2008).

Chapter 15

the householder's duties because of his swollen leg. Liu Qie in Example I was in her prime at the age of thirty-seven, an age at which the majority of women were wives. The composition of her family is unknown but the tally slip for the household indicates that she had four other family members who were male. These two women carried out part of their official responsibilities as householders; they were among a small number of women who directly dealt with the official realm.

In later periods, female householders became even less common. While women became householders even when there was a male member of the household in the examples from the state of Wu during the Three Kingdoms period, women were no longer able to become householders if there was a male member in the household during the Tang period.[28] This was a marked shift from the earlier situation. Women's access to the householder position became even narrower and women became even more segregated from the official realm under the institution of the household.

In closing

In China, household registration was instituted because rulers believed that it was important to keep information about the people as human resources and to protect and develop the 'household' in which they lived. The state endeavored to preserve the household as the support structure for people's livelihoods while keeping individuals under control through the household registration system.

Humans were considered to be a resource with feelings and great care was required in nurturing and maintaining them; they could only live in the context of relationships with other people. Humans were not just bodies but also wives, husbands, fathers and mothers. In the system of that time it is possible to observe the intention to maintain order with an emphasis on human relationships that existed in the private realm. While this intention was reflected in the rules governing the family hierarchy through laws and regulations, the family register also functioned to determine the inside-outside or official-private roles of husband and wife and entrench the hierarchical relationship between

---

28 Nakada Kaoru (1926). Han Shufeng (2011) argues that this rule had been inherited from the Northern Dynasties system.

them. Consequently, women in general were placed in relative isolation from the official realm of the state.

I have thus far attempted to highlight parts of the diverse implications of the household registration system in China. Although many questions remain about the household register, it can be said with certainty that household registration was an important means for policymakers to pry into the relatively 'private' space of each household. Examining the household register and the household has enormous significance for the study of the official-private relationship as well as the state's intervention into the family relationships of its people.

16. Perceptions of 'Talented Women'

— *ITAHASHI Akiko*

Introduction

It is well known that scholars commanded more respect than soldiers in traditional Chinese culture. In the realm of classical fiction, however, it is the women with spectacular military exploits who exude presence. Representations of these women – including Mulan, who joined the army in place of her aging father, as well as the female generals in *Water Margin* – have become widely popular outside of China through films and literature. In Chinese history, however, many of the women recorded and remembered for their 'talent' achieved eminence because of their aptitude for literature (*wen* / 文) rather than military (*wu* / 武) prowess.

How have talented women (*cainü* / 才女) been defined, positioned and recognized in Chinese history? There is a well-known saying about Chinese women and 'talent': 'A woman without talent is virtuous' (*Nüzi wucai bian shi de*). Has this notion prevailed throughout the history of China? Drawing on previous studies, this chapter focuses on discourses from ancient to modern times (Han onward) surrounding the 'talented' women themselves rather than examining their achievements.

While the general understanding in the modern period is that the term 'talented women' in traditional Chinese society refers to those who displayed their capacity mainly in the literary field, there is no established definition in the Chinese classics. According to indices in encyclopedias, which are a useful resource in understanding how the Chinese classified and systematized all things in the universe, entries that are similar to but different from 'talented women' such as 'wise wife' (*xianfu*) and 'wise daughter or woman' (*xiannü*) can be found even in relatively older volumes among the extant encyclopedias, including *Literature Arranged by Topic* (*Yiwen leiju*) from the early Tang period and *Mr. Bai's Categorized Reference Collection for Passing the Examinations* (*Baishi liutie shilei ji*) from the middle Tang. On the other hand, the term 'talented women' is virtually absent as a headword in encyclopedias across the ages. Although the term itself appears sporadically in encyclopedias and Chinese classics, it never became a common expression. This was the case even in the Tang and Song periods that saw increased publication of private essays. The usage of 'talented women' rose dramatically only in the Ming and Qing periods. In comparison with the early dissemination of many Chinese expressions for women with certain attributes such as 'filial daughter' (*xiaonü*), 'faithful maiden' (*zhennü*) and 'lecherous woman' (*yinfu*), 'talented woman' appears to be a relatively late-maturing category.

Before and during the Han dynasty

It is said that *Biographies of Exemplary Women* (*Lienü zhuan*) by Liu Xiang (77–6 BCE) of the Former Han period is the oldest Chinese classic that categorizes the achievements of Chinese women. Seven of the eight extant scrolls are thought to have been composed by Liu Xiang (the *Gu Lienü zhuan*) and contain a total of 104 biographical accounts, with each scroll organized according to a specific theme. The heroines of these stories are categorized according to themes that correspond to their achievements. While those who can be regarded as what were later called 'talented women' are included in the sixth scroll entitled 'Biographies of accomplished speakers' (*Bian tong zhuan*) which presents their wit and eloquence, all of the women included in the scrolls – except Scroll No. 7, 'Biographies of depraved favorites' (*Nie bi zhuan*) – are generally assumed to have been intelligent and thoughtful. We can speculate that Liu Xiang was motivated to compile the collection of biographies at the end of the Former Han period at a time when male relatives of the empress dowager's family played a dominant role in politics because he wanted to establish strict models for women's lives within the harem or quarters of the emperor's wives, disseminating the models throughout the country. The ideal role models pursued by Liu Xiang can be classified as 'wise mother' (*xianmu*) and 'wise wife/wise daughter or woman' (*xianfu/xianü*) (Yamazaki 1996). However, this was not dictated solely by the peculiar

Chapter 16

circumstances immediately prior to the overthrow of the Former Han dynasty. Conforming to the Confucian orthodoxy of the Han period, the *Biographies of Exemplary Women* is underlain by Liu Xiang's belief that both women and men should play their part in upholding social order through the practice of ritual (Nakajima 2001). The thoughtfulness of the heroines in the *Biographies of Exemplary Women* is portrayed as an attribute that benefits the societies and communities to which they belong – within the harems of various princes and the households of everyday people and between warring states – although it also sometimes helps them to overcome difficulties in their own lives. The clear exemplification of how female intelligence ought to function in society in this Han-era text has had a long-lasting effect on the Chinese view of women that extended over generations.[1]

Most of the heroines included in the *Biographies of Exemplary Women* lived in the part of Chinese history that spanned the Mythical period to the Warring States period and were not Liu Xiang's contemporaries. When it comes to 'talented women' representing the four hundred years of the Han dynasty, contemporary and modern/pre-modern observers would probably be in accordance with the nomination of Ban Zhao (mid-first century to early second century) and Cai Yan (or Cai Wenji; c. 177–249). However, their reputations do not accord, as one has enjoyed admiration for two millennia whereas the other has drawn both praise and censure. Ban Zhao, who lived in the early days of the Later Han period, took over the unfinished task of her older brother, Ban Gu (32–92), in completing the *History of the Former Han* (*Hanshu*) and blazed a trail in the field of what later came to be known as 'textbooks of morals for women' by writing *Precepts for My Daughters* (*Nüjie*) to prepare her daughters for married life. On the whole, her reputation has been consistently positive through the generations (even though in modern times *Precepts for My Daughters* was criticized for 'having oppressed her fellow women' (Chen Dongyuan 1928)). On the other hand, Cai Yan, the daughter of a famous scholar of the late Eastern Han period named Cai Yong (c. 132/133–192), was not only

---

[1] In terms of the actual reception of the *Biographies of Exemplary Women*, shortly after publication its readership spread from the inner palace to ordinary citizens from the end of Former Han to the Later Han period, but evidence that women were reading it in person diminished gradually. However, cases involving the use of the *Biographies of Exemplary Women* in education and learning began to appear in 'Biographies of women', *History of the Ming Dynasty* (*Mingshi*), Vols. 301–303. In the Qing period, commentaries by female scholars of evidential research emerged (Yamazaki 1996). It is possible that the composition of the main text of the *Biographies of Exemplary Women* was also intended for the education of illiterate women, as the beginning of each scroll and the end of each biographical account were versified to suit recitation (Kakehi 1978).

learned enough to be able to restore some of the ancient books in her father's lost collection, just as was Ban Zhao, but was also known for her mastery of literature and music, the two pillars of the culture of scholars, as demonstrated in her two poems: 'Poem of grief' (*Beifen shi*), contained in 'Biography of Dong Si's wife' (*Dong Si qi zhuan*) in 'Collected biographies of women', the *History of the Later Han* ('*Lienü zhuan*', *Houhanshu*), Vol. 84 and 'Eighteen songs of a nomad flute ' (*Hujia shiba pai*) in *Collection of the Music Bureau Poems* (*Yuefu shiji*), Scroll No. 59. While her authorship of these works has been disputed,[2] it is important to note that later generations have shown strong enough faith in Cai Yan's intellect to prompt supportive arguments whenever such doubts have been raised (suspicions were first raised by the Northern Song literary giant Su Shi (1036–1101)). Nevertheless, her personal reputation was heavily burdened by another facet that made her life extraordinary – the fact that she was widowed, abducted by a nomadic tribe and bore mixed-race children, before being returned to Han and remarrying. About the women portrayed in 'Collected biographies of women' in the *History of the Later Han*, including Cai Yan, its compiler Fan Ye (398–445) made the following appraisal: 'Proper chastity leaves vestiges and graceful silence offers much to see. Let us cast light on the talents and accomplishments of these women to bring the history recorded by female historians into sight'. Fan Ye of the Liu Song states in his 'Introduction' that he deliberately included the biographies of women in the biographies section of the *History of the Later Han* in view of the fact that the earlier official history books – such as the *History of the Former Han* and the *Records of the Three Kingdoms* – contain no categorized biographies of women. His decision was based on a policy whereby he would 'merely seek out women whose talent and conduct were exceptional and not necessarily give priority to only those who kept their chastity'.[3]

On the other hand, Liu Zhiji (661–721) from the Tang dynasty period argues as follows in Chapter Thirty, 'Personalities' (*Renwu*), of the Inner Chapters of the *Principles of Writing History Books* (*Shitong*), the oldest systematic critique of Chinese historiography.

---

2 The research history of her works, including such allegations, are systematically reported in Iriya Yoshitaka (1960) and Fukuyama Yasuo (2005), among others.

3 Fan Ye's intention behind the inclusion of the biography of Cai Yan in *Collected Biographies of Women* is discussed in Nishimura Fumiko (1996).

Chapter 16

Among wise women of the Later Han period, there is Xu Shu, the wife of Qin Jia. [...] a lady equipped with talent and virtue. Cai Yan, the wife of Dong Si, gave birth to barbarian children and was shamed in an alien court. Of literary merit she had more than enough, but her moral behavior was defective. This is a woman of contradicting words and actions. Yet, Cai Yan's biography is included in Fan Ye's 'Collected biographies of women' in the *History of the Later Han* while Xu Shu is omitted. When [Fan Ye] states [in his 'Introduction'] his intent to present the records of female scholars, his standards [for recording] appear to be inappropriate.

The particular point of contention here with regard to Cai Yan's track record is the fact that (after she had been widowed) she married a barbarian man and bore his children. Liu Zhiji nominated 'disfiguring herself and declining to remarry' as one of the virtues of Qin Jia's wife Xu Shu, whose poems are contained in the *New Songs from a Jade Terrace* (*Yutai xinyong*) and *Literature Arranged by Topic* (*Yiwen leiju*), on the assumption that remarriage itself was a shameful act that disqualified a woman from being included in the biographies. It is well known that constraints on women's activities were relatively weak in the Tang period and remarriage was not particularly frowned upon in real life. At the level of public discourse on scholarship, however, it seems that women's 'literary' talent was thought to be deserving of being called 'wisdom' only when it coexisted with 'fidelity'. Prominent literary figures have frequently made reference to Cai Yan since the Tang period. For example, Su Xun (1009–1066), Su Shi's father and one of the Eight Masters of Literature between the Tang and Song dynasties (Tang Song *badajia*), criticized Fan Ye's approach from the same perspective as Liu.[4] The 'appraisal of Cai Yan' was primarily an assessment of the way she lived rather than of her works, evident in comments such as those made by Zhu Xi (1130–1200) that 'Disloyalty [shown by Yang Xiong (53 BCE–18 CE), a major scholar during the transition from the Former to Later Han periods] is equivalent to that shown by Cai Yan. At least Cai Yan had a sense of shame and blamed herself'.[5]

---

4 The later chapter of 'Theory of historiography' in *Jiayou ji*, Scroll No. 9.
5 The foreword for the table of contents, 'The later commentary on songs of Chu' (*Chuci houyu*), in the *Collected Works of Huian* (*Hui'an ji*), Scroll No. 76.

The Wei, Jin, Southern and Northern Dynasties period

The period of the Wei, Jin, Southern and Northern Dynasties that followed the Later Han dynasty was a time when 'conferring status on people' was pursued in both the public and private domains, as symbolized by the nine-rank bureaucratic system (*jiupin guanren fa*). A compilation of novels recording words and deeds titled *A New Account of the Tales of the World* (*Shishuo Xinyu*) is a collection of anecdotes from the lives of prominent figures from the Han dynasty to the Jin-Song transition period compiled during the Liu Song period in the name of Liu Yiqing (403–444), a member of the imperial family who hosted a literary salon. The anecdotes are categorized according to the key words and deeds of each story in a manner similar to the composition of *Biographies of Exemplary Women* (*Lienü zhuan*). In other words, the deeds and words and the person to whom they were attributed were judged and evaluated according to the relevant chapter title under the prevailing value system at the time of compilation. One chapter entitled 'Wise women' (*Xian yuan*) exclusively deals with women. What is meant by 'wise' in this case? According to Hayashi Kana (2004), many textbooks providing instruction on female and family morals compiled during and after the Tang and Song periods prescribe various criteria for being considered 'wise' and define 'wise women' as those with the ability to contribute to the survival and preservation of household order. On the other hand, the wisdom portrayed in 'Wise women' in *A New Account of the Tales of the World* does not necessarily fit this definition, as some stories are devoted to presenting the accomplishments and shrewdness of individual women – often involving outsmarting their husbands and brothers – and praise from others. This is in contrast to the importance placed on fidelity and the practice of normative rites outlined in 'Collected biographies of women' in the *History of the Jin* (*Jinshu*), Vol. 96, compiled during the Tang period (Toyofuku 1976). One pertinent example from 'Wise women' tells of an Eastern Jin aristocrat named Xie Daoyun (mid-fourth century to early fifth century) who came to be considered as the leading 'talented woman' of the Six Dynasties period. Her brilliant mind and free-spirited speech and action attracted deep admiration even from the likes of Qiu Jin (1875–1907), a late Qing female revolutionary, one and a half millennia later (Xia Xiaohong 1999). *A New Account of the Tales of the World* included a certain type of universal image of 'talented woman', which struck a chord even in the age of transition toward the disintegration of normative rites. This was likely made possible by the peculiar social circumstances of the Wei-Jin period that preceded the compilation of *A New Account of the Tales of the World*.

In a society based on the hereditary aristocracy system developed in the Wei-Jin period, men came to seek a new kind of humanity outside of the traditional paradigm while it became possible for women of the same social class to enjoy educational and cultural opportunities and develop a kind of self-awareness distinct from that of previous generations (Shimomi 2008). In other words, the groundwork had been laid for men to positively and sometimes proudly accept the awakening of women. This is corroborated by reactions from male characters in 'Wise women' as well as the way these stories were passed on to others: it is probable that prior to their inclusion in *A New Account of the Tales of the World*, the male family members of these heroines disclosed to their aristocratic communities the anecdotes concerning their mothers, wives and sisters, which would otherwise have remained within the walls of their households.

The Sui-Tang dynasties period

The level of political participation among upper-class women increased during the Sui-Tang period when norms imposed on women became less rigid. In a certain sense, Wu Zetian (624–705), who ascended to the summit of her dynasty (see Essay 2), and Shangguan Wan'er,[6] who almost reached the apex of officialdom, can be regarded as the epitome of 'talented women'. However, later generations appraised 'the hens that crowed louder than the cock' unfavorably, and this tone basically remained unchanged until the modern era. Other than Wu Zetian and those who succeeded on the political stage, surprisingly few upper-class Tang women were celebrated for their literary or scholarly achievements. Nonetheless, the period of the Tang dynasty, during which a sophisticated political system and culture that set the standard for ancient East Asia were developed, was also the age that spawned a courtesan

---

6 Shangguan Wan'er was in charge of writing imperial commands and advising on propositions or petitions to the emperor during the reigns of Empress Wu Zetian and Emperor Zhongzong and contributed to the promotion of scholarship.

culture that served as a model for the practice of entertaining or having romantic relationships with courtesans in East Asia. For the first time in the history of China, the courtesan class began to produce 'talented women' separately from the cohort of upper-class women who had access to education at home or at the court. For example, Xue Tao (c. 770–c. 832) and Yu Xuanji (c. 844–c. 871) stand out from their peers as 'talented women' of the Tang period who made their mark purely due to their literary skills based on the quality and volume of their works included in *All the Poems Written in the Period of the Tang Dynasty* (*Quan Tangshi*) (Matsuura 1982). Both women were reportedly courtesans, although Yu Xuanji produced her extant poems mostly after her ordination as a Daoist/Taoist nun (some say that she grew up in an ordinary household before her ordination; see Chapter Three).

The Song-Yuan dynasties period

After the collapse of the Tang empire and the subsequent fragmentation into Five Dynasties and Ten Kingdoms, the Song dynasty period brought unification, albeit conditional, and saw the emergence of a new phase of politics led by scholar-officials. As a natural consequence of this shift, one of the most 'talented women' in the entire history of China appeared during this time. This was Li Qingzhao (1084–mid-twelfth century), who came to occupy a pre-eminent position in the field of *ci* (a type of classical Chinese poetry). She is also well known for her high level of learning and sincere pursuit of scholarship, evident in her 'Later foreword' to the *Record of Inscriptions on Bronze and Stone* (*Jinshi lu*), a collaboration with her late husband Zhao Mingcheng (1081–1129), that described the process of artefact collection and later dispersion. After the fall of the Northern Song and the turmoil of the Zhao Song court's retreat to the south of the Yangtze, Li Qingzhao reportedly remarried amid the hardship that followed the death of her beloved husband (even though she soon divorced her second husband). This 'remarriage issue' was often viewed as problematic after her death. According to a detailed study by Matsuo Hatsuko (2003) that traced the various critiques of Li Qingzhao from the Southern Song period to contemporary China, there is a correlation between the critiques and the rise and fall of *ci* poetry culture. Li's remarriage was often the target of criticism in the early Ming period, when fidelity was absolutely valued while *ci* poetry almost died out. The publication of her collected poems in the late Ming period increased appreciation of her works, and the revival of *ci* poetry culture during the Qing period led to the establishment of the appraisal of Li Qingzhao while a theory denying her remarriage became the widely accepted view. The Qing-era theory was not revised during the Republic of China period. The spotlight was once again focused on the remarriage issue and many of the Qing-era contentions were carried on after the formation of the People's Republic of China, with an intermission during the Cultural Revolution period. In any case, the fact that a widow's remarriage continued to be a focus of debate for such a long time indicates the strengthening of the fidelity norm during the Ming and Qing periods, and at the same time demonstrates the consolidation of Li's status in Chinese literary history alongside the requisite correlation with 'blamelessness'.

The Ming-Qing dynasties period

The period of the Ming and Qing dynasties, especially the latter, can be referred to as the age of 'talented women' as the use of the term proliferated, as noted at the start of this chapter. While keeping to their respective lineages from the Tang-Song period, the talented women of the Ming-Qing period came to be divided more clearly into two categories: the so-called *guixiu* (cloistered ladies) who received education at their scholar-official households and continued to write as the wives of scholar-officials, and the courtesans who developed academic and cultural sophistication as well as artistic skills in music and dance in order to entertain their scholar-official clients. Courtesans were more conspicuous in the Ming period while the *guixiu* were more active during the Qing period. Courtesan culture went into decline after the end of the Ming dynasty, as legal restrictions on courtesans were introduced in the Qing dynasty, including the abolition of the system in which courtesans who were female musicians and dancers were affiliated with government institutions (*guanji*) and the frequent issuance of orders prohibiting courtesans (Wang Shunu 1934).

It is said that the adage cited above – 'A woman without talent is virtuous' – appeared at the end of the Ming period at the earliest and came into general use during the Qing period (Chen Dongyuan 1928). The saying can be regarded as a counterpart created precisely because the presence and activity of talented women had gained a certain level of social recognition. Based on the *Study of the Works of Women throughout History* (*Lidai funü zhuzuo kao*), a groundbreaking study published by Hu Wenkai after the birth of the People's Republic of China, Ming-Qing-era women account for 93% of all female writers in several thousand years of China's history, from the Mythical period to the Republic of China. Even on the assumption that more recent works had a better chance of survival, the level of literary activity among women of the Ming-Qing dynasties[7] was remarkable (Gōyama 2006).

A high percentage of Ming and Qing female writers hailed from the Jiangnan region to the south of the lower reaches of the Yangtze River that boasted a particularly high level of culture. The *guixiu* were cultivated by the regional environment at the macro level and at the micro level by the educational environment of the birth family as well as understanding and support provided by the matrimonial home. Amid the proliferation of the formation and activities of scholars' associations in Jiangnan at the end of the Ming dynasty, the mothers, wives and daughters of scholar-officials built and deepened their own social networks through their writing and publishing activities while fulfilling their domestic responsibilities and performing normative rites. Where a network spread beyond the confines of their kinship, their male relatives often acted as intermediaries and used their own connections to actively support the expansion of the women's activities – and men sometimes used the *guixiu* networks to expand their own scholar networks in turn (Ko 1994 [English]). After surviving the cultural control and oppression policies of the Ming-Qing transition period, Jiangnan society managed to maintain its high cultural standard throughout the eighteenth century, which was known as the Kangxi-Qianlong Flourishing Age or High Qing (*Kang-Qian shengshi*), and supported further progress in the writing and publishing activities of upper-class women. Susan L. Mann (1997) depicts the values and social environment of Qing women based on their own writings, including *Precious Records* (*Lan gui bao lu*), a collection of biographies of women compiled by Yun Zhu (Wanyan Yun Zhu) who produced many works as a female poet and editor in the early nineteenth century. It vividly shows that the mothers, wives and daughters of scholar-officials were not merely enduring 'oppression' deep in

---

[7] Many of these works have not been published in punctuated edition and access to their original editions is not readily available. However, a considerable number of digitized reprints have been released on the *Ming Qing Women's Writings* website (http://digital.library.mcgill.ca/mingqing/english/index.php) of McGill University in collaboration with Harvard-Yenching Library and other institutions (as at October 2017).

Chapter 16

their domestic compounds as imagined by Westerners; instead they nurtured self-respect and as a result experienced a sense of intellectual and ethical fulfillment through Confucian learning and writing endeavors. Mann's other work (2007) is set in a scholar-official household in Yun Zhu's home province of Jiangsu, Changzhou, during the nineteenth century and narrates the lives of women of the Zhang family who maintained a family culture through a local marriage custom in which the husband lived with his bride's family, presenting the world of the very wide-ranging and independent intellectual activities of the Qing *guixiu*. Conversely, the Qing-era scholar-official society's approval of and demand for 'talented women' must have been one of the factors that enabled the continuance and development of the *guixiu* culture within individual households and local communities.

In the case of courtesans, their sophistication in learning and culture directly stemmed from their need to entertain and socialize with scholars, but it was ultimately a result of the region's cultural standard that produced and attracted excellent intellectuals, as in the case of the *guixiu*. *Figures and Poems Devoted to Eight Beauties in Qinhuai* (*Qinhuai bayan tuyong*), an illustrated anthology published at the end of the Qing period, features the top eight famed courtesans produced by the Qinhuai pleasure quarters that had prospered in Nanjing since the early Ming era. All of them were active from the end of the Ming to the early Qing period (Ōki 2001). Liu Rushi (1618–1664) is the most renowned and acclaimed among them. Although her connection with Qinhuai was not deep as she was described as a famed courtesan of Wuzhong (present Suzhou) by a Qing biographer, it was in the mature culture of the lower reaches of the Yangtze River that she made her name. Overflowing with brilliance, Liu not only freely associated with Jiangnan scholar-officials of the late Ming dynasty but also tried to commit suicide in response to the imminent fall of Nanjing and provided assistance to the resistance movement against the Qing dynasty to restore the Ming. After her tragic death under pressure from the relatives of her late husband Qian Qianyi (1582–1664), she drew much admiration and sympathy from her contemporaries who had survived the regime change, leading to the writing of various records and biographies (Gu Huizhi 2000). Among many Ming and Qing courtesans, Liu's name and conduct are well known today thanks largely to the publication of *Unofficial Biography of Liu Rushi* (*Liu Rushi biezhuan*), authored by Chen Yinke (1890–1969), a leading historian of the Republic of China and the People's Republic of China. While Chen did not complete the book until 1964, several years before his death under persecution during the Cultural Revolution, he reportedly began writing it around 1954 (Jiang Tianshu 1981), less than a decade after the end of the Anti-Japanese War. He experienced the semi-colonization of China during his adolescence and moved from place to place, adhering to the resolve to resist Japanese occupation during the war. Chen must have felt a strong affinity with the determination Liu Rushi demonstrated throughout her life. Chen explains his motivation to write Liu's biography in Chapter One, 'The beginning':

> Aspirations to avenge the loss of their country or words of mourning for the demise of their country should be regarded as an expression of the spirit of independence and free thinking and given respect even if they were expressed by scholar-officials of the time [who ought to take responsibility for their country's fate as a matter of duty]. The showing of such a spirit by a fragile young woman deserves even greater respect. (Chen Yinke 1980, Vol. 1, p. 4)

It is clear that he valued Liu's Ming restoration action against the Qing as a 'spirit calling for Chinese people's independence'. Chen Yinke sincerely praises the fact that Liu came to think that 'a common "woman"' (*pi 'fu'*) is also responsible for defending her country (Cai Hongsheng 1995).[8] For Chen Yinke, one of modern China's greatest intellectuals, this 'talented woman' produced by the turbulence of the Ming-Qing transition period was sublimated into an identifiable comrade by her principles rather than remaining a mere object of literary critique.

Conclusion

During Emperor Guangxu's reign at the end of the Qing dynasty, Liang Qichao (1873–1929) exhorted the need for the education of women in 'Argument on women's learning' ('Lun nüxue') in Vol. 1 of his *General Discussions on Reform* (*Bianfa tongyi*). He criticized traditional 'talented women' as follows:

---

8 The original version of this expression is 'Even a common, humble man is also responsible for defending his country', penned by Gu Yanwu, a scholar who declined to serve the Qing dynasty for life as a *Mingchao yichen* (people declaring their loyalty to the Ming dynasty even after its overthrow) ('*Zhengshi*'), *Record of Knowledge Daily Acquired* (*Rizhi lu*), Vol. 13.

What is called the talented woman in ancient times is the woman who toys with ditties on the wind and the moon, the flowers and the grass, the woman who makes ditties on spring sorrow and sad departures, the woman who even composes several volumes of poems. Now this sort of thing really cannot be called learning at all[9] [...]. What I call scholarship is something that clarifies one's thinking internally while benefiting people's lives externally and continues to produce achievements once acquired.

As if to grant his wish, education was extended to women in the Republic of China. Terms such as 'new women' (*xin funü*) came to be used to describe women who received higher education and advanced in society.[10] When people became aware of China's 'backwardness' through contact with the West and began to call for reform during the transition period from the Qing to the Republic of China, the norms and values about women preserved in traditional Chinese society also became symbols of China's 'backwardness' and were considered problems to be challenged and overcome as far as China's intelligentsia and youth were concerned. As a result, the limitations of traditional 'talented women' also came to be clearly recognized.

The 'new women', who walked a much wider path to intellectual activities than traditional 'talented women', were no longer satisfied with expressing 'spring sorrow and sad departures' (*shangchun xibie*) and endeavored to acquire expert knowledge and skills in order to participate in society and take part in the nation-building project in the same way as men. From the viewpoint of both the nature and application of the 'talent' to be appraised, there is a large gap between pre-modern 'talented women' and modern/contemporary 'new women'. For a majority of the pre-modern 'talented women', the type of activity criticized by Liang Qichao was the only kind of opportunity they could access in order to express their intelligence. Nevertheless, they sometimes impressed male scholar-officials with their exceptionally brilliant words expressing 'spring sorrow and sad departures' to the extent that they also forced these men to recognize the importance of women's learning. Furthermore, their reputation for words expressing 'spring sorrow and sad departures' helped spark interest in the way they lived their lives outside of 'spring sorrow and sad departures',

---

9 English translation before the omission is based on Hu Ying (2000 [English]: 7).
10 Strictly speaking, the connotations of the term 'new women' vary in different periods. The variation is detailed in Egami (2006 [Chinese]).

igniting debates in history books and the literary world. Even though many of such debates were dominated by the fidelity doctrine, some put forward interpretations and voices of support to avoid conflict with the doctrine and even appraisals that transcended the doctrine itself – based on the criteria of pure wit, literary skill or loyalty to endangered Chinese civilization.

Perceptions of 'talented women' in Chinese history, the feelings of respect, fraternity, disappointment and contempt toward them and the dismantling and rebuilding of the concept of 'talented women' in modern times have closely reflected the trajectory of Chinese civilization's progress, vacillation and quest to overcome crises.

17. Healthcare, the Body and Gender in Chinese Medicine

— *YAO Yi*

Introduction

In medicine and healthcare, what have been the discourses about people's bodies and diseases and what have been the definitions of people's behavioral standards, social norms, gender roles and body images in a given society? Who have been considered to be the appropriate people to be involved in healthcare? These questions have been some of the main concerns of gender studies as well as medical sociology and have also drawn attention in the field of Chinese studies in recent years. These fields of study cover very wide ground but their main interests from a gender perspective can be summarized as follows. Firstly, medicine and healthcare corroborated the theory of 'female vulnerability' positing that women were physiologically and psychologically weaker beings than men which was used as a basis for male dominance and female subordination in society. Secondly, medicine contributed to the formulation of behavioral standards for men and women and the division of gender roles by classifying and defining physical characteristics as masculine or feminine. Thirdly, the modernization of medicine accompanied occupational gender division, with doctors being male and nurses and midwives female – this process not only excluded women from the medical profession but also made them the object of treatment and monitoring and alienated them from their own bodies (Yao Yi 2011 [Japanese]). These three tendencies have been conspicuous especially in the process of the establishment of modern Western medicine. In short, the 'science' of medicine in modern times together with the establishment of the capitalist system and the formation of modern states constituted the holy trinity in marking clear boundaries between men's and women's bodies, assigning a new meaning to each and facilitating the establishment of a modern order.

Curiously, it is no exaggeration to say that the fervent interest shown in Chinese medicine and the body from the 1980s emanated from the 'bafflement' about China that eluded Western conceptualization rather than a desire to prove the applicability of the female 'vulnerability/alienation' theory in China. For instance, surgeons in the Ming-Qing period at the end of Imperial China did not use their advanced 'skills' to move into the field of obstetrics as their Western counterparts had done. Chinese medical descriptions were not only unclear about distinction between the sexes but also paid scant attention to the physical body itself. Moreover, people dutifully adhered to postnatal recuperation in the 'delicate month' in a state of near confinement despite the absence of a rationale. The People's Republic of China (PRC) provides special protection and preferential treatment for women even though it upholds gender equality as a state policy. Researchers turned their attention to healthcare and the body when they 'discovered' that almost all of these numerous phenomena were tied to healthcare and the body when they analyzed them. In this sense, it was no coincidence that many studies chose menstruation as their subject.

Charlotte Furth's early study that sparked research into the body and gender was about menstrual blood. Furth (1986) argued that the menstrual taboo from the seventeenth to nineteenth centuries certainly brought with it the restriction and oppression of women, but at the same time it created a symbolic value system for women to use as a medium for cooperation with the power structure in negotiating and challenging male authority. The number of studies on menstruation and childbirth gradually increased from the 1980s. Francesca Bray (1997) analyzed how science and technology formed the gender relationship in China's traditional society from three aspects, namely, architecture, spinning and child/healthcare from the Song to Qing dynasties. In the twentieth century, three major studies on the history of medicine and the body were published one after another and caused a spike in the interest in this field. Lee Jen-Der, Furth and Wu Yi-Li each used a vast number of medical documents to discuss changes in the traditional Chinese view of pregnancy, childbirth and the body, the establishment of gynecology and obstetrics and the distinction between the male and female bodies and relationships between various healthcare workers centering on the Sui-Tang period, the Sui-Tang to Ming-Qing period and the Ming-Qing period respectively (Lee Jen-Der 2008; Furth 1999; Wu Yi-Li 2010

Chapter 17

[English]). Chou Chun-Yen of Taiwan studied the changes that had been brought by modern Western medicine with a focus on menstruation (Chou Chun-Yen 2010). Yao Yi published a thesis on body politics and the relationship between healthcare workers from late Qing to the present (Yao Yi 2010a [Japanese]; 2010b [Japanese]; 2011 [Japanese]; 2015 [Japanese]; 2016 [Japanese]). Leung Angela Ki Che and Yi Jo-Lan published leading studies on pre-modern female healthcare workers (Leung Angela Ki Che 2005; Yi Jo-Lan 2002).

This chapter offers outlines of the views of the body and gender in Chinese healthcare and sketches out a Chinese history from the perspective of healthcare and gender. More specifically, the first part describes the characteristics of the traditional views of the body and reproduction and traces changes in these views up to the end of the nineteenth century. In doing so, I focus on whether a Chinese understanding of the body was different from that of the West, looking at what were the differences and how they influenced China's social norm of strict segregation between men and women. The second section discusses the changes in the Chinese views of the body and reproduction and the gender awareness that resulted from the introduction of modern Western medicine at the end of the nineteenth century and how a series of issues concerning the reproducing body were interpreted mainly in the area of women's physical education. The third section casts light on gender relations between childbirth professionals, especially modern obstetricians and midwives. My own studies did not find that the phenomenon of excluding women from childbirth-related professions was particularly notable in modern China. This chapter summarizes the study findings and raises new questions.

View of the body and gender in traditional Chinese medicine

The human body in traditional Chinese medicine

Chinese medicine is predicated on the philosophy of '*qi*', which is a principle to explain the genesis, change and demise of all things, and exists as a complete knowledge system that includes a cosmology and moral and ethical values. *Qi* is an extremely difficult concept to understand. It arises from '*dao*', which is the highest category of being, and is split into *yin* and *yang*. *Yin* and *yang* are the forces that are generated by continuous interactions between heaven and earth, light and shadow, sun and moon, male and female, strength and weakness, lightness and darkness and so on, which are mutually complementary and change dynamically.[1] *Yin* and *yang* are applied in the exposition of all sciences, natural phenomena and the order of human society. The view of the body on the basis of this system of medicine has a highly symbolic value with indivisible completeness and invisibility and clearly differs from the anatomically-based biological body. Furth has discovered this metaphorical body and called it the 'Yellow Emperor's Body', explaining that although *yin* and *yang* are two opposing elements, they coexist in the human body as well as in meridians and organs. In other words, the Yellow Emperor's Body is also 'the androgynous body of generation' (Furth 1999). Furth has built a framework that enables a comparison between the gendered obstetric knowledge of Europe and China's unique history of the body by proposing 'the female body gestation' concept as opposed to the Yellow Emperor's Body and deftly corresponding it to Thomas Laqueur's one-sex and two-sex model.

Although this framework offered a stimulating way to explain the Chinese view of the body which was different from the European model, it gave rise to a range of problems. One is the association between medicine and women's behavioral norms. As Mann pointed out, there is a tacit common belief that *yang* is superior to *yin* even though *yang* and *yin* are mutually complementary and indivisible. In other words, the *yin-yang* concept itself contains a hierarchy. This concept came to support the oppressive Confucian order of male dominance and female subordination as Confucianism from the Han dynasty period onward constructed a sophisticated system of morals and ethics (Mann 2011). What reasoning did medicine provide and what role did it play in that process? Let us look at the famous Confucian canon, 'Men and women are different', that profoundly defined China's social and gender order.

The origin of the saying goes back to a phrase in 'The pattern of the family' (*Neize*) in the *Records of Ritual* (*Liji*) which ruled that 'At the age of seven, boys and girls did not occupy the same mat nor eat together'. The reasoning for it can be found in 'The plain conversation' (*Suwen*) of a classical medical text, the *Yellow Emperor's Inner Cannon* (*Huangdi neijing*).

---

[1] Medical historians translate the word '*qi*' as vital energy, while in philosophical studies the same term is usually translated as 'material force'. For comparison see the Focal Point associated with Chapter Six.

Chapter 17

> At seven years of age a girl's kidney *qi* is flourishing; her adult teeth come in and her hair grows long. At fourteen she comes into her reproductive capacities; her Conception pulse moves and her Highway pulse is abundant; her menses flow regularly and she can bear young. [...] At forty-nine her Conception pulse is exhausted and her main Highway pulse withers; her sex hormones stop and she goes into menopause; her body shape changes and she is no longer reproductive.
>
> At eight a boy's kidney *qi* is replete; his adult teeth come in and his hair grows long. At sixteen his kidney *qi* is abundant, and he comes into his reproductive capacities; his seminal essence overflows and drains; he can unite *yin* and *yang* and so beget young. [...] At sixty-four, he has declining functions of the five organs, runs out of sex hormones and loses his reproductive capacities.

Interestingly, Furth takes note of this canonical argument and uses it to explain the Yellow Emperor's Body.

> At the same time male and female are homologous partners in generative function; their complementarity as a yin yang pair is evoked through the convention of correlative cosmology that odd numbers are yang in resonance and even numbers are yin. In this way, the two sexes develop parallel and equivalent bodies and capacities. (Furth 1999: 45)

Furth's interpretation sounds logical. In reality, however, this canonical argument provided the reasoning behind the social norm of 'gender segregation' that has had a profound effect on later generations in China by ruling that girls and boys should be spatially separated because their bodies began preparations for reproduction at age seven in the former and eight in the latter instead of promoting the idea of 'equivalent bodies and capacities'. It was inherited by later medical texts and provided grounds for various popular beliefs. One example is the idea that the kidneys are much more important than the uterus: the kidneys store vital energy and therefore people must avoid strenuous exercise or study, overusing the eyes and unstable lifestyle or mental conditions so as not to exhaust it. This has had a deep influence on people's behavioral norms. Thus, one of the future tasks is to find out the process by which the classical medical texts defined people's behavioral norms.

Wu Yi-Li offers a different view to Furth's Yellow Emperor's Body. Wu points out that the body is simultaneously sexless and sexed and that this should be understood as the 'prototype model' ('infinitive body') (Wu Yi-Li 2010: 230–235). This 'infinitive body' is the basis for all human bodies that can be conjugated into not only male and female but also young and old, Southern and Northern, robust and delicate or other bodily configurations depending upon circumstance. Changes in medical theory represent diverse variations to this universal body rather than divergence from and regression to a certain canonical body. Wu explains the historical changing process of the body in this way. She also casts aside the long-standing stereotypical view that Chinese medical texts stress physical functions and neglect anatomy on the basis that the uterus was regarded as important by classical medical texts.

How did traditional medical texts explain distinctions between the sexes? How did they reconcile the idea of the androgynous Yellow Emperor's Body with the 'reproductive body' that menstruated, gestated and delivered young? What contributions did they make to the formulation of the view of the body that formed part of the Confucian world order? As the medical texts approach the female body from a reproductive viewpoint, I discuss the establishment of and change in the field of medicine for women in detail.

Women's medicine and the discovery of the female body

In traditional medical texts, gynecology and obstetrics are called the 'department of medicine for women' (*nüke*) which is generally believed to have been established in the Sui-Tang period. Numerous books about childbirth have been compiled since then and the *Prescriptions for Emergencies Worth a Fortune* (*Qian jin fang*) by Sun Simiao is regarded as one of the most comprehensive. The book devotes the first three volumes to 'Prescriptions for women' (*Furen fang*) and argues that female characteristics must be understood before treatment. Sun explains the reason for the need for special formulas and therapies for women as follows (Vol. 2, '*Qiuzi diyi*').

> There are formulas for women's diseases separately from men's because there are conditions peculiar to women such as pregnancy, childbirth and abnormal vaginal bleeding. It is ten times more difficult to treat women's diseases than men's.

Chapter 17

> [It is because] women have more sensual desires than men and are twice as likely to fall ill. With added compassion, love, likes and dislikes, melancholy, anger and hysteria, their illnesses are deep-rooted and intractable.

This statement clearly demonstrates that Sun paid attention to women's psychological characteristics as well as physiological phenomena and reproductive functions and perceived that their abundant pathos and emotions and mood instability were the main factors in their higher susceptibility to diseases than men. Another of his statements, 'Four virtues [*side*] are the key to women's success, and childbirth and childrearing are women's strengths', points to his understanding that childrearing as well as pregnancy and birth were women's special functions.

Sun considered that general diseases were common to men and women and should be treated the same way. In other words, he perceived women's reproductive function as a marker that differentiated them from men and treated childbirth and childrearing as the responsibilities that only women could fulfill because of these reproductive functions, although he repeatedly emphasized the essential similarity between men and women. In the Han-Tang period, the science of obstetrics was consolidated and systematized and the natal and postnatal care regimen was established as a norm, prompting the formation of various childbirth-related taboos, the notion of uncleanness and behavioral rules such as the segregation of pregnant women. In this context, Lee Jen-Der argues that medicine provided grounds for the 'fragile women' theory and accentuated women's childbearing role, and points out that a gender element was introduced into the field of women's medicine (Lee Jen-Der 2008).

On the other hand, some researchers place the formation of women's medicine in the Song dynasty period on the grounds that physical distinction in the Sui-Tang period was limited to physiological phenomena and reproductive functions and that scant attention was paid to uniquely female reproductive organs such as the uterus and ovaries while the common organ of the kidneys was considered more important than the uterus. Furth is among them.

Furth argues that the appearance of *Complete Effective Prescriptions for Women's Diseases* (*Furen daquan liangfang*) with detailed descriptions of women's medicine in general by Chen Ziming in 1237 was one of the signs, in addition to the establishment of the Bureau of Imperial Physicians and the separation of obstetrics and gynecology from internal medicine in 1060. Chen

Ziming stated that 'men regulate their *qi* whereas women regulate their blood' and that 'women are dominated by blood'. He used 'blood' to differentiate the female body from the male body and attempted to explore and rationalize physical differences between men and women by the internal structure in addition to their reproductive differences. Under the Neo-Confucianism of the Song dynasty period that sought to understand laws of all things, medicine emphasized the risks and uncertainties involved in childbirth, explored drugs to supplement *qi* and blood (*qixue*) and investigated techniques and technologies such as fetal position adjustment and induction in order to prevent and solve difficult labor and unforeseen contingencies. Furth argues that the shift from a homologous body model to a model emphasizing differences took place in the Song period when sex differences were sought inside the body. However, the Ming-Qing period saw another transition in the discourse of sex differences which challenged the prevalent Song notion that 'Women are dominated by blood' and regressed to the one-sex model of the Yellow Emperor's Body that highlighted the similarity between male and female bodies (Furth 1999).

Certainly, the description that 'The female body is essentially the same as the male body except for menstruation, pregnancy and birth' is repeated more widely than ever in Ming-Qing medical texts. In the Qing period, physicians became more assertive about taking no action and more disapproving of human intervention and drug use. For instance, the famous 1715 publication, *Treatise on Easy Birth* (*Dasheng bian*), states the following about childbirth.

> Childbirth is part of the spontaneous generation of the universe [...] very simple and not difficult unless it is forced. In today's world, however, difficult births are common because human errors spoil the natural dynamics of it.

Furth sees this change as a regression from the two-sex model to the one-sex Yellow Emperor's Body model, as mentioned earlier, whereas Wu re-examines it and views it as the infinitive body that is capable of more diverse morphological variations than the Yellow Emperor's Body.

Both Furth and Wu Yi-Li clearly have in mind Laqueur's famous argument on the establishment of the modern Western view of the body. According to a summary by Miho Ogino, Laqueur argues that the one-sex model prevailed until around the eighteenth century and treated the male and female reproductive organs as essentially the same, with the ovaries being called 'female testicles'.

Chapter 17

In the process of the formation of modern society from the eighteenth century, however, the two-sex body model that viewed men and women as entirely different and dissimilar in body, mind and lifestyle emerged. This transition coincided with not only the period when male obstetricians entered and gradually dominated the previously women's domain of childbirth but also the period during which the capitalist system was established and the division of gender roles was formed in modern society (Ogino 2002: 154–155).

Several questions about Laqueur's argument give rise to even more fundamental concerns in relation to discussions on China. For example, the transition to the two-sex body was predicated by not only the establishment of the nation-state and capitalist systems but also the development of modern sciences such as anatomy and physiology. Did these conditions exist in the Ming-Qing period? The change from the one-sex to the two-sex model accompanied the theory underpinning the oppression of women that maintained that women were inferior to men. Did the same phenomenon occur in China? In any case, the earnest and detailed work undertaken by Furth and Wu Yi-Li offered new research methods and angles to the field of traditional Chinese medicine and gender. The most refreshing and interesting among them is the question of why the Ming-Qing period followed a different path from sixteenth-to-eighteenth-century Europe, despite the presence of strong capitalist elements and advanced women's medical technologies. Before I discuss this in detail below, I look at the similarity between the male and female bodies depicted in Ming-Qing medical texts. Assuming the regression to the one-sex model occurred in the Ming-Qing period, was it identical to the pre-Sui-Tang model? Let us examine a commentary written by Zhang Jingyue, a leading Ming medical practitioner, in his *Discourses on Women* (*Furen gui*).

In 'Women's nine conditions' (*Furen jiuzheng*) and 'Discourses of difficulty' (*Lun nanyi*) in *Discourses on Women*, Zhang Jingyue expresses a similar view to the aforementioned view of Sun Simiao that men's and women's diseases are basically the same aside from menstruation, pregnancy and birth and that women's diseases are more difficult to treat. However, his reason for the difficulty involved in treating women is different: 'Women's emotions are different from men's; for women live in seclusion and suffer from much melancholy'. He recognizes spatial isolation as the cause of melancholy and attributes the difficulty in treating women's diseases to 'human problems' (social customs etc.). Zhang provides a detailed explanation regarding human problems in particular and methodically lays out a logic. Zhang laments that the women's segregation rule forces women to live in the seclusion of their inner chambers and stops them from 'telling others of their illness'; three of the four treatment methods – 'looking, listening/smelling, asking, palpating the pulse' – cannot be used because of the importance of the rules of conduct based on the difference between men and women, and even a medical practitioner's consummate skills are rendered useless in this situation.

We must pay attention here to the way the commentator perceives the association between 'women's emotions' as the uniquely female cause of diseases and the uniquely female physiological phenomena and structures such as menstruation, pregnancy and birth. Zhang considers that the high incidence of melancholy in women is caused by living in seclusion rather than female physiological phenomena. He also appears to criticize the rules of conduct that segregate men and women as if to defend the medical skills of male medical practitioners, implying that the custom of isolating women should be discarded for the purpose of active medical treatment for women.

Changing view of the body and construction of physical knowledge

As mentioned above, what attracted a great deal of attention from researchers was the fact that medical practitioners were not actively involved in childbirth in China, unlike in Europe. In fact, researchers made mention of this from early on. However, instead of delving into its cause, they simply attributed it to such things as a 'sense of pollution' involved in childbirth, the custom of 'segregating women' that shunned direct interference by men and a disregard for surgical medicine performed with one's hands (Yao Yi 2011 [Japanese]). In recent years, some studies have burrowed deeply into its cause and Wu Yi-Li (2010 [English]) is the most notable among them. Wu calls the natural, non-interventionist approach represented by *Treatise on Easy Birth* 'cosmologically resonant childbirth' and makes the following argument in comparison with the West (especially the U.K.). Firstly, in Europe, obstetric technologies were used by practitioners as a means to advance their professional careers and acquire medical authority as well as economic benefits. In China, manual skills for child delivery did not lead to career progression or profits. Secondly, medical practitioners were afraid that midwives might misuse the technologies. Prior to the development of safe procedures such as Caesarean section, it was common in both China and Europe to remove a dead fetus from the womb by crushing it. Chinese male medical practitioners gave this method little credit and looked for more advanced and less risky alternatives. Thirdly, Chinese male medical practitioners maintained their authority over childbirth by providing methodological and epistemological knowledge and shifted their domain from specialized problems such as difficult births (midwives' province) to female reproductive health more broadly (medical practitioners' province), whereas doctors in Europe pushed midwives aside and sought to supervise delivery themselves.

Wu Yi-Li advanced her argument with the process of the specialization of physicians in England in mind and her analysis is highly thought-provoking and convincing. Nonetheless, it is hard to say that her argument answers the fundamental questions of why childbirth skills did not lead to career enhancement or profit in China and why Chinese medical practitioners did not seek to supervise delivery, even though they tried to maintain their authority. Medical specialization in Europe would have required two background factors in the first place: one was that the authoritative knowledge taught at universities was textbook knowledge rather than practical knowledge; the other was that the state and laws were involved in the establishment of the new textbook form of knowledge. It is unlikely that these factors existed in Ming-Qing China. Accordingly, it is my view that the fundamental reason behind medical practitioners' non-intervention should be investigated from two standpoints: the historical backdrop of the Ming-Qing period and the strained relationship between 'medicine' and Confucianism (Yao Yi 2011 [Japanese]).

Let us discuss the historical background first. It is common knowledge that the School of Mind (*Xinxue*) flourished in the field of thought and philosophy in the Ming dynasty, especially from the mid-Ming period, and drove a shift from *li-qi* dualism to *qi*-monism. In the social and economic domains, this age featured the expansion of commerce, the development of printing, the appearance of a gentry class, a boom in textual studies and book collections and population growth. This diversification trend was even more prominent in the medical field. Large quantities of medical texts were circulated, boosting the number of men who took an interest in medicine. Editors and promoters of medical texts came from diverse backgrounds and specialties. Behind this diversification, a revivalist current strengthened, as suggested by the popularity of textual studies, which emphasized the orthodoxy of classical teachings and demanded the integration and systematization of medical principles by Confucian medical practitioners.

The emphasis on agency in reproduction needs to be considered on the basis of this background. People feared the prevalence of hedonism and materialism and the erosion of proprieties and called for Neo-Confucianism that stressed moral and ethical codes for moderation and self-control. Medical texts preached that the cause of diseases was associated with not only internal bodily processes but also sexuality and everyday temperance and required men to be responsible in reproduction, to discharge their Confucian duty by producing offspring and to become ideal persons with cultural and moral accomplishments (sage). Medical texts repeatedly asserted that 'feeling' (*qing*) and 'desire' (*yu*) had a 'fire' (*huo*) quality and caused 'weakness' (*xu*) in the body and promoted the development of techniques for a health regimen through the control of feelings and desire. Thus, knowledge of women's medicine was interlocked with health regimens and sexuality and provided techniques for men to achieve inner sagehood (*nei sheng*). Of course, this responsibility to attain inner sagehood and raise healthy sons was placed on women as well. Medical practitioners claimed that appropriate behavior, conduct and mindset would guarantee easy birth and healthy young.

The diversification and unification trends observable in the Ming-Qing period seem to have emanated from the tension between medicine and Confucianism on a fundamental level. In traditional China, medicine was ranked below Confucianism. To become a 'Confucian medical practitioner' (*Ru yi*), one had to be an 'erudite' person with mastery of not only medical knowledge but also the ideology and rules of Confucianism that governed the entire society and personally live according to Confucian morals. This meant that one had to respect the rule of gender segregation in practicing medicine. On the other hand, the ideal and belief of the medical practitioner was to improve one's skills, provide better care and enhance one's value in society. In a society that was permeated by the view of life and death or value judgment represented by the doctrine 'To starve to death is a small matter, but to lose one's chastity is a great matter', the value of the medical practitioner was well below that of the Confucian. In this sense, there was always conflict and contradiction between the social norms of proprieties and morals and the medical practitioner's ideal and belief in protecting life. This strained relationship was not resolved before China's encounter with Western medicine.

Chapter 17

The 'science' of the body in modern medicine and gender

Introduction of Western knowledge of women's medicine

The introduction of modern Western medicine into China by missionaries began in the mid-nineteenth century. The first Chinese-language book on Western women's medicine by English physician B. Hobson, *On the Theory and Practice of Midwifery and Infant Care* (*Fuying xinshuo*), was published in Shanghai in 1858 and was followed by the construction of many obstetrics and gynecology hospitals and medical schools by missionaries, resulting in a gradual increase in the number of Western medicine practitioners. As mentioned earlier, however, the acceptance of Western medicine and improvement in physicians' status required a new system of knowledge that was distinct from Confucian thinking. The theory of evolution paradigm imported in late Qing fit the bill perfectly. Frank Dikötter, in his many pioneering studies on the theory of evolution and modern medicine in China, described in detail how the new form of medicine presented a new order that contrasted with China's traditional cosmic order by concretizing the obscure notion of the body as a quasi-universe by linking itself with new concepts such as the citizen, nation and state (Dikötter 1992, 1995, 1998). The new medicine declared that truth was found in nature that only science could decipher rather than in Confucian and other scriptures and that people needed biogenesis and genetics research as well as medicine to cure diseases and restore health instead of Confucianism.

What enabled and supported this conceptual shift in the background was an intense nationalism and the need for swift nation-building (see Chapter Nine). In order to realize national wealth and military strength through its transformation from inferior (*liebai*) to superior status (*yousheng*), China needed medical science that could stop racial degeneration, treat diseases, maintain health and exert control over society, including sexuality and reproduction. Thus, the nationalist discourse gave legitimacy and value to modern medicine while medical science assumed the role of national development and gained authority. For example, Liang Qichao, who published a manifesto on 'new citizens' (*xin min*), asserted that Chinese people had to improve their physical condition as well as their intellectual condition in order to avoid extinction and that the intellectual and physical renovation should start with motherhood. Because the children of physically and mentally strong women were expected to be healthier and stronger, all women should learn to practice gymnastics (Liang Qichao 1897, 1902). The focus on the mother's body was an important factor in Liang's idea of nation-building and it is no exaggeration to say that the motherhood and fatherhood that would produce a better generation of people (*chuan zhong*) were the keystones of Liang's vision for a new nation. It was a way of thinking that pressed for a substantive change in the Confucian tradition that had long monopolized 'knowledge'. After the abolition in 1905 of the imperial examinations which were closely linked to the long-standing civil service selection system, the awarding of the title of *jinshi*, which had been the highest degree in the imperial examinations, to those who passed the medical examination was a symbolic event that opened up a path for career advancement in the field of science/medicine. What shifts did modern medicine, especially women's medical science, experience and what impacts did it have on gender? This topic is very complex and controversial, but we shall have a brief look at it in the next section.

Anatomical scrutiny and the 'pathologization' of reproduction

A review of numerous texts of modern Western women's medicine that have circulated in China from the end of the nineteenth century to the 1940s would readily find the following characteristics. Firstly, menstruation and pregnancy, which are now part of everyday life, came to be exaggeratedly described as 'illnesses' in the scientific discourse. These texts enumerate in minute detail the physical and psychological changes in the uterus, breasts, skin, complexion and emotions during gestation and the rectal and bladder problems caused by pregnancy. In this view, pregnancy not only leaves permanent skin blemishes but also causes pain in all organs, including the stomach, spine, head and teeth, turning the body into a 'repository' of pain. From this perspective, an invisible and frightening 'dark force' takes hold of the body until labor and delivery are over (Yao Changxu and Yu Yunyou [1920] 1927). The texts gradually pathologized pregnancy in this way even though they stated that pregnancy was a normal physiological phenomenon. Of course, the pathologization of pregnancy and birth was not an entirely modern phenomenon, but it did take a dramatic turn in modern times. The medical texts sent this message to all women, regardless of whether they were pregnant or not or whether they were experiencing pregnancy-related disorders or not, and spread the perception that women were potential 'weaklings'. As pointed out by Chou Chun-Yen, this situation sharply contrasts with the descriptions in traditional medical texts that tended to be confined to the identification, symptoms and treatment of diseases and rarely made reference to physiological symptoms appearing during normal menstruation or pregnancy (Chou Chun-Yen 2010). A persistent inquiry into menstruation in girls also offers a glimpse into this transition.

The second characteristic is the anatomical, iconographical and mathematical scrutinizing of the body. Penis size, the number of sperm in one ejaculation, the number of eggs released during ovulation, male and female bone structures, skull size, brain size and so on were measured and subjected to mathematical studies. Modern medical scientists proclaimed that pregnancy was a phenomenon that could be represented by numbers rather than a concretion of a mysterious *yin-yang qi* or blood and endeavored to disseminate this new knowledge. In addition to numbers, modern medical texts made liberal use of graphic representations and provided detailed descriptions of the skeleton, cranium, brain, nerves, uterus, ovaries and other body parts in photographs and illustrations. This anatomical viewpoint not only allowed the exploration and discovery of invisible body parts under the skin which had not been graphically represented before, but also made a visual impact and reinforced the potential pathologization of pregnancy at the same time. This kind of anatomical scrutiny and the pursuit of mathematical precision have had a tremendous impact on people's perception of the body, because they emphasized the heterogeneity of the male and female bodies, created the impression that there was an obvious difference between men and women psychologically and intellectually and associated the body with labor force as an economic value. More importantly, they furnished the body with the external appearance of 'natural phenomena'. As pointed out by German scholar Barbara Duden, the biological identity of the female body was defined and hypostatized as conforming to a law of nature (Duden 1998).

To China's traditional medicine, the mathematical and anatomical perspective of the body meant a dismantling and degrading which consequently stripped the body of its highly symbolic value of integrity as well as its purposeful ambiguity or hidden nature. While there is a need to examine the actual impact of this qualitative change on the body and the history of gender in China, this chapter next looks specifically at the implications of the 'modern body' in the discourse about the introduction of women's physical education.

Women's physical education and the girl's body

Women's physical education was strongly advocated by not only Liang Qichao and other reformists but also the governments from the early twentieth century. The Regulations for Normal Colleges for Women (*Nüzi shifan xuetang zhangcheng*) and the Regulations for Girls' Schools (*Nüzi xiaoxuetang zhangcheng*), promulgated in 1907, contained clauses concerning physical education. In summary, they claimed 'It shall promote balanced development of all parts of the body, agility of limb movements, discipline and the public propriety of cooperation'. Moreover, 'The level of lesson in girls' elementary schools shall entail appropriate play, sometimes accompanying music and proceed to normal gymnastics. In girls' senior schools, normal gymnastics and play shall be taught. Play shall be taught actively and cheerfully. However, they must not be too unrestrained. The learned posture must be maintained at all times'. The 1912 school system (*renzi xuezhi*) after the founding of the Republic of China in 1912 also included physical education in the curricula of elementary and middle schools.

The physical education program for women was introduced for the purpose of involving girls in active exercise and overcoming the pathological physical backwardness caused by footbinding so that girls would grow up to be strong mothers. Nevertheless, its curricula, the amount of exercise and activity types and levels were entirely different from those for boys. Various restrictions were imposed in order to avoid the promotion of women's rights through unisex physical education as well as to preserve women's physical beauty and traditional roles by adopting less strenuous exercises, dance and play (Yu Chien-Ming 2009). In particular, there was heated debate on the topic of physical education during menstruation. Many of the arguments sought to ban physical education, especially during menstruation, on the grounds that it would lead to infertility and miscarriage. Famous eugenicist Pan Guangdan pointed out that 'Excessive exercise in girls would decrease the birthrate and have genetically disadvantageous effects' (Pan Guangdan 1929). Medical science provided a potent rationale for these arguments.

> The girl's internal reproductive organ is positioned between the rectum and the bladder and in suspension. The position is shifted in strenuous exercise. During menstruation, the uterus becomes congested and hypersensitive to even minor shaking or becomes retroflexed. The retroflexion of the uterus

hampers pregnancy. This would condemn the woman to an unhappy life marred by the disorder. (Xu Fulin 1921)

This statement was published in a prestigious pedagogical journal. Schools conducted surveys about the age of menarche, the duration of menstruation and physiological and psychological changes before and after menstruation including abdominal pain, sleepiness, listlessness, hypersensitivity, irritability and loss of mental and sensory acuity. The repeated surveys and data collation were useful in terms of painting a picture of the average girl's body. Schools paid careful attention to allowing menstruating girls to ask for exemptions from physical education lessons while pedagogists formulated curricula for female students in consideration of their delicate bodies (Yu Chien-Ming 2009).

It is notable here that the focus shifted from the build of the body as a visible aspect of the girl's physicality to the constitution and strength of her body as its invisible aspect. According to the advocates of women's physical education, exercises should be helpful for orderly menstruation, pelvic development, easy childbirth and physical beauty. They referred to the female skeletal structure, musculature, resistance, endurance, constitution and even psychological characteristics and expounded how female bodily characteristics were different to those of males anatomically and biologically and that the intrinsic traits and reproductive function of the female body were the very factors that threatened its life and health.

The aforementioned *Inner Canon of the Yellow Emperor* advises the avoidance of strenuous exercise in order to preserve reproductive energy stored in the kidneys. This applies to men as well as women. Nevertheless, the introduction of the anatomical perspective gave more objective scientific authority to the notion that the female body was inherently delicate and weak.

It is interesting to note that the imagination that was aroused by gymnastics led to the formation of subjectivity in seeking pleasure and liberty, despite the governments' effort to carefully remove de-gendering elements from physical exercise and constantly tether it to daintiness and beauty. China's discourse on 'national salvation' (*jiuguo*) actually led the nation in two directions at the same time: guiding women to reproduction while opening up a path for their liberation. The 'female citizens' (*nüguomin*) discourse that spread in the 1900s encouraged women to step out of their homes and participate in society directly rather than staying behind as 'mothers of citizens' (see Chapter Nine). The rise of freedom and democracy in the 1920s together with some advancement in women's education contributed to the climate of women's liberation. Spurred by this social milieu, women freed themselves from physical restraints such as footbinding and breast-binding (to limit breast development) and in some cases began to argue for the legitimacy of pleasures that did not lead to reproduction. Yu Chien-Ming and Wan Qionghua paint vivid pictures of women who developed self-awareness and tried to enjoy their own lives through physical education and sports (Yu Chien-Ming 2009; Wan Qionghua 2010). Based on their own physical experience, the women rejected the image of a typically fragile girl created by medical and educational experts and demanded respect for their bodies on the basis of their individuality rather than gender.

In this section, we have seen how the perception of the human body changed from the rather obscure physicality replete with philosophical and cultural meanings that formed part of a cosmology to the biological system which was measured and visualized mathematically and anatomically in modern times in the area of girls' sports. While anatomy and physiology were used for the 'scientific' verification of the differences between men and women, women with uterus and ovaries were guided by the glorification of motherhood and femininity toward the reproductive role as their 'natural calling'. At the same time, women's reproductive organs and physiological functions such as gestation and menstruation were in themselves deemed pathological and the myth of female fragility was used as the logic behind the exclusion of women from the world of public interest. Ironically, this modern Western body not only stereotyped the reproducing body but also gave women a path to assert their rights and enjoy their own lives.

Male physicians' intervention in and retreat from birthing

The emergence of obstetrics and gynecology professions

We have seen that the ideas about the body and gender changed markedly in modern times and that the distinction between men and women came to be emphasized in scientific discourses. The extent of the impact of this change on China is yet to be fully examined. In the area of reproduction, resistance to modern physical knowledge was intense, as demonstrated by traditional doctors' refusal to perform Caesarean sections and women's resistance to hospital births

Chapter 17

(Yao Yi 2011 [Japanese]). This section discusses a modern Chinese phenomenon which contrasted with the professional exclusion of women that became common in the process of the modernization of childbirth in the West, Japan and Taiwan which divided the field into male physicians and female midwives and examines the prescriptive nature of traditional Chinese medicine.

From the early twentieth century, the Chinese male physicians who had studied obstetrics in Japan or the West actively entered and revolutionized the field of childbirth. Consequently, the birthing assistance role was transferred from traditional midwives to modern midwives/physicians with the division of labor between obstetricians and midwives in China just as it was in Western countries and Japan. However, male physicians were not welcomed to the frontline of birth assistance as they were hampered by the barrier of proprieties. For example, Yu Songyun, a male physician who had trained and received his medical degree in Germany, was not accepted even when he offered to assist at births free of charge (Yao Yi 2011 [Japanese]). His repeated lamentations were no different from those of Zhang Jingyue, the Ming medical practitioner mentioned earlier. Why did male obstetricians continue to be rejected throughout the ages?

The 'gender segregation' (*nannü geli*) rule is certainly one of the factors that barred male physicians from attending childbirth. However, the situation in Taiwan which has the same custom indicates that the 'barrier of proprieties' was not a decisive factor. The midwives of colonial Taiwan succeeded in turning midwifery into a women's profession on the back of the 'Men and women are different' (*nannü youbie*) gender norm, but the career path to become a physician was almost closed to women (Wu Chia-Ling 2000). Cheng Ling-Fang probed its cause by comparing the situation in Taiwan with that in mainland China and conducted a thought-provoking analysis on how a colonial policy defined medicine and the gender relationship in the former (Cheng Ling-Fang 2002). So, why did female physicians succeed in breaking into the medical profession in China? It is likely that the following two among various factors had a major impact. One was the intent of the government. One of the biggest challenges for modern China was to cultivate good citizens and therefore lowering the rates of infant and maternal mortality as well as raising healthy new generations were imperative. The government served women's needs, promoted training for female doctors, especially obstetricians, and opened the doors of medical schools and medical licensing to women. Unlike other parts of the world, China institutionally guaranteed the entry of women into the medical profession (Yao

Yi 2010a [Japanese]; 2011 [Japanese]). The other factor was women physicians' strategy for social participation. I look at this in detail next.

Medical treatment by and for women: Women physicians' strategy

I begin with the case of Zhang Zhujun (1876–1964), China's prominent first-generation female physician. Besides medical treatment, she was an advocate for women's liberation and social activities such as hospital development and charitable work. As the founder of the earliest medical school with Chinese involvement, the College of Chinese and Western Medicine for Women (*Nüzi zhongxi yixueyuan*), Zhang stated as follows in the founding history of the school.

> There are more diseases affecting women than men and many of them are considered unmentionable and not talked about. Only five out of ten women's diseases are treated by male physicians. Diseases in the lower half of the body are even worse. Innumerable women have died unnecessary deaths since ancient times. Is this not a lamentable situation? [...] While good doctors stand by helplessly in difficult childbirth, midwives do things haphazardly and let the mother and baby die; this is particularly tragic. Accordingly, obstetrics is the cornerstone of women's medicine, about which only women can learn everything, and they ought to train in both Chinese and Western modalities. This is the reason for our endeavor to establish the women's medical school. (Zhang Zhujun 1905)

Zhang also stated that the purpose of the school was to 'give top priority to women's medicine and to have women's diseases diagnosed and treated by women physicians' (Zhang Zhujun 1905).

It is clear from her comment that she perceived that there were more women's diseases than men's and that they were more complex; she explained that male physicians were limited in what they could do to treat women mainly because of 'private circumstances' (which could not be discussed publicly). This is very similar to the aforementioned views of Sun Simiao and Zhang Jingyue in particular. However, Zhang Zhujun used this as the reason to assert that women should be in charge of obstetrics and gynecology and advocated for the 'treatment of women by women for women'. In other words, she put forward

Chapter 17

the same view of women's diseases as male physicians' but took advantage of the limitations of male physicians by using the 'gender segregation' rule as the need and justification for women's entry into the medical profession.

'Treatment by women for women' was inherited by Yang Chongrui and other female physicians. Yang was a prominent modern obstetrician in charge of maternity healthcare and midwifery training during the nationalist government period. Like Zhang Zhujun, who had endeavored to give women medical training before her, she argued that employment was the key to women's liberation and endeavored to help women have professions. In order to establish midwifery as a women's profession, Yang incorporated maternity healthcare, which was of paramount importance in the then government's nation-building plan, in the midwife's duties. Her idea was a success. The midwives who had received rigorous training in this capacity went beyond their authority and assumed a quasi-physician role amid the serious obstetrician shortage from the second half of the 1930s. After the founding of the PRC, many of these midwives were upskilled to become obstetricians through additional training.

The 'barefoot doctors' in the PRC

As we have seen above, women's entry into the medical profession in China was greatly assisted by the demand from patients for female physicians, women's strategy for social participation in compliance with the traditional gender norm and the rise of the women's liberation movement and the government policy that supported it.

In reality, the mass production of women obstetricians had to wait until the founding of the PRC. Its government upheld the ideal of equality between men and women and adopted the social policy to promote and mobilize women's participation in production labor and society (see Chapters Twelve and Thirteen). In order to resolve the shortage of healthcare personnel, the government not only invested much effort into training women physicians but also substantially increased the ratio of female doctors in women's medicine by promoting the Republic-trained midwives to medical doctors (Yao Yi 2010b [Japanese]). In rural areas, the government endeavored to train female 'barefoot doctors' with a focus on birthing assistance (Yao Yi 2016 [Japanese]). Consequently, a large majority of obstetricians are women in present-day China, where the obstetrics department has been 'feminized' and the obstetrician has become one of the typical gendered professions. The active training of women physicians by the government is largely attributable to criticisms of the traditional gender segregation norm and the advancement of the gender equality policy. However, a review of the process of the formulation and advancement of the policy clearly finds an aspect of compromise with and concession to China's enduring and strong patriarchal mindset and its preservation and exploitation. In other words, it is a highly pragmatic aspect in which women's social participation was promoted and the space for women's activity was created with minimal protest from men by translating the normally objectionable patriarchal norm into women's need (Yao Yi 2016 [Japanese]).

In closing

This chapter has offered a brief account of Chinese history from a medical and gender viewpoint. Problematizing China's medical practices from a gender perspective is closely associated with the concept of the 'gendered body', a concept that has been at the center of many scholarly discussions in recent years. Engagement with this concept has simultaneously generated many new perspectives and raised awareness of many issues that had previously received little attention. For example, the meticulously constructed Yellow Emperor's Body, one-sex and two-sex models, Wu Yi-Li's revision of them, the formation of women's medicine, changes caused by the acceptance of Western medicine and so on are all large-scale subjects.

China's traditional medicine was a complete knowledge system including a cosmology and a set of moral and ethical values. I await further detailed studies on how the body and the reproductive body specifically in terms of pregnancy and birth were understood according to traditional Chinese medicine. The traditional perception of the body was deeply shaken by the arrival of modern Western medicine. The mathematical and anatomical measurement and visualization of the body stripped it of its integrity with highly symbolic value, philosophical and cultural ambiguity and meaningful hiddenness. We have only just begun to examine how the two knowledge systems underpinned by different systems of medicine contrasted and coalesced and in what forms their relationship manifested. Researchers have been advancing their work to decipher China's medicine and perception of the body on the understanding that they form the undercurrent that defines China itself. Part of this prescriptive nature can be seen in the 'feminization' of women's medicine. The norm of 'gender segregation' is the keystone of the preservation of social and family orders that has occupied a central position in politics and been used for the achievement of political goals in every era. The emphasis on the body's cultural and symbolic meanings has led to the disregard of corporality as well as the view of the body as being simultaneously sexual and asexual, both of which are still alive in contemporary society. However, the modern view of the body has also infiltrated Chinese society and opened up a path to women's liberation as we can see in the case of women's physical education and sports. It is interesting to consider today's 'disassembling of reproduction' in the context of the 'dismantling of the body' that took place in the modern age. The disassembling of reproduction refers to the phenomenon generated by the emergence of assisted reproductive technologies in which the long process of reproduction that could previously only happen inside a woman's body is broken into separate parts – ovulation, fertilization, pregnancy and birth – which can now be combined in various ways as required (Ogino 2014; Yao Yi 2015 [Japanese]). The body that can be sold and bought can be regarded as the ultimate consequence of the 'dismantling and downgrading of the body' as a cosmology but it is also possible to weave a story of 'women's liberation' from it. While there are concerns that it may pose an unparalleled threat to the existing concept of 'the human' and bioethics, it is welcomed by some sections of society as an opportunity to liberate women from the inherence and restrictiveness of their reproductive body. The body is becoming an increasingly compelling research theme.

18. The History of Women's/Gender Studies and Feminism in China

—*AKIYAMA Yōko*[1]

The birth of women's studies in China

The concept of 'gender' was born in the midst of the second wave of feminism. This idea/movement emerged in the U.S. in the second half of the 1960s and spread from the West to Asia in the first half of the 1970s. The phenomenon was more a series of chained combustions of women's issues that had accumulated in these countries than the transmission of an idea. Feminism as an ideology gave rise to the academic discipline of women's studies, which gave new meanings to terms such as 'patriarchy' and 'gender' and shaped them into weapons to be used in analyzing and reforming the traditional androcentric social structure.

Its spread, however, remained on the western side of the Cold War and made no impact on the Eastern Bloc. Even in the Soviet Union and Eastern European countries that were more permissive toward Western culture than China, which was thrown into the Cultural Revolution and all but culturally isolated, there was a strong feeling of rejection toward 'bourgeois feminism' due to the firmly stated

---

[1] Akiyama Yōko (1942–2016) was a feminist activist, scholar of Chinese literature, member of the Japanese Chinese Women's History Association and professor at Surugadai University. In the 1970s, she was one of the leaders of a pioneering group of second-wave feminists in Japan named after Virginia Woolf. She was one of the first Japanese scholars to introduce contemporary Chinese women's literature, and also played a major role in building networks between students of women's studies and feminism in China and Japan. Her works include *My Experiences with China and Feminism* (*Watashi to Chūgoku to feminism*; 2004) and *Personal Notes on Feminist History* (*Femi shishi nōto*; 2016a). She produced many academic papers and translations: the 2017 issue of the journal of the Chinese Women's History Association, *Chūgoku joseishi kenkyū*, includes a bibliography of her works. Akiyama Yōko passed away in 2016, after completing the draft of this chapter for the Japanese edition of this book.

principle that women's liberation could be realized only through class struggle/ socialist revolution (and hence it had already been realized in socialist countries). The impact of second-wave feminism was not felt by the Eastern Bloc countries until after the 1980s when the socialist regimes began to destabilize.

During the 1980s, following the end of the Cultural Revolution, China embarked on the Deng Xiaoping-led reform and opening-up policies, which saw a flurry of new social problems. They included women's issues such as the restructuring of the female labor force, the rising divorce rate, trafficking in women and the commercialization of sex which became rife after the introduction of the market economy as the women's liberation and gender equality that had been promised at the founding of the PRC failed to materialize.

Until then, a quasi-government agency called the All-China Women's Federation (ACWF) had been the one-stop shop for all Chinese women's issues. After a period of forced inactivity during the Cultural Revolution, it resumed its operations and came under pressure to respond to emergent women's issues. Despite much effort made by the central and local Women's Federations to organize study meetings on 'marriage and family issues', the orthodox Marxist ideology for women's liberation alone was no longer able to deal with social changes. A theoretical basis to respond to this situation and a movement/organization to put it into practice entered the picture in the form of the establishment of the discipline of women's studies.

Women's studies came into being in the U.S. during the 1970s and soon crossed the sea to Japan to spawn the Women's Studies Association of Japan and other societies and groups by the late 1970s. Women's studies (*fünuxue*)[2] was introduced to China with the publication of a Chinese-language edition of a Japanese essay written by Atsushi Shirai, 'The history of feminism and women's studies', in 1982.

Separately, a proposal to establish China's own women's studies was put forward by Li Xiaojiang, a professor at Zhengzhou University, Henan Province, which was far away from China's political center. She published 'Human evolution and women's liberation' in 1983, arguing that women's liberation

---

2 The English word 'women' is generally translated as either *fünü* (婦女) or *nüxing* (女性) in Chinese. Both words have been used in China since the late 1990s and the traditional *fünü* tends to carry connotations of officialdom or a tone of Marxist women's liberation theory whereas *nüxing*, which was popularized via Taiwan and Hong Kong, has come to have a feminist tone. Also, 'feminism' is translated as either *nüquan zhuyi* (女權主義) or *nüxing zhuyi* (女性主義). They are generally used in a manner similar to that of the previous two words but some feminists (such as Wang Zheng) intentionally use *nüquan zhuyi* implying women's rights.

needed to be won through a long battle fought by women themselves rather than via social revolution (Li Xiaojiang 1983).

Li founded the first non-government research organization, the Henan Women's Studies Center, in 1985 and held a conference for researchers interested in the discipline as well as establishing a course of lectures on women's studies (women's literature) at Zhengzhou University in the same year. She set up the Women's Studies Center, Zhengzhou University, in 1987. The founding of an academic society and the convening of a conference led by a single university academic outside of Beijing was unprecedented in China, where everything was carried out under the government's initiative.

In parallel with organizing, Li proposed the establishment of women's studies as an academic discipline and began to plan the publication of *Women's Studies Book Series* that encompassed all fields of women's studies. She convened the Symposium for Founding Women's Studies that involved around forty prospective contributors to the series in 1987. The publication was launched in 1988 and covered diverse fields from women's studies theory to history, sexual science, jurisprudence, population studies and literary history. The contributing authors were pioneers of women's studies who served as the backbone for the network and sowed the seeds of women's studies across China.[3]

Meanwhile, the ACWF mobilized its subsidiary organizations throughout China to collect historical materials concerning the women's movements in the country in the early 1980s and published six volumes of *Historical Records of the Chinese Women's Movement* (*Zhongguo funü yundong lishi ziliao*), used as the basis of *History of the Chinese Women's Movement* (*Zhongguo funü yundongshi*) (Zhonghua quanguo funü lianhehui funü yundong lishi yanjiushi 1986, 1991a, b, c, d; Zhonghua quanguo funü lianhehui 1989). The book reflects the ACWF's belief that it is the legitimate successor of the Chinese women's movement and the rightful author of its history. On the other hand, the move toward ideological liberalization under the reform and opening-up policies began to engender an attitude that was more receptive to the new women's studies within the ACWF. At the Symposium on the Theory of Women's Studies in China hosted by the ACWF in 1986, Li Xiaojiang proposed the founding of women's studies and ignited a lively debate on the issue.

---

3 The founding of Chinese women's studies by Li Xiaojiang and others is described in Li Xiaojiang (1995), Akiyama (1996) and Akiyama et al. (1998), among others.

Chapter 18

The move toward ideological liberalization was frozen, however, with the occurrence of the Tiananmen Incident in 1989 in which student-led pro-democracy protests were met with a military crackdown. In this oppressive climate, the Women's Studies Center of Zhengzhou University hosted a symposium on Chinese women's social participation and development in March 1990 which attracted 150 attendees, including women's studies researchers from Hong Kong and Taiwan. It was reportedly the first large conference in China since the crackdown on the pro-democracy movement. The passion and courage of Li and her fellow researchers were of course behind the successful organization of the conference in this politically tense period, but another factor was that the independent women's movement still in its infancy was overlooked as a minor activity that would not pose a threat to the government with its stated gender equality principle.

Feminine consciousness and sinicization in 1980s women's studies

Li Xiaojiang and others called the push to establish Chinese women's studies the 'women's studies movement'. In China, where all movements were government-initiated campaigns and no independent citizen-led activism existed, the women's studies network paved the way for the involvement of non-governmental organizations (NGOs).

The move to establish Chinese women's studies can be placed in the history of the evolution of second-wave feminism on a global scale. However, its social background and the idea behind it were unique to China.

In her advocacy of women's studies in *Searching for Eve*, Li calls for the breaking of the three taboo areas that had been imposed on Chinese studies on women in the past (Li Xiaojiang 1988).

The first is the 'sex/gender taboo'. Besides the taboo regarding sex in a narrow sense that restricts sexual expression, this norm includes a 'taboo on femininity' that ignores the physical and social differences between men and women. This stems from a desire to redress the situation in which the gender equality policy from the early PRC to the Cultural Revolution era ignored sexual differences and forced heavy labor on women and suppressed their natural expression of emotions.

The second is the 'Marxist taboo'. Li claimed that women's liberation was a long-term struggle which did not end with the socialist revolution and that Marxist women's liberation theory should therefore evolve to fit with reality. This argument was closer to the Marxist feminism of the West than to the orthodox Marxist theory of women's liberation and was naturally regarded as heretical by the conservative cadres of the ACWF.

The third is the 'feminism taboo'. Although first-wave feminism was introduced to China in the early twentieth century and had some influence during the 1920s and 1930s, it was rejected by the Chinese Communist Party (CCP) as 'bourgeois feminism'. Li's stance on Western feminism has been one of ambivalence. She introduced the feminist thoughts of Simone de Beauvoir and others and criticized the ACWF for rejecting them on one hand but refused to identify herself as feminist by arguing that feminism originated in the West and that China has a unique history and climate on the other. (Many scholars from the West, including myself, consider Li's definition of feminism too narrow and regard her as a feminist in the broad sense of the term; she has so far shown no adverse reaction to this.)

So, what was at the heart of the Chinese women's studies movement advanced by Li and others? In short, it was the awakening of 'feminine consciousness'.

Behind the rise of feminine consciousness was the shared experience of Li's generation of Chinese women who were born after the Second World War. They spent their youth in the so-called decade of turmoil of the Cultural Revolution (1966–1976) and tried to embrace it alongside men inspired by Mao Zedong's words, 'Whatever men comrades can do, women comrades can do, too'. When they were pulled back to the mundane world after the Cultural Revolution, however, they were brought back to reality by the same old gender structure of Chinese society of the past. Li Xiaojiang's call to awaken their feminine consciousness resonated strongly with those who had been trapped in the 'women's pitfall' of childbirth, childcare and the double burden of employment and domestic work.

Li urged women to affirm their feminine identities before reaching out to society because feminine consciousness included the subject's consciousness as an individual and group consciousness as women, which expanded to become social consciousness. In response, young researchers embarked on the task of analyzing and restructuring the genderless worldview of each academic field from a women's point of view – a process through which they regained their self-confidence and fostered a sense of solidarity. While the feminine consciousness advocated in the 1980s went on to be criticized for being essentialist, it is undeniable that it had a strong enough impact on women of China's intellectual class at the time to change their consciousness and allow them to take ownership of women's issues.

Along with feminine consciousness, 'sinicization' (*bentuhua*) was another keyword of the founding phase of Chinese women's studies. As mentioned in relation to the third area of taboo above, the sinicization argument claims that Chinese women's studies is bound to be different from Western women's studies because it has been developed in China's unique history and social climate. The notion of sinicization has maintained its currency whereas feminine consciousness has become the target for criticism. However, it is hard to say whether the meaning of the term has been hammered into consensus as it is sometimes used in the context of the rejection of Western feminist theory or the revival of Marxist women's liberation theory (Akiyama 2001).

It has been argued that China's reform and opening-up policies and move toward a market economy were important background factors for the emergence of Li Xiaojiang's theory. Tani Barlow, an American scholar of Chinese history, calls the Chinese feminism of the 1980s championed by Li 'market feminism' in her voluminous book, *The Question of Women in Chinese Feminism* (Barlow 2004). When the advance of market orientation in the 1980s resulted in the breakdown of the previously government-guaranteed women's employment, labor protection and public childcare system, the ACWF and a majority of women scholars voiced criticisms, but Li Xiaojiang gave recognition to its positive aspect in that the market economy presented new opportunities to women despite its problems.[4] Barlow's definition of 'market feminism' is somewhat one-sided and open to misunderstanding, but there is no doubt that Chinese women's studies of the 1980s was fostered in the struggle to deal with the new economic and social milieu.

---

4 Although Li Xiaojiang disapproved of the definition of 'market feminism', she recognized the significance of Barlow's study and lent her support to the publication of its Chinese edition (2012; translated by Shen Qiqi).

Encounter between Eastern/Western feminisms and UN Conference

The first contact between Chinese women's studies and its Western counterpart took place at a 1992 conference held at Harvard University entitled 'Engendering China'. The leading scholars involved in the founding of Chinese women's studies,[5] including Li Xiaojiang and Du Fangqin, were invited and sat down with American scholars and Chinese students in the U.S. to exchange views and engage in debate, at times intensely. The collection of conference papers was published in both the English and Chinese languages and provided a starting point for the subsequent Chinese studies from a gender perspective (Gilmartin et al. 1994; Li Xiaojiang, Zhu Hong and Dong Xiuyu 1994).[6]

While the communities of thinkers and academics in China were holding their breath at the time in the aftermath of the Tiananmen Incident, activities surrounding women were comparatively spirited. In 1991, the ACWF set up the Women's Studies Institute of China, which launched its journal, *Funü Yanjiu Lunzong (Collection of Women's Studies)*. This was the ACWF's attempt to regain the initiative after it had fallen behind the non-governmental sector in establishing women's studies. Other women's studies centers were established across China, among which the Women's Studies Center of Peking University (1990) and the Women's Studies Center of Tianjin Normal University (1993) have been the driving force behind Chinese women's studies through to the twenty-first century. The United Nations' decision to convene the 1995 Fourth World Conference on Women in Beijing sparked a flurry of activity with the publication of women-related books, the establishment of women's studies centers and women's professional associations and the staging of various women's studies symposia.[7]

There was another trend involving women during this period, as the stifling political situation made people turn their attention toward the economy. China's

---

5 Attendees from China included Li Xiaojiang, Du Fangqin, Qi Wenying, Chen Yiyun, Tan Shen, Wang Xingjuan, Tan Lin, Dong Xiuyu and Li Ziyun (according to Cai Qingyuan (2011)).

6 The English edition and the Chinese edition contain a few different studies.

7 For example, the Women's Studies Center of Peking University hosted the International Symposium on Women's Issues three times between 1992 and 1994, which were also attended by Japanese researchers. Tianjin Normal University hosted a two-week workshop entitled 'Chinese Women and Development: Status, Health and Employment' jointly with the Society for the Studies of Chinese Women Overseas where more than 100 researchers, including Americans, and women's issue activists held discussions.

transition to a market economy led to the commercialization of sexuality in a broad range of industries from advertising to service and adult entertainment. Anti-establishment and avantgarde cultures receded into the background while traditional customs and classical femininity were celebrated. After elevating a wide range of issues to social consciousness in the 1980s, women's literature shifted to 'personal novels' that explored one's inner sexuality. Thus, the first half of the 1990s became the 'women boom' era with friends and foes boarding the same boat.

The nineties' women's boom peaked at the 1995 UN Fourth World Conference on Women held in Beijing (Akiyama 1999). The World Conference on Women was organized for the first time in Mexico City in 1975, which was designated as the International Women's Year, followed by the Copenhagen Conference in 1980 and the Nairobi Conference in 1985. Ten years later, Beijing became the first Asian city to host the conference. China was determined to stage a successful conference in order to cleanse its international image tarnished by the pro-democracy movement crackdowns. For this purpose, it supported the aforementioned women's boom while attempting to eliminate dissenters and make unified efforts to prepare for the conference. The women's studies movement led by Li Xiaojiang's network was suspected of dissidence and Li's workplace was visited by 'thought investigators' while her books were removed from the display of publications on women's issues next to the main hall where the conference was being staged.

The conference was held from 4 to 15 April 1995, including the intergovernmental conference and the NGO forum, with the participation of almost 30,000 people comprising a large contingent of Chinese attendees, support staff and the media and nearly 15,000 international attendees. The Chinese government had difficulty in handling the NGO forum. It designated the ACWF as China's women's NGO to be the forum organizer, but this was a somewhat awkward approach since it involved presenting a governmental organization as an NGO on the international stage. There was much discord between the Chinese side and foreign NGOs from the preparatory stage and the venue for the NGO forum was eventually moved from central Beijing to Huairou County, a one-hour drive from the city. This change caused various problems such as poor access to transportation, inadequate conference facilities and accommodation and excessive security, but once it began the NGO forum itself was full of enthusiastic debates and presentations. Li Xiaojiang was critical of the organizational process and did not attend the conference. She later released an essay entitled 'Why I refused to participate in the NGO Forum of the Fourth World Conference on Women' (Li Xiaojiang 2000 [Japanese]).[8]

The conference was closed after the adoption of the Beijing Declaration and the Beijing Platform for Action. A fifth world conference on women has not been held to date (2015), while other anniversary conferences and events have been organized at the UN headquarters and in other parts of the world known by names such as Beijing+5 and Beijing+10. In a sense, the Beijing conference marked the beginning of a new era of thinking about women's issues on a global scale.

Beijing+10: ACWF-led building of a women's studies network

Despite many contradictions, the Fourth World Conference on Women became a major turning point for women's studies and the women's movement in China. It provided a springboard for Chinese women, who had been cut off from the world, to be 'brought into the orbit of the rest of the world', to use a Chinese expression. The existence of NGOs that were neither 'pro-government' nor 'anti-government' gained official recognition and concepts such as 'gender', 'reproductive health' and 'the empowerment of women' found acceptance. The adoption of the Beijing Declaration and the Beijing Platform for Action at the Conference and the release of the Outline for the Development of Chinese Women (1995–2000) immediately before the conference have since served as an endorsement for women to advance their movement and put forward their demands.

The women's studies centers at various universities that had been set up in the lead up to the conference prepared themselves to take the next step while the activities of women's NGOs (e.g., centered on violence against women, health, poverty, media monitoring etc.) increased, inspired by the conference's momentum (Liu Bohong 2007 [Japanese]). After successfully sponsoring the NGO forum at the conference, the ACWF endeavored to invigorate its research activity along with reform of the ACWF itself by taking advantage of the connections it had made in China and overseas in the process of organizing the forum to construct a national women's studies network. As a result, the Chinese Women's Research Society (CWRS) was founded under the initiative

---

8 It was originally written by Li Xiaojiang as a statement submitted to a symposium held at Harvard University in the fall of 1995. Only the Japanese version is published in 2000. See Li Xiaojiang (2000 [Japanese]).

of the ACWF in 1999. This is a national network that unifies the channels of party-schools, social science academies, women's federations and higher education institutions and has a total of 110 member organizations as at 2015.[9] Its headquarters are situated at the ACWF Women's Studies Institute of China, whose *Funü Yanjiu Lunzong* (*Collection of Women's Studies*) journal became the official journal of the CWRS.

This process can be regarded as the reorganization of the non-governmental-sector women's studies movement orchestrated by the state. In fact, the rules of the CWRS reveal its true colors as a state-run organization by stating, 'Under the guidance of Marxism-Leninism, Maoism and Deng Xiaoping's and Jiang Zemin's Theories, efforts have been made in resolving major problems and difficulties Chinese women have faced since the reform and opening-up policies and during the period of socialist modernization [...]'. However, the core personnel in this network-building process were the new generation of ACWF cadres who gained a deeper understanding of feminism and NGOs through contact with foreign women during the preparation for the Fourth World Conference on Women as well as the researchers who had run research centers and programs since the pioneering days of Chinese women's studies. Of course, the Marxist theory of women's liberation upheld by the ACWF and feminism-based women's/gender studies are incompatible in certain aspects and their copresence is apparent in the terminology used in *Funü Yanjiu Lunzong* (*Collection of Women's Studies*).[10] It is likely that the researchers who joined this network with knowledge of the situation employed the strategy of influencing the state's women's policy while utilizing government resources to the extent permitted by the state.

Naturally, there are maverick individuals who would not fit in a coalition of this sort. Li Xiaojiang, the founder of Chinese women's studies, left Zhengzhou University after the ideological clampdown around the time of the Fourth World Conference on Women and took a position at Dalian University in 2002 to undertake women's studies symposia and Chinese women's oral histories projects on her own terms. Other maverick feminist scholars include

---

9 'Women's studies network', 26 August 2015, *The Fourth Annual Conference Report of the Chinese Women's Research Society*.

10 As mentioned in Note 1 above, all four words (*funü* / 婦女, *nüxing* / 女性, *nüquan zhuyi* / 女權主義 and *nüxing zhuyi* / 女性主義) are used in the studies and it is possible in some cases to infer the author's stance on the basis of the terminology used.

Dai Jinhua[11] who employs postmodernism in her incisive analysis of films and literature and Li Yinhe who pioneered the study of sexual minorities in China.

Foreign-funded development projects and women's/gender studies

Another entity that exerted as much influence over Chinese women's studies/movement as the ACWF after the Fourth World Conference on Women was a group of Chinese women's studies researchers living outside of China: the Chinese Society for Women's Studies (CSWS) which was formed in the U.S. in 1991. Its core members such as Bao Xiaolan and Wang Zheng left China during the 1980s and studied and earned their degrees in feminism/women's studies. Shocked by the changes in women's status that accompanied the reform and opening-up policies and the 1989 Tiananmen Incident in their home country, they wished to promote mutual understanding between the West and China through feminism/women's studies and make contributions to the resolution of women's issues and democratization in China (Wang Danning, Wang Zheng and Xu Wu 2014 [Japanese]).

The aforementioned Engendering China symposium at Harvard University in 1992 set up the first face-to-face meeting between CSWS members and women's studies researchers inside China. In the following year, seven members of the CSWS attended the summer workshop at Tianjin Normal University and engaged with over 100 Chinese women's studies researchers. The concept of 'gender' was presented there and '*shehui xingbie*' (社會性別) was proposed as its Chinese equivalent to replace '*xingbie*' (性別) that carried the connotation of traditional sexual distinction.[12] An introductory book on feminist theories edited by CSWS members was well-received as an important source of information around the time of the Fourth World Conference on Women.

Although the problems of women's poverty, health and violence and harassment against women were raised and the need for women's advocacy was recognized at the 1995 conference, official support for these activities after the conference was limited. For this reason, various research institutions as well as

---

11 In her 2004 study, Tani Barlow devotes a whole chapter to Dai Jinhua as a representative of 'post-structuralist feminism' of the 1990s in contrast to Li Xiaojiang as representing the 1980s. See Barlow (2003 [Japanese]), Dai Jinhua (2006 [Japanese]) and Meng Yue and Dai Jinhua (1989).

12 See Wang Zheng (1997) for the Chinese translation of the term 'gender'.

Chapter 18

Women's Federations and the CSWS jointly sponsored large-scale workshops across China during the Beijing+10 review. These activities received funding from the Ford Foundation as a gender and development (GAD) project. The Ford Foundation with an office in Beijing has been the largest sponsor of Chinese women's studies since its early days. International cooperation projects like this supported activities for women and trained personnel in less developed provinces such as Sichuan, Guizhou and Yunnan. On the other hand, the situation in which Chinese women's studies researchers were mobilized for development projects under foreign formulae and funding was criticized by Li Xiaojiang as 'postcolonialism' (Li Xiaojiang 2006 [Japanese]).

Following the development projects, another international cooperation project began at the end of the 1990s: the Developing Women's and Gender Studies in China project led by Du Fangqin of Tianjin Normal University and Wang Zheng of the University of Michigan. After groping her way forward in studying women's history from the start of Chinese women's studies, Du gained experience in international exchange and became aware of a shift in the research framework from women's history to gender history. When she felt the need to improve women's studies theory and establish women's studies as a specialized academic discipline in China, she sought cooperation from CSWS members in establishing the project. This ran from 1999 to 2006 over three phases with the Ford Foundation's sponsorship and produced good results, including the hosting of conferences, workshops and training courses for young researchers, as well as participation in international conferences, interuniversity exchanges and publications. The work has been taken over by the Network for the Development of Chinese Women's/Gender Studies since the project ended.

Du Fangqin made her most significant contribution in her own area of interest, women's history, which began with the implementation of the reading and discussion school program in Tianjin in 1999 and 2000. A limited number of participants (around fifty people) were given material to read and engaged in free discussion afterward. This formula was new to China. CSWS members supplied many diverse materials, ranging from gender theory to oral history methodology and the work of Susan Mann and Gail Hershatter and others. The reading and discussion school program became a turning point from women's history to gender history as well as a training ground for the next generation of researchers in China.[13] (See Du Fangqin (2008) and Gao Shiyu (2015) for detailed accounts of the development of women's/gender history in China. It is said that they deliberately retained the word 'women's' so as not to forget the aspirations they had in the early days of Chinese women's studies.)

On the back of these nationwide activities, the women's studies researchers of Chinese universities endeavored to institutionalize women's studies as an official curriculum. Peking University set up a woman studies course within the graduate school of sociology in 1997. China Women's University (*Zhonghua Nüzi xueyuan*: formerly a cadre training school for the ACWF which was opened at the time of the Fourth World Conference on Women) is the only state-owned women's university; it attached great importance to research and education in women's studies and became the first university in China to offer an undergraduate degree in women's studies beginning in 2006 (Ōhama 2007). The aforementioned Women's Studies Center of Peking University hosted the Seminar for the Development of Women's Studies Departments at Chinese Universities in 2001, and the participating educational institutions formed the Group for the Development of Women's Studies Departments at Chinese Universities.

Digital age feminism: 'Smiling feminism', street performance

China experienced a rapid development of information technology (IT) in the latter half of the 1990s and became a full-fledged IT society by the early twenty-first century. It is highly significant that individuals have acquired the ability to disseminate information in China where the mass media is controlled by the state. Chinese women's advocacy NGOs that flourished after the Fourth World Conference on Women have developed their own websites from which to transmit information.

As these activities are too numerous to mention here, I look at the activity of *Chinese Feminism* by Huang Lin and others as one example of feminist activism that has adapted to the digital age.[14]

---

13 The activity of the reading and discussion school is explained in Cai Yiping, Wang Zheng and Du Fangqin (2000) and Du Fangqin (2001).
14 See Akiyama (2013) for details on the activities of Huang Lin and others.

Huang Lin is a professor in literature at Capital Normal University who engaged in her own feminist network activity from around 2004 to 2010, including publishing the website '*Liangxing Shiye*' (*Two-Sex Vision*), founding the general feminist journal *Zhongguo Nüxing Zhuyi* (*Chinese Feminism*), publishing a series of women's studies books and hosting the Academic Salon on Feminism.

The term '*nüxing zhuyi*' (女性主義) used by Huang Lin above was introduced via Hong Kong and Taiwan as an alternative translation of 'feminism' to *nüquan zhiyi* (女權主義) in the late 1990s. This softer sounding term came into wide use in the 2000s. In China with Marxism as its creed, however, while it may be acceptable to introduce foreign feminism, creating any other 'ism' independently is regarded as taboo. Huang made a point of naming it 'Chinese Feminism' and used the catchphrase 'smiling feminism' to promote dialogue with men who were hostile to feminism. The novelty of the movement of Huang and others lay in the fine balance between their strength of character to declare feminism in spite of the taboo and their suppleness to present it with a smile.

The Academic Salon on Feminism was hosted by a Beijing bookstore, providing a venue where participants listened to Chinese and international guest speakers and engaged in discussion freely on a wide range of cutting-edge subjects from feminist theory to men's studies, sexuality and the body, films, literature and paintings. The salon was publicized on the website and the discussions were turned into books. Their network activity combining the three modes of communication was appropriate for the twenty-first century as a new era.

In the 2010s, a group of young feminists called Young Feminism Activists launched a new form of activism called performance art. The movement to stage *The Vagina Monologues* was a precursory activity. The play, written by Eve Ensler of the U.S., consists of monologues about sexuality and the body given by women. It began to be performed around the world in the late 1990s, with adaptations to fit the experiences of local women. The staging of the play itself became a global movement. In China, it was first performed by the students of Ai Xiaoming, a professor at Zhongshan University, Guangzhou, who is a friend of Huang Lin, in 2003 and was subsequently performed mostly by students in places such as Beijing, Wuhan and Xiamen. In 2013, a documentary film entitled *From Vaginas* was produced to mark the tenth anniversary of the first performance. Feminist performance artists emerged from the movement to stage local performances (Ohashi 2014).

The use of performance art as protest began in 2012 with the Occupy Men's Toilet Movement to highlight the fact that only women had to queue up at public lavatories as there were always fewer women's toilets than men's. This was followed by creative and humorous performances that captured the public eye, including an anti-domestic violence protest in blood-stained wedding dresses, the protest against employment discrimination dressed in the costume of the legendary female warrior Hua Mulan and the protest by shaved-headed performers against the practice of disqualifying female students from university entrance examinations. These performances were disseminated through the internet and inspired further reactions (Tōyama 2013).[15] It is very interesting that Chinese feminism, which originated from the women's studies movement, spawned direct actions by the younger generation while at the same time advancing academic institutionalization.

Activism through performance art caught the government off guard by using an art form in conjunction with the new medium of the internet, but it failed to circumvent regulations that were being tightened under Xi Jinping's regime. Five feminist-activists were detained in March 2015, not at the scene of a protest-performance but for allegedly hatching a 'plan' to mount a campaign to protest against sexual harassment on buses on the 8 March International Women's Day. News of their detention was immediately reported worldwide and sparked international petitions and protest actions. They were released from detention one month later as a result, but they reportedly continue to be on the watchlist of China's public security organs (Ohashi 2015a, 2015b).

The above is a brief overview of the development of feminism and women's/gender studies in China over the last three decades. Although the activity started ten years behind the West and Japan, it has been making remarkable progress. Nevertheless, there are some concerns that China's increasingly tighter thought control may have an impact on the women's/gender studies area. Now that the pioneering generation, who paved the way for women's/gender studies in the face of internal and external pressure, is stepping back from the front line, the next generation is being tested as to whether they can carry on the legacy of critique and creativity.

---

15 See Ohashi's '*Chūgoku femiteki kenbunroku*' (Feminist observations of China), serialized since No. 71 (2012) of *Onnatachi no 21 seiki* (*Women's Asia 21*).

Column 5

Sexual Minorities

TŌYAMA Hideya

Pre-modern times

This column deals with people presently called 'sexual minorities' (LGBT = lesbian, gay, bisexual, transgender). However, such designation is based on heteronormativity, premised upon modern society's discourse of a gender binary, while historically, it was not necessarily 'minority' groups that engaged in same-sex sexual activity and sexual border transgression. Moreover, there was no clear terminology to refer to such people.

In Confucian ethics in pre-modern China, the utmost importance was placed upon forming a family and having sons in order to carry on the paternal line. For that reason, sexuality aimed at reproduction was the legitimate kind. Yet, as long as it did not hinder that goal, there was also tolerance towards same-sex sexual relations and suchlike. Some researchers describe such circumstances in terms of homosexuality existing in an 'ambiguous condition' (Zhang Zaizhou 2001). What is more, homosexuality was purely a matter of 'acts' and 'preference' and was not understood as the status of being 'a homosexual' (Hinsch 1990: 7).

In the Ming and Qing dynasties, it is also said that homosexuality became a common ethos among the upper classes. However, at the time, patrilineality was strengthened all the more, and it was also a period when women were extolled for chastity and forced to practice abstinence. Men's ability to behave as their passions dictated, including engaging in homosexual activity, was because women's acceptance of such male activities was deemed a virtue. Men's homosexuality also involved discrimination between superior and inferior, master and subordinate and older and younger, and while the side that took the initiative had higher status and sought stimulation and satisfaction, the passive side had lower status and was in a position of servitude – in this sense, homosexual activity was also often inseparable from prostitution. Moreover, gender constructs were maintained in the sense that the side with lower status would be the one to be penetrated and was also described as a feminine presence (Wu Cuncun 2000: 1–16).

During the Qing dynasty, however, legal penalties for homosexuality and same-sex rape against children were intensified. There is no accepted explanation as to the cause for this, but it has been pointed out that the emphasis on women's chastity at that time was also expanded to include male victims (Guo Xiaofei 2007: 20–33).

There are few records of sexual relations between women. Reasons for this lie, for example, in the fact that men, who were the authors of much of the writing, were unable to recognize female homosexuality because women had few activities outside the home and female sexual desire was denied. On the other hand, there is also the view that the segregation of men from women supported not only male homosexuality, but female homosexuality as well (van Gulik 1961). In such male literary works as *Women in Love* (Li Yu, 1610–1680), two women manifest homosexuality through marrying the same husband. Of course, this is a form of female homosexuality in an androcentric society, and because it was such a society, female homosexuals often chose death (Sang 2003 [English]: 46–60; Nomura 2015). However, in Canton from the late Qing into the Republican period, there was a mode of marriage called 'delayed-transfer marriage' (*bu luo fu jia*) in which the wife did not join her husband's household; and there were also some so-called 'self-combed women' (*zishunü*) who, even while remaining unmarried, asserted that they would not marry by putting their hair up (*faji*) in the style symbolic of a married woman. They frequently formed sister-in-law relationships called 'unions of sisters' (*jinlan hui*), lived together in so-called 'spinster houses' (*gupowu*) and sometimes developed homosexual relationships (Stockard 1992; Narita 2004, and so forth).

Takeda Masaya gives an account of cross-dressing from ancient times to the present day, and while this centers upon males in female clothing, it also touches upon females in male dress (Takeda 2007). Cross-dressing spread especially during the Ming and Qing dynasties through the idealization of feminine, beautiful men, and in plays, cross-gender performance (*fanchuan*) in which men played female roles became a fixed model (Wu Cuncun 2000: 4).

One example of well-arranged literary research is Shi Ye's (2008) discussion of pre-modern works focusing on Ming and Qing. Shi also discusses a historical change, namely, how the depiction in the *Book of the Chen Dynasty* (*Chenshu*) of Emperor Wen's (?–566) lover, a valiant and handsome youth, was rewritten during the Ming dynasty into the tale of an obsequious 'male queen' (*nan wanghou*) or 'male empress' (*nan huanghou*). Other research includes a paper discussing the 'male homosexuality poems' (*nanse shi*) of the Wei, Jin and Northern and Southern Dynasties, which describe the beauty of the appearance of men who received affection from other men (Cang Yachen 2016 [Japanese]), and one dealing with Li Yu's homosexual novel (Shiau Han-Chen 2009 [Japanese]).

As a collection of historical materials, Zhang Jie (2013) compiles descriptions of mainly male homosexuality from pre-Qin to the Qing dynasty.

Republican period

In the Republican period, due to the influence of Western sexology and the like, homosexuality came to be seen as 'abnormal' and an 'illness'. In this period, it was acknowledged that women also had sexual desire, but under the ideology of romantic love which viewed love, marriage and sex as one entity, sexual desire was placed beneath love and marriage, and women were impounded within a new norm, namely to be 'good wives [and] wise mothers' (Shirouzu 2015: 213–216). Naturally, there were various debates about homosexuality in the Republican period, and in the 1920s, there were also arguments in its favor, including those on women's homosexuality, but gradually homosexuality began to be seen in a negative light. Such a change was not merely due to Western influence, but while on the one hand male intellectuals of the time defended free love and marriage between men and women, this was also the result of using Western sexology to deny sexual love between women. Male writers such as Yu Dafu depicted sexual relations between women, but these examples, too, championed nationalism, seeing female homosexuality as social decadence, or as something that served male sexual desire (Sang 2003 [English]: 99–126, 156–158).

However, the woman writer Lu Yin's *Old Friends from the Seaside, Lishi's Diary* and so forth were critical of heterosexual marriage and affirmed love between women; and Ling Shuhua and Ding Ling also penned such works. There is also a study relating to the bond between women in Ding Ling's *Miss Sophie's Diary* (Gao Yuan 2011 [Japanese]). However, works by female writers in this period, unlike those from the 1990s onwards, still did not clearly affirm long-term female same-sex partnerships that continued past adolescence, nor sexual desire between women (Sang 2003 [English]: 127–160; Shirouzu 2015: 219–220).

The term '*tongqinglian*' (same-sex love) came into existence in the Republican period. This was due to the recognition of the binary of homosexuality and heterosexuality, and simultaneously because (romantic) love (*lian ai*) was a new concept. However, the identity of being 'a homosexual' had still not become widespread at the time (Sang 2003 [English]: 102–106, 123). Moreover, Kiyochi Yukiko demonstrates the process of establishment of the term *dōseiai* for homosexuality in Japan versus *tongqinglian* in China, arguing that the difference between them arose because the word for 'love' in Japanese, '*ai*', and '*lian*' in Chinese, had the ability to generate new terms (Kiyochi 2013).

After the establishment of the People's Republic

After the founding of the People's Republic of China, extra-marital sex was repudiated, and topics relating to homosexuality disappeared from publications. Persons who engaged in same-sex sexual activity were labelled 'hooligans' (*liumang*), 'morally corrupt' or the like, and received such administrative penalties as demotion, dismissal, being sent to the countryside or undergoing reform through labor.

The early years of the People's Republic, however, also saw cases of sexual relations with close members of the same sex. There is a survey showing that if discovered, those engaging in same-sex relations were criticized as having a 'lifestyle' problem, but were not punished. In 1957, a legal interpretation saying that homosexuality should not be the object of punishment also emerged.

Once the mid-1960s arrived, however, extra-marital sexual relations became the target of 'class struggle' as a manifestation of 'bourgeois thought'. During the Cultural Revolution, no small number of male homosexuals were driven to suicide, having been beaten, stripped naked or dragged around the streets. On the other hand, sexual activity did take place among educated youth who were sent to rural areas (Tong Ge 2005: 95–100; 2008: 81–90).

From 'reform and opening-up' to the 1990s

After China's 'reform and opening-up' policies, sexual minority movements spread, and those involved began once more to be recognized. The difference between this period and the pre-modern and Republican periods was that the concept of 'homosexuality' arrived, as well as various kinds of information relating to homosexuals. There was also a dawning recognition of the membership of a group who self-identified as homosexual.

This did not become a reality immediately, however. Firstly, when sexology was revived after the Cultural Revolution, homosexuality was viewed as a mental illness or psychological disorder and became the target of treatment.

However, in the 1990s, attention was drawn to male homosexuals in terms of the prevention of AIDS, and in 1992, the ministry of health's National Health Education Institute initiated social activities for male homosexuals. This salon was forced to close by the Communist Party group from the ministry of health, for the reason that it 'encouraged homosexuality and advocated human rights'. Nevertheless, in 1997 a telephone counselling service began in the private sector, and in 1998 homosexuals from all over China gathered secretly in Beijing and engaged in social interaction and debates (Tōyama 2010).[1]

On the occasion of the 1995 UN Fourth World Conference on Women in Beijing, Chinese authorities tried to prevent Chinese women from coming into contact with the activities of lesbians from outside China, but they were unable to completely prevent contact, and the conference became the impetus for the birth of a small lesbian group. In 1998, lesbians held a gathering in Beijing, established a hotline, and in the following year, they published a magazine, *Tiankong* (*Sky*) (He Xiaopei 2001 [English]; Wei Tingting 2014).

When reform of the penal code took place in 1997, homosexuality was 'decriminalized' through the abolition of 'hooliganism', once deemed grounds

---

1 On factual developments hereafter, see the 'Sexual minorities' category in my blog 'Chinese women, gender news+': http://genchi.blog52.fc2.com/.

for the punishment of same-sex sexual activity (in a legal interpretation, within same-sex sexual activity, only that which was forced or that vis-a-vis minors was the target of punishment, but the interpretation was often extended).[2] In addition, in 2001 the *Classification and Diagnostic Criteria for Psychiatric Disorders in China (3rd Edition)* determined by the Chinese Society of Psychiatry ceased viewing homosexuality as a mental illness.[3]

In the 1990s, survey research relating to urban male homosexuals also began, and by means of interviews, etc., Li Yinhe and Wang Xiaobo examined their feelings, sex, marriage, social interaction, values and so on (Li Yinhe and Wang Xiaobo 1993; Li Yinhe 1998 is the enlarged and revised edition). Female homosexuality, too, began to be taken up in literary works. In the 1980s, also, Wang Anyi's *Brothers* depicted a close relationship between women. Hamada Maya situates this in the lineage of school stories since the founding of the People's Republic (Hamada 2013). In the 1990s, works including Lin Bai's *One Person's War* and Chen Ran's *Private Life* explicitly depicted female homosexuality (Sang 2003 [English]: 175–222).

Post-2000

Due to the growing seriousness of the AIDS epidemic in the late 1990s, from around 2000 the Chinese government began to permit the establishment of gay men's groups that touted the aim of preventing AIDS. However, it continued its repressive response towards lesbians, such as instructing the police to halt the First Lesbian Cultural Arts Festival in 2001.

In societal terms, from around 2000, gay and lesbian communities appeared. Behind this lay such factors as the dilution of traditional family and kinship relations due to the increasing mobility of the population and urbanization, the emergence of venues for socialization such as tea houses,

---

2 However, this was not a repeal for the sake of homosexuals' human rights, but merely the result of a dismantling of the crime of hooliganism into six charges, including indecent assault, as the range of application of hooliganism was ambiguous (Guo Xiaofei 2007: 66–93).

3 However, in cases where persons themselves did not desire to be homosexual, and it was accompanied by anxiety, depression and mental anguish, it was seen as a 'disorder', and it was an inconsistent 'depathologization' of homosexuality.

bath houses, saunas and bars accompanying the transition towards a market economy, growing opportunities for socialization through the internet and so on. Previously, short-term relationships not based on love, such as searching for sexual partners in parks or public toilets, were numerous, but since the 2000s, the number of stable same-sex relationships has grown. In addition, the term '*tongzhi*' ('comrade' = sexual minority, especially used to indicate gay men) has come to be widely used. As indicated by the fact that the terms '*tongzhi*' and '*lala*' (lesbian or female bisexual) originated in Hong Kong and Taiwan, the impact that interchange with Hong Kong and Taiwan has exerted on China has also been significant (Wei Wei 2012: 10–11, 38–39, 46–52, 166–167; Kam 2013 [English]: 19–37).

Moreover, from 2000, Li Yinhe started making proposals for the recognition of same-sex marriage to the National People's Congress and National Committee of the Chinese People's Political Consultative Conference. In 2001, the inaugural Beijing Gay & Lesbian Film Festival (renamed the Beijing Queer Film Festival in 2007) was held (Yu Ning 2017 [Japanese]). From 2003 to 2005, a lecture series on homosexuality was given at Fudan University (contents recorded in Gao Yanning 2006); and in 2006, Fudan University and Yale University jointly held an academic symposium relating to sexual orientation (Zhou Dan 2006). In 2008, various groups in Beijing jointly established the Beijing LGBT Center, and in 2012 and 2013, an LGBT parade was also held in Changsha City in Hunan Province.

However, the organizers of the LGBT parade were sentenced to twelve days' administrative detention. Furthermore, even now there are many university textbooks that describe homosexuality as 'abnormal' (Tōyama 2015: 168–169). In response to such circumstances, LGBT people call attention to their existence and their claims through group participation in marathons instead of parades, and mounted a court case (defeated in 2017) to bring the ministry of education to account over the issue of negative descriptions in textbooks.

Fieldwork focusing on gay men since 2000 includes a survey by Tong Ge about their sexual activity and partners, self-identification, social conditions and so on (Tong Ge 2005), and a survey by Fu Xiaoxing on such issues as their spaces of activity and marriage (Fu Xiaoxing 2012). Fieldwork aimed at lesbians has also recently emerged (Kam 2013 [English]; Engebretsen 2014).

As gay men often hide their sexual orientation and marry women, their wives (*tongqi* = heterosexual wives of gay men) are placed in a difficult position. This is similar to the situation in pre-modern times when married men engaged in extramarital sexual activity. The difference is that in 2009, *tongqi* held the 'First Chinese Conference of Heterosexual Wives of Gay Men' in Qingdao, and have instituted a movement that has published a joint statement calling for unmarried gay men not to marry women (Xing Fei 2012).

Trends in sexual minority movements

Lastly, I shall bring together some key points that have emerged as issues in the movements and the trends relating to them.

Firstly, within sexual minority movements, there is a tendency to create an image of 'model' homosexuals (those who, for example, maintain a stable one-to-one relationship, contribute to society and so on) in an attempt to gain the acceptance of society at large. In the case of China, in particular, as cooperation with governmental mechanisms is crucial for political stability and financial gain, such a tendency has readily arisen (Kam 2013 [English]: 89–99).[4]

However, as this tendency gives rise to fresh exclusion and marginalization, Tong Ge has criticized the propensity to pander to the norms of heterosexual society, such as to emphasize homosexuals' 'excellence', or to disdain effeminate gay men (Shirouzu 2007: 544–547). Additionally, Tong conducted a survey of one of the marginalized groups – male sex workers who are paid to have sex with men – and pointed out that unlike in pre-modern times, there is no relationship akin to human trafficking between them and their managers or clients, and that the occurrence of discrimination and violence is due to social prejudice (Tong Ge 2007a).

Secondly, sexual minority movements tend to focus upon gay men, while lesbian, transgender and bisexual people tend to be disregarded (Tōyama 2010). As economic independence is difficult for lesbians to achieve, they experience unique hardships such as being strongly pressured to marry (Kam 2013 [English]:

---

[4] The fact that the authorities and suchlike take the lead in AIDS-prevention activities has brought about such contradictions as gay men's own initiatives being disregarded (Tong Ge 2007b).

60–62). Moreover, surveys have revealed that 'marriage-in-form-only' is sometimes entered into by gays and lesbians in order to allow them to avoid such marriage pressure (Kam 2013 [English]: 99–103; Engebretsen 2014: 104–123).

Lesbians created the 'Beijing Lesbian Salon' in 2004, and an organization called 'Common Language' (*Tongyu*) in 2005 (Engebretsen 2014: 135–153); further, from around 2011, they intensified criticism towards the gay-centrism of the LGBT movement (Tōyama 2010, 2015). Moreover, 2003 saw the publication of a book in which Zhang Kesha, who underwent China's first sex-reassignment surgery in 1983, spelled out her past life (Lin Qi et al. 2006 [Japanese]); and in recent years, transgender and bisexual people, too, have developed their own movements. In 2000, Li Yinhe introduced queer theory to China (Li Yinhe 2000), and Cui Zien is said to be 'China's first queer writer' (Shirouzu 2007: 548–557).

Thirdly, the women's movement has conventionally seldom taken up homosexual issues. The same can be said of men's liberation discourse (Tōyama 2010). However, a movement calling itself 'Feminist Activists' which arose in 2012 had lesbians' movements as one of its foundations, and since 2013 it has begun to engage to a certain extent with lesbian issues (Tōyama 2015: 170–174; 2016: 160, 168–169, 175).

In recent years, collections of papers about various activities and culture relating to sexual minorities (creative works, including those on the internet, independent films, BL, pop culture, etc.) and about their communities have also been published (Engebretsen, Shroeder and Bao 2015).

However, beginning from the middle of the last decade, under the Xi Jinping regime there has been increasing pressure on movements for improvement in the status of sexual minorities. At present, this pressure has not only made it difficult to carry out demonstrations in the street, but has also endangered public lectures and university classes related to these issues.

Column 6

Theatre and Gender

NAKAYAMA Fumi

Introduction

In October 2015, the 'Fifth Red Crane International Arts Circle' was held in Nanjing to consider traditional theatre. The theme on that occasion was 'An attempt towards acting techniques that transcend gender and character', and traditional 'cross-dressing' drama from the Nanjing Kunqu company[1] was introduced, along with that from Japan, India, Indonesia and Thailand.

In the West, as well as in East Asia, there was a tradition in the theater of male actors playing female roles as we can see in Elizabethan-period performances of Shakespearean plays. However, this was due to a prohibition on actresses; in the West we rarely see the kind of cross-dressing traditional theatre that is found throughout Asia. It is often said with regard to Japan's Noh theatre that 'the pursuit of beauty is manifested in the very switching of gender' (Hori 1998), but what about the situation in China? This column looks at the emergence of actresses in the history of Chinese theatre from a gender perspective.

Actresses in Chinese traditional theatre

Actresses were originally part of traditional theatre in China. More than 100 actresses' names are recorded in a commentary on stage performers, *Qing Lou Ji*, by Yuan dynasty writer Xia Tingzhi, revealing that there were actresses who performed *laosheng* (roles of males of middle age and older) and *wusheng* (acrobatic male roles). Moreover, there is an illustration of an actress dressed as

---

1 In 2008, this company made a success of a joint Sino-Japanese production of *The Peony Pavilion* in collaboration with the Japanese *kabuki* actor, Bandō Tamasaburō.

a man depicted in a Yuan dynasty mural at the Hongdong Mingyingwangdian in Shanxi Province.[2]

In terms of theatre, performers' bodies do not necessarily conform to their actual gender as we can see when one considers the issue of actresses in male dress and male actors in female dress. Audiences at the time, also, probably thought that the characters in the plays were unrelated to the actors' own physiological sex and appreciated the way in which gender was expressed on stage as an artistic performance. Through changes in costume and gesture, actors freely performed not only social position or occupation, but also gender.

Actors, who frequently moved from place to place, appeared to be a menace with the capacity to corrupt social stability and disturb public morals. As a result, officials enacted various laws and tried to crush the potential for the transgression of social boundaries contained in expressive activities. Yuan dynasty laws deemed actors to be of low social status, and strictly constrained elements of their everyday lives such as clothing and means of travel. Furthermore, the laws forbade marriage with those of higher status, as well as actors taking civil-service examinations. The treatment of actresses who flaunted themselves in public spaces was even harsher, along the same lines as the treatment of prostitutes.

Throughout the Ming and Qing dynasties, when the segregation of the sexes was tightened as a social norm, actresses were banned from performing in public places. In the eighteenth century, Emperor Qianlong forcefully promulgated a ban on actresses, and they finally disappeared from China's stages. In all-male theatre groups, characters termed '*qiandan*' who specialized in playing female roles attracted attention, and Wei Changsheng (1744–1802) developed the art of the '*qiao*' (raised foot).[3] This was a technique that involved wearing shoes that replicated the shape of bound feet, expressing women's delicate manner of moving, and from then on, bound feet became a code that signified women (Zhou Huiling 2000).

---

2 Onstage, five actors were lined up, with this actress at the center, while five musicians and others formed the back row. A banner hanging above makes it understood that a starring actress called Zhong Duxiu was present (Zhou Huiling 2000: 6; Tan Fan 2002: 20; Liao Ben and Liu Yanjun 2006: 118).

3 On *qiao*, see Huang Yufu (1998).

From female-role players to actresses

In the early twentieth century, Qing dynasty regulations began to slacken in cities like Shanghai, and laws forbidding actresses from performing in public were gradually relaxed. In 1912, the edict banning actresses was revoked and, even in Beijing, actresses returned to the stage of traditional theatre. In a reflection of the times, the personalities and circumstances of female protagonists depicted on stage also changed markedly. There was a relative decrease in female images from old moral codes, and the depiction of female characters who endured hardship and pursued love increased dramatically (Matsuura 2003).

In the Xinhai Revolution period, Chinese students who were studying in Japan were influenced by Japanese 'new drama' (*shinpa* and *shingeki*). Inventing a new dramatic form, they performed works that criticized the old society. This new form, created by young artists who admired Western romanticism and were passionate about the ideals of social revolution, was called '*xinju*' (new drama) or '*wenmingxi*' (civilized drama). In 1907, the Spring Willow Society (*Chunliu She*), a theater troupe created by Chinese students in Japan, performed *La Traviata* and *Uncle Tom's Cabin* in Japan, and in China, there was a boom in 'new drama' centered on Shanghai. However, the 'new drama' was performed as a kind of improvisation with no fixed script, and the female roles were played by men using gestures from Peking opera.[4]

When the May Fourth period arrived, the enlightenment magazine *Xin Qingnian* (*New Youth*) was launched, advocating the promotion of Westernization and criticism of Confucianism, emphasis on science and democracy and reform of the writing system and literature. At roughly the same time, *xinju* (new drama) began to employ scripts and a directorial system, and further evolved into '*huaju*' (spoken drama) that pursued realism.

When Hu Shi published a translation of Ibsen's *A Doll's House* in *New Youth*, the new image of a woman who develops an awareness of her own ego caused a sensation. New themes required new drama techniques since it was

---

4 Li Shutong, who founded the theatre group, was a man who learned how to play Japanese *shinpa*-style female roles and also studied the new female image by searching Western paintings for female models in Western dress. Iizuka argues, 'Even by merely looking at his [*shingeki*] script, one can infer he had a powerful fetish for dressing in women's clothing and for cross-dressing' (Iizuka 2014: 17).

impossible to represent a 'new woman' by means of old-style drama's so-called 'orchid-flower fingers'[5] and imitation of the way of walking with bound feet. The best strategy for solving this problem was to turn female students who had a new way of thinking into actresses. In this manner, in the 1920s, when female education was progressing and ideas of women's liberation were spreading, actresses of the new age finally took to the stage in spoken drama performances.[6]

From their emergence, actresses took on the role of embodying male writers' ideal images and political messages. Let me introduce Hu Shi's early-period spoken drama, *The Main Event of One's Life* (*Zhongshen dashi*). Influenced by Ibsen, in this work the protagonist Tian Yamei is caught between the marriage urged by her parents and her lover. However, she awakens through a letter from her lover which says, 'You should decide for yourself', and she resolutely leaves her parents' home. Just like Snow White, who was kissed by a prince, a woman is awakened by means of a man's words.

Throughout the periods of the war of resistance against Japan in the 1930s and the war between the Nationalists and Communists in the 1940s, spoken drama became a vital medium for spreading patriotism and communism. In a street-theatre play by Chen Liting, *Put down Your Whip*, which was chiefly performed prior to the establishment of the PRC, a girl street-performer who is whipped by her father speaks of the miserable conditions in the Northeast (Dongbei) region, which was colonized by Japan. A young worker called to the onlookers to band together and appeal to the father to 'Strike down the enemy with that whip!' The father also realizes who his real enemy is and joins forces with the spectators. This drama represented another example of a woman, who was being oppressed, being saved by a new man. In the spoken drama of the

---

5 In Peking opera, female-role players gesture with their hands in a manner called '*lan hua zhi*' (orchid-flower fingers) because the expression of their fingers resembles an orchid flower. Performers express various emotional states through the shape of their fingers.

6 In 1923, when Hong Shen staged Hu Shi's *The Main Event of One's Life* with a mixed cast, followed by *A Valiant Housewife* by Ouyang Yuqian in which males played the female roles, the audience felt that the old-style mode of acting was unnatural and accepted the realism of the actresses. The success of actresses was confirmed the following year with the production of Oscar Wilde's *Lady Windermere's Fan*.

day, women were objects used by male writers to express their ideas on social reform and the modernization of China.[7]

Around the time when spoken-drama stage actresses were playing 'new women', female *Yue* opera (*yueju*) in which women were the subjects of the creation of works came into being in Shanghai. Once a regional operatic form begun by male peasants in Zhejiang Province, *yueju* grew into the greatest form of entertainment for Shanghai women through its style of performing with an all-female cast targeting a female audience. In 1942, when Yuan Xuefen launched a reform of *yueju* calling for artistic progress and enhancement of the status of actresses, actresses from other theatre groups responded. The activities of the 'Ten Sisters of *Yueju*', top actresses who had banded together to escape exploitation from theatre owners and endeavored to build their own theatre and school, are remembered as spectacular achievements in the history of Chinese theatre.[8]

Conclusion

A century has passed since the advent of spoken drama. What picture of gender can be seen in contemporary Chinese theatre?

In July 2015, the Eighth National Congress of the China Theatre Association was held, and a new chair and officers were elected. The chair was male actor and deputy director of the Beijing People's Art Theatre Pu Cunxin. Of the fifteen deputy chairs, six were women, accounting for 37.5% of the total number. In China, which took ninety-first place in the 2015 Gender Gap Index ranking (eighty-seventh the previous year), the theatrical world can be considered an industry where women are comparatively active.

Going into more detail, those six female deputy chairs were all famous actresses representing different theatre genres. On the other hand, among the male deputy chairs there was one Communist Party cadre, one academic, one

---

[7] Even in the operas that postdate the establishment of New China, *The White-haired Girl* (*Bai mao nü*) and *The Red Detachment of Women* (*Hongse niangzi jun*), weak, immature females are rescued by male Communist Party members, receive instructions and grow into maturity (Matsuura 2000).

[8] On *yueju*, see Jiang (2009 [English]), Nakayama (2015) and Nakayama ed. (2019).

director and two dramatists, in addition to three actors. From this data it is clear that in the domain of playwriting and directing, which comprise the core of theatrical creation, women are not seen as the equals of men. This is not to say that women are not involved in the creation of new dramas. For example, the female playwright Qian Jue introduced three major female dramatists (Shen Hongguang, Liao Yimei and Xu Fen), and discussed their commonalities as follows:

> In female dramatists' works, hardly any characters that have women's negative sides appear. 'Bad women' seldom come into view, and there are very few androgynous female images, 'tomboys' or lesbians. The women whom female dramatists depict are all extremely feminine. Whether they be old or young, female dramatists all unconsciously adhere to mainstream moral norms and aesthetic standards. (Nakayama, Qian Jue and Ushida 2012: 11–21)

The People's Republic of China was established with calls for equality of the sexes. However, political issues were always prioritized over gender issues. What had been sought from stage actresses for many years was not to express their real selves; and it did not necessarily follow that a new view of women would come into being if female dramatists depicted them. In order to liberate women from the existing view of their gender, female dramatists' own ideas are needed (Mizuta 1982).

However, the advent of new media has made it easier for everyone to freely talk about themselves through blogging, and inevitably this will have an influence on drama. I wait in anticipation to see what kind of female images the stage will show us in the future.

Bibliography

Japanese

Akiyama Yōko 秋山洋子 (1996). 'Chūgoku no joseigaku: Li Xiaojiang no "Josei kenkyū undō" o chūshin ni' 中国の女性学―李小江の「女性研究運動」を中心に [Women's studies in China: A study of 'Women's Studies Movement' by Li Xiaojiang]. *Joseigaku* 女性学, 4.

Akiyama Yōko 秋山洋子 (1999). 'Dai 4 kai kokuren sekai josei kaigi o megutte: Chūgoku ni okeru kokka to josei' 第四回国連世界女性会議をめぐって―中国における国家と女性 [On the UN Fourth World Conference on Women: The state and women in China]. In: Chūgoku joseishi kenkyūkai 中国女性史研究会 (ed.), *Ronshū Chūgoku joseishi* 論集 中国女性史 [Collected papers on the history of women in China]. Tokyo: Yoshikawa Kōbunkan.

Akiyama Yōko 秋山洋子 (2001). 'Chūgoku josei gaku ni okeru sisō keisei' 中国女性学における思想形成 [Thought formation in Chinese women's studies]. *Joseigaku* 女性学, 8.

Akiyama Yōko 秋山洋子 (2004). *Watashi to Chūgoku to feminizumu* 私と中国とフェミニズム [My experiences with China and feminism]. Tokyo: Inpact Shuppankai.

Akiyama Yōko 秋山洋子 (2013). 'Bishō suru Chūgoku joseishugi: 2000 nendai no Kō Lin ra ni yoru nettowāku katsudō 微笑する中国女性主義―2000年代の荒林らによるネットワーク活動 [Chinese feminism with a smile: The network activities of Huang Lin and others in the 2000s]. *Chūgoku joseishi kenkyū* 中国女性史研究, 22.

Akiyama Yōko 秋山洋子 (2016a). *Femi shishi nōto* フェミ私史ノート [Personal notes on feminist history]. Tokyo: Inpact Shuppankai.

Akiyama Yōko 秋山洋子 (2016b). 'Nihon ni okeru Chūgoku josei/jendāshi kenkyū: Chūgoku joseishi kenkyūkai no ayumi o jiku to shite' 日本における中国女性／ジェンダー史研究―中国女性史研究会の歩みを軸として [Japanese research on Chinese women's/gender history: Centering around the footsteps of the Society of Historical Studies on Chinese women]. In: Chūgoku joseishi kenkyūkai 中国女性史研究会 (ed.), *Chūgoku no media hyōshō to jendā* 中国のメディア・表象とジェンダー [Media, representations and gender in China]. Tokyo: Kenbun Shuppan.

Akiyama Yōko 秋山洋子, Egami Sachiko 江上幸子, Tabata Sawako 田畑佐和子 and Maeyama Kanako 前山加奈子 (eds. and trans.) (1998). *Chūgoku no joseigaku* 中国の女性学 [Women's studies in China]. Tokyo: Keisō Shobō.

Aoki Atsushi 青木敦 (2003). 'Nansō joshi bunpō saikō' 南宋女子分法再考 [Reconsidering Southern Song's daughter's half-share law]. *Chūgoku: Shakai to bunka* 中国―社会と文化 [China: Society and culture], 18. Revised and augmented version in Aoki (2014) *Sōdai minji hō no sekai* 宋代民事法の世界 [The society of Civil Law in the Song dynasty]. Tokyo: Keio Gijuku Daigaku Shuppankai.

Aoki Atsushi 青木敦 (2014). *Sōdai minji hō no sekai* 宋代民事法の世界 [The society of Civil Law in the Song dynasty]. Tokyo: Keio Gijuku Daigaku Shuppankai.

Asanuma Kaori 浅沼かおり (2005). 'Shindai no joseizō to shakai: Josei no saika o megutte' 清代の女性像と社会―女性の再嫁をめぐって [The image of women and society in Qing]. *Kyōritsu Joshi Daigaku Sōgō Bunka Kenkyūjo kiyō* 共立女子大学総合文化研究所紀要, 11.

Barlow, Tani E. タニ・E・バーロウ (2003). *Kokusai feminizumu to Chūgoku* 国際フェミニズムと中国 [International feminism and China], translated by Ito Ruri 伊藤るり and Kobayashi Eri 小林英里. Tokyo: Ochanomizu Shobō.

Cang Yachen 倉雅晨 (2016). 'Gi Shin Nanbokuchō ki no danshokushi ni okeru jōyoku hyōgen' 魏晋南北朝期の男色詩における情欲表現 [The manifestation patterns of passion in male homosexual poems in Wei, Jin, Northern and Southern Dynasties]. *Tōtetsu* 饕餮, 24.

Chen Ching-Feng 陳青鳳 (1988). 'Shin chō no fujo seihyō seido ni tsuite: Seppu, retsujo o chūshin ni' 清朝の婦女旌表制度について―節婦・烈女を中心に [Qing's *funü jingbiao* system: Chaste widows and chastely martyred wives and daughters]. *Kyūshū Daigaku Tōyōshi ronshū* 九州大学東洋史論集, 16.

Chen Ching-Feng 陳青鳳 (1990). 'Shin dai no keihō ni okeru fujo sabetsu: Toku ni shōgai satsujin, kan'in zai ni okeru' 清代の刑法における婦女差別―特に障害殺人、姦淫罪における [Discrimination against women in Qing criminal law: With special attention to assault, murder and fornication charges]. *Kyūshū Daigaku Tōyōshi ronshū* 九州大学東洋史論集, 18.

Ching May-Bo 程美宝 (2012). 'Kindaiteki dansei sei to minzoku shugi' 近代的男性性と民族主義 [Modern masculinity and nationalism]. In: Shingai kakumei 100 shūnen kinen ronshū henshū iinkai 辛亥革命百周年記念論集編集委員会 (ed.), *Sōgō kenkyū Shingai kakumei* 総合研究辛亥革命 [A multidisciplinary study on the Xinhai Revolution]. Tokyo: Iwanami Shoten.

Chūgoku joseishi kenkyūkai 中国女性史研究会 (ed.) (2004). *Chūgoku josei no 100 nen: siryō ni miru ayumi* 中国女性の100年―史料にみる歩み [A hundred years of Chinese women: Tracing their steps in historical documents]. Tokyo: Aoki Shoten.

Dai Jinhua 戴錦華 (2006). *Chūgoku eiga no jendā poritikusu: Posuto reisen jidai no bunka seiji* 中国映画のジェンダー・ポリティクス ― ポスト冷戦時代の文化政治 [Gender politics in Chinese cinema: Cultural politics in the post-Cold War era], edited by Tachi Kaoru 舘かおる and translation supervised by Miyao Masaki 宮尾正樹. Tokyo: Ochanomizu Shobō.

Du Fangqin 杜芳琴 (2011). '30 nen no kaiko; Tairiku Chūgoku ni okeru josei/jendāshi kenkyū to senmon ryōiki to shite no hatten (1978–2008)' 三十年の回顧―大陸中国における女性／ジェンダー史研究と専門領域としての発展 (1978–2008) [Thirty years in review: Women's/gender history research and its development as a discipline in mainland China (1978–2008). *Chūgoku joseishi kenkyū* 中国女性史研究, 20.

Egami Sachiko 江上幸子 (1993). 'Kōsenki no henku ni okeru Chūgoku kyōsantō no josei undo to sono hōshin tenkan: Zasshi *Chūgoku fujo* o chūshin ni' 抗戦期の辺区における中国共産党の女性運動とその方針転換―雑誌『中国婦女』を中心に [The Chinese Communist Party's women's movement and its policy shift in the liberated zone during the anti-Japanese resistance period: Centering on the *Chinese Women* magazine]. In: Yanagida Setsuko Sensei koki kinen ronshū henshū iinkai 柳田節子先生古稀記念論集編集委員会 (ed.), *Chūgoku no dentō shakai to kazoku* 中国の伝統社会と家族 [Traditional society and family in China]. Tokyo: Kyūko Shoin.

Egami Sachiko 江上幸子 (2003). 'Mō Takutō no "Shin Chūgoku" ni okeru "jinmin, katei, jōsei"–Tei Rei no "*Yoru*" saidoku' 毛沢東の「新中国」における「人民・家庭・女性」—丁玲の『夜』再読 ['The people, the family and women' in Mao Zedong's 'New China': A rereading of Ding Ling's *The Night*]. In: Ferris Jōgakuin Daigaku フェリス女学院大学 (ed.), *Pen o toru josei tachi* ペンをとる女性たち [Women who take up the pen]. Tokyo: Kanrin Shobō.

Egami Sachiko 江上幸子 (2007). 'Chūgoku no "kensai ryōbo" shisō to "modan gāru": 1930 nendai chūki no "onna wa ie ni kaere" ronsō kara' 中国の賢妻良母思想と「モダンガール」—一九三〇年代中期の「女は家に帰れ」論争から [China's wise wife and good mother ideology and 'modern girls': From the 'Women go home' debate in the mid-1930s]. In: Hayakawa Noriyo 早川紀代 et al. (eds), *Higashi Ajia no kokumin kokka keisei to jendā: Jōseizō o megutte*. 東アジアの国民国家形成とジェンダー—女性像をめぐって [Gender and the formation of the nation-state in East Asia: Discourses on the ideal woman]. Tokyo: Aoki Shoten.

Egami Sachiko 江上幸子 (2013). 'Tei Rei: Kindai Chūgoku no jendā chitsujo eno aragai' 丁玲—近代中国のジェンダー秩序への抗い [Ding Ling: Resisting gender order in modern China]. *Kōza Higasiajia no chishikijin 3* 講座 東アジアの知識人3 [East Asian intellectuals 3]. Tokyo: Yushisha. (The Chinese version of this article is published in Akiyama 秋山 et al. (2017).)

Egami Sachiko 江上幸子 (2014). '1920 nendai Chūgoku no sekushuariti rongi: Chō Kyōsei, Tei Rei ra ni yoru iron' 1920年代中国のセクシュアリティ論議—張競生、丁玲らによる異論 [Sexuality controversy in 1920s China: Objections from Zhang Jingsheng, Ding Ling and others]. *Chūgoku: Shakai to bunka* 中国—社会と文化, 29.

Egami Sachiko 江上幸子 (2015). '"Tetsu no musume" to josei minpei' 『鉄の娘』と女性民兵 ['Iron girls' and women's militia]. In: Kohama Masako 小浜正子 (ed.), *Jendā no Chūgokushi* ジェンダーの中国史 [Gender in Chinese history]. Tokyo: Bensei Shuppan.

Egawa Shikibu 江川式部 (2010). 'Tōdai no jōbo girei: Bosai shūzoku no reiten hennyū to sono igi ni tsuite' 唐代の上墓儀禮—墓祭習俗の禮典編入とその意義について [Tang tomb-visiting rites: The incorporation of tomb-visiting practices in the ritual code and its significance]. *Tōhōgaku* 東方学, 120.

Egawa Shikibu 江川式部 (2013). 'Tōdai no kaisō girei to sono seido' 唐代の改葬儀禮とその制度 [Tang reburial rites and its system]. *Tōyōshi kenkyū* 東洋史研究, 72(2).

Engels Friedrich エンゲルス、フリードリッヒ ([1884] 1965). *Kazoku, shiyū zaisan, kokka no kigen* 家族・私有財産・国家の起源 [The origin of the family, private property and the state], translated by Tohara Shirō 戸原四郎. Tokyo: Iwanami Shoten.

Feng Yuan 馮媛 (2016). 'Jendā o meguru feminisuto, kokka, dansei no kyōdō/fu kyōdō: Han-DVhō seitei katei o rei ni' ジェンダーをめぐるフェミニスト・国家・男性の協働／不協働—反DV法制定過程を例に [Feminists, states and men's cooperation/non-cooperation over gender: The case of the anti-DV legislation process]. In: Kohama Masako 小浜正子 and Akiyama Yōko 秋山洋子 (eds), *Gendai Chūgoku no jendā poritikusu: Kakusa, sei baibai, "ianfu"* 現代中国のジェンダー・ポリティクス—格差・性売買・「慰安婦」 [Gender politics in contemporary China: Economic disparity, sex trade, 'comfort women']. Tokyo: Bensei Shuppan.

Fujikawa Masakazu 藤川正数 (1958). 'Tōdai ni okeru hahaoya shugi teki bukki kaisei ni tsuite' 唐代における母親主義的服紀改制について [Reforms of regulations on mourning garments and rituals for mothers in Tang China]. *Tōhōgaku* 東方学, 16.

Fujikawa Masakazu 藤川正数 (1960). *Gi Shin jidai ni okeru sōfukurei no kenkyū* 魏晋時代における喪服礼の研究 [Studies in regulations on mourning garments and rituals during the Wei-Jin period]. Tokyo: Keibunsha.

Fujikawa Masakazu 藤川正数 (1968). 'Shō kōshu no sei ni tsuite' 尚公主の制について [System of marriage between imperial princess and vassal]. *Kandai ni okeru reigaku no kenkyū* 漢代における礼学の研究 [A study of ritual learning in the Han period]. Tokyo: Kazama Shobō.

Fukamachi Hideo 深町英夫 (2013). *Shintai o shitsukeru seiji: Chūgoku Kokumintō no Shin seikatsu undō* 身体を躾ける政治―中国国民党の新生活運動 [Politics to discipline the body: The Kuomintang's New Life Movement]. Tokyo: Iwanami Shoten.

Fukuhara Akirō 福原啓郎 (2015). 'Chōsa Go kan no shōbyō kiroku no tokuchō' 長沙呉簡の傷病記録の特徴 [The characteristics of medical records in the Changsha bamboo slips of Wu]. In: Itō Toshio 伊藤敏雄 et al. (eds), *Konan shutsudo kandoku to sono shakai* 湖南出土簡牘とその社会 [A study of the wooden-bamboo manuscripts and community of Hunan Province]. Tokyo: Kyūko Shoin.

Fukuyama Yasuo 福山泰男 (2005). '"Hifunshi" shōkō: Kenkyūshi to sono mondaiten' 「悲憤詩」小考―研究史とその問題点 [An essay on '*beifen shi*': A history of its studies and their problems]. *Yamagata Daigaku Daigakuin Shakai Bunka Shisutemu Kenkyūka kiyō* 山形大学大学院社会文化システム研究科紀要, 1.

Fuma Susumu 夫馬進 (1993). 'Chūgoku Min Shin jidai ni okeru kafu no chii to kyōsei saikon no fūshū' 中国明清時代における寡婦の地位と強制再婚の風習 [Status of widows and customs of forced remarriage of widows in Ming-Qing China]. In: Maekawa Kazunari 前川和也 (ed.), *Kazoku, setai, kamon: Kōgyōka izen no sekai kara* 家族・世帯・家門―工業化以前の世界から [Family, household and lineage: From the pre-industrialized world]. Kyoto: Minerva Shobō.

Fuma Susumu 夫馬進 (1997). *Chūgoku zenkai zendō shi kenkyū* 中国善会善堂史研究 [A study of the history of charitable halls and associations in China]. Kyoto: Dōhōsha Shuppan.

Furukawa Sueki 古川末喜 (2008). *Toho nōgyōshi kenkyū* 杜甫農業詩研究 [A study of Du Fu's farming poems]. Tokyo: Chisen Shokan.

Gao Yuan 高媛 (2011). '*Sophī joshi no nikki* ni katarareru onna dōshi no kizuna' 『ソフィ女士の日記』に語られる女同士の絆 [Bonds between women as told in *Miss Sophie's Diary*]. *Tagen bunka* 多元文化, 11.

Gomi Tomoko 五味知子 (2008). 'Teisetsu ga towareru toki: "*Monshin ichigū*" ni miru chiken no saiban o chūshin ni' 貞節が問われるとき―『問心一隅』に見る知県の裁判を中心に [The moment one's chastity is questioned: Focusing on local magistrate trials in *Wenxin yiyu*]. *Chūgoku joseishi kenkyū* 中国女性史研究, 17.

Gomi Tomoko 五味知子 (2011). 'Kindai Chūgoku no ottogoroshi enzai jiken to media: Yō Daibu to Shō Hakusai' 近代中国の夫殺し冤罪事件とメディア―楊乃武と小白菜 [Cases of false accusations of mariticide and the media in modern China: Yang Naiwu and Xiao Baicai]. In: Yamamoto Eishi 山本英史 (ed.), *Kindai Chūgoku no chiikizō* 近代中国の地域像 [Images of modern Chinese regions]. Tokyo: Yamakawa Shuppansha.

Gomi Tomoko 五味知子 (2012). '"Bukan" no imisuru mono: Min Shin jidai no hantoku kanshinsho no kijutsu kara' 「誣姦」の意味するもの—明清時代の判牘・官箴書の記述から [The meaning of 'false accusations of adultery', from the records of judgements and manuals for the administration of the Ming and Qing dynasties]. *Tōyōshi kenkyū* 東洋史研究, 70(4).

Gomi Tomoko 五味知子 (2014). 'Min Shin jidai no kohi ni kakawaru shakai tsūnen' 明清時代の錮婢にかかわる社会通念 [The conventional wisdom about bondwoman incarceration in the Ming and Qing dynasties]. *Tōyō Bunka Kenkyū* 東洋文化研究, 16.

Gomi Tomoko 五味知子 (2015). 'Shin dai no haigūsha satsujin no kiroku ni miru joseizō to sono jittai' 清代の配偶者殺人の記録に見る女性像とその実態 [Image and reality of women from the Qing dynasty's spousal homicide case reports]. *Shigaku* 史学, 85(1–3).

Gōyama Kiwamu 合山究 (2006). *Min Shin jidai no josei to bungaku* 明清時代の女性と文学 [Women and literature in the Ming-Qing period]. Tokyo: Kyūko Shoin.

Grove, Linda リンダ・グローブ (1997). 'Chūgoku ni okeru josei rōdōsha san sedai no kiseki' 中国における女性労働者三世代の軌跡 [Tracing the footsteps of three generations of Chinese women workers]. In: Ajia joseishi kokusai symposium jikkō iinkai (ed.), *Ajia joseishi: Hikakushi no kokoromi* アジア女性史—比較史の試み [Asian women's history: An attempt for comparative history]. Tokyo: Akashi Shoten.

Grove, Linda リンダ・グローブ (2020). 'Senjiki Chūgoku no shokugyō josei: "*Shanhai fujo*" sono ta no zasshi keisai kiji ni miru "byōdō" no tsuikyū' 戦時期中国の職業女性—『上海婦女』その他の雑誌掲載記事に見る「平等」の追求 [The struggle for 'equality' in wartime China as seen in articles in *Shanghai Funü* and other contemporary journals]. *Chūgoku joseishi kenkyū* 中国女性史研究, 29.

Hamada Maya 濱田麻矢 (2013). 'Haruka na yūtopia: Ō An'oku *Teikeimon* ni okeru rezubian renzokutai' 遥かなユートピア—王安憶『弟兄門』におけるレズビアン連続体 [A distant utopia: The lesbian continuum in Wang Anyi's *Brothers*]. *Gendai Chūgoku* 現代中国, 87.

Harada Norio 原田憲雄 (2001). *Miwaku no shijin Ri Seishō* 魅惑の詩人 李清照 [Li Qingzhao: An enchanting poet]. Kyoto: Hōyū Shoten.

Hayashi Hiroshi 林博史 (2015). *Nihongun 'ianfu' mondai no kakushin* 日本軍「慰安婦」問題の核心 [At the heart of the 'comfort women' issue with the Imperial Japanese Army]. Tokyo: Kadensha.

Hayashi Kana 林香奈 (2004). 'Ken narazaru fu to wa: Jokunsho ni miru ie to onna' 賢ならざる婦とは—女訓書に見る家と女 [Unwise woman: Family and women in textbooks on female conduct]. In: Kansai chūgoku joseishi kenkyūkai 関西中国女性史研究会 (ed.), *Jendā kara mita chūgoku no ie to onna* ジェンダーからみた中国の家と女 [The Chinese family and women from a gender perspective]. Tokyo: Tōhō Shoten.

Hori Mariko 堀真理子 (1998). 'Engeki to jendā: Iseisō no yakuwari to sono konnichi teki imi ni tsuite no ichikōsatsu' 演劇とジェンダー—異性装の役割とその今日的意味についての一考察 [Theatre and gender: A consideration of cross-dressing roles and their present-day meaning]. *Aoyama Gakuin Daigaku sōgō kenkyū sōsho gakusai kenkyū project* 青山学院大学総合研究叢書学際研究プロジェクト, 3.

Hori Toshikazu 堀 敏一 (1996). 'Chūgoku kodai no kazoku keitai' 中国古代の家族形態 [Family forms in ancient China]. In: *Chūgoku kodai no ie to shūraku* 中国古代の家と集落 [The family and settlements in ancient China]. Tokyo: Kyūko Shoin.

Hoshina Sueko 保科季子 (2002). 'Tenshi no kōkyū: Kan dai no jukyō teki kōgō ron' 天子の好逑—漢代の儒教的皇后論 [The emperor's ideal spouse: A Han Confucian discourse on the empress]. *Tōyōshi kenkyū* 東洋史研究, 61(2).

Iijima Wataru 飯島渉, Kubo Tōru 久保亨 and Murata Yūjirō 村田雄二郎 (eds) (2009). *Shirīzu 20 seiki Chūgokushi* シリーズ20世紀中国史 [Twentieth-century China], 4 vols. Tokyo: Tokyo Daigaku Shuppankai.

Iizuka Yutori 飯塚容 (2014). *Chūgoku no 'shin geki' to Nihon* 中国の「新劇」と日本 [China's 'New Drama' and Japan]. Tokyo: Chūō Daigaku Shuppanbu.

Ikeda Yūichi 池田雄一 (2014). 'Shin Kan jidai no koseki ni tsuite' 秦漢時代の戸籍について [Household registration in Qin and Han China]. In: Tōyō Bunko Chūgoku kodai chiiki kenkyū 東洋文庫中国古代地域史研究 (ed.), *Chōkazan Kankan 'Ninen ritsuryō' no kenkyū* 張家山漢簡『二年律令』の研究 [A study of the '*Ernian lüling*' in Zhangjiashan Han Bamboo slips]. Tokyo: Tōyō Bunko.

Imamura Yoshiko 今村佳子 (2002). 'Chūgoku shin sekki jidai no gūzō, dōbutsuzō' 中国新石器時代の偶像・動物像 [Idols and animal figurines in China's Neolithic Age]. *Chūgoku kōkogaku* 中国考古学, 2.

Inohara Tatsuo 猪原達生 (2015). 'Kangan' 宦官 [Eunuchs]. In: Kohama Masako 小浜正子 (ed.), *Jendā no Chūgokushi* ジェンダーの中国史 [Gender in Chinese history]. Tokyo: Bensei Shuppan.

Inoue Masato 井上雅人 (2001). *Yōfuku to Nihonjin: Kokuminfuku to iu mōdo* 洋服と日本人—国民服というモード [Western clothing and the Japanese: Men's fashion in wartime civilian uniform]. Tokyo: Kōsaido Shuppan.

Inoue Tōru 井上徹 (2000). *Chūgoku no sōzoku to kokka no reisei: sōhō shugi no shiten kara no bunseki* 中国の宗族と国家の礼制—宗法主義の視点からの分析 [Lineages and the state ritual system in China: An analysis from a patriarchist viewpoint]. Tokyo: Kenbun Shuppan.

Iriya Yoshitaka 入矢義高 (1960). '"Koka Jūhappaku" ronsō'「胡笳十八拍」論争 [Debates on *Eighteen Songs of a Nomad Flute*]. *Chūgoku bungakuhō* 中国文学報, 13.

Ishida Yoneko 石田米子 and Uchida Tomoyuki 内田知行 (eds) (2004). *Kōdo no mura no seibōryoku: Dā'nyan tachi no sensō wa owaranai* 黄土の村の性暴力—大娘たちの戦争は終わらない [Sexual violence in yellow-earth villages: War never ends for the aunties]. Tokyo: Sōdosha.

Iwama Kazuhiro 岩間一弘 (2011). *Shanhai kindai no howaito karā: Yureru shin chūkansō no keisei* 上海近代のホワイトカラー—揺れる新中間層の形成 [The rise of a 'white collar' in modern Shanghai: The formation of an unstable new middle class]. Tokyo: Kenbun Shuppan.

Iwama Kazuhiro 岩間一弘 (2012). *Shanhai taishū no tanjō to henbō: Kindai shin chūkansō no shōhi, dōin, ibento* 上海大衆の誕生と変貌—近代新中間層の消費・動員・イベント [The appearance and transformation of the masses in Shanghai: Consumption, mobilization and events of the modern new middle class]. Tokyo: Tokyo Daigaku Shuppankai.

Jin Jung-Won 陳姃湲 (2006). *Higasi Ajia no ryōsaikenbo ron; Tsukurareta dentō* 東アジアの良妻賢母論—創られた伝統 [The good wife and wise mother ideal in East Asia: The creation of a tradition]. Tokyo: Keisō Shobō.

Jin Yihong 金一虹 (2010). 'Furikaeri saikō suru: Chūgoku bunka daikakumei ki no jendā to rōdō, soshite "Tetsu no musume" undō' ふりかえり再考する―中国文化大革命期のジェンダーと労働、そして「鉄の娘」運動 [Reflect and rethink: Gender, labor and 'iron girls' during China's Cultural Revolution]. *Jendā shigaku* ジェンダー史学, 6.

Jin Yihong 金一虹 (2014). 'Ku'nan no uchi ni tachidomatte; Nihon-gun seibōryoku panel ten no Nankin ni okeru zasetsu to naisei' 苦難のうちに立ち止まって―日本軍性暴力パネル展の南京における挫折と内省 [Standing still in distress: Frustration and soul-searching in the panel exhibition of sexual violence by the Imperial Japanese Army in Nanjing]. *Chūgoku joseishi kenkyū* 中国女性史研究, 23. (Reprinted in Kohama and Akiyama (eds) (2016).)

Jin Yihong 金一虹 (2016). 'Chūgoku shakai no henyō to josei no keizai-sankaku: Pekin kaigi kara 20 nen' 中国社会の変容と女性の経済参画―北京会議から二〇年 [Transformation of Chinese society and women's economic participation: Twenty years after the Beijing Conference]. In: Kohama Masako 小浜正子 and Akiyama Yōko 秋山洋子 (eds), *Gendai Chūgoku no jendā poritikusu: Kakusa, seibaibai, 'ianfu'* 現代中国のジェンダー・ポリティクス ―格差・性売買・「慰安婦」 [Gender politics in contemporary China: Economic disparity, sex trade, 'comfort women']. Tokyo: Bensei Shuppan.

Kakehi Kumiko 筧久美子 (1978). '"*Retsujo den*" nōto' 「列女伝」ノート [Notes on *Biographies of Exemplary Women*]. *Kindai* 近代, 53.

Kami Yuki 上悠紀 (2009). '*Ikenshi*' ni okeru josei' 『夷堅志』における女性 [Women in *Records of the Listener*]. *Jōchi shigaku* 上智史学, 54.

Kamiya Noriko 神矢法子 (1994). '*Haha' no tame no sōfuku: Chūgoku kodai shakai ni miru fuken-fuken, tsuma=haha no chii, ko no gimu* 「母」のための喪服: 中国古代社会に見る夫権・父権・妻＝母の地位・子の義務 [The mourning dress for the 'mother': Husband's and father's authority, wife-mother's status and children's duties in ancient Chinese society]. Tokyo: Kindai Bungeisha.

Kaneko Shūichi 金子修一 (2009a). 'Sokuten Bukō to To Shisen boshi: Awata-no-Mahito no kentōshi to kanren shite' 則天武后と杜嗣先墓誌―粟田真人の遣唐使と関連して [Empress Wu and the epitaph of Du Cixian: In association with the Awata-no-Mahito embassy to the Tang dynasty]. *Kokushigaku* 国史学, 197.

Kaneko Shūichi 金子修一 (2009b). 'Tōdai shōchokubunchū no Sokuten Bukō no hyōka ni tsuite' 唐代詔勅文中の則天武后の評価について [The appraisal of Empress Wu in the imperial edicts of the Tang dynasty]. *Tōyōshi kenkyū* 東洋史研究, 68 (2).

Kaneko Shūichi 金子修一 (2015). 'Sokuten Bukō: Jotei to saishi' 則天武后―女帝と祭祀 [Empress Wu Zetian: Empress regnant and rituals]. In: Kohama Masako 小浜正子 (ed.), *Jendā no Chūgokushi* ジェンダーの中国史 [Gender in Chinese history]. Tokyo: Bensei Shuppan.

Kaneko Shūichi 金子修一 (2016). 'Gensō no saishi to Sokuten Bukō' 玄宗の祭祀と則天武后 [Emperor Xuanzong's rituals and Empress Wu Zetian]. In: Furuse Natsuko 古瀬奈津子 (ed.), *Higashi Ajia no rei, gishiki to shihai kōzō* 東アジアの礼・儀式と支配構造 [East Asian ceremonies and rituals, and dominance structure]. Tokyo: Yoshikawa Kōbunkan.

Kansai Chūgoku joseishi kenkyūkai 関西中国女性史研究会 (ed.) (2014). *Chūgoku joseishi nyūmon: onna tachi no ima to mukashi (zōho kaitei ban)* 中国女性史入門―女たちの今と昔 (増補改訂版) [Introduction to the history of Chinese women: The past and present (enlarged and revised edition)]. Kyoto: Jinbun Shoin.

Karashima Takeshi 辛島驍 (1964). *Gyo Genki, Setsu Tō* 魚玄機・薛涛 [Yu Xuanji and Xue Tao]. Tokyo: Shūeisha.

Katō Mihoko 加藤美穂子 (2001). *Shōkai Chūgoku kon'in, rikonhō* 詳解中国婚姻・離婚法 [Chinese marriage and divorce law]. Tokyo: Nihon Kajo Shuppan.

Katsumura Tetsuya 勝村哲也 (1974). 'Nanchō monbatu no kasan: Monzen shoin *sōdan Ryū Sei* no shin kaishaku' 南朝門閥の家産―文選所引「奏弾劉整」の新解釈 [Family properties of great clans in the Southern Dynasties: A new account of 'The memorial impeaching Liu Zheng' collected in *Selection of Refined Literature*]. Jinbungaku ronsyū 人文学論集 Bukkyo Diagku gakkai (仏教大学学会), 8.

Katsuyama Minoru 勝山稔 (2007). *Chūgoku Sō, Mindai ni okeru kon'in no gakusaiteki kenkyū* 中国宋―明代における婚姻の学際的研究 [Interdisciplinary research into marriage in Song-Ming China]. Sendai: Tohoku Daigaku Shuppankai.

Kawai Yasushi 川合安 (2015). 'Nanchō no kōshu: Kizoku shakai no naka no kōtei no musume tachi' 南朝の公主―貴族社会のなかの皇帝のむすめたち [The princesses of the Southern dynasties: Emperors' daughters in aristocratic society]. In: Kohama Masako 小浜正子 (ed.), *Jendā no Chūgokushi* ジェンダーの中国史 [Gender in Chinese history]. Tokyo: Bensei Shuppan.

Kegasawa Yasunori 氣賀澤保規 (2005). *Kenran taru sekai teikoku: Zui Tō jidai* 絢爛たる世界帝国: 隋唐時代 [Glorious cosmopolitan empires: Rise and fall of the Sui and Tang dynasties]. Tokyo: Kōdansha.

Kikuchi Toshio 菊池敏夫 et al. (2002). *Shanhai shokugyō samazama* 上海職業さまざま [Various occupations in Shanghai]. Tokyo: Bensei Shuppan.

Kinoshita Tetsuya 木下鉄矢 (2007). *Shushigaku no ichi* 朱子学の位置 [The position of the Cheng-Zhu school]. Tokyo: Chisen Shokan.

Kishimoto Mio 岸本美緒 (1998). 'Tsuma o utte wa ikenai ka? Min Shin jidai no baisai-tensai kankō' 妻を売ってはいけないか?―明清時代の売妻・典妻慣行 [Shouldn't I sell my wife?: The practice of wife-selling and wife-pawning in Ming-Qing China]. *Chūgoku shigaku* 中国史学, 8.

Kishimoto Mio 岸本美緒 (2003). 'Shin dai ni okeru "sen" no kannen: Bōenbōkō mondai o chūshin ni' 清代における「賤」の観念 ― 冒捐冒考問題を中心に [The concept of '*jian*' in the Qing period: An analysis of regulations on the capacity for taking examinations and purchasing degrees]. *Tōyō Bunka Kenkyūjo kiyō* 東洋文化研究所紀要, 144.

Kishimoto Mio 岸本美緒 (2005). 'Mindai no shakai shūdan to "sen" no kannen' 明代の社会集団と「賤」の観念 [Social groups and the concept of '*jian*' in the Ming period]. In: Inoue Tōru 井上徹 and Tsukada Takashi 塚田孝 (eds), *Higashi Ajia kinsei toshi ni okeru shakaiteki ketsugō* 東アジア近世都市における社会的結合 [Social cohesion in early-modern East Asian cities]. Osaka: Seibundō.

Kita Mika 喜多三佳 (2010). 'Sasshi kanpu no ri: Shin ritsu "Sasshi kanpu jō" no engen to sono hatten' 殺死姦夫の理―清律「殺死姦夫条」の淵源とその発展 [Rationale behind adulterer killings: The origin and development of 'the adulterer killing provisions' (*Shasi jinfu tiao*) of the Ming code]. *Hōshigaku kenkyūkai kaihō* 法史学研究会会報, 15.

Kitahara Kaoru 北原 薫 (1980). 'Tōdai Tonkō seki no sanjō chūki kara mita kyōdai kan no sekiko to gōko 唐代敦煌籍の三状注記から見た兄弟間の析戸と合戸 [The division and combination of households between siblings as seen in annotations to Dunhuang household registers during the Tang era]. In: Nakajima Satoshi Sensei koki kinen ronshū, jō kan 中嶋敏先生古稀記念論集 上巻 [Studies on Asian history for Professor Satoshi Nakajima on his 70th birthday, Vol. 1]. Tokyo: Kyūko Shoin.

Kiyochi Yukiko 清地ゆき子 (2013). '"Dōseiai" to "tongxinglian" no seiritsu to teichaku: Kindai no Nicchu goi kōryū o shiten ni' 「同性愛」と"同性恋"の成立と定着―近代の日中語彙交流を視点に [The formation and establishment of the terms for homosexuality in Japanese and in Chinese: From the perspective of vocabulary exchange in modern Japan and China]. *Tsukuba Daigaku chiiki kenkyū* 筑波大学地域研究, 34.

Ko, Dorothy ドロシー・コー (1997). 'Chūgoku, Minmatsu Shinsho ni okeru tensoku to bunmeika katei' 中国・明末清初における纏足と文明化過程 [Footbinding and civilization process in late Ming and early Qing China], translated by Shinno Kazuko 秦和子. In: Ajia joseishi kokusai shinpojiumu jikkō iinkai アジア女性史国際シンポジウム実行委員会 (ed.), *Ajia joseishi: Hikakushi no kokoromi* アジア女性史：比較史の試み [Asian women's history: A comparative attempt]. Tokyo: Akashi Shoten.

Kohama Masako 小浜正子 (2015). 'Gendai Chūgoku no kazoku no hen'yō: Shōshika to bokei nettowāku no kengen' 現代中国の家族の変容―少子化と母系ネットワークの顕現 [Transformation of the family in contemporary China: A declining birthrate and the emergence of the matrilineal network]. In: Kohama Masako (ed.), *Jendā no Chūgokushi* ジェンダーの中国史 [Gender in Chinese history]. Tokyo: Bensei Shuppan.

Kohama Masako 小浜正子 (2016). 'Jendāshi: Kazoku, dōin, shintai' ジェンダー史―家族・動員・身体 [Gender history: Family, mobilization and the body]. In: Nakamura Motoya 中村元哉 and Ōsawa Hajime 大澤肇 (eds), *Gendai Chūgoku no kigen o saguru: Shiryō handobukku* 現代中国の起源を探る―史料ハンドブック [Search for the origins of contemporary China: A handbook of historical materials]. Tokyo: Tōhō Shoten.

Kohama Masako 小浜正子 (2020). *Hitorikko seisaku to Chūgoku shakai* 一人っ子政策と中国社会 [One child policy and the society of China]. Kyoto: Kyoto Daigaku Gakujutsu Shuppannkai.

Kohama Masako 小浜正子 (ed.) (2015). *Jender no Chūgokushi* ジェンダーの中国史 [Gender in Chinese history]. Tokyo: Bensei Shuppan.

Kohama Masako 小浜正子 and Akiyama Yōko 秋山洋子 (eds) (2016). *Gendai Chūgoku no jendā poritikusu; Kakusa, seibaibai, 'ianfu'* 現代中国のジェンダー・ポリティクス ― 格差・性売買・「慰安婦」 [Gender politics in contemporary China: Economic disparity, sex trade, 'comfort women']. Tokyo: Bensei Shuppan.

Kohama Masako 小浜正子 and Matsuoka Etsuko 松岡悦子 (eds) (2014). *Ajia no shussan to kazoku keikaku: "umu, umanai, umenai" shintai o meguru seiji* アジアの出産と家族計画―「産む・産まない・産めない」身体をめぐる政治 [Childbirth and family planning in Asia: The politics on women's reproductive bodies]. Tokyo: Bensei Shuppan.

Kotera Atsushi 小寺敦 (2008). *Senshin kazoku kankei shiryō no shin kenkyū* 先秦家族関係史料の新研究 [A new study on historical resources of pre-Qin family relations]. Tokyo: Kyūko Shoin.

Koyama Shizuko 小山静子 (1991). *Ryōsaikenbo to iu kihan* 良妻賢母という規範 [Ryosai Kenbo: The educational ideal of 'Good wife, wise mother' in modern Japan]. Tokyo: Keisō Shobō.

Kusamori Shin'ichi 草森紳一 (2013). *Ri Ga: Suishi no kyaku* 李賀—垂翅の客 [Li He: A broken-hearted traveler]. Tokyo: Geijutsu Shuppansha. (First published in *Gendaishi techō* 現代詩手帖, April 1973.)

Li Xiaojiang 李小江 (1998). 'Kōkyō kūkan no sōzō: Chūgoku no josei kenkyū undo ni kakawaru jiko bunseki' 公共空間の創造—中国の女性研究運動にかかわる自己分析 [Creation of public space: Self-analysis involved in the women's studies movement in China]. In: Akiyama Yōko 秋山洋子 et al. (eds. and trans.) (1998), *Chūgoku no joseigaku: Byōdō gensō ni idomu* 中国の女性学—平等幻想に挑む [Women's studies in China: Challenging the illusion of equality]. Tokyo: Keisō Shobō.

Li Xiaojiang 李小江 (2000). *Onna ni mukatte: Chugoku joseigaku o hiraku* 女に向かって—中国女性学をひらく [Toward women: Developing Chinese women's studies], translated by Akiyama Yōko 秋山洋子. Tokyo: Inpact Shuppankai.

Li Xiaojiang 李小江 (2006). 'Grōbaruka no moto de no Chūgoku joseigaku to kokusai kaihatsu purojekuto: Awasete hondo no shigen to "hondoka" no mondai o kataru' グローバル化のもとでの中国女性学と国際開発プロジェクト—あわせて本土の資源と『本土化』の問題を語る [Chinese women's studies and international development projects under globalization: Discourse on mainland resources and localization issue]. *Kikan pīpuruzu puran* 季刊ピープルズ・プラン, 34. (Republished in Kohama and Akiyama (eds) (2016).)

Lin Hong 林紅 (2007). *Chūgoku ni okeru baibaishun konzetsu seisaku* 中国における売買春根絶政策 [Prostitution eradication policy in China]. Tokyo: Akashi Shoten.

Lin Qi 林祁 and Shirouzu Noriko 白水紀子 (ed.) (2006). *Meshibe no nai hana: Chūgoku hatsu no sei tenkansha Shasha no monogatari* めしべのない花—中国初の性転換者莎莎の物語 [A flower without a pistil: The story of Shasha, China's first transsexual]. Tokyo: Shinpūsha.

Liu Bohong 劉伯紅 (2007). 'Chūgoku josei NGO no hatten shōyaku' 中国女性NGOの発展抄訳 [Development of Chinese women's NGOs: Extract translation]. *Kokuritsu Josei Kyōiku Kaikan kenkyū jānaru* 国立女性教育会館研究ジャーナル, 11.

Liu Hsin-Ning 劉欣寧 (2011). 'Shin Kan ritsu ni okeru dōkyo no renza' 秦漢律における同居の連坐 [Collective responsibility of co-inhabitants under the statutes of Qin and Han]. *Tōyōshi kenkyū* 東洋史研究, 70(1).

Machida Takayoshi 町田隆吉 (2007). 'Chōsa Go kan yori mita "ko" ni tsuite: Sangoku Go no kazoku kōsei ni kansuru shohoteki kōsatsu' 長沙呉簡よりみた「戸」について—三国呉の家族構成に関する初歩的考察 ['Households' in the Changsha bamboo slips of Wu: A preliminary study on family composition in Wu of the Three Kingdoms]. *Chōsa Go kan kenkyū hōkoku* 長沙呉簡研究報告, Vol. 3.

Maeda Hisami 前田尚美 (2009). 'Mindai kōkyū to kōhi, Nyokan seido' 明代後宮と后妃・女官制度 [The inner palace, empresses and maids of honor in the Ming dynasty]. *Kyoto Joshi Daigaku Daigakuin Bungaku Kenkyūka kenkyū kiyō, shigaku hen* 京都女子大学大学院文学研究科研究紀要・史学編, 8.

Maeyama Kanako 前山加奈子 (1993). 'Lin Godō to "fujo kaika" ronsō: 1930 nendai ni okeru joseiron' 林語堂と「婦女回家」論争——一九三〇年代に於ける女性論 [Lin Yutang and the 1930s debates about 'Women go home']. In: Yanagida Setsuko Sensei koki kinen ronshū henshū iinkai (ed.), *Chūgoku no dentō shakai to kazoku* 中国の伝統社会と家族 [Traditional society and family in China]. Tokyo: Kyuko Shoin.

Maeyama Kanako 前山加奈子 (2000). 'Kindai Chūgoku josei to kokka tono kakawari' 近代中国女性と国家とのかかわり [Women in modern China and their connection to the state]. In: Igeta Midori 井桁碧 (ed.), *'Nihon' kokka to onna* 「日本」国家と女 [The 'Japanese' state and women]. Tokyo: Seikyūsha.

Maeyama Kanako 前山加奈子 (2005). 'Kakumei to gendā: Chūgoku joseishi no saikouchiku ni mukete' 革命とジェンダー－中国女性史の再構築に向けて [Revolution and gender: Towards a reconstruction of Chinese women's history]. *Jendā shigaku* ジェンダー史学1, inaugural issue.

Mann, Susan L. (1986). 'Shin dai no shakai ni okeru kafu no ichi' 清代の社会における寡婦の位置 [Status of widows in Qing society], translated by Kishimoto Mio 岸本美緒. *Ochanomizu shigaku* お茶の水史学, 29.

Maruta Takashi 丸田孝志 (2013). *Kakumei no girei: Chūgoku kyōsantō konkyochi no seiji dōin to minzoku* 革命の儀礼—中国共産党根拠地の政治動員と民俗 [Revolutionary rites: Political mobilization and folk customs in areas controlled by the Chinese Communist Party]. Tokyo: Kyūko Shoin.

Matsuo Hatsuko 松尾肇子 (2003). 'Ri Seishō zō no hensen: Nido no kekkon o megutte' 李清照像の変遷—二度の結婚をめぐって [The changing image of Li Qingzhao: Surrounding her two marriages]. *Josei shigaku* 女性史学, 13. (Reprinted in Matsuo (2008). *Shiron no seiritsu to hatten: Cho En o chūshin to shite* 詞論の成立と発展—張炎を中心として [The birth and evolution of poetic theory of *ci*: Centering on Zhang Yan]. Tokyo: Tohō Shoten.)

Matsuura Tomohisa 松浦友久 ([1982] 1986). 'Tōshi ni arawareta joseizō to joseikan: "Keienshi" no imi suru mono' 唐詩に表われた女性像と女性観:「閨怨詩」の意味するもの [The image of womanhood and the view of women in Tang poems: The meaning of 'boudoir lament' poetry]. In: Matsuura, *Chūgoku shika genron* 中国詩歌原論 [Principles of Chinese poetry]. Tokyo: Taishūkan Shoten. (First published in Ishikawa Tadahisa 石川忠久 (ed.) (1982), *Chūgoku bungaku no joseizō* 中国文学の女性像 [Women in Chinese literature]. Tokyo: Kyūko Shoin.)

Matsuura Tsuneo 松浦恆雄 (2000). 'Kageri naki hyōshō: Yankō geki kara kakumei mohan geki e' 翳りなき表象—秧歌劇から革命模範劇へ [Unclouded representation: From *Yangge* opera to revolutionary model operas]. In: Maki Yōichi 牧陽一, Matsuura Tsuneo 松浦恆雄 and Kawata Susumu 川田進 (eds), *Chūgoku no puropaganda geijutsu* 中国のプロパガンダ芸術 [China's propaganda arts]. Tokyo: Iwanami Shoten.

Matsuura Tsuneo 松浦恆雄 (2003). '20 seiki no kyōgeki to Mei Ranfan' 20世紀の京劇と梅蘭芳 [Peking opera in the twentieth century and Mei Lanfang]. In: Unoki Yō 宇野木洋 and Matsuura Tsuneo 松浦恆雄 (eds), *Chūgoku 20 seiki bungaku o manabu hito no tame ni* 中国二〇世紀文学を学ぶ人のために [For those who study Chinese literature in the twentieth century]. Kyoto: Sekai Shisōsha.

Mitamura Taisuke 三田村泰助 ([1963] 2012). *Kangan: Sokkin seiji no kōzō* 宦官—側近政治の構造 [Chinese eunuchs: The structure of intimate politics]. Tokyo: Chūkō Shinsho.

Mitsunari Miho 三成美保, Himeoka Toshiko 姫岡とし子 and Kohama Masako 小浜正子 (eds) (2014). *Rekishi o yomikaeru: Jendā kara mita sekaishi* 歴史を読み替える—ジェンダーから見た世界史 [Reinterpreting world history: From the gender perspective]. Tokyo: Ōtsuki Shoten.

Miyajima Hiroshi 宮嶋博史 (1995). *Yanban: Richō shakai no tokken kaisō* 両班—李朝社会の特権階層 [Yangban: A privileged class in Joseon society]. Tokyo: Chūkō Shinsho.

Miyamoto Kazuo 宮本一夫 (2005). *Chūgoku no rekishi 01: Shinwa kara rekishi e* 中国の歴史01—神話から歴史へ [History of China 01: From mythology to history]. Tokyo: Kōdansha.

Mizoguchi Yūzō 溝口雄三 et al. (eds) (2001). *Chūgoku shisō bunka jiten* 中国思想文化事典 [Encyclopedia of Chinese thought and culture]. Tokyo: Tokyo Daigaku Shuppankai.

Mizubayashi Takeshi 水林彪 (1987). *Hōkensei no saihen to Nihonteki shakai no kakuritsu* 封建制の再編と日本的社会の確立 [The reorganizing of the feudal system and the establishment of Japanese society]. Tokyo: Yamakawa Shuppansha.

Mizubayashi Takeshi 水林彪 (1992). 'Hikaku kokuseishi, bunmei shiron taiwa' 比較国制史・文明史論対話 [Dialogue on comparative history of government and civilization theories]. In: Suzuki Masayuki 鈴木正幸 et al. (eds), *Hikaku kokuseishi kenkyū josetsu: Bunmeika to kindaika* 比較国制史研究序説 — 文明化と近代化 [Introduction to a comparative study of regimes: Civilization and modernization]. Tokyo: Kashiwa Shobō.

Mizuta Noriko 水田宗子 (1982). *Hiroin kara hīrō e: Josei no jiga to hyōgen* ヒロインからヒーローへ—女性の自我と表現 [From heroine to hero: Women's selfhood and representation]. Tokyo: Tabata Shoten.

Mori Noriko 森紀子 (1999). 'Ryō Keichō no butsugaku to Nihon' 梁啓超の仏学と日本 [Liang Qichao's studies of Buddhism and Japan]. In: Hazama Naoki 狭間直樹 (ed.), *Kyōdō kenkyū Ryō Keichō: Seiyō kindai sisō juyō to Meiji Nihon* 共同研究梁啓超—西洋近代思想受容と明治日本 [Liang Qichao: The absorption of Western modern thought and Meiji Japan]. Tokyo: Misuzu Shobō.

Mori Noriko 森紀子 (2005). *Chūgoku tenkanki ni okeru jukyō undo* 中国転換期における儒教運動 [The Confucian movement in China's transitional stages]. Kyoto: Kyoto Daigaku Gakujutstu Shuppankai.

Moriya Mitsuo 守屋美都雄 (1955). '*Furō*' 父老 [Village elders]. *Tōyōshi kenkyū* 東洋史研究, 14(1–2). (Reprinted in Moriya (1968). *Chūgoku kodai no kazoku to kokka* 中国古代の家族と国家 [Family and state in ancient China]. Kyoto: Tōyōshi Kenkyūkai.)

Moriya Mitsuo 守屋美都雄 (1968). *Chūgoku kodai no kazoku to kokka* 中国古代の家族と国家 [Families and the state in ancient China]. Kyoto: Tōyōshi Kenkyūkai.

Murata Yūjirō 村田雄二郎 (2009). 'Chūka minzokuron no keifu' 中華民族論の系譜 [Genealogy of discourses on Chinese people as a nation]. In: Iijima Wataru 飯島渉, Kubo Tōru 久保亨 and Murata Yūjirō 村田雄二郎 (eds), *Chūka sekai to kindai* 中華世界と近代 [Qing China and the modern world]. Tokyo: Tokyo Daigaku Shuppankai.

Nagata Hidemasa 永田英正 (ed.) (1994). *Kandai sekkoku shūsei* 漢代石刻集成 [Compilation of stone inscriptions in the Han dynasty]. Kyoto: Dōhōsha Shuppan.

Nagata Hidemasa 永田英正 and Umehara Kaoru 梅原郁 (trans. and annots.) (1988). *Kanjo shokka, Chiri, Kōkyokushi* 漢書食貨・地理・溝洫志 [Treatises 'on economic matters', 'geography' and 'on rivers and canals' in *History of the Former Han*]. Tokyo: Heibonsha Tōyō Bunko.

Nakada Kaoru 中田 薫 ([1926] 1943). 'Tō Sō jidai no kazoku kyōsan sei' 唐宋時代の家族共産制 [The system of 'common family property' in Tang-Song China]. *Kokka gakkai zasshi* 国家学会雑誌, 40(7–8). (Reprinted in Nakada (1943). *Hōseishi ronshū* 法制史論集 [A collection of essays on legal history], Vol. 3. Tokyo: Iwanami Shoten.)

Nakajima Midori 中島みどり (trans. and annot.) (2001). *Retsujo den* 列女伝, 3 vols. [*Biographies of Exemplary Women* by Liu Xiang]. Tokyo: Heibon Sha.

Nakasuna Akinori 中砂明徳 (1993). 'Tōdai no bosō to boshi' 唐代の墓葬と墓誌 [Tombs and epitaphs in Tang China]. In: Tonami Mamoru 礪波護 (ed.), *Chūgoku chūsei no bunbutsu* 中國中世の文物 [Cultural relics in medieval China]. Kyoto: Kyoto Daigaku Jinbunkagaku Kenkyūsho.

Nakayama Fumi 中山文 (2015). 'Jendā no etsugeki shi: Chūgoku no josei engeki' ジェンダーの越劇史—中国の女性演劇 [A gendered history of *yueju*: China's female theatre]. In: Kohama Masako 小浜正子 (ed.), *Jendā no Chūgokushi* ジェンダーの中国史 [Gender in Chinese history]. Tokyo: Bensei Shuppan.

Nakayama Fumi 中山文 (ed.) (2019). *Etsugeki no sekai: Chūgoku no josei engeki* 越劇の世界—中国の女性演劇 [The world of *yueju*: China's female theatre]. Wakayama: NKStation.

Nakayama Fumi 中山文, Qian Jue 錢珏 and Ushida Hiroko 牛田博子 (2012). '21 seiki no josei engeki o motomete (1): Qian Jue *Chūgoku josei sakka no egaku josei keishō*' 21世紀の女性演劇を求めて（1）―銭珏「中国女性作家の描く女性形象」 [Seeking female theatre for the twenty-first century (1): Qian Jue, '*The figure of women depicted by Chinese female dramatists*']. *Kobe Gakuin Daigaku Jinbun Gakubu kiyō* 神戸学院大学人文学部紀要, 32.

Nakayama Yoshihiro 中山義弘 (1983). *Kindai Chūgoku ni okeru josei kaihō no shisō to kōdō* 近代中国における女性解放の思想と行動 [Feminist philosophy and action in modern China]. Kitakyushu: Kitakyushu Chūgoku Shoten.

Namba Junko 難波純子 (2005). 'Chūgoku kodai no jendā rōru: Jokō no kigen' 中国古代のジェンダーロール – 女工の起源 [Gender roles in ancient China: The origin of female workers]. *Chūgoku bunka kenkyū* 中国文化研究, 21.

Narita Shizuka 成田靜香 (2004). 'Jisojo no ie: Kanton no kon'in bunka' 自梳女の家—広東の婚姻文化 [Self-combing sisters' house: Marriage cultures of Canton]. In: Kansai Chūgoku joseishi kenkyūkai 関西中国女性史研究会 (ed.), *Jendā kara mita Chūgoku no ie to onna* ジェンダーから見た中国の家と女 [The Chinese family and women from a gender perspective]. Tokyo: Tōhō Shoten.

Niida Noboru 仁井田陞 ([1937] 1983). *Tō Sō hōritsu monjo no kenkyū* 唐宋法律文書の研究 [Studies in Tang-Song legal documents]. Tokyo: Tokyo Daigaku Shuppankai.

Niida Noboru 仁井田陞 ([1959] 1962). 'Tonkō hakken no Tō Sō kazokuhō kankei monjo' 敦煌発見の唐宋家族法関係文書 [Dunhuang legal documents for the family in Tang-Song China]. *Chūgoku hōseishi kenkyū* 中国法制史研究 [Studies in Chinese legal history]. Tokyo: Tokyo Daigaku Shuppankai.

Niida Noboru 仁井田陞 (1942). *Shina mibunhōshi* 支那身分法史 [A history of Chinese status law]. Tokyo: Tōhō Bunka Gakuin. (Reprinted by Tokyo Daigaku Shuppankai in 1983.)

Nishimura Fumiko 西村富美子 (1996). 'Chūgoku josei bungaku no keifu: Sai En ron: "Hifunshi" no igi, Fu "Koka Jūhappaku" ni tsuite' 中国女性文学の系譜―蔡琰論:「悲憤詩」の意義 付「胡笳十八拍」について [Genealogy of women's literature in China: On Cai Yan: The significance of '*beifen shi*' and about *Eighteen Songs of a Nomad Flute*]. *Jimbun rongi Mie Daigaku Jinbun Gakubu Bunka Gakka kenkyū kiyō* 人文論叢 三重大学人文学部文化学科研究紀要, 13.

Nishimura Shigeo 西村成雄 (ed.) (2003). *Nashonarizumu: Rekishi kara no sekkin* ナショナリズム: 歴史からの接近 [Chinese nationalism: Institutional changes in Republican China]. Tokyo: Tokyo Daigaku Shuppankai.

Noda Tōru 野田徹 (1993). 'Minchō kangan no seiji teki chi'i ni tsuite' 明朝宦官の政治的地位について [A study on the political position of eunuchs in the Ming dynasty]. *Kyushu Daigaku tōyōshi ronshū* 九州大学東洋史論集, 21.

Nomura Ayuko 野村鮎子 (2007). 'Chūgoku shitaifu no domesutikku baiorensu: Shukka no musume no gyakutaishi to chichi no aikoku' 中国士大夫のドメスティック・バイオレンス―出嫁の女の虐待死と父の哀哭 [Domestic violence committed by a Chinese scholar-official: Death of a wife by physical abuse and her father's grief]. *Nara Joshi Daigaku Bungakubu kenkyū kyōiku nenpō* 奈良女子大学文学部研究教育年報, 3.

Nomura Ayuko 野村鮎子 (2015). 'Tomo ni totsugu ka, tomo ni sinu ka?: Zen kindai Chūgoku no josei dōseiai' ともに嫁ぐか、ともに死ぬか?―前近代中国の女性同性愛 [To marry men, or to die together?: Lesbianism in pre-modern China]. In: Mitsunari Miho 三成美保 (ed.), *Dōseiai o meguru rekishi to hō: Songen toshite no sekushuariti* 同性愛をめぐる歴史と法―尊厳としてのセクシュアリティ [History and law on homosexuality: Sexuality and dignity]. Tokyo: Akashi Shoten.

Ochi Shigeaki 越智重明 (1997). *Sengoku Shin Kanshi kenkyū 3* 戦国秦漢史研究3 [Historical analysis of the Warring States period, Qin and Han eras, Vol. 3]. Fukuoka: Chugoku Shoten.

Ochiai Atsushi 落合淳思 (2015). In: *Chūgokushi saiko no ōchō* 殷―中国史最古の王朝 [Yin: China's oldest dynasty]. Tokyo: Chūō Kōron Shinsha.

Ogawa Yoshiyuki 小川快之 (2015). 'Sōdai joshi zaisanken ronsō ni tsuite' 宋代女子財産権論争について [The debate on Song women's property rights]. *Jōchi shigaku* 上智史学, 60.

Ogino Miho 荻野美穂 (2002). *Jendā ka sareru shintai* ジェンダー化される身体 [Genderized bodies]. Tokyo: Keisō Shobō.

Ogino Miho 荻野美穂 (2014). *Onna no karada: Feminizumu igo* 女のからだ ―フェミニズム以後 [Woman's bodies: Post-feminism]. Tokyo: Iwanami Shoten.

Ōhama Keiko 大浜慶子 (2007). 'Chūgoku ni okeru joseigaku seidoka no ayumi: Pekin sekai josei kaigi igo no shin dōkō' 中国における女性学制度化の歩み―北京世界女性会議以後の新動向 [History of institutionalization of women's studies in China: New direction after the World Conference on Women in Beijing]. *Ningen kenkyū* 人間研究, 43.

Ohashi Fumie 大橋史恵 (2011). *Gendai Chūgoku no ijū kaji rōdōsha: Nōson-toshi kankei to sai seisan rōdō no jendā poritikusu* 現代中国の移住家事労働者―農村―都市関係と再生産労働のジェンダー・ポリティクス [Migrant domestic workers in contemporary China: The politics of reproductive labor in rural-urban relations]. Tokyo: Ochanomizu Shobō.

Ohashi Fumie 大橋史恵 (2014). 'Chūgoku femiteki kenbunroku' 中国フェミ的見聞録 [Feminist observations of China], No. 6. *Onnatachi no 21 seiki* 女たちの21世紀, 77.

Ohashi Fumie 大橋史恵 (2015a). '"Kaigai josei nyūsu" Chūgoku: Sekushuaru harasumento hihan kyanpein wo keikaku shita feminisuto katsudōka ra ga kōryū shobun' [海外女性ニュース] 中国―セクシュアル・ハラスメント批判キャンペーンを計画したフェミニスト活動家らが拘留処分 [Overseas news on women, China: 'Feminism activists detained for planning anti-sexual harassment campaign']. *Onnatachi no 21 seiki* 女たちの21世紀, 82.

Ohashi Fumie 大橋史恵 (2015b). 'Chūgoku femiteki kenbunroku' 中国フェミ的見聞録 [Feminist observations of China], No. 11. *Onnatachi no 21 seiki* 女たちの21世紀, 82.

Okabe Toshiyoshi 岡部利良 (1992). *Kyū Chūgoku no bōseki rōdō kenkyū: Kyū Chūgoku no kindai kōgyō rōdō no ichibunseki* 旧中国の紡績労働研究―旧中国の近代工業労働の一分析 [Studies on workers in the pre-liberation Chinese spinning industry: An analysis of pre-liberation Chinese labor]. Fukuoka: Kyushu Daigaku Shuppankai.

Okamura Hidenori 岡村秀典 (2008). *Chūgoku bunmei: Nōgyō to reisei no kōkogaku* 中国文明: 農業と礼制の考古学 [Chinese civilization: An archaeology of farming and rituals]. Kyoto: Kyoto Daigaku Gakujutsu Shuppankai.

Okano Makoto 岡野誠 (1976). 'Tōdai ni okeru kinkonshin no han'i ni tsuite: Gaiin mufuku sonpi ikon no baai' 唐代における禁婚親の範囲について―外姻無服尊卑為婚の場合 [The scale of marriage prohibition in Tang: A case study of marriage between collateral relatives who should not observe mourning practices for each other but are of a higher and lower generation]. *Hōseishi kenkyū* 法制史研究, 25.

Okano Makoto 岡野誠 (1990). 'Tō kokonritu riccyaku ihō jō ni tsuite' 唐戸婚律立嫡違法條について [A case study of the Tang articles dealing with 'Violating the law by not selecting the eldest son of the principal wife to be heir']. In: Tōdaishi kenkūkai 唐代史研究会 (ed.), *Higashi Ajia komonjo no shiteki kenkyū* 東アジア古文書の史的研究 [Studies in the history of East Asian manuscripts and documents]. Tokyo: Tōsui Shobō.

Ōki Yasushi 大木康 (2001). *Chūgoku yūri kūkan: Min Shin Shinwai gijo no sekai* 中国遊里空間―明清秦淮妓女の世界 [Pleasure quarters in China: Courtesans in Qinhuai during the Ming-Qing period]. Tokyo: Seidosha.

Ōki Yasushi 大木康 (2010). *Bō Jō to "Eibaian okugo" no kenkyū* 冒襄と『影梅庵憶語』の研究 [A study of Mao Xiang and *Memories from the Yingmei Nunnery* (*Yingmeian yiyu*)]. Tokyo: Kyūko Shoin.

Ono Kazuko 小野和子 (1968). 'Shinmatsu no fujin kaihō shisō' 清末の婦人解放思想 [Women's liberation thought in the late Qing]. *Shisō* 思想, 525.

Ono Kazuko 小野和子 (1977). 'Kon'inhō kantetsu undo o megutte' 婚姻法貫徹運動をめぐって [China's campaign for the implementation of the Marriage Law]. *Tōhōgakuhō* 東方学報, 49.

Ono Kazuko 小野和子 (1978). *Chūgoku joseishi: Taihei tengoku kara gendai made* 中国女性史―太平天国から現代まで [Chinese women in a century of revolution: From the Taiping Rebellion to the present day]. Tokyo: Heibonsha.

Ono Kazuko 小野和子 (1992). *Goshi jiki kazoku ron no haikei* 五四時期家族論の背景 [Background of family theory during the May Fourth period]. Kyoto Daigaku Jinbun Kagaku Kenkyūsho kyōdō kenkyū hōkoku 京都大学人文科学研究所共同研究報告, 5(15). Kyoto: Dōhō Shuppan.

Ono Kazuko 小野和子 (2005). 'Hakkin ni natta watashi no *"Joseishi"'* 発禁になった私の『女性史』 [On my *Women's History* that was banned]. *Chikaki ni arite* 近きに在りて, 48.

Onodera Shirō 小野寺史郎 (2011). *Kokki, kokka, kokkei: Nashonarizumu to shinboru no Chūgoku kindaishi* 国旗・国家・国慶―ナショナリズムとシンボルの中国近代史 [Flags, anthems and national days: Nationalism and symbols in modern Chinese history]. Tokyo: Tokyo Daigaku Shuppankai.

Osabe Yoshihiro 長部悦弘 (1990). 'Hokuchō Zui Tō jidai ni okeru Kanzoku shitaifu no kyōiku kōzō' 北朝隋唐時代における漢族士大夫の教育構造 [The education system of Han-Chinese elites (*shidafu*) during the Northern Dynasties, Sui and Tang]. *Tōyōshi kenkyū* 東洋史研究, 49(3).

Ōsawa Masaaki 大澤正昭 (1997). '"*Seimeishū*" no sekai e: Teiryō bunseki no kokoromi' 『清明集』の世界へ―定量分析の試み [The world of *Collection of Enlightened Judgments*: A quantitative study]. *Jōchi shigaku* 上智史学, 42. (Reprinted in Ōsawa Masaaki 大澤正昭 (2015).)

Ōsawa Masaaki 大澤正昭 (2005a). *Tō Sō jidai no kazoku, kon'in, josei: Tsuma wa tsuyoku* 唐宋時代の家族・婚姻・女性―婦は強く [Family, marriage and women in Tang and Song: Strong wives]. Tokyo: Akashi Shoten.

Ōsawa Masaaki 大澤正昭 (2005b). 'Tō Sō jidai no kazoku to josei: Aratana siten no mosaku' 唐宋時代の家族と女性 ― 新たな視点の模索 [The family and women in Tang-Song China: Searching for a new perspective]. *Chūgoku shigaku* 中国史学, 15.

Ōsawa Masaaki 大澤正昭 (2008). *Rekishika no sanpo michi* 歴史家の散歩道 [Historian's promenade]. Tokyo: SUP Jōchi Daigaku Shuppan.

Ōsawa Masaaki 大澤正昭 (2015). *Nansō chihōkan no shuchō: 'Seimeishū', 'Enshi sehan' no sekai* 南宋地方官の主張―『清明集』『袁氏世範』の世界 [Ideologies of Southern Song regional officials: The world of '*Collection of Enlightened Judgments*' and '*Yuan Clan Hereditary Rules*']. Tokyo: Kyūko Shoin.

Ōsawa Masachi 大澤真幸 (ed.) (2002). *Nashonarizumu ron no meicho 50* ナショナリズム論の名著50 [Fifty masterpieces on nationalism]. Tokyo: Heibonsha.

Ōshima Ritsuko 大島立子 (1997). '"*Genshi*" retsujoden o yomu' 『元史』列女伝を読む [Biographies of exemplary women in the *History of the Yuan*]. *Aidai shigaku* 愛大史学, 6.

Otagi Hajime 愛宕元 (2002). 'Tōdai ni okeru kōkyū no joseitachi' 唐代における後宮の女性たち [The women's quarters of Chang'an palace in the Tang dynasty]. *Kyoto Daigaku Sōgō Ningen Gakubu kiyō* 京都大学総合人間学部紀要, 9.

Qu Yajun 屈雅君 (2013). 'Josei, heiwa, minzoku jisei: Sensei shihan daigaku de Nihongun seibōryoku panel ten o kaisai shite' 女性・平和・民族自省―陝西師範大学で日本軍性暴力パネル展を開催して [Women, peace, national self-reflection: On hosting the panel exhibition on sexual violence by the Japanese army at Shanxi Normal University]. *Chūgoku joseishi kenkyū* 中国女性史研究, 22. (Reprinted in Kohama and Akiyama (eds) (2016).)

Raijō Kōhei 頼城航平 (2013). 'Min dai shōren kō' 明代粧奩考 [An essay on dowry in the Ming period]. Master's thesis, Hokkaido University Graduate School.

Rekishigaku kenkyūkai and Nihonshi kenkyūkai 歴史学研究会・日本史研究会 (eds) (2014). *"Ianfu" mondai o/kara kangaeru: Gunji seibōryoku to nichijyō sekai* 「慰安婦」問題を/から考える―軍事性暴力と日常世界 [Thinking of/from the 'comfort women' issue: Sexual violence under the military and everyday life]. Tokyo: Iwanami Shoten.

Saga Takashi 嵯峨隆 (2001). *Chūgoku kokushoku kakumei ron: Shifuku to sono sisō* 中国黒色革命論―師復とその思想 [China's Black Revolution: Shifu and his anarchism]. Tokyo: Shakai Hyōronsha.

Saitō Shigeru 齋藤茂 (1992). *Kyōbōki, Hokurishi* 教坊記・北里志 [*Jiaofangji* and *Beilizhi*]. Tokyo: Heibonsha.

Sakai Keiko 酒井恵子 (2006). 'Kōshi kara seppu e: Gendai ni okeru seihyō seido to seppu hyōka no tenkan' 孝子から節婦へ―元代における旌表制度の節婦評価の転換 [From filial sons to faithful wives: The change in *jing biao* and the evaluation of fidelity during the Yuan period]. *Tōyōgakuhō* 東洋学報, 87(4).

Sakai Keiko 酒井恵子 (2007). 'Mindai kōhan ki no seihyō: Kitei kaitei o megutte' 明代後半期の旌表―規定改定をめぐって [The *jingbiao* of late Ming: Surrounding law reform]. *Nagoya Daigaku Tōyōshi kenkyū hōkoku* 名古屋大学東洋史研究報告, 31.

Sakamoto Hiroko 坂元ひろ子 (2000). 'Ashi no disukōsu: Tensoku, tensoku, kokuchi' 足のディスコース: 纏足・天足・国恥 [Discourse on feet: Footbinding, natural feet and national disgrace]. *Shisō* 思想, 907. (Later reproduced in Sakamoto (2004a).)

Sakamoto Hiroko 坂元ひろ子 (2001). 'Shō Heirin ni okeru dentō no sōzō' 章炳麟における伝統の創造 [Zhang Binglin's creation of tradition]. In: Hazama Naoki 狭間直樹 (ed.), *Seiyō kindai bunmei to Chūka sekai* 西洋近代文明と中華世界 [Modern Western civilization and the universe of China]. Kyoto: Kyoto Daigaku Gakujutsu Shuppankai. (Revised edition later published in Sakamoto (2009).)

Sakamoto Hiroko 坂元ひろ子 (2004). *Chūgoku minzokushugi no shinwa: Jinshu, shintai, jendā* 中国民族主義の神話: 人種・身体・ジェンダー [The myth of Chinese nationalism: Race, body and gender]. Tokyo: Iwanami Shoten.

Sakamoto Hiroko 坂元ひろ子 (2009). *Rensa suru Chūgoku kindai no 'chi'* 連鎖する中国近代の「知」 [Chain of 'knowledge' in modern China]. Tokyo: Kenbun Shuppan.

Sakamoto Hiroko 坂元ひろ子 (2010). 'Manga hyōshō ni miru Shanhai modan gāru' 漫画表象に見る上海モダンガール [Shanghai modern girls depicted in cartoons]. In: Ito Ruri 伊藤るり, Sakamoto Hiroko 坂元ひろ子 and Tani Barlow (eds), *Modan gāru to shokuminchiteki kindai: Higashi Ajia ni okeru teikoku, shihon, jendā* モダンガールと植民地的近代―東アジアにおける帝国・資本・ジェンダー [The Modern Girls and colonial modernity: Capital, empire and gender in East Asia]. Tokyo: Iwanami Shoten.

Sakiyama Masaki 崎山政毅 (2002). 'P. Chatajī: *Nashonarisuto no shisō to shokuminchi sekai*' P. チャタジー『ナショナリストの思想と植民地世界』 [On Partha Chatterjee's *Nationalist thought and the colonial world*, 1986, London: Zed Books]. In: Ōsawa Masachi 大澤真幸 (ed.), *Nashonarizumu ron no meicho 50* ナショナリズム論の名著 50 [Fifty masterpieces on nationalism]. Tokyo: Heibonsha.

Sasagawa Yūji 笹川裕史 and Okumura Satoshi 奥村哲 (2007). *Jūgo no Chūgoku shakai: Nicchū sensoka no sōdōin to nōson* 銃後の中国社会―日中戦争下の総動員と農村 [Chinese society behind the line: General mobilization and rural villages in the Sino-Japanese Wars]. Tokyo: Iwanami Shoten.

Sasaki Megumi 佐々木愛 (1998). 'Mō Kirei no "Shushikarei" hihan: Tokuni sōhō o chūshin to shite' 毛奇齢の『朱子家礼』批判―特に宗法を中心として [Mao Qiling's criticism of Zhu Xi's *Family Rituals*: Centering on the descent-line system]. *Jōchi shigaku* 上智史学, 43.

Sasaki Megumi 佐々木愛 (2000a). 'Chō Sai, Tei I no sōhō ron ni tsuite' 張載・程頤の宗法論について [Zhang Zai's and Cheng Yi's discourse on the descent-line system]. *Shirin* 史林, 83–85.

Sasaki Megumi 佐々木愛 (2000b). 'Tei I, Shuki no saika hihan no gensetsu o megutte' 程頤・朱熹の再嫁批判の言説をめぐって [Cheng Yi's and Zhu Xi's criticisms of remarriage]. *Jōchi shigaku* 上智史学, 45.

Sasaki Megumi 佐々木愛 (2008). 'Furin shita tsuma wa koroseru no ka? Min Shinritsu, sasshi kanpuritsu to sono unyō' 不倫した妻は殺せるのか?―明清律・殺死姦夫律とその運用 [Is it acceptable to kill an adulterous wife?: Provisions for adulterer killing in the Ming-Qing code and their operation]. *Jōchi shigaku* 上智史学, 53.

Sasaki Megumi 佐々木愛 (2009). 'Min dai ni okeru Syushigaku teki sōhō fukkatsu no zasetsu: Kyū Shun "Kareigisetsu" o chūshin ni' 明代における朱子学的宗法復活の挫折―丘濬『家礼儀節』を中心に [A failure to revive the Neo-Confucian patriarchal system in Ming China: Centering on *Propriety of Family Rituals* by Qiu Jun]. *Shakai bunka ronsyū* 社会文化論集, 5.

Sasaki Megumi 佐々木愛 (2015a). 'Haka kara mita dentō Chūgoku no kazoku: Sōdai Dōgakusha ga tsukutta haka' 墓からみた伝統中国の家族―宋代道学者がつくった墓 [What tombs tell us about families in traditional China: Tombs built by Song Neo-Confucianists]. *Shakai bunka ronsyū* 社会文化論集, 11.

Sasaki Megumi 佐々木愛 (2015b). 'Musume no haka, haha no haka: Haka kara mita dentō Chūgoku no kazoku' むすめの墓・母の墓―墓からみた伝統中国の家族 [Daughter's tomb, mother's tomb: What tombs tell us about families in traditional China]. In: Kohama Masako 小浜正子 (ed.), *Jendā no Chūgokushi* ジェンダーの中国史 [Gender in Chinese history]. Tokyo: Bensei Shuppan.

Sasaki Megumi 佐々木愛 (2020). '"Fushi dōki" gainen no seiritsu jiki ni tsuite: "Chūgoku kazokuhō' no genri" saikō' 「父子同氣」概念の成立時期について―「中國家族法の原理」再考 [The concept of 'father and sons sharing the same *qi*': A reconsideration of Shiga Shūzō's *Principles of Chinese Family Law*]. *Tōyōshi kenkyū* 東洋史研究, 79(1).

Satake Yasuhiko 佐竹靖彦 (1980). 'Chūgoku kodai no kazoku to kazoku teki shakai chitsujo' 中国古代の家族と家族的社会秩序 [Family and familial social order in ancient China]. *Jinbun gakuhō (Tokyo Toritsu Daigaku)* 人文学報 (東京都立大学), 141.

Satake Yasuhiko 佐竹靖彦 (2007). "'*Seimei jōga zu*" nanisurezo sennan ichijo: Kōryōiki shakai to dangai jonai' 《清明上河図》為何千男一女 – 広領域社会と男外女内 ['Traveling Upstream at the Qingming Festival' Why are there 1,000 men and only one woman?: Men work outside, women work inside]. *Sōdaishi no kiso teki kenkyū* 宋代史の基礎的研究 [Fundamental study of the history of the Song dynasty]. Kyoto: Hōyū Shoten.

Satō Taketoshi 佐藤武敏 (1977). *Chūgoku kodai kinu orimonoshi kenkyū* 中国古代絹織物史研究 [A study of silk goods in ancient China], Vol. 1. Tokyo: Kazama Shobō.

Sechiyama Kaku 瀬地山角 (1996). *Higasi Ajia no kafuchōsei: Jendā no hikaku shakaigaku* 東アジアの家父長制―ジェンダーの比較社会学 [Patriarchy in East Asia: A comparative sociology of gender]. Tokyo: Keisō Shobō.

Sengoku Tomoko 仙石知子 (2011). *Min Shin shōsetsu ni okeru joseizō no kenkyū: Zokufu ni yoru bunseki o chūshin ni* 明清小説における女性像の研究―族譜による分析を中心に [A study of female images in Ming-Qing novels: Centering on analysis of clan genealogies]. Tokyo: Kyūko Shoin.

Sengoku Tomoko 仙石知子 (2015). 'Kō to teisetsu: Chūgoku kinsei ni okeru josei no kihan' 孝と貞節―中国近世における女性の規範 [Filiality and chastity: Norms for women in pre-modern China]. In: Kohama Masako 小浜正子 (ed.), *Jendā no Chūgokushi* ジェンダーの中国史 [Gender in Chinese history]. Tokyo: Bensei Shuppan.

Seo Tatsuhiko 妹尾達彦 (2002). 'Koi o suru otoko: 9 seiki no Chōan ni okeru atarashii danjo ninshiki no keisei' 恋をする男 – 九世紀の長安における新しい男女認識の形成 [Men in love: The formation of a new gender perception in ninth century Chang'an]. *Chūō Daigaku Ajiashi kenkyū* 中央大学アジア史研究, 26.

Seo Tatsuhiko 妹尾達彦 (2003). 'Ren'ai: Tōdai ni okeru atarashii ryōsei ninshiki no kōchiku' 恋愛 – 唐代における新しい両性認識の構築 [Romance: The formulation of a new gender consciousness in Tang China]. *Tōdaishi kenkyū* 唐代史研究, 6.

Shiau Han-Chen 蕭涵珍 (2009). 'Ri Gyo no shōsetsu ni okeru dōseiai: Shinjō to reikyō no kakudo kara' 李漁の小説における同性愛―真情と礼教の角度から [Homosexuality in Li Yu's fiction: From the perspectives of genuine feelings and the doctrine of ritual propriety]. *Nihon Chūgokugaku kaihō* 日本中国学会報, 61.

Shiga Shūzō 滋賀秀三 (1950). *Chūgoku kazokuhō ron* 中国家族法論 [A study of Chinese family law]. Tokyo: Kōbundō.

Shiga Shūzō 滋賀秀三 (1967). *Chūgoku kazokuhō no genri* 中国家族法の原理 [Principles of Chinese family law]. Tokyo: Sōbunsha.

Shiga Shūzō 滋賀秀三 (1979). 'Tōritsu sogi yakuchūhen 1 (Myōrei)' 唐律疏議譯註篇 1 (名例) [Tang Code with commentary and explanations translated and annotated 1 (Penalties and application rules)]. In: Ritsuryō kenkyūkai 律令研究会 (ed.), *Yakuchū Nihon ritsuryō 5* 譯註日本律令 5 [Translated and annotated Japanese law codes 5]. Tokyo: Tokyodō Shuppan.

Shiga Shūzō 滋賀秀三 (1984). *Shindai Chūgoku no hō to saiban* 清代中国の法と裁判 [Law and trial in Qing China]. Tokyo: Sōbunsha.

Shiga Shuzo 滋賀秀三 (2003) *Chūgoku hōseishi ronshū: Hōten to keibatsu* 中国法制史論集 – 法典と刑罰 [Essays on the history of Chinese law: Legal codes and penalties]. Tokyo: Sōbunsha.

Shiga Shūzō 滋賀秀三 (2009: posthumous publication). *Zoku Shindai Chūgoku no hō to saiban* 続 清代中国の法と裁判 [Law and trial in Qing China, supplementary volume]. Tokyo: Sōbunsha.

Shiga Shūzō 滋賀秀三 (ed.) (1993). *Chūgoku hōseishi: Kihon shiryō no kenkyū* 中国法制史－基本資料の研究 [History of the Chinese legal system: Study of basic materials]. Tokyo: Tokyo Daigaku Shuppankai.

Shimada Kenji 島田虔次 (1967). 'Shinchō makki ni okeru gakumon no jōkyō' 清朝末期における学問の情況 [The condition of learning at the end of the Qing dynasty]. In: *Kōza Chūgoku* 講座中国 [Studies on China], Vol. 2. Tokyo: Chikuma Shobō.

Shimizu Ken'ichirō 清水賢一郎 (trans.) (1992). 'Owarai kigeki kekkon sōdō' お笑い喜劇結婚騒動 [Uproarious comedy 'Marriage turmoil']. In: Fujii Shōzō 藤井省三 (ed.), *Warai no kyōwakoku: Chūgoku yūmoa bungaku kessaku sen* 笑いの共和国―中国ユーモア文学傑作選 [The republic of laughter: Selection of masterpieces of Chinese humorous literature]. Tokyo: Hakusuisha.

Shimokura Wataru 下倉渉 (2001). 'Kandai no haha to ko' 漢代の母と子 [Mother and child in the Han dynasty]. *Tōhoku Daigaku Tōyōshi ronshū* 東北大学東洋史論集, 8.

Shimokura Wataru 下倉渉 (2005). 'Shin Kan kan'inzai zakkō' 秦漢姦淫罪雑考 [Thoughts on the crime of adultery in the Qin and Han periods]. *Tōhoku Gakuin Daigaku ronshū (rekishigaku, chirigaku)* 東北学院大学論集 (歴史学・地理学), 39.

Shimokura Wataru 下倉渉 (2015). 'Ifu dōbo toiu kankei: Chūgoku fukei shakaishi kenkyū josetsu' 異父同母という関係―中国父系社会史研究序説 [Maternal half-siblings: Introduction to the history of patrilineal society in China]. In: Kohama Masako 小浜正子 (ed.), *Jendā no Chūgokushi* ジェンダーの中国史 [Gender in Chinese history]. Tokyo: Bensei Shuppan.

Shimomi Takao 下見隆雄 (1994). *Jukyō shakai to bosei: Bosei no iryoku no kanten de miru Kan Gi Shin Chūgoku joseishi* 儒教社会と母性：母性の威力の観点でみる漢魏晋中国女性史 [Confucian society and motherhood: A history of Chinese women in Han, Wei and Jin from the viewpoint of maternal power]. Tokyo: Kenbun Shuppan.

Shimomi Takao 下見隆雄 (2008). *Jukyō shakai to bosei: Bosei no iryoku no kanten de miru Kan Gi Shin Chūgoku joseishi (zōho ban)* 儒教社会と母性―母性の威力の観点でみる漢魏晋中国女性史（増補版）[Confucian society and materialism: A history of women in Han, Wei, Jin China from the perspective of maternal power (augmented edition)]. Tokyo: Kenbun Shuppan.

Shio Takugo 塩卓悟 and Kawamura Kōtarō 河村晃太郎 (eds) (2004). *Yakuchū Taiheikouki fujinbu* 譯注太平廣記婦人部 ['Section of women' in the *Extensive Records Assembled in the Taiping Era*, translated and annotated edition]. Tokyo: Kyūko Shoin.

Shirouzu Noriko 白水紀子 (2001). *Chūgoku josei no 20 seiki: Kingendai kafuchōsei kenkyū* 中国女性の20世紀―近現代家父長制研究 [Chinese women in the twentieth century: A study of modern patriarchy]. Tokyo: Akashi Shoten.

Shirouzu Noriko 白水紀子 (2003). 'Chūgoku bungaku ni miru "kindai kazoku" hihan' 中国文学にみる「近代家族」批判 [Criticism of the 'modern family' in Chinese literature]. *Tōyō Bunka Kenkyūjo kiyō* 東洋文化研究所紀要, 143.

Shirouzu Noriko 白水紀子 (2004a). 'Chūgoku ni okeru "kindai kokka" no keisei: Josei no kokuminka to nijū yakuwari no rekishi' 中国における『近代家族』の形成 – 女性の国民化と二重役割の歴史 [The formation of the 'modern family' in China: The history of women's citizenship and dual roles]. *Yokohama Kokuritu Daigaku Kyōiku Ningen Kagakubu kiyō 2, jinbun kagaku* 横浜国立大学教育人間科学部紀要Ⅱ人文科学, 6.

Shirouzu Noriko 白水紀子 (2004b). 'Chūgoku no sekushuaru mainoritī' 中国のセクシュアル・マイノリティー [Sexual minorities in China]. *Higashi Asia hikaku bunka kenkyū* 東アジア比較文化研究, 3.

Shirouzu Noriko 白水紀子 (2007). 'Chūgoku dōseiai shōsetsu no sakka to sono shūhen' 中国同性愛小説の作家とその周辺 [Writers of homosexual novels in China and their periphery]. In: Yamada Keizō Sensei koki kinen ronshū kankōkai 山田敬三先生古稀記念論集刊行会 (ed.) *Nankō hokuchō ronshū: Chūgoku bunka no dentō to gendai* 南腔北調論集: 中国文化の伝統と現代 [Tradition and present of Chinese culture]. Tokyo: Tōhō Shoten.

Shirouzu Noriko 白水紀子 (2015). 'Sekushariti no disukōse: Dōseiai o meguru gensetsu o chūshin ni' セクシャリティのディスコース—同性愛をめぐる言説を中心に [Discourses of sexuality: Focusing on discourses on homosexuality]. In: Kohama Masako 小浜正子 (ed.), *Jendā no Chūgokushi* ジェンダーの中国史 [Gender in Chinese history]. Tokyo: Bensei Shuppan.

Soda Saburō 曽田三郎 (1994). *Chūgoku kindai seishigyōshi no kenkyū* 中国近代製糸業史の研究 [Studies on the history of the silk industry in modern China]. Tokyo: Kyūko Shoin.

Sommer, Matthew H. (1997). 'Banki teisei Chūgoku ni okeru baishun: 18 seiki ni okeru mibun pafōmansu kara no ridatsu' 晩期帝制中国における売春—18世紀における身分パフォーマンスからの離脱 [Prostitution in late imperial Chinese law: The eighteenth century shift away from status performance], translated by Terada Hiroaki 寺田浩明. *Chūgoku: Shakai to bunka* 中国—社会と文化, 12.

Song Shaopeng 宋少鵬 (2016a). 'Gendai Chūgoku no jendā gensetsu to sei no seiji keizaigaku' 現代中国のジェンダー言説と性の政治経済学 [Gender discourse and the political economy of sex in contemporary China]. In: Kohama Masako 小浜正子 and Akiyama Yōko 秋山洋子 (eds), *Gendai Chūgoku no jendā poritikusu; Kakusa, seibaibai, 'ianfu'* 現代中国のジェンダー・ポリティクス – 格差・性売買・「慰安婦」 [Gender politics in contemporary China: Economic disparity, sex trade, 'comfort women']. Tokyo: Bensei Shuppan.

Song Shaopeng 宋少鵬 (2016b). 'Media no naka no "ianfu" disukōsu; Kigōka sareta "ianfu" to "ianfu" jojutsu ni okeru kioku/bōkyaku no mekanizumu' メディアの中の「慰安婦」ディスコース—記号化された「慰安婦」と「慰安婦」叙述における記憶/忘却のメカニズム [The 'comfort women' discourse in the media: The encoded *'ianfu'* and the recalling/forgetting mechanism in the *'ianfu'* narrative]. In: Kohama Masako 小浜正子 and Akiyama Yōko 秋山洋子 (eds), *Gendai Chūgoku no jendā poritikusu; Kakusa, seibaibai, 'ianfu'* 現代中国のジェンダー・ポリティクス – 格差・性売買・「慰安婦」 [Gender politics in contemporary China: Economic disparity, sex trade, 'comfort women']. Tokyo: Bensei Shuppan.

Sudō Mizuyo 須藤瑞代 (2002). 'Nihon ni okeru Chūgoku jōseishi kenkyū dōkō' 日本における中国女性史研究動向 [Trends in research on Chinese women's history in Japan]. *Junggugsa yeongu* 中國史研究, 18.

Sudō Mizuyo 須藤瑞代 (2007). *Chūgoku 'joken' gainen no henyō: Shinmatsu minsho no jenken to jendā* 中国「女権」概念の変容―清末民初の人権とジェンダー [Transformation of 'women's rights' (*nüquan*) in China: Human rights and gender in the late Qing to early Republican period]. Tokyo: Kenbun Shuppan.

Suetsugu Reiko 末次玲子 (2000). 'Josei no kurashi to ryōsei kankei' 女性のくらしと両性関係 [Women's lives and the gender relationship]. In: Mitani Takashi 三谷孝 et al., *Mura kara Chūgoku o yomu: Kahoku nōson 50 nen shi* 村から中国を読む―華北農村五十年史 [China from a rural perspective: Fifty years of northern Chinese villages]. Tokyo: Aoki Shoten.

Suetsugu Reiko 末次玲子 (2009). *20 seiki Chūgoku joseishi* 20世紀中国女性史 [History of Chinese women in the twentieth century]. Tokyo: Aoki Shoten.

Suetsugu Reiko 末次玲子 and Enomoto Akiko 榎本明子 (1995). 'Joseishi' 女性史 [Women's history]. In: Nozawa Yutaka 野澤豊 (ed.), *Nihon no Chūka minkokushi kenkyū* 日本の中華民国史研究 [The historical studies on Republican China in Japan]. Tokyo: Kyūko Shoin.

Taga Akigorō 多賀秋五郎 (1981). 'Sōfu seiritsu no fukusen toshiteno kofu no kenkyū' 宗譜成立の伏線としての古譜の研究 [Research on ancient genealogies as a clue to the emergence of genealogies of lineage groups]. In: *Chūgoku sōfu no kenkyū, jō kan* 中国宗譜の研究 上巻 [Studies in Chinese genealogies], Vol. 1.

Taga Futoshi 多賀太 (2001). *Dansei no jendā keisei: 'Otokorashisa' no yuragi no naka de* 男性のジェンダー形成―＜男らしさ＞の揺らぎのなかで [The gender formation of men]. Tokyo: Tōyōkan Shuppansha.

Taga Futoshi 多賀太 (2006). *Otokorasisa no shakaigaku: Yuragu otoko no raifu kōsu* 男らしさの社会学―揺らぐ男のライフコース [Sociology of masculinities: Changing men's life courses]. Kyoto: Sekai Shisōsha.

Tajima Miki 田嶋美喜 (1999). 'Sōdai no shōnō keiei ni okeru josei rōdō' 宋代の小農経営における女性労働 [Women's labor in small-scale farming operations in Song]. In: *Ronshū Chūgoku joseishi* 論集中国女性史 [Collected essays on Chinese women's history]. Tokyo: Yoshikawa Kōbunkan.

Takahashi Nobuo 高橋伸夫 (2010). 'Tō, nōson kakumei, ryosei kankei' 党、農村革命、両性関係 [Political party, rural revolution and the gender relationship]. In: Takahashi Nobuo 高橋伸夫 (ed.), *Kyūkoku, dōin, chitsujo: Henkakuki Chūgoku no seiji to shakai* 救国、動員、秩序―変革期中国の政治と社会 [National salvation, mobilization, social order: Politics and society in China's period of reform]. Tokyo: Keio Gijuku Daigaku Shuppankai.

Takahashi Yoshirō 高橋芳郎 (2007). 'Shōren wa dare no mono ka: Nansōdai o kiten ni shite' 粧奩は誰のものか―南宋代を起点にして [Who owns the dowry: From the Southern Song period]. *Shihō* 史朋, 40.

Takashima Kō 高嶋航 (2003). 'Tensoku kai to fu tensoku kai' 天足会と不纏足会 [The Natural Foot Society and the *Buchanzu hui*]. *Tōyōshi kenkyū* 東洋史研究, 62(2).

Takashima Kō 高嶋航 (2004). 'Kyōkai to shinja no aida de: Josei senkyōshi ni yoru tensoku kaihō no kokoromi' 教会と信者の間で―女性宣教師による纏足解放の試み [Between the church and the followers: Attempts to unbind feet by a female missionary]. In: Mori Tokihiko 森時彦 (ed.), *Chūgoku kindaika no dōtai kōzō* 中国近代化の動態構造 [Dynamic structure of Chinese modernization]. Kyoto: Kyoto Daigaku Gakujutsu Shuppankai.

Takashima Kō 高嶋航 (2010). '1920 nendai no Chūgoku ni okeru josei no danpatsu: Giron, fasshon, kakumei' 1920年代の中国における女性の断髪―議論・ファッション・革命 [Women's hairstyles in 1920s China: Debate, fashion and revolution]. In: Ishikawa Yoshihiro 石川禎浩 (ed.), *Chūgoku shakaishugi bunka no kenkyū* 中国社会主義文化の研究 [A study of Chinese socialist culture]. Kyoto: Kyoto Daigaku Jinbun Kagaku Kenkyūsho.

Takashima Kō 高嶋航 (2013). '"Tōa byōfu" to supōtsu: Koroniaru masukyuriti no shiten kara' 「東亜病夫」とスポーツ: コロニアル・マスキュリニティの視点から ['Sick man of East Asia' and sports: From the lens of colonial masculinity]. In: Ishikawa Yoshihiro 石川禎浩 and Hazama Naoki 狹間直樹 (eds), *Kindai Higashi Ajia ni okeru honyaku gainen no tenkai* 近代東アジアにおける翻訳概念の展開 [Development of translational concepts in modern East Asia]. Kyoto: Kyoto Daigaku Jinbunkagaku Kenkyūsho.

Takashima Kō 高嶋航 (2015a). 'Guntai to shakai no hazama de: Nihon, Chōsen, Chūgoku, Firipin no gakkō ni okeru gunji kunren' 軍隊と社会のはざまで―日本・朝鮮・中国・フィリピンの学校における軍事訓練 [Between the military and society: Military training at schools in Japan, Korea, China and the Philippines]. In: Tanaka Masakazu 田中雅一 (ed.), *Guntai no bunka jinruigaku* 軍隊の文化人類学 [Cultural anthropology of the military]. Tokyo: Fūkyōsha.

Takashima Kō 高嶋航 (2015b). 'Benpatsu to Gunpuku: Shin matsu no gunjin to danseisei no saikōchiku' 辮髪と軍服―清末の軍人と男性性の再構築 [The *queue* and the military uniform: Late Qing soldiers and the restructure of masculinity]. In: Kohama Masako 小浜正子 (ed.), *Jendā no Chūgokushi* ジェンダーの中国史 [Gender in Chinese history]. Tokyo: Bensei Shuppan.

Takashima Kō 高嶋航 (2016a). 'Naze baseball wa *bangqiu* to yakusareta ka: Honyaku kara miru kindai Chūgoku supōtsu' なぜbaseballは棒球と訳されたか―翻訳から見る近代中国スポーツ [Why baseball was translated as *bangqiu*: Modern Chinese sports from a translation perspective]. *Kyoto Daigaku Bungakubu kiyō* 京都大学文学部紀要, 55.

Takashima Kō 高嶋航 (2016b). '"Tōa byōfu" to kindai Chūgoku (1896-1949)' 「東亜病夫」と近代中国 (1896–1949) [Modern China and the 'Sick man of East Asia',1896–1949]. In: Murakami Ei 村上衛 (ed.), *Kingendai Chūgoku ni okeru shakai keizai seido no saihen* 近現代中国における社会経済制度の再編 [Reorganization of social and economic institutions in modern China]. Kyoto: Kyoto Daigaku Jinbun Kagaku Kenkyūsho.

Takeda Masaya 武田雅哉 (2007). *Yōkihi ni naritakatta otoko tachi: 'Ifuku no yōkai' no bunkashi* 楊貴妃になりたかった男たち―〈衣服の妖怪〉の文化誌 [Men wanted to be Yang Guifei: A study on cross-dress culture in China]. Tokyo: Kōdansha.

Takeda Ryūji 竹田龍兒 (1995). 'Tōdai shizoku no kahō ni tsuite' 唐代士族の家法について [Family rules of the Tang aristocracy]. *Shigaku* 史學, 28(1).

Takenami Takayoshi 竹浪隆良 (1995). 'Chūgoku kodai no fuken to fuboken ni tsuite' 中国古代の夫権と父母権について [Husband's rights and parental rights in ancient China]. In: 'Chūgoku kodai no kokka to minshū' henshū iinkai 「中国古代の国家と民衆」編集委員会編 (ed.), *Chūgoku kodai no kokka to minshū: Hori Toshikazu Sensei koki kinen* 中国古代の国家と民衆―堀敏一先生古稀記念 [The state and people in ancient China: Commemoration of Professor Toshikazu Hori's seventieth birthday]. Tokyo: Kyūko Shoin.

Tanigawa Michio 谷川道雄 (1976). 'Hokuchō kizoku no seikatsu rinri' 北朝貴族の生活倫理 [The 'community' ethic of the Northern Dynasties aristocracy]. *Chūgoku chūsei shakai to kyōdōtai* 中国中世社会と共同体 [Medieval Chinese society and the local community]. Tokyo: Kokusho Kankōkai.

Terada Hiroaki 寺田浩明 (2018). *Chūgoku Hōseisshi* 中国法制史 [China's traditional legal order]. Tokyo: Tokyo Daigaku Shuppankai.

Tokunaga Yōsuke 德永洋介 (1998). 'Sōdai no gyohitsu shushō' 宋代の御筆手詔 [Imperial edicts from the emperor himself during the Song period]. *Tōyōshi kenkyū* 東洋史研究, 57(3).

Tokyo Teikoku Daigaku 東京帝国大学 (ed.) (1919). *Tokyo Teikoku Daigaku ichiran ju Taishō 7 nen shi Taishō 8 nen* 東京帝国大学一覧 従大正七年至大正八年 [Tokyo Imperial University Yearbook 1918–1919]. Tokyo: Tokyo Teikoku Daigaku.

Tōyama Hideya 遠山日出也 (2010). 'Chūgoku ni okeru sekushuaru mainoriti o meguru seisaku to undo' 中国におけるセクシュアル・マイノリティをめぐる政策と運動 [Policy and movements of sexual minorities in China]. *Chikaki ni arite* 近きに在りて, 58.

Tōyama Hideya 遠山日出也 (2013). 'Chūgoku no wakai kōdōha feminisuto no katsudō to sono tokuchō: "Jendā byōdō syōdō, akushon nettowāku" o megutte' 中国の若い行動派フェミニストの活動とその特徴―「ジェンダー平等唱導・アクションネットワーク」をめぐって [Activism of young Chinese feminists and its characteristics: On the 'gender equality advocacy and action network']. *Joseigaku nenpō* 女性学年報, 34.

Tōyama Hideya 遠山日出也 (2015). 'Kinnen no Chūgoku ni okeru LGBT undo to feminisuto kōdō ha' 近年の中国におけるLGBT運動とフェミニスト行動派 [LGBT movements and feminist activists in China in recent years]. *Gendai shisō* 現代思想, 43–16.

Tōyama Hideya 遠山日出也 (2016). 'Feminisuto kōdō ha no undo to sono tokuchō: 2012-nen 2 gatsu ~ 2016-nen 4 gatsu' フェミニスト行動派の運動とその特徴−2012年2月~2016年4月 [Feminist activist movements and their characteristics: February 2012–April 2016]. In: Kohama Masako 小浜正子 and Akiyama Yōko 秋山洋子 (eds), *Gendai Chūgoku ni okeru jendā poritikusu: Kakusa, seibaibai, 'ianfu'* 現代中国のジェンダー・ポリティクス：格差・性売買・「慰安婦」 [Gender politics in contemporary China: Economic disparity, sex trade, 'comfort women']. Tokyo: Bensei Shuppan.

Toyofuku Kenji 豊福健二 (1976). '*Sesetsu* "Ken'en" hen to *Shinjo* "Retsujo den"' 世説「賢媛」篇と晋書「列女伝」['Wise women' in *A New Account of the Tales of the World* and 'Collected biographies of women' in the *History of the Jin*]. In: Obi Hakushi taikyū kinen ronbunshū henshū iinkai 小尾博士退休記念論文集編集委員会編 (ed.), *Obi Hakushi taikyū kinen Chūgoku bungaku ronshū* 小尾博士退休記念中國文學論集 [Collected essays on Chinese literature commemorating Dr. Obi's retirement]. Hiroshima: Daiichi Gakushūsha.

Ueda Sanae 上田早苗 (1979). 'Kandai no kazoku to sono rōdō: Fukō fuseki ni tsuite' 漢代の家族とその労働―夫耕婦續について [Family and labor in the Han period: Men till and women weave]. *Shirin* 史林, 62(3).

Umemura Keiko 梅村恵子 (2007). *Kazoku no kodaishi: Ren'ai kekkon kosodate* 家族の古代史―恋愛・結婚・子育て [The ancient history of the family: Love, marriage, child-rearing]. Tokyo: Yoshikawa Kōbunkan.

Uno Nobuhiro 宇野伸浩 (2014). 'Mongoru teikoku no kōgō to Chingisuke no kon'in senryaku' モンゴル帝国の皇后とチンギス家の婚姻戦略 [Empresses of the Mongolian Empire and the marriage strategy of Genghis's family]. In: Mitsunari Miho 三成美保 Himeoka Toshiko 姫岡とし子 and Kohama Masako 小浜正子 (eds), *Rekishi o yomikaeru: Jendā kara mita sekai shi* 歴史を読み替えるジェンダーから見た世界史 [Reinterpreting world history: From the gender perspective]. Tokyo: Ōtsuki Shoten.

Usui Sachiko 臼井佐知子 (2007). 'Saiban kankei bunsho kara mita Kishū shakai no ichi sokumen: Otto no shigo, kafu wa ikani shite ikita ka' 裁判関係文書からみた徽州社会の一側面—夫の死後、寡婦はいかにして生きたか [An aspect of Huizhou society seen in judicial documents: How widows lived after their husbands' death]. In: Futaki Hiroshi 二木博史 (ed.), *Monjo shiryō kara mita zen kindai Ajia no shakai to kenryoku* 文書史料からみた前近代アジアの社会と権力 [Pre-modern Asian society and power seen in historical documents]. http://repository.tufs.ac.jp/bitstream/10108/24609/1/zaichi_web.pdf. Tokyo: Tokyo Gaikokugo Daigaku Daigakuin Chiikibunka kenkyūka 21 seiki COE puroguramu 'Shi shiryō habu chiiki bunka kenkyū kyoten' honbu 東京外国語大学大学院地域文化研究科21世紀COEプログラム「史資料ハブ地域文化研究拠点」本部.

Wakabayashi Keiko 若林敬子 (2005). *Chūgoku no jinkō mondai to shakaiteki genjitsu* 中国の人口問題と社会的現実 [Population problems and social reality in China]. Kyoto: Minerva Shobō.

Wakabayashi Keiko 若林敬子 (ed.) (2006). *Chūgoku jinko mondai no ima: Chūgokujin kenkyūsha no siten kara* 中国人口問題のいま—中国人研究者の視点から [The current state of Chinese population problems: A Chinese researcher's perspective]. Kyoto: Minerva Shobō.

Wang Danning 王丹凝, Wang Zheng 王政 and Xu Wu 徐午 (2014). 'Grōbaru to rōkaru o kakyō suru koto: Diasupora no Chūgoku feminiusto' グローバルとローカルを架橋すること—ディアスポラの中国フェミニスト [Bridging the local with the global: Chinese feminists in diaspora]. *Jendā shigaku* ジェンダー史学, 10.

Wang Hui 汪暉 (2011). *Kindai Chūgoku shisō no seisei* 近代中国思想の生成 [Rise of Chinese modern thought], translated by Ishii Tsuyoshi 石井剛. Tokyo: Iwanami Shoten. (Japanese abridged translation of Wang (2008) and full translation of selected essays in Wang (2010).)

Wang Zheng 王政 (2016). '"Josei ishiki" to "shakai seibetsu ishiki": Gendai Chūgoku feminizumu shisō no ichibunseki' 〈女性意識〉と〈社会性別意識〉 –現代中国フェミニズム思想の一分析 ['Women's consciousness' and 'social gender consciousness': An analysis of feminist thought in contemporary China]. In: Kohama Masako 小浜正子 and Akiyama Yōko 秋山洋子 (eds), *Gendai Chūgoku no jendā poritikusu: Kakusa, seibaibai, 'ianfu'* 現代中国のジェンダー・ポリティクス－格差・性売買・「慰安婦」 [Gender politics in contemporary China: Economic disparity, sex trade, 'comfort women']. Tokyo: Bensei Shuppan.

Washino Masaaki 鷲野正明 (1995). '"Teijo" no hakken: Ki Yukō no "Teijo ron" to seppu reppuden' 「貞女」の発見—帰有光の「貞女論」と節婦・烈婦伝 [Discovery of 'faithful maidens': Gui Youguang's '*Zhengnü lun*' (discourse on faithful maidens) and '*Jiefu liefu zhuan*' (biographies of chastely martyred wives)]. *Kokushikan Daigaku Bungakubu Jinbun Gakkai kiyō* 国士舘大学文学部人文学会紀要, 27.

Washio Yūko 鷲尾祐子 (2015). 'Bun'i no jiki to kazoku kōsei no henka ni tsuite: Chōsa Go kan ni yoru kentō' 分異の時期と家族構成の変化について—長沙呉簡による検討 [The timing of family branching and change in family composition: An examination of the Changsha bamboo slips of Wu]. In: Itō Toshio 伊藤敏雄 et al. (eds), *Konan shutsudo kandoku to sono shakai* 湖南出土簡牘とその社会 [A study of the wooden-bamboo manuscripts and community of Hunan Province]. Tokyo: Kyūko Shoin.

Watabe Takeshi 渡部武 (1987). *Chūgoku nōsho 'Koshokuzu' no ruden to sono eikyō ni tsuite* 中国農書「耕織図」の流伝とその影響について [Propagation of agronomic book '*Pictures of Tilling and Weaving*' and its impact]. Grant-in-Aid for Scientific Research Report, No. 60510185.

Watanabe Hiroshi 渡辺浩 (2016). *Higashi Ajia no ōken to shisō zōho shinsō ban* 東アジアの王権と思想 増補新装版 [Confucianism and after: Political thoughts in early-modern East Asia, augmented and renewed version]. Tokyo: Tokyo Daigaku Shuppankai.

Watanabe Shinichirō 渡辺信一郎 (1986). *Chūgoku kodai shakairon* 中国古代社会論 [Ancient Chinese society]. Tokyo: Aoki Shoten.

Wong Yu-Hsuan 翁育瑄 (2000). '7 seiki kara 10 seiki hajime no Chūgoku ni okeru jōryū kaikyū no kazoku keitai: Boshi o chūshin ni' 七世紀〜十世紀初の中國における上流階級の家族形態—墓誌を中心に [Elite family forms in seventh to early tenth century China as seen in epitaphs]. *Ochanomizu shigaku* お茶の水史学, 44.

Wong Yu-Hsuan 翁育瑄 (2001). 'Tōdai ni okeru kannin kaikyū no konin keitai: Boshi o chūshin ni' 唐代における官人階級の婚姻形態—墓誌を中心に [Marriage forms of Tang officials as seen in epitaphs]. *Tōyōgakuhō* 東洋学報, 83(2).

Wong Yu-Hsuan 翁育瑄 (2003). 'Tō Sō boshi kara mita josei no shusetsu to saikon ni tsuite: Mibōjin no sentaku to sono seikatsu' 唐宋墓誌から見た女性の守節と再婚について—未亡人の選択とその生活 [Female chastity and remarriage as seen in Tang-Song epitaphs: Choices for widows and their widowed life]. *Tōdaishi kenkyū* 唐代史研究, 6.

Wong Yu-Hsuan 翁育瑄 (2006). 'Sōdai no kanzai' 宋代の姦罪 [Sex crimes in Song]. *Ochanomizu shigaku* お茶の水史学, 50.

Wong Yu-Hsuan 翁育瑄 (2012). 'Tōdai no shuboku kankei: Hikki shōsetsu o rei toshite' 唐代の主僕関係—筆記小説を例として [The master-servant relationship in Tang China: Reading miscellaneous stories]. *Hikaku Nihongaku Kyōiku Kenkyū Sentā kenkyū nenpō* 比較日本学教育研究センター研究年報, 8.

Yamazaki Jun'ichi 山崎純一 (1967). 'Shinchō ni okeru setsuretsu seihyō ni tsuite: Dōki retsujo den kankō no haikei' 清朝における節烈旌表について—同期列女伝刊行の背景 [*Jielie jingbiao* of Qing: Backgrounds of publishing biographies of exemplary women in the Qing dynasty]. *Chūgoku koten kenkyū* 中国古典研究, 15.

Yamazaki Jun'ichi 山崎純一 (1996–97). *Retsujo den* 列女伝, 3 volumes. [*Biographies of Exemplary Women* by Liu Xiang]. Tokyo: Meiji Shoin.

Yanagida Setsuko 柳田節子 (1993). 'Sōdai no joko' 宋代の女戸 [Women's households in Song]. In: Yanagida Setsuko Sensei koki kinen ronshū henshū iinkai 柳田節子先生古稀記念論集編集委員会 (ed.), *Chūgoku no dentō shakai to kazoku* 中国の伝統社会と家族 [Traditional society and family in China]. Tokyo: Kyūko Shoin. (Reprinted in Yanagida Setsuko 柳田節子 (2003). *Sōdai shomin no onnatachi* 宋代庶民の女たち [Common women in Song]. Tokyo: Kyūko Shoin.)

Yao Yi 姚毅 (2010a). 'Kindai Chūgoku ni okeru josan ryōiki no senmonshokuka to jendā' 近代中国における助産領域の専門職化とジェンダー [Professionalization of birth assistance and gender in modern China]. *Chūgoku: Shakai to bunka* 中国—社会と文化, 25.

Yao Yi 姚毅 (2010b). 'Boshi eisei shisutemu no renzoku to tenkan: Kenkoku zengo no Pekinshi o chūshin ni' 母子衛生システムの連続と転換—建国前後の北京市を中心に [Continuity and change in the maternal and child healthcare system in China: A case of Beijing City before and after the foundation of the PRC]. *Chikaki ni ari te* 近きに在りて, 58.

Yao Yi 姚毅 (2011). *Kindai Chūgoku no shussan to kokka, shakai: Ishi, josanshi, sesseiba* 近代中国の出産と国家・社会—医師・助産士・接生婆 [Childbirth, state and society in modern China: Doctors, professional midwives (*zhuchanshi*) and midwifery practitioners (*jieshengpo*)]. Tokyo: Kenbun Shuppan.

Yao Yi 姚毅 (2015). 'Chūgoku ni okeru dairi shussan to "bosei": Gendai no "karibara"' 中国における代理出産と『母性』 — 現代の『借り腹』 [Surrogacy and 'motherhood' in China: 'Borrowed womb' at the present day]. In: Kohama Masako 小浜正子 (ed.), *Jendā no Chūgokushi* ジェンダーの中国史 [Gender in Chinese history]. Tokyo: Bensei Shuppan.

Yao Yi 姚毅 (2016). '"Hadashi no isha" no shikaku hyōshō to jendā' 「はだしの医者」の視角表象とジェンダー [A visual representation of 'barefoot doctors' and gender]. In: Chūgoku joseishi kenkyūkai 中国女性史研究会 (ed.), *Chūgoku no media hyōshō to jendā* 中国のメディア・表象とジェンダー [Media, representations and gender in China]. Tokyo: Kenbun Shuppan.

Yoshida Kōichi 吉田浤一 (2012). *Chūgoku sensei kokka to kazoku, shakai ninshiki* 中国専制国家と家族・社会認識 [Chinese authoritarian state and perceptions of family and society]. Kyoto: Bunrikaku.

Yoshida Yutaka 吉田豊 and Arakawa Masaharu 荒川正晴 (2009). 'Sogudo no josei to kekkon (8 seiki hajime)' ソグドの女性と結婚（八世紀初） [Sogdian women and marriage (early eighth century)]. In: Rekishigaku kenkyūkai 歴史学研究会 (ed.), *Sekaishi shiryō 3: Higashi Ajiia, Nairiku Ajia, Tōnan Ajia I* 世界史史料3—東アジア・内陸アジア・東南アジアI [World history: Historical materials 3: East Asia, Inner Asia, Southeast Asia I]. Tokyo: Iwanami Shoten.

Yoshizawa Seiichirō 吉澤誠一郎 (2003). *Aikoku shugi no sōsei: nashonarizumu kara kindai Chūgoku o miru* 愛国主義の創成—ナショナリズムから近代中国をみる [Formation of patriotism: Modern China from the perspective of nationalism]. Tokyo: Iwanami Shoten.

Yoshizawa Seiichirō 吉澤誠一郎 (2014). 'Shin matsu Chūgoku ni okeru dansei sei no kōchiku to Nihon' 清末中国における男性性の構築と日本 [Construction of masculinity in late Qing China and Japan]. *Chūgoku: Shakai to bunka* 中国—社会と文化, 29.

Yu Ning 于寧 (2017). 'Peking Kuia eiga ten: Gendai Chūgoku ni okeru seiteki shōsūsha no bunka seiji ni tsuite' 北京酷児映画展—現代中国における性的少数者の文化政治について [Beijing Queer Film Festival: On the cultural politics of sexual minorities in present-day China]. *Onnatachi no 21 seiki* 女たちの21世紀, 90.

Yu Ping 虞萍 (2010). *Hyōshin kenkyū: Josei, shi, kekkon* 冰心研究—女性・死・結婚 [Study of Bingxin: Women, death, marriage]. Tokyo: Kyūko Shoin.

Yuasa Yukihiko 湯浅幸孫 (1981). *Chūgoku rinri shisō no kenkyū* 中国倫理思想の研究 [A study of Chinese ethics]. Kyoto: Dōhōsha.
Zhao Lingzhi 趙令志 (2006). 'Shindai no shūjo senbatsu seido ni tsuite' 清代の秀女選抜制度 について [The system of selection of *xiunü* in the Qing dynasty]. *Daito Ajiagaku ronshū* 大東アジア学論集, 6.

Chinese

Akiyama Yōkō 秋山洋子, Egami Sachiko 江上幸子, Maeyama Kanako 前山加奈子 and Tabata Sawako 田畑佐和子 (2017). *Tansuo Ding Ling* 探索丁玲 [Searching for Ding Ling]. Taipei: Renjian chubanshe.
Barlow, Tani E. 汤尼 白露 (2012). *Zhongguo nüquan sixiang zhong de funü wenti* 中国女权思想中的妇女问题 [The question of women in Chinese feminism], translated by Shen Qiqi 沈齐齐 and supervised by Li Xiaojiang 李小江. Shanghai: Shanghai renmin chubanshe.
Beijing daxue kaoguxuexi Shang Zhou zu, Shanxi sheng kaogu yanjiusuo 北京大学考古学系商周组·山西省考古研究所 (ed.) (2000). *Tianma: Qucun 1980-1989* 天马一区村 1980-1989 [Tianma – Qucun 1980–1989], Vol. 2. Beijing: Kexue chubanshe.
Beijing daxue kaoguxuexi, Shanxi sheng kaogu yanjiusuo 北京大学考古学系·山西省考古研究所 (1994). 'Tianma: Qucun yizhi Beizhao Jin Hou mudi disici fajue' 天马一区村遗址北赵晋侯基地第四次发掘 [The fourth excavation study of Beizhao Jin Hou cemeteries at the Tianma-Qucun site]. *Wenwu* 文物, 8.
Cai Hongsheng 蔡鸿生 (1995). '"Songhongzhuang" song' "颂红妆"颂 [Ode for 'an Ode for a Beauty']. In: Zhongshan daxue lishixi 中山大学历史系·Hu Shouwei 胡守为 (eds), *Liu Rushi biezhuan yu guoxue yanjiu; jinian Chen Yinke jiaoshou xueshu taolunhui lunwenji*《柳如是别传》与国学研究—纪念陈寅恪教授学术讨论会论文集 [*Unofficial biography of Liu Rushi* and Chinese national studies: Collected essays based on presentations at the symposium commemorating Prof. Chen Yinke]. Zhejiang: Zhejiang renmin chubanshe.
Cai Qingyuan 蔡庆远 (ed.) (2011). *Du Fangqin xueshu huodong nianbiao (1985–2009)* 杜芳琴学术活动年表 (1985–2009) [Chronology of Du Fangqin's academic career (1985–2009)], self-published.
Cai Yiping 蔡一平, Wang Zheng 王政 and Du Fangqin 杜芳琴 (eds) (2000). *Fu lishi yanjiu yi shehui xingbie* 赋历史研究以社会性别 [Historical studies by gender]. Tianjin: Funüshi xueke jianshe shoujie dushu yantaoban zhuanji (restricted publication).
Ch'en Chieh-Hsien 陈捷先 (1989). 'Tangdai zupu lueshuo' 唐代族谱略说 [An overview of Tang genealogy]. In: *Tangdai yanjiu xuezhe lianyihui* 唐代研究学者联谊会 (ed.), *Diyijie guoji Tangdai xueshu huiyi lunwenji* 第一届国际唐代学术会议论文集 [Papers from the first International Tang Studies Conference]. Taipei: Zhonghua minguo Tangdai yanjiu xuezhe lianyihui.
Chang Wen-Chang 张文昌 (2012). *Zhi li yi jiao tianxia: Tang-Song lishu yu guojia shehui* 制礼以教天下—唐宋礼书与国家社会 [Establishing *li* to civilize *tianxia*: Ritual books and historical changes in Tang-Song China]. Taipei: Taida chuban zhongxin.

Chang Yu-Fa 张玉法 (1992). 'Xinwenhua yundong shiqi dui Zhongguo jiating wenti de taolun 1915–1923' 新文化运动时期对中国家庭问题的讨论 1915–1923 [The Chinese family debate in the New Culture Movement era 1915–1923]. In: *Jinshi jiazu yu zhengzhi bijiao lishi lunwen ji xia* 近世家族与政治比较历史论文集 下 [Family process and political process in modern Chinese history], Vol. 2. Taipei: Zhongyang yanjiuyuan jindaishi yanjiusuo.

Changsha jiandu bowuguan 长沙简牍博物馆, Zhongguo wenwu yanjiusuo 中国文物研究所 and Beijing daxue lishixuexi 北京大学历史学系 (2003). 'Zhujian 1' 竹简 壹 [Bamboo slips One], (1–3). In: *Changsha zoumalou sanguo Wujian* 长沙走马楼三国吴简 [Wu state's wooden and bamboo slip documents unearthed in Zoumalou, Changsha City]. Beijing: Wenwu chubanshe.

Changsha jiandu bowuguan 长沙简牍博物馆, Zhongguo wenwu yanjiusuo 中国文物研究所 and Beijing daxue lixuexi 北京大学历史学系 (2007). 'Zhujian 2' 竹简 貳 [Bamboo slips Two], (1–3). In: *Changsha zoumalou sanguo Wujian* 长沙走马楼三国吴简 [Wu state's wooden and bamboo slip documents unearthed in Zoumalou, Changsha City]. Beijing: Wenwu chubanshe.

Changsha jiandu bowuguan 长沙简牍博物馆, Zhongguo wenwu yanjiusuo 中国文物研究所 and Beijing daxue lishixuexi 北京大学历史学系 (2008). 'Zhujian 3' 竹简 叄 [Bamboo slips Three], (1–3). In: *Changsha zoumalou sanguo wujian* 长沙走马楼三国吴简 [Wu state's wooden and bamboo slip documents unearthed in Zoumalou, Changsha City]. Beijing: Wenwu chubanshe.

Chen Chao-jung 陈昭容 (2009). 'Xingbie, shenfen yu caifu' 性别、身份与财富 [Gender, status and wealth]. In: Lee Jen-der 李贞德 (ed.), *Zhongguoshi xinlun Xingbieshi fence* 中国史新论 性别史分册 [New perspectives on Chinese history: Gender history]. Taipei: Lianjing chuban.

Chen Dezheng 陈德徵 (1921). 'Jiazu zhidu de pochan guan' 家族制度的破产观 [The bankruptcy of the family institution]. *Funü zazhi* 妇女杂志, 7(5). (Compiled in Mei Sheng (1923), Vol. 3.)

Chen Dongyuan 陈东原 (1928). *Zhongguo funü shenghuoshi* 中国妇女生活史 [A history of the lives of Chinese women]. Shanghai: Shangwu yinshuguan.

Chen Gaohua 陈高华 (2008). 'Yuanchao de gongnü' 元朝的宫女 [Royal palace maidservants in the Yuan dynasty]. *Wenshi zhishi* 文史知识, 326.

Chen Gaohua 陈高华 (2011). *Zhongguo funü tongshi: Yuan dai pian* 中国妇女通史·元代篇 [The general history of Chinese women: The Yuan dynasty]. Hangzhou: Hangzhou chubanshe.

Chen Gaohua 陈高华 and Tong Shaosu 童芍素 (eds) (2010–2011). *Zhongguo funü tongshi* 中国妇女通史 [The general history of Chinese women]. Hangzhou: Hangzhou chubanshe.

Chen Guidi 陈桂棣 and Chun Tao 春桃 (2004). *Zhongguo nongmin diaocha* 中国农民调查 [An investigative report on the Chinese peasantry]. Taipei: Dadi chubanshe.

Chen Guyuan 陈顾远 (1920). 'Jiazu zhidu di piping' 家族制度底批评 [Criticism of the family system]. *Jiating yanjiu* 家庭研究, 1(1). (Compiled in Mei Sheng (1923), Vol. 3.)

Chen Hwei-Syin 陈惠馨 (2005). '*Tanglü* zhong jiating yu geren de guanxi: Touguo jiaoyu yu fazhi jiangou "jianei zhixu"' 《唐律》中家庭与个人的关系—透过教育与法制建构「家内秩序」 [The relationship between family and individual in the *Tanglü*: Reconstructing 'family order' through analysis of education and laws]. In: Kao Ming-Shih 高明士 (ed.), *Dongya chuantong jiali, jiaoyu yu guofa (2): Jianei zhixu yu guofa* 东亚传统家礼、教育与国法 (二): 家内秩序与国法 [Traditional family rituals, education and state law in East Asia (2): Family order and state law]. Taipei: Taida chuban zhongxin.

Chen Jing 陈敬 (ed.) (1984). *Wu-zhengfu zhuyi zai Zhongguo* 无政府主义在中国 [Anarchism in China]. Changsha: Hunan renmin chubanshe.

Chen Jo-Shui 陈弱水 (1997). 'Shitan Tangdai funü yu benjia de guanxi' 试探唐代妇女与本家的关系 [Women and their natal families in Tang China: A preliminary investigation]. *Zhongyang yanjiuyuan lishi yuyan yanjiusuo jikan* 中央研究院历史语言研究所集刊, 68(1).

Chen Jo-Shui 陈弱水 (2003). 'Taiwan xuehui Tang-Song funü shi yanjiu de keti yu quxiang' 台湾学会唐宋妇女史研究的课题与取向 [Trends and challenges for the study of the history of Tang-Song women in Taiwan]. *Tangdaishi yanjiu* 唐代史研究, 6.

Chen Jo-Shui 陈弱水 (2004). 'Xiaoshuo suojian de Tangdai funü yu benjia' 小说所见的唐代妇女与本家 [Married Tang women and their natal families in novels]. In: Pao Chia-Lin 鲍家鳞 (ed.), *Zhongguo funü shilunji* 中国妇女史论集 [Studies in the history of Chinese women], Vol. 6. Taipei: Daoxiang chubanshe.

Chen Jo-Shui 陈弱水 (2007). *Tangdai de funü wenhua yu jiating shenghuo* 唐代的妇女文化与家庭生活 [Women's culture and family life in Tang China]. Taipei: Yunchen wenhua.

Chen Peifen 陈佩芬 (2004). *Xia-Shang-Zhou qingtong qi yanjiu: Xizhou pian* 夏商周青铜器研究 西周篇 [Studies of Xia-Shang-Zhou bronzes]. Shanghai: Shanghai guji chubanshe.

Chen Wenhua 陈文华 (ed. and annot.) (1984). *Tang nü shiren ji sanzhong* 唐女诗人集三种 [Three women poets of Tang]. Shanghai: Shanghai guji chubanshe.

Chen Wenlian 陈文联 and Li Guimei 李桂梅 (2003). 'Lun Wusi-shiqi tanqiu jiating biange de shehui sichao' 论五四时期探求家庭变革的社会思潮 [Social trends seeking family reform in the May-Fourth era]. *Shehui kexue jikan* 社会科学辑刊, 146.

Chen Xiefen 陈撷芬 (1903). 'Duli pian' 独立篇 [Essay on independence]. *Nüxue bao* 女学报, 1.

Chen Yan 陈雁 (2006). '"Dayuejin" yu 1950-niandai Zhongguo chengshi nüxing zhiye fazhan: yi Shanghai Baoxingli wei zhongxin de yanjiu' '大跃进'与1950年代中国城市女性职业发展—以上海宝兴里为中心的研究 [The great leap forward and the development of women's occupations in Chinese cities in the 1950s: A study of Baoxing-li, Shanghai]. In: Wu Jingping 吴景平 and Xu Siyan 徐思彦 (eds), *1950-niandai de Zhongguo* 1950年代的中国 [China in the 1950s]. Shanghai: Fudan daxue chubanshe.

Chen Yingke 陈寅恪 (1980). *Liu Rushi biezhuan* 柳如是别传 [Unofficial biography of Liu Rushi], 3 vols. Shanghai: Shanghai guji chubanshe.

Cheng Ling-Fang 成令方 (2002). 'Xingbie, yishi zhuanye he geren xuanze' 性别·医师专业和个人选择 [Gender, medical profession and personal choice]. *Nüxue xuezhi* 女学学志, 14.

Cheng Ya-Ju 郑雅如 (2001). *Qinggan yu zhidu: Wei-Jin shidai de muzi guanxi* 情感与制度: 魏晋时代的母子关系 [Emotions and institutions: The bond between mothers and sons in Wei-Jin China]. Taipei: Taida chuban zhongxin.

Cheng Ya-Ju 郑雅如 (2009). 'Zhongguo shiqi de muzi guanxi: Xingbie yu Han-Tang zhijian de jiatingshi yanjiu' 中国时期的母子关系—性别与汉唐之间的家庭史研究 [Mothers and sons in early Imperial China: Rethinking family history]. In: Lee Jen-Der 李贞德 (ed.), *Zhongguo shi xinlun: Xingbieshi fence* 中国史新论: 性别史分册 [New perspectives on Chinese history: Gender history]. Taipei: Lianjing chuban.

Cheng Ya-Ju 郑雅如 (2010). '"Zhongyanghua" zhihou: Tangdai Fan-yang Lu-shi dafang baosuxi de juzhu xingtai yu qianyi' 「中央化」之后—唐代范阳卢氏大房宝素系的居住形态与迁移 [After 'centralization': The inhabitation and migration of the Fan-yang Lu family *paosu fang* in Tang China]. *Zaoqi zhongguoshi yanjiu* 早期中国史研究, 2(2).

Cheng Ya-Ju 郑雅如 (2016). 'Tangdai shizu nüer yu jiazu guangrong: Cong Tianbao si'nian "Chen Zhao muzhi" tanqi' 唐代士族女儿与家族光荣—从天宝四年<陈照墓志>谈起 [Aristocratic daughters and family pride in the Tang dynasty: A study over the epitaph of Chen Zhao]. *Zhongyang yanjiuyuan lishi yuyan yanjiusuo jikan* 中央研究院历史语言研究所集刊, 87(1).

Cheng Yu 程郁 (2003). 'Jin ershinian Zhongguo dalu Qing dai nüxingshi yanjiu zongshu' 近二十年中国大陆清代女性史研究综述 [A review of studies of the history of Qing women in mainland China in the last twenty years]. *Jindai zhongguo funüshi yanjiu* 近代中国妇女史研究, 10.

Cheng Yu 程郁 (2006). '80 niandai hou kaipi de xin lingyu: Song dai shehui yanjiu' 八〇年代后开辟的新领域—宋代社会研究 [A new field opened up after the 1980s: Studies of Song society]. In: Zhu Ruixi 朱瑞熙 and Cheng Yu 程郁, *Song shi yanjiu* 宋史研究 [Studies of Song history]. Fuzhou: Fujian renmin chubanshe.

Chou Chun-Yen 周春燕 (2010). *Nüti yu guozu: Qiangguoqiangzhong yu jindai Zhongguo de funü weisheng (1895–1949)* 女体与国族—强国强种与近代中国的妇女卫生 (1895–1949) [Women's bodies and the nation's folk: 'Strong nation, strong race' and modern Chinese women's hygiene (1895–1949)]. Taipei: Guoli zhengzhi daxue lishi xuexi.

Deng Xiaonan 邓小南 (2004). '"Neiwai" zhi ji yu "zhixu": Songdai funü, Fulu: Song dai funüshi yanjiu huigu' "内外"之际与"秩序" — 宋代妇女 附录: 宋代妇女史研究回顾 [The border of 'inner and outer' and the gender 'order': Song women, Appendix: Review of studies on Song women]. In: Du Fangqin 杜芳琴 and Wang Zheng 王政 (eds), *Zhongguo lishi zhong de funü yu xingbie* 中国历史中的妇女与性别 [Women and gender in Chinese history]. Tianjin: Tianjin renmin chubanshe.

Deng Xiaonan 邓小南 (2009). 'Yanying zhijian: Songdai shangshu neisheng guankui' 掩映之间—宋代尚书内省管窥 [Amidst the shadows: A glance at the inner court secretariat in the Song period]. *Hanxue yanjiu* 汉学研究, 27(2).

Ding Yizhuang 定宜庄 and Guo Songyi 郭松義 (2005). *Qing dai minjian hunshu yanjiu* 清代民间婚书研究 [A study of marriage contracts in Qing China]. Beijing: Renmin chubanshe.

Du Fangqin 杜芳琴 (2008). 'Sanshi nian huimou: Funü/xingbieshi yanjiu he xueke jianshe zai Zhongguo dalude fazhan' 三十年回眸—妇女/性别史研究和学科建设在中国大陆的发展 [Reflecting on the last thirty years: Women's/gender studies and its development as an academic discipline in mainland China]. *Shanxi shida bao (shehui kexue ban)* 山西师大报 (社会科学版), June.

Du Fangqin 杜芳琴 (ed.) (2001). *Yinru shehui xingbie: Shixue fazhan xin qushi* 引入社会性别—史学发展新趋势 [Introducing gender: New trend in the development of historical studies]. Tianjin: Funüshi xueke jianshe shoujie dushu yantaoban zhuanji (restricted publication).

Du Fangqin 杜芳琴 and Wang Zhen 王政 (eds) (2004). *Zhongguo lishi zhong de funü yu xingbie* 中国历史中的妇女与性别 [Women and gender in Chinese history]. Tianjin: Tanjin renmin chubanshe.

Egami Sachiko 江上幸子 (2006). 'Xiandai Zhongguo de "xinfunü" huayu yu zuowei "modeng nülang" daiyanren de Ding Ling' 现代中国的"新妇女"话语与作为"摩登女郎"代言人的丁玲 ['Xin funü' discourse in contemporary China and Ding Ling as a spokesperson of 'modern girls']. *Zhongguo xiandai wenxue yanjiu congkan* 中国现代文学研究丛刊, 109.

Eluosi kexueyuan dongfang yanjiusuo 俄罗斯科学院东方研究所 et al. (ed.) (1992–2001). *Eluosi kexueyuan dongfang yanjiusuo Sheng Bidebao fensuo cang Dunhuang wenxian* 俄罗斯科学院东方研究所圣彼得堡分所藏敦煌文献 [Dunhuang Documents held at the St Petersburg Branch of the Russian Academy of Sciences Eastern Studies Institute], 1(17). Shanghai: Shanghai guji chubanshe.

Fang Gang 方刚 (2008). *Nanxing yanjiu yu nanxing yundong* 男性研究与男性运动 [Men's studies and men's movements]. Jinan: Shandong renmin chubanshe.

Fu Xiaoxing 富晓星 (2012). *Kongjian, wenhua, biaoyan: Dongbei A-shi nan tongxinglian qunti de renleixue guancha* 空间, 文化, 表演: 东北A市男同性恋群体的人类学观察 [Space, culture, performance: An anthropological study of gay men's communities in a city in northeast China]. Beijing: Guangming ribao chubanshe.

Fujii Shizue 藤井志津枝 (ed.) (1995). *Jindai Zhongguo funüshi riwen ziliao mulu* 近代中国妇女史日文资料目录 [Catalogue of Japanese-language materials on the history of women in modern China]. Taipei: Zhongyang yanjiuyuan jindaishi yanjiusuo.

Gansu sheng wenwu dui 甘肃省文物队 et al. (1985). *Jiayuguan bihuamu fajue baogao* 嘉峪关壁画墓发掘报告 [Jiayuguan tomb murals excavation report]. Beijing: Wenwu chubanshe.

Gao Shiyu 高世瑜 (1988). *Tangdai funü* 唐代妇女 [Women in the Tang dynasty]. Xi'an: Sanqin chubanshe.

Gao Shiyu 高世瑜 (2015). 'Cong funü shi dao funü/xingbieshi: Xin shiji funü shi xueke de xin fazhan' 从妇女史到妇女/性别史—新世纪妇女史学科的新发展 [From women's history to women's/gender history: New development in the women's history department in the new millennium]. *Funü yanjiu luncong* 妇女研究论丛, 3.

Gao Xiaoxian 高小贤 (2005). '"Yinhua sai": 20-shiji 50-niandai nongcun funü de xingbie fengong' "银花赛"—20世纪50年代农村妇女的性别分工 [The silver flower contest: Rural women in 1950s China and the gendered division of labor]. *Shehuixue yanjiu* 社会学研究, 2005(4).

Gao Yanning 高燕宁 (2006). *Tongxinglian jiankang ganyu* 同性恋健康干预 [Health intervention for homosexuals]. Shanghai: Fudan daxue chubanshe.

Geng Huamin 耿化敏 (2015). *Zhongguo gongchandang funü yundongshi (1921-1949)* 中国共产党妇女运动史 (1921–1949) [The history of women's work in the Chinese Communist Party 1921–1949]. Beijing: Shehui kexue wenxian chubanshe.

Gomi Tomoko 五味知子 (2009). '"Wujian" yu zhenjie: Yi wan-Ming zhi Qing qianqi de pandu wei zhongxin「诬奸」与贞节—以晚明至清前期的判牍为中心 ['False accusations of adultery' and chastity: Based on the records of judgements from late Ming to early Qing]. *Jindai Zhongguo funüshi yanjiu* 近代中国妇女史研究, 17.

Gong Yanming 龚延明 (1997). *Songdai guanzhi cidian* 宋代官制辞典 [Dictionary on the government system of the Song dynasty]. Beijing: Zhonghua shuju.

Gu Huizhi 谷辉之 (2000). *Liu Rushi shiwenji* 柳如是诗文集 [Collected poems of Liu Rushi]. Shanghai: Shanghai guji chubanshe.

Gu Xiulian 顾秀莲 (ed.) (2008, 2013). *20-shiji Zhongguo funü yundongshi* 20世纪中国妇女运动史 [The twentieth-century history of the Chinese women's movement], 3 volumes. Beijing: Zhongguo funü chubanshe.

Guei Chi-Shun 桂齐逊 (2003). 'Woguo guyoulü guanyu "tongju xiangwei yin" de lilunmian yu shiwumian: Yi Tanglü wei hexin' 我国固有律关于「同居相为隐」的理论面与实务面—唐律为核心 [Tang Code: Theory and practice regarding our country's unique penal code stipulating to 'conceal crimes committed by one's family member']. In: Kao Ming-Shih 高明士 (ed.), *Tangdai shenfen fazhi yanjiu: Yi Tanglü minglilü wei zhongxin* 唐代身分法制研究—以唐律名例律为中心 [Study of Tang status law: Centering on Tang Code terminology of precedents and laws]. Taipei: Wunan tushu.

Guei Chi-Shun 桂齐逊 (2005). 'Tanglü "Jiaren gongfan, zhizuo zunzhang" fenxi' 唐律「家人共犯、止坐尊长」分析 [Analysis of the Tang Code provision that 'Only the family patriarch is punishable for a joint offense committed by a family']. In: Kao Ming-Shih 高明士 (ed.), *Dongya chuantong jiali, jiaoyu yu guofa (2): Jianei zhixu yu guofa* 东亚传统家礼、教育与国法 (二): 家内秩序与国法 [Traditional family rituals, education and state law in East Asia (2): Family order and state law]. Taipei: Taida chuban zhongxin.

Guo Jing 郭晶 (2020). *Wuhan fengcheng riji* 武汉封城日记 [Diary of the Wuhan lockdown]. Taipei: Lianjing.

Guo Xiaofei 郭晓飞 (2007). *Zhongguo fa shiye xia de tongxinglian* 中国法视野下的同性恋 [Homosexuality from a Chinese legal perspective]. Beijing: Zhishi chuaquan chubanshe.

Han Shufeng 韩树峰 (2011). 'Han-Tang chenghu zhidu de bianqian' 汉唐承户制度的变迁' [Change in the household succession system between Han and Tang]. In: *Han-Wei falü yu shehui: Yi jiandu, Wenshu wei zhongxin de kaocha* 汉魏法律与社会—以简牍·文书为中心的考察 [Law and society from Han to Wei: A study of bamboo and wooden slips and texts]. Beijing: Wenwu chubanshe.

He-Yin Zhen 何殷震 (震述 Zhenshu) (1907a). 'Nüzi fuchou lun' 女子复仇论 [Women's revenge]. *Tianyi bao* 天义报, 2–5, 8–10.

He-Yin Zhen 何殷震 (震述 Zhenshu) (1907b). 'Nüzi jiefang wenti' 女子解放问题 [Women's liberation question]. *Tianyi bao* 天义报, 7–10. (Compiled in Zhang Nan and Wang Renzhi (1963).)

Hee Wai-Siam 许维贤 (2015). *Cong Yanshi dao Xingshi: Tongzhi shuxie yu jinxiandai Zhongguo de nanxing jiangou* 从艳史到性史—同志书写与近现代中国的男性建构 [From erotic history to the history of sexuality: Homosexual texts and the modern and contemporary Chinese structure of masculinity]. Taipei: Zhongyang-daxue chuban zhongxin.

Hou Xudong 侯旭东 ([2004] 2005). 'Han-Wei liuchao fuxi yishi de chengzhang yu "zongzu"' 汉魏六朝父系意识的成长与"宗族" [The development of patrilineal consciousness and "lineage" in Han, Wei and Six Dynasties]. *Beichao cunmin de shenghuo shijie: Chaoting, zhouxian yu cunli* 北朝村民的生活世界—朝廷、州县与村里 [The life-world of villagers in Northern Dynasties: Court, state, county and village]. Beijing: Shangwu yinshuguan.

Hsiang Shu-Yun 向淑云 (1991). *Tangdai hunyinfa yu hunyin shitai* 唐代婚姻法与婚姻实态 [Tang marriage law and the true state of marriage]. Taipei: Taiwan shangwu yinshuguan.

Hu Fan 胡凡 and Wang Wei 王伟 (1999). 'Lun Mingdai de xuan xiunü zhi zhi' 论明代的选秀女之制 [On the system of selection of *xiunü* in the Ming dynasty]. *Xi'nan shifan daxue xuebao, zhexue shehuike xueban* 西南师范大学学报·哲学社会科学版, 25(6).

Hu Pingsheng 胡平生 (2011). 'Xin chu Hanjian hukou buji yanjiu' 新出汉简户口簿籍研究 [A study of household registers in newly excavated Han bamboo slips]. *Chutu wenxian yanjiu* 出土文献研究 [Studies of excavated texts], 10. (Also published in Hu Pingsheng 胡平生 (2012), *Hu Pingsheng jiandu wenwu lun gao* 胡平生简牍文物论稿 [Hu Pingsheng's essays on bamboo and wooden artifacts]. Shanghai: Zhongxi shuju.)

Hu Pingsheng 胡平生 and Zhang Defang 张德芳 (eds) (2001). *Dunhuang Xuanquan Hanjian shicui* 敦煌悬泉汉简释粹 [Selected explications of Hanjian from Xuanquan, Dunhuang]. Shanghai: Shanghai guji chubanshe.

Hu Shi 胡适 (1923). 'Kexue yu renshengguan xu' 科学与人生观序 [Preface to science and the philosophy of life]. *Kexue yu renshengguan* 科学与人生观 [Science and the philosophy of life]. Shanghai: Yadong tushuguan.

Hu Wenkai 胡文楷 (ed.) (1985). *Lidai funü zhuzuo kao (zengdingben)* 历代妇女著作考 (增订本) [Study of the works of women throughout history (revised edition)]. Shanghai: Shanghai guji chubanshe. (Original edition published by Shangwu yinshuguan in 1957.)

Hu Yun-Wei 胡云薇 (2008). 'Qianli huanyou cheng dishi, meinian fengjing shi taxiang: Shilun Tangdai de huanyou yu jiating' 千里宦游成底事、每年风景是他乡—试论唐代的宦游与家庭 [Official travels and family life in Tang China]. *Taida lishi xuebao* 台大历史学报, 41.

Hu Yun-Wei 胡云薇 (2014). 'Tangdai de ji-muzi guanxi: Yi Wang Wan, Wei Chengqing wei zhongxin' 唐代的继母子关系—以王婉、韦承庆为中心 [Stepmother-son relationships in the Tang dynasty: A case study of Wang Wan and Wei Chengqing]. *Zaoqi Zhongguoshi yanjiu* 早期中国史研究, 6(2).

Huang Biyao 黄碧遥 (1948). 'Du Pan Guangdan xiansheng funü wenti de lunwen hou' 读潘光旦先生妇女问题的论文后 [After reading Mr. Pan Guangdan's paper on women's issues]. *Guancha* 观察, 5(8).

Huang Chih-Yen 黄旨彦 (2013). *Gongzhu zhengzhi: Wei, Jin, Nan-beichao zhengzhishi de xingbie kaocha* 公主政治—魏晋南北朝政治史的性别考察 [The politics of princesses' social networks: A gendered investigation into the political history of Medieval China]. Taipei: Daoxiang chubanshe.

Huang Mei-Yin 黄玫茵 (2003). 'Tangdai sanfubamu de falü diwei' 唐代三父八母的法律地位 [Legal status of three fathers and eight mothers in Tang]. In: Kao Ming-Shih 高明士(ed.), *Tangdai shenfen fazhi yanjiu: Yi Tanglü minglilü wei zhongxin* 唐代身分法制研究—以唐律名例律为中心 [Study of Tang status law: Centering on Tang Code terminology of precedents and laws]. Taipei: Wunan tushu.

Huang Shaoming 黄少明 (2007). 'Guanyu wo guo zaoqi gonggong tushuguan de bumen shezhi' 关于我国早期公共图书馆的部门设置 [The establishment of China's early public library sector]. *Fujian tushuguan lilun yu shijian* 福建图书馆理论与实践, 28(1).

Huang Shengzhang 黄盛璋 (1994). 'Jiangling Gaotai Hanmu xinchu "gaodice", Qiance yu xiangguan zhidu' 江陵高台汉墓新出"告地策",遣策与相关制度 [The 'Gaodice' and 'Qiance' newly discovered from Han-period tombs at Gaotai in Jiangling and the associated system]. *Jianghan kaogu* 江汉考古, (2).

Huang Shi 黄石 (1923). 'Jiating zuhe lun' 家庭组合论 [Family configuration]. *Funü zazhi* 妇女杂志, 9(12).

Huang Tsuimei 黄翠梅 (2013). 'Liuguangyicai, Cuiraozhuwei: Xizhou zhi Chunqiu zaoqi de tixing pailian chuanshi' 流光溢彩、翠绕珠围—西周至春秋早期的梯形牌联串饰 [Gleaming and exuberant: Bead-strings with trapezoidal plaque from Western Zhou to the early Spring and Autumn Period]. In: Chen Kwang-tzuu 陈光祖 (ed.), *Jinyujiaohui: Shangzhou kaogu; Yishu yu wenhua lunwen ji* 金玉交辉—商周考古、艺术与文化论文集 [Radiance between bronze and jade: Archaeology, art and culture of the Shang and Zhou dynasties]. Taipei: Zhongyang yanjiuyuan lishi yuyan yanjusuo.

Huang Yanli 黄嫣梨 (1993). *Handai funü wenxue wujia yanjiu* 汉代妇女文学五家研究 [A study of the five female writers of Han]. Kaifeng: Henan daxue chubanshe.

Huang Yufu 黄育馥 (1998). *Jingju: Qiao he Zhongguo de xingbie guanxi* 京剧—跷和中国的性别关系 [Peking opera: 'Raising the foot' and China's gender relations]. Beijing: Sanlian shudian.

Hunansheng wenwukaogu yanjiusuo 湖南省文物考古研究所 (2007). *Liye fajue baogao* 里耶发掘报告 [Liye excavation report]. Changsha: Yuelu chubanshe.

Jiang Tianshu 蒋天枢 (1981). *Chen Yinke xiansheng biannian shiji (Chen Yinke wenji fulu)* 陈寅恪先生编年事辑（陈寅恪文集附录）[Chronicles of Prof. Chen Yinke, appendix to Chen Yinke collection]. Shanghai: Shanghai guji chubanshe.

Jiang Weiqiao (Zhuzhuang) 蒋维乔 (竹庄) (1904). 'Lun Zhongguo nüxue buxing zhi hai' 论中国女学不兴之害 [Discussion on the harm stemming from not promoting women's education in China]. *Nüzi shijie* 女子世界, 3.

Jin Meilan 金美兰 (2011). '1953-nian Zhongguo hunyin zizhu yundong de liangmianxing: Guanche fangshi he lengzhan zhixia de wenhua chonggou' 1953年中国婚姻自主运动的两面性—贯彻方式和冷战之下的文化重构 [Two sides of the marriage autonomy movement in 1953 China: Method of implementation and cultural restructuring under the Cold War]. In: Luo Xiaoming 罗小茗 (ed.), *Zhizao "Guomin": 1950-70 niandai de richang shenghuo yu wenyi shijian* 制造"国民"—1950-70年代的日常生活与文艺实践 [Manufacturing a 'nation': Everyday life and literary practice from the 1950s to the 1970s]. Shanghai: Shanghai shudian chubanshe.

Jingzhou bowuguan, Hubei Province 湖北省荆州博物馆 (ed.) (2000). *Jingzhou Gaotai Qin-Han mu: Yihuang gonglu jingzhouduan tianye kaogu baogao zhiyi* 荆州高台秦汉墓—宜黄公路荆州段田野考古报告之一 [Excavation of the Qin-Han dynastic tombs at Gaotai in Jingzhou: Report 1 of the archaeological reports from the Jingzhou section of the Yu-Huang highway project]. Beijing: Kexue chubanshe.

Kan Huai-Chen 甘怀真 (1991). *Tangdai jiamiao lizhi yanjiu* 唐代家庙礼制研究 [A study of ancestral temples and rituals in Tang]. Taiwan: Shangwu yinshuguan.

Kan Huai-Chen 甘怀真 (1995). 'Tangdai guanren de huanyou shenghuo: Yi jingji shenghuo wei zhongxin' 唐代官人的宦游生活—以经济生活为中心 [Job relocations and lives of Tang bureaucrats: Centering on economic life]. In: Zhongguo Tangdai xuehui 中国唐代学会 (ed.), *Dierjie Tangdai wenhua yantaohui lunwenji* 第二届唐代文化研讨会论文集. Taipei: Zhongguo Tangdai xuehui.

Kan Huai-Chen 甘怀真 (2012). 'Zai sikao shizu yanjiu de xiayibu: Cong tongzhi jieji guanxian chufa' 再思考士族研究的下一步：从统治阶级观点出发 [Rethinking the study of the aristocracy: Ruling class as the starting point]. In: Kan Huai-Chen 甘怀真 (ed.), *Shenfen, wenhua yu Quanli: Shizu yanjiu xintan* 身分、文化与权力—士族研究新探 [Status, culture and power: A new quest in aristocracy study]. Taipei: Taida chuban zhongxin.

Kao Ming-Shih 高明士 (2003). 'Tanglü zhong de jiazhang zeren' 唐律中的家长责任 [Responsibilities of the master of the house under the Tang Code]. In: Kao Ming-Shih 高明士 (ed.), *Tangdai shenfen fazhi yanjiu: Yi Tanglü Minglilü wei zhongxin* 唐代身份法制研究—以唐律名例律为中心 [Study of Tang status law: Centering on Tang Code terminology of precedents and laws]. Taipei: Wunan tushu.

Kao Ming-Shih 高明士 (2009). 'Yihe yu yijue: Jianlun Tangchao lüling de fei xueyuan fazhi zhixu' 义合与义绝—兼论唐朝律令的非血缘法制秩序 [Yihe and yijue: Judicial order of the Tang Code and statutes concerning non-consanguineous relationships]. In: Zeng Yi-Min 曾一民 (ed.), *Lin Tianwei jiaoshou jinian wenji* 林天蔚教授纪念文集 [Essays commemorating Professor Lin Tien-Wei]. Taipei: Wenshizhe chubanshe.

Ke Jisheng 柯基生 (2013). *Jinlian xiaojiao: Qiannian chanzu yu Zhongguo xing wenhua* 金莲小脚—千年缠足与中国性文化 [Lotus step: Shoes for bound feet – Footbinding in the thousand years and sexual history of China]. Taipei: Duli zuojia.

Kohama Masako 小滨正子 (2010). 'Jihua shengyu de kaiduan: 1950-1960 niandai de Shanghai' 计划生育的开端—1950-1960年代的上海 [The beginning of family planning: Shanghai from the 1950s to the 1960s]. *Zhongyang yanjiuyuan jindaishi yanjiusuo jikan* 中央研究院近代史研究所集刊, 68.

Kohama Masako 小滨正子 (2011). 'Zhongguo nongcun jihua shengyu de puji: Yi 1960-1970 niandai Q-cun weili' 中国农村计划生育的普及—以1960-1970年代Q村为例 [Dissemination of family planning in rural China: The case of Q village from the 1960s to the 1970s]. *Jindai zhongguo funüshi yanjiu* 近代中国妇女史研究, 19.

Lai Liang-Chun 赖亮郡 (2011). 'Cong fangqishu kan Tangdai de heli' 从放妻书看唐代的合离 [A study of Tang-style divorce by consent based on a bill of divorce]. In: Huang Yuan-Sheng 黄源盛 (ed.), *Tanglü yu chuantongfa wenhua* 唐律与传统法文化 [*Tang Code and traditional legal culture*]. Taipei: Yuanzhao chuban.

Lee Jen-Der 李贞德 (1999). 'Wei-Liuchao de rumu' 魏六朝的乳母 [Wet-nurses in late antiquity and early medieval China]. *Zhongyang yanjiuyuan lishi yuyan yanjiusuo jikan* 中央研究院历史语言研究所集刊, 70(2). (Revised as Chapter 5, 'Significant supporting figures: Wet-nurse', in Lee Jen-Der (2008).)

Lee Jen-Der 李贞德 (2001). *Gongzhu zhi si: Ni suo buzhidao de Zhongguo falü shi* 公主之死—你所不知道的中国法律史 [*The death of a princess: Codifying classical family ethics in early medieval China*]. Taipei: Sanmin shuju.

Lee Jen-Der 李贞德 (2008). *Nüren de Zhongguo yiliaoshi: Han Tang zhijian de jiankang zhaogu yu xingbie* 女人的中国医疗史—汉唐之间的健康照顾与性别 [*A history of women's medicine in China: Gender and healthcare from Han to Tang*]. Taipei: Sanmin shuju.

Lee Shwu-Yuan 李淑媛 (2005a). 'Tangdai de jiating baoli: Yi nueqi, Oufu wei zhongxin zhi sikao' 唐代的家庭暴力—以虐妻、殴夫为中心之思考 [Domestic violence in Tang China: A discussion about the abuse of the wife and violence against the husband]. In: Kao Ming-Shih 高明士 (ed.), *Dongya chuantong jiali, jiaoyu yu guofa (2): Jianei zhixu yu guofa* 东亚传统家礼、教育与国法 (二): 家内秩序与国法 [Traditional family rituals, education and state law in East Asia (2): Family order and state law]. Taipei: Taida chuban zhongxin.

Lee Shwu-Yuan 李淑媛 (2005b). 'Tangdai de yuanzuo: Yi fanni yuanzuo xia de funü wei hexin zhi kaocha' 唐代的缘坐—以反逆缘坐下的妇女为核心之考察 [Kin punishment in Tang: A study of married women involved in collective punishment for treason]. In: Kao Ming-Shih 高明士 (ed.), *Dongya chuantong jiaoyu yu fazhi yanjiu (2): Tanglü zhu wenti* 东亚传统教育与法制研究 (二): 唐律诸问题 [Study of traditional education and the legal system in East Asia (2): Tang Code issues]. Taipei: Taiwan daxue chuban zhongxin.

Lee Shwu-Yuan 李淑媛 (2010). 'Xiuqi qifang: Tangdai lihunfa "Qichu" "Yijue" wenti zaitan' 休妻弃放—唐代离婚法「七出」、「义绝」问题再探 [A study on divorcing and abandoning the wife: Focusing on Chi-Chu and Yi-Chueh in statutes of the T'ang dynasty]. *Fazhishi yanjiu* 法制史研究, 17.

Lei Sean Hsiang-Lin 雷祥麟 (2011). 'Xiguan cheng siwei: Xinshenghuo yundong yu feijiehe fangzhi zhong de lunli, jiating yu shenti' 习惯成四维—新生活运动与肺结核防治中的伦理、家庭与身体 [Habituating the four virtues: Ethics, family and the body in the anti-tuberculosis campaigns and the New Life Movement]. *Zhongyang yanjiuyuan jindaishi yanjiusuo jikan* 中央研究院近代史研究所集刊, 74.

Leung Angela Ki Che 梁其姿 (2005). 'Qian jindai Zhongguo de nüxing yiliao congshi zhe' 前近代中国的女性医疗从事者 [Female medical practitioners in pre-modern China]. In: Lee Jen-Der 李贞德 and Leung Angela Ki Che 梁其姿 (eds), *Funü yu shehui* 妇女与社会 [*Women and society*]. Beijing: Zhongguo baikequanshu chubanshe.

Li Chuo 李绰 (1920). 'Hunyin keyi dang fei' 婚姻可以当废 [Marriage can be abolished]. *Minguo ribao, Juewu* 民国日报·觉悟, 22 May 1920. (Compiled in Mei Sheng (1923), Vol. 4.)

Li Guimei 李桂梅 (2008). 'Luelun jindai Zhongguo jiating lunli de shanbian jiqi qishi' 略论近代中国家庭伦理的嬗变及其启示 [Change in family ethics and its revelation in modern China]. *Zhongguo jiating yanjiu* 中国家庭研究 [Research on the Chinese Family], Vol. 3. Shanghai: Shanghai shehui kexueyuan chubanshe.

Li Jingheng 李競恒 (2014). 'Yiguan zhi shang: Wanqing Minchu zhengzhi sichao yu shijian zhong de "hanyiguan"' 衣冠之殇: 晚清民初政治思潮与实践中的"漢衣冠" [Short-lived national costumes: Political trends in the late Qing to early Republic period and the practice of 'Han-style fashion']. *Tianfu xinlun* 天府新论, 5.

Li Rui 李锐 (1993). *Zaonian Mao Zedong* 早年毛泽东 [Mao Zedong in the early years]. Shenyang: Liaoning renmin chubanshe.

Li Xiaojiang 李小江 (1983). 'Renlei jinbu yu funü jiefang' 人类进步与妇女解放 [Human evolution and women's liberation]. *Makesi zhuyi yanjiu* 马克思主义研究, 1983(2).

Li Xiaojiang 李小江 (1988). *Xiawa de tansuo: Funü yanjiu lungao* 夏娃的探索—妇女研究论稿 [Searching for Eve: Essays on women's studies]. Zhengzhou: Henan renmin chubanshe.

Li Xiaojiang 李小江 (1995). *Zouxiang nüren: Xin shiqi funü yanjiu jishi* 走向女人—新时期妇女研究纪实 [Toward women: The new era of Chinese women's studies]. Zhengzhou: Henan renmin chubanshe.

Li Xiaojiang 李小江, Zhu Hong 朱虹 and Dong Xiuyu 董秀玉 (eds) (1994). *Xingbie yu Zhongguo* 性别与中国 [Gender and China]. Beijing: Sanlian shudian.

Li Yinhe 李银河 (1998). *Tongxinglian ya wenhua* 同性恋亚文化 [Homosexual subculture]. Beijing: Jinri zhongguo chubanshe.

Li Yinhe 李银河 (2000). *Kuer lilun* 酷儿理论 [Queer theory]. Beijing: Shishi chubanshe.

Li Yinhe 李银河 and Wang Xiaobo 王小波 (1993). *Tamen de shijie: Zhongguo nan tongxinglian qunluo toushi* 他们的世界—中国男同性恋群落透视 [Their world: Looking into the male homosexual group in China]. Hong Kong: Tiandi tushu.

Li Zehou 李泽厚 (1987). 'Qimeng yu jiuwang de shuangchong bianzou' 启蒙与救亡的双重变奏 [The double variation of enlightenment and national salvation]. In: *Zhongguo xiandai sixiangshi lun* 中国现代思想史论 [A treatise on the contemporary history of thought in China]. Beijing: Dongfang chubanshe.

Li Zheng-Yu 李正宇 (2005). 'Cong "Tufan zinian(gongyuan 808 nian) Shazhou Zuoerjiang baixing Fan Lüqing deng wuhu huji shoushi canjuan" kan Tufan huhun fangmian ruogan wenti' 从「吐蕃子年 (公元808年) 沙洲左二将百姓氾履倩等五户户籍手实残卷」看吐蕃户婚方面若干问题 [A study of a few issues concerning the Tufan family and marriage according to 'Tufan zinian (808) Shazhou Zuoerjiang baixing Fan Lüqing deng wuhu huji shoushi canjuan']. In: Kao Ming-Shih 高明士 (ed.), *Dongya chuantong jiali, Jiaoyu yu guofa(1): Jiazu jialiu yu jiaoyu* 东亚传统家礼、教育与国法 (一): 家族、家礼与教育 [Traditional family rituals, education and state law in East Asia (1): Family, family rituals and education]. Taipei: Taida chuban zhongxin.

Li Zhongqing 李中清, Ding Yizhuang 定宜庄 and Guo Songyi 郭松義 (2000). *Hunyin jiating yu renkou xingwei* 婚姻家庭与人口行为 [Marriage, family and demographic behavior]. Beijing: Bejing daxue chubanshe.

Liang Jinghe 梁景和 (1991). 'Lun Wusi-shiqi de jiating gaizhi guan' 论五四时期的家庭改制观 [Family system reform ideas in the May Fourth era]. *Liaoning shifan daxue xuebao (shekeban)* 辽宁师范大学学报 (社科版), 1991 (4).

Liang Jinghe 梁景和 (1994). 'Lun Qing mo de "Jiating geming"' 论清末的'家庭革命' ['Family revolution' in late Qing China]. *Shixue yuekan* 史学月刊, 1994 (1).

Liang Jinghe 梁景和 (1998). 'Wuxu-weixin pai de hunyin wenhua guan' 戊戌维新派的婚姻文化观 [Wuxu Reformists' view of marriage culture]. *Jianghai xuekan* 江海学刊, 1998 (6).

Liang Jinghe 梁景和 (1999). 'Wusi shiqi de "Feihun zhuyi"' 五四时期的'废婚主义' ['Marriage abolitionism' in the May Fourth era]. *Ershiyi-shiji shuangyuekan* 二十一世纪双月刊, 53.

Liang Jinghe 梁景和 (2009). 'Wusi shiqi shehui wenhua shanbian lungang: Yi Hunyin, Jiating, Nüxing, Xinglun wei zhongxin' 五四时期社会文化嬗变论纲：一以婚姻、家庭、女性、性伦为中心 [Socio-cultural change in the May Fourth era: Centering on marriage, family, women and sexual morals]. *Renwen zazhi* 人文杂志, 2009 (4).

Liang Jinghe 梁景和 (2011). 'Lun Xinhai-geming yu Minchu shiqi hunyin wenhua de bianhe' 论辛亥革命与民初时期婚姻文化的变革 [Marriage culture reform in the Xinhai Revolution era and the early Republic period]. *Ming-Qing luncong* 明清论丛, 11.

Liang Qichao 梁启超 (1897). 'Nüxue' 女学 [Education for women]. In: Liang Qichao, 'Bianfa tongyi' 变法通议 [General discussion on reform]. *Shiwu bao* 时务报 23 and 25. (Later reproduced in *Yinbingshi wenji* 饮冰室文集 [Collected works of Yinbingshi] (1936), Vol. 1.)

Liang Qichao 梁启超 (1901). 'Diwujie, "Renzhong"' 第五节〈人种〉 [Section 5, 'Race']. *Zhongguoshi xulun* 中国史叙论 [Introductory discussion on Chinese history]. Shanghai: Zhonghua shuju. (Later reproduced in *Yinbingshi wenji* 饮冰室文集 [Collected works of Yinbingshi] (1936), Vol. 6.)

Liang Qichao 梁启超 (1902). 'Jin zaohun yi' 禁早婚议 [Discussion on forbidding early marriages]. *Xinmin congbao* 新民丛报, 23, 1 December.

Liang Qichao 梁启超 (1936). *Yinbingshi wenji (heji)* 饮冰室文集（合集） [Collected works of Yinbingshi], Vol.1. Shanghai: Shanghai zhonghua shuju.

Liang Siyong 梁思永 and Gao Quxun 高去寻 (1962). *Houjiazhuang dierben 1001 hao damu* 侯家庄第二本1001号大墓 [Houjiazhuang, Vol. 2, Tomb 1001]. Taipei: Zhongyang yanjiuyuan lishi yuyan yanjiusuo.

Liang Siyong 梁思永 and Gao Quxun 高去寻 (1976). *Houjiazhuang dibaben 1550 hao damu* 侯家庄第八本1550号大墓 [Houjiazhuang, Vol. 8, Tomb 1550]. Taipei: Zhongyang yanjiuyuan lishi yuyan yanjiusuo.

Liao Ben 廖奔 and Liu Yanjun 刘彦君 (2006). *Zhongguo xiqu fazhan shi Di 2 juan* 中国戏曲发展史 第2卷 [History of the development of Chinese theatrical plays, Vol. 2]. Taiyuan: Shanxi jiaoyu chubanshe.

Liao Xichen 廖熹晨 (2012). 'Xinzhongguo chengli chuqi Beijing diqu xinglun wenhua yanjiu (1949-1966)' 新中国成立初期北京地区性伦文化研究 (1949—1966年) [A study of sex culture in the Beijing area in the early phase of New China (1949–1966)]. In: Liang Jinghe 梁景和 (ed.), *Hunyin, jiating, xingbie yanjiu (di er ji)* 婚姻·家庭·性别研究 (第二辑) [Study of marriage, family and gender (2nd edition)]. Beijing: Shehui kexue wenxian chubanshe.

Liao Yi-Fang 廖宜方 (2009). *Tangdai de muzi guanxi* 唐代的母子关系 [The mother-son relationship in Tang China]. Taipei: Daoxiang chubanshe.

Lin Jialin 林嘉琳 (2006). 'Anyang Yin-mu zhong de nüxing: Wangshi zhufu, jisi, Muqin, junshi jiangling he nubi' 安阳殷墓中的女性—王室诸妇、祭祀、母亲、军事将领和奴婢 [Women in Anyang Yin tombs: Female royals, priestesses, mothers, military leaders and slaves]. In: Lin Jialin 林嘉琳 and Sun Yan 孙岩 (eds), *Xingbie yanjiu yu Zhongguo kaoguxue* 性别研究与中国考古学 [Gender and Chinese archaeology]. Beijing: Kexue chubanshe.

Lin Jiling 林吉玲 (1999). 'Wusi shiqi jiating guannian de chonggou jiqi tixian' 五四时期家庭观念的重构及其体现 [Reconstruction of the family concept and its manifestation in the May Fourth era]. *Ji'nan daxue xuebao* 济南大学学报, 9(3).

Lin Liyue 林丽月 (2005). 'Cong xingbie faxian chuantong: Ming dai funüshi yanjiu de fansi' 从性别发现传统：明代妇女史研究的反思 [Revealing tradition from a gender perspective: A review of studies on Ming women's history]. *Jindai zhongguo funüshi yanjiu* 近代中国妇女史研究, 13.

Lin Zhensheng 林振声 (1920). 'Jiating zhidu de zuie he gaige de fangfa' 家庭制度的罪恶和改革的方法 [The ills of the family system and its reform strategy]. *Jiating yanjiu* 家庭研究, 1(2).

Liu Dapeng 刘大鹏 (1990). *Tuixiang zhai riji* 退想斋日记 [Diary of the study of reclusive thoughts], punctuated and annotated by Qiao Zhiqiang 乔志强. Taiyuan: Shanxi renmin chubanshe.

Liu Huiying 刘慧英 (2006). 'Cong Nüquan zhuyi dao Wu-zhengfu zhuyi: He Zhen de yinxian yu *TianYi* de bianqian' 从女权主义到无政府主义—何震的隐现与《天义》的变迁 [From feminism to anarchism: The appearance and disappearance of He Zhen and the variance of the periodical *Tianyi*]. *Zhongguo xiandai wenxue yanjiu congkan* 中国现代文学研究丛刊, 2.

Liu Huiying 刘慧英 (2013). *Nüquan, Qimeng yu Minzu guojia huayu* 女权、启蒙与民族国家话语 [Feminism, enlightenment and nationalist discourse]. Beijing: Renmin wenxue chubanshe.

Liu Huiying 刘慧英 and Chen Yangu 陈燕谷 (2012). 'Fan minzu-guojia de huayu de jueqi: Wu-zhengfu nüquan zhuyi de lishi yiyi' 反民族国家的话语的崛起—无政府女权主义的历史意义 [The rise of anti-nationalism discourse: Historical significance of anarcho-feminism]. *Nankai xuebao (zhexue shehui kexue ban)* 南开学报 (哲学社会科学版), 2012 (6).

Liu Renfeng 刘人锋 (2012). 'Xinhai geming shiqi de funü kanwu *Tianyi bao* yu Wu-zhengfu zhuyi sixiang' 辛亥革命时期的妇女刊物《天义报》与无政府主义思想 [Women's publication *Natural Justice* and anarchism in the Xinhai Revolution era]. *Chuanshan xuekan* 船山学刊, 2012 (2).

Liu Shifu 刘师复 (1912). 'Fei Hunyin-zhuyi' 废婚姻主义 [Marriage abolitionism] and 'Fei Jiazu-zhuyi' 废家族主义 [Family abolitionism]. *Shifu Wencun* 师复文存 [Collected writings of Shifu] (1928). Guangzhou: Gexin shuju. (Also included in Chen Jing (1984)).

Liu Tseng-Kuei 刘增贵 (1980). *Handai hunyin zhidu* 汉代婚姻制度 [The marriage system of the Han dynasty]. Taipei: Huashi chubanshe.

Liu Xiaoli 刘晓丽 (2014). *1950-nian de Zhongguo funü* 1950年的中国妇女 [Chinese Women in the 1950s]. Taiyuan: Shanxi jiaoyu chubanshe.

Liu Yen-Lih 刘燕俪 (2003). 'Cong falü mian kan Tangdai de fu yu diqi guanxi' 从法律面看唐代的夫与嫡妻关系 [A study of the relationship between husband and legal wife in Tang from a legal perspective]. In: Kao Ming-Shih 高明士 (ed.), *Tangdai shenfen fazhi yanjiu: Yi Tanglü minglilü wei zhongxin* 唐代身份法制研究—以唐律名例律为中心 [Study of Tang status law: Centering on Tang Code terminology of precedents and laws]. Taipei: Wunan tushu.

Liu Yen-Lih 刘燕俪 (2005a). 'Tanglü sijian jieceng de fuqi guanxi yu shitai zhi tantao' 唐律私贱阶层的夫妻关系与实态之探讨 [A study of the husband-wife relationship among privately subordinated people under the Tang Code and its realities]. In: Kao Ming-Shih 高明士 (ed.), *Dongya chuantong jiaoyu yu fazhi yanjiu (2): Tanglü zhu wenti* 东亚传统教育与法制研究（二）：唐律诸问题 [Study of traditional education and the legal system in East Asia (2): Tang Code issues]. Taipei: Taida chuban zhongxin.

Liu Yen-Lih 刘燕俪 (2005b). 'Tanglü zhong de muzi guanxi' 唐律中的母子关系 [The mother-son relationship in the Tang Code]. In: Kao Ming-Shih 高明士 (ed.), *Dongya chuantong jiali, Jiaoyu yu guofa (2): Jianei zhixu yu guofa* 东亚传统家礼、教育与国法（二）：家内秩序与国法 [Traditional family rituals, education and state law in East Asia (2): Family order and state law]. Taipei: Taida chuban zhongxin.

Liu Yen-Lih 刘燕俪 (2007). *Tanglü zhong de fuqi guanxi* 唐律中的夫妻关系 [The husband-wife relationship in the Tang Code]. Taipei: Wunan tushu.

Lo Tung-Hwa 罗彤华 (2000). '"Tongju" xilun: Tangdai jiating gongcai xingzhi zhi tantao' 「同居」析论 – 唐代家庭共财性质之探讨 [Analysis of 'co-residence': Joint property ownership among Tang families]. *Dalu zazhi* 大陆杂志, 100(6).

Lo Tung-Hwa 罗彤华 (2015). *Tongju gongcai: Tangdai jiating yanjiu* 同居共财—唐代家庭研究 [Co-residence and joint property ownership: A study of Tang-era families]. Taipei: Zhengda chubanshe.

Lu Chien-Lung 卢建荣 (1993). 'Tangdai Pengcheng Liushi zongzu tuanti zhi yanjiu' 唐代彭城刘氏宗族团体之研究 [Research on the lineage of Peng-cheng Liu in the T'ang dynasty]. *Zhongyang yanjiuyuan lishi yuyan yanjiusuo jikan* 中央研究院历史语言研究所集刊, 63(3).

Lu Chien-Lung 卢建荣 (1997). 'Cong zaishinü muzhi kan Tang-Song xingbie yishi de yanbian' 从在室女墓志看唐宋性别意识的演变 [Shifts in gender consciousness from the T'ang to the Sung as revealed in the funerary inscriptions of unmarried women]. *Guoli Taiwan shida lishi xuebao* 国立台湾师大历史学报, 25.

Lu Liancheng 卢连成 Hu Zhisheng 胡智生 (1988). *Baojiguo mudi* 宝鸡国墓地 [Baopaguo cemetery]. Beijing: Wenwu chubanshe.

Luo Zhitian 罗志田 (1999). *Quanshi zhuanyi: Jindai Zhongguo de sixiang, shehui yu xueshu* 权势转移—近代中国的思想、社会与学术 [Transition of power: Modern Chinese thought, society and scholarship]. Wuhan: Hubei renmin chubanshe.

Mao Han-Kuang 毛汉光 (1988). *Zhongguo zhonggu shehui shilun* 中国中古社会史论 [A discussion of Chinese medieval social history]. Taipei: Lianjing chuban.

Mao Han-Kuang 毛汉光 (1995). 'Tangdai funü jiating juese de jige zhongyao shiduan: Yi muzhiming wei li' 唐代妇女家庭角色的几个重要时段—以墓志铭为例 [Important stages in Tang women's role transition within the family: A case study on epitaphs]. In: Pao Chia-Lin 鲍家麟 (ed.), *Zhongguo funüshi lunji* 中国妇女史论集 [Studies in the history of Chinese women], Vol. 4. Taipei: Daoxiang chubanshe.

Mei Sheng 梅生 (ed.) (1923). *Zhongguo funü wenti taolun ji* 中国妇女问题讨论集 [Collected discussions on the woman question in China], Vols. 3 & 4. Shanghai: Xin wenhua shushe.

Meng Yue 孟悦 and Dai Jinhua 戴锦华 (1989). *Fuchu lishi dibiao: Xiandai funü wenxue yanjiu* 浮出历史地表—现代妇女文学研究 [Emerging from the horizon of history: A study of contemporary Chinese women's literature]. Zhengzhou: Henan renmin chubanshe.

Menghuan 梦幻 (pseud.) (1912). 'Lun nüzi yaoqiu canzhengquan zhi guaixiang' 论女子要求参政权之怪象 [On the strange phenomenon of women demanding suffrage]. *Dagong bao* 大公报, March 30.

Miao Lijuan 苗利娟 (2013). 'Shi xi Jiagu jishi keci zhong de "Fumoulai"' 试析甲骨记事刻辞中的"妇某来" [An analysis of 'certain woman came' in the inscriptions on oracle bones]. *Shixue yuekan* 史学月刊, 13.

Mou Runsun 牟润孙 ([1952] 1987). 'Han chu gongzhu ji waiqi zai dishi zhi diwei shishi' 汉初公主及外戚在帝室之地位试释 [A study of the status of imperial princesses and maternal relatives in the imperial court in early Han China]. *Zhushi zhai conggao* 注史斋丛稿 [Collected historical commentaries]. Beijing: Zhonghua shuju.

Mu Xuan 穆烜 and Yan Xuexi 严学熙 (eds) (1994). *Dasheng shachang gongren shenghuo de diaocha (1899-1949)* 大生纱厂工人生活的调查 (1899–1949) [A survey of workers' lives at the Da Sheng spinning mill]. Nanjing: Jiangsu renmin chubanshe.

Nie Xiaohong 乜小红 (2009). *E cang Dunhuang qiyue wenshu yanjiu* 俄藏敦煌契约文书研究 [Dunhuang documents held in Russia]. Shanghai: Shanghai guji chubanshe.

Ning Xin 宁欣 (2003). 'Tang dai funü de shehui jingji huodong: Yi *Taiping Guangji* wei zhongxin' 唐代妇女的社会经济活动—以《太平广记》为中心 [Socioeconomic activity of Tang women – Focus on the *Extensive Records Assembled in the Taiping Era*]. In: Deng Xiaonan 邓小南 (ed.), *Tang-Song nüxing yu shehui* 唐宋女性与社会 [Women and society in the Tang-Song period]. Shanghai: Shanghai cishu chubanshe.

Niu Shishan 牛世山 (2011). 'Zhongguo gudai ducheng de guige moshi chubu yanjiu' 中国古代都城的规格模式初步研究 [A preliminary study on the specification pattern of ancient Chinese capitals]. In: Zhongguo shehui kexueyuan kaogu yanjiusuo 中国社会科学院考古研究所 (ed.), *Yin-xu zhong yu Shang wenhua: Yin-xu kexue fajue 80 zhounian ji'nian wenji* 殷墟中与商文化—殷墟科学发掘80周年纪念文集 [Yinxu site and Shang culture – 80th anniversary collection of Yinxu scientific excavations]. Beijing: Kexue chubanshe.

Ono Kazuko 小野和子 (1987). *Zhongguo nüxingshi 1851-1958* 中国女性史1851—1958 [History of Chinese Women 1851–1958], edited and translated by Gao Dalun 高大伦 and Fan Yong 范勇. Chengdu: Sichuan daxue chubanshe.

Pan Guangdan 潘光旦 (1924). 'Zhongguo zhi yousheng wenti' 中国之优生问题 [Issues of eugenics in China]. *Dongfang zazhi* 东方杂志, 21. (Later reproduced in his *Yousheng gailun* 优生概论 [Eugenics overview] (1936).)

Pan Guangdan 潘光旦 (1929). 'Nüzi yundong yingxiang shengyu' 女子运动影响生育 [Impact of women's sports on childbirth]. *Shenbao* 申报, 18 June.

Pan Wei-He 潘维和 (1965). *Tanglü shang jiazu zhuyi zhi yanjiu* 唐律上家族主义之研究 [A study of familism in the Tang Code]. Taipei: Zhongguo wenhua xueyuan chubanbu.

Peng Hui 彭慧 (1948). 'Kang-Ri zhanzheng Zhong zhanqu funü de zaoyu' 抗日战争中战区妇女的遭遇 [Calamities of women in the battlefields during the anti-Japanese war]. *Xiandai funü* 现代妇女, 12(1). Shanghai: Xiandaifunüshe.

Qian Qianyi 錢謙益 ([n.d.] 1969). *Jiangyunlou shumu* 絳雲樓書目 [Catalogue of Jiangyunlou], annotated by Chen Jingyun. Shanghai: Hongwen shuju, reprint of Yueyatang congshu.

Qiao Yigang 乔以钢 and Liu Kun 刘堃 (2010). 'Wan Qing "nü guomin" huayu ji qi nüxing xiangxiang' 晚清"女国民"话语及其女性想象 [Discourse on 'female citizens' in late Qing and its images of women]. *Zhongshan daxue bao (shehui kexue ban)* 中山大学学报 (社会科学版), 50 (1).

Qiu Chung-Lin 邱仲麟 (2004). 'Huangdi de canzhuo: Mingdai de gongshan zhidu jiqi xiangguan wenti' 皇帝的餐桌: 明代的宫膳制度及其相关问题 [The emperor's dining table: The serving system of palace meals and related problems in the Ming dynasty]. *Taida lishi xuebao* 台大历史学报, 34.

Qiu Chung-Lin 邱仲麟 (2012). 'Yinqiyuji: Mingdai gongren de caixuan yu fangchu' 阴气郁积—明代宫人的采选与放出 [The selection and discharge of royal palace maidservants in the Ming dynasty]. *Taida lishi xuebao* 台大历史学报, 50.

Qiu Chung-Lin 邱仲麟 (2014). 'Yongrenzirao: Qingdai caixuan xiunü de eyan yu shehui konghuang' 庸人自扰—清代采选秀女的讹言与社会恐慌 [Ignorant people disturb themselves: Societal panic and rumors about the selection of *xiunü* in the Qing dynasty]. *Qinghua xuebao* 清华学报, 44(3).

Satake Yasuhiko 佐竹靖彥 (2003). '*Qingming shanghe tu* weihe qian nan yi nü' 《清明上河图》为何千男一女 [Why there is one woman in a thousand men in *Traveling Upstream at the Qingming Festival*]. In: Deng Xiaonan 邓小南 (ed.), *Tang-Song nüxing yu shehui* 唐宋女性与社会 [Women and society in the Tang-Song period]. Shanghai: Shanghai cishu chubanshe.

Shao Lizi 邵力子 (1920). 'Feichu hunzhi taolun zhong de ganxiang' 废除婚制讨论中的感想 [Impressions of the marriage abolition debate]. *Minguo ribao, Juewu* 民国日报·觉悟, 21 May 1920.

Shen Shaogen 沈绍根 and Yang Sanping 阳三平 (1999). 'Wusi-shiqi xinshi zhishifenzi de jiating biange sichao' 五四时期新式知识分子的家庭变革思潮 [Views on family reform among new intellectuals in the May Fourth period]. *Qiusuo* 求索, 2.

Shi Cuntong 施存统 (1920). 'Feichu hunzhi wenti' 废除婚制问题 [Marriage system abolition issue]. *Minguo ribao, Juewu* 民国日报·觉悟, 25 May 1920. (Compiled in Mei Sheng (1923), Vol. 4.)

Shi Ye 施晔 (2008). *Zhongguo gudai wenxue zhong de tongxinglian shuxie yanjiu* 中国古代文学中的同性恋书写研究 [Studies in homosexual writings in ancient Chinese literature]. Shanghai: Shanghai renmin chubanshe.

Shiga Shūzō 滋賀秀三 (2003). *Zhongguo jiazu fa yuanli* 中国家族法原理 [Principles of Chinese family law], translated by Zhang Jianguo 張建国 and Li Li 李力. Beijing: Falü chubanshe.

Shimoda Utako (Xiatian Gezi) 下田歌子 (1902). 'Jishu: Riben huazu nüxuexiao jiandu Xiatian Gezi zhi lun xing Zhongguo Nüxue shi' 寄书: 日本华族女学校监督下田歌子之论兴中国女学事 [Contributed writing: Shimada Utako, supervisor of the high school for women aristocrats, discusses promotion of Chinese women's education]. *Dalu bao* 大陆报, 1, December 9.

Shirai Atsushi 白井厚 (1982). 'Zhengqu nüquan yundong de lishi he funüxue' 争取女权运动的历史和妇女学 [The history of feminism and women's studies], translated by He Peizhong 何培忠. *Guowai shehui kexue*, 4.

Song Jiaoren 宋教仁 (2008). 'Jiandao wenti' 间岛问题 [On the Gando issue]. In: Song Jiaoren, *Song Jiaoren ji* 宋教仁集 [Collection of Song Jiaoren's writings], Vol. 1, edited by Chen Xulu 陈旭麓. Changsha: Hunan renmin chubanshe. (Originally published in 1908.)

Song Qiang 宋强, Zhang Zangzang 张藏藏 and Qiao Bian 乔边 et al. (1996). *Zhongguo keyi shuo bu: Lengzhanhou shidai de zhengzhi yu qinggan jueze* 中国可以说不: 冷战后时代的政治与情感抉择 [The China that can say no: Political and emotional choices in the post Cold-War era]. Beijing: Zhonghua gongshang lianhe chubanshe.

Song Shaopeng 宋少鹏 (2011). 'Gong zhong zhi si: Guanyu jiating laodong de guojia huayu (1949-1966)' 公中之私—关于家庭劳动的国家话语 (1949—1966) [Private in public: National discourse on the shackles of housework (1949–1966)]. *Jindai zhongguo funüshi yanjiu* 近代中国妇女史研究, 19.

Song Shaopeng 宋少鹏 (2016b). 'He-Yin Zhen de "Nüjie geming": Wu-zhengfu zhuyi de funü jiefang lilun' 何殷震的'女界革命'—无政府主义的妇女解放理论 [He-Yin Zhen's 'women's revolution': Anarchist theory of women's liberation]. *Funü yanjiu luncong* 妇女研究论丛, 133.

Sudō Mizuyo 须藤瑞代 (2012). 'Riben de Zhongguo nüxingshi yanjiu' 日本的中国女性史研究 [Japanese studies on Chinese women's history]. *Jindai zhongguo funüshi yanjiu* 近代中国妇女史研究, 20.

Sun Wen 孙文 (1985). 'Jianguo fanglüe' 建国方略 [Nation-building strategy]. In: Guangdongsheng shehuikexueyuan lishi yanjiushi, Zhongguo shehuikexueyuan jindaishi yanjiusuo zhonghuaminguoshi yanjiushi and Zhongshan daxue lishixi Sun Zhongshan yanjiushi 广东省社会科学院历史研究室 中国社会化学院近代史研究所中华民国史研究室 中山大学历史系孙中山研究室 (eds), *Sun Zhongshan quanji* 孙中山全集 [The complete works of Sun Zhongshan]. Beijing: Zhonghua shuju.

Tai Guangdian 邰光典 and Bao Zhen 宝贞 (1921). 'Xin jiating' 新家庭 [New family]. *Funü zazhi* 妇女杂志, 7(1). (Compiled in Mei Sheng (1923), Vol. 3.)

Tan Fan 谭帆 (2002). *Youling: Gudai yanyuan beihuan lu* 优伶—古代演员悲欢录 [Actors: Memories of actors in pre-modern China with their joy and sorrow]. Shanghai: Baijia chubanshe.

Tan Sheying 谈社英 (1936). *Zhongguo funü yundong tongshi* 中国妇女运动通史 [A comprehensive history of the Chinese women's movement]. (Contained in Minguo congshu bianji weiyuanhui 民国丛书编辑委员会 (ed.) (1990). *Minguo congshu 20* 民国丛书 20 [Collected books of the republic 20]. Shanghai: Shanghai shudian.)

Tang Guizhang 唐圭璋 (ed.) (1986). *Cihua Congbian* 詞話叢編 [Collection of *ci* comments]. Beijing: Zhonghua shuju.

Tao Jing-Shen 陶晋生 (2013). 'Song dai gongnü chutan' 宋代宫女初探 [Royal palace maidservants of the Song dynasty]. In: *Song Liao Jin shi lunji* 宋辽金史论集 [Collection of historical papers on Song, Liao and Jin]. Taipei: Lianjing Chuban Shiye Gongsi.

Tian Xueyuan 田雪原 and Wang Guoqiang 王国强 (eds) (2004). *Quanmian jianshe xiaokang-shehui zhong de renkou yu fazhan* 全面建设小康社会中的人口与发展 [Population and development in building a moderately affluent society in all aspects]. Beijing: Zhongguo renkou chubanshe.

Tie Aihua 铁爱花 (2011). *Song dai shiren jieceng nüxing yanjiu* 宋代士人阶层女性研究 [A study of scholar-class women in Song China]. Beijing: Beijing renmin chubanshe.

Tong Ge 童戈 (2005). *Zhongguoren de nan-nan xingxingwei: Xing yu ziwo rentong zhuangtai diaocha* 中国人的男男性行为——性与自我认同状态调查 [Chinese male-to-male sexual activity: Survey on the situation of sex and self-identity]. Beijing: Beijing ji'ande zixun zhongxin.

Tong Ge 童戈 (2007a). *Zhongguo nan-nan xingjiaoyi zhuangtai diaocha* 中国男男性交易状态调查 [Survey on the situation of male-to-male prostitution in China]. Beijing: Beijing ji'ande zixun zhongxin.

Tong Ge 童戈 (2007b). *MSM Renqun aizibing fangzhi gongzuo de 'tizhi zhangai"* MSM 人群艾滋病防治工作的'体制障碍' ['Institutional obstruction' to AIDS prevention efforts for men who have sex with men]. Beijing: Beijing ji-ande zixun zhongxin.

Tong Ge 童戈 (2008). 'Tongzhi shequn: Xingcheng de beijing he huodong xingshi de fazhan' 同志社群：形成的背景和活动形式的发展 [The gay community: The background of its formation and the development of various forms of activities]. In: He Xiaopei 何小培, Guo Yaqi 郭雅琦, Cui Zi'en 崔子恩, Mao Yanling 毛燕凌 and Guo Xiaofei 郭晓飞 (eds), *Zhongguo 'tongzhi' renqun shengtai baogao (1)* 中国·同志·人群生态报告（一）[Report on the way of life of China's *tongzhi* crowd (1)]. Beijing: Beijing ji-ande zixun zhongxin.

Tong Xin 佟新 (2003). *Yihua yu kangzheng: Zhongguo nügong gongzuo shi yanjiu* 异化与抗争—中国女工工作史研究 [Alienation and resistance: A study of the lives of Chinese women workers]. Beijing: Zhongguo shehui kexue chubanshe.

Tsai Mei-Fen 蔡玫芬, Zhu Naicheng 朱乃诚 and Chen Kwang-tzuu 陈光祖 (eds) (2012). *Shangwang Wu Ding yu hou Fu Hao* 商王武丁与后妇好 [Shang King Wu Ding and his wife Fu Hao]. Taipei: Guoli Gugong Bowuyuan.

Tu Cheng-Sheng 杜正胜 (1992). 'Chuantong jiazu jiegou de dianxing' 传统家族结构的典型 [Model for the traditional family structure]. *Gudai shehui yu guojia* 古代社会与国家 [Ancient society and state]. Taipei: Yunchen wenhua.

UM-Fudan Joint Institute for Gender Studies (Fudan-Mixiegen daxue shehui xingbie yanjiusuo) 复旦—密歇根大学社会性别研究所 (ed.), Wang Zheng 王政 and Chen Yan 陈雁 (chief eds) (2005). *Bainian Zhongguo nüquan sichao yanjiu* 百年中国女权思潮研究 [A century of research into the currents of thought on Chinese women's rights]. Shanghai: Fudan daxue chubanshe.

Wan Qionghua 万琼华 (2010). *Jindai Zhongguo nüzi jiaoyu sichao he nüxing zhuti shenfen goujian* 近代中国女子教育思潮和女性主体身份构建 [Trends in women's education and the construction of women's subjective identity in modern China]. Beijing: Zhonguo shehui kexue chubanshe.

Wang Dongxia 王东霞 (ed.) (2003). *Bainian Zhongguo shehui tupu: Cong changpao magua dao xizhuang gelü* 百年中国社会图谱—从长袍马褂到西装革履 [Illustrated book of a century of Chinese society: From *magua* to Western clothing and leather shoes]. Chengdu: Sichuan renmin chubenshe.

Wang Fansen 王汎森 (2013). '"Fanmen" de benzhi shi shenme: "Zhuyi" yu jindai Zhongguo siren lingyu de zhengzhihua' 「烦闷」的本质是什—「主义」与近代中国私人领域的政治化 [The essence of 'dysphoria': 'Ideology' and the politicization of the modern Chinese private sphere]. *Sixiangshi* 思想史, 1.

Wang Guimei 王桂妹 (2008). 'Zhongguo wenxue zhong de "tieluhuoche" yixiang yu xiandaixing xiangxiang' 中国文学中的"铁路火车"意象与现代性想象 ['Railway train' images in Chinese literature and the modern imagination]. *Xueshu jiaoliu* 学术交流, 176.

Wang Hui 汪晖 (2008). *Xiandai Zhongguo sixiang de xingqi* 现代中国思想的兴起 [The rise of Chinese modern thought], Vol. 1, Part 1, 2nd edition. Beijing: Shenghuo, dushu, xinzhi sanlian shudian. (Originally published in 2004.)

Wang Hui 汪晖 (2010). *Yazhou shiye: Zhongguo lishide Xushu* 亚洲视野: 中国历史的叙述 [Perspectives on Asia: Narratives of Chinese history]. Hong Kong: Oxford University Press.

Wang Jianhua 王建华 and Cao Jing 曹静 (2014). 'Qianzhang da mudi renkou xingbie yanjiu' 前掌大墓地人口性别研究 [Qianzhangda cemetery population and gender study]. In: Zhongguo shehui kexueyuan kaogu yanjiusuo 中国社会科学院考古研究所 (ed.), *Xia-Shang duyi yu wenhua* 夏商都邑与文化 [Cities and culture of the Xia and Shang dynasties], Vol.1. Beijing: Zhongguo Shehui Kexue chubanshe.

Wang Jing 王晶 (2015). 'Tangdai de fangfen yu jiazu de fenhua' 唐代的房分与家族的分化 [Fangfen and family division in the Tang dynasty]. *Chengda lishi xuebao* 成大历史学报, 49.

Wang Shen 王申 (2012). 'Jin 10nian Tang Song funüshi yanjiu de huigu yu fansi' 近10年唐宋妇女史研究的回顾与反思 [A review of studies of the history of Tang-Song women in the last ten years]. *Funü yanjiu luncong* 妇女研究论丛, 2.

Wang Shih-Ying 王诗颖 (2011). *Guomin geming jun yu jindai Zhongguo nanxing qigai de xingsu: 1924-1945* 国民革命军与近代中国男性气概的形塑: 1924–1945 [The national revolutionary army and the formation of modern Chinese masculinity: 1924–1945]. Taipei: Guoshi guan.

Wang Shou-Nan 王寿南 (1992). 'Tangdai gongzhu zhi hunyin' 唐代公主之婚姻 [The marriages of the Tang princesses]. *Tangdai yanjiu lunji* 唐代研究论集 [Collected studies on the Tang dynasty], Part 1. Taipei: Xinwenfeng chuban gongsi.

Wang Shu-Hwai 王树槐, Cheng Lucie 成露茜, Lu Fang-Shang 吕芳上, Susan Mann 曼素恩, Chang Jui-Te 张瑞德, Yu Chien-Ming 游鉴明 and Pao Chia-Lin 鲍家麟 (eds) (1995). *Jindai Zhongguo funüshi zhongwen ziliao mulu* 近代中国妇女史中文目录 [Catalogue of Chinese-language materials on the history of women in modern China]. Taipei: Zhongyang yanjiuyuan jindaishi yanjiusuo.

Wang Shunu 王书奴 (1934). *Zhongguo changji shi* 中国娼妓史 [The history of prostitutes in China]. Shanghai: Shenghuo shudian.

Wang Xiaoqing 王晓清 (2005). *Yuan dai shehui hunyin xingtai* 元代社会婚姻形态 [Forms of marriage in Yuan society]. Wuhan: Wuhan chubanshe.

Wang Yuesheng 王跃生 (2003). *Qing dai zhongqi hunyin chongtu touxi* 清代中期婚姻冲突透析 [Analysis of marriage troubles in the mid-Qing period]. Beijing: Shehui kexue wenxian chubanshe.

Wang Yun 王云 (1997). 'Ming dai nüguan zhidu tanxi' 明代女官制度探析 [Study on the court ladies in the Ming dynasty]. *Qilu xuekan* 齐鲁学刊, 1997(1).

Wang Zheng 王政 (1997). '"Nüxing yishi" yu "shehui xingbie yishi" bianyi' '女性意识'与 '社会性别意识'辩异 [Difference between 'feminine consciousness' and 'gender consciousness']. *Funü yanjiu longcong* 妇女研究论丛, 1.

Wang Zheng 王政 (2004). *Yuejie: Kuawenhua nüquan shijian* 越界—跨文化女权实践 [Crossing borders: Trans-cultural feminist practices]. Tianjin: Tianjin renmin chubanshe.

Wang Zheng 王政, Gao Yanyi (Dorothy Ko) 高彦颐 and Liu He (Lydia H. Liu) 刘禾 (2004). '(Dingtan) Cong *Nüjie zhong* dao *Nanjie zhong*: Nanxing zhuti, guozu zhuyi yu xiandaixing' (鼎谈) 从《女界钟》到《男界钟》: 男性主体、国族主义与现代性 [(Dialogue) From *Bell of the Women's World* to *Bell of the Men's World*: Male subjectivity, nationalism and modernity]. In: Du Fangqin 杜芳琴 and Wang Zheng 王政 (eds), *Shehui xingbie* 社会性别 [Gender studies], 2. Tianjin: Tianjin renmin chubanshe.

Wang Zhongwen 王仲闻 (1979). *Li Qingzhao ji jiaozhu* 李清照集校注 [Collected works of Li Qingzhao, corrected and annotated edition]. Beijing: Renmin wenxue chubanshe.

Wei Tingting 韦婷婷 (2014). 'Yi nü-tongxinglian de yanjing kan Beijing shifuhui' 以女同性恋的眼睛看北京世妇会 [The Beijing World Conference on Women seen from a lesbian perspective]. *Zhongguo fazhan jianbao* 中国发展简报, 3.

Wei Wei 魏伟 (2012). *Gongkai: Dangdai Chengdu 'tongzhi' kongjian de xingcheng he bianqian* 公开—当代成都'同志'空间的形成和变迁 [Making public: Formation and transition of contemporary Chengdu *'tongzhi'* space]. Shanghai: Shanghai sanlian shudian.

Wong Yu-Hsuan 翁育瑄 (2003). 'Cong Tanglü de guiding kan jiating nei de shenfen dengji: Tangdai de zhupu guanxi' 从唐律的规定看家庭内的身份等级—唐代的主仆关系 [Status rank within the family according to the Tang Code: The master-servant relationship in Tang]. In: Kao Ming-Shih 高明士 (ed.), *Tangdai shenfen fazhi yanjiu: Yi Tanglü Minglilü wei zhongxin* 唐代身份法制研究—以唐律名例律为中心 [Study of Tang status law: Centering on Tang Code terminology of precedents and laws]. Taipei: Wunan tushu.

Wong Yu-Hsuan 翁育瑄 (2005a). 'Huhunlü yu jianei zhixu: Tangdai jiazu de tantao' 户婚律与家内秩序—唐代家庭的探讨 [Study of the Tang family: The household and marriage section of the Code and family order]. In: Kao Ming-Shih 高明士 (ed.), *Dongya chuantong jiali, jiaoyu yu guofa (2): Jianei zhixu yu guofa* 东亚传统家礼、教育与国法 (二): 家内秩序与国法 [Traditional family rituals, education and state law in East Asia (2): Family order and state law]. Taipei: Taida chuban zhongxin.

Wong Yu-Hsuan 翁育瑄 (2005b). 'Tang-Song youguan qinshu xiangfan anjian de shenli' 唐宋有关亲属相犯案件的审理 [Judicial examination of cases concerning disputes between kinspersons in Tang and Song]. In: Kao Ming-Shih 高明士 (ed.), *Dongya chuantong jiaoyu yu fazhi yanjiu (1): Jiaoyu yu zhengzhi shehui* 东亚传统教育与法制研究 (一): 教育与政治社会 [Study of traditional education and the legal system in East Asia (1): Education and political society]. Taipei: Taida chuban zhongxin.

Wong Yu-Hsuan 翁育瑄 (2012). *Tang-Song de jianzui yu liangxing guanxi* 唐宋的奸罪与两性关系 [The crime of illicit sexual relationships and gender relationships in Tang and Song]. Taipei: Daoxing chubanshe.

Wu Chia-Ling 吳嘉苓 (2000). 'Yiliao zhuanye, xingbie yu guojia: Taiwan zhuchanshi xingshuai de shehuixue fenxi' 医疗专业、性别与国家—台湾助产士兴衰的社会学分析 [Medical profession, gender and state: A sociological analysis of the rise and fall of midwives in Taiwan]. *Taiwan shehuixue yanjiu* 台湾社会学研究, 4.

Wu Cuncun 吴存存 (2000). *Ming-Qing shehui xing'ai fengqi* 明清社会性爱风气 [Sexual mores in Ming and Qing society]. Beijing: Renmin wenxue chubanshe.

Xia Xiaohong 夏晓虹 (1995). *Wan-Qing wenren funü guan* 晚清文人妇女观 [Literati's views on women in the late Qing]. Beijing: Zuojia chubanshe.

Xia Xiaohong 夏晓虹 (1999). 'Qiu Jin yu Xie Daoyun' 秋瑾与谢道韫 [*Qiu Jin and Xie Daoyun*]. *Beijing daxue xuebao (zhexue shehui kexue ban)* 北京大学学报 (哲学社会科学版), 1.

Xia Xiaohong 夏晓虹 (2002). 'Lishi jiyi de chonggou: Wan Qing "Nan xiang nü buxiang" shiyi' 历史记忆的重构：晚清"男降女不降"释义 [The invention of historical memory: Explaining the late Qing 'Men surrendered, women did not']. In: Chen Pingyuan 陈平原 et al. (eds), *Wan Ming yu wan Qing: Lishi chuancheng yu wenhua chuangxin* 晚明与晚清：历史传承与文化创新 [Late Ming and late Qing: Historical heritage and cultural innovation]. Wuhan: Hubei jiaoyu chubanshe.

Xia Xiaohong 夏晓虹 (2006). 'He Zhen de Wu-zhengfu zhuyi "Nüjie geming" lun' 何震的无政府主义'女界革命'论 [*Tianyi bao* and He Zhen's views on the 'women's revolution']. *Zhonghua wenshi luncong* 中华文史论丛, 83.

Xia Xiaohong 夏晓虹 (2014). 'WanQing nübao zhong de guozu lunshu yu nüxing yishi: 1907-nian de duoyuan chengxian' 晚清女报中的国族论述与女性意识—1907年的多元呈现 [Nationalism and feminism in women's newspapers in late-Qing China: Multiple presentation in 1907]. *Beijing daxue xuebao (zhexue shehui kexue ban)* 北京大学学报 (哲学社会科学版), 51(4).

Xiang Jingyu 向警予 (1920). 'Nüzi jiefang yu gaizao de shangque' 女子解放与改造的商榷 [The discussion of women's liberation and reform]. *Shaonian zhongguo* 少年中国, 2(2). (Compiled in Zhonghua quanguo funü lianhehui (1981).)

Xiang Jingyu 向警予 (1923). 'Zhongguo zhishi funü de sanpai' 中国知识妇女的三派 [Three factions of educated Chinese women]. *Funü zhoubao* 妇女周报, 15. (Compiled in Zhonghua quanguo funü lianhehui funü yundong lishi yanjiushi (1986).)

Xie Wuliang 谢无量 (ed.) (1979). *Zhongguo funü wenxueshi* 中国妇女文学史 [The history of women's literature in China]. Taipei: Taiwan zhonghua shuju.

Xing Fei 邢飞 (2012). *Zhongguo 'tongqi' shengcun diaocha baogao* 中国「同妻」生存调查报告 [Survey on China's 'gay-straight marriage' lifestyle]. Chengdu: Chengdu shidai chubanshe.

Xu Fulin 徐傅霖 (1921). 'Xuexiao ticao gaishan an' 学校体操改善案 [Proposal for improvement in school gymnastics]. *Jiaoyu zazhi* 教育杂志, 13(4), April.

Xu Jialiang 徐家良 (2003). *Zhidu, Yingxiangli yu Boyi: Quanguo Fulian yu gonggong zhengce zhiding* 制度·影响力与博弈：全国妇联与公共政策制定 [Institution, influence and contest: All-China Women's Federation and public policy formulation]. Beijing: Zhongguo shehui chubanshe.

Xu Peijun 徐培均 (2013). *Li Qingzhao ji jianzhu: xiudingben* 李清照集笺注：修订本 [Collected works of Li Qingzhao annotated edition: Revised version]. Shanghai: Shanghai guji chubanshe.

Xu Qiu 徐釚 ([n.d.] 1981) *Ciyuan congtan* 詞苑叢談 [Collection and discussions of *ci* comments], corrected and annotated by Tang Guizhang 唐圭璋. Shanghai: Shanghai guji ghubanshe, 1981.

Yan Bin (Lianshi) 燕斌 (炼石) (1907a). 'Nüquan pingyi' 女权平议 [Fair discussions on women's rights]. *Zhongguo Xinnüjie* 中国新女界, 1.

Yan Bin (Lianshi) 燕斌 (炼石) (1907b). 'Nüjie yu guojia zhi guanxi' 女界与国家之关系 [Relationship between women's world and the nation-state]. *Zhongguo Xinnüjie* 中国新女界, 2.

Yan Yiping 严一萍 (ed.) (1983). *Yin-Zhou Jinwen zongji* 殷周金文总集 [Collection of bronze inscriptions of the Shang and Zhou dynasties], Vol. 9. Taipei: Yiwen yinshuguan.

Yang Xingmei 杨兴梅 (2012). *Shenti zhi zheng: Jindai Zhongguo fanchanzu de licheng* 身体之争：近代中国反缠足的历程 [The contested body: The anti-footbinding movement in modern China]. Beijing: Shehui kexue wenxian chubanshe.

Yang Zhenhong 杨振红 ([2004] 2009). 'Longgang Qinjian zhu "tian" "zu" jian shiyi bu: Jiehe Zhangjiashan Hanjian kan mingtianzhi de tudi guanli he tianzu zhengshou' 龙岗秦简诸'田''租'简释义补—结合张家山汉简看名田制的土地管理和田租征收 [Supplementary exegesis of 'tian' and 'zu' bamboo slips among the Longgang bamboo slips of Qin: A connection between land management and rice-field tax collection under the land registration system recorded in the Zhangjiashan bamboo slips of Han]. In: *Chutu jiandu yu Qin-Han shehui* 出土简牍与秦汉社会 [Excavated bamboo and wooden slips and society of the Qin-Han dynasties]. Guilin: Guangxi shifan daxue chubanshe.

Yao Changxu 姚昶绪 and Yu Yunyou 余云岫 (eds) ([1920] 1927). *Taichan xuzhi* 胎产须知 [Pregnancy guidebook]. Beijing: Shangwu yinshuguan.

Yao Lingxi 姚灵犀 (ed.) (1936a). *Caifeilu: Zhongguo funü chanzu shiliao* 采菲录：中国妇女缠足史料 [Record of picking radishes: Sources on women's footbinding in China]. Reproduced from Tianjin: Tianjin shidai gongsi.

Yao Lingxi 姚灵犀 (ed.) (1936b). *Caifeilu xubian* 采菲录续编 [Continuation of the record of picking radishes]. Reproduced from Tianjin: Tianjin shidai gongsi.

Yao Ping 姚平 (2004). *Tangdai funü de shengming licheng* 唐代妇女的生命历程 [Life histories of Tang women]. Shanghai: Shanghai guji chubanshe.

Yao Ping 姚平 (2018). *Tangdai de shehui yu xingbie wenhua* 唐代的社会与性别文化 [Tang society and gender culture]. Beijing: Beijing daxue chubanshe.

Yen Ju-Ting 颜汝庭 (2005). 'Jin ershinian lai liang'an Song dai funüshi yanjiu gaikuang (1985-2004)' 近二十年来两岸宋代妇女研究概况 (1985—2004) [An overview of studies on the history of Song women in the last two decades in China and Taiwan (1985–2004)]. *Shiyun* 史耘, 11.

Yi Jiayue 易家钺 (1921). 'Jiating zhidu miewang lun de yige yinzi' 家庭制度灭亡论的一个引子 [Introduction to the discourse on the end of the family system]. *Jiating yanjiu* 家庭研究, 1(4).

Yi Jo-Lan 衣若兰 (1999). 'Bei yiwang de gongting funü: Qianlun Ming dai gongzhu de shenghuo' 被遗忘的宫廷妇女—浅论明代公主的生活 [The forgotten court women: On the life of princesses in the Ming dynasty]. *Fujen lishi xuebao* 辅仁历史学报, 10.

Yi Jo-Lan 衣若兰 (2002). *Sanguliupo: Ming dai funü yu shehui de tansuo* 三姑六婆—明代妇女与社会的探索 [Three spinsters and six dames: An investigation of women and society in Ming China]. Taipei: Daoxiang chubanshe.

Yu Chien-Ming 游鉴明 (2009). *Jindai huadong diqu de nüzi tiyu (1895—1937)* 近代华东地区的女子体育 (1895–1937) [Women's physical education in the modern Eastern China region (1895–1937)]. Taipei: Zhongyang yanjiuyuan jindaishi yanjiusuo.

Yu Huaqing 余华青 (1993). *Zhongguo huanguan zhidu shi* 中国宦官制度史 [History of the system of Chinese eunuchs]. Shanghai: Shanghai renmin chubanshe.

Yu Hui-Yuan 游惠远 (1998). *Song dai minfu de juese yu diwei* 宋代民妇德角色与地位 [The role and status of ordinary women in Song China]. Taipei: Xinwenfeng chuban gongsi.

Yu Hui-Yuan 游惠远 (2003). *Song Yuan zhiji funü diwei de bianqian* 宋元之际妇女地位的变迁 [Change in the status of women in Song and Yuan China]. Taipei: Xinwenfeng chuban gongsi.

Zhang Bangwei 张邦炜 (1989). *Hun-hun yu shehu: Song dai* 婚婚与社会 — 宋代 [Marriage and society in Song China]. Chengdu: Sichuan renmin chubanshe.

Zhang Bangwei 张邦炜 ([1990] 2003). 'Song dai de gongzhu' 宋代的公主 [Song princesses]. *Song dai hunyin jiazu shi lun* 宋代婚姻家族史论 [History of marriage and family in the Song dynasty]. Beijing: Renmin chubanshe.

Zhang Bangwei 张邦炜 (2003). *Song dai hunyin jiazushi lun* 宋代婚姻家族史论 [Marriage and family in the Song dynasty period]. Beijing: Renmin chubanshe.

Zhang Bangwei 张邦炜 (2011). '"Tang-Song bian'ge" lun yu Song dai shehuishi yanjiu' "唐宋变革"论与宋代社会史研究 [A study of the history of Song society and the Tang-Song transition theory]. *Zhongguo jingjishi luntan* 中国经济史论坛, 2011 (8)3.

Zhang Feng 张凤 (2007). 'Jin shinian lai Song dai hunyin wenti yanjiu tanshu' 近十年来宋代婚姻问题研究探述 [Studies of the marriage issue in Song China in the last ten years]. *Gansu lianhe daxue xuebao (Shehui kexue ban)* 甘肃联合大学学报 (社会科学版), 4.

Zhang Guogang 张国刚 (ed.) (2007). *Zhongguo jiatingshi* 中国家庭史 [History of the family in China]. Guangdong: Guangdong renmin chubanshe.

Zhang Jie 张杰 (ed.) (2013). *Duanxiu wen bian: Zhongguo gudai tongxinglian shiliao jicheng* 断袖文编—中国古代同性恋史料集成 [A 'cut sleeve' selection: Corpus of historical materials on homosexuality in ancient China]. Tianjin: Tianjin guji chubanshe (in 3 volumes).

Zhang Jishun 张济顺 (2015). *Yuanqu de dushi: 1950-niandai de Shanghai* 远去的都市—1950年代的上海 [The city in the distant past: Shanghai in the 1950s]. Beijing: Shehui kexue wenxian chubanshe.

Zhang Nan 张柟 and Wang Renzhi 王忍之 (eds) (1963). *Xinhai-geming qian shinian jian shilun xuanji* 辛亥革命前十年间时论选集 [Anthology of editorial articles in the decade before the 1911 Revolution], Vol. 2. Beijing: Shenghuo, dushu, xinzhi sanlian shudian.

Zhang Nan 张柟 and Wang Renzhi 王忍之 (eds) (1977). *Xinhai-geming qian shinian jian shilun xuanji* 辛亥革命前十年间时论选集 [Anthology of editorial articles in the decade before the 1911 Revolution], Vol. 3. Beijing: Shenghuo, dushu, xinzhi sanlian shudian.

Zhang Renlan 张纫兰. (1912). Zhang Renlan nüshi lai han 张纫兰女史来函 [Ms. Zhang Renlan's letter to the editor]. *Minli bao* 民立报, March 9.

Zhang Ruoming 张若名 (1920). "'Jixianfeng" de nüzi' '急先锋'的女子 [Woman 'vanguard']. *Juewu (Tianjin)* 觉悟 (天津), 1. (Reprinted by Renmin chubanshe, 1980.)

Zhang Yu 张羽 (2014). *Minguo nanxing fushi wenhua yanjiu* 民国男性服饰文化研究 [A study of men's dress culture in the Republic]. Ph.D. thesis, Shanghai Theater Academy [上海戏剧学院].

Zhang Yumu 张于牧 (2005). *Minguo ziran kexue yu minzu zhuyi* 民国自然科学与民族主义 [Natural science and nationalism in the Republic]. Ph.D. thesis, Wuhan University [武汉大学].

Zhang Zaizhou 张在舟 (2001). *Aimei de licheng: Zhongguo gudai tongxinglian shi* 暧昧的历程——中国古代同性恋史 [An ambiguous course: History of homosexuality in ancient China]. Zhengzhou: Zhongzhou guji chubanshe.

Zhang Zhibin 张志斌 (2000). *Gudai zhongyi fuchanke jibingshi* 古代中医妇产科疾病史 [History of women's diseases in ancient Chinese medicine]. Beijing: Zhongyi guji chubanshe.

Zhang Zhujun 张竹君 (1905). 'Shanghai nüzi zhong-xiyi xueyuan jianzhang' 上海女子中西医学院简章 [General regulations of the College of Chinese and Western Medicine for Women]. *Jingzhong ribao* 警钟日报, 24 January.

Zhao Lingzhi 赵令志 (2008). 'Lun Qingdai zhi xuan xiunü zhidu' 论清代之选秀女制度 [On the system of selection of *xiunü* in the Qing dynasty]. In: Zhongguo diyi lishi dang'an guan 中国第一历史档案馆 (ed.), *Ming-Qing dang'an yu lishi yanjiu lunwenji: Qingzhu Zhongguo diyi lishi dang'an guan chengli 80 zhounian* 明清档案与历史研究论文集：庆祝中国第一历史档案馆成立80周年 [Collection of Ming and Qing archives and historical dissertations: Celebrating the 80th anniversary of the establishment of the first national historical archives in China]. Beijing: Xinhua chubanshe.

Zhao Mingcheng 赵明诚 (1985). *Jinshilu jiaozheng* 金石录校证 [Record of epigraphy, corrected edition], corrected by Jin Wenming 金文明. Shanghai: Shanghai shuhua chubanshe.

Zheng Guanying 郑观应 (1880). *Yiyan* 易言 [Frivolous words]. (Reproduced in his *Zheng Guanying ji, Jiushi jieyao, wai bazhong* 郑观应集：救时揭要，外八种 [Collection of Zheng Guanying's writings: Important guidelines for saving the world and eight other books], edited by Xia Dongyuan 夏东元 (2013). Beijing: Zhonghua shuju.)

Zheng Guanying 郑观应 (1885). *Shengshi weiyan* 盛世危言 [Bold words during a prosperous age], 14 *juan* edition. (Reproduced in his *Zheng Guanying ji, Shengshi weiyan* 郑观应集：盛世危言 [Collection of Zheng Guanying's writings: Bold words during a prosperous age], edited by Xia Dongyuan 夏东元 (2013). Beijing: Zhonghua ganbu.)

Zhongguo funü guanli ganbu xueyuan 中国妇女管理干部学院 (ed.) (1987, 1988). *Zhongguo funü yundong wenxian ziliao huibian* 中国妇女运动文献资料汇编 [Chinese women's movement documentary records edition], 2 volumes. Beijing: Chunqiu chubanshe.

Zhongguo nongye bowuguan 中国农业博物馆 (ed.) (1995). *Zhongguo gudai gengzhi tu* 中国古代耕织图 [Pictures of tilling and weaving in ancient China]. Beijing: Zhongguo nongye chubanshe.

Zhongguo qingtongqi quanji bianji weiyuanhui 中国青铜器全集编辑委员会 (ed.) (1997). *Zhongguo qingtongqi quanji* 中国青铜器全集 [Bronze treasures of China], Vol. 2. Beijing: Wenwu chubanshe.

Zhongguo shehui kexueyuan kaogu yanjiusuo Anyang gongzuodui 中国社会科学院考古研究所安阳工作队 (2009). 'He'nan Anyang shi Yin-xu Xiaomintun dongnandi Shang dai muzang 1989–1990 nian de faxue' 河南安阳市殷墟孝民屯东南地商代墓葬1989–1990年的发掘 [1989–1990 Excavations of Shang era tombs at Xiaomintun dongnandi in Yinxu, Anyang, Henan Province], *Kaogu* 考古, 9.

Zhongguo shehui kexueyuan kaogu yanjiusuo 中国社会科学院考古研究所 (ed.) (1980). *Yin-xu Fu-hao Mu* 殷墟妇好墓 [Tomb of Fu Hao at Yinxu in Anyang]. Beijing: Wenwu chubanshe.

Zhongguo shehui kexueyuan kaogu yanjiusuo 中国社会科学院考古研究所 (ed.) (1987). *Yin-xu fajue baogao 1958–1961* 殷墟发掘报告 1958-1961 [Report on Yinxu excavations 1958–1961]. Beijing: Wenwu chubanshe.

Zhongguo shehui kexueyuan kaogu yanjiusuo 中国社会科学院考古研究所 (ed.) (1994). *Yin-xu de faxian yu yanjiu* 殷墟的发现与研究 [Excavations and studies of Yinxu]. Beijing: Kexue chubanshe.

Zhongguo shehui kexueyuan kaogu yanjiusuo 中国社会科学院考古研究所 (ed.) (2000). *Shandong Wang Yin* 山东王因 [Excavations of the Wangyin site in Shandong]. Beijing: Kexue chubanshe.

Zhonghua quanguo funü lianhehui 中华全国妇女联合会 (ed.) (1981). *Wusi-shiqi funü wenti wenxuan* 五四时期妇女问题文选 [Selected writings on women's issues in the May Fourth era]. Beijing: Zhongguo funü chubanshe.

Zhonghua quanguo funü lianhehui 中华全国妇女联合会 (1989). *Zhongguo funü yundongshi (Xin minzhu zhuyi shiqi)* 中国妇女运动史 (新民主主义时期) [History of the Chinese women's movement (the new democratic era)]. Beijing: Chunqiu chubanshe.

Zhonghua quanguo funü lianhehui funü yundong lishi yanjiushi 中华全国妇女联合会妇女运动历史研究室 (ed.) (1986). *Zhongguo funü yundong lishi ziliao: 1921–1927* 中国妇女运动历史资料: 1921–1927 [Historical records of the Chinese women's movement: 1921–1927], 2 volumes. Beijing: Renmin chubanshe.

Zhonghua quanguo funü lianhehui funü yundong lishi yanjiushi 中华全国妇女联合会妇女运动历史研究室 (ed.) (1991a). *Zhongguo funü yundong lishi ziliao: 1840–1918* 中国妇女运动历史资料: 1840–1918 [Historical records of the Chinese women's movement: 1840–1918]. Beijing: Chunqiu chubanshe.

Zhonghua quanguo funü lianhehui funü yundong lishi yanjiushi 中华全国妇女联合会妇女运动历史研究室 (ed.) (1991b). *Zhongguo funü yundong lishi ziliao: 1927–1937* 中国妇女运动历史资料: 1927–1937 [Historical records of the Chinese women's movement: 1927–1937]. Beijing: Chunqiu chubanshe.

Zhonghua quanguo funü lianhehui funü yundong lishi yanjiushi 中华全国妇女联合会妇女运动历史研究室 (ed.) (1991c). *Zhongguo funü yundong lishi ziliao: 1937–1945* 中国妇女运动历史资料: 1937–1945 [Historical records of the Chinese women's movement: 1937–1945]. Beijing: Zhongguo funü chubanshe.

Zhonghua quanguo funü lianhehui funü yundong lishi yanjiushi 中华全国妇女联合会妇女运动历史研究室 (ed.) (1991d). *Zhongguo funü yundong lishi ziliao: 1945–1949* 中国妇女运动历史资料: 1945–1949 [Historical records of the Chinese women's movement: 1945–1949]. Beijing: Zhonggue funü chubanshe.

Zhou Dan 周丹 (ed.) (2006). *Tongxinglian yu fa: 'Xing, zhengce yu fa guoji xueshu yantaohui' lunwen ji ziliao* 同性恋与法——'性·政策与法国际学术研讨会'论文及资料 [Homosexuality and law: Papers and materials from the 'International Symposium on Sex, Policy and Law']. Guilin: Guangxi shifan daxue chubanshe.

Zhou Huiling 周慧玲 (2000). 'Nüyanyuan, Xieshi zhuyi, "Xinnüxing" lunshu: Wanqing zhi Wusi shiqi Zhongguo xiandai juchang zhong de xingbie biaoyan' 女演员, 写实主义, '新女性'论述——晚清至五四时期中国现代剧场中的性别表演 [Female acting, realism, [and] the 'new woman' discourse: Gender performance in Chinese modern theatres from late Qing to the May Fourth period]. *Xiju Yishu* 戏剧艺术, 2000 (1).

Zhou Yiliang 周一良 (1985). *Wei-Jin-Nan-Beichao zhaji* 魏晋南北朝札记 [Notes on the history of the Wei, Jin and Southern and Northern Dynasties]. Beijing: Zhonghua shuju.

Zhu Fenghan 朱凤瀚 (1992). 'Lun Buci yu Shang-Zhou Jinwen zhong de "Hou"' 论卜辞与商周金文中的「后」 [About '*hou*' in Shang and Zhou oracle inscriptions]. *Guwenzi yanjiu* 古文字研究, 19.

Zhu Hanmin 朱汉民 and Chen Songchang 陈松长 (eds) (2013). *Yuelu shuyuan cang Qinjian* 岳麓书院藏秦简 [Qin bamboo strips held by the Yuelu academy], 3. Shanghai: Shanghai cishu chubanshe.

Zhu Ruixi 朱瑞熙 (1994). 'Songchao de gongting zhidu' 宋朝的宫廷制度 [The inner palace system of the Song dynasty]. *Xueshu yuekan* 学术月刊, 1994 (4).

Zhu Ziyan 朱子彦 (1998). *Hougong zhidu yanjiu* 后宫制度研究 [A study on the inner palace system]. Shanghai: Huadong shifan daxue chubanshe.

Zhu Zongzhen 朱宗震 (2000). 'Shidafu chuantong dui "Wusi-shiqi" Xinqingnian de yingxiang' 士大夫传统对'五四时期'新青年的影响 [The influence of the scholar-official tradition on May Fourth period *New Youth*]. *Shanghai xingzheng xueyuan xuebao* 上海行政学院学报, 1.

English

Anderson, Benedict (1983). *Imagined Communities: Reflections on the Origin and Spread of Nationalism*. London: Verso.

Balibar, Etienne and Immanuel Wallerstein (1991). *Race, Nation, Class: Ambiguous Identities*, translated by Chris Turner. London: Verso. (Originally published in 1988 as *Race, Nation, Classe: Les Identités Ambiguës*. Paris: La Découverte.)

Banerjee, Sikata (2012). *Muscular Nationalism: Gender, Violence, and Empire in India and Ireland, 1914–2004*. New York: New York University Press.

Barlow, Tani E. (2004). *The Question of Women in Chinese Feminism*. Durham: Duke University Press.

Bederman, Gail (1995). *Manliness and Civilization: A Cultural History of Gender and Race in the United States, 1880–1917*. Chicago: University of Chicago Press.

Birge, Bettine (1989). 'Chu Hsi and women's education'. In: de Bary, William Theodore and John W. Chaffee (eds), *Neo-Confucian Education: The Formative Stage*. Berkeley: University of California Press.

Bossler, Beverly (2002). 'Faithful wives and heroic martyrs'. In: Association of Chinese Historians (ed.), *The World of Chinese History: Unified Systems and Pluralistic Developments*. Tokyo: Tokyo Metropolitan University Press.

Bray, Francesca (1997). *Technology and Gender: Fabrics of Power in Late Imperial China*. Berkeley: University of California Press.
Chan, Anita et al. (1984). *Chen Village: The Recent History of a Peasant Community in Mao's China*. Berkeley: University of California Press.
Chang, Kang-i Sun and Haun Saussy (eds) (1999). *Women Writers of Traditional China: An Anthology of Poetry and Criticism*. Stanford: Stanford University Press.
Chang, Leslie T. (2009). *Factory Girls: From Village to City in a Changing China*. New York: Spiegel & Grau.
Chatterjee, Partha (1986). *Nationalist Thought and the Colonial World: A Derivative Discourse?* London: Zed Books.
Chen Yu-Shih (1996). 'The historical template of Pan Chao's Nü Chieh'. *T'oung Pao*, Vol. 82, Livre 4.5.
Chou Wahshan (2009). *Tongzhi: Politics of Same-Sex Eroticism in Chinese Societies*. London: Routledge.
Connell, Raewyn (1995). *Masculinities*. Cambridge: Polity Press.
Connell, Raewyn (2005). *Masculinities*, 2nd ed. Stanford: Stanford University Press.
Connell, Raewyn and Rebecca Pearse (2014). *Gender: In World Perspective (Short Introduction)*, Third Edition. Cambridge: Polity.
Culp, Robert (2006). 'Rethinking governmentality: Training, cultivation, and cultural citizenship in nationalist China'. *The Journal of Asian Studies*, 65(3): 529–554.
Dautcher, Jay (2009). *Down a Narrow Road: Identity and Masculinity in a Uyghur Community in Xinjiang China*. Cambridge: Harvard University Asia Center.
Diamant, Neil J. (2000). *Revolutionizing the Family: Politics, Love, and Divorce in Urban and Rural China, 1949–1968*. Berkeley: University of California Press.
Dikötter, Frank (1992). *The Discourse of Race in Modern China*. London: Hurst & Company.
Dikötter, Frank (1995). *Sex Culture and Modernity in China*. London: Hurst & Company.
Dikötter, Frank (1998). *Imperfect Conceptions: Medical Knowledge, Birth Defects and Eugenics in China*. New York: Columbia University Press.
Duden, Barbara (1998). *The Woman Beneath the Skin: A Doctor's Patients in Eighteenth-Century Germany*, translated by Thomas Dunlap. Cambridge: Harvard University Press. (English translation of Duden (1987). *Geschichte unter der Haut: Ein Eisenacher Arzt und seine Patientinnen um 1730*. Stuttgart: Klett-Cotta.)
Dunch, Ryan (2001). *Fuzhou Protestants and the Making of a Modern China, 1857–1927*. New Haven: Yale University Press.
Ebrey, Patricia Buckley (1978). *Aristocratic Families of Early Imperial China: A Case Study of the Po-ling Ts'ui Family*. Cambridge: Cambridge University Press.
Ebrey, Patricia Buckley ([1991] 2014). *Confucianism and Family Rituals in Imperial China: A Social History of Writing about Rites*. New Jersey: Princeton University Press.
Ebrey, Patricia Buckley (1992). 'Women, money, and class: Sima Guang and Neo-Confucian views on women'. In: Academia Sinica (ed.), *Papers on Society and Culture in Early Modern China* [中国近世社会文化史论文集]. Taipei: Zhongyang yanjiuyuan lishi yuyan yanjiusuo.
Ebrey, Patricia Buckley (1993). *The Inner Quarters: Marriage and the Lives of Chinese Women in the Sung Period*. Berkeley: University of California Press.

Edwards, Louise (1994). *Men and Women in Qing China: Gender in the Red Chamber Dream*. Leiden: E. J. Brill.
Elias, Norbert (2000). *The Civilizing Process: Sociogenetic and Psychogenetic Investigations, Revised Edition*. Oxford: Blackwell.
Engebretsen, Elisabeth L. (2014). *Queer Women in Urban China: An Ethnography*. New York: Routledge.
Engebretsen, Elisabeth L., William F. Schroeder and Bao Hongwei (eds) (2015). *Queer/Tongzhi China: New Perspectives on Research, Activism and Media*. Copenhagen: NIAS Press.
Enloe, Cynthia (1990). *Bananas, Beaches and Bases: Making Feminist Sense of International Politics*. Berkeley: University of California Press.
Epstein, Israel (1993). *Woman in World History: Life and Times of Soong Ching Ling (Mme Sun Yatsen)*. Beijing: New World Press.
Evans, Harriet (1997). *Women and Sexuality in China: Dominant Discourses of Female Sexuality and Gender since 1949*. New York: Continuum.
Friedman, John and Michael John Rowlands (1978). 'Notes towards an epigenetic model of the evolution of "civilization"'. In: John Friedman and Michael John Rowlands (eds), *The Evolution of Social Systems*. Pittsburgh: University of Pittsburgh Press.
Furth, Charlotte (1986). 'Blood, body and gender: Medical images of the female condition in China, 1600–1850'. *Chinese Science*, 7.
Furth, Charlotte (1999). *A Flourishing Yin: Gender in China's Medical History, 960–1665*. Berkeley: University of California Press.
Geertz, Clifford (1983). *Local Knowledge: Further Essays in Interpretive Anthropology*. New York: Basic Books.
Gellner, Ernest (1983). *Nations and Nationalism*. Ithaca: Cornell University Press.
Gerth, Karl (2003). *China Made: Consumer Culture and the Creation of the Nation*. Cambridge: Harvard University Asia Center.
Gilmartin, Christina, Gail Hershatter, Lisa Rofel and Tyrene White (eds) (1994). *Engendering China: Women, Culture and the State*. Cambridge: Harvard University Press.
Glosser, Susan L. (2003). *Chinese Visions of Family and State, 1915–1953*. Berkeley: University of California Press.
Greenhalgh, Susan (2008). *Just One Child: Science and Policy in Deng's China*. Berkeley: University of California Press.
Greenhalgh, Susan and Edwin A. Winckler (2005). *Governing China's Population: From Leninist to Neoliberal Biopolitics*. Stanford: Stanford University Press.
Grove, Linda (2018). 'Prostitution in a small North China town in the 1930s'. *Nan Nü*, 20(2).
Harsgor, Michael (1978). 'Total history: The Annales School'. *Journal of Contemporary History*, 13(1).
He Xiaopei 何小培 (2001). 'Chinese queer (*tongzhi*) women organizing in the 1990s'. In: Hsiung Ping-Chun, Maria Jaschock and Cecilia Milwertz (eds), *Chinese Women Organizing: Cadres, Feminists, Muslims, Queers*. Oxford: Berg Publishers.
Henriot, Christian (2001). *Prostitution and Sexuality in Shanghai: A Social History, 1849-1949*. Cambridge: Cambridge University Press.

Hershatter, Gail (1986). *The Workers of Tianjin, 1900-1949*. Stanford: Stanford University Press.
Hershatter, Gail (1997). *Dangerous Pleasures: Prostitution and Modernity in Twentieth-Century Shanghai*. Berkeley: University of California Press.
Hershatter, Gail (2011). *The Gender of Memory: Rural Women and China's Collective Past*. Berkeley: University of California Press.
Hillman, Ben and Lee-Anne Henfry (2006). 'Macho minority: Masculinity and ethnicity on the edge of Tibet'. *Modern China*, 32(2): 251–272.
Hinsch, Bret (1990). *Passions of the Cut Sleeve: The Male Homosexual Tradition in China*. Berkeley: University of California Press.
Hinsch, Bret (2013). *Masculinities in Chinese History*. Lanham: Rowman & Littlefield.
Hobsbawm, Eric and Terence Ranger (1983). *The Invention of Tradition*. London: Cambridge University Press.
Honig, Emily (1986). *Sisters and Strangers: Women in the Shanghai Cotton Mills, 1919-1949*. Stanford: Stanford University Press.
Howell, Jude (2003). 'Women's organizations and civil society in China: Making a difference'. *International Feminist Journal of Politics*, 5(2).
Hsiung, Ping-Chun, Maria Jaschok and Cecilia Milwertz, with Red Chan (eds) (2001). *Chinese Women Organizing: Cadres, Feminists, Muslims, Queers*. Oxford and New York: Berg.
Hu Ying (2000). *Tales of Translation: Composing the New Woman in China, 1899-1918*. Stanford: Stanford University Press.
Huang, Martin W. (2006). *Negotiating Masculinities in Late Imperial China*. Honolulu: University of Hawai'i Press.
Huang, Philip C. C. 黄宗智 (2006). 'Court mediation in China, past and present'. *Modern China*, 32(3).
Jiang, Jin (2009). *Women Playing Men: Yue Opera and Social Change in Twentieth-Century Shanghai*. Seattle: University of Washington Press.
Jing Tsu (2005). *Failure, Nationalism, and Literature: The Making of Modern Chinese Identity, 1895–1937*. Stanford: Stanford University Press.
Judd, Ellen (2002). *The Chinese Women's Movement between State and Market*. Stanford: Stanford University Press.
Judge, Joan (2008). *The Precious Raft of History: The Past, the West, and the Woman Question in China*. Stanford: Stanford University Press.
Kam, Lucetta Yip Lo (2013). *Shanghai Lalas: Female Tongzhi Communities and Politics in Urban China*. Hong Kong: Hong Kong University Press.
Kang, Wenqing (2009). *Obsession: Male Same-Sex Relations in China, 1900–1950*. Hong Kong: Hong Kong University Press.
Keesing, Roger M. (1976). *Cultural Anthropology: A Contemporary Perspective*. New York: Holt, Rinehart and Winston.
Keightley, David N. (1999). 'At the beginning: The status of women in Neolithic and Shang China'. *Nan Nü*, 1(1).
Ko, Dorothy (1994). *Teachers of the Inner Chambers: Women and Culture in Seventeenth-Century China*. Stanford: Stanford University Press.
Ko, Dorothy (1997b). 'The body as attire: The shifting meanings of footbinding in seventeenth-century China'. *Journal of Women's History*, 8(4).

Ko, Dorothy (2001). *Every Step a Lotus: Shoes for Bound Feet*. Berkeley: University of California Press.

Ko, Dorothy (2005). *Cinderella's Sisters: A Revisionist History of Footbinding*. Berkeley: University of California Press.

Lang, Olga (1946). *Chinese Family and Society*. New Haven: Yale University Press.

Lee, James (1990). 'Capital punishment and violent crime in late imperial China: A preliminary statistical analysis'. *Jindai Zhongguoshi yanjiu tongxun* 近代中国史研究通讯 [Newsletter for modern Chinese history], 10.

Lee, Swann Nancy (1932). *Pan Chao: Foremost Woman Scholar of China*. New York: Century.

Li Jun (2014). 'The growth and dilemma of women's NGOs in China: A case study of the Beijing Zhongze Legal Consulting Service Center for Women'. In: Hao Zhidong and Chen Sheying (eds), *Social Issues in China: Gender, Ethnicity, Labor, and the Environment*. New York: Springer.

Liu Bohong 刘伯红, Li Ling 李玲 and Yang Chunyu 杨春雨 (2014). *Gender Equality in China's Economic Transformation*. New York: UN Women.

Liu, Lydia H. (1995). *Translingual Practice: Literature, National Culture, and Translated Modernity: China, 1900–1937*. Stanford: Stanford University Press.

Liu, Lydia H., Rebecca E. Karl and Dorothy Ko (2013). *The Birth of Chinese Feminism*. New York: Columbia University Press.

Louie, Kam (2002). *Theorising Chinese Masculinity: Society and Gender in China*. Cambridge: Cambridge University Press.

Louie, Kam (2015). *Chinese Masculinities in a Globalizing World*. London: Routledge.

Louie, Kam (2016). *Changing Chinese Masculinities: From Imperial Pillars of State to Global Real Men*. Hong Kong: Hong Kong University Press.

Louie, Kam and Morris Low (2003). *Asian Masculinities: The Meaning and Practice of Manhood in China and Japan*. London: RoutledgeCurzon.

Lu Weijing (2008). *True to Her Word: The Faithful Maiden Cult in Late Imperial China*. Stanford: Stanford University Press.

Mann, Susan L. (1987). 'Widows in the kinship, class, and community structures of Qing dynasty China'. *Journal of Asian Studies*, 46(1).

Mann, Susan L. (1991). 'Grooming a daughter for marriage: Brides and wives in the mid-Ch'ing Period'. In: Rubie S. Watson and Patricia Buckley Ebrey (eds), *Marriage and Inequality in Chinese Society*. Berkeley: University of California Press.

Mann, Susan L. (1997). *Precious Records: Women in China's Long Eighteenth Century*. Stanford: Stanford University Press.

Mann, Susan L. (2007). *The Talented Women of the Zhang Family*. Berkeley: University of California Press.

Mann, Susan L. (2011). *Gender and Sexuality in Modern Chinese History*. Cambridge: Cambridge University Press.

McMahon, Keith (1994). 'The classic "beauty-scholar" romance and the superiority of the talented woman'. In: Angela Zito and Tani E. Barlow (eds), *Body, Subject, and Power in China*. Chicago: University of Chicago Press.

Meijer, Marinus J. (1991). *Murder and Adultery in Late Imperial China: A Study of Law and Morality*. Leiden: E. J. Brill.

Morgan, Lewis H. (1877). *Ancient Society: Or Researches in the Lines of Human Progress from Savagery through Barbarism to Civilization*. London: MacMillan & Company.
Morris, Andrew D. (2004). *Marrow of the Nation: A History of Sport and Physical Culture in Republican China*. Berkeley: University of California Press.
Mosher, Steven Westley (1990). *China Misperceived: American Illusions and Chinese Reality*. New York: HarperCollins.
Mosher, Steven Westley (1993). *A Mother's Ordeal: One Woman's Fight against China's One-Child Policy*. New York: Harcourt.
Moskowitz, Marc L. (2013). *Go Nation: Chinese Masculinities and the Weiqi in China*. Berkeley: University of California Press.
Mosse, George L. (1996). *The Image of Man: The Creation of Modern Masculinity*. Oxford: Oxford University Press.
Nagel, Joane (1998). 'Masculinity and nationalism: Gender and sexuality in the making of nations'. *Ethnic and Racial Studies*, 21(2): 242–269.
Ng, Vivien W. (1984). 'Ideology and sexuality: Rape laws in Qing China'. *Journal of Asian Studies*, 46(1).
Nishijima Sadao (1984). 'The formation of the early Chinese cotton industry'. In: Linda Grove and Christian Daniels (eds), *State and Society in China: Japanese Perspectives on Ming-Qing Social and Economic History*. Tokyo: University of Tokyo Press.
Ochiai Emiko (1996). *The Japanese Family System in Transition: A Sociological Analysis of Family Change in Postwar Japan*. LTCB International Library Foundation.
Ono Kazuko, and Joshua A. Fogel (ed.) (1989). *Chinese Women in a Century of Revolution, 1850–1950*. Stanford: Stanford University Press.
Pomeranz, Kenneth (2013). 'Labour-intensive industrialization in the rural Yangzi Delta: Late imperial patterns and their modern fates'. In: Gareth Austin and Sugihara Kaoru (eds), *Labour-Intensive Industrialization in Global History*. London: Routledge.
Pun Ngai (2006). *Made in China: Woman Factory Workers in a Global Workplace*. Durham: Duke University Press.
Remick, Elizabeth J. (2014). *Regulating Prostitution in China: Gender and Local Statebuilding 1900-1937*. Stanford: Stanford University Press.
Rhodes, J. M. Edward (2000). *Manchus and Han: Ethnic Relations and Political Power in Late Qing and Early Republican China, 1861–1928*. Seattle: University of Washington Press.
Ross, Robert (2008). *Clothing: A Global History*. Cambridge: Polity Press.
Sakamoto Hiroko (2004b). 'The cult of "love and eugenics" in May Fourth movement discourse', translated by Rebecca Jennison. *Positions: east asia cultures critique*, 12(2).
Sakamoto Hiroko (2004c). 'The relationship between national identity formation and gender in Liang Qichao', translated by Matthew Fraleigh. In: Joshua Fogel (ed.), *The Role of Japan in Liang Qichao's Introduction of Modern Western Civilization to China*. Berkeley: Institute of East Asian Studies, University of California-Berkeley.

Sakamoto Hiroko (2004d). 'Chinese nationalism, the gaze of Japan, and China's national history'. *Social Science Japan: Newsletter of the Information Center for Japanese Social Studies, Institute of Social Science, University of Tokyo*, 30 (December).

Sakamoto Hiroko. (2017). 'The impact of Versailles on Chinese nationalism as reflected in Shanghai graphic and urban culture, 1919–31', translated by Hiromi Sasamoto-Collins. In: Urs Matthias Zachmann (ed.), *Asia after Versailles: Asian Perspectives on the Paris Peace Conference and the Interwar Order, 1919–33*. Edinburgh: Edinburgh University Press.

Sang, Tze-lan D. (2003). *The Emerging Lesbian: Female Same-sex Desire in Modern China*. Chicago: University of Chicago Press.

Scharping, Thomas (2003). *Birth Control in China 1949–2000: Population Policy and Demographic Development*. London: Routledge Curzon.

Schillinger, Nicholas (2016). *The Body and Military Masculinity in Late Qing and Early Republican China: The Art of Governing Soldiers*. Lanham: Lexington Books.

Scott, Joan Wallach ([1988] 1999). *Gender and the Politics of History*. New York: Columbia University Press.

Sedgwick, Eve Kosofsky (1985). *Between Men: English Literature and Male Homosocial Desire*. New York: Columbia University Press.

Shiga Shūzō (1978). 'Family property and law of inheritance in traditional China'. In: David C. Buxbaum (ed.), *Chinese Family Law and Social Change in Historical Comparative Perspective*. Seattle: University of Washington Press.

Sinha, Mrinalini (1995). *Colonial Masculinity: The 'Manly Englishman' and the 'Effeminate Bengali' in the Late Nineteenth Century*. Manchester: Manchester University Press.

Sinha, Mrinalini (1999). 'Giving masculinity a history: Some contributions from the historiography of colonial India'. *Gender and History*, 11(3): 445–460.

Smith, Anthony D. (1986). *The Ethnic Origins of Nations*. Oxford: Basil Blackwell.

Sommer, Matthew H. (2000) *Sex, Law, and Society in Late Imperial China*. Stanford: Stanford University Press.

Sommer, Matthew H. (2015) *Polyandry and Wife-Selling in Qing Dynasty China: Survival Strategies and Judicial Interventions*. Oakland: University of California Press.

Song Geng (2004). *The Fragile Scholar: Power and Masculinity in Chinese Culture*. Hong Kong: Hong Kong University Press.

Song Geng and Derek Hird (2014). *Men and Masculinities in Contemporary China*. Leiden: Brill.

Spivak, Gayatri (1988). 'Can the subaltern speak?' In: Carey Nelson (ed.), *Marxism and the Interpretation of Culture*. Urbana: University of Illinois Press.

Spivak, Gayatri (2010). *Nationalism and the Imagination*. London: Seagull Books.

Stacey, Judith (1983). *Patriarchy and Socialist Revolution in China*. Berkeley: University of California Press.

Stockard, Janice E. (1992). *Daughters of the Canton Delta: Marriage Patterns and Economic Strategies in South China, 1860–1930*. Hong Kong: Hong Kong University Press.

Stoler, Ann Laura (1995). *Capitalism and Confrontation in Sumatra's Plantation Belt, 1870–1979*, revised edition. New Haven: Yale University Press.

Stoler, Ann Laura (2002). *Carnal Knowledge and Imperial Power: Race and the Intimate in Colonial Rule.* Berkeley: University of California Press.
Sudō Mizuyo (2007b). 'Japanese research on the history of women in modern China'. *Asian Research Trends,* New Series, 2.
Sun, Yan and Yang Hongyu (2004). 'Gender ideology and mortuary practice in Northwestern China'. In: Katheryn M. Linduff and Yan Sun (eds), *Gender and Chinese Archaeology.* Walnut Creek: Alta Mira Press.
T'ien, Ju-K'ang (1988). *Male Anxiety and Female Chastity: A Comparative Study of Chinese Ethical Values in Ming-Ch'ing Times.* Leiden: E. J. Brill.
Tang, Jigen (2004). *The Social Organization of Late Shang China: A Mortuary Perspective.* Ph.D. thesis for London University.
Teng, Emma Jinhua (2004). *Taiwan's Imagined Geography: Chinese Colonial Travel Writing and Pictures, 1683–1895.* Cambridge: Harvard University Press.
Theiss, Janet M. (2004). *Disgraceful Matters: The Politics of Chastity in Eighteenth-Century China.* Berkeley: University of California Press.
Uberoi, Patricia (1995). 'Body, state and cosmos: Mao Zedong's "Study of physical education" (1917)'. *China Report,* 31(1): 109–133.
Ueno Chizuko (2009). *The Modern Family in Japan: Its Rise and Fall.* Melbourne: Trans Pacific Press.
van Gulik, Robert Hans (1961). *Sexual Life in Ancient China: A Preliminary Survey of Chinese Sex and Society from ca. 1500 B.C. till 1644 A.D.* Leiden: Brill.
Vitiello, Giovanni (2011). *The Libertine's Friend: Homosexuality and Masculinity in Late Imperial China.* Chicago: University of Chicago Press.
von Falkenhausen, Lothar (2006). *Chinese Society in the Age of Confucius (1000–250BC): The Archaeological Evidence.* Los Angeles: Cotsen Institute of Archaeology, University of California.
Wang Hui (2014). *China from Empire to Nation-State,* translated by Michael Gibbs Hills. Cambridge: Harvard University Press. (Translation of the introduction to Wang Hui (2008).)
Wang Zheng 汪铮 (2012). *Never Forget National Humiliation.* New York: Columbia University Press.
White, Tyrene (2006). *China's Longest Campaign: Birth Planning in the People's Republic, 1949–2005.* Ithaca: Cornell University Press.
WHO (2015) *World Health Statistics 2015.* http://www.who.int/gho/publications/world_health_statistics/2015/en/
Wu Yi-Li (2010). *Reproducing Women: Medicine, Metaphor, and Childbirth in Late Imperial China.* Berkeley: University of California Press.
Wu, Juiman (2004). 'The late Neolothic cemetery at Dadianzi, Inner Mongolia Autonomous Region'. In: Katheryn M. Linduff and Yan Sun (eds), *Gender and Chinese Archaeology.* Walnut Creek: Alta Mira Press.
Yamamoto Tatsurō et al. (1978–1987, 2001). *Tun-huang and Turfan Documents Concerning Social and Economic History I–IV & Supplements.* Tokyo: Toyo Bunko.
Ying, Wang (2004). 'Rank and power among court ladies at Anyang'. In: Katheryn M. Linduff and Yan Sun (eds), *Gender and Chinese Archaeology.* Walnut Creek: Alta Mira Press.

Zarrow, Peter Gue (1988). 'He Zhen and anarcho-feminism in China'. *Journal of Asian Studies*, 47(4).
Zheng, Tiantian (2009). *Red Lights: The Lives of Sex Workers in Postsocialist China*. Minneapolis: University of Minnesota Press.
Zhong Xueping (2000). *Masculinity Besieged? Issues of Modernity and Male Subjectivity in Chinese Literature of the Late Twentieth Century*. Durham: Duke University Press.

Other

Foucault, Michel (1976). *L'Histoire de la sexualité Volume I: La volonté de savoir* [The history of sexuality I: The will to knowledge]. Paris: Editions Gallimard.
Kim Yong-suk (1987). *Joseonjo gungjung pungsok yeongu* [A study of royal court customs of the Joseon period]. Seoul: Iljisa.
Kühne, Thomas (ed.) (1996). *Männergeschichte-Geschlechtergeschichte: Männlichkeit im Wandel der Moderne*. Frankfurt/Main: Campus.
Ono Kazuko (1985). *Hyeondae jung-gug-yeoseongsa* [A history of women in present-day China], translated by Lee Dong-Yoon. Seoul: Jeongusa.

Index

Terms

1898 Reform Movement	229, 247, 251, 266–268, 270
1943 Decision	232, 319, 323
1989 Tiananmen Square incident	235, 239, 346, 416, 419, 423

Academic Salon on Feminism 426
Agrarian Reform Law 320
AIDS 432, 433, 435
All-China Federation of Trade Unions 323, 339
All-China Women's Federation (ACWF) 232–233, 235, 323–324, 332–336, 338–345, 348–349, 414–415, 417–423
ancestor goddess 妣 48
ancestral shrines/halls/temples 104, 110, 190–191
attire
    cross-dressing 10, 429
    Han clothing 228, 235, 270
    Mao suits 233
    military uniforms 231, 269–270
    qipao dress 旗袍 228, 233
    Tang clothing 228, 235
    Western clothing 269–270
    Zhongshan suit 231, 276–278

'barbaric' 夷 (*yi*) / 蛮夷 *see* 'civilized' 华 (*hua*) and 'barbaric' 夷 (*yi*)
Beijing Qianqian Law Firm 348
Beijing Queer Film Festival 434
Beijing Women's Higher Normal School 289
Beijing Zhongze Women's Legal Consulting Services Center 348–349
bio-power 228, 317, 324, 330
birth planning 计划生育 234, 257, 324, 326–330
    see also reproduction
blood 176, 254, 397, 404 *see also qi*
bondservants 奴婢 112–114, 122–123, 202, 208, 212, 367
Buddhism 33, 108, 187, 267

capitalism 233, 247, 258, 272, 295, 390, 398
Center for Women's Law and Legal Services, Peking University 347–348
chastity
    charitable halls and associations 216
    chaste widows and chastely martyred wives and daughters 148, 194, 201, 207, 379
    chaste/faithful widows 节妇 122, 148, 194, 201, 206, 215, 241
    chastely martyred women 烈女 148, 201, 241
    martyrdom 148, 151, 194, 201, 207
    'To starve to death is a small matter, but to lose one's chastity is a great matter' 饿死事极小, 失节事极大 16, 148–149, 192–193, 401
childbirth 59–60, 63, 68, 109, 169, 178, 235, 253, 292, 309, 327–328, 369, 391–392, 395–400, 406, 408–409, 417
    see also reproduction
    maternal mortality rate 59, 408
    revolution of — 408
    'sense of pollution' 399
China Women's University 425
Chinese Communist Party (CCP) 11, 231–236, 270, 275–277, 279, 310–311, 318–324, 332–336, 339–342, 345–346, 348, 417, 432, 441
Chinese Nationalist Party (Kuomintang) 231, 268, 275–277, 279, 305–306, 318–319, 335
Chinese Society for Women's Studies (CSWS) 423–424
Chinese Women's Research Society (CWRS) 421
Chinese world order
    see 'civilized' 华 (*hua*) and 'barbaric' 夷 (*yi*)
Christian
    — activists 335
    — churches 273
    — missionary 241, 251, 304
    — societies 21
    — world 200

citizens 229–230, 278
   citizens' bodies 249
   female — 女国民 229, 253–255, 406
   mothers of the — 229, 252–253, 406
   new — 268, 272, 402
   soldier-citizen 军国民 268, 270, 274, 276, 279–280
Civil Code 318
'civilized' 华 (hua) / 华夏 see 'civilized' 华 (hua) and 'barbaric' 夷 (yi)
'civilized' 华 (hua) and 'barbaric' 夷 (yi) (Chinese world order) 215, 242, 266
cloistered ladies (guixiu) 闺秀 214, 216, 384–386
   see also gender segregation, spatial
   guixiu networks 385
College of Chinese and Western Medicine for Women 409
colonialism 23, 242, 254, 263, 267, 387, 408
   colonial modernity 19, 22–23, 258
'comfort women' of the Japanese military 23, 231, 236, 259
commerce/business 14, 62, 161–163, 168–171, 305, 310–311, 400
commercialization of sex 414, 420
'common living, common budget' 104, 175–178, 181–182, 366
Common Program of the Chinese People's Political Consultative Conference 319, 340, 349, 434
Confucianism 13, 16–19, 32–35, 83, 108, 110, 112–116, 136, 144, 147, 150, 153, 188, 204, 209, 211, 217–218, 224, 230, 250, 258, 266, 271–272, 276, 283, 371, 378, 386, 393, 395, 400, 402–403, 428, 439
   Cheng-Zhu school 15, 144, 149, 184, 187–197
   Neo-Confucianism 12, 17, 146, 148, 189, 194–195, 197, 397, 401
   three principles and five virtues 三纲五常 23, 271
   two views of — 34
cosmology 392, 394, 407, 411–412
court ladies 152, 221–226
Cultural and Developing Center for Rural Women 347

Cultural Revolution 18, 233–234, 323–326, 328, 334–335, 341, 352, 413, 416–417, 431
   iron girls 铁姑娘 233, 325
   Sent-down Youth Movement 上山下乡 341

'debased' 贱 (jian) 122, 212, 216–218 see also 'good' 良 (liang) and 'debased' 贱 (jian)
debt of gratitude 义 115
democratization 105, 235, 258, 274, 406, 416, 420, 423, 439
descent
   — line system 宗法 195–196
   bilateral — 16, 330
divorce 35, 39, 113, 121, 126–130, 132, 159, 163–164, 169–170, 199, 318, 321, 373, 414 see also marital freedom for freedom of —
   bills of divorce 117, 126–127, 129–130
   compulsory — 113, 115
   female-initiated — 130, 132
   form for divorcing the wife 113
   husband-initiated — 113
   marriage breakdown 330
   seven reasons for — 113
domestic violence 110, 113, 122, 330, 349–350, 427 see also violence and harassment against women
   Anti-Domestic Violence Law 342, 348
   Anti-Domestic Violence Network 349
dominance of men over women 148, 295, 318
double burden of paid and domestic work 两勤 20, 290, 324–325, 327, 417
dowry 14, 146, 150, 178, 180–181, 205–207, 371, 373 see also marriage
Dunhuang 15, 126, 132
   — Documents 39, 112–113, 117, 126–134
   — household register 118, 124

economic disparity see income
   — between men and women 20, 60, 332, 337, 344 see also gender wage gap
   — between urban and rural 20, 272, 332–333
elites 士 (shi) and commoners 庶 (shu) 211–212
'Engendering China' 419, 423
Enlightenment Society 272, 275

Index

entertainment
  — trades   310–311
  courtesan culture   382–384
  courtesans/female entertainers 妓女
     93, 144–145, 216–218, 383–384, 386
  entertainers (*changyou*)   212
ethnic minorities   10, 246, 262, 353
eugenics   258
eunuchs   221–226, 265

family 家/家庭/家族   14, 102, 119, 366–367
     see also lineage
  — reform and revolution   20, 282, 292, 297, 318, 320, 323
  composite — form   118
  Han —   28, 103, 121
  modern —   19, 230, 232, 283–284, 287, 290–291, 299, 321
  nuclear —   19, 36–37, 67, 370
  small families   19–20, 36, 103, 144, 257, 272, 283–285, 287–291, 295–300
  Tang —   40, 102–124
  three relationship —   118
  three-family system   34
family businesses 家业   161–163
family relations
  affinal relatives   65
  stepmother-stepson relationship   108
  uncle-nephew relationships   74–75
     see also matrilineal uncle-nephew relationships
family rituals   110, 121, 193
Fan Clan's Charitable Estate   196–197
farm work   45, 155–157, 164–167, 169, 171, 235, 303
female physicians/medical professionals   249, 408–410
female writers   17, 84–85, 88, 100, 288–290, 385, 431 *see also* literature
feminine consciousness   417–418 *see also* women's studies in China
feminism
  Chinese Feminism   425–426
  nüquan zhuyi 女权主义 as Chinese translation   414, 426
  nüxing zhuyi 女性主义 as Chinese translation   414, 422, 426
  second-wave —   9, 10, 413–414, 416
  third wave of —   11
feudalism   148, 232–233, 256, 276, 319–320, 324
first-born legitimate sons   195–196
'Five good families' 五好家庭   342
Five Peoples Under One Union 五族共和   229, 242–243, 248
filiality
  filial daughter 孝女   107, 377
  filial piety   108, 114, 193
  filial son 孝子   201
  'There are three unfilial matters and to have no posterity is the greatest of them' 不孝有三, 无后为大   193
footbinding   11, 16, 22, 145, 148, 151, 194, 214–215, 241, 249–256, 264–267, 308, 405, 407, 438, 440 *see also* health
  anti-footbinding movement   229, 241, 249–251, 253, 255–257, 284, 336
  Anti-Footbinding Society   250–251
fuma (husband of an imperial princess)   76–83

gender
  — and development (GAD) project   424
  — equality 13, 20, 232, 257, 305, 311, 313, 316, 318–319, 325, 391, 411, 414, 416
  — gap   23, 325, 337
  — norms   16–17, 19–20, 22–23, 196–197, 209, 212, 216–218, 220, 249–258, 290, 306, 308, 408, 410
  — order 8, 12–13, 16, 19, 21–24, 213–215, 228–229, 231, 317, 319, 321–324, 326, 332–334, 339, 342, 345, 347–350, 393
  — roles   272, 284, 390, 398
  — segregation 350, 394, 401, 408, 410–411
     see also sex-based segregation
  — segregation, occupational   332, 344, 350, 410
  — segregation, spatial   17, 19, 372
  — wage gap   235, 307 *see also* women's economic independence
Gender Gap Index   441
sexual morality   202, 279, 285–286
translation of —   9, 423

gender aphorisms
   'Men and women are different' 男女有别 393, 408
   'Men surrendered, women did not' 男降女不降 215
   'Men till and women weave' 男耕女职 61–62, 156, 302
   'Men work outside, women work inside' 男外女内 17, 19, 145, 284, 296, 372
gender equality
   'Whatever men comrades can do, women comrades can do, too' 233, 325, 417
   'Women hold up half the sky' 315, 325
girls' schools 269
   physical education 405–406
   Regulations for Girls' Schools 405
goddess worship 44
'good' 良 (*liang*) 208, 211–212, 216 *see also* 'good' 良 (*liang*) and 'debased' 贱 (*jian*)
'good' 良 (*liang*) and 'debased' 贱 (*jian*) 208, 211–212
'good wife and wise mother' 良妻贤母 23, 284, 430
Great Leap Forward 232, 311, 324, 327

Han society 15, 65–66, 68, 79, 131–132, 150, 265
haohan (brave men) 好汉 264
health 254, 258, 276, 327, 340, 401–402, 406, 421, 423
hereditary 29, 105, 122, 144, 208, 210–211, 218–219, 382
'Heroine's contributions' 巾帼建功 342, 344
heterosexuality 21, 285, 431
   heteronormativity 10, 249, 428, 435
   heterosexual marriage 321
homosexuality 10, 18, 21, 232, 262, 278–279, 428–429, 431–434
   bisexuals 428, 434–436
   gays 428, 433–436
   heterosexual wives of gay men 同妻 435
   homosexuals 21, 429, 431–433, 435
   homosociality 18, 264, 273
   lesbians 428, 432–436
   same-sex love 431
   same-sex relationships 21, 428, 431

household
   — head 户主 111, 159, 163, 370
   — register 30, 117–118, 358–359, 361, 364–367, 369–370, 375
   Dunhuang — register 118, 124
   — registration (system) 30, 111, 218, 311, 324, 359, 364, 371, 374–375
   householder 户人 30–31, 360, 366, 370–371
   female-headed households 370, 373–374
illicit sex 奸 202–203, 205, 219
   consensual — 203
   fornication by husbandless women 无夫奸 205, 318
   same-sex rape against children 203, 429
   sex crimes 202–204
imperial examinations 14, 18, 22, 138, 144–145, 150, 211–213, 215, 224, 245, 264, 272, 276, 403, 438
imperial princess 公主 16, 32, 67, 70, 75–83, 157
imperialism 19, 244, 247, 250, 263, 279
income 167, 181–182, 303–304, 308, 313, 332–333, 337, 343, 368, 372
individualism 210–211, 258, 277
inheritance *see also* patrimony
   property — rights 14, 80–81, 131–132, 160, 174–175, 181–182, 196
   women's — 14–15, 126, 131–132, 180–182, 318, 373

labor market 235, 315
land reform 232, 320
lecherous woman 377 *see also* chastity
LGBT 21, 428, 434, 436
   see also love; sexual minorities
   — parade 434
   Beijing LGBT Center 434
lineage 宗族 57–58, 60, 65, 67, 75, 82–83, 87, 90, 102–106, 110, 116, 119–120, 136, 138, 144, 176, 188, 196–197, 199, 330
   see also family
literacy 10, 145–146, 225, 323, 342, 378
literati 士大夫 18, 83, 90, 110, 123, 145, 211, 213, 216–218, 245, 250, 264, 266, 270, 383–388

Index

literature *see also* poetry
— on female relationships 431, 433
— on heterosexual marriage 430
— on homosexuality 430
collected biographies of women
    157, 378–381, 385
novels 16, 82, 93, 107, 252, 289–290, 420
romance (literature) 144
scholar and beauty — 18
local leaders
grassroots cadres 328, 338
women's heads 340, 343–345
love
— supremacism 21
discussion on — 285
discussion on the rules of — 286
free — 292, 296–298, 430
ideology of romantic — 430
love-based marriage 20, 257, 285, 289, 322
romantic — 217, 219, 285–288, 297–298, 320, 322, 431
romantic relationships 287, 297, 383
romanticists faction 291

Maoism 311–312, 422
market economy 234–235, 329–342, 344–345, 349–350, 414, 418, 420, 434
market feminism 418
marriage
— alliances 58, 60, 63, 121
— arranged by parents 282, 319, 322
— between equal social status families 門当戸对 322
— between people bearing the same surname 14
— between the good and the debased 212, 217
— prohibition 117
bride-buying 282, 319–320
delayed-transfer — 429
'getting a husband to support a husband' 招夫养夫 219
'Husband is superior, wife is inferior' 夫尊妻卑 31–32, 66–67, 78, 82–83
legal wife 11, 72, 87, 122, 177–178, 180

marital freedom 232, 294, 319–321
marriage system abolition issue, debate on the 295–299
matrilocality/uxorilocality 151, 321, 386
matrimonial relationship 15, 29, 46, 58, 60, 63, 68, 107, 112, 287, 385
mistress 106, 168, 171, 190, 310–311
monogamy 36, 48, 121, 145, 232, 287, 293, 296–297, 318–319
monogamy with many concubines 178
patrilocality 16
penalty imposed on spousal assaults 31, 66, 113, 204
polyandry 151, 218–219
polygamy 219, 282, 330
same-sex — 434
sororal — 146
wife-selling 151, 218–219
Marriage Law
— campaign 320–321, 338
— of the People's Republic of China
20, 231–232, 319, 321–322, 326, 330
Marriage Code 318–319
Marriage Code of the Border Area 319
Marxism 422, 426
Marxist women's liberation theory
334, 414, 417–418, 422
masculinity 8, 17–18, 145, 231, 236, 260–269, 271–273, 275–280
hegemonic masculinity 18–19, 260, 263, 265, 269, 276
masculinist culture 236
masculinization of women 233
remasculinization 263, 266–268, 270, 274, 277, 279
maternal relatives 15, 65, 70, 72–73, 75, 121, 151
matriarchal society 145
matrilineal *see also* patrilineal
— kinship 14–15, 32, 65–66, 70, 72–73, 75, 121, 151, 176, 183, 189, 330
— society 12, 44, 188
uncle-nephew relationship 32, 68, 72–73, 75
May Fourth/New Culture Movement
10, 19, 147, 213, 230, 250, 255, 257, 274, 295, 318

– 509 –

medical doctors 402, 408–410
medical practitioners
    barefoot doctors 325, 328, 410
    Confucian medical practitioner 400–401
    midwives 216, 338, 390, 392, 399–400, 408–410
menstruation 391–392, 395, 397–399, 403–407
middle class 20, 53, 305–306, 313
migrant workers 309, 314–316, 331–332, 344–345, 347, 350
    Migrant Women's Club 347, 349
mother
    birthmother 69–70, 72, 81, 113
    divorced — 113
    remarried — 113
    stepmother 108, 113
    'The son's honor increases as his mother's position rises and the mother's honor increases as her son's position rises' 子以母贵 母以子贵 58, 60
motherhood 291, 402–403, 407
    childrearing 109, 235, 284, 289, 292, 299, 312, 315–316, 341–342, 396, 417
    communal childrearing 298–299, 418
    mother-child relationship 72–73, 81, 83

national salvation 229–230, 277, 406
National Women's Congress 334–335, 340, 345–346
nationalism 230–231, 235–236, 239–245, 247–249, 253, 255–256, 259, 263, 275, 278, 291, 402, 430 *see also* patriotism
    nationalist discourse 257, 402
Nationalist Party (Guoming dang) 244
neighborhood committees 323
Network for the Development of Chinese Women's/Gender Studies 424
New Life Movement 231, 258, 275–276
NGO 339, 341, 346–347, 416, 420–421

obstetrics and gynecology 109, 391, 393, 395–396, 399, 402, 407–410
    see also reproduction
Occupy Men's Toilet Movement 427
one child policy 16, 234, 315, 326–330
    see also reproduction

oracle bone inscriptions 甲骨文字 15, 48, 51, 61, 63
oral history 235, 308–309, 336–349, 354, 422, 424
overseas study
    female students 253, 353
    students in Japan 229, 268–269, 287, 439

patriarch 111, 160
patriarchy 12, 15–16, 23, 32–34, 111, 122, 145, 160, 209, 231, 250, 278, 320, 326, 411
patrilineal *see also* matrilineal
    — kinship 14–16, 21, 30, 48, 57, 65–68, 83, 104, 108–109, 112–113, 160, 176, 179, 187–190, 195, 197, 199, 330, 428
    patrilinealization 14–15, 19, 35, 46, 48, 54, 62–63, 65, 67–69, 72, 75, 81, 83, 108, 146, 151, 160, 197, 214, 330, 428
patrimony 118 *see also* inheritance
patriotism 235, 247, 272, 278, 440
    see also nationalism
performance art 350, 426–427
poetry *see also* literature
    — about freedom and comfort 闲适诗 94, 96
    boudoir lament (*guiyuan*) 闺怨 39, 85–88, 90–93, 95, 100–101
    ci 词 84, 96–97, 99, 101, 383–384
    fu 赋 84, 88–90, 94
    male homosexuality poems 430
    ode 颂 89
    poem of grief 89, 379
    shi 词 84–85, 93–94, 96, 100
    spring sorrow and sad departures 388
    waiting women 39, 86, 88, 93, 100
population 203, 215, 246, 257, 327–329, 400
    aging — 234, 329
    imbalance in the sex ratio 203, 234, 329
    infanticide, female 18, 203, 251
poverty 17, 180, 235, 257, 331, 421
    see also income
    feminization of — 331
    women's — 423
prostitution 145, 169, 207, 216, 218–219, 310–311, 428
    Anti-Prostitution Movement 232, 322

Protection of Rights and Interests of Women, Law of the People's Republic of China 349

qi (material force or vital energy) 气 66, 176–177, 189–190, 254, 392–394, 397, 400
   brothers 177
   father and son 175, 177, 184
   father and son sharing — 15, 72, 175–177, 184, 188–189
   forming one body 176–177
   husband and wife 119, 175, 177–180, 184
   principle and material (*li* and *qi*) dualism 188–190
   the same *qi* 14–15, 66, 175–176, 184, 188–190, 195
   unification of spirit and flesh 285, 290
qiqin 期亲 115
queue, the Manchu hairstyle 215, 265–270
   — cutting 245, 247, 266–267, 269

races 243, 246, 251, 253–254, 257, 261
Red Guards 280
reform and opening-up policies 20, 28, 234, 321, 328, 330, 332, 341, 414–415, 418, 422–423
religion 57, 148, 261, 271, 273
remarriage 16–17, 35, 68–89, 97, 107, 109, 112–113, 122, 128–129, 148–150, 163, 192–194, 199–202, 204–207, 216, 380, 383–384 *see also* marriage
reproduction 234, 249, 257, 322, 327–328, 369, 394, 401–403, 406, 412, 428
   birth planning 计划生育 234, 257, 324, 326–330
   childbirth 59–60, 63, 68, 109, 169, 178, 235, 253, 292, 309, 327–328, 369, 391–392, 395–400, 406, 408–409, 417
   obstetrics and gynecology 109, 391, 393, 395–396, 399, 402, 407–410
   one child policy 16, 234, 315, 326–330
   reproductive health 329, 400
restructuring the female labor force 414
righteousness 义 258

sericulture 61, 166–167, 171 *see also* gender aphorisms; weaving industry
sex-based segregation 146–147, 192, 195, 197, 392, 399, 438
sexual minorities 423, 428, 432, 434–436 *see also* LGBT
sexuality 10–11, 261, 285–286, 297–298, 322–323, 352, 401–402, 420, 426, 428–431
Shuihudi Qinjian 睡虎地秦简 31, 66, 68, 368–369
siblings *see also* family
   agnate — 34, 68, 72
   uterine — 32, 68, 75
'Sick Man of East Asia' 东亚病夫 254, 263
'Silver flower contest' 232, 337
Simuwu ding 司母戊鼎 48–50
singlehood 10, 287–288
   bare sticks 光棍 18, 214, 264
   men 264
   spinster houses 321, 429
   unions of sisters 321, 429
   women 193–194, 287–288, 296–297, 429
sinicization 416, 418
Sino-Japanese relations 139–140, 231, 236, 245, 253, 257–259, 266–267, 275, 278–279, 306, 353
Sino-Korean relations 139, 196, 222, 226, 243–244
social Darwinism 245, 263
socialism 20–21, 231, 257–258, 313–314, 322, 324, 332, 334–335, 337–338, 414, 417
Society of Historical Studies on Chinese Women 10, 353
Society to Preserve National Scholarship 246
sports 272–274, 280, 407, 412
Survey of the Social Status of Women in China 332

'talented women' 才女 85, 213, 376–378, 380–384, 386–389
Taoism 33, 187, 189, 383
'ten abominations' 115

theatre
    actors 437, 441
    actresses 437–438
    cross-dressing 437, 439
    cross-gender performance 429
    dan 旦 (female roles played by male actors) 278–279
    lan hua zhi (orchid-flower fingers) 440
    laosheng 老生 (roles of males of middle age and older) 437
    Peking opera 278–279, 439–440
    Ten Sisters of — 441
    wusheng 武生 (acrobatic male roles) 437
    Yue opera 越剧 441
'three spinsters and six dames' 三姑六婆 216
Tianjin Awakening Society 288
transgenderism 10, 428, 435–436
transgression 94, 216, 258, 428, 438
'Two studies, two competitions' 双学双比 340, 342–344
two-sex model 393, 397–398, 411

UN Fourth World Conference on Women 329, 331, 346, 419–423, 425, 432

violence and harassment against women 308, 421, 423, 427
    domestic violence 110, 113, 122, 330, 349–350, 427

wage labor 169, 313, 315 *see also* income
weaving industry 303
    spinning and weaving factories 304, 307
wen (cultural attainment) 文 18, 261, 264–267, 269, 276, 376 *see also wen* 文 and *wu* 武
wen 文 and *wu* 武 262–264, 266–280
widow 17, 106–107, 135, 150, 160, 162, 170, 177, 179, 200, 204–205, 209, 215, 241, 289, 372
'wise wife and good mother' 贤妻良母 20, 284, 287, 290, 296
    'new —' 259, 284, 287, 289–291, 295, 300
    'new wise husband and good father' 291
wise wife/wise daughter or woman 162–163, 377, 380–382

women and natal families 65–66, 72, 75, 106–107, 109, 114, 121, 177–178, 180, 189–191, 193, 207, 225, 385
    returning to her natal lineage 归宗 207
'women return home' 妇女回家 20, 231, 258, 291, 306, 341
women's career 290, 304, 312–313, 315, 408, 427
women's earning 162, 168, 170, 175, 178, 181–182
women's economic independence 20, 163–164, 230, 232, 282, 290, 292–293, 313, 319, 354, 435 *see also* gender wage gap
women's education 213, 251, 253, 323, 407
    campaign for — 229, 254, 269, 284, 293, 299, 336
    physical — 251, 392, 403–406, 412
    Regulations for Normal Colleges for Women 405
women's employment 108, 290, 306–307, 310, 314, 324, 341, 344–345, 410, 418
women's independence 163–164, 170, 283, 296, 299, 318, 416
women's lib 10, 293
women's liberation 20, 148, 230–232, 285, 291, 296–297, 318–319, 336, 352–354, 406–407, 409–410, 412, 414, 417, 440, 442
    — movement 231–234, 253, 257, 288, 318, 410
    history of — 231, 256, 354
    Marxist theory of — *see under* Marxism
women's livelihoods 35, 46, 61–63, 132, 154, 161–172, 372
    spindle whorl 46, 47, 61–62
    spinning and weaving 17, 61–63, 155, 168, 171, 303
women's mobilization 232, 258–259, 319, 324, 333–335
women's rights 252, 305, 414
    calls for — 253, 254, 405
Women's Rights Recovery Association 293–294
women's social status 35–37, 44, 53, 55, 63, 65, 163, 177, 180
Women's Studies Center, Peking University 419, 425
Women's Studies Center, Tianjin Normal University 419, 423, 424

Women's Studies Center,
   Zhengzhou University   414–416, 422
women's studies in China   234, 414–420,
   422–424, 427 *see also* feminine
                              consciousness
women's tombs/tombstone epitaphs
           29, 45–46, 53, 56, 106–107,
           109, 122, 125, 192–193
women's virtue
   'A woman without talent is virtuous'
   女子无才便是德   376, 384
   state's system of commendation for —
   旌表   16, 148–149, 201–202, 215, 342
work force   232, 306–307
wu (martial valor) 武   18, 264–267, 275,
   279–280, 376 *see also wen* 文 and *wu* 武

yang 阳 *see yin* 阴 and *yang* 阳
Yellow Emperor's Body   393–395, 397, 411
yin 阴 and *yang* 阳   392–394, 404
yin 阴 *see yin* 阴 and *yang* 阳
YMCA   272–273, 276
Young Feminism Activists   426

Personal names

Ai Xiaoming 艾晓明   426
Ai, Emperor of Former Han 哀帝   70
Anle, Princess 安乐公主   135, 140
Awata-no-Mahito 粟田真人   139–140
Ba Jin 巴金   279
Bai Juyi 白居易   94
Ban Gu 班固   87–88, 378
Ban Jieyu 班婕妤   88, 94
Ban Zhao 班超   88–90, 92, 94, 97–98,
                 100, 378–379
Bao Linghui 鲍令晖   91
Bao Xiaolan 鲍晓兰   423
Bao Zhao 鲍照   91
Cai E 蔡锷   271
Cai Yan 蔡琰 (Cai Wenji 蔡文姬)   88–90,
               99–100, 378–380
Cai Yong 蔡邕   89, 378
Cai Yuanpei 蔡元培   274
Cao Cao 曹操   85, 89, 361
Cao Pi 曹丕   85–87, 189
Cao Zhi 曹植   85–87, 189

Chao Cuo 晁错   367
Chen Dongyuan 陈东原   10, 125, 147–148,
   150–151, 187, 192, 197,
   229–231, 351, 378, 384
Chen Duxiu 陈独秀   270–271, 274
Chen Hengzhe 陈衡哲   289
Chen Jingyun 陈景云   98
Chen Liting 陈鲤庭   440
Chen Tingchuo 陈廷焯   97
Chen Xiefen 陈撷芬   253
Chen Ying 沉樱   217, 289
Chen Yinke 陈寅恪   386–387
Chen Zhao 陈照   109
Chen Zilong 陈子龙   217
Chen Ziming 陈自明   396
Cheng Hao 程颢   189, 193
Cheng Ling-Fang 成令方   408
Cheng Yi 程颐   148–149, 180, 189,
               191–195, 200
Chiang Kaishek (Jiang Jieshi) 蒋介石
           269, 276–277
Chunyu Chang 淳于长   71, 73–75
Cixi, Empress Dowager 慈禧太后   135
Dai Jinhua 戴锦华   423
Deng Xiaoping 邓小平   235, 328, 414, 422
Ding Ling 丁玲   290, 431
Dong Xiaowan 董小宛   217
Du Fangqin 杜芳琴   12, 354, 419, 424–425
Du Sixian 杜嗣先   139–140
Ebrey, Patricia B.   11, 40, 119, 125,
             145–147, 149, 194
Fan Zhongyan 范仲淹   197
Feng Guozhang 冯国璋   270
Feng Yuanjun 冯沅君   289
Fengzi 凤子   287
Fu Hao 妇好   48–52, 61–62
Fu Jing 妇妌   48–49
Fu Zhaoyi 傅昭仪   70
Gao Susu 高素素   287
Gou Can 苟参   70–71
Gu Yanwu 顾炎武   387
Guan Yu 关羽   264–265
Han Feizi 韩非子   267
He(-Yln) Zhen 何(殷)震   253, 293–294
Hexi, Empress Dowager 和熹太后   136
Hobson, B. 合信   402

Hong Mai 洪邁	158
Hu Shi 胡適	273–274, 439–440
Hu Yaobang 胡耀邦	342
Huang Biyao 黃碧遙	258
Huang Fumei 皇甫枚	93
Huang Lin 荒林	425–426
Huangdi (Yellow Emperor) 黃帝	245–246, 393
Huizong, Emperor of Song 徽宗	222–223
Ji Kang 嵇康	91
Jia Yi 賈誼	359
Jiajing, Emperor 嘉靖帝	225
Jiang Qing [wife of Mao Zedong] 江青	326
Jiang Weiqiao 蔣維喬	252–253
Jin Tianhe 金天翮 (Jin Yi 金一)	252
Kang Youwei 康有為	251, 266–267
Kangxi, Emperor of Qing 康熙帝	155, 156, 201, 385
Ko, Dorothy 高彥頤	147, 151, 213–215, 217, 219, 250, 252, 256
Kōtoku Shūsui 幸德秋水	247
Lanling, Princess 蘭陵長公主	110
Lee Jen-Der 李貞德	12, 40, 76, 108–110, 391, 396
Li Chao 李綽	299
Li Chongmao, King Wen 溫王李重茂	140
Li Gefei 李格非	95, 98
Li Qingzhao 李清照	39, 95–99, 101, 383–384
Li Xiaojiang 李小江	234, 414–424
Li Yinhe 李銀河	423, 433–434, 436
Li Yuanhong 黎元洪	270
Li Yu 李漁	270, 429–430
Liang Ji 梁冀	136, 293
Liang Qichao 梁啟超	229, 246, 251, 253, 267–268, 270–271, 387–388, 402–403, 405
Liang, Empress 梁皇后	136
Lianshi 煉石 see Yan Bin	
Liu Bei 劉備	18
Liu Rushi 柳如是	217–218, 386–387
Liu Shaoqi 劉少奇	233
Liu Shifu 劉師復	292–293, 295, 297
Liu Xiang 劉向	89, 372, 377–378
Liu Xiaochuo 劉孝綽	92
Liu Yiqing 劉義慶	381
Liu Zhiji 劉知幾	379–380
Lu, Empress (dowager) 呂后	28
Lu Xun 魯迅	16, 257
Lu Yin 廬隱	289, 430
Luo Qiong 羅瓊	341–342
Ma Rong 馬融	88
Ma Zhemin 馬哲民	295–296, 298–299
Mann, Susan L.	11, 16, 147, 151, 183, 213–215, 219, 229, 385, 393, 424
Mao Xiang 冒襄	217
Mao Zedong 毛澤東	233, 271–273, 277, 280, 320, 324–326, 417
Mei Lanfang 梅蘭芳	279
Mulan (花)木蘭	376, 427
Ono Kazuko 小野和子	10, 234, 319–320, 351–355
Ouyang Yuqian 歐陽予倩	440
Pan Guangdan 潘光旦	257, 283, 405
Qian Jue 錢珏	442
Qian Qianyi 錢謙益	98, 217, 386
Qianlong, Emperor of Qing 乾隆帝	201–203, 385, 438
Qiu Jin 秋瑾	253, 381
Ruizong, Emperor of Tang 睿宗	38, 135, 138–142
Shangguan Wan'er 上官婉兒	92, 100, 382
Shangguan Yi 上官儀	92
Shao Lizi 邵力子	298–299
Shen Qionglian 沈瓊蓮	224
Shen Yue 沈約	92
Shiga Shūzō 滋賀秀三	14–15, 72, 117, 131, 173–178, 181–191, 195, 197–198
Shimoda Utako 下田歌子	253
Sima Guan 司馬光	147
Song Jian 宋健	18, 328
Song Jiaoren 宋教仁	244
Song Ruozhao 宋若昭	222
Song Yu 宋玉	94–95
Su Shi 蘇軾	379–380
Su Xun 蘇洵	380
Suetsugu Reiko 末次玲子	10–11, 318, 324, 352–355
Sun Simiao 孫思邈	395, 398, 409
Taiping, Princess 太平公主	35, 81, 135, 141
Taizong, Emperor of Tang 太宗	141
Tan Lin 譚琳	419
Tan Shen 譚深	419
Tan Sheying 談社英	290–291, 351

Tan Sitong 谭嗣同	267
Tang Qunying 唐群英	287
Tian Fen 田蚡	69–70, 72
Tianqi, Emperor of Ming 天启帝	225
Wan Qiong-hua 万琼华	407
Wang Feng 王凤	71, 73–75
Wang Guangmei 王光美	233
Wang Ji 王济	59, 71, 75, 80, 105, 369
Wang Lang 王朗	78–79
Wang Mang 王莽	74–75
Wang Pu 王溥	82
Wang Wan 王婉	69, 71, 108
Wang Xizhi 王羲之	91
Wang Zheng 王政	233, 235, 252, 354, 414, 423–425
Wang Zhuo 王灼	97
Wang, Empress (wife of Emperor Jing of Former Han) 王皇太后	69–70
Wang, Empress (wife of Emperor Yuan of Former Han) 王皇后	71, 73
Wanyan Yun Zhu 完颜恽珠	385–386
Wei Changsheng 魏长生	438
Wei Ran 魏冉	70–72
Wei Zhongxian 魏忠贤	225
Wei, Empress 韦后	92, 121, 135, 140, 142
Wen, Emperor of Han 文帝	364–365, 367
Wu Song 武松	264–265
Wu Zetian, Empress 武则天	15, 28, 35, 38, 92, 135, 137, 140–142, 157, 382
Xi Jinping 习近平	236, 348, 427, 436
Xia Tingzhi 夏庭芝	437
Xiang Jingyu 向警予	290–291, 296–297, 299
Xiao Hong 萧红	278
Xie Daoyun 谢道蕴	90–91, 94, 96, 100, 381
Xie Lihua 谢丽华	347, 349
Xu Qiu 徐釚	100
Xu Shu 徐淑	380
Xuan, Queen Dowager 宣太后	70–71, 107, 123
Xuanzong, Emperor of Tang 玄宗	38, 135, 138, 140–142
Xue Tao 薛涛	93, 383
Xun Shuang 荀爽	79–80
Yan Bin 燕斌	253–254, 287
Yan Fu 严复	266
Yan Zhenqing 颜真卿	163
Yanagida Setsuko 柳田節子	10, 131
Yang Chongrui 杨崇瑞	410
Yang Jinying 杨金英	225
Yang Weizhen 杨维贞	97
Yongle, Emperor of Ming 永楽帝	224, 226
Yongzheng, Emperor of Qing 雍正帝	201–203, 218
Yu Chien-Ming 游鉴明	12, 407
Yu Xuanji 鱼玄机	39, 93–97, 100, 383
Yuan Cai 袁采	161–163
Yuan Shikai 袁世凯	205, 230, 270
Yuan Xuefen 袁雪芬	441
Zhang Jian 张謇	267
Zhang Jingsheng 张竞生	286
Zhang Jingyue 张景岳	398, 408–409
Zhang Kesha 张克沙	436
Zhang Ruoming 张若名	288
Zhang Zai 张载	189, 191, 195
Zhang Zhujun 张竹君	249, 409–410
Zhao Mingcheng 赵明诚	95, 97–98, 383
Zhaoxiang, King of Qin 秦昭襄王	70–72
Zheng Guanying 郑观应	251
Zheng Yun 郑恽	70
Zhezong, Emperor of Song 哲宗	223
Zhongzong, Emperor of Tang 中宗	38, 135, 137–142, 382
Zhou Enlai 周恩来	272
Zhou Jianren 周建人	257
Zhu Xi 朱熹	110, 180, 188–197, 200, 380
Zhuang Jiang 庄姜	87
Zuo Fen 左棻	90, 92, 100
Zuo Si 左思	90

Titles

A Flower in a Sinful Sea 孽海花	252
A History of the Lives of Chinese Women 中国妇女生活史	10, 125, 147, 187, 230
A New Account of the Tales of the World 世说新语	17, 33, 381–382
A Place for Life and Death 生死场	278
A Sketch Story from the Qing Dynasty 清代野记	76
A Way of Life Based on Beauty 美的人生观	286
Aching for the Departed 伤逝	288
After the Wedding Reception 喜宴之后	289
After Victory 胜利以后	289

All the Poems Written in the Period of the Tang Dynasty 全唐诗	383	*Draft Recovered Edition of the Essential Documents and Regulations of the Song* 宋会要辑稿	77
Analects 论语	86	*Extensive Records Assembled in the Taiping Era* 太平广记	93, 122, 157, 164, 166, 168
Annals of Lü Buwei 吕氏春秋	62	*Family Rituals* (文公)家礼	110, 190–191, 193, 196
Awakening, a supplement of *Republican Daily News* 觉悟 (民国日报副刊)	295–299	*Funü gongming* 妇女共鸣	291
Balanced Discourses 中论	361	*Funü zazhi* 妇女杂志	286, 296
Biji manzhi 碧鸡漫志	97	*Gender and Sexuality in Modern Chinese History*	11, 214
Biographies of Exemplary Women 列女传	89, 372, 377–378, 381	*General Discussions on Reform* 变法通议	251, 387
Book of the Chen Dynasty 陈书	430	*Gongyang Commentary on the Spring and Autumn Annals* 春秋公羊传	58, 199, 366
Brothers 弟兄们	433	*Great Qing Code with Substatutes* 大清律例	206
Bushido of China 中国之武士道	267	*Guocui xue bao* 国粹学报	246
Catalogue of Jiangyunlou 绛云楼书目	98	*History of Chinese Women in the Twentieth Century* 二〇世纪中国女性史	11, 353
Catalogue of the Complete Library of the Four Branches 四库全书总目提要	96	*History of the Former Han* 汉书	32, 69, 73–74, 87–88, 367, 369, 371, 378–379
Chinese Feminism 中国女性主义	426	*History of the Jin* 晋书	80, 90, 381
Chinese Women in a Century of Revolution	10, 234, 351–354	*History of the Later Han* 后汉书	79–80, 89, 366, 379–380
Church News 教会新报 (later *Wanguo gongbao* 万国公报)	251	*History of the Song* 宋史	79, 82, 157
Classic of Changes 易经/周易	90–91	*History of the Sui* 隋书	168
Classic of Songs 诗经	39, 62, 84, 86, 88, 94, 100	*History of the Yuan* 元史	149
Collected Statutes of the Great Ming 大明会典	79	*Jishenlu* 稽神录	164
Collected Works of Baishi 白氏文集	94	*Laozi* 老子	90–91
Collected Works of Huian 晦庵集	380	*Lishi's Diary* 丽石的日记	430
Collected Works of Li Qingzhao 李清照集校注	95	*Literature Arranged by Topic* 艺文类聚	90–92, 377, 380
Collection of Enlightened Judgments by Celebrated Judges 名公书判清明集	158–160, 164, 182	*Main Event of One's Life* 终身大事	440
Collection of Music Bureau Poems 乐府诗集	92, 379	*Mencius* 孟子	18, 193
Complete Effective Prescriptions for Women's Diseases 妇人大全良方	396	*Mingbaoji* 冥报记	167
Complete Writings of the Two Cheng Brothers 二程全书	200	*Miss Sophie's Diary* 莎菲女士的日记	290, 431
Comprehensive Discussions in the White Tiger Hall 白虎通	372	*Mr. Bai's Categorized Reference Collection for Passing the Examinations* 白氏六帖事类集	377
Criminal Laws of the Song Classifed by Category 宋刑统	205	*New History of the Tang* 新唐书	92, 157
Dadaili 大戴礼	199	*New Songs from a Jade Terrace* 玉台新咏	91–92, 380
Dalu bao 大陆报	253	*New Year Sacrifice* 祝福	17
Discourse on the New Citizen 新民说	267–268, 270	*Ni Huanzhi* 倪焕之	288
Discourses on Women 妇人规	398	*Nongjianü baishitong* 农家女百事通	347
		Notes on Poetry from Four Seas 四溟诗话	92
		Nü bao 女报	253

Index

Nüjie zhong 女界钟	252
Nüxue bao 女学报	253
Nüzi shijie 女子世界	252
Observances and Rituals 仪礼	187
Old Friends 旧雨	289
Old Friends from the Seaside 海滨故人	289, 430
Old History of the Tang 旧唐书	92, 139, 142
'On the origin of strength' 原强	266
On the Theory and Practice of Midwifery and Infant Care 妇婴新说	402
One Person's War 一个人的战争	433
Original Meaning of Zhouyi 周易本义	192
Pictures of Tilling and Weaving 耕织图诗	154–157, 166
Precepts for My Daughters 女诫	89, 94, 378
Precious Records 兰闺宝录	385
Prescriptions for Emergencies Worth a Fortune 千金方	395
Principles of Chinese Family Law 中国家族法的原理	14, 72, 173–176, 181–186
Principles of Writing History Books 史通	379
Private Life 私人生活	433
Propriety of Family Rituals 家礼仪节	196
Put down Your Whip 放下你的鞭子	440
Qing Lou Ji 青楼集	437
Qingnian zazhi 青年杂志	270–271
Qiu Shu 訄书	267
Question of Rogers 洛绮丝的问题	289
Record of Important Events in Chronological Order since the Jianyan Era 建炎以来系年要录	223
Record of Inscriptions on Bronze and Stone 金石录	95, 383
Record of Knowledge Daily Acquired 日知录	387
Records of Ritual 礼记	187, 371, 393
Records of the Grand Historian 史记	32, 69–70
Records of the Listener 夷坚志	122, 157–160, 165–167, 169–170
Records of the Three Kingdoms 三国志	18, 361, 379
Red Detachment of Women 红色娘子军	441
Renmin ribao (People's Daily) 人民日报	324–325
School Sayings of Confucious 孔子家语	199
Searching for Eve 夏娃的探索	416
Selections of Refined Literature 文选	85, 89, 94
Separation 隔绝	289
Sex Histories 性史	286
Song History 宋书	78, 85
Songs of Chu 楚辞	87
Statutes and Precedents of the Yuan 元典章	206
Statutes of the Great Ming 大明令	79, 206
Stories from Amidst the Court 中朝故事	77
Study of the Works of Women throughout History 历代妇女著作考	385
Su bao 苏报	253
Sunzi 孙子	359
Supper Discussions of the Stone Forest 石林燕语	77
Tang Code with Commentary and Explanation 唐律疏议	31, 68, 205
Tang Poetry Chronicle 唐诗纪事	92
Tianyi (bao) 天义(报)	253, 291–294
Traveling Upstream at the Qingming Festival 清明上河图	145, 154
Treatise on Easy Birth 达生编	397, 399
Tuhua ribao 图画日报	254
Unofficial Biography of Liu Rushi 柳如是别传	386
Unofficial Matters from the Wanli Period 万历野获编	76
Vagina Monologues 阴道独白	426
Water Margin 水浒传	18, 264, 376
White-haired Girl 白毛女	441
Women in Love 怜香伴	429
Women's Studies Book Series 妇女研究丛书	415
Xin qingnian 新青年	270–271, 295
Xin shiji 新世纪	291–292
Xingqi pinglun 星期评论	295
Yuan Clan Hereditary Rules 袁氏世范	161
Zhongguo funü 中国妇女	10, 12, 125, 147, 187, 230, 235, 324, 347, 349, 415
Zhongguo funü bao 中国妇女报	347, 349
Zhongguo nü bao 中国女报	253
Zhongguo xin nüjie 中国新女界	254
Zhuangzi 庄子	90–91

www.ingramcontent.com/pod-product-compliance
Lightning Source LLC
Chambersburg PA
CBHW071408160426
42814CB00037B/100